THE PARKING GARAGE

THE PARKING GARAGE

DESIGN AND
EVOLUTION OF
A MODERN
URBAN FORM

SHANNON SANDERS McDONALD

Urban Land Institute

The development and production of this publication were underwritten
in part through the generosity of Walker Parking Consultants.

ULI–the Urban Land Institute
1025 Thomas Jefferson Street, N.W.
Suite 500 West
Washington, D.C. 20007-5201

Library of Congress Cataloging-in-Publication Data

McDonald, Shannon Sanders.
The parking garage : design and evolution of a modern urban form / Shannon Sanders McDonald.
    p. cm.
Includes bibliographical references.
1. Parking garages. 2. Public architecture. 3. Architecture, Modern.
I. Title.
  TL175.M385 2007
  725'.38–dc22   2007038301

ISBN: 978-0-87420-998-3

Printed in the United States of America

10 9 8 7 6 5 4 3 2 1 10 09 08 07

Visit www.uli.org/parkinggarage for updates and additional resources.

Design and Composition
Marc Alain Meadows, Meadows Design Office, Inc.
Washington, D.C. www.mdomedia.com

Frontispiece: Nash Motors display, Century of Progress Exhibition, Chicago, 1933.

Project Staff

Rachelle L. Levitt
Executive Vice President, Global Information Group
Publisher

Dean Schwanke
Senior Vice President, Publications and Awards
Project Director

Nancy H. Stewart
Director, Book Program
Managing Editor

Lori Hatcher
Director, Publications Marketing

Sandra F. Chizinsky
Editor/Consultant

Betsy VanBuskirk
Art Director

Craig Chapman
Director, Publishing Operations

About ULI–the Urban Land Institute

The mission of the Urban Land Institute is to provide leadership in the responsible use of land and in creating and sustaining thriving communities worldwide. ULI is committed to

■ Bringing together leaders from across the fields of real estate and land use policy to exchange best practices and serve community needs;

■ Fostering collaboration within and beyond ULI's membership through mentoring, dialogue, and problem solving;

■ Exploring issues of urbanization, conservation, regeneration, land use, capital formation, and sustainable development;

■ Advancing land use policies and design practices that respect the uniqueness of both built and natural environments;

■ Sharing knowledge through education, applied research, publishing, and electronic media; and

■ Sustaining a diverse global network of local practice and advisory efforts that address current and future challenges.

Established in 1936, the Institute today has more than 38,000 members worldwide, representing the entire spectrum of the land use and development disciplines. ULI relies heavily on the experience of its members. It is through member involvement and information resources that ULI has been able to set standards of excellence in development practice. The Institute has long been recognized as one of the world's most respected and widely quoted sources of objective information on urban planning, growth, and development.

About the Author

Shannon Sanders McDonald is a practicing architect licensed in Georgia and Illinois, as well as an author and frequent speaker on architecture, parking, transportation, and related issues. She is a 1992 graduate of the Yale School of Architecture, where she was awarded a Business and Professional Women's Scholarship. In 1994–1995, Ms. McDonald worked with Carol Ross Barney in designing the award-winning Little Village Academy, in Chicago. She has also worked on many other public and transportation-related projects.

Ms. McDonald has written numerous articles on various aspects of parking and movement, and has given presentations at the meetings of a number of organizations, including the Advanced Transit Association, the American Institute of Architects, the American Society of Civil Engineers, the Association of Collegiate Schools of Architecture, the Construction Specifications Institute, the International Parking Association, the National Transportation Research Board, and the Vernacular Architecture Forum. She has taught architecture at many levels across the country.

PREFACE

It was in 1992, during an urban planning class at the Yale School of Architecture, that I first developed an interest in the parking garage as a research subject. The professor, Dolores Hayden, asked the class to write about "the most important piece of architecture in urban planning." I decided to focus on the parking garage—the one piece of architecture that brings together transportation, planning, aesthetics, and the environment.

In the course of writing that short paper, I became aware that very little had been written about the parking facility from the perspective of architectural design. This book is a beginning attempt to understand an architectural type that, without having been considered part of the "art of architecture," has been placed at the center of most of the design decisions of the 20th century.

Understanding the parking garage requires a multidimensional approach: thus, each chapter of the book focuses on one key aspect of the design process for this building type. One of the interesting facts that emerged, as my work on the book unfolded, is that in each decade, the evolution of the parking garage had a specific emphasis that mirrored—and sometimes led—the design strategies of the period. The order of the chapters reflects this progression. Although each chapter can be read independently, the book as a whole will provide the most complete understanding of the evolution of the building type. I believe that this approach will allow a broad readership to understand the complexity of the design process.

Because so little research has been undertaken about the parking garage, most of the information and images are drawn from primary sources—in particular, the magazines of the time. I hope that my research will set in motion more detailed investigations, in cities large and small, to provide a more thorough understanding of the building type. It is my further hope that as communities nationwide face the challenges of growth and development, this book will raise as many questions as it answers, inspire new solutions, and foster greater understanding of movement, of the nature of design, and of the role of the parking facility in modern life.

ACKNOWLEDGMENTS

Since 1992, many people have assisted in my understanding of the parking garage. Without their encouragement and support, this book would never have come into being. If I attempt to thank every single person with whom I have spoken in the course of my years of work, I'm sure I'll miss someone. Instead, I offer my heartfelt gratitude to all those who have shared their passion for parking with me—and, most importantly, those who encouraged me to pursue my research. Of course, I am solely responsible for any errors or omissions in this work.

I would like to thank the following organizations for their support, and for giving me the opportunity to write articles, present papers, and discuss my ideas with others: the Advanced Transit Association, the American Institute of Architects, the American Public Transportation Association, the American Society of Civil Engineers, the Association of Collegiate Schools of Architecture, the Automated People Movers Group of the American Society of Civil Engineers, the California Public Parking Association, the Construction Specifications Institute, the Georgia Institute of Technology, the International Parking Institute, the National Parking Association, the New Jersey Institute of Technology, the Transportation Research Board, the Vernacular Architecture Forum, and a small, unofficial group of personal rapid transit aficionados.

I would also like thank the many educational institutions, private firms, and governmental and nongovernmental organizations that shared their knowledge of unique parking solutions, including the American Automobile Association, the Eno Transportation Foundation, and *Parking Today*. I'd like to extend special thanks to Damien Kulash, of the Eno Transportation Foundation, for providing leads to some key sources and for allowing me access to his personal library, and to George Nassar, editor emeritus, *PCI Journal,* for all his advice and encouragement. I'd also like to thank the offices of Albert Kahn Associates, Inc.—in particular, Amy Russeau, manager, marketing and public relations; Donald Bauman, manager of specifications; James Boufford, archivist; and Larry Raymond. Thanks, too, to Sandra Stanton, property manager, and Robin Zohoury, director of marketing and tenant relations, Farbman Group, who graciously granted permission to reproduce images of the Fisher Building. I am also grateful to the members of the Detroit Athletic Club for granting permission to reproduce images of the club. I would especially like to thank the universities where I was given the opportunity to interact with students: Montana State University, North Dakota State University, and the University of Nebraska. I would also like to thank the staff of historical societies, and of public, private, and university libraries across the country; in particular, I am grateful to the following staff at the main library of the Georgia Institute of Technology—who, over a number of years, have patiently (and repeatedly) provided me with every single bound volume of many different journals: Temitayo Bamidele, Charlie Bennett, Andrew Blakely, Joey Fones, Carolyn Gill, Karen Glover, Richard Holland, Laurie Judd, Robert Luck, Stella Richardson, Crit Stuart, and Thomas Teshome. I'd also like to thank Kathryn Brackney and Kevin Quick, at the Georgia Institute of Technology Architecture Library, for their assistance and support. I am especially grateful to Constance Carter and John Buydos, of the Library of Congress, for their assistance over many years. Constance Carter provided a level of personal service rarely found in today's world. I'd also like to thank Barbara Thompson, of the National Automotive History Collection at the Detroit Public Library, and Karen L. Jania, reference archivist head, Bentley Historical Library, University of Michigan.

I would like to thank the Science and Technology Division of the Library of Congress, the Price-Gilbert Library and Information Center and the Architecture Library at the Georgia Institute of Technology, and the National Parking Association for allowing me unique access to their many holdings. I am also grateful to the many individuals and organizations that delved into their files—many of which had not seen the light of day since their creation—to assist with providing images for the book. I'd also like to thank the many photographers whose visions of parking garages are reproduced here.

I am deeply grateful to all the members of the parking industry who granted me access to their facilities, tolerated my many questions at conventions, spent time showing me the details of their operations, and talked with me about their companies. I would especially like to thank Forrest Hibbard, of the Atlanta office of Carl Walker, Inc., for allowing me to spend time in the office to see what is involved in an actual parking project. Thanks also to the offices of Gordon Chong and Partners, Watry Design, Inc., and International Parking Design, Inc., who introduced me to parking "California style." I'd also like to thank Tom Feagins, principal and managing director, and Jerry Marcus, principal and executive director, Walter P. Moore, for the grand tour of Texas. A number of people have provided constant support and encouragement and have always been ready to answer an e-mail or a phone call: Kim Clawson, of Goettsch Partners; Dale Denda, director of research, Parking Market Research Company; Larry Donoghue, of Donoghue and Associates; Kevin Haggerty, manager, customer access department, Bay Area Rapid Transit; James Hunnicutt, former president of the International Parking Institute; Richard C. Rich, president, Rich and Associates, Inc.; Carl Walker, of CW Consulting, LLC; and Nick Watry, lecturer, Department of Architectural Engineering, California Polytechnic State University, San Luis Obispo. Most importantly, I would like to thank the late George Devlin, who enthusiastically shared his zest for parking.

I'd like to extend my gratitude to the volunteer reviewers who read the entire first draft and provided valuable insight and encouragement: Monroe Carrell Jr., the founder of Central Parking; Donald Shoup, professor of urban planning, University of California at Los Angeles; Larry Donoghue, of Donoghue and Associates; James Hunnicutt, former president of the International Parking Institute; and Robert Dunphy, senior resident fellow, Transportation and Infrastructure, Urban Land Institute. I'd also like to thank the following people for providing comments on the text: Jim Anderson, of Carl Walker, Inc.; Robert Jurasin, of CH2M HILL; Paul Spero Kitsakos, of Parsons; Mark Santos, of Timothy Haahs & Associates; and Saleh Srouji, of Parsons Brinckerhoff Quade & Douglas.

A number of people reviewed, or made contributions to, individual chapters: John Purinton, of Watry Design, Inc. (Chapter 3); Michael Klein, executive director, Albany Parking Authority, and Richard Mobley, of Wilbur Smith Associates (Chapter 4); Sy Gage, of Gage Engineers; Peggy Guignon, of Robotic Parking Systems; Gerald Haag, of Robotic Parking Systems; and Lee Lazarus, of A.P.T. Parking Technologies (Chapter 5); Scott Humphreys, of Concrete Reinforcing Steel Institute; Michael Jolliffe, Zaldastani Associates, Inc.; Bill Pascoli, senior regional engineer, AISC Marketing, LLC; John Purinton, of Watry Design, Inc.; Edward K. Rice, former president, T.Y. Lin & Associates; and Saleh Sourji, of Parsons Brinckerhoff Quade & Douglas (Chapter 6); Kent Bloomer, Yale University School of Architecture (Chapter 7); Kent Bloomer, Yale University School of Architecture, and Michelle Wendler, principal, Watry Design, Inc. (Chapter 8); Patrick Pinnell, of Patrick L. Pinnell, Architecture and Town Planning (Chapter 9); Dale Denda, director of research, Parking Marketing Research Company, and Michele Wendler, principal, Watry Design, Inc. (Chapter 10). I would also like to thank the students, assistants, and editors who helped me during the past seven years, as I developed and wrote this book.

A special thanks is due to Walker Parking Consultants and to Chairman Frank M. Transue for the generous financial support they provided to help develop and produce this publication. Many thanks are also due to several experts at Walker Parking Consultants, including Mary Smith for her support and advice during the early book development stages and throughout the project, and Anthony Chrest, Don Monahan, and Mark A. Zelepsky for their specific technical contributions and advice.

I'm deeply grateful to Dean Schwanke, senior vice president, publications and awards, Urban Land Institute, for his time, patience, and support in bringing this project to fruition. Dean had long envisioned a new approach to a book about parking, to complement *The Dimensions of Parking,* and his knowledge and experience in this area were invaluable to me. I would like to thank my editor, Sandy Chizinsky, for her excellent editing and advice and for her patience with my questions and with an architect's approach to writing. I'd also like to thank ULI staff members who contributed to the production of this book: Rachelle Levitt, executive vice president, global information group; Nancy H. Stewart, director, book program; and Betsy VanBuskirk, art director. I really appreciate the work of Marc Alain Meadows, of Meadows Design Office, who designed the book, and who had to deal with images from so many different sources, which made layout and design a challenge. I would also like to thank my family for their support throughout the years, and for encouraging me to express my thoughts and creativity.

Finally, I would like to dedicate this book to my cousin, Wendy Friedman, who inspires me every day through the humor, grace, and intelligence with which she has met—and continues to meet—extraordinary challenges. A flair for language is among Wendy's many gifts, and without our daydreaming and "punfests," it would have been impossible to complete this book.

Contents

When Noah sailed the ocean blue

He had his problems just like you

For forty days he sailed his ark

Before he found a place to park.

—Anonymous

The Parking Garage
Design and Evolution of a Modern Urban Form

Why take the time to study the history, the evolution, and the architectural and urban development of a building type that most people want to ignore, cover up, put underground, and hurry through? Precisely because it has become such a ubiquitous—and indispensable—part of everyday life. In the numerous discussions that took place during the development of this book, many people enthusiastically shared their favorite "parking-garage stories"—despite the fact that none of these people would be likely to want one in their backyard. The parking garage, a largely unrecognized building type, defines how people live and what industrialized society has become: it is a crucial building form that lies at the intersection of architecture, transportation, sustainability, and urban design. A typological study of best practices in the design, development, and construction of parking garages is long overdue.

Complexities and Contradictions

Independent movement poses a dilemma: it is important to the well-being of society, but too much can be detrimental to a sense of community. Nevertheless, people are reluctant to part with the independence, freedom, and thrill that individual travel provides. The parking garage represents, in built form, an unresolved tension about modern life: on the one hand, the movement system on which most people in the industrialized world depend—the automobile—provides unique and unparalleled mobility. On the other hand, the parking garage is a large, imposing, desolate, and often stark structure—a physical manifestation of the realities of an automobile-dependent culture. But this is not the fault of the buildings so much as of ourselves. Both the designers and the users of garages have allowed them to take on often unwelcome forms.

Architecture interweaves many different elements to create a functioning whole. Over time, buildings that are used for the same purpose develop unique characteristics—their own

Facing page: Motor Mart Garage, Boston, 1926. This handsome parking facility and civic structure replaced the original five-sided garage built in 1905; recently restored, it is continuing to give life and service to the city.

3

"design logic"; the result is known as a building type. Almost from its inception, the parking garage was a unique building type, with its own set of construction parameters and design elements. Because it is possible, in the case of the parking garage, to trace both theoretical and physical development, the garage offers an ideal opportunity to explore the notion of a building type.

As technology gave rise to new movement systems during the 20th century, several new building types emerged, among them the parking garage and the train station. Both functioned as places of transition from one environment or experience to another, and both therefore played a civic role. But only the train station has been recognized as a civic space. The parking garage, in contrast, has been placed well outside the pantheon of civic buildings. Perhaps this is because the experience of being in a parking garage tends to be private, or because the buildings themselves often lack architectural expression. But it is a mistake to believe that successful public places must be group gathering spaces: they can just as easily be spaces that all people experience privately, and at their own pace. Within Central Park, New York City's "front yard," Frederick Law Olmsted designed both types of public spaces. And just as varieties of civic space can occur within a designed landscape, they can also occur within architecture.

The garage is a unique combination of human transition space and mechanical storage space. This combination, which had never occurred until the advent of the car, ultimately helped create and define modern architecture and the American psyche alike. This consummately practical building has been the focus of innovation and experimentation—and has, on occasion, yielded extraordinary beauty. Despite never having been acknowledged as part of the "art of architecture," the garage has often exemplified the best of what cities and towns can be.

The garage is singular in the scope of its requirements, which range from unforgiving functional issues, such as traffic planning, to the realm of aesthetics. Because the parking garage is so central to the urban environment, misperceptions and miscalculations dramatically affect urban life. The hitherto silent struggle to solve this key architectural design problem, now given voice in this volume, offers fresh insights to aspiring and practicing designers. Observing how history, function, style, aesthetics, engineering, and urban planning merge to create actual built solutions provides a unique opportunity to learn about design.

The Birth of Sprawl

The parking garage has been at the center of development and redevelopment in American cities since before the turn of the 20th century. By the mid- to late 1800s, American cities were difficult places to live: mass immigration from Europe and the influx of rural residents in search of work had led to overcrowding; the burning of coal and wood made urban environments dirty and unhealthy; and the horse, the principal form of transportation, was the environmental hazard of its time.

When the horse population was almost annihilated in the 1870s by an epidemic, the lack of horses to power the fire vehicles allowed fires to spread; as a result, inventors began working to develop a mechanical replacement. The automobile brought the solution to a number of problems: it eliminated the environmental issues associated with horses, and offered access to the bucolic countryside, which was then still abundant throughout the country.

Downtowns—architecturally definable districts with a concentration of business, commerce, and entertainment—developed in the United States during the late 19th and early 20th century, and were viewed as crucial to a successful business environment. They were also viewed as inevitable—as part of the natural evolution of cities. It was assumed that downtown and "uptown" (the residential complement of downtown), would always exist, as they were both complementary and interdependent: one very crowded and busy, and the other typified by what Frederick Law Olmsted referred to as the "'cleanliness and purity'...of domestic life."[1]

With the advent of steam power, electricity, and the internal combustion engine came the ability to travel farther within the same amount of time, and to escape many of the environmental hazards of the expanding and industrializing city. The fact that homes could be located much farther from workplaces, on land that was less expensive than what was available downtown, encouraged the horizontal expansion of the city and the complete separation of home and work. This development pattern was set in motion several decades before the automobile by trains, trolleys, and streetcars—but the automobile solidified it.

Frederick Law Olmsted saw a "'strong and steadily increasing tendency'...toward the separation of business and residences, although he created for New Yorkers a wonderful front yard—Central Park."[2] Nevertheless, most of Olmsted's plans, along with those of other designers and architects of the time, encouraged the physical separation of home and work. A few people—including Carter H. Harrison Sr., mayor of Chicago; George A. Lespinasse, a New York real estate broker; Helen Campbell, who later organized the Consumers' League of New York; and Reverend Amory H. Bradford—yearned for the compact and integrated spatial relationships of European cities, and fought against the emerging architecture of separation. But they were very much in the minority. The negative results of excessive horizontal development, now referred to as "sprawl"—which include social isolation; traffic congestion; restricted mobility for children, elderly people, and citizens with physical limitations; and environmental, financial, and land use burdens—have been apparent for several decades, but are now receiving serious attention from designers.

At the World Parking Symposium, held it Canada in 1999, mobility was defined as a "personal right." This notion can sometimes be in conflict with an equally powerful vision of a community where everyone strives together for the betterment of the whole. Even with the advent of new communication technologies like the Internet, which promise to relieve people of the need to travel, it turns out that meeting face to face—that is, creating community—may not only be a source of enjoyment, but essential to mental and physical health. The parking facility is an important public-use building type and reflects many complex issues that are crucial to emotional, environmental, and physical well-being.

In an effort to create sustainable environments that balance individual and collective needs, architects, planners, and citizens are trying to create vital, livable urban forms. One essential element in this effort involves providing as many transportation, work, and living options as possible. The parking garage is at the center of this discussion. How can these new connections be achieved? How can linkages to "new" transit, automobile, bicycle, and walking solutions be provided? Fortunately, many historic examples offer complex, aesthetic, and integrated solutions that have been forgotten.

What Can Be Learned from This Study?

The parking garage is a familiar space to almost everyone in industrial society. That the garage is central to the arrival and departure experience for most buildings and cities suggests that it is a common transition space, eliciting complex emotions that people often choose to ignore. What makes a suc-cessful parking garage is the creation of a positive transition experience, regardless of whether the garage is being viewed from the outside or experienced from within.

The parking garage was not always perceived as an eyesore. The early excitement associated with the car—the sense of mobility, freedom, and power—gave rise to many beautiful and imaginative garage structures. But as cars became commonplace, so did garages—until recently. Within the past decade, many parking garages have addressed the issues discussed in this book: in some places, parking garages have become functioning parts of mixed-use projects, contributing to civic life and expanding the future possibilities of transportation, architecture, and design.

Some of the solutions presented in this volume have been forgotten since the early years of the automobile; some are old ideas that can be revived to solve new issues; and some were so visionary at the time they were developed that they can only now be put into practice. Still others have provided object lessons in what not to build. The goal of this volume is to stimulate fresh insights and solutions—new visions that can contribute to a more holistic, sustainable future. It is essential to shape the landscape in a sustainable and realistic way that will meet the needs of all citizens: the parking garage will continue to play a key role in the evolution of design to meet current demands.

This volume offers a sweeping tour of the long-forgotten history and fascinating evolution of this most unpopular of building types. Each chapter addresses a key issue in the evolution of the parking garage: psychological and emotional aspects of the building type; the development of the parking garage "form"; the connection between the garage and other building uses; the relationship between form and function in the parking garage; the integration of new technologies; the structure of the parking garage; the garage in the context of architectural theory; the aesthetics of the parking garage; urban planning and land use; and the future of the garage.

The parking garage has tremendous potential to integrate the disparate elements of the American city—to continue to support mobility for all. As the building type continues to evolve, its civic role—as a link between different types of travel—will become even more evident and vital. Form follows parking.

CONCRETE GARAGE FOR PALMER & SINGER MFG. CO., BROADWAY, NEAR
50TH STREET, NEW YORK

Marvin & Davis, Architects

CHAPTER 1

A Time of Excitement
A New Building Form

The first several decades of parking garage design were marked by a struggle to define a new building type—one that would have profound implications for architecture, urban design, and the American way of life. The starting points for garage design were existing buildings and the standard architectural and construction practices at the turn of the 19th century, but the emerging technology of the automobile demanded new solutions. Some of the early solutions—such as elevators, flat floor plates, classical proportions, and seamless integration into the urban fabric—are drawing attention today. Many of the early designs incorporated features that would now be referred to as sustainable: mechanization, new electric-vehicle technology, a mix of uses, the creation of a sense of place, and sensitivity to the needs of the human user. The early years of the parking garage offered a wealth of ideas, many long since forgotten, that can be viable once again.

The first parking garages arose from an immediate practical need: both personal automobiles and the vehicles of the burgeoning cab industry required heat and protection from the weather. However, the design of the parking garage, unlike that of its many precursors—the roundhouse, the bicycle shop, the barn, the stable, and the carriage house—had to respond to a completely new technology, and to the emotions that it engendered. Early garages were not just for storage and maintenance, but provided a range of services for motorists and their vehicles: changing rooms, restrooms, long-term storage, pickup and delivery, retail facilities, chauffeurs' quarters, and car washing and detailing.

The parking garage started as a single-story structure whose characteristics were related to those of all its antecedents; however, it quickly took on the unique, multistory form that is familiar today. The terms for the new building type also changed over time: the early parking garage was referred to as a barn, stable, station, livery, hotel, parkway, and even arcade. Later terms included those still in use today: structure, ramp, deck. ("Parking facility" is currently a popular term.)

Facing page: Palmer & Singer Manufacturing Company garage, New York City, 1910.

7

Movement Facts, 1823–1919

The turn of the 20th century brought rapid change to the American landscape: new technologies were changing the American way of life, and none had greater impact than the automobile.

- The first macadam roads built in the United States were constructed in 1823. Asphalt paving was first used in American cities in 1876.

- The Bicycle Wheelman's Association, founded in 1880, initiated the Good Roads Movement, which promoted the construction of paved roads in the United States.

- In 1889, in New York City's Tenth Ward, population density was estimated at 757 people per acre (1,870 per hectare)—the highest in the world at that time. Many other areas in New York had densities higher than those of Paris or Berlin.

- In 1891, New Jersey enacted road-aid laws to support road construction.

- In 1898, large-scale production of automobiles first began in Germany.

- Between 1900 and 1910, American cities added 11,826,000 new residents: 41 percent were immigrants, and 29.8 percent were migrants from rural America. In five years alone—from 1905 to 1910—5 million immigrants came to the United States.

- The Ford Model T was first put into production in 1908 and became widely available soon thereafter.

- By 1910, it cost less to drive a Maxwell automobile than a horse and buggy: 1.8 cents per passenger mile (2.9 cents per passenger kilometer) for the car, versus 2.5 cents (4.0 cents) for the horse and buggy.

- In 1913, construction began on the Lincoln Highway, which would eventually connect the United States from coast to coast.

- By 1914, 1,644,003 automobiles were registered in the United States (many more existed but were not registered). Two years later, when the Federal Roads Act was passed (to coordinate the principal interstates and to construct all roads on which mail was transported), there were 3,367,889 automobiles registered.

The ornamentation on early garages gave physical expression to the feelings of excitement and adventure associated with auto travel, but the practical needs of the car changed the architectural language as well. New physical features became common, such as oversized mechanized doors, and large glass windows that allowed the cars to be seen from the street. The new multistory garages also included other emerging technologies: elevators to move cars from floor to floor, and turntables to minimize the amount of space needed to rotate the automobile.

The Horse, the Car, and the Parking Garage

In 1890, when the U.S. population numbered just under 63 million, horses and mules numbered 20 million. In 1900, the 23 largest U.S. cities combined had 1,454,000 stables. And as late as 1907, Chicago alone had over 61,000 horse-drawn vehicles.[1]

Horse traffic was essentially uncontrolled: there were no stop signs, no traffic lights, no parking regulations; in 1900, horses were involved in 750,000 accidents nationwide. City streets were dirty and crowded, with animal carcasses and feces lying alongside the carts of food vendors. The horse, the principal means of transportation, was also the principal source of pollution. Disease was common, and easily spread by splashed mud. In the late 19th and early 20th centuries, life in America's cities was both difficult and unhealthy. Then the automobile arrived on the scene.[2]

Almost immediately, this new technology was viewed as the solution to a host of problems. By 1909—the peak year for travel by horsepower—the ascendance of the gasoline-powered automobile was already well underway, and thousands of automobile garages had been built in the United States alone. Although other means of transportation (the bicycle, the streetcar, and the trolley among them) had already addressed the need for safe, reliable, and nonpolluting vehicles, it was the automobile that captured the popular imagination: the horse was viewed as a source of pollution, and the car as an environmental savior—a new machine that would transform cities into cleaner and healthier places to live.[3]

Public health concerns, rising prices for animal care (which made it cheaper to own an automobile), and traffic jams—caused by the intersection of horse-drawn vehicles, trolleys, and streetcars—led people to embrace this new

movement device. In 1900, there were 8,000 cars registered in the United States (in addition to the many that were not registered), and 300 factories producing them. In 1904, 21,281 autos were built in the United States, and there were 60 factories for steam-powered cars, 40 for electric cars, and hundreds for gasoline-powered vehicles. But it was in 1912, with the advent of Henry Ford's assembly line, that cars became widely affordable—promising, at least at first, a better future and a cleaner, healthier way of life for all.[4]

This one object, the automobile, had the power to change the built environment and people's lives—and, in combination with other forces already in motion, it did just that. In 1905, it was already being written that "there is hardly a village of any importance in the thickly peopled parts of the country which does not boast of one or more storage stations."[5] By the 1920s, examples of the parking garage—the built form that both supported and represented the automobile—were too numerous to count.

Facing page: Joscelyn Garage, New York City, 1909.

Above: Hoyt & DeMallie garage, New York City, 1911.

The Car, the City, and the Parking Garage

Even though the car was first developed in Europe (Paris issued its first automobile license in 1893), European cities and towns were already fully formed, and the car was forced to adapt to an existing environment. In the United States, in contrast, most cities were undergoing rapid growth, and the automobile therefore affected the design of American cities far more than it did their older European counterparts. A 2002 study of Lincoln, Nebraska, for example, found that nearly 40 percent of the buildings in Lincoln's early core were auto-related, including garages, production shops, and accessory shops. Thus did the automobile literally build American cities and towns—while simultaneously clogging their streets.[6]

At the same time, those on farms needed access to the markets and the amenities of the city, and those in cities wanted easy access to the bucolic countryside; the car provided for both. A 1917 garage built in Jacksonville, Texas, is a mixed visual metaphor that clearly symbolizes the country's transition from a rural and agricultural society to an urban and industrial one: although the building proclaimed itself to

Above: New York City, circa 1900. At the beginning of the 20th century, urban streets in the United States were often unpaved, unsanitary, and unpleasant.

Right: Campus Martius, Detroit, circa 1920. With the advent of the bicycle, the trolley, and the automobile, city streets were eventually paved, and order and cleanliness emerged.

be a garage, it took the form of a barn decorated with vines on its front.[7]

By the mid-1920s, automobile traffic was already a problem in most American cities:

Down to 1950, thanks to the revolution Ford had wrought, America was the only country in the world that could boast mass car ownership. By 1927, building 85% of the world's cars, it could already boast one car for every five Americans: a car-ownership level of one to approximately two families.... As a result, mass motorization had already begun to impinge on American cities by the mid-1920's, in a way the rest of the world would not know until the 1950's and 1960's. By 1923 traffic congestion in some cities was already so bad there was talk of barring cars from some downtown streets; by 1926, Thomas E. Pitts had closed his cigar store and soft drink bar at a major intersection in the center of Atlanta because congestion made it impossible to operate.[8]

By 1920, 8,132,000 autos and 1,108,000 trucks were registered in the United States, and the problem of where to park them had become critical.[9]

Nor was the United States the only country grappling with the question of where to place parked automobiles. In 1901, there were more automobiles in Paris than in any other city in the world, but autos were excluded from the Champ de Mars because there was no proper place to park them. The colonial minister of France had a room fitted for his automobile under the Rubens Gallery at the Louvre—a move that was greeted by a public outcry.[10]

The need for parking garages presented an obvious opportunity for entrepreneurs and designers. Despite early creative solutions in France—such as the Garage Rue de Ponthieu—it was in the United States that the parking garage developed into the building type that is most familiar today.[11]

Top left: Jackson Motor Company, Jacksonville, Texas, 1916. The facade of this garage is a visual expression of the transition from an agricultural to an industrial economy.

Above: Garage Rue de Ponthieu, Paris, 1905. Designed by Auguste Perret, this garage was a pivotal structure that combined fireproof construction, ornament, and classical proportions.

The Parking Garage and the Train Station

In the earliest parking garages, passengers did not move through the inside of the building: the only people who entered the interior of a garage were the garage owners, cabbies, chauffeurs, and mechanics. Eventually, however, parking garages evolved into places that passengers moved through as well, a shift that made the new building type unique, and that also brought it into closer relation to the train station, a well-established civic building type.[1]

However, the landmark quality of the great train hall, which announced the entrance into a city, never found its way into parking garage design. Perhaps the auto garage could have evolved more like the train station (which was itself a new building type in the 19th century), with a public gathering hall that was separate from storage and maintenance areas. But the more individualized nature of driving did not suggest this architectural form, so the parking garage evolved according to its own internal logic, in a way that stressed functionality and the independence of the passenger. Nevertheless, the parking garage has always functioned as a gateway or arrival and departure space for cities, towns, and buildings, and the designs of some new facilities are attempting to reflect this civic role.[2]

Grand Central Station, New York City, constructed 1903–1913.

Early Garages and Their Sources

Although the owners of horses and stables may have regarded the parking garage as an unwelcome symbol of change, to others it was a new and exciting architectural type—a visual symbol of mechanized mobility, healthy living, and the modern city. Because cars, unlike horses, could be housed in large numbers and combined with living spaces, architects, designers, and entrepreneurs could think in a completely new way about what to do when the car was stopped. However, a building design that would accommodate the new and complex requirements of the automobile—that would provide the right "fit"—was not something that would develop overnight.

The first requirement was for large, open spaces—not only for movement, but also for repair, maintenance, and fueling. Second, early cars were open vehicles, featuring sensitive internal mechanisms and nonweatherproof materials; thus, the buildings designed to house them had to be heated and fully enclosed. Some of the first parking garages were located in existing buildings: stables, coach houses, or car-

riage houses (which is why parking spaces are often still referred to as "stalls"). The initial appeal of stables was based simply on their availability: stables had been linked to illnesses (including smallpox), and were under attack by insurance companies as both fire hazards and public health hazards (particularly when many horses were gathered in one location). Thus, simply replacing the horses with automobiles was an appealing way to make use of these buildings—although, because of the stables' small size, such reuse was not often practical.

Some stables, however, were large, multistory masonry or concrete structures that could accommodate the new horseless vehicles. For example, a 1909 article noted that the Imperial Motor Vehicle Company, in New York City, had purchased a stable and was making extensive alterations to allow for the movement of vehicles (which must have been a major undertaking, as the building—with six floors and a basement—was one of the city's largest stables). The Joscelyn Garage, also in New York City, underwent a thoroughly modern conversion from stable to garage: floors were rebuilt out of concrete, and many new rooms and services were added. In Memphis, the E.K. Keck & Bros. Livery Stable, a fireproof structure built in 1868, had been converted to parking use by 1920, and continued to operate as a garage until 1934.[12]

Conversions were not always possible, of course. Some ramps were too steep for automobiles—rendering even large, fireproof stables inappropriate for adaptation. In New York City, for example, where the average stable held only 16 horses, most stables were too small to convert to garages, and did not necessarily have room for expansion. Even when the stable was large enough, the unique requirements of the automobile required extensive changes; moreover, existing stables were not necessarily in the best locations for garages. Finally, conversion often met with resistance from stable owners, who viewed the automobile as a threat to their established businesses.[13]

When stable conversions did occur, they were not without risk—principally from fire, since many stables were constructed of wood. Combustion was a particular concern during the transition from stable to garage, when horses and steam-, electric-, and gasoline-powered vehicles were housed together, and wood, hay, gasoline, and greasy rags were brought under one roof. (In fact, the fire hazards associated with converting stables to garages prompted many new regulations in cities.) One example of a fireproof building that was a combination stable and garage was the People's Garage and Livery Company, in Chicago. Many such combinations already existed when the new construction laws for "parking hotels" went into place.[14]

The documentation on these early stable/garages is not as straightforward as one might wish: many early garages were called stables even though they actually housed automobiles. The "stable" designed by York & Sawyer Architects for a residence at 213 West 58th Street, for example, was an elaborately designed structure worthy of New York City: of fireproof construction, it featured a tiled, barrel-vaulted ceiling. A photo of the building proudly depicts the owners' preferred method of transportation: the automobile—which, unlike the horse, could be stored inside the home.[15]

One of the most famous stable conversions was undertaken for the White House. Because the president's stables were separate from his dwelling, he had to travel to reach them. And because this arrangement was perceived as a security risk, the Secret Service began using automobiles in 1901. However, it was William Howard Taft, whose term began in 1913, who converted the stable on the South Lawn into a garage. Taft's successor, Woodrow Wilson, moved the executive automobiles to 19th Street, where he constructed a new garage between the existing stables.[16]

Another early model for the parking garage was the roundhouse, a behind-the-scenes building where railway cars were stored, maintained, and moved into position to be used again. (The word *garage* is actually derived from the French word for roundhouse. The words *car* and *motorcar* also derive from railroad terminology, and were first used to refer to the parts of the train that were pulled by the engine.) Movement in roundhouses was not linear: the railroad cars could be moved easily in any direction, and could turn around

People's Garage and Livery, Chicago, 1907. In the early 20th century, many of the newly built fireproof garages housed both horses and automobiles.

Presidential garage, Washington, D.C., 1913. The first presidential garage was a converted stable on the South Lawn of the White House.

if necessary in order to enter or exit, providing a great deal of flexibility for parking purposes. The storage sheds (often called car barns), used for steam-powered and electric trolleys could also be considered part of the roundhouse category; although they were not round in form, they served a similar purpose.[17]

In 1898, in Boston, a Civil War cyclorama (a round building containing an "in-the-round" painting—a popular form of entertainment in the pre-cinema era) was transformed into a cab station for the New England Electric Vehicle & Transportation Company. One of the first parking stations in Washington, D.C., was also a former cyclorama. When these entertainment centers fell on hard times, the large, open spaces in their interiors were a natural fit for parking. It is likely that the familiar roundhouse design prompted the use of cycloramas for automobile storage.[18]

Initially, bicycle repair shops were often used to store autos: many early automobiles were mechanized bicycles, and bicycle mechanics therefore had the expertise to maintain them. In Philadelphia in 1902, the Century Wheelman bike club transformed a large portion of its wheel room—where bicycles were stored and repaired—into an automobile garage. On May 24, 1899, when W.T. McCullough established the Back Bay Cycle and Motor Company, in Boston—the

first public garage on record—he advertised it as "a stable for renting, sale, storage, and repair of motor vehicles."[19] However, just as the needs of the auto diverged from those of the horse, bicycle shops failed to meet all of the unique design requirements of the emerging auto technology.[20]

Being open vehicles, early autos often needed interior repair; thus, upholstery shops also housed automobiles. In 1917, for example, an upholstery shop in Detroit charged patrons to park in its shop.[21]

The first recorded parking garage in the United States was created, in 1897, out of an old skating rink. Owned by the Electric Vehicle Company, an electric cab company in New York City, and located at 1684 Broadway, the garage immediately gained an international reputation, and set the tone for the innovation that was to come. According to a French news article about the opening of the station, "New York has no motor vehicle exhibition such as recently drew all of Paris to its doors, nor does she as yet count the motor vehicles in her streets by thousands, but she has something which even Paris, the mother of the motor vehicle, cannot boast—a complete electric cab installation."[22] The station was 75 by 200 feet (23 by 61 meters); the battery room—which housed several hundred batteries, charging or charged—took up half the interior. The cab storage area,

Left: Cyclorama, Boston, circa 1870. In both Boston and Washington, D.C., former cycloramas were among the earliest parking structures.

Below left: Electric Vehicle Company garage, New York City, 1897. The first documented commercial parking structure was built for the Electric Vehicle Company in an old skating rink.

Below right: Moutoux Automobile Garage (location and date unknown). A typical combination found in early garages: a single shop offering bicycle and automobile repair.

accessible by elevator, was raised above the battery room. Business offices were housed in the front portion of the building, and drivers' rooms and a machine shop in the rear.[23]

In sum, the sources of the first parking stations were many and varied—from stables to bicycle shops, upholstery shops, cycloramas, and skating rinks—all in an attempt to accommodate the requirements of a new and rapidly changing technology. What the first parking stations had in common were characteristics already present in the very first documented garage: large, open spaces for the autos, and smaller, adjoining support spaces to allow for the maintenance and other services that the new technology required. Thus did a new building type emerge.

New Structures for a New Technology

Initially, automobile storage was based on existing models of transit, horse, and bicycle storage—buildings used strictly for the storage and maintenance of movement devices. However, from the beginning of the 20th century, the need for specialized buildings drew the attention of architects, engineers, and entrepreneurs, all of whom attempted to solve the complex problems that arose as the new building type evolved.

Garages for Electric Vehicles

The first personal electric vehicle was developed by William Morrison in 1891, in Des Moines, Iowa. Although they had a limited range, electric vehicles were very reliable and were operating well into the 1920s. Many of the cars manufactured before 1910 were electric-powered, and the electric companies naturally encouraged the proliferation of the technology. Thus, many of the earliest garages were for electric automobiles (either cabs or privately owned vehicles), and by the first decade of the 20th century, garages for electric vehicles were quite numerous.[24] As early as 1899, "a coin-controlled mechanism" was being tested for use on the street curb "such that the driver of an electric vehicle, after having deposited the necessary coin in a slot, can draw upon it for a certain number of watt hours."[25]

In 1894, Henry Morris and Pedro Salom, of Philadelphia, began commercial production of an electric vehicle called the Electrobat, which was built as a taxicab; that company later evolved into the Electric Vehicle Company, which in 1898 became the owner of the first structure in the United States that was constructed solely as a parking garage. Little is known about the building, other than the fact that it was located in Chicago and was advertised in *The Horseless Age*, a magazine of the time.[26]

In 1900, several parking stations were constructed in Pittsburgh by D.N. Seely, president of the Seely Manufacturing Company. Seely organized a scheme to erect charging stations for electric automobiles throughout Pittsburgh and Allegheny County, Pennsylvania, and also operated a for-hire motor delivery company. The arrangement was described in *The Horseless Age*:

A livery building is being erected at Baum and Beaty Sts. that will be capable of housing 40–50 automobiles. Over 180 ft. of plate glass will be used in the front, and it will be arranged that automobiles can be taken in and out easily. It is the intention to have owners of automobiles keep their vehicles in the stable, and upon a telephone call the automobiles will be taken to the owner's residence as liveried carriages now are. A gas engine and dynamo will be installed in the stable so as to charge all electric vehicles and gasoline vehicles will also be cared for as well. Mr. Seely intends establishing a charging station at the city end of the Grant Boulevard, at Grant St. And Seventh Ave., for the East End residents who desire to come to town on shopping expeditions on their automobiles. The vehicles will be recharged and kept there until the owners are ready to return home.[27]

In 1902, the magazine *Automobile Topics* noted that there were over 30 charging stations in northern New Jersey. Entrepreneurship flourished: a doctor in Brooklyn was just one among many individuals who allowed privately owned electric vehicles to be parked and charged on their property.[28] In 1913, *The Horseless Age* noted that the monthly rate for a "prominent electric garage recently established in Philadelphia was $15.00, which included storage, cleaning, washing, polishing, flushing of batteries with distilled water, and inspection of the car."[29]

The Edison Electric Garage, in Boston, constructed in 1913, is another example of an early garage for electric vehicles. The Edison Electric Company built seven buildings on 17 acres (seven hectares) of land, including a parking garage for electric vehicles and an adjacent garage for gasoline-powered vehicles (the latter was designed so that it could be transformed for electric automobile parking if necessary). At the time, this garage was viewed as the most modern in the United States. It was constructed of brick and reinforced concrete, with glass on three sides and in the roof, and was 110 feet (34 meters) wide and 260 feet (79 meters) long, with 108 charging plugs. The garage's many safety features included a fire pump and an overhead sprinkler system. The adjacent three-story garage for gasoline-powered vehicles included dormitories for chauffeurs. (Since automobiles were used round the clock, the mechanics and chauffeurs needed living space, so this was a typical arrangement at the time.)[30]

Garages for Steam- and Gasoline-Powered Vehicles

Early parking garages for automobiles powered by other sources, such as steam and gasoline, followed patterns of architectural development that were similar to those of the garages for electric cabs. In fact, electric-, gasoline-, and steam-powered vehicles were often housed together.

Steam-powered cars were first developed in 1796; the first self-propelled road vehicle was built in 1866, although commercial production did not begin until 1897. Both the Locomobile Company and the Steam Vehicle Company of America had garages for steam-powered vehicles in New York City by 1901. Although the electric vehicle survived longer than the steam vehicle, the gasoline vehicle outlasted both, largely because of its longer range, and because Henry Ford made it affordable. Although the earliest garages accommodated all three types of vehicles, eventually the building type evolved solely to meet the needs of the gasoline-powered auto.[31]

The first time on record that a gasoline-powered automobile drove down a city street in the United States was in Baltimore, in 1890. The machine frightened everyone. Eventually, the auto burned down the building that it had been stored in—an inauspicious beginning for a brand-new building type.[32]

Parking for a Variety of Users

The rise of the automobile eventually led to the emergence of distinct user groups with their own parking needs. These users ranged from automobile clubs to municipalities to manufacturers, and early garages emerged to serve each of these markets and user groups.

Clubs and Parking

In the early years of auto travel, parking was often limited, if not banned entirely, in parks and on certain streets. Automobile drivers soon found that they needed to band together to create places to store and care for their recently purchased motor carriages. In 1905, in Sydney, Australia, it was illegal to leave a carriage without a horse parked on a city street—so car owners joined forces to build a garage, which eventually became the Royal Automobile Club of Australia. In the United States, auto clubs evolved to address the travel-related needs that were arising throughout the country—specifically, to provide places to park. The first such club in the United States, the American Motor League, started in Chicago in 1895 but was unable to sustain itself. In 1899, the Automobile Club of America was founded in New York to protect users of motor carriages from park boards and to establish a depot for the proper storage and care of vehicles; the club was also a center of information.[33] An early publication of the club castigated stable owners for their "stupid hostility" in refusing to cater to the demand for storing autos.[34]

By the early 20th century, local automobile clubs had formed in many cities across the country, building garages and meeting places for the exclusive use of their members. In 1899, the Cleveland Automobile Club retrofitted an ath-

Chicago Automobile Club, 1907. Because parking was one of the main reasons for the formation of automobile clubs, virtually every club offered vehicle storage.

letic club and transformed it into a clubhouse, driving school, and "motor livery business."[35] The Massachusetts Automobile Club, headquartered in Boston, offered a full-service, multilevel garage in 1902. It was followed by the New York Clubhouse, near Central Park, that same year. Chicago's first automobile clubhouse, which opened in 1902, was a residential-looking building that contained storage space and a small repair shop in the back; the club's new clubhouse and garage opened five years later. Hartford, Connecticut, had its own automobile club and garage by the 1920s. Early business clubs, such as the Jonathan Club, in Los Angeles, eventually purchased the land around their clubhouses to provide parking for members.[36]

Despite the successful efforts of automobile and business clubs to provide member parking, reliable storage and maintenance remained hard to come by. As reported in *Scientific American* in 1902, potential car buyers were deterred by the dearth of well-located garages, "close to the city's business heart," and by "the lack of repair shops able to do good responsible work."[37]

Early Public Garages

As noted earlier, the first public garage on record was the Back Bay Cycle and Motor Company, built in Boston in 1899. In 1900, the St. Nicholas Rink Building, in New York City, was converted to the city's first public parking garage and renamed the Automobile Storage and Repair Company. In 1901, *The Horseless Age* listed seven major automobile storage and repair shops (and a few others) in New York; by 1915, the number had grown to 600. (All garages that opened were tracked in a regular feature of the magazine, as well as in other publications of the time, such as *The Garage* magazine.) In 1906, a public garage was advertised in Baltimore. By 1910, parking had begun to emerge as an industry, and New York City's White Garage was setting its rates according to the recommendations of the New York Automobile Trade Association—which is to say that chauffeurs received no commissions, and fees depended on the style and size of the car. The White Garage consisted of two buildings, three and six stories high, and included a complete auto-service shop and a five-ton elevator. The Acton Garage, built in New York City in 1906 and now called the Monterey Garage, is still in operation today.[38]

As towns competed to become major centers, public garages began to appear all across the country. Although many public garages were built to meet the demand—and although those that *were* built prospered—parking spaces were still needed in specific locations. In 1902, New York was considered the only city with enough parking garages for the number of automobiles.[39]

Women Drivers and the Parking Garage

Some early motorists were women—a fact that helped fuel the women's rights movement by allowing women to travel to every part of the country in support of women's suffrage. However, in order for parking garages to be accepted and used by women, they had to provide the necessary amenities, especially in retail and commercial areas. Particularly as it became clear that short-term parkers were often women, addressing women's needs became a specialized aspect of the parking industry. At Baltimore's St. Paul Garage, for example, built in 1930, the entire first level was reserved for female customers.[1]

In the era of open, unprotected vehicles, both men and women wore special clothing while driving or riding, and women required a place to change into and out of these motoring costumes. Once women began to drive downtown to shop, parking was needed not only for the cars of businessmen, but for their wives as well, as they went about their errands for the family. Thus, early garages often included lounges where owners would wait for the retrieval of their cars, and to which packages could be delivered after shopping. Other services, such as baby sitting and stroller rental, also appeared.[2]

YOU AUTO BE WITH ME

Top: Postcard, circa 1910.
Right: St. Paul Garage, Baltimore, 1930.

Then as now, location was of foremost importance, but architectural design also played an important role in the early development of the parking garage. The Dupont Garage, at 2020 M Street, N.W., in Washington, D.C., constructed in 1906, offers an excellent example. Built on one of the busiest crosstown streets in the city and convenient to both chauffeurs' residences and a wealthy residential neighborhood, the garage had a handsome, classically detailed brick and stone facade. The entry and exit bays were given architectural prominence, and the main facade had large expanses of operable glass windows. Three stories high, fireproof, and constructed of reinforced concrete, the structure was a proud, civic architectural statement that added to the beauty of the

Above left: Acton Garage, New York City, 1906. Now known as the Monterey Garage, the Acton Garage is probably the oldest garage in continuous operation in the country.

Top right: Dupont Garage, 2020 M Street, N.W., Washington, D.C., 1906. Known as "the neighborhood garage," the Dupont served residents of the surrounding area.

Above: Clinton Garage, New York City, 1912. Early multistory garages could be found all across the country.

street and the city as a whole. The location of the garage, and its focus on good service, made it quite a success.[40]

Like the Dupont Garage, Atlanta's Georgian Terrace Hotel Garage, constructed in 1913, and Williams Parking Garage, constructed in 1917, were used by local residents; however, they lacked the grand civic presence of the Dupont. Many other cities also had well-located garages that were close to prominent neighborhoods and often convenient to hotels, yielding an early version of shared parking. Among the garages that attempted to blend in with the surrounding streetscape and to be good architectural neighbors were Connart's Garage, in Savannah, Georgia, and Leavitt Garage and Service Building, in Seattle, Washington, both constructed in 1909. Other similar garages were built in Cincinnati, Knoxville, Portland, and Toledo. In 1915, on Detroit's Woodward Avenue, Smith, Hinchman, & Grillis—one of the oldest architectural firms in continuous operation in the country—built two public garages.[41]

Early Municipal Garages

Along with cab companies and private citizens, municipalities were among the first purchasers of motorized vehi-

cles. In fact, the storage needs of municipally owned vehicle fleets (fire trucks, ambulances, mail trucks, and delivery vehicles) helped spur the standardization of garages. By the first year of the 20th century, "New York City had its first automobile ambulance; a railroad motor bus was used for the first time, and gasoline engine wagons were tried out for the distribution and collection of the mails."[42] Detroit, the first city to centralize control of its motor vehicles (in 1919), built main and branch municipal garages throughout the city.[43]

Motorized vehicles were a particular priority for fire stations. At the time that a destructive fire broke out in Boston in 1872, an outbreak of distemper had killed or incapacitated all of the city's fire horses: 14 people died, and 776 buildings were destroyed. All the damage was attributed to the lack of horses to power the fire vehicles—hence the importance of seeking a safe new movement device for cities. Fire departments were among the first municipal agencies to use mechanized vehicles in downtowns.[44]

The first fire-station garages emerged just after the turn of the 20th century, and took on many visual forms—from modest, houselike buildings to grand civic structures.

Fire station, Amarillo, Texas, 1915. Municipalities were among the first to adopt mechanized vehicles, and fire stations were among the earliest parking garages.

The Parking Garage

Bungalow-style fire stations, built in Denver in 1915, and a neoclassical station, built in Ocean City, New Jersey, are two examples of the range of architectural styles. Whatever their style, local fire stations were a source of civic pride. From Amarillo, Texas, to New York City, fire departments displayed their new motorized vehicles in photographs, always positioning them out in front of their garages.[45]

In 1916, the city of Cleveland came up with a concept that was ahead of its time: a garage for city vehicles that also served as a public parking garage, creating income for the city. This is the earliest example of municipal provision of public parking.[46]

Garages for Competing Manufacturers

Early automobiles were not stored for sale, as they are today. Instead, many were produced on demand, with minimal overhead. Thus, early parking garages often had two purposes—to provide storage space for current owners and to provide advertising and sales spaces for manufacturers: "Walter Stearn's New York Automobile Exchange at 114 Fifth Avenue was a successful garage with sales agencies for Packard, the International Company, Locomobile, the United Power Vehicle Company, and Adams and McMurtie."[47] The garage owners generally had nothing to do with the sale of autos, nor were they associated with the manufacturers in any other way.[48]

The new technology created a market crowded with competing manufacturers: of the 5,000 companies that attempted to get into the business, 3,000 succeeded—at least for a while. At the beginning of the 20th century, chains of automobile storage and repair stations began to emerge, to meet the growing demand. The Manhattan Automobile Company, for example, offered garage services, maintenance, and repair for cars of any manufacture. The Banker Brothers Company, the eastern distributor for nine automobile manufacturers, had public garages in New York, Philadelphia, and Pittsburgh. In 1903, its garage in Philadelphia employed 35 people, had room for 150 automobiles, and was considered one of the largest and best storage and maintenance garages in the United States.[49]

John Wanamaker, owner of Wanamakers, the Philadelphia-based department store chain, began selling motor vehicles in his stores and pioneered garages in New York and Philadelphia. His Philadelphia automobile station, opened in 1901, occupied a city block; in addition to providing emergency service for breakdowns, the station offered driving lessons.[50]

Times Square Auto Company, New York City, circa 1925. An example of a combination dealership and garage.

Parking Garage Design Emerges

Very early in the 20th century, competitions and exhibits exploring the architectural opportunities presented by the parking garage began to appear. The first, in 1904, was for automobile clubhouses and was sponsored by the Department of Architecture at Washington University in St. Louis; the winning design was published in *Architectural Review.*[51]

In 1910, *The American Architect* published the winning entries for a competition in which participants had been asked to design a seven-car garage and chauffeur's quarters for a wealthy homeowner living in the countryside. (Because early automobiles were unreliable, well-to-do owners often owned many vehicles, so as to always have one at the ready.) In this competition, designers were beginning to explore a larger building type, but still within a residential context.[52]

In a 1913 competition sponsored by *The Brickbuilder,* the requirements included a garage, long-term storage, an automobile salesroom, a repair shop, and a chauffeurs' recreation room. Entries were to combine modern technology, such as elevators and turntables, with a beaux-arts terra-cotta facade. The elaborate bas-relief ornamentation on the facades—often featuring touring cars with winged wheels, occupied by ladies whose scarves billowed in the wind—reflected the sense of excitement about automobile travel that dominated the popular imagination then, and continues to do so today.[53]

Thus, the first coherent approach to the design of a parking garage was beginning to take form: it involved thinking of the building as a machine for the automobile, and creating designs that combined new technologies with an established architectural language. The second-prize entry for the 1913 *Brickbuilder* competition, submitted by Valere de Mari, of Chicago, did just that: mounted on the traditional facade was an oversized electrical sign that used large, simple letters to announce the building's presence. The sign—easily viewed from a moving car—was a direct response to the automobile's speed, and reflected the transformative power of the new automobile technology.

Garages for the Landed Gentry

Like urban stables, barns were often used to store automobiles, but without being designed for their unique needs. And, as might be expected, multicar garages designed for the landed homeowner were related to typical barn structures in size and scale; however, the new garages were specifically designed to accommodate the automobile. They were also integrated into the homes' architectural aesthetic: the relationship between the garage and the main home was similar to that of Italian villas and their functional buildings, except that the emphasis was on movement between the garage, the chauffeur's residence, and other functional buildings.

The designs for this new building type were presented in lavish ink renderings that showed how the garage could be integrated into both the landscape and the overall design of the residence. The facades and the massing of the structures were not modern in style—that is, they did not reflect the mechanistic character of the automobile—but their interior plans reflected the modern practical needs of the automobile and chauffeur.[1]

Brandon Smith, first-prize entry, 1910 design competition.

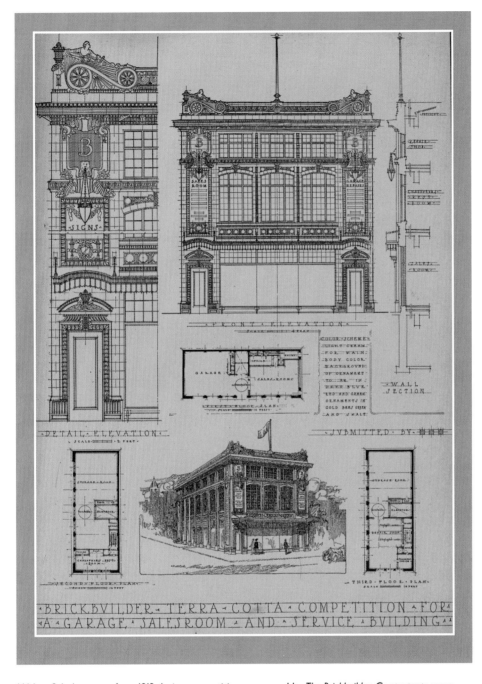

Walter Scholer, entry for a 1913 design competition sponsored by *The Brickbuilder*. Contestants were asked to design a combined showroom and garage.

- Parking facility design today is as important and exciting as it was in its early years.

- The building type is currently subject to new pressures, and is again having tremendous influence on the built environment.

- Early designs that incorporated elevators, turntables, and integrated facades can be revitalized for today.

- Location, size, and scale are just as important today as they were in the early years of the parking garage.

- The automobile, once regarded as the solution to urban environmental problems, was designed both to be part of, and to improve, the urban environment. It can play this role again.

CHAPTER 2

Early Design Issues
The Utilitarian versus the Symbolic View of the Car

What is the relationship of the automobile to man? Is the auto a machine used principally for utilitarian purposes, or is it a symbol of personal freedom? The answer to these questions defined two different spatial approaches to the design of the parking garage, one based on the elevator and the other on the ramp.

A designer formulating ideas for a project must first understand what the client wants and needs; this understanding informs the creation of the design. In the case of the parking garage, an understanding of client needs was complicated by two factors: first, by the presence of a mechanical "client"—the auto, which had its own set of needs; and second, by the fact that the ultimate clients were automobile drivers, a diverse and rapidly expanding group. The emergence of a building type mirrors the design process, but with factors other than client needs coming into play—including history, aesthetics, planning, theory, structure, function, and ideas about the future. New spatial ideas for the parking garage emerged because of the combination of all these factors.

Initially, mechanics, chauffeurs, and garage attendants (also known as car jockeys) were the only ones who parked vehicles in a garage, an arrangement that allowed significant flexibility in garage design. Cars were often parked back-to-back, or in no particular arrangement; in either case, it was necessary to move one car in order to free another. At the time, however, this was not considered a major disadvantage, as it was rarely necessary to move many cars simultaneously. In multistory garages, elevators were used to move vehicles vertically between floors, and the top floors were typically reserved for long-term storage (also known as "dead storage"). Many automobiles were stored for long periods, and the use of attendants made it possible to maximize storage space, even when the first ramp garages appeared.

As cars proliferated, however, drivers began to enjoy the freedom that automobiles provided, along with a new sense of control over their environment. The emotions aroused by this new sense of freedom and mobility became an overwhelming force in shaping garage

Facing page: Facade of Eliot Street Garage, Boston, 1927. This structure featured circular ramps.

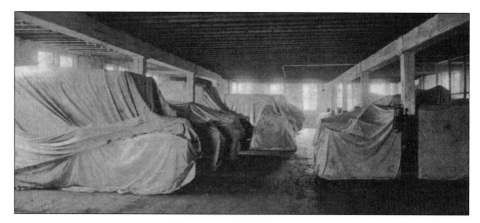

Top: White Garage, New York City, 1910. Long-term storage (known as "dead storage") was common in early garages and was typically located on the up-permost levels.

Right: Old Post Road Garage, Tarrytown, New York, 1909. This garage added an elevator in the back to increase the avail-able storage area.

design. This effect was most obvious in the 1920s, when the burgeoning car population created the need for numerous multilevel garages, and the phenomenon of self-parking first appeared.[1]

The principal design debate of the time centered on a single issue: whether the vertical movement system would be the ramp or the elevator. Ultimately, of course, the ramp became the system of choice—but not without a debate. The technology of the car demanded a new way of thinking about and designing space. This was true not just in the broad sense—designing cities to allow for the greater mo-

bility associated with the automobile—but was also reflected in the practical specifics of a built form: the parking garage. The solutions to two principal design problems—how the auto would move through the confined space of this build-ing type, and how the number of cars could be maximized—tapped both technology and emotion.

The first solution, the elevator, was grounded solely in the world of technology. The ramp, however, had appeal on a number of historical and emotional grounds: it was linked to the landscape (both because it mimicked natural forms, and because some of the earliest ramp garages were built on

- The invention of safety glass in the late teens made safety-glass windshields practical and allowed the development of hard tops, providing some protection from the elements for both the car and its passengers.

- In 1920, the U.S. fatality rate per 100 million vehicle-miles (160,934,400 vehicle-kilometers) was approximately 30 for horse-drawn vehicles and approximately 20 for automobiles.

- By 1920, 3,191 miles (5,135 kilometers) of federal-aid roads—that is, roads built with federal assistance—had been improved or constructed, making dust less of a drawback to driving.

- In 1921, William Eno established the Eno Foundation for Highway Traffic Regulation; its mission was to address the complex traffic issues of the automobile age.

- During the 1920s, the natty movie star with the fast convertible roadster became a popular image.

- The Long Island Motor Parkway, a private toll road constructed by William K. Vanderbilt between 1906 and 1911, was the first limited-access road in New York. It inspired Robert Moses, Long Island Park Commissioner, to build parkways across Long Island. To obtain land to do so, Moses relied on a 1924 state law that gave powers of appropriation.

- Writer Lewis Mumford was so impressed by three limited-access roads built in Westchester County, New York, in the 1920s, that he wrote (with Benton Mackaye, in *Harper's Magazine*) of a day when a motorist could drive "with less anxiety and more safety at 60 miles per hour than he used to have in the old roadtown confusion at 25."

- In 1924, Secretary of Commerce Herbert Hoover convened the first National Conference on Street and Highway Safety.

- In 1925, both Washington and Los Angeles banned horses from their downtowns.

- By 1925, the average auto had been driven over 25,000 miles (40,233 kilometers) before it reached the junkyard.

- By 1929, there were between 5 and 5.5 million autos and trucks on 6.5 million farms. Rural residents had more need for private transportation than city dwellers.

- By the end of the 1920s, belt highways were being built around congested areas; the resulting increase in traffic led to a 5 percent jump in traffic fatalities.

- A survey conducted by Hanff-Metzger, Inc., found that in the late 1920s, 24.3 percent of all drivers were women.

- Everything was in the auto's favor: by 1924, the horse and carriage was virtually obsolete.

Movement Facts of the 1920s

In the United States, the decade after World War I was one of expansion, experimentation, and emancipation. The country was developing at a rapid rate, amid tremendous optimism.

---

sloping sites); it was a familiar structure that had already been used in barns and stables; it was in keeping with the sense of individual freedom that had become associated with auto travel; and it met drivers' increasingly strong demands to move rapidly—and independently—through the garage.

The Elevator Garage

In the 1920s, modern technologies such as the elevator and the turntable allowed designers to view the car as just another piece of modern machinery, to be manipulated and moved about. Then as now, technology offered freedom from physical drudgery, represented the promise of a better life, and held great fascination for the popular imagination. Even workers on auto assembly lines, who witnessed daily the emotional limitations of a world dominated by machines, lined up to buy cars—symbols of freedom from the repetitiveness of their daily lives.

The Otis safety elevator, in use for passengers and freight since 1852, seemed like a logical choice for transporting the automobile. Because elevators had been designed to handle heavy loads from the beginning and were already being used to move goods in manufacturing, they were a practical choice for moving cars. There were other advantages as well: an elevator could easily handle an inoperable car, whereas the same car would have to be towed up a ramp. The elevator also allowed garage construction to meet traditional building standards for floor-to-floor heights, and permitted the use of the new technologies used in warehouse construction. Finally, the elevator garage had the cachet of being "modern": it used new technology to meet the needs of the newest machine.

Examples of smaller, two-story elevator garages include the garage designed by Kirchhoff & Rose, Architects, for a location on Eighth Street, in Milwaukee, and the garage designed by Bernard Ebeling for the Boulevard Auto Company, in the Bronx. Both were built before 1911. Multistory elevator garages were also common; the garage designed by Marvin & Davis, Architects, for the Palmer and Singer Manufacturing Company, on Broadway in New York City, is an example. The J.A. McCaddon Garage, in San Diego, was typical for a small elevator garage: it had shops in front, parking

and an elevator in the back, and no turntable. Other small garages, such as the Waterville Garage, in Waterville, Maine, incorporated a turntable. The placement of the elevator and the turntable were design variables in early garages; several locations could be used, but no particular pattern or relationship became typical. And, since cars were not necessarily stored in rows, elevators were placed in every possible position.[2]

Regardless of the elevator's other advantages, however, the decisive issue became the number of cars that could be parked on a floor plate: because elevators allowed more space for parked cars than ramps, they were the more popular solution well into the 1920s. One elevator could handle the work for a 125-car garage—and, since large numbers of cars did not, in the early years, require retrieval simultaneously, one elevator was usually enough.

Nevertheless, by 1925, garages served by elevators alone had begun to disappear, as the ramp gained acceptance in parking garage design. The plans for the Portland Street Garage and the Eliot Street Garage, both in Boston, combine

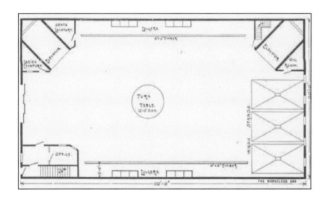

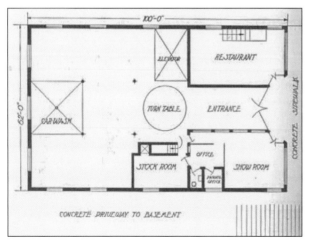

As designers sought the most efficient plan, elevators and turntables were positioned in many different ways.

Above left: Plan of White Garage, Boston, 1909.

Above right: Boulevard Auto Company Garage, Bronx, New York, pre-1911.

Left: Plan of Waterville Garage, Waterville, Maine, 1913.

The Parking Garage

an elevator with a ramp, an arrangement that had become typical by the mid- to late 1920s. By the end of the decade, garages that relied solely on elevators for vertical movement existed only in dense urban environments like New York, where land was a more valuable commodity, sites were smaller, and an extensive transit system rendered the newer, more efficient ramp garages less essential to the viability of the area.[3]

The Ramp Garage

Individual freedom was one of the founding principles of the United States, and Americans pride themselves on being independent thinkers and lovers of freedom. Especially in the early decades of the 20th century, the car was the perfect technological match for Americans' ideals, desires, and way of life. As the combination of the assembly line and creative financing techniques made the car affordable to the emerging middle class, the automobile came to represent physical and economic mobility, both symbolically and in reality. The car, the great social equalizer, held out the promise of freedom and success, fostering the independence that was instrumental in propelling the country's development.

This essentially emotional relationship between the automobile and its driver led to a design process—and, ultimately, to a garage structure—that was very different from that of the elevator garage. The new design emphasized the connection between the automobile, the driver, and the landscape—in a way that echoed the relationship between horse, rider, and landscape—and its premise was that the driver could completely control the movement of the car, *even when it was inside a building.* Thus, two factors led to the ultimate ascendance of the ramp design: the connection to the land, and the sense of personal freedom. Of course, as discussed in this book, many practical concerns also contributed to this evolution, but at bottom was a link between driver and automobile that was in many ways analogous to that between rider and horse. Although the differences between the two movement devices were profound, the auto, like the horse before it, met many emotional needs. Nevertheless, an auto, unlike a horse, is not a living being—and this fact led the parking garage, over the years, to become a place largely for machines, not living beings—a problem that persists to this day.

The major practical hurdle was to find a ramp design that would provide more parking spaces, and thus defeat the

Portland Street Garage, Boston, 1920. In the 1920s, larger garages often featured both a ramp and an elevator; elevators were useful for meeting peak demand and moving inoperable vehicles.

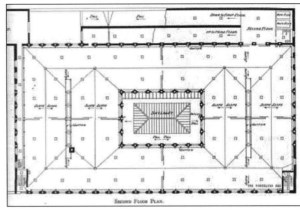

Top left: Fenway Garage, Boston, 1914. This early ramp garage minimized the length of the ramp through an innovative design: one parking level was positioned one-half floor above the street, and the other was positioned one-half floor below. The facade allowed this innovative parking design to be a part of the urban experience.

Top right: New York Taxicab Company garage, New York City, 1909. This was the first ramp garage recorded in the magazines of the time.

Above: Brown Garage, Des Moines, Iowa, 1915. In this early garage, which had an exterior ramp on the side and back of the structure, alarms signaled that an automobile was on the ramp.

elevator garage on the theoretical battlefield.[4] A four-story garage built for the New York Taxicab Company in 1909 was the earliest ramp recorded in the magazines of the time. The design of this facility, which featured "radical departures from the regular practice in garage construction," was in response to two factors: the cost of elevator equipment, and the need to move cabs rapidly into and out of the structure.[5] (During the two peak periods of the day, 700 cabs had to be transported almost simultaneously.) Although the garage did include two elevators, cabs moved from floor to floor by means of two straight, inclined, parallel ramps. Because maximizing speed of movement, rather than storage area, was the priority, the floor plan was 250 feet by 144 feet (76 meters by 44 meters). Another taxicab garage, described at the time as one of the most innovative of garage designs, housed only 175 cabs. Elevators were present in both of these garages because cars tended to slip when the floors of the inclines became greasy; elevators were also used to move inoperable vehicles.[6]

A 1989 article in The Parking Professional refers to another early ramp structure: a parking garage in Columbus, Ohio, reported to have been built in 1909, that was constructed of heavy timber with a ramp of wood. The garage faced a hotel and was two blocks from the state capitol building.[7]

Boston's Fenway Garage, an early, two-story public garage that did not have an elevator, was constructed in 1914. Built of reinforced concrete, the building offered 50,000 square feet (4,646 square meters) on each floor and was designed to house 400 cars in live storage and 100 in dead storage. The first-floor parking area was actually below street level, and the second was one half-story above street level. Access was provided by two 30-foot (nine-meter) ramps, with two lanes each, at an 8 percent grade. (At this stage of parking garage design, no rules had been set to determine grade, so it was shaped by the nature of the site, the limits of the automobile, and the designers' understanding.) As envisioned by the owners of the garage, the benefits of this ramp design were speed and freedom of movement: "no congestion on days when hundreds of cars are garaged temporarily."[8] Another innovative aspect of the Fenway Garage was the way the cars were parked: they were placed in rows, with a large clearance circle in front of every car. Thus, any car could be moved without bumping or moving any other car, an arrangement that also allowed the cars to be maintained and serviced without being moved.

Many early two-story ramp garages were built where the land sloped naturally, allowing access to each level from either end. Because this arrangement did not require cars to move between floors within the garage, no space was sacrificed to movement between levels. The Brown Garage, in Des Moines, Iowa, built in 1915, was one of the first recorded garages to have an exterior ramp. The building was 130 feet (40 meters) deep and three stories high. The 15-foot- (4.5-meter-) wide, two-way ramp had a 6 percent grade and a rise of eight feet (2.4 meters), and went around two sides

of the building, creating a blind turn for drivers. The design relied on the fact that the land was sloped, which meant that the second-floor entrance was very close to street grade, and that the first floor was on the lowest level, below street grade. When a car was driven onto the ramp that led to the third-floor entrance, the door opened automatically and an alarm sounded. This prevented conflict between two drivers who both wished to use the ramp. Thus did technology weave its way into every aspect of the new building type, even in the ramp garage.[9]

Another early ramp garage, the A.C.A. Annex Garage, built in 1917 in New York, was four stories high, with long-term storage on the top floor. Like many other early ramp garages, this garage contained an elevator as well, although it was typically used only for access to the fourth level. The ramps were straight, had a 10 percent grade, and were 18 feet (5.5 meters) wide, to allow for two-way traffic.[10]

In Chicago in 1918, Holabird & Roche, Architects and Engineers, created the Hotel La Salle Garage, an innovative six-story structure designed for both rapid movement and maximum storage capacity. As was typical for a garage of the time, flat-slab construction was used for the floors; the concrete

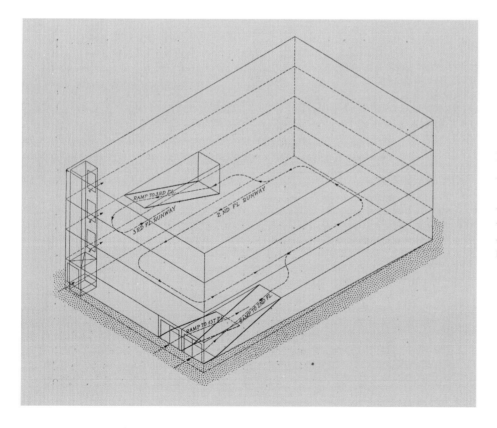

A.C.A. Annex Garage, New York City, 1917. This garage featured three levels connected by straight, 18-foot- (5-meter-) wide ramps that allowed two-way traffic. The two levels were one-half floor above and one-half floor below street level.

ramp that connected the floors, however, was a half-circle design, and the space within the curve of the ramp was used for elevator shafts, heating and ventilating shafts, and a stairway. Since the automobile elevators were used primarily to supplement the ramp, only two were required. The elevators were called into service when traffic was light, and to carry cars for painting or repair, but would not have been able to handle the full capacity of the garage. Like the A.C.A. Annex Garage, the Hotel LaSalle Garage relied mostly on the ramp for peak traffic times, and on the elevators for other purposes. The Hotel LaSalle Garage provided easy access for people who drove to work in the business district, and was well designed to fit into the character of the city.[11]

Ordinarily, the inclusion of a ramp—and of elevators, heating and ventilating shafts, and stairways—reduces the area available for storage. But the design of the Hotel LaSalle Garage, which placed all functional uses, including washrooms and other accessory areas, within the helical ramp, yielded more parking space than the typical, straight-ramp garage. Even with this space-saving design, however, which clustered functional uses within a single block of space at one end of the building, the garage had fewer parking spaces than would have been found in a facility served only by elevators.

When a building is designed, especially in the beaux-arts tradition, it is standard to create a "poche"—a block of spaces clustered together—to accommodate mechanical, plumbing, and elevator systems. Such a space is normally thought of as merely functional, not as one for daily human occupation. But in the design of a ramp garage, this basic architectural precept was eventually turned inside out: both the poche *and* the open space came to be used by both humans and automobiles. This new way of thinking, which was in line with the discussions of function and design taking place in the architectural community at the time, allowed designers to focus primarily on functionality.

The Elevator versus the Ramp

In the early years of the multistory garage, no ramp design could provide as many parking spaces within the same amount of floor area as an elevator garage, making the elevator the movement system of choice. But as the debate continued and the demand for parking spaces increased,

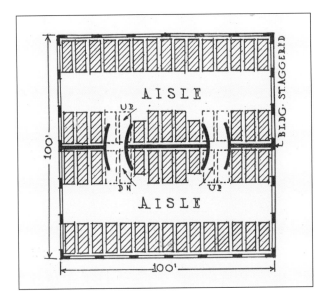

The ramp configuration of the patented D'Humy system maximized the number of parking spaces in a 100-foot by 100-foot (30-meter by 30-meter) floor plan, changing the garage building type forever. In the D'Humy system, splitting and staggering the floors yielded a more efficient layout, shorter ramps, better views for drivers, and a simple fire door arrangement.

Above: D'Humy ramp system.

Right: D'Humy ramp, section.

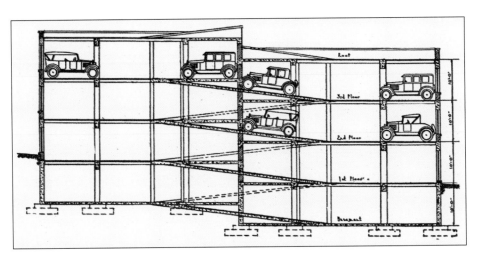

The Parking Garage

other plusses and minuses emerged. Elevators were costly to operate and to maintain, and often broke down; they also required the use of an attendant to park the cars. Moreover, because only one car could be brought up or down at a time (a factor that became of increasing importance), elevators were also slower during periods of peak automobile use. Ramps were difficult and expensive to build and hard for drivers to maneuver, but they allowed more cars to move simultaneously and created the potential for drivers to park their own cars.[12]

In 1921, writing in *The Architectural Forum,* Harold F. Blanchard, an automotive engineer for the Ramp Buildings Corporation and one of the most vocal participants in discussions of parking garage design, identified the ramp versus the elevator as the "major technical issue" in the quest for parking. Blanchard regarded the ramp as the older solution—even older than the stair—and also saw that its appeal stemmed, in part, from the freedom associated with driving one's own car. In Blanchard's view, the individual nature of the driver's experience dictated different spatial arrangements than, for example, the great gathering rooms of train terminals.[13]

Using a floor area of 100 feet by 100 feet (30 meters by 30 meters) as the basis for his calculation, Blanchard compared the number of parking spaces allowed by the elevator and the ramp. He found that the elevator would take up only six car spaces per floor, whereas a typical ramp would take up 12. However, Blanchard also found that when he compared an elevator garage, two other ramp designs, and an innovative design known as the D'Humy system, the D'Humy system allowed more cars to be parked than the elevator garage, by two cars per floor. As an example of the D'Humy system at work, Blanchard pointed to Boston's Portland Street Garage: the garage, which was built in 1920, housed 444 cars on six floors. (The garage still retained three elevators, without which it would have had even more storage space for cars.)[14]

It was the D'Humy system, an innovative and functional new ramp design, that finally started to tip the scales in favor of the ramp and that ultimately shaped the future direction of garage design. This new system was created under four influences: the evolving technology of the automobile; new explorations of ramp structure; the notion that form follows function; and the driver's emotional connection to the automobile as a symbol of freedom and movement. It was a perfect spatial expression of modern architectural innovation.

The D'Humy Ramp Garage

The D'Humy ramp system, first introduced in 1918 by Fernand D'Humy, the designer, and his partner, Fred Moe, was based in part on the Fenway Garage. (The patent was issued in 1920.) The plan of the garage was split in half, and the floors were staggered halfway above each other; this design reduced the difference in height between one floor and the next and allowed the ramps to be shorter. There were two ramps, each 30 feet (nine meters) long and at an 8 percent grade. To allow direct traffic flow up and down, the ramps had two lanes. At the time the D'Humy system was designed, some cities had already implemented fire codes for parking garages, and these codes required ramps to be closed off from parking floors. The D'Humy system met this requirement through automatic fire doors positioned at the split at the end of each floor, at either the top or the bottom of the ramp. This arrangement eliminated the need to surround the ramps with walls (the design approach used in most other ramp garages). By allowing the driver a clear view within the garage, the open design of the system resolved another early problem with ramp garages.[15]

The Book Tower Garage, in Detroit, designed by Louis Kamper, Inc., Architects, in the late 1920s, was an early example of the D'Humy system, as was the Baker Garage, in Minneapolis. In a minor twist on the original design, the Book Tower Garage featured slightly curving ramps, which created even more parking spaces. The Baker Garage, built in 1927 and operated successfully for many years, was a ten-level, city-owned garage with an expansion capability of 18 additional levels—an indication of the heights to which it was assumed the D'Humy system could be designed. (It is now known that no matter what the ramp design, navigating this many levels is not a comfortable experience for the average driver.) The footprint of the Baker Garage was 100 feet by 155 feet (30 meters by 47 meters).[16]

The D'Humy system reduced long-term operating costs, allowed more rapid traffic flow during peak demand periods, provided better fire protection, improved sight lines, and maximized the number of parking spaces by reducing the length of the ramp and eliminating the elevator completely. The approach gained wide acceptance, bringing the construction of elevator garages almost to a halt. The splitting of the floors was a breakthrough in internal spatial relationships that encouraged a new way of thinking about movement—both in general, and in practical terms for the parking garage.

Baker Garage & Baker Bldg.
2nd Ave. Side.

77768

The Parking Garage

Other Ramp Designs

Other ramp systems in use at the time of the D'Humy design were the straight, single-ramp system; the two-way ramp system; the elliptical ramp; the concentric spiral ramp; and the double-spiral ramp.[17]

The most basic design, the straight, single-ramp system, was found in many early garages. In this simple plan, upward and downward ramps were separate, and were located on opposite sides of the garage. The disadvantage was that a driver had to travel around the entire floor plate to gain access to another level. The two-way ramp system solved this problem by locating the ramps right next to each other, so that a car could bypass a floor and move to the next level without circling through the entire garage.[18]

The elliptical ramp system created more parking spaces than the straight, single-ramp system but required 140 feet (43 meters) along one dimension. This design, as implemented in New York's Commodore-Biltmore Garage, which was constructed in 1919, easily accommodated a flow of traffic both up and down. In one of the first uses of what proved to be the most efficient approach, the designers of the Commodore-Biltmore Garage laid out the parking-space pattern first, then integrated the ramp system and the column spacing.[19]

Boston's Eliot Street Garage is an example of the concentric spiral ramp, which had both inner and outer circular ramps. The disadvantage of this design was that to allow sufficient turning radius for the nested ramps, a very large floor plate was required: the autos of the time required an inside circle 60 feet (18 meters) in diameter and an outside circle 90 feet (27 meters) in diameter. In the Richmond Garage, in Richmond, Virginia, designed by Lee, Smith & Vandervoort and constructed in 1928, the two ramps are interlaced in a double-spiral pattern that was invented by Horace L. Smith, one of the partners in the firm. The arrangement reduced the amount of space required for the ramps.[20]

Innovations in Ramp Design

In 1922, Albert Kahn, Inc., Architects, the architectural firm that worked with Henry Ford and almost every other auto manufacturer, built a continuous sloping floor system in the Fort Shelby Garage, in Detroit. The entire floor had an incline of 4 percent, creating a continuous ramp from the ground to the top; the result was a precursor to Frank Lloyd

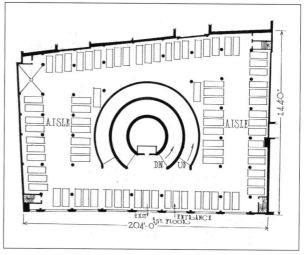

Facing page: Baker Garage, Minneapolis, 1927. Another early example of the D'Humy ramp system, this garage was ten stories high and designed to accommodate an additional 18 stories.

Top: Commodore-Biltmore Garage, New York City, 1927. At this garage, the parking pattern was designed first, and the elliptical ramp was chosen to fit at the back of the building.

Above: Eliot Street Garage floor plan, Boston, 1927. Inner and outer circular ramps required a great deal of space.

Wright's vision for Sugarloaf Mountain. Garages with continuously sloping floors provided the maximum number of parking spaces, eliminated the attendant, maintained a constant flow of movement throughout the garage, and allowed the driver of the automobile to remain in control of the car at all times. Once this design evolved to the point where it was easy for both cars and drivers to navigate, it would become one of the most familiar designs in the history of the parking garage.[21]

In 1924, Frank Lloyd Wright was commissioned to design a "structure on the summit of Sugarloaf Mountain," in Maryland, that would "serve as an objective for short motor trips."[22] Wright responded initially by designing continuous spiraling helicoids (round ramps) around a domed core. The automobile ascended on one spiraling helicoid and then descended on the other. The descending ramp provided parking for 200 to 500 hundred vehicles; the surrounding mountainside offered space for an additional 1,000 vehicles. Although it was never built, this vision granted the ultimate wish of every parking garage designer: to completely merge the ramp and the parking area, maximizing the number of parking spaces and integrating storage space and traffic flow. Wright later used the same approach to design a self-service garage in Pittsburgh, adjacent to the Kauffman Department Store, but that design was never constructed either. Still later, Wright's design for New York's Guggenheim Museum reflected his continued fascination with the construction of a spiral ramp—in this case a pedestrian ramp. By the time the Guggenheim was constructed, space (the shape that would appear if you poured gelatin into a building, and then removed the building), and flow (the experience of moving through space) had merged: the museum is not a series of discrete rooms, but an integration of space and flow. The emergence of a ramp design that was integral to the parking area contributed to breakthroughs in the notions of space and time.[23]

This important breakthrough in ramp construction was also reflected in the Kehler Garage, which was constructed in Louisville, Kentucky, in the early 1920s. Four stories high, 50 feet (15 meters) wide, and capable of storing 160 automobiles, the garage featured a design that was patented by the Garage Experts Association of Louisville. Each floor was sloped at a 7 percent grade, and the connecting ramps were sloped at 10 percent. Cars could be parked on the sloped floor plates, and the design minimized the length of the ramps. Modifications of this design were later built in Detroit and Cleveland.[24]

During the early years of parking garage design, architectural firms began to specialize in this building type. In the late 1920s, for example, the Richmond, Virginia, firm of Lee, Smith & Vandervoort, Architects and Engineers, worked in conjunction with the Auto Ramp Corporation to design the double helix (screw) ramp, which could be entered from any level and allowed the driver to go either up or down from the point of entry. (The modern version of this design is called an express ramp, or speed ramp.) The ramp had a 13 percent grade and was located at the back of the building, allowing the front facades to remain part of the existing streetscape; for its time, the design was an extraordinary architectural accomplishment, although Da Vinci's sketchbooks had envisioned a similar form several centuries earlier. Cherished and still in use today, the garage is now connected to a new parking facility.[25]

Early Standardization

Because early autos varied widely in size, weight, and turning radius, designing parking layouts to any standard was initially very difficult. Moreover, ensuring that the parking garage could accommodate the largest autos and turning radii added to the structure's size and cost, compromising feasibility. However, by the end of the 1920s, the number of auto manufacturers had been reduced to a few, and the resulting standardization of cars allowed the standardization of parking garages to begin.[26]

Studies showing optimum layouts were published as early as 1927. The building block for internal dimensions was the one-row, two-row, three-row, or four-row arrangement of cars. By this time, designers had begun to approach the parking garage as an interrelated system, combining structural, functional, technological, and urban-design considerations. Since such interrelationships are the backbone of any good architectural design, it might be assumed that the parking garage needed no further tinkering. But as the 1930s arrived, the challenges of that decade, including changes in the automobile, led the parking garage in new directions.[27]

In a 1929 article in *The Architectural Record,* a group of expert engineers and parking garage designers wrote that "because the parking garage business is still in its infancy, commercial garages must necessarily be extremely efficient from the economic standpoint if they are to compete with future buildings of improved character and with subsidized garages which will rapidly increase in number within the next

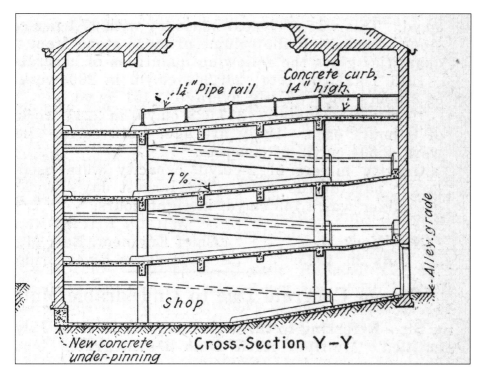

Left: Kehler Garage, Louisville, Kentucky, 1925. The completely sloped floors of this garage were patented and constructed by the Garage Experts Association, of Louisville.

Below: Fort Shelby Garage, Detroit, 1922. By the mid-1920s, the completely sloped floor had become a feature of garage design. This garage was designed by Albert Kahn.

Albert Kahn (1869–1942)

Albert Kahn, the most important industrial architect of all time, designed many early and significant parking garages, although this aspect of his career is rarely discussed. Kahn's firm built garages all over the country, but his best-known parking facility is the 13-story ramp garage that is part of Detroit's 28-story Fisher Building, an art deco–style National Historic Landmark that is still in use.[1]

In 1891, while working for the architectural firm of Mason and Rice, Kahn was awarded a one-year scholarship to study in Europe. In 1895, several years after his return, Albert and his brother Julius, an engineer, founded an architectural firm that still practices worldwide today. The brothers first achieved recognition in 1907, for the Packard Motor Car Company building #10, a multistory structure based on the Kahn system of internally reinforced concrete and the Kahn steel-trussed bar. Concrete construction improved fire protection while creating larger expanses of unobstructed space. (The interior columns in the Packard building were spaced 30 feet [nine meters] apart, quite a large span at the time.) In another improvement developed by Kahn, who wanted to increase the flow of light into the building interior, enormous windows filled the concrete-framed grid that served as the building's facade. Kahn and his brother continued to design innovative buildings with long spans between columns. These efforts culminated in the Willow Run Factory, in Ypsilanti, Michigan, which was designed to hold the B-24 bomber. Kahn also designed many private homes, offices, apartments, university buildings, and civic buildings in a range of styles.[2]

Unlike his contemporaries, Kahn was not inclined to "romanticize the machine";[3] instead, his designs for auto showrooms and garages relied on both his trained aesthetic vision and his understanding of function. One of Kahn's first garage structures, created for the Standard Auto Company between 1905 and 1908, was considered the most elaborate structure of its kind in Detroit. In addition to storage space, the one-story structure included showrooms, and provided repair and cleaning services. The beautifully proportioned facade was designed to blend in with the surrounding urban fabric. The Kahn Realty Garage was a simple, factory-style structure with brick walls and wood posts. The front was two stories high, and the back section was a 12-foot- (3.7-meter-) high, one-story structure with lantern windows at the peak of the facade.[4]

Kahn's early multistory parking garages had concrete frames, were built using factory-construction methods, and relied on elevators for vertical movement of cars. In the garage built in 1910 for the Chicago Motor Car Company, simple ornamentation on the beautifully proportioned facade created a visual link between the utilitarian structure within and the more traditionally detailed facades of the surrounding office buildings. Other garage designs were more heavily ornamented, depending upon their location, their use, and whether they were connected to other buildings.[5]

In the late teens, just as the tide was turning in favor of the ramp garage, Kahn began work on an elevator garage for the

Detroit Athletic Club. Although he shifted in mid-design to create a ramp garage, he retained the original ornamented facade. The building, which opened in 1921, was six stories high, had capacity for 800 automobiles, and included an automatic passenger elevator. Although the interior parking ramp was recently rebuilt, the beautiful facade of this parking garage was maintained and still graces downtown Detroit today.[6]

Kahn often incorporated parking garages within his large office structures. The first "skyscraper" garage—with 11 floors of parking, each of which held 80 cars, and offices above—was part of Detroit's First National Bank building, which Kahn designed in 1919–1922. The S.S. Kresge Administration Building, built in Detroit in 1931, was another example of an incorporated garage, in this case underground.[7]

In 1926, a garage featuring an innovative ramp design was attached to Detroit's Fort Shelby Hotel; it was yet another example of Kahn's ability to design storage structures that were as beautiful as his other buildings. The Detroit News Garage, built in 1931, was considered a

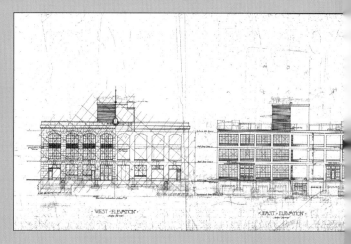

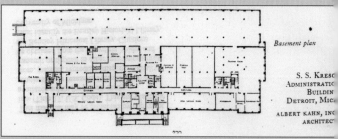

Top: Detroit Athletic Club, 1915–1921.

Above: S.S. Kresge Administration Building, Detroit, 1931.

Opposite, top: Fort Shelby Garage, Detroit, 1926.

Opposite, bottom: Detroit News Garage, 1931.

fine example of an "honest" parking garage—one that didn't look like a "Renaissance Palace."[8] By today's standards, the garage looks like most other buildings of the time, with a beautifully proportioned brick facade that highlights the frame structure behind it, and draws the eye to the vertical tower of the elevator shaft.

Kahn, a man who built 2,000 factories, received little recognition from his peers because of their lack of respect for the utilitarian building. In their view, the factory and the parking garage were not building types that fit within the "art of architecture," which was associated with the public, residential, or civic space and form. However, utilitarian buildings are often opportunities for experimentation with new ideas about space and form. Kahn understood that the parking garage is a public building, and part of the civic space of the city. Although it was not until the late 1920s that his contributions were recognized, Kahn revolutionized every architectural building type by understanding the importance of parking within the world of modern design.[9]

few years."[28] Calculating efficiency ratios and the required square footage per car for all the basic ramp systems, the authors of the article found, once again, that the D'Humy design was the most efficient, requiring only 218 square feet (20 square meters) per car and achieving an efficiency ratio (parking area to other areas of the floor plate) of 51 percent, based on a parking floor of 100 feet by 200 feet (30 meters by 61 meters). The purpose of the article was not to suggest that one ramp system was better than another regardless of site constraints, but to provide designers, builders, and owners with enough information to decide for themselves what was best for a given situation. As is clear from the quotation, one of the authors' main concerns was competition from the "subsidized garage"—that is, a garage that was part of another building. Because zoning codes had begun to require a certain number of parking spaces for each building type, garages were more and more likely to be combined with other building uses, such as offices, hotels, and apartment buildings. This change would become a key issue in garage construction and in the evolution of parking garage design.[29]

The Modern Garage Emerges

Two hallmarks of the parking facilities of today emerged between 1930 and 1950: the first was the open-air deck, which developed when autos no longer required protection from the weather; the second was the complete shift to self-parking. These two developments led to a complete shift in design thinking—to a focus on functionality and practicality at the expense of many other concerns, such as visual appeal and integration into the urban environment. But this practical focus was also very much in keeping with the essence of modernism: if form follows function, then why not allow the interior of the building—the ramp—to be exposed and expressed on the exterior?

The Open-Deck Garage

It was not until the advent, in 1935, of an all-steel turret top, more durable paints, gasoline suitable for year-round driving, and engines that could withstand the cold that it became possible to construct the open-deck parking garages that are typical today.[30] Boston's Cage Garage—commissioned by Sam Eliot, designed by Coolidge, Shepley, Bulfinch and Abbott, and erected by the Business Men's Garage, Inc.—was a pioneering effort in the development of open-deck parking.

Built in 1933, the garage was razed in 1985, to make room for an office building.

Particularly with the advent of the underground garage, the provision of mechanical ventilation became one of the principal design issues of the day. This problem was solved in the Cage Garage by simply eliminating the walls, which allowed the car exhaust to escape naturally. This first open-deck garage was followed by another, constructed in 1936 by Kauffman's Department Store, in Philadelphia. The increasing acceptance of the open-deck garage eventually led to new fire codes.[31]

The Self-Park Garage

Although some early garages had allowed auto drivers access to the floors above the entry level (typically theater patrons, or businessmen who were regular customers), in most garages before 1950, cars were parked by attendants. The attendants were fast and efficient, but there were only so many of them; moreover, the man-lift (the mechanical device used by the attendants to move quickly between floors) was only so fast. Waiting for the attendant, especially after large events, was often very time-consuming, and the completely self-park garage was viewed as a way of solving this problem. Most important, however, was the perception of drivers, who now preferred to remain in control of their vehicles at all times, and who believed not only that the attendants slowed down the process, but that they caused damage to vehicles. Attempts to create self-park facilities that were easy to access and to navigate yielded some unique designs; one example is the parking garage built in the early 1960s for the Texas Bank and Trust Company, which has multiple entry and exit ramps nested one on top of the other and consecutive, street-level entries.[32]

Given the assumption that the driver would park the car, the goals of ramp design were to provide shorter travel times, easy entry and exit, user-friendly ramps, and more parking spaces. One of the first self-park garages to be advertised as such was built by J.C. Nichols, in 1948, at Kansas City's Country Club Plaza. Constructed on a sloping site, the three-level structure was free to patrons and provided direct entrances to the adjacent buildings from the second and third levels.[33]

The General Petroleum Corporation Garage, in Los Angeles, designed by Welton Becket and built in 1948, was a re-thinking of the continuous spiral, rectangular in plan, that brought renewed attention to that form. Two garages—one designed by Robert Law Weed and Associates in Miami, and

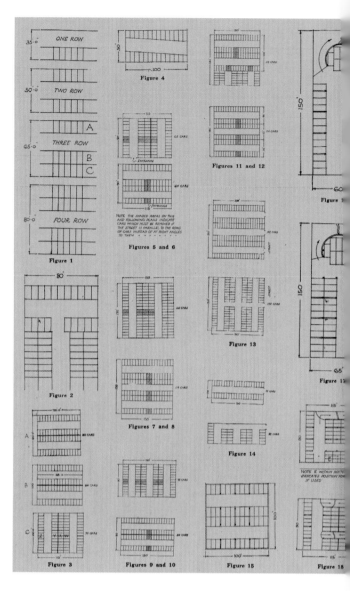

Examples of garage layouts. In the 1920s, designers experimented with different ramp and parking layouts to discover the most efficient arrangement for specific site conditions.

the other designed by Walter Wurdeman and Welton Becket, for Los Angeles Power and Light—featured updated versions of the D'Humy system's staggered floor. Weed retained the simplicity of the original split-level system, but modified the design by slightly overlapping the floor plates (which was possible because fire walls were not required) and reducing the overall building width. This approach, which allowed ramp garages to be built on smaller sites than ever before, also appeared in Atlanta in 1954, at the Williams Parking Deck, a self-park facility designed by Richard Aeck; in this structure, there was even greater overlap of the split levels.[34]

Many self-park garages followed in cities around the country.[35] The Dennison Garage, built in 1954 in Indianapolis, was "the fifth purpose-built self-park garage in the U.S."; its park-it-yourself design also included passenger elevators.[36] Grant Park North, developed by Ralph Burke Associates and built in Chicago in 1954, was an underground, 2,800-space garage designed for self-parking; however, because self-parking had not yet been fully accepted by the market, especially in underground facilities, 15 percent of the spaces were designated for customer assistance. San Francisco's Downtown Center Garage, built in 1955 by George Applegarth, was one of the earliest garages to advertise self-parking architecturally, by placing its speed ramp on the structure's most prominent street corner; the building also featured a large sign indicating that it was a self-park facility. By the end of the 1950s, the self-park garage was everywhere: it had become the garage of the decade.

Not all self-park garages were new construction; some were conversions of existing garages. Such conversions faced a number of difficulties: older ramps were often too tightly configured for the newer, larger automobiles; ramp slopes were often excessive; and the actual number of parking spaces available between the columns was often limiting. Striping and bright colors could improve these tight and often dangerous conditions, but only minimally. Since self-parking created the need for revenue control, ticket dispensers had to be installed, but this was a relatively simple improvement if space was available at the entry points. The Cleveland Plaza Hotel Garage, originally built in the late 1930s and early 1940s, was first converted to a movie theater; in the 1960s, it became an attended parking facility to serve the original 1912 hotel next door. The building's conversion to self-park, in 1977, required the addition of a passenger elevator and a pedestrian fire stair, and new striping on a steep ramp. Even though 30 parking spaces were lost

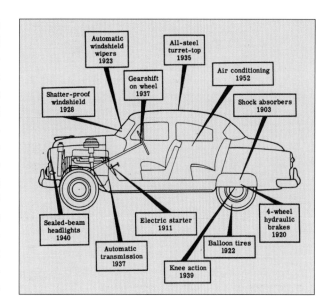

Top: Advances in the automobile. The development of the car influenced the evolution of parking garage design, leading ultimately to the modern ramp garage that is familiar today.

Above: Cage Garage, Boston, 1933. The first open-deck parking garage in the United States was commissioned by Sam Eliot; designed by Coolidge, Shepley, Bulfinch and Abbott; and erected by the Business Men's Garage, Inc.

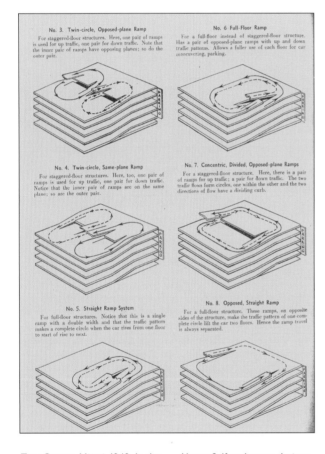

No. 3. Twin-circle, Opposed-plane Ramp

For staggered-floor structures. Here, one pair of ramps is used for up traffic, one pair for down traffic. Note that the inner pair of ramps have opposing planes; so do the outer pair.

No. 6. Full-Floor Ramp

For a full-floor instead of staggered-floor structure. Has a pair of opposed-plane ramps with up and down traffic patterns. Allows a fuller use of each floor for car maneuvering, parking.

No. 4. Twin-circle, Same-plane Ramp

For staggered-floor structures. Here, too, one pair of ramps is used for up traffic, one pair for down traffic. Notice that the inner pair of ramps are on the same plane; so are the outer pair.

No. 7. Concentric, Divided, Opposed-plane Ramps

For a staggered-floor structure. Here, there is a pair of ramps for up traffic; a pair for down traffic. The two traffic flows form circles, one within the other and the two directions of flow have a dividing curb.

No. 5. Straight Ramp System

For full-floor structures. Notice that this is a single ramp with a double width and that the traffic pattern makes a complete circle when the car rises from one floor to start of rise to next.

No. 8. Opposed, Straight Ramp

For a full-floor structure. These ramps, on opposite sides of the structure, make the traffic pattern of one complete circle lift the car two floors. Hence the ramp travel is always separated.

Top: Garage, Miami, 1949. In the late 1940s, the D'Humy ramp design was still in use, but to minimize the size of the lot and maximize the space available for parking, designers overlapped parking rows.

Above: Self-park ramp designs. In the 1950s, many new ramp designs emerged for the new self-park garage.

in the process, the conversion prolonged the life of the handsome seven-story building.[37]

The self-park garage required a new approach and new design considerations. For example, the interior of the garage now had to accommodate not only self-parkers (both skilled and not so skilled), but also pedestrians moving into, through, and out of the garage. To allow passengers to travel from floor to floor in the larger multistory garages, passenger elevators and fire stairs were added.

In the Parkit, a ramp design introduced in 1955 by the architect M.R. Beckstrom, two spiral ramps were joined on one side by a flat floor plate. One spiral led up and the other down, and parking spaces were provided along the ramp. This configuration allowed for easy traffic flow, and even novice drivers could readily navigate from one floor to the next and in and out of the garage. The flat floor plate allowed the facade facing the street to be similar to that of other buildings. Circ-L-Park, an innovative design for a small site, consisted of two identical spirals made of a single concrete unit; it was an innovative example of the use of prefabricated concrete.[38]

Art students contributed their own unique suggestions to these explorations of ramp configurations. For an event sponsored by the Portland Cement Association, one student created a model that featured a flat floor plate with an integrated express ramp, allowing light into the interior. In his Self-Service Garage Project, Frank Lloyd Wright had also allowed light to penetrate into the interior; in Wright's design, however, a separate pedestrian ramp was integrated with the automobile ramp, so that even new users—whether on foot or behind the wheel—could easily understand where they were at all times. Typically, however, the focus of new ramp

The Parking Garage

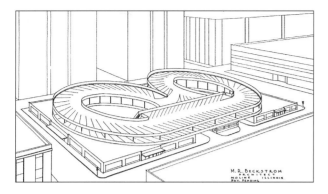

Top left: M. Beckstrom, Parkit design, 1955. As the self-park garage proliferated, designers explored many new combinations of ramp and parking.

Left: Philip R. Weary, Circ-L-Park, Los Angeles, 1966. In this ramp design, two identical spirals

were constructed from a single concrete unit.

Above: Thomas D. Rebek, entry for a 1965 competition sponsored by Portland Cement. Even art students contributed ideas for parking and ramp configurations.

designs was on ensuring smooth traffic flow and ease of use for the driver, rather than on the pedestrian experience.[39]

Post-1950s Ramp Design

By the 1950s, there were three different means of getting the car into and out of the structure: full attendant, customer/attendant, and self-park. In addition, there were seven typical ramp designs: straight ramps, which included the D'Humy system; two-way ramps; ramps with sloping floor plates; curved ramps; elliptical ramps; double-helix (also known as double-spiral) ramps; and concentric spiral ramps. The early history of ramp design produced the fundamental structures that are typical today; after 1950, larger garages, larger vehicles, and the advent of self-parking led to some new approaches that have since become standard, and to some reconfigurations of earlier designs. In the 1960s, for example, in a design first envisioned by E.M. Khoury, a sloped internal ramp connected concentric flat floor plates; the result was a structure with a modern interior that nevertheless allowed a more traditional facade. Khoury's design was actually im-

plemented in a 1975 garage designed by Carl Walker for Grand Rapids Community College.[40]

The Allen Center Garage, which served a mixed-use development in downtown Houston, had four decks that operated independently of each other but were part of the same structure: in essence, the design created four separate garages, each with its own entry, exits, and ramps. This arrangement, which was assumed to be easier for shoppers, was used in three garages in the late 1970s, including the garage for the Macy's department store in New Rochelle, New York.[41]

Although the speed ramp is the most efficient way of providing rapid entry and exit to a garage, its constant turns can be difficult for drivers to manage. One solution was the double-drop ramp, which dropped two floors at a time instead of one, creating curves that were easier for drivers to negotiate. However, this approach created another problem: ensuring ramp access from each floor. At the Parkade Garage, in San Diego, the designers, led by George Devlin, addressed this problem by using a spare piece of land to connect the garage to the speed ramp on every other floor. At the Lazarus Company and National Garage project, in

Columbus, Ohio, a double-drop ramp was used within the context of a square floor plan.[42]

Other innovative ramp designs included the Park-A-Back and the Silo parking systems, both designed in the 1960s by William Gleckman. The Park-A-Back system, a modification of the standard parking lot, increased parking capacity by 66.6 percent. In this configuration, cut and fill was used to create two vertically interlocking parking levels, each with a slope of 15 percent. Parking could be accessed from driveways adjacent to either of the sloped spaces. The prototype structure was built in Oerlikon, a suburb of Zurich, Switzerland. (In 1954, William Brower had created a similar configuration, using a sawtooth design to maximize parking space in a lot configured as a one-way lane.)[43]

Gleckman's Silo garage was "characterized by an access ramp in the form of a rising helicoid with parking spaces on both sides, turning about a central axis, and concentrically surrounding a helicoidal exit ramp, which in turn surrounds the central opening."[44] One-way circulation patterns have two advantages: they are easier for drivers to use, and they facilitate smooth traffic flow during peak periods. Gleckman noted that because the Silo ramp had a constant radius, the use of movable, track-mounted form work and the reuse of metal forms would allow economical construction. Gleckman

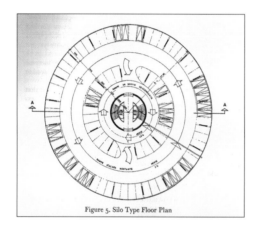

Figure 5. Silo Type Floor Plan

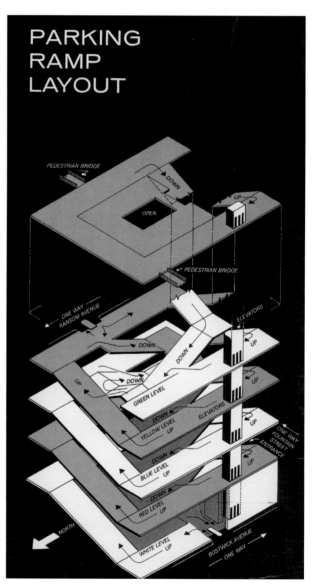

Top: William Gleckman, Silo proposal, 1960. Old ideas about how to design a ramp to maximize parking continue to resurface: this idea was considered fantastic in 1920; by 1960, it was a potential reality.

Above: William Gleckman, Park-A-Back prototype, Oerlikon, Switzerland, 1960. This modification of the standard parking lot, built outside Zurich, doubled the amount of parking space.

Right: Grand Rapids Community College Garage, Grand Rapids, Michigan, 1975. Placing a ramped garage in the center of a facility and surrounding it with flat floor plates makes it possible to preserve flat floor plates on the exterior portion of the structure.

The Parking Garage

The Elevator Garage: A New Old Idea

The Lofts of Merchants Row, a modern garage that opened in 2003 in downtown Detroit, advertises a "high-tech vehicle elevator parking garage" for the 157 renovated loft units next door. This garage, however, harks back to the building type's earliest form: it is the first newly built elevator garage in many decades. (The facility is valet parked.) The structure features a flat floor plate, and offers the option of later adaptive use if the need arises. The punched window openings, strip window openings, traditional massing, and habitable space on the first level allow the garage to fit into the city block. The building is evidence that when circumstances are right, a good idea can be revived.[1]

Below and right: Lofts of Merchants Row, Detroit, 2003.

also noted that this system would work equally well underground: he imagined the new metropolis as a vertically oriented environment, with "ziggurat blocks." The large, open interior space of the Silo ramp contained elevators, stairs, and a pedestrian bridge. Interestingly, a similar idea had been designed and patented by Eugene Higgins, of New York, around 1920; in Higgins's vision, an 18-story parking garage sat atop an office block.[45]

Even today, new ramp forms are still being explored as designers attempt to reconcile the many conflicting demands of the parking garage. The Watry warp, an innovative design created by Nick Watry, an architect and engineer, is one example of such explorations; it was first used in a garage constructed for Stanford University in 1986–1987 by C. Overaa and Company, of Richmond, California. The 300-foot (91-meter) length of a typical parking garage is dictated by three features: a floor-to-floor height of 10.5 feet

(3.2 meters), a 2 percent slope on the end bays (toward the parking split), and a 5 percent slope on the ramp. The Watry warp keeps the exterior elevation of the end parking bays flat, and still meets the slope requirements of the Uniform Building Code (a maximum of 5 percent for ramps, and a minimum of 2 percent for decks, to facilitate drainage). The design succeeds by the following means: the standard ramp, with its 5 percent slope, is reduced in length to 150 feet (45 meters), and the additional three feet (one meter) required to achieve standard height are added to the 2 percent slope of the end bay, which is also sloped 2 percent toward the center. The end bays parallel to the sloped bay and level to the exterior are made up of 60-foot (18-meter) beams that are straight in plan and warped to accommodate both the internal slope of 2 percent and the exterior flat elevation within a minimal lot size. This design allows a flat elevation at either end, thus mitigating the effects of the

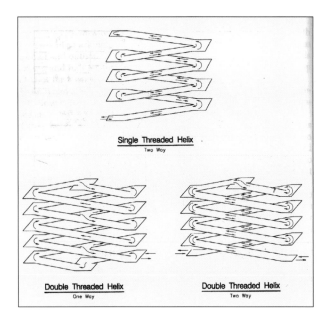

Current ramp designs. Today, new ramp designs are developed for specific purposes, depending on the building types to which they are connected and the anticipated user groups.

Single Threaded Helix
Two Way

Double Threaded Helix
One Way

Double Threaded Helix
Two Way

modern parking structure in the urban context.[46]

Other new ramp designs have improved the efficiency of the parking garage by accommodating different categories of self-parkers. For example, daily, long-term users can "learn" the relatively more complex configurations of interconnecting or overlapping helix systems, whereas short-term parkers require simpler and more immediately understandable ramp systems.[47]

Ramp design today is both a science and an art. The particular design chosen depends on a number of factors, including the site, the topography, the type of building to which the garage is connected, the nearby traffic patterns, and the types of users. The "Parking" section of the list of further readings at the end of this book includes a number of sources that address these complex conditions.[48]

The Ramp Garage as a Civic Presence

As the older, open vehicles left the road, as fire and auto-emissions regulations became codified, and as cost became one of the driving factors in design, the "purely" functional garage—a stripped-down version of a building, with only the structural skeleton required—appeared more and more fre-

quently in cities. The modernist credo "form follows function" became an overriding dictate—and, as new spatial relationships were revealed in the structure of the parking garage, architecture's traditional civic responsibility was lost. In the hands of talented designers and enlightened clients, the new aesthetic of "form follows function" yielded many excellent creations, but it also yielded many starkly designed garages with little or no architectural merit. An unexpected and problematic result of the focus on the ramp was the realization that a facade was no longer necessary: it was not required for structural support, for protection from weather, for ventilation, or for fire protection. Although the open-air ramp was efficient and functional, the elimination of the facade—the mediating force of architecture—had a dramatic effect on the relationship between the parking structure and the urban fabric.

One of the lessons of this book is that architectural design cannot occur in a vacuum: everything in the urban fabric is interconnected, and the disappearance of the facade eventually created a backlash. The parking garage came to be perceived as an aesthetic threat—and in order to save the city, architects and planners were compelled to focus on integrating parking into the urban aesthetic. The simultaneous emergence of suburban development patterns, with their expansive parking lots, created a temporary diversion from the dilemma of the facade, but not from the issue of how to handle the parked car. The search for solutions continues today: how can these very large (and often out of scale) pieces of architecture be aesthetically integrated into urban environments? With the increasing density of development patterns, this challenge is even more urgent: hiding the garage is not always feasible, and transit, while necessary, cannot serve all movement needs.

Man, Machine, and Building

The creation of a new building type requires the exploration of a variety of important issues, from the psychological to the mechanical. Most importantly, however, it requires a fit between the use, the user, the facility, and the setting. The early years of the parking garage were spent attempting to achieve this fit, within the context of a new technology and the emotions it evoked. By the 1930s, a straightforward functional building type had emerged that was then refined over the next several decades. But many of the early explorations of the relationship between man and machine continue to

Current Perceptions of Time and Space

Because garages have become so large, self-parking is rarely faster than attendant parking. Moreover, drivers and passengers must absorb all the other unpleasant realities of the self-park garage: the sense of emptiness, the coldness and harshness, and the lack of pedestrian amenities. And because garages are often directly connected to destinations, they keep people away from the active life of the street—a pattern that has defined the experience of arrival and departure in the American city as an isolating one.

Much of modern design has been shaped by the quest for efficiency and speed. But how fast is the modern-day parking garage? For example, retrieving a car today typically requires a walk from the entry, a ride up or down in an elevator, a walk to the car, a drive around and out of the facility, a stop at the payment booth, and whatever time it takes to get into the street. Because the retrieval process involves constant motion, it may appear to go relatively quickly. But perhaps the time could be better spent waiting in an air-conditioned or heated lobby while an automobile—summoned by a simple call from a cell phone—is delivered by machine. Like the modern highway—designed for speed but now cluttered with automobiles crawling at a snail's pace—the modern parking garage may be less than efficient. The time that is now spent parking or retrieving cars—circling through the garage—might be better spent in a parking lobby, communicating with others. Linking automobile movement with transit, walking, and bicycling could make better use of limited time and resources while still providing the freedom and social interaction that everyone desires. Thinking of simultaneity and overlap—a weaving of different forms of movement—might help reveal new solutions.

Lobby, Downtown Center Garage, San Francisco, 1955.

reappear. In fact, one of the most fascinating aspects of this building type is its fluidity and its ongoing evolution.

Solutions to the puzzle of parking garage design were rooted in science and technology, in historical precedent, and in emotion, though these influences were not necessarily in balance. The psychological expression of freedom that the auto embodied was shared by an entire nation, especially in the 1920s. This provided the emotional foundation for the solution that finally became dominant in this country: the self-park ramp garage. But in the creation of a new building type, competing visions are inevitable.

Past Lessons for the Present and Future

⊃ The flat floor plate can be a desirable design option: it facilitates adaptive use and helps integrate the facade of the parking facility into the urban fabric.

⊃ The ramp is still a viable and practical solution for parking efficiency and ease of use; the challenge is to celebrate or integrate its form, instead of allowing it to conflict with other design considerations.

⊃ Early design strategies—using the land to create natural connections between ramps and parking decks, shorter ramp lengths, and configurations that have minimal impact on the surrounding topography—remain important and viable today.

⊃ In certain situations, especially to facilitate future adaptive use, the elevator garage is a design worth considering.

⊃ In some circumstances, attendant or valet parking still makes sense.

⊃ The design of the ramp needs to be sensitive to the pedestrian experience.

⊃ The placement of the ramp can be used to integrate light into a parking facility and to assist with way-finding.

CHAPTER 3

Synergistic Land Use Connections

The early garage was a living place, simultaneously supporting the automobile user, other buildings, and the larger transportation system of the city. Unlike the stable or the carriage house, the garage played multiple roles and incorporated multiple functions, enjoyed synergistic relationships with many other building types, and was crucial to the economic and geographic growth of developing cities and towns. This chapter considers these synergistic relationships: how does the parking structure connect, how should it connect, and how have these connections changed over time?

For the first several decades of their history, garages were integral parts of the urban fabric: they harmonized architecturally with their surroundings, and were sometimes physically connected to other building types. Then a number of things began to change. The city itself became more diffuse and suburbanized; where land was plentiful, lots often replaced structured garages.[1] (Meanwhile, the fact that vast stretches of asphalt were unlikely to develop synergistic connections to *anything* went virtually unnoticed.) In both the cities and the suburbs, self-park structures eventually replaced the attended garage, a shift that transformed the garage from a "service-based" building type to a simple holding bin for automobiles. At the same time, the ever-increasing demand for parking made its way into local ordinances and zoning codes. Such codes—which shape parking garage design even today—link the number, size, and location of spaces to the particular building type (for example, so many spaces per unit for residential, per room for a hotel, or per gross leasable area for offices and retail).[2]

In many cases, the combination of code requirements and simple economic necessity—the realization that, without parking, no project can succeed—led to the excessive proliferation of parking garages, and to the construction of garages that were out of scale in relation to nearby buildings, further undermining the possibility of synergistic connections. Nevertheless, the history of garage design has been marked by strong, creative, and sometimes

Facing page: Saks Fifth Avenue parking facility, Kansas City, Missouri, 2001. Ornament was used at this new parking structure at Country Club Plaza to enliven the streetfront; the structure also includes streetfront retail and is part of a larger mixed-use district.

1180 Peachtree Street, Atlanta, Georgia. Giving a garage facade a treatment that is similar to that of the building that it serves is an excellent architectural design strategy.

even fanciful links to other uses. A garage can be much more than a place to put the car, and innovative designers, owners, and entrepreneurs have never lost sight of that fact. Successful synergies emerge when the whole is greater than the sum of its parts: when a waterfall built into the side of a medical center garage offers a calming environment for visitors; when a garage lined with first-floor shops links a residential development to the life of the street; and when a landscaped garage roof becomes an after-hours gathering space for local residents.

As the demand for parking continues to grow, the issue of where and how to integrate parking with other uses becomes ever more pressing. In many urban areas, the combination of increasing density and increasing land values means that structured parking is essential to meeting demand. These structures must be conceived as dynamic assets that contribute both functionally and aesthetically to the property and to the area as a whole, rather than as necessary evils that must be hidden. Their design and placement must respect both the use being served and the surrounding context.

The fundamental principle is simple: every parking facility is a gateway experience. Fortunately, the options for connecting the garage to other uses are almost infinite, and the building type is generous in its ability to shelter many functions that can enhance everyday life and strengthen the surrounding urban fabric. Creative approaches to achieving synergy will unquestionably yield better parking garages, but they will also yield better communities.[3]

The Showroom Connection

The link between the parking garage and the automobile showroom, a juxtaposition that appeared almost from the beginning, was the most visually exciting aspect of early garage design. Showrooms were designed to seduce the potential buyer by expressing and encouraging every fantasy implied by travel and automobile ownership. *The Horseless Age,* an early auto magazine, even ran a regular column devoted to the garage-salesroom combination, indicating where such facilities were located and what brands of automobile were sold in each. Typically, the automobile salesroom was combined with public parking. The showroom-garage combination remained an important building type into the 1930s, after which it persisted only in a few large city centers.[4]

Connerat's, an early example of a garage-showroom combination, was built in Savannah in 1909. A three-story elevator garage located close to the city center, the structure was plain by the standards of other cities, but had a facade of imitation marble—and, unlike the other buildings on the street, featured a large glass display window. In 1913, the Locomobile Salesroom, on Peachtree Street, in Atlanta, was described by *The Horseless Age* as the "most pleasing" of the auto showrooms on that street, despite its limited storage space.[5] One of the showroom's unusual features was concealed lighting, which gave the building a distinctive appearance at night and showcased the automobiles within. The electric-vehicle showroom of William F.V. Neumann and Company, built in Detroit in 1909, had a large, attractive facade and a garage in the back designed so that cars could be driven freely in and out without backing up.[6]

The Parking Garage

- In 1929, the total number of automobiles manufactured in the United States was 5 million; by the end of the 1930s, that number had dropped to 1 million.

- The 1930s were a slow period for the parking garage industry; most garage owners were just trying to pay their taxes.

- Until 1930, a majority of states did not require drivers' licenses.

- By 1930, the average car had been driven over 40,000 miles (64,374 kilometers) before it reached the junkyard.

- In 1930, 26,750,000 motor vehicles were registered, and $2.5 billion was expended on highways.

- The Institute of Traffic Engineers was established in 1930.

- In 1931, in a move that pointed the way to the future, North Carolina assumed financial and managerial responsibility for the 40,000 miles (64,374 kilometers) of county roads in the entire state. (Three other states did so that same year.)

- The National Recovery Act, passed in 1933, provided money for secondary and "farm-to-market" roads and required landscaping of the roadsides along main highways.

- Between 1933 and 1941, as a result of federal "make-work" programs, the number of miles of paved roads in the United States more than doubled.

- As funding became available for new highway systems, two new design ideas came to be viewed as important for safety: grade separations and controlled entrance and exit ramps. The designs were pioneered in portions of New Jersey that were near Philadelphia and New York City.

- By the 1930s, automobiles were appearing in movies and were developing a character all their own.

- Although most auto owners drove big, boxy black Fords, the cars of movie stars became fancier and even larger, fueling the desire for luxury vehicles.

- Despite the power of the Pierce-Arrow as a status symbol, the company went out of business in 1938.

- In the early 1930s, a Chrysler Airflow sold for $1,535, but $445 was enough to purchase a less exciting—but practical—Chevrolet model.

- Reflective paints, which improved safety and gave added protection from the weather, were introduced in 1935; this and other changes to automotive technology appeared almost simultaneously with the first open parking decks.

- Chrysler introduced overdrive in 1934, and Oldsmobile perfected the automatic transmission in 1937. Cars were rapidly becoming more efficient and easier to operate.

- The first Park-O-Meter (parking meter), which was invented by Carl C. Magee, was installed in Oklahoma City in 1935.

- Through competition and merger, the thousands of automobile manufacturing companies that had come into being since the turn of the 20th century essentially evolved into the Big Three: General Motors, Ford, and Chrysler. (A few smaller manufacturers, such as Nash and Studebaker, still remained.)

- The first commercial television broadcast was in 1939; the area covered by the first television signals stretched from Boston, Massachusetts, to Washington, D.C.

Movement Facts of the 1930s

Despite the economic depression of the 1930s, life went on: although auto production practically ceased, people still needed mobility, and the car maintained its allure.

Preserving Early Showrooms

Early automobile districts, where the combination of showroom and garage yielded fabulous architectural monuments to the adventurous spirit of the automobile, still exist in many cities. Those that remain are important remnants of the historic urban form, and provide a sharp contrast to the miles of homogenized showrooms and surface lots lining today's suburban arteries.[1]

Albert Kahn designed many early automobile showrooms across the country, and managed to successfully meet their various requirements. In a 1927 article in *The Architectural Forum*, Kahn identified the "business of transportation" as the "keystone of our whole industrial structure" and its "greatest single factor" as the "self-propelled private motor car."[2] The two-story building Kahn designed for the New York showroom of the Packard Motor Car Company combined display space with a parking garage, and featured an elevator and wood floors. Other designs, such as the Cadillac Sales Building and the Ford Motor Company Sales Building, both in Detroit, and the Packard Motor Car Service Building, in Chicago, were notable for meeting the functional demands for interior parking while exhibiting sensitivity to the aesthetic requirements of proportion and scale.[3]

The Capital Garage, in Washington, D.C., was demolished in 1974; however, its external ornamentation was preserved and is in the Smithsonian Institution. Recently, a 1929 Ford dealership in Washington, D.C., that had been used for parking was renovated as a Barnes & Noble bookstore, a move that preserved it as a handsome and functional part of the neighborhood.[4]

In April 2000, the city's Commission on Landmarks urged landmark status for Chicago's Motor Row, a series of buildings built between 1905 and 1915 and located primarily along three blocks of Michigan Avenue. Motor Row includes, among many other striking examples of early automotive architecture, the first car dealership Henry Ford ever opened in Chicago. A few of the buildings are still used today as showrooms, but most have been turned over to manufacturing, commercial, or mixed use. Nevertheless, the names "Buick," "Hudson," "Locomobile," and "Premier" remain proudly displayed on the facades.[5]

Clockwise from top left: Cadillac Salon, New York City, 1927; Cullen-Thompson Motor Company, Denver, 1927; combination salesroom and garage designed by Albert Kahn, New York City, 1929; De Soto Motors, Hollywood, California, 1927.

Albert Kahn, an architect famous for his work on industrial buildings, designed showrooms for almost every major manufacturer, including one of the first automobile salesrooms for the Chicago Motor Car Company, which was constructed in 1910. In keeping with the emerging modernist aesthetic, this large structure featured a functional exterior with a visible concrete frame, and glass and brick between the structural supports; the facade was simply ornamented with terra cotta. The design reflected the grandeur, the permanence, and the practicality of the new machine it was designed to house.[7]

By 1927, the automobile showroom was being discussed as a specific building type: an article in *The Architectural Forum,* for example, described the showroom as "a spacious and beautifully appointed gallery, different by far from a garage." The article further noted that "it is not safe to shut our eyes to the inherent nature of the wares displayed or to the importance of maintaining in the setting a character which will accord with that of the article itself. It is an instance in which good taste counts for much, taste not only in actual designing but also in choosing the character of the setting."[8]

Today, a resurgence of interest in downtowns is yielding building formats that refer back to earlier times. In an echo of the way that cars were once sold and marketed, a proposed vertical auto mall in the center of Los Angeles will feature individual showrooms on each level. Designed by Kanner Architects and housed in a renovated office building, the facility will depend on elevators (elevators again!) to transport cars through the structure. Customer parking will be provided on the roof. No structural upgrades will be required—but, in an ironic twist, one curtain wall will be removed to make the building look like a garage. The auto mall will be wrapped in glass panels to provide a five-story screen for video advertising of the vehicles. In what may be a trend, other car showrooms are being added to downtown Orlando, Florida, and St. Helena, California.[9]

Municipal Storage Solutions and Public Parking Garages

As noted in chapter 1, municipalities switched to gasoline-powered fleets very early in the 20th century; hence, municipal garages were among the first to be built. Although municipal garages were initially constructed for the sole purpose of storing municipal equipment, they were eventually combined with many other uses and building types. As early as 1910, for example, a municipal garage in Boston was combined with a boys club: in this innovative design, the garage was situated at the entrance to the complex, directly under the ballroom, and gave direct access to the swimming pool and locker rooms. Twenty years later, in St. Louis, the police department constructed a six-story facility that also housed a gymnasium and a parking garage.[10] Later public garages were developed to support diverse business needs in downtowns and other commercial areas.

Because fire departments were usually the first public agencies to adopt gasoline-powered vehicles, they often led the way in designing spaces for vehicle storage. In the words of Arthur Aungst, chief of the East Liverpool, Ohio, fire department, the first consideration in designing a fire station should be "the comfort of the men"; the second should be "the neatness and beautification of buildings and their surroundings... so as to make the station as homelike as possible"; finally, "the building should be a credit to the neighborhood."[11] In residential districts, stations were generally either one-story structures of various design, or bungalow designs. The advantage of the bungalow design was that it easily accommodated the needs of both the motorized equipment and the firefighters, while blending in with local neighborhood forms. A bungalow-style station built in 1914 in Alliance, Ohio, was believed at the time to be the first to use this design. A station in Amarillo, Texas, another fine example of the bungalow design, featured two porte-cocheres and a Spanish flair.[12]

The advent of motorized fire equipment also changed the design of fire stations in downtown locations. The Ocean City, New Jersey, fire station, built in 1915, was designed in a classical style that made it look more like a courthouse, except for the large garage-door openings. Smaller stations in places such as Tampa and New Orleans were more restrained, but their designs—with classical proportions, and simple detailing on the base, middle, and cornice—still reflected their civic importance.[13]

Road-building equipment, sanitation equipment, and other municipal vehicles also became motorized at the beginning of the 20th century, requiring proper storage and a great deal more space for maintenance and repair. By 1915, the city of Oakland, California, was operating a "systematized" municipal garage where the use, maintenance, and costs of each vehicle were tracked.[14] By 1916, the city of Cleveland had transformed a vacant lot into a maintenance building and municipal storage facility that also served as a public parking

Kanner Architects, vertical auto mall, Los Angeles, 1998. This structure combines the older approaches to parking—flat floor plates and an elevator—with modern architectural language.

garage, creating an income stream for the city. In 1928, the city of Schenectady, New York, built a two-story masonry structure as its municipal garage. The facility could accommodate between 17 and 100 vehicles and was considered one of the most modern in the state. Like fire stations, municipal garages were often built with aesthetics in mind. The curved, sawtooth roof structure of a garage for street equipment built in Miami in 1953, for example, created a distinctive architectural presence for a practical building.[15]

Although steam- and electric-powered trolleys persisted well into the 1950s, motorized buses were in operation in many American cities early in the 20th century. Although buses were at first a supplementary form of transportation (because they could go where trains could not), in some cases they supplanted trains, particularly where tracks had begun to interfere with motorized travel. An early terminal garage in Newark, New Jersey, was six stories high and classically designed.[16]

Bus garages were of two types: those used to store and maintain buses only, and those used to store both buses and cars. The first type was typically located away from the downtown, in an area where the newly emerging municipal regulations allowed both maintenance activities and on-site gasoline storage. An Atlanta bus garage, designed by Stevens & Wilkinson in 1948 for "trackless trolleys," was a simple, steel-framed structure; glass-in-steel sashes, with varying grid proportions, added to the modern aesthetic. Located one mile (1.6 kilometers) from downtown, the structure could hold 254 buses. Along with the typical offices and maintenance areas, the facility also featured a clinic, a barbershop, a uniform-pressing room, and locker rooms. Above the shop was an auditorium/gymnasium that was open to the public.[17]

The second type of bus garage was a multimodal facility that linked the bus, a form of mass transit, to the car, a form of private transportation. New York's Port Authority Bus Terminal, for example, which was built in 1949, was directly connected to the Lincoln Tunnel, through which 2,500 intercity buses arrived daily. The Port Authority roof was a parking deck offering space for 450 cars.[18]

Large buildings, municipal and otherwise—including courthouses, auditoriums, and stadiums—generated needs for large concentrations of parking. A 1950 article in *The American City* noted that "in 1940, more auditoriums were completed in cities than in any other single year."[19] Visitors were increasingly likely to arrive at such facilities by car, and cities began to address the resulting parking needs. In 1949, an information report created by the American Society of Planning Officials—*Municipal Auditoriums and the City Plan*—stressed the importance of providing adequate parking spaces near public buildings. In 1945, Hartford's city engineer planned an "attractive parking plaza" that would accommodate between 2,500 and 3,300 cars.[20] The plaza was to be accessible from all directions by car, and connected to the central places of business by electric trains and a proposed subway.[21]

In 1960, the first municipally funded public parking garage in New York City opened in midtown Manhattan to serve the New York Coliseum; it was the first of 16 such garages constructed in the city.[22] The Mountain View Parking Complex,

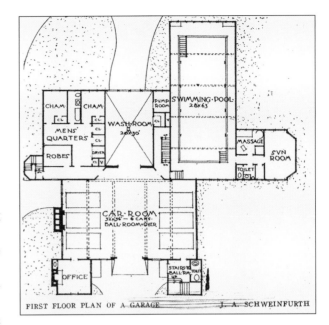

FIRST FLOOR PLAN OF A GARAGE — J. A. SCHWEINFURTH

Top: Boys Club House, Boston, 1910. This combination of parking garage and boys' club featured an architecturally interesting layout and was innovative for its time.

Above: Fire station, Ocean City, New Jersey, 1915. Fire stations came in many styles and sizes, and were often proud civic statements.

Left: Port Authority Terminal, New York City, 1949. As cities took on broader responsibilities for transportation, they began to construct multimodal facilities.

Above: Forbes Field, Pittsburgh, 1909. In the first example of a combined sports facility and parking garage, cars were stored under the grandstands.

built in 1976 in Knoxville, Tennessee, to meet the needs of the civic auditorium and coliseum, had to accommodate 4,000 cars in three structures. Parking at large stadiums remains a challenge: even demountable parking structures have been tried. One of the earliest examples of a municipal mixed-use project incorporating a sports facility was Pittsburgh's Forbes Field, built in 1909, which not only had an automobile garage under the bleachers but also included a Studebaker showroom and salesroom.[23]

The construction of many new courthouses has focused attention not only on the necessity of providing adequate parking, but also on the importance of safety and security. Garages that are physically connected to courthouses require safe means of transferring inmates and quick access for police and other officials—requirements that make the design of such facilities a specialized area within the industry. In 2004, when the city of Orlando expanded the parking garage of the Orlando County Courthouse, the garage won an award from the Precast Prestressed Concrete Institute; among the many reasons for the award was the building's civic presence.[24]

In the late 1960s, many municipalities attempted to address the needs of multiple users while respecting the surrounding urban context. One approach to meeting large-scale, time-specific parking needs was to position garages to serve more than one purpose or patron in the course of a day—an early version of shared parking. In Mankato, Minnesota, in 1967, for example, a downtown parking lot and condemned hotel were demolished to make room for a parking garage large enough to support the business life of the county. Similar approaches are being used in new town centers; in redeveloped downtowns, suburban villages, and malls; and in mixed-use developments and "entertainment zones" in urban downtowns. Whatever the venue, the principle is the same: if the code-based parking requirements for different buildings overlap, but there is little overlap in parking demand, it is possible to build smaller, but still adequate, parking structures.[25]

In a new twist on an old favorite among municipal solutions—the underground garage—Chicago's Museum of Science and Industry has an underground garage that is actually the entrance to the museum. In 1930, when the Palace of Fine Arts—built for the World's Columbian Exposition of 1893—was renovated to house the science museum, the great lawn that the Olmsted brothers had designed for the exposition became a surface parking lot. In 1998, the architectural firm of A. Epstein and Sons, along with the museum's master planner and landscape architects, developed a plan to move parking underground, which made it possible to restore the great lawn.[26]

The Parking Garage

Visitors entering the garage find themselves in a replica of a train station that bisects the facility. The Zephyr, a train that first went into operation in 1934 and that once set a land-speed record of 13 hours from Denver to Chicago, is set on tracks within the garage. The nose of the streamlined, stainless-steel electric-diesel engine points visitors toward the Great Hall, a three-story subterranean space inspired by the futuristic form of the train. The design succeeds on two levels: it assists with way-finding, and it successfully integrates the garage into the museum experience from the moment visitors enter. Partially funded by the Federal Highway Administration and the Illinois Department of Transportation, this project—like many municipal parking projects—also benefited from funds available through ISTEA (the Intermodal Surface Transportation Efficiency Act).[27]

The Queensway Bay Parking Structure, which is owned by the city of Long Beach, California, and opened in 1998, offers a different approach to the garage entry. A joint venture with private developers, the facility accommodates 1,471 cars and was designed by International Design Group. It is part of a 300-acre (121-hectare) complex that incorporates a convention center, an aquarium, a marina, a ferry terminal, and the Queen Mary ocean liner, now a historic attraction. Designed primarily to serve the Aquarium of the Pacific, the main attraction of the complex, the garage immediately engages the arriving visitor in the aquarium experience. The traffic circle through which visitors enter the garage features a sculpture of dolphins. Circles of different sizes cut into the garage facade create a "bubbly" appearance, and the facility's circular ramp resembles the prow of a ship. Elevators with backlit images of marine life give visitors the sense of being on an underwater dive. Adding to the ambience, the lobby gives visitors the sense of being within the sails of a ship. Visitors enter the parking structure by passing through a 65-foot- (20-meter-) high metal sculpture of a breaking wave, which is constructed of blue neon and gold-anodized aluminum panels.[28]

The garage lobby features green glass tiles and fiber-optic lighting. The adjacent aquarium is visible through the circular cutouts in the walls of the garage. The interior is very open, with high ceilings and gleaming white walls, and offers level floor plates. Fish carved into the concrete floors help visitors find their way toward the aquarium; columns exhibiting graphics of the Pacific Ocean help identify parking spaces. The open and flowing spaces direct visitors to the lobby. This imaginative approach provides a safe and inviting

Museum of Science and Industry, Chicago (top, circa 1930; above, 1998). Through the construction of an underground parking facility, this museum reclaimed green space and created a wonderful new gateway experience.

experience, and allows visitors to feel connected to the destination the moment they see it. It is an excellent example of parking design complementing a specific building type.[29]

To preserve the vitality of the sidewalk experience in redevelopment projects, some municipalities are reviving the idea of integrated parking. The city of Lodi, California, in cooperation with a private developer, completed preliminary designs for a project that was to have included a 12-screen, 1,900-seat, 46,000-square-foot (4,274-square-meter) theater with stadium seating, and 9,000 square feet (836 square meters) of retail space on two levels. The complex was to be topped by a two-level, 277-space parking facility. While the combination of shopping, entertainment, and parking is not new, what set the project apart was its re-creation, on a much larger scale, of the art deco movie palaces of the past. As in the early automobile showrooms, which were also "fantasy" environments, parking was to be hidden behind the theater facade. Although the project was not built in accordance with these preliminary plans, the parking structure that was ultimately included is within walking distance of a new, multimodal transit station that features retail along the street.[30]

Other municipal uses are increasingly being combined with parking. A colorful modernist structure in the Lincoln Heights district of Los Angeles, for example, houses the offices of the Department of Water and Power, microwave transmission and communication towers, and parking for 1,000 cars. The appearance of the facility belies its use. In downtown Minneapolis, the Minneapolis Energy Center, which generates electricity, chilled water, and steam for downtown buildings, also provides much-needed parking for the downtown retail and entertainment district. The architectural forms are simple and balanced, creating a modern feel without disguising the building's use, and are a good fit for the eclectic neighborhood. One corner of the structure is a round tower, a form that is echoed in the round openings for exhaust that appear within a decorative brick band above the garage entry. Angled screens allow the cooling towers to be viewed as part of the architectural form (this is a different building from that depicted on the facing page).[31]

In other new municipal facilities, parking is being combined with cultural uses. The Academy for the Performing Arts, in Bethesda, Maryland, for example, is located in the northern third of a parking garage built by the Montgomery County Department of Public Works and Transportation. The facility features a double-height entry with a curved vestibule and backlit facade panels that draw the visitor in.

Below, left and right: Queensway Bay Parking Structure, Long Beach, California, 1998. Today's parking facilities are often designed to engage the visitor from the moment of entry.

The Parking Garage

Minneapolis Energy Center, 1972. Parking is often linked to other municipal uses: in addition to housing a garage, this building generates electricity, chilled water, and steam for downtown buildings.

Along with 905 parking spaces are 34,000 square feet (3,158 square meters) devoted to the academy, including a 450-seat theater, a theater café, a store, classrooms, and administrative offices.[32]

The Garage and the Workplace

As early as 1924, *The American City* noted that "city governments cannot be expected to furnish parking space in the streets for the increasing number of automobiles being used by employees of large industrial plants. . . . The heads of such industries are giving more attention than heretofore to the solution of this problem."[33] Initially, workplace garages were built by entrepreneurs, often as stand-alone structures. Cincinnati's Government Square Garage, for example, a ramp garage built in 1916, was "ideal for . . . catering to the car owners in the office building neighborhood."[34] Often, early garages in business districts were called "hotel" garages;

one example is Chicago's now-demolished Hotel LaSalle Garage, built in 1918. An early example of a ramp garage, the LaSalle was a private facility built to serve workers in the downtown business district.[35]

In time, however, employers and building owners saw the need to provide workers with dedicated parking. In 1924, on land adjacent to its industrial facility, the C.L. Best Tractor Company, in San Leandro, California, created a 35,000-square-foot (3,252-square-meter) covered parking lot for the exclusive use of its employees. The lot, which held 150 automobiles, was monitored by an attendant and featured wash racks so that employees could keep their vehicles clean. One purpose of this "parking station" was to keep automobiles from parking on the surrounding streets; another was to make it easier for autos to enter and leave the grounds of the industrial facility.[36] Eventually, to keep streets clear, zoning codes required the construction of parking spaces to serve newly built office or manufacturing facilities.[37]

One of the earliest and most comprehensive examples of the integration of workplace and parking garage was Detroit's Fisher Building, built in 1928. The Fisher brothers, who owned and built the facility, had made a fortune in the auto-body industry, and spared no expense in its construction, devoting approximately $2.2 million to art and luxury materials alone. The building featured an 11-story garage attached to a 28-story office tower; above the fourth floor, each level of the garage was directly connected to a floor of the office building, so that most employees could go straight from their cars to their work stations. Other amenities included a corner bank, sidewalk shops, and a theater, all connected by an arcade. A pedestrian tunnel that led to the General Motors Building, across the street, made the Fisher Building an important element in the city's developing transportation system.[38] An office building that also housed doctor, dentist, banker, and broker, the Fisher Building was a supremely functional, architecturally coherent, urbanistic whole. It is now a National Historic Landmark, and the garage is still in operation.[39]

In 1954, the combination of office and parking reached new heights in the Cafritz Office Building, in Washington, D.C. From the outside, the 11-story structure looked like any other office building, but the office portion of the building concealed a completely internal garage. In office building design, the depth of the building is limited by the amount of light that can penetrate to the interior. In a nearly square building such as the Cafritz, with its large floor plates, the lack

The Fisher Building, 1927 to the Present

Conceived by the Fisher Brothers Carriage Maker Company and designed by Albert Kahn, the great architect of the industrial age, the Fisher Building was brought into being as both a commercial and a philanthropic venture. Often referred to as "the Fisher Brothers' gift to the city of Detroit," the building was met with great enthusiasm from the time its construction was announced, in 1927.[1]

Because no site large enough could be found in thriving downtown Detroit, the project was to be built in three phases in an area north of the downtown, known as New Center, where the General Motors Building was already located. An expression of continuing optimism about Detroit, New Center was eventually to be linked with downtown by subway. But the Great Depression intervened.[2]

Although only the first phase of the Fisher Building was actually constructed, it is regarded as a symbol of Detroit's golden age. An early example of mixed use, the building housed a cinema of "Aztec" design; 99,000 square feet (9,197 square meters) of retail; 500,000 square feet of office space; and an 11-story garage with space for 1,100 cars. One of the most beautiful and elaborate buildings ever built in the United States (some say the world), it featured decorative mosaics, granite finishes, marble from around the globe, extensive ornamentation, artwork, gold leaf, and gold fixtures in the restrooms. The building cost $10 million to build and was designated a National Historic Landmark in 1989.[3]

The 150-by-160-foot (46-by-49-meter) art deco parking garage, with its granite and marble facades, was an integral part of the main structure and was given equal design attention. Albert Kahn had been integrating parking into his downtown structures for many years, and one of the goals of the Fisher Building garage was to improve on these early designs, for both attendant parking and for self-parking. The purpose of the garage was not only to provide parking for occupants of the entire structure but to relieve traffic congestion on the streets. Beginning with the steel-frame reinforcement, Kahn applied every possible new technology and approach. For example, the combination of steel columns with concrete beams and slabs made possible the 52-foot- (16-meter-)

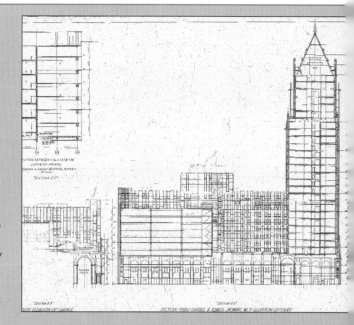

wide parking aisles. The garage was positioned on the side of the building that was away from the sunlight, allowing the stronger light to enter the main building while shielding drivers' eyes from direct sun. The ramps in the self-park facility were designed for the convenience of the average driver, and to accommodate the large crowds entering and leaving the theater.[4]

Safety and service were the key priorities. Existing ramp designs did not meet the designer's standards, so a full-scale model of a special ramp system was built and tested, by drivers with various levels of skill, at the General Motors Proving Ground. There are two ramps (one on each end of the building), and each ramp accommodates movement in one direction only. The ramps are elongated double helixes that rise one full floor with each turn. Floor-to-floor height is 12 feet, creating a grade of 12.2 percent. Automatic door openers and efficient checkers at the double-lane entrances and exits permit a smooth and continuous flow of traffic into and out of the building. Waiting rooms and service rooms are near the checkers' offices, and connect to the arcade that runs the length of the build-

of daylight would have made the building's center undesirable for human occupation. But the designers of the Cafritz came up with the perfect solution: by relegating all the functional portions of the building to its center, they maximized the space available for offices on the perimeter of the building, while providing a continuous, shallowly sloped parking ramp in the interior. Each floor of the building is approximately 190 by 170 feet (58 by 52 meters), and the garage portion is approximately 100 by 100 feet (30 by 30 meters). The

structure was originally designed with a man-lift to serve the attendants who parked the cars. Self-parking was available for workers who wanted to drive directly to their office floor, and walk to their offices on the same level.[40]

By the 1950s, most industrial plants had moved to the suburbs, which led to extensive studies of how best to move large numbers of cars in and out of such facilities. Once a few basic configurations had been settled on, these were adapted to other, similar situations. One of the most so-

Far left: Fisher Building garage and offices, 1928.

Left: Entrance, Fisher Building garage.

ing. The cashiers' office is connected to every floor by telephone and by pneumatic tube.[5]

The garage is designed so that pedestrian movement does not intersect with automobile traffic; patrons use automatic elevators to reach their cars, and can travel from car to street in an average of 3.5 minutes. Moreover, the parking floors are connected directly to the office building, which means that office occupants can park on the same floor as their offices and need never use an elevator once they have parked their car. A pedestrian tunnel was designed to allow easy access to the General Motors Building across the street.[6]

Each floor of the garage had its own gasoline station and uniformed service worker. Gasoline and oil were stored underground, in basement tanks, and delivered by hydraulic systems to each floor. A service area in the basement provided brake service and other repairs, and there was a wash rack on the 11th floor. One of the most advanced parking facilities of its time, the Fisher Building garage is still in use today.[7]

phisticated suburban solutions was the parking structure created for the John Manville Company, in Jefferson County, Colorado, in 1976. Parking is integrated at each end of the office complex, in an arrangement that maintains a functional traffic flow, allows workers to enjoy a pleasant arrival experience, and preserves unobstructed views from the offices to the landscape beyond.[41]

Despite the departure of manufacturing to the suburbs, the demand for downtown office parking only increased. In 1965, it was reported that 73.2 percent of all garages served office buildings, and that 42.3 percent of those garage were located within the buildings. At the Pacific Guardian Center (formerly the Grosvenor Center), built in 1982 in downtown Honolulu, the dense urban environment called for an innovative solution: the double-helix parking structure is integrated into the base of the building and, on the first ten levels, serves as the connector between the twin glass towers. The parking facility is almost invisible from the exterior. At the East Bay Garage, in Charleston, South Carolina, built in 1986, the architect faced a different challenge: providing modern structured parking within a historic waterfront district. As it happened, the surrounding 19th-century warehouses provided the perfect foundation, as has often been the case in the course of the garage's history. With street-level office space and room for 343 cars, the renovated warehouse-turned-garage is a sensitive approach to maintaining the character of the neighborhood and enhancing the user's experience.[42]

In today's central business districts, parking garages are usually found on the lower levels of office buildings, either above or below ground, or on adjoining property. They may also be located in adjacent private or municipal facilities. Only occasionally are parking garages located on the tops of buildings. In suburban office locations, designers are incorporating parking areas—usually lots—into more natural, campuslike settings. What both urban and suburban solutions have in common, however, is the isolation of both the parking facility and the parking experience. As workers speed back and forth from home to work, they almost never encounter a parking experience that is linked, synergistically, to any other experience. Recently, however, downtown offices have begun to forge links with hotel and retail uses, and with alternative forms of transportation. For example, the 1991 renovation of Cleveland's Terminal Tower complex yielded a mixed-use project that revitalized the entire central business district. In addition to a department store, a hotel, a baseball stadium, and a basketball arena, the project offers a 3,150-space garage connected to a renovated transit station.[43]

In another innovative solution, a three-story parking structure (half of which is underground) sits between three office buildings in the International Center Complex on the outskirts of downtown Dallas. Although the principal appeal to employees is the generous amount of parking space provided (more than is required by code), what makes the office complex special is the beautifully designed, 1.5-acre (0.60-

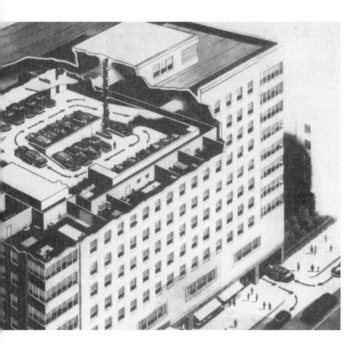

Cafritz Office Building, Washington, D.C., 1954. The parking garage was located in the center of this square office building and was surrounded by offices; workers could drive straight to their office doors.

hectare) garden that sits atop the parking structure. Employees can dine on the roof, and the facility is used after hours as a music venue, providing unique benefits to the community as well. Although the complex was in an excellent location, with access to all forms of transportation, it was the roof of the parking facility—along with the adjoining 15-acre (six-hectare) park—that sold the project to tenants, investors, and the city council.[44]

In addition to integrating the parking garage with other uses, designers are once again attempting to integrate the garage architecturally. At the Comerica Tower, completed in downtown Detroit in 1991, the aesthetic quality of the office building was carried over to the parking garage, a separate, six-story structure that is off to one side. The garage facade includes gently arched, windowlike openings accented by pierced iron grillwork. A glass-covered skyway with a gabled roof connects the parking structure to the office tower. In Atlanta, the designers of a recently completed office tower took another approach, integrating the parking facility seamlessly and invisibly within the glass skin of the structure. The tightness of the site dictated the solution; however, the decision not to differentiate between office and parking is an old strategy made visually new.[45]

The Retail Connection

The need for a practical connection between shopping and parking began almost immediately upon the advent of the automobile. The parking garage became necessary as soon as cars outnumbered the available spaces on the street (which were often taken up by the owner and employees), and the resulting congestion began to inhibit business activity.[46] Over the years, many combinations of shopping and parking have appeared; typically, location is the key driver in determining design solutions. For example, to maintain the aesthetic integrity of the street facade, designers of early garages established an architectural link between shopping and parking: most garages included street-level retail along their sidewalk edges. The Park Square Garage, built in 1905 and one of the first garages constructed in Boston, was among the many garages that had shops lining the exterior of the first level. Although the notion of integrating street-level retail and garages fell out of favor until recently, it did persist in unique cases, such as the Rampark garages, which were built in the 1950s in Lincoln and in Omaha, Nebraska. In these facilities, the shops along the sidewalk edge were maintained, but with a twist: the ramp itself formed a modernistic awning above the sidewalk. At the Gala Garage, built in Spokane, Washington, in 1968, stores were similarly sheltered by a second-story pedestrian skyway that encircled the building. Large, bubblelike canvas awnings covered an adjacent skyway, creating a wonderful visual addition to the city.[47]

As early as 1901, Wanamakers, a Philadelphia-based department store that was also an auto retailer, built a garage connected to the store; soon thereafter, the company did the same for its New York store. Wanamakers was one of the first companies to realize that shoppers were beginning to arrive by automobile; providing parking for patrons of the store (as well as storage space for vehicles that were being sold) was a smart business decision. In San Francisco, the Crystal Palace, a 68,000-square-foot (6,317-square-meter) supermarket established in 1923, offered parking for 4,350 cars and one hour of free parking. Nevertheless, most cities and businesses struggled constantly to meet the need for short-term off-street parking.[48]

The first floor of the Union Market, built in St. Louis, Missouri, in 1926, offered fish, meat, produce, and a general grocery store. But the rest of the building served as a hub for both auto travel and mass transit: the three upper stories operated 12 hours a day as a public garage, and in the basement was a terminal for 22 bus lines that connected St. Louis to other cities; this underground area also included a large public restroom. The public garage was so successful that it paid for itself.[49]

When banks discovered that they could gain customers by providing parking, garages became an integral part of bank design. As early as 1928, a Denver bank leased a garage for its customers. Drive-up banking, which began in 1940, reduced the need for parking spaces, but it was nevertheless logical to combine banking service with a garage. One of the leaders in the drive-up banking trend was the Exchange National Autobank of Chicago, a U-shaped structure whose ten windows and driveways easily accommodated a smooth flow of customers. At the American National Bank of Austin, banking was on the second and third levels; parking was on the fourth and fifth floors, on the roof, and in the basement. The basement also offered drive-in-windows for bank patrons.[50]

One way of relieving street overcrowding was to provide parking on the roof of a retail facility. The Seattle Public Market offered rooftop parking as early as 1930. The nine-department-store chain run by Fred Meyer, Inc., in Portland, Oregon, also offered rooftop parking in the 1930s. In 1936, for the "Hollywood" store of the Meyer chain, local architects Claussen & Claussen created a cantilevered design that overlapped the sidewalk: in addition to providing more parking spaces, the canopy facilitated window shopping by protecting pedestrians from the elements.[51] In Wilkes-Barre, Pennsylvania, a large retail store built in 1954 combined rooftop parking and street-level retail, thus mixing an older approach (retail integrated into garages) with a somewhat newer one (rooftop parking). The State Bank and Trust, constructed in St. Louis in 1954, also provided rooftop parking.[52]

Rooftop parking was also found in early first-ring suburbs, as part of an effort to better integrate parking structures into neighborhoods and to avoid the vast surface lots that were beginning to proliferate in suburban areas. In Evanston, Illinois, in 1936, the Marshall Field store offered rooftop parking on the top of the Firestone retailer next door. The Macy's

Above left: Rampark Garage, Lincoln, Nebraska, 1950. In this visually intriguing design, the sidewalk is lined with storefronts, while the ramp flies above, providing a modernistic awning above the sidewalk.

Above: Gala Garage, Spokane, Washington, 1968. Pedestrian connections of various types, linking parking and city structures, enliven the entire downtown experience.

Left: Union Market, St. Louis, Missouri, 1926. In an early example of a use mix that is reappearing today, this structure combined a garage, a market, and transit.

Synergistic Land Use Connections

Sears, Roebuck & Company store, Los Angeles, 1939. Rooftop parking was a popular mid-20th-century solution.

in Jamaica, New York, built in 1948, had rooftop parking for 150 vehicles. Rooftop parking was common in Sears stores around the country: in the Houston Sears, an attendant operated traffic lights to control the flow of cars on the ramps.[53]

In the never-ending quest for adequate parking, every conceivable spatial arrangement was tried. At the Gay Street Stores, for example, built in Knoxville, Tennessee, in 1959, second- and third-level pedestrian promenades, featuring glass display windows, were constructed above the alley behind the stores, while the alley itself continued to afford passage for cars and trucks. This approach provided some relief from congestion without requiring the streets to be widened. In addition, the mechanical speed ramp that gave pedestrians access to the second-level promenade created a walkable shopping experience.[54]

Country Club Plaza, in Kansas City, which opened in 1929, offers an example of the integration of parking and shopping in the newly developing suburbs. An early instance of the master-planned shopping center, Country Club Plaza was designed specifically to extend the urban street grid of downtown Kansas City and to address the needs of the automobile. The shopping center's two parking lots featured extensive ornamental treatments such as plantings, tile work, and fountains. Later additions to the area—including modern, multistory parking facilities—reflected the same attention to detail that distinguished the original construction. Country Club Plaza demonstrates the value of a good urban design scheme: the basic plan allowed additional development, increased density, and the effective and aesthetic integration of new parking facilities.[55]

Another interesting example of the shopping-parking connection is Pittsburgh's McCann Building built in 1933. In this design, a spiral ramp led inside and looped around one end of the building, providing access only to the upper parking levels, but passing a grocery store and a restaurant en route. The integrated garage—an attended facility—provided parking for 600 cars. The thoughtful integration of store, restaurant, parking, and delivery space within one structure made this facility unique. On the restaurant floor, for example, the kitchen buffered restaurant patrons from the movement of vehicles, but on the market floor, auto users could directly access the market.[56]

San Francisco's Union Square Garage was developed and constructed through a public/private partnership of retailers and city government. Downtown businesses had been harmed by the scarcity of parking and by the reduction in the various types of public transit that had existed prior to the proliferation of the automobile. Given the density of the area and the surrounding land uses, however, the only solution was to go underground. Union Square Garage, a self-park fa-

The Parking Garage

Country Club Plaza: From the 1920s to the Present

Country Club Plaza, developed by J.C. Nichols, was innovative when it was first built, in the 1920s, and is still at the forefront of real estate design and development. In 1993, it received the Heritage Award from the Urban Land Institute. Originally begun as a predominantly retail development at the heart of the larger community known as the Country Club District, the Plaza today is a diverse town center that includes retail, hotel, office, residential uses, and parking structures. Nichols believed that in every city, the downtown retail area should remain dominant; thus, his intent in developing the suburban center was not to compete with downtown Kansas City but to promote stability and further development there. Country Club Plaza was designed to relate to the downtown area and to the city as a whole. It was also meant to create an urban experience that was in keeping with the modern era of man and machine.[1]

Nichols grasped a fundamental principle that is often ignored today: planning must balance the needs of both people and vehicles. He was interested in scientific approaches to handling automobile traffic and the increasing need for parking. The design of the Plaza included streets that channeled unnecessary traffic away from the center, and the Plaza's parking lots were linked to bus transportation. The Plaza's elegant and pedestrian-friendly plan included wide streets and boulevards, and landscaped parking lots that were defined by low walls and featured fountains and seating areas. Some of the fountains and landscape features built in the 1920s remain today. In the 1940s, the *Saturday Evening Post* described the parking stations at Country Club Plaza as being "sunken and landscaped around the edges to resemble parks."[2] The article also noted that "the streets are laid out to create esplanades and parks of every shape, on which Mr. Nichols has mounted art objects from all over Europe."[3] Soon after this article appeared, Nichols again innovated by constructing a three-level self-park garage, free to patrons, with the same Spanish-style exterior used elsewhere in the Plaza. To make parking more convenient, the parking spaces were angled; and to minimize the possibility of contact with car doors, supporting columns were located in front of, rather than between, vehicles. The structure had six entrances for automobiles, and the second and third levels provided direct entry into neighboring buildings.[4]

Despite its many years of successful growth, by the late 1990s Country Club Plaza faced competition from suburban districts even farther from the city, and the city council had to create a tax-increment financing district to fund redevelopment. The project required $240 million, of which $58 million was for parking structures and public amenities. Although the plan was initially met with a public outcry, once Kansas City residents, school officials, and other interested parties understood that the area was in decline, they agreed to the use of public funds for redevelopment. Just as J.C. Nichols had advocated the protection of downtown retail districts when he created Country Club Plaza, his project was protected from decline in the face of even more far-flung suburban growth.[5]

In the redevelopment, the shortage of land made structured parking a necessity. One of the new garages, Saks Parking Garage, reflected the early tradition of ornamented parking facilities: a lively structure with traditional massing and colorful tiles, the garage is visually exciting from all angles and provides a fine complement to the Plaza.[6]

Country Club Plaza was conceived as a pedestrian-friendly suburban business district. Its original thoughtful plan allowed for sustained growth, and for its continuation as a vital part of Kansas City today.

Above: The first parking structure built at Country Club Plaza, 1948.

Below: Saks Fifth Avenue parking facility, 2001.

Bottom: Valencia Place at Country Club Plaza, 2003.

cility built in 1942, was the first garage to be built beneath an existing public park and in the heart of a downtown shopping district. It was also the garage that popularized the notion of underground parking as *the* solution for downtowns.[57]

Union Square Garage was also known as the Garage for Women. Because the architects wanted the garage users, most of whom were women, to feel at ease in such an unfamiliar environment, they included a number of amenities designed to make the facility more comfortable, to make shoppers feel less harried, and to make it easier to cope with the physical distance between the garage and the shops. The floor just below ground level featured offices, an auto-accessories salesroom, and elegantly decorated waiting rooms and restrooms. Valet parking was available, as were private telephone lines linked to nearby department stores. (Each level of the garage also offered public telephones.) But the nursery was perhaps the most important amenity. For the shoppers of today, whose lives are even more hectic, such comforts should certainly be given serious consideration.[58]

The shopping-parking connection also spawned other creative solutions. For example, a 1954 proposal for a supermarket consisted of a wheel-shaped building surrounded by parking lots for easy access for all parkers. At Milliron's Department Store, in Los Angeles, the parking garage (built in 1949) was linked with an auditorium, a kindergarten, and a beauty parlor, creating a kind of one-stop shopping experience for women. San Francisco's Self-Park Garage, built in 1955 to serve the downtown area rather than a single store, not only allowed the driver complete control of parking, but also featured elegant, well-lit merchandise displays on the interior walkway that led from the entrance to the garage, creating a pleasant environment for pedestrians making their way to or from their cars. The facility also provided lounge areas and parcel-checking stations, where packages delivered from the local shops could be stored until the patron was ready to retrieve them.[59]

By 1951, in Arlington, Virginia, the Hecht Company had built what was then the world's largest parking garage, a 2,000-car facility with entrances from each level of the garage directly into the store. (Surface parking provided space for an additional 10,000 cars.) In 1955, Zion's Cooperative Mercantile Institution built what was then Salt Lake City's largest self-park garage. This five-story, ten-level ramp structure measured 300 by 100 feet (91 by 30 meters), provided space for 550 automobiles, and allowed shoppers to walk directly into the store from any parking level. The garage was constructed as an alternative to building a new suburban store. However, the size of the facility was quickly outstripped by demand: soon after it opened, the expanding volume of customers made it once again almost impossible to find a place to park.[60]

In the 1950s and 1960s, as downtown stores attempted to compete with the new suburban malls, designs that allowed customers to enter the store from any level of the parking facility became increasingly common; examples included Rich's Department Store, built in Atlanta in 1955, and People's Department Store, built in Roseland, Illinois, in 1956. Peoples Department Store was a particularly interesting case: in an area where competing stores did not provide parking, owner Jim Gately realized that free parking made

---

Unique Proposals and Initiatives

In the course of the development of the garage as a building type, some of the ideas that emerged were eminently practical; others were ahead of their time; and still others, although they were not implemented, embodied valuable insights that would eventually reemerge, sometimes in unexpected forms.

In the mid-1920s, the architect Raymond Hood developed a design for a church for the Columbus, Ohio, downtown business district. Because the land was so valuable, the congregation wanted the facility to include revenue-producing components: a hotel, a YMCA, an apartment house with a swimming pool, street-level retail spaces, and the city's largest underground garage. The garage was seen as particularly important, since "in giving his congregation a place to park their cars on coming to work weekdays the pastor would indeed make the church the center of their lives."[1] Hood and the pastor understood that function and practicality were just as important as symbols, and could give rise to new ways of living. As a consequence, the design for this multipurpose building was indifferent to programmatic hierarchy: in other words, a parking garage is not normally considered a foundation for a church. In his plan, Hood felt free to engage in a modern practice: "to stack... disparate activities directly on top of each other without any concern for their symbolic compatibility."[2]

Although the Columbus project was never actually built, other combinations of church and garage were. The First Church of Christ, Scientist, erected on Central Park West, in New York City, had an automobile room in its basement as early as 1901. In 1954, the First Baptist Church, in Dallas, built a 300-car parking garage that incorporated not only a chapel, offices, and classrooms, but a gymnasium, a bowling alley, and a roller-skating rink. And at the Calvary Baptist Church, in Washington, D.C., Raymond Hood's 1920s vision for a church as a mixed-used structure is alive and

for good business: patrons who parked in his garage had to walk through his store in order to shop at the establishments across the street. Thus, the garage was essentially an advertising expense. The Gala Garage, which opened in Harrisburg, Pennsylvania, in 1970, was a large garage that offered all the modern features designed to make shoppers' lives easier: angled parking, neon signs directing patrons to open spaces, and express exit ramps.[61]

Recognizing that providing parking was essential to maintaining their businesses, some merchants formed corporations to purchase land and build garages. In 1950, for example, 38 merchants in Wilmington, Delaware, formed such a corporation with the intent of building a parking structure. In other instances, businesses felt that parking was partially a municipal responsibility. In 1936, merchants in Quincy, Massachusetts, asked the city to purchase a vacant lot for public parking. By 1963, 67 percent of department stores and major specialty stores offered some form of parking; however, these structures were not typically community expenses but were constructed at a cost to the owner and developer: thus, costs were eventually passed on to the shopper.[62]

Every shift in how and where people live entails a shift in how and where they shop—and park. Today, parking and retail connections are undergoing tremendous changes, as older towns and first-ring suburbs are being revitalized; town centers are being created or renewed in outer-ring suburbs; seniors, young singles, and families with young children are moving back into downtowns; and development is continuing on the fringes of existing metropolitan centers. As the population expands, suburban malls are being surrounded—

Portrait Square Building and Calvary Baptist Church, Washington, D.C., 2005.

well: the church jointly developed a multifunctional building that includes four levels of parking, all below grade; offices; and a church school with classrooms, assembly space, and a gymnasium. The facility also features street-level retail space developed by Trammell Crow and designed by Leo A. Daly Architects.[3]

Another interesting idea was the combination of auto-rental and parking facilities. In 1922, in Columbus, Ohio, the founders of the U-Drive-It Company, a short- and long-term car-rental company, realized that they could create a logical addition to their business by renting out the spaces that were vacated when cars were in use. By 1954, this company offered 2,100 parking spaces in 12 midwestern cities. Most of these parking garages were near hotels and in the heart of downtown. When the Budget Rent-A-Car Company was founded, in 1962, many parking garage owners added the rental franchise to their primary businesses. During the late 1970s, Share-A-Cab, another innovative idea, linked the parking garage at Boston's Logan Airport to 21 suburban cities by providing cabs that could be shared by travelers going to the same destination.[4]

Visual ideas often find their expression well ahead of their time. In a design proposed by Mies van der Rohe for the 1930 Krefeld Golf Club competition, individual parking garages were the point of entry to the entire facility. Although the project was never built, probably for aesthetic reasons (the effect was reminiscent of the faceless communities where all that can be seen from the street are the blank faces of garage doors), it nevertheless represented a new vision for its time.[5]

In Atlanta in the 1960s, another one-of-a-kind garage combination was conceived: the Varsity, a favorite downtown hamburger joint, erected a two-story parking garage called the Launching Pad just to handle its business volume. This arrangement allowed a typically suburban form—the drive-in hamburger joint—to survive and thrive in a downtown location. By this time, parking had become inseparable from commerce and everything else in the American architectural scene, whether in an urban or suburban location.[6]

and in some cases hidden—by parking structures built on the original surface lots: demand is so great that a 3:1 ratio of parking square footage to building square footage is not unusual. Not only are patrons visually cut off from their destination—the shopping center—but they are compelled to pass through a space that is often daunting and unpleasant, and may be perceived as unsafe. At Old Orchard Shopping Center, for example, one of the earliest open-air shopping centers in suburban Chicago, some of the original surface parking lots now host multilevel garages. Although bridges connect the parking to the stores' original entries, the new structures were designed with little consideration for the pedestrian or for the overall shopping experience. At Miami's Aventura Mall, an attached, five-level, 2,519-space parking structure, built in 1997, visually overwhelms the shopping center. Moreover, the front entrance of the complex is cut off from the nearest road by water retention ponds, creating the impression that the mall is surrounded by a moat. Although express ramps allow for easy entry and exit from the garage, and there are good pedestrian linkages to the shops, the water retention ponds—necessitated by the drainage requirements for the large paved areas—have replaced the original salt marshes. Similarly, the overwhelming parking structures at Atlanta's Lenox Mall have virtually hidden the shopping center on its three public sides.[63]

Interestingly, when Honolulu's Ala Moana Center was built, in 1964, the density of the city *required* the complex to be surrounded by parking structures. The solution was to design a wide sidewalk along the facades of the stores, and to create glass display windows facing into the garage. Skylights make the environment even more open and inviting. Dadeland Station, in Dadeland, Florida, a more recent example of a creative response to site constraints, offers multilevel parking integrated with multilevel shopping. Instead of the typical horizontal arrangement common to power centers, Dadeland Station is structured vertically; escalators and pedestrian and cart elevators provide access to all five anchor stores, and a covered promenade links the parking and shopping areas.[64]

At some existing malls, the designers of new parking structures have succeeded in making the garages more appealing. At the Mall in Columbia, in Maryland, for example, the new garages feature higher floor-to-floor heights and decorative suspended lighting, creating a sense of greater openness—and setting what amounts to a tone of elegance, for a garage. At Tysons Corner Center, outside Washington, D.C., a recent renovation and expansion not only added new parking facilities, but also a children's play area, free valet parking for patrons of selected stores, and a customer service center.[65]

Ala Moana Center, Honolulu, 1964. This suburban shopping center is surrounded by parking garages—but in this case, the arrangement was deliberate: shopfronts face the interior of the garage.

The Parking Garage

At the Promenade at Westlake, in Westlake, California, completed in 1996, the designers reversed the typical relationship between parking and shopping by placing the parking in the center of the landscaped site and ringing it with retail stores. A small number of parking spaces are also provided on the outside perimeter. Because parking is in close proximity to the shops, patrons do not have to cross vast asphalt deserts to reach their destination. In addition, the placement of the retail facilities helps the shopping center blend into the surrounding community and provides a more pleasant pedestrian experience. Although simply reversing the standard layout of mall and parking falls short of creating or supporting a city or a town environment, it can nevertheless benefit both shoppers and the community. Unless it is undertaken with care, however, such an approach can create its own unique problems: if parking, pedestrians, and delivery trucks are compelled to share the same space in the unregulated environment of the parking lot, havoc may result.[66]

To take advantage of their existing amenities, some downtowns have attempted to reposition themselves as urban retail entertainment complexes (UREs), which combine entertainment attractions and retail facilities. A 1996 list of trendsetting UREs included the redeveloped 42nd Street, in New York City; Circle Center, in downtown Indianapolis; and the Mall of America, near Minneapolis.[67] Naturally, UREs depend on good parking—and often on shared parking. At the CambridgeSide Galleria, in Cambridge, Massachusetts, for example, the garage was placed above grade, so that pedestrians would encounter pleasing architectural details as they passed by the facility. It is not uncommon, in UREs, to find sidewalk shops on the ground floor of parking facilities—an old idea that enriches and supports urban street life.[68]

The environments, connections, experiences, and amenities at places like Ala Moana Center, the Mall in Columbia, Tysons Corner Center, and the Promenade at Westlake are examples that garage designers might do well to emulate. There is also much to be learned from Kansas City's Country Club Plaza, which has successfully integrated new parking structures within a well-designed urban plan that is well-connected to the broader urban fabric. A number of new town centers and new urbanist mixed-use developments—including CityPlace, in West Palm Beach, Florida; Reston Town Center, in Reston, Virginia; and Santana Row, in San Jose, California—have drawn on Country Club Plaza and

Above and left: Dadeland Station, Dadeland, Florida, 1993. In this vertical power center, every level of shopping is directly connected to a level of parking.

other early models to create pedestrian-oriented urban parking solutions.[69]

On a site that is perpendicular to the community's original retail strip, Boca Raton's Mizner Park has effectively integrated parking into a coherent urban design scheme. The development offers retail and office space, a multiplex theater, and townhouses and apartments. A public auditorium is the focus of the closed end of the street. On the outer edge of one side of the complex are multilevel public parking facilities connected directly to a divided highway. Large, open, and lavishly appointed stairways lead from these facilities to the movie theaters or to an activated breezeway. Lined with shops, and offering tables and chairs where visitors can sit and relax, the breezeway creates a pleasant transition to the main street of the complex.[70]

On the other side of the project, parking facilities for the office, residential, and retail uses are integrated between the townhouses, creating a buffer between the residential areas and the shopping/office core. Access is by means of a beautifully landscaped alley that has more of the feeling of a side street. The facilities themselves were designed to meet the needs of their various users: private enclosed garages for homeowners are built into the lower level of the garage, and office users have keyed access to separate areas of the garage. Bicycle parking is provided, and retailers and other businesses have delivery zones within the parking facilities.

Every effort to link parking and retail faces the same challenges that arose in the earliest decades of the 20th century: where and how to integrate vehicle storage for shoppers. New retail centers, such as lifestyle centers and retail-oriented towns, have the opportunity to seek new connections to parking and transportation, and to address broader planning concerns. Older centers that are being revitalized always face larger constraints. Regardless of whether the project is a renovation or new construction, however, determining the appropriate relationship between parking and building type is key. Some projects have adopted the strategies employed at Mizner Park. Additional techniques for successfully integrating parking include extensive street parking; multiple small surface lots; parking structures that are visually and physically integrated with nearby buildings; placement of retail or other uses at the ground level of parking structures; and garage designs that are visually distinctive and complement the surrounding architecture. It is the sensitivity of the solution—its ability to integrate the needs of man, machine, and movement—that determines whether a project will be successful in the long term.

Residential Links

Residential uses were first combined with garages on private estates, in urban townhouses, and in the new suburbs that emerged at the turn of the 20th century. Public garages close to residential areas were also part of the solution.

Early designs integrated garages and townhouses, often placing the garage at ground level and the living spaces above. The New York City townhouse garage designed by Whitfield & King for Andrew Carnegie, for example, provided space for parking and for an electric charging station at grade level. Some townhouses of this period included chauffeurs' quarters on this level as well, and some included elevators to move the automobile to an upper level.

Larger-scale combinations of apartment house and parking garage appeared as early as the 1920s, with the garage typically located on the lower levels. Columbus, Ohio, established off-street parking requirements for multifamily dwellings in 1923; other cities followed. Generally, garages

Transition space, Mizner Park, Boca Raton, Florida, 1990. Today, the most popular approach to combining retail and parking is to start from scratch, recreating small-town environments by offering a mix of retail, residential, and public uses. Parking is generally provided on the street; in small, scattered surface parking lots; and in garages that are fully integrated into the overall plan.

for multifamily housing provided no more than one parking space per apartment unit. The Garden Court Garage, built in 1928 in Philadelphia, is an excellent early example of the integration of parking and multifamily housing. Set beneath a garden courtyard in the midst of seven apartment buildings, all of which were at least 14 stories tall, the two-level, 400-vehicle garage was illuminated and ventilated by light wells set into the ground, along the edges of the landscaped courtyard that topped the garage. One parking level was at grade and one was below, and drivers accessed the garage from an adjoining street, moving from one level to another by means of a ramp.[71]

Typically, basement garages for smaller-scale apartment houses were designed to be entered at grade, to take advantage of a slope in the land. One of the early examples of this type was the Massellton, in Atlanta, now on the National Register of Historic Places. The five-story building, constructed in 1925, was one of the first fireproof apartment buildings in Atlanta. It was recently restored and is now a condominium complex. In 2004, the Massellton's parking spaces were selling for $10,000.[72]

In Omaha in the 1920s, a strategically placed and architecturally complementary garage was built across the street from an apartment complex to serve the growing number of automobile owners who lived in the apartments. The surrounding residential area was just distant enough from downtown for residents to need some form of transportation to get to work, but was far enough from the center city to have a leafy, suburban feel: gardens and a fountain sit at the center of the clustered, three-and-a-half-story units. Because of the excellent location and the solid and attractive architecture, this complex remains a functioning part of the city today. The garage sits unused, however, because residents would have to cross a busy four-lane street to obtain access to it. This is a less-than-ideal arrangement that would not be acceptable today in most locations, or in new construction.[73]

At Marina City Towers, designed by Bertrand Goldberg and built in Chicago in 1962, structured parking within a residential building took on a whole new dimension. An early mixed-use complex, the project consists of two cylindrical 65-story towers, in which the 17 stories above the two-story base are devoted to parking. This arrangement elevates the apartments, creating wonderful views, while allowing the garage to become a prominent part of the design from the perspective of the street. The entire structure—referred to locally as "the corncobs"—seems to float above the Chicago River; the garage floors are so open, and so lacking in any observable horizontal restraints, that one can almost imagine a car driving right off and flying, Jetson-style, into the city. When it first opened, the helical ramp garage offered attendant parking; it was later changed to self-park.[74]

In the early 1980s, parking condominiums became one solution for crowded cities. A parking condominium is typically a separate building that is not associated with any particular apartment or housing structure, although it can be. The parking condominium has its own association and is run under the same rules as a residential condominium; as is the case with any other purchase of property, owners may

Above: Andrew Carnegie townhouse, New York City, 1906. In major cities, connections between parking and residential uses started quite early. Often, city townhouses were raised above garages; chauffeurs' quarters were sometimes included within the garage, and some designs used elevators to move the car to another level within the townhouse.

Below: Garden Court Apartments, Philadelphia, 1928. By the 1920s, a strategy was being explored that would eventually become one of the most sought-after of parking solutions: the underground garage with a landscaped courtyard above.

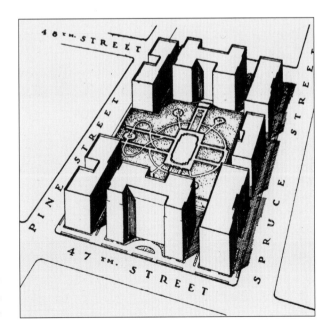

Marina City Towers, Chicago, 1962. The proliferation of the automobile created some strong visual solutions, such as this one: 17 stories of parking supporting 40 stories of apartments in a unique "corncob" design.

benefit from appreciation in value. In Chicago, for example, between 1980 and 1998, apartments increased in value 150 percent, whereas parking spots increased in value by 1,000 percent; in 2000, parking spots were selling for as much as $30,000. Parking condominiums can be found in many cities where real estate values are high and where there are few alternatives.[75]

Boston's Brimmer Street Garage, considered the first parking condominium conversion, was originally built in 1907 as a stable. It has three stories and 110 parking spaces. Cars are still moved by means of an electric lift. Owners whose spaces are unoccupied during the day are permitted to rent them out for short-term parking, which reduces the costs to the owners and makes the most efficient use of the facility. The parking spaces at the Founders Garage, built in 2005 in a prime downtown location in Vail, Colorado, were sold to fund the garage itself and the park above. Seventy-five buyers lived within walking distance of the much-needed parking; each space sold for $100,000, and some spaces now rent during the day for $1,000 a month. The village has several other projects in progress to address the shortage of parking.[76]

Another approach is to construct municipal parking to serve existing residential and retail uses. San Francisco's Lombard Street Parking Garage, built in 1988, was one of the first such garages introduced into an existing neighborhood and designed to blend into the surrounding community. The project was created by Kevin Hagerty, assistant director of the San Francisco Parking Authority; Gordon Chong, president of Gordon Chong and Associates; and Sam Nunes, a design architect, and was built by the San Francisco Parking Authority. Local citizens' groups participated in the design process. Because the main objective was revitalization of the commercial district, cost was a secondary consideration.[77]

The garage has two distinct facades: one faces housing, and is residential in scale and appearance, with peaked roofs, balconies, and windowlike openings covered by decorative screens. The other side of the parking facility, which faces a four-lane retail arterial, features the bay windows typical of San Francisco, and planter boxes that relate to the retail scale but that are still residential in feel. A neighborhood post office, relocated to the first floor of this side of the garage, features a neon and glass-block sculpture on its facade.

In some locations, such as the Cotton Mill Apartments, in New Orleans, a separate parking facility may be the only option. The apartments were converted from a historic mill,

72

The Parking Garage

and there was no land available on the site. Because of nearby transit options, the complex was required to provide only a limited amount of parking—0.66 spaces per unit; nevertheless, young people who appreciated the unique quality of the neighborhood still purchased the units.[78]

As residential projects become increasingly dense, finding land for parking is often a challenge, and the public garage down the street is unlikely to be a viable option for a large development, unless it happens to be in a downtown environment. Moreover, most people today want a direct connection from their parking to their home. In the search for space, elevator garages—which do not need to devote space to ramps—are being considered once again. The approach used in turn-of-the century townhouses—integrating parking on the first level, with living space above—remains common in new townhouse communities all over the

Brimmer Street Garage Condominium, Boston, 1970. One solution to residential parking needs is the parking condo, which can be a neighborhood garage where each car owner purchases a spot.

country, although it has been visually updated to suit modern tastes. And in some warehouse buildings that have been converted to residential use, designers can take advantage of the large floor plates by devoting the center of the building to parking.[79]

On the assumption that residents who live near transit need fewer cars, code-based residential parking requirements are being reduced near transit stations. And as mixed-use projects become more common, shared parking is becoming increasingly viable. In shared parking arrangements, different uses at different times of day (office workers from nine to five, for example, and cinema and restaurant patrons in the evenings) make it possible to reduce the overall number of spaces. Shared parking can work particularly well where residences are located above shops, a once-common urban development pattern that is now being revived.[80]

To keep garage structures hidden from street view, designers sometimes place them within the center of residential developments; however, this arrangement disengages residents from the experience of the street as they make their way between the parking structure and their homes, heightening the isolation of the entry and exit experience. Centering the parking structure can also have a number of other disadvantages: especially in hilly terrain, the result is often visually incongruous. And parking structures can create undesirable views within the development. At the Jefferson at Lenox Park Project, in Buckhead, Georgia, for example, apartment terraces face directly onto exposed parking decks. One option is to "soften" parking facilities with landscaping and to provide access by means of a well-designed alleyway. However, unless the streetfront sidewalk is activated—by being adjacent to a park or other urban amenity, for example—parking the car within the center of the block is an isolating experience. Although placing a tennis court or a swimming pool atop a garage goes some distance toward integrating these "hidden" structures by transforming them into amenities, a more important goal is to fully integrate parking structures not only with housing, but also with other elements of the urban fabric: that is, ensuring that parking structures address the residences, the city, and the street.[81]

Gramercy on the Park, in downtown Cincinnati, is one of the best examples of how to integrate parking within a residential project without sacrificing an active street experience. The result of a partnership between the municipal

Gramercy on the Park, Cincinnati, 1996. Completely integrating parking within a mixed-use project can yield a successful merger of form and function. In this urban example, the parking garage is located at the center of the site, the residential/retail buildings abut the street on the edges, and a courtyard and swimming pool are located atop the parking structure on the third level, creating a pleasant visual and recreational amenity for the residents. Top: First-floor plan. Bottom: Third-floor plan.

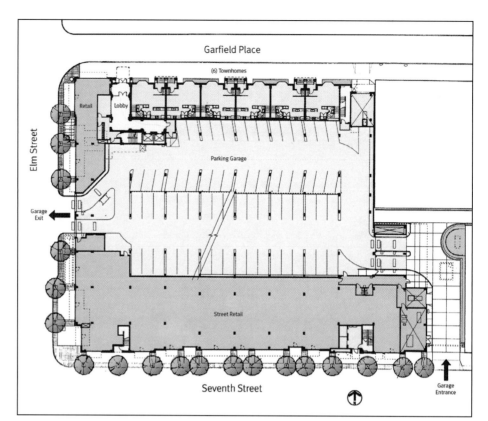

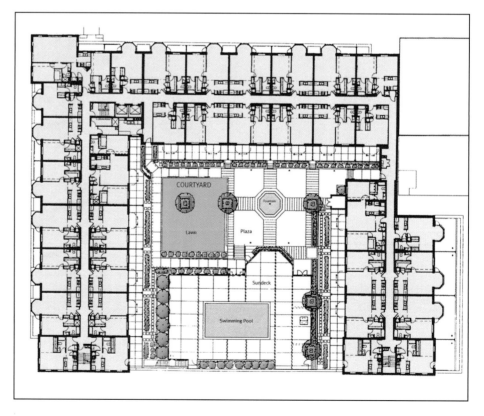

The Parking Garage

government and private developers, Gramercy on the Park is a midrise rental apartment complex opposite the oldest park in the city. The complex replaced a parking lot that had been on the site. The parking structure was used to create an amenity: the roof is an outdoor courtyard with a swimming pool. One side of the parking garage is fronted by street-level retail, making the entire project an excellent neighbor. Apartment residents also have some priority in parking on the generously landscaped street.[82]

Often, new linkages between garages and other uses are in dense locations, where space constraints result in the construction of tall buildings. Because operable windows in such buildings would be unsafe, designers must find ways to bring in fresh air. At 301 Mission Street, a 60-story condominium in San Francisco, tiny holes in the mullions provide air flow. To dampen vibration from automobile movement, particularly where parking facilities are structurally connected to residences, shock absorbers and thicker concrete are now being used.[83]

Hotels, Resorts, Casinos—and the Garage

It did not take long for the parking garage to become a requirement—and a selling point—for the hotel. Kirk's Garage, in New Haven, Connecticut, was operating in 1914 as the garage for the Hotel Taft, New England's largest year-round hotel. W.A. Kirk, who had previously run a livery stable, made an agreement with the Taft to erect and maintain a modern garage, in exchange for the exclusive right to provide parking for the hotel. An elevator garage, Kirk's Garage accommodated 250 cars on four parking floors and offered a number of amenities: a cloakroom, storage for travelers' belongings, private telephone booths, a ladies' lounge, a chauffeurs' lounge, and an auto-accessory showroom. The garage also provided auto maintenance and other services, including fueling, washing, and polishing, and charging stations were available for electric vehicles. A fleet of 14 taxis and a 20-seat motor bus provided shuttle service between the hotel and the railroad station, allowing the hotel to remain closely linked to the station despite the distance. The garage was a practical-looking structure with some brick detailing. But it was also much larger than neighboring buildings, and sported a 40-foot- (12 meter-) long electric sign that exuberantly proclaimed its allegiance to the modern age.[84]

Atlanta's Georgian Terrace Hotel was one of the best-known tourist hotels in the South, and the public garage that,

by 1913, had been connected to it was one of the largest in the region, holding at least 200 vehicles. The garage also provided a taxicab service for the hotel. In what appears to have been a unique effort to shelter the driver from the nitty-gritty aspects of the early automobile, the garage employed only women to polish cars and deliver them to customers—keeping the male mechanics, in their greasy overalls, out of sight. The single-story, 25,000-square-foot (2,323-square-foot) wood-truss garage was located behind the hotel; cars entered through a brick archway that, according to a 1913 article in *The Horseless Age,* was "not at all displeasing."[85] It was here, in the middle of the Peachtree Street facade of the main building, that the automobile was polished and delivered to the owner. Although the initial purpose of the garage was to serve the hotel and the surrounding residences, it quickly outgrew that function and was turned over to an independent operator who managed the growing operation. Especially after the construction of an 11-story apartment hotel, on the corner opposite the Georgian Terrace Hotel, parking in the area was at a premium.[86]

In 1923, Morris Baker, a parking garage pioneer in the Minneapolis–St. Paul area, built the first integrated hotel garage in the Twin Cities area, for the Sheridan Hotel. The billboards advertising the garage read, "You and Your Car at the Sheridan for only $3.00," and were located at some distance from what was then the center of downtown. This early downtown ramp garage housed 645 cars and eventually became part of what would now be called a mixed-use complex.[87]

Early hotel garages were generally designed to be architecturally distinctive. For example, in 1926, a small but elegant garage was built to complement the Mediterranean Revival style of the Biltmore Hotel, in Los Angeles.[88] At around the same time, a five-story brick and limestone garage, also reflecting an urbane sensibility, was built for Buffalo's Hotel Statler. The facade of the Hotel Statler's garage belied its purpose: cars entered the facility through an opening that had been astutely designed to match a shopfront opening in size; another such opening accommodated the gas station, creating wonderful architectural rhythms of solid and void along the street and blending the building successfully into the surrounding urban fabric. These openings had awnings, just like the rest of the shops on the street, and were marked only by small signs. Examples of similarly designed garages, carefully planned to blend into their surroundings, could be found in cities, rural vacation spots, and tourist areas throughout the country.[89]

As early as the 1920s, hotels began to spring up on popular travel routes outside of cities. Since land was more plentiful in these rural areas and emerging suburbs, the typical parking arrangement consisted of a "motor hotel" (motel) alongside a surface lot: guests drove right up to the doors of their rooms. In addition to offering privacy and convenience, this arrangement provided travelers with the comfort of being able to see the car at all times—a must in an era when a car was a source of personal pride. Once travelers became accustomed to this spatial relationship and level of convenience, some downtown hotels—even those in dense urban locations—tried to match it.[90] San Francisco's Hilton Hotel, for example, built in 1959, offered an internal parking garage that allowed guests on the fourth through the tenth floors to walk directly from their cars to their rooms.[91]

The 1960s was the era of the "skyscraper" hotel, where rooms were stacked above parking. Here the design approach of choice was to accentuate the garage, as at the Howard Johnson Motor Hotel in Chicago's Loop. Integrating the latest hotel amenities—pools, restaurants, lounges, observation decks, *and* garages—wasn't easy, but it did offer some terrific design opportunities. In one example of innovative integration, the Royal Orleans Garage, in New Orleans, allowed patrons to register at a special desk within the garage itself, then proceed directly to their rooms.[92]

Hotels in dense urban environments, such as the Washington Statler, used fully automated garage systems such as the Park-O-Mat (discussed in chapter 5). In 1965, *Innkeeping* magazine described a new hotel design in which patrons placed their cars in an automated parking system, then walked immediately through a set of glass doors into a beautifully appointed lobby. The transition to the lobby was marked by a row of little green plants atop a glass wall; the article regarded the juxtaposition of mechanization and modern aesthetics as the perfect modern solution.[93]

Resorts, casinos, and hotels must attract customers—and thus, by definition, must offer attractive facilities and experiences. And since the parking garage is often the first environment patrons encounter, it should be a legitimate focus of attention: a resort or a hotel should make the guest feel taken care of from the moment of arrival. Nevertheless, hotel parking (unless it's valet) has often been an unpleasant experience involving badly lit garages and poor pedestrian connections to the rest of the facility.[94]

However, the tide has begun to turn. Hotels, resorts, and other entertainment facilities are attempting to integrate garages, both aesthetically and experientially, into the overall experience. At the Turning Stone Casino Resort, in Verona, New York, for example, the six-story, 2,401-space parking facility features large-scale graphics and neon signs; decorative lighting; and curved, Le Corbusier–style roofs. Nor have the innovative owners of Las Vegas casinos spared any effort in making their parking facilities as glitzy as the rest of the city, in an effort to immediately connect their visitors to the fantasy experience of Las Vegas. The parking facility at Caesar's Palace, for example, would look right at home near the Parthenon; the garage has received a design award from the International Parking Institute.[95]

In all of Las Vegas, 32 parking garages, with 175 parking floors, serve the casinos. Parking is free in the casinos, but because of overwhelming demand, there is a charge for parking almost everywhere else in the city. To alleviate congestion on the Strip and to free up spaces in existing garages, local investors, the city of Las Vegas, and a St. Louis construction company have been exploring the construction of large new parking facilities at some distance from the hotels. The structures, which would have as many as 25,000 spaces, would serve hotel and casino workers, who would then be shuttled to their jobs. Although some of the casinos are already connected by a raised transit system, unless further efforts are made to integrate non-auto transportation, the parking problem will only continue to escalate.[96]

Completed in 2001 and designed by Walker Parking Consultants and Harry Wolfe, the Disney Resort garage, in Anaheim, California, is one of the largest parking facilities in the United States, serving over 10,000 vehicles a day. This one structure incorporates many unique solutions, but one of the most instructive is its relationship to its neighbors. The goals of the design were to minimize the impact of traffic on the surrounding streets and to limit the visual impact of the massive parking structure; both were accomplished. One facade of the facility, which faces a neighborhood of small, single-family homes, is stepped and beautifully landscaped to create the impression of a low-rise wall. The garage fits easily within the residential context, and the facade gives virtually no clue that 10,000 cars are parked beyond the landscaping. Moreover, the circulation patterns and the arrangement of the garage entrances are such that the resort traffic never enters the residential community. The structure exemplifies the best in creative solutions for the mega-facility.[97]

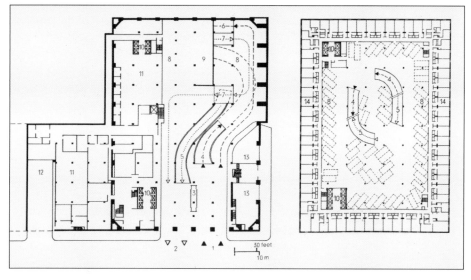

Top left: Commodore-Biltmore Hotel and garage, Los Angeles, 1926. By the 1920s, hotels across the country—in towns large and small, and even in the most remote locations—had their own garages. The garage is the beautifully detailed building adjacent to the hotel in the lower left of this photo.

Above right: Howard Johnson Motor Hotel, Chicago, 1971. In an urban form that emerged during the 1970s, the garage was a plinth on which to perch a hotel.

Bottom left: Hilton Hotel and garage, San Francisco, 1959. Because travelers had become accustomed to the convenience of parking directly in front of their motel rooms, multilevel urban garages eventually began to provide the same amenity, allowing visitors to drive right up to their hotel rooms.

Synergistic Land Use Connections

New Challenges:
The Airport and the Hospital

Many land uses are facing parking shortages; among these are hospitals and airports. What these land uses have in common is typically urban locations, limited open land, and the need to expand.

Airport Parking

The airport has a unique and important connection to parking. Many airports have grown piecemeal, and the resulting complexity, and sheer size, can make navigation difficult. At its best, the parking garage can bring a pedestrian-friendly experience to the airport environment, providing design features that assist with way-finding and "parking memory" ("Where did we leave the car?"). Although signs are still important navigational aids, architectural "messages" may be easier to grasp: a well-placed skylight, or a separate path with distinctive paving, can do wonders for the confused pedestrian. At a new parking garage at the Louisville International Airport, in Louisville, Kentucky, two interior light wells with barrel-vaulted skylights serve as cues, directing pedestrians to the terminal building. At San Francisco International Airport, the automated people-mover system, which can transport 3,400 people per hour in each direction, now connects the parking structures, the terminal, and the regional rail system, eliminating the need for as many as 200,000 car trips per year.[98]

Disney parking facility, Anaheim, California, 2001. This massive facility was designed with two goals in mind: first, to avoid overwhelming the adjacent small-scale residential area; and second, to accommodate the large number of drivers who arrive simultaneously and are unfamiliar with the structure.

A relatively new arrival on the airport parking scene is the consolidated rental car facility (also known as a RAC, CONRAC, or CRCF),[99] a parking structure that gathers all the rental agencies and their associated vehicles into a single building, an arrangement that saves customers time, makes better use of scarce airport land, and offers potential connections with shuttles, limousines, and hotels (both on and off the airport site). In addition, this type of garage facility could become an entry point for the screening and transfer of luggage to the airport terminal, an idea that was originally proposed for the Los Angeles airport (LAX) as early as 1967. (As of 2006, LAX will allow luggage to be checked at remote locations.)[100]

The Dallas–Fort Worth International Airport was one of the first to consolidate all its rental facilities into a single, well-appointed parking structure with spacious lobbies and walkways and elegant terrazzo floors. The CONRAC at McCarran International Airport, in Las Vegas, serves 11 agencies, all of which share bus service from the airport to the facility. A CONRAC has been in operation at the San Francisco airport since 2000. Such facilities are now being built even in smaller airports that face increasing constraints on the availability of land. In San Jose, for example, HNTB designed a 10,000-car facility that will be the first thing the driver encounters upon entering the airport complex.[101]

Hospital Parking

Particularly in dense urban settings, parking garages have long been essential elements in hospital design. One early example is the Cornell University Medical College and Main Hospital, in New York City, which included a parking facility in its 1933 master plan; the structure is still used by hospital employees. So that employees, patients, and vehicles can move easily and safely between the parking garage and the hospital facility, the hospital and the garage need a close and direct relationship, but site constraints often make it difficult to meet this need.[102]

Funding for hospital garages often competes directly with funding for other necessities, such as modernized equipment. One way to address both site constraints and uncertainty about the direction of future needs is to build in flexibility: at Erlanger Medical Center, in Chattanooga, Tennessee, completed in 1981, the "old" idea of converting a flat-floored garage to other uses was revived: flat floor plates and an easily removed external speed ramp allow easy renovation or expansion. Floor-to-floor heights in the parking structure range from ten to 16 feet, and are in line

Left: Louisville International Airport, Louisville, Kentucky, 1998. At this airport parking facility, pedestrians are drawn to a central atrium, then guided to the terminal by a series of architectural and design cues.

Below: Dallas–Fort Worth consolidated rental car facility, 2000. The consolidated rental car facility (CRCF) is among the newest variations on the parking garage. CRCFs are often multimodal facilities and commonly feature large, well-designed lobbies.

with those of other buildings in the hospital complex.[103]

Today's hospital garages often incorporate special designs and uses. Houston's John P. McGovern Texas Medical Center Commons, for example, designed by Walter P. Moore and built in 2003 with private funds, is a multifunction facility offering a restaurant and other services. The facility's most striking feature, however, is the waterfall at the entry, which redefines the entry and exit experience by offering a visually calming element rarely associated with parking structures. Moreover, the numerous amenities of the Commons—including a food court, conference rooms, a lounge, retail space, and a roof terrace—create a welcome refuge from the hospital environment.[104]

At the Royal Jubilee Hospital, in Saanich, British Columbia, the presence of some mature, heritage Garry Oaks presented a challenge to the construction of a new parking garage. The designers saved the trees by creating a therapeutic garden between the garage and an adjacent acute-care facility for seniors. The solid wall of the garage serves as a pleasant visual backdrop, creating a walled garden that is shielded from noise. The garden is a successful element in the hospital's care plan for its patients.[105]

Parking at Colleges and Universities: A Unique Opportunity

Colleges and universities, microcosms of larger and more diffuse urban (or suburban) environments, offer self-contained planning opportunities—ideal laboratories for the exploration of parking, planning, and transportation synergies and solutions.[1] Parking problems arose at institutions of higher education in the 1950s; reminiscing about the period, Clark Kerr, chancellor of the University of California, Berkeley, commented that "the great administrative problems of the day were sex for the students, athletics for the alumni, and parking for the faculty."[2]

Older campuses typically required parking only for sports stadiums or other large gatherings, as automobiles were rarely used on campus. Today, however, more students own cars and bring them to campus; more students commute by car; and campuses are growing, making cars more necessary. All these factors combine to increase the demand for parking. By the 1990s, the average campus parking garage (and there is often more than one) held 1,000 cars; four decades earlier, the typical campus facility held between 300 and 500 vehicles.[3]

Urban campuses often lack land that can be used for parking, and even suburban and small-town campuses are pressed to keep up with demand. Some colleges and universities have become

ringed with surface parking facilities, in order to maintain their centers as predominantly pedestrian areas. However, this arrangement requires expensive investments in transportation systems to carry students from the lots to the center of campus. Some institutions have had to build structured parking, which is also costly.[4]

Because colleges and universities must deal with complex issues of topography, growth, and restricted land area, many have become laboratories for parking and transportation solutions. For example, the Mountain View Student Center Parking Garage—designed by McCarty Bullock Church and Holsaple, and built in 1973 at the University of Tennessee at Knoxville—combines a parking facility and a student center on a sloped site. Terraced parking levels and a screen covering the top of the structure create a pleasing exterior; pedestrian walkways connect the highest level of the parking facility to the entry level of the student center. A masterful balance of functionality, modern aesthetics, and pedestrian connections enabled this very modern structure to be situated among historic campus buildings.[5]

Old Dominion University, in Norfolk, Virginia, has proposed a more unusual solution to the parking problem: the nation's first magnetic levitation train, which would run on an elevated track above roads and walkways, and link the convocation center and residence halls with academic buildings and parking garages.[6]

In many cases, colleges and universities collaborate with surrounding communities to construct parking facilities and/or trans-

portation systems that will meet both their needs; examples include Hillsborough Community College and the city of Tampa, and the University of Michigan and the city of Ann Arbor. In 2003, in a historic district of Ybor City, Florida, Tampa and Hillsborough Community College constructed a 1,200-space brick garage that includes a ground-level pedestrian colonnade. In the 1970s, the city of Morgantown, West Virginia, and West Virginia University collaborated on an innovative personal rapid transit system. The system is still in place today, but is not as effective as it could be because it is not connected to parking. In 2002, Emory University, in Atlanta, built a six-story, 1,897-space, neoclassically styled parking facility that is connected to the main campus by means of an electric shuttle that passes through the otherwise sacrosanct woods surrounding the president's house. The facility also houses 50 charging stations and a storage area for the electric shuttles, and serves as a parking hub for a new housing complex on the other side of campus.[7]

College and university buildings are often steeped in history, and one of the most difficult challenges for campus parking facilities is maintaining the existing aesthetic. At the University of Virginia, in Charlottesville, a new, classically styled parking facility nestles into a hillside, blending in with the surrounding historic buildings. Thanks to a well-conceived design, the building also comfortably houses the school bookstore.[8]

By attempting to meet all their everyday needs, some colleges and universities are trying to encourage students and employees to live on or near campus. Parking facilities are being combined with dormitories, and elaborate, on-campus apartment complexes are being constructed. The campus of the University of Pennsylvania, in Philadelphia, features an 11-story, 800-space combination parking facility and supermarket. A pay-on-foot station is conveniently located in the elevator lobby near the supermarket entrance.[9]

Some institutions have placed grass playing fields on top of garages—a strategy that not only saves land, but also helps to reduce runoff and alleviate the heat island effect. Other campuses—such as the University of British Columbia, which created the Rose Garden Parkade—have combined parking with gardens or parklike settings. Still others, such as the University of Kansas, in Lawrence, have taken advantage of hilly terrain to situate the parking facility neatly in the center of campus.[10]

Colleges and universities have explored all the solutions that have been tried in cities; however, because institutions of higher education often have more autonomy, their solutions are more likely to be integrated into complete planning strategies. Although this can be an advantage when it comes to sensitively constructing parking facilities, autonomy also means absorbing all costs. In other words, colleges and universities face the same issues as municipalities, but often without the opportunity to share costs with private enterprise.[11]

From left (on facing page) to right: Grocery and parking garage, University of Pennsylvania, Philadelphia, 2002; parking garage, Arizona State University, Tempe, 2004; parking garage, University of Virginia, Charlottesville, 1994; parking garage, Emory University, Atlanta, 2002.

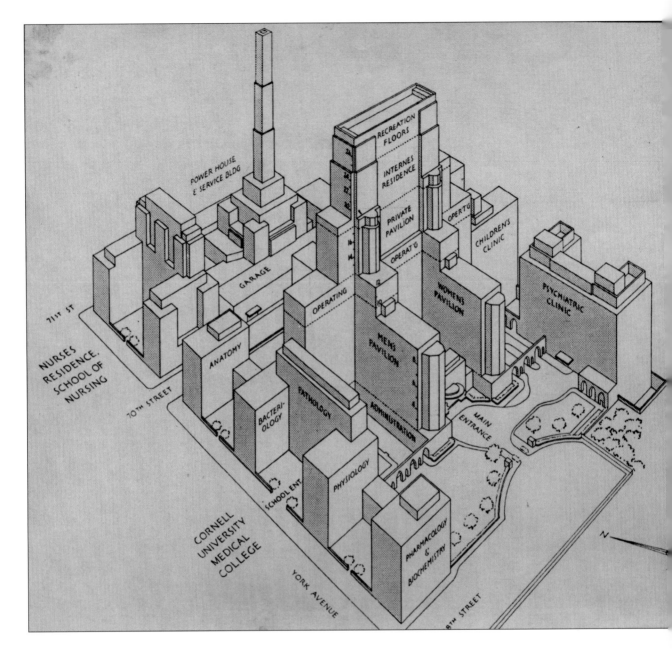

Cornell University Medical
College and Main Hospital,
New York, 1933. Large, multistory parking facilities were included as part of the overall
plan for this hospital campus.

The Parking Garage

At Huntsville Hospital East, in Huntsville, Alabama, a teaching facility with 901 beds and 3,981 parking spaces, the decision to build a parking structure on an existing parking lot, rather than on open land, left land available for a new medical office building. Rick Kinnell, a parking consultant on the project, noted that parking was "one of the key factors in the success of the hospital's expansion" and "played a direct role in the hospital's ability to grow."[106] The Huntsville medical campus is so large that a light-rail system was built to link the medical buildings and the parking facilities, cutting down on vehicle traffic and sparing visitors the inconvenience of having to negotiate the large distances between facilities on foot. The light-rail service reflects a holistic view of the overall movement system, in which each element—including the parking garage—plays an important part.

Integrated Parking Solutions

The traditional relationships between parking and the workplace, parking and retail, and parking and residential uses are becoming increasingly complex. At the same time, growing demand for parking is overwhelming other land uses—from airports to hospitals to entertainment complexes. As the history of parking combinations continues to unfold, the possibilities are infinite, and many of the solutions already put into practice have been both creative and successful. The key question, as always, is how best to integrate parking.

Parking exists in a dynamic relationship with every conceivable land use and building type: a change in one side of the equation will inevitably produce a change in the other. For a significant portion of the 20th century, the social, aesthetic, and urbanistic context of the parking garage was not adequately taken into account. In the past decade, however, the designers of parking facilities have become increasingly aware of the garage's potential to forge synergistic connections with other uses. Cities, towns, and suburbs alike are seeking more sustainable forms of development. Parking garages that are architecturally integrated with other building types, that feature a mix of uses, and that take into account future movement patterns can support this effort.[107]

Past Lessons for the Present and Future

➔ The parking garage has always been linked with other building types, and how this connection occurs is one of the key aspects of parking garage design. At best, the garage fully supports the uses to which it is linked, and also serves as a place of transition between experiences. New designs must acknowledge the importance of the parking garage as a gateway—to another building, to a particular set of uses, and to the city itself.

➔ In a spirit of integration that harks back to early garage designs, a new relationship is emerging between the hotel and the parking garage: beautiful interior car lobbies are now just steps away from the main hotel lobby.

➔ Automobile showrooms are returning to downtown centers. Integrating them with parking for local uses—as was the case when automobile showrooms first appeared—makes sense once again.

➔ Creating complementary exteriors for the garage and its primary use is a step in the right direction; however, the pedestrian experience within the garage is of equal importance. A truly successful experience for the user means that every aspect of the garage and the associated facilities must work in combination, both practically and aesthetically.

➔ Municipal parking facilities can and should be integrated into the community as part of an overall, pedestrian-centered design strategy that balances the needs of both man and machine.

➔ Synergistic connections between uses can reduce the need for parking (by facilitating shared parking) and offer more options for the placement of parking facilities. Reversing the typical spatial relationship between the suburban mall and parking can completely transform projects into pedestrian-friendly environments designed for humans as well as machines.

➔ The most sustainable results derive from thinking of the parking garage as a connector to other building types, and providing a rich and complex set of experiences and choices for the user.

CHAPTER 4

Form and Function

The parking garage sprang from a unique set of utilitarian needs that had never before existed. As the building type evolved, functionality was one of the driving factors. In the earliest purpose-built garages, the emphasis on functionality was limited to the interior; eventually, however, changes in the automobile, in society, and in architectural thinking led to designs in which the exterior expressed the utilitarian purposes of the interior. The dreary, cavernous, overwhelming, unadorned concrete boxes that resulted are the bane of many a city today. Nevertheless, an understanding of the functional needs that a parking structure serves remains inseparable from successful design.

This chapter considers a very basic question: How did the parking garage become the thing especially fitted *only* for storing the car?

Functionality and the Early Garage

For the early parking garage, functionality meant meeting the needs not only of vehicles but of their owners and users. Boston's Fenway Garage, for example, built in 1914, was designed specifically to accommodate the expectations of automobile owners. The full-service garage offered a machine shop, a repair room, and an area for charging the batteries of electric vehicles. The garage was also heated, and had lounges for customers. The chauffeurs' rooms had pool and billiard tables, a barber shop, and places to read and relax. Because vehicles required constant servicing, good lighting was essential: for maximum daylight, Fenway had floor-to-ceiling plate-glass windows; it also had electric lights, then a new technology. The unique layout of the garage allowed automobiles to be cleaned and maintained without being moved: each bay was fitted with all the necessary equipment. The entry and exit doors were controlled manually, so that cars' movements could be recorded, and all chauffeurs had to sign a log. A telephone connection with the main office allowed for easy retrieval of vehicles.[1]

Above: Clinton Garage, New York City, 1912. The chauffeurs' room was an integral part of the early parking garage. Some chauffeurs' rooms were very simple; others offered numerous amenities for comfort and relaxation.

Facing page: Clayton Lane Parking Structure, Boulder, Colorado, 2006. Glass stairwells, now a common design element, increase the sense of security in parking facilities.

The U.S. Post Office Garage, designed by Ballinger & Perrot, Architects, and constructed in 1918, was built to accommodate a fleet of identical vehicles, a rare situation in the early years of automotive travel. Thus, the designers had the opportunity to explore the maximum integration of function and efficiency. Every design decision originated with the dimensions of the mail truck. On the basis of those dimensions, parking spaces of a particular size were designed. And once the size of the parking spaces had been determined, other decisions followed: for example, in order to maximize the number of stored vehicles, structural elements had to be separated by a particular distance. Thus, the two-story garage was conceived as an architecturally complete system of interrelated parts: parking stalls were uniform, driving aisles and turning radii were consistent, and the structure used a ramp, the most efficient movement system available.

As part of the effort to make the best use of available space, the designers situated a locker room above the exit ramp. Floors were pitched to facilitate drainage. Water and waste runoff were collected, channeled, and drained through a gutter system. Curbs and raised platforms separated parking and maintenance areas from traffic flow. Equipment for washing vehicles was provided at the parking stalls. Operable windows allowed fresh air to enter the structure, and sawtooth skylights admitted light into the top floor of the garage and into the top-floor sewing room of the adjoining three-story building, where auto upholstery was repaired.[2]

Not until the 1930s was the functionality of garage interiors fully expressed on their exteriors. In this respect, the Post Office Garage was a transitional structure: the exterior was simple but well proportioned, reflecting both a modern sensibility and the influence of traditional aesthetics. The combination of industrial plate-glass windows; a traditional base, middle, and cornice; and decorative brick patterns yielded a style that might be called "industrial beaux-arts." However, the garage was a long and imposing structure, and did not include shops or other ground-floor amenities.

Lighting, Safety, and Way-Finding

To meet the need for maneuverability, early garages needed vast, unencumbered expanses of space. And to meet the need for maintenance, they needed light. Thus, designers had to find a way to bring natural light into the interior of these large spaces. The first solution was large expanses of glass. Ads for Boston's Fenway Garage, for example, trumpeted the advantages of an open facade with "large plate glass windows," where the supporting columns were virtually the only masonry work. In one early garage, light from the exterior windows was supplemented by a central, skylit two-story space above the ramp, which not only provided light for the ramp itself, but also allowed light to spill into the center of the garage.[3]

For supplemental lighting, incandescent electric lamps were generally the choice, because of their low fire risk. At San Francisco's Ford Service Building, which was built in 1916, 100-watt tungsten lamps were placed 11.5 feet (3.5 meters) above the floor in a 12.5-foot by 14-foot (3.8-meter by 4.3-meter) grid, an arrangement that provided uniform illumination of 4.13 foot-candles (44.5 lux) three feet (0.9 meters) above the floor.[4] The lamps were equally spaced and hung by cords from the ceiling.[5]

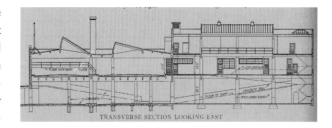

TRANSVERSE SECTION LOOKING EAST

Top: U.S. Post Office Garage, New York City, 1918. The structure of this early parking garage was based on standardized parking spaces and conceived as an efficient, integrated system. The design included a skylight.

Above: Packard Garage, Philadelphia, Pennsylvania, 1927. Because light was important for both maintenance and navigation, skylights of all varieties were common in early parking garages.

Another early source of artificial light was the RLM fixture (so called because it had the endorsement of the Reflector and Lighting Equipment Manufacturers), a single lightbulb with a porcelain reflector. Indirect lighting and other types of specialty lighting were also used; for example, auto showrooms located within garages were lit round the clock, to display the automobiles inside.[6]

Sufficient light for maintenance remained an important design issue until about 1930, when most localities began requiring complete separation of parking and maintenance services, and when the open-deck parking structure did away with the facade altogether. Although open-deck garages allowed less natural light into the interior than had been admitted by skylights and large expanses of glass, this was not considered a problem: the attendants who parked the cars were familiar enough with the facility to maneuver in low light—and, even with the advent of self-park facilities, garages were still typically used only during the day.[7]

Maneuvering a vehicle in low light, however, was not the only safety issue associated with garages. As early as 1925, the entire first floor of a Baltimore garage had been designated for the use of women only—partly for safety reasons, and partly because women were typically short-term parkers.[8] But it was not until the 1950s that Ethel E. Brimmer, of St. Louis, Missouri, made security a priority. Brimmer's reasoning was that the garage was central to the community. At Brimmer's 18th Street Garage, the emphasis was on service to the public—which meant creating an environment that was welcoming, pleasant, and safe, and that considered user needs beyond parking. Gradually, other garages followed suit. By offering the same kinds of services provided at Brimmer's garage—such as stroller rental and daycare—and by giving more attention to details such as lighting, maintenance, and aesthetics, garage owners and designers hoped to create environments that were both comfortable and secure.[9]

The major catalyst in the transition from the purely functional to the pedestrian-oriented facility was the self-park garage. In the era of attendant parking, personal security for garage patrons had not been considered a major issue. But as self-park ramps proliferated, and as nighttime use of parking decks became common, the kinds of safety concerns that are associated with any large public space began to arise.[10]

Because the parking garage is often a large, vacant space, it can create the potential both for actual crime and for a feeling of discomfort and insecurity. Thus, in parking garage design, perceived safety is as important as actual safety; in fact, safety is both researched and discussed in terms of what makes people feel "comfortable."[11] For the garage designer, light is one means of combating both actual crime and the sense of insecurity—which, in turn, affects the amount of light that is required and the ways in which it is provided. For example, the high light levels that are often needed for safety tend to spill over into nearby buildings and even entire neighborhoods, creating yet another problem that designers must address. At Emory University, in Atlanta, 24-hour parking garages on the perimeter of campus back up to a historic, Olmsted-designed residential district. To deflect light and noise to the inside of the structures, the designers placed louvers within the openings on the sides of the garages that face the residential district.[12]

18th Street Garage, St. Louis, Missouri, 1955. Ethel E. Brimmer, of St. Louis, believed that the parking garage was central to the community and should provide services to the public. Many in the garage industry followed her lead.

The Parking Garage

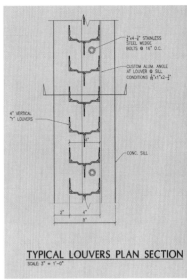

Left: Moana Pacific Condominium Tower, Honolulu, 2005. Properly designed, louvers screen light, limit views to the interior, create the "look" of a building (not simply a garage), and allow parking garages to meet ventilation requirements.

Above: Moana Pacific condominium, plan section, typical louver.

In the late 1940s and 1950s, when underground garages became common, lighting naturally became a key consideration in making the structures usable and safe. The self-park underground garage built in 1961 for the Brooklyn Civic Center, for example, had a specially designed fixture that improved light output by directing the light downward, and that also featured a dust-proof, vandal-resistant cover.[13]

In garage interiors, the combination of low ceilings and exposed structural elements can block light; thus, it can be difficult to place lighting fixtures so as to obtain the maximum possible level of illumination and light coverage. Moreover, because of tight construction tolerances and the minimum clearances required for vehicles, lowering the fixtures below the beams is generally not an option. In the parking area of a garage, 15 foot-candles (161 lux) is the industry standard for level of illumination; however, higher levels may be desirable in entry, exit, and pedestrian areas. The most appropriate lighting choices also depend on weather conditions, as lighting sources behave differently in cold and in hot environments.[14]

A number of efforts are currently underway to develop new approaches to lighting parking structures. New fixture designs, for example, use less energy and have the capacity to provide more or less light, depending on what is needed.

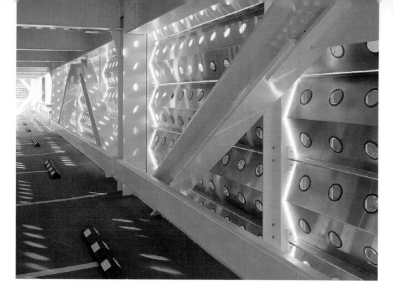

Above left: Station Place Parking Facility, Portland, Oregon, 2004. In this structure, an innovative use of exterior baffles creates different-colored lights on each level, which helps drivers remember where they parked their cars.

Above right: Nashville International Airport, Nashville, Tennessee, 2001. The best approach to way-finding relies not on signs or maps but on art and architecture to guide users to their destination.

An architecture student at the University of Nebraska has proposed placing automated louvers on garage facades; the system would reflect natural light farther into the garage during the day (and thereby reduce dependence on electricity), and would redirect sound and unwanted light at night. Another student at the same university has proposed placing curved reflective strips within the hollow areas of the precast structural system. When combined with uplighting, this approach provides better coverage from fewer watts over a broader area. Both of these ideas are simple, passive, energy-efficient means of increasing overall light levels while channeling more light where it is most needed: toward pedestrian walking paths.[15]

The garage at Lexington Bluegrass Airport, in Lexington, Kentucky, which opened in 2002, features excellent use of prismatic (glass optics) lighting: 100-watt high-pressure sodium lamps are located on a 23-foot by 30-foot (seven-meter by nine-meter) grid; the lights are mounted 15 feet (4.5 meters) high on the first floor and 12 feet (3.7 meters) high on the second floor; in addition, the entire garage is painted white, which intensifies but also diffuses the light from the fixtures. Depending on ceiling height, the light levels range from 5.8 foot-candles (62.4 lux) to 12.3 foot-candles (132.3 lux). At all vehicle and pedestrian entrances and exits, 175-watt metal halide lamps provide more light than is typical for a garage, to help ease the visual transition from exterior to interior. The lighting on the roof parking deck is controlled by a photocell, which turns the fixtures on and off in response to the amount of daylight; all other lighting fixtures remain on at all times, providing safety and security throughout the structure. (An environmentally desirable alternative might be to install lights that are triggered by motion, or that are turned on and off by timers.)[16]

In addition to lighting, a number of other architectural approaches can be used to increase safety and security: high floor-to-ceiling heights, light-colored or high-reflectivity paints, carefully planned entrances and exits, and dedicated pedestrian paths that are well lit and open to the exterior as much as possible. Glass-enclosed stairwells and elevators are an option that is now considered standard. One of the earliest glass-backed elevators ever used in a parking garage was in the Western Michigan Community College parking deck, which was designed by Carl Walker and built in Kalamazoo in 1969.[17]

Although glass is used in stairwells and elevators primarily as a passive security measure, it also creates an excellent opportunity for architectural expression. Historically, however, technology, rather than architecture or human connections, has been used to address safety and security in garages. Closed-circuit television was an early approach that is still in use today. (Such systems were also used in parking lots, once the tower attendants—whose job it was to locate empty stalls in large parking areas—had been eliminated.) Other technologies include intercoms and telephones. A facility built in Harrisburg, Pennsylvania, in 1971 incorporated

TV monitors, two-way intercoms, and random patrols at all hours. A Des Moines, Iowa, garage—built in 1985 and designed, owned, and managed by Richard C. Rich—was one of the earliest facilities to use both cameras and an intercom system. Today, many parking structures feature direct telephone lines to local police, or blue-light systems that connect the user directly to security services at the touch of a single button. The parking facility at BWI Airport, outside Baltimore, features more than 350 two-button hands-free speakerphones that are compliant with the Americans with Disabilities Act.[18]

In the wake of the attacks of September 11, 2001, security has become a particular challenge for the designers of airport garages. After September 11, U.S. airports were required to comply with the "300-foot [91-meter] rule," an emergency directive from the Federal Aviation Agency under which unauthorized vehicles were not permitted to park within 300 feet (91 meters) of a terminal building. Under current directives, if the alert level is elevated or severe, no airport parking facilities within 300 feet (91 meters) of a terminal may be used unless they have undergone a blast analysis, or unless each vehicle is inspected before entry.[19] At Hartsfield-Jackson Atlanta International Airport, as at many others, the blocked sections of the parking decks closest to the terminal create yet another empty, isolated, and unpleasant zone for passengers to walk through, and are a constant reminder of the threat of terrorism.[20]

Airports are exploring a number of innovative security solutions. At Los Angeles International Airport and at six other airports around the country, for example, "cell phone parking lots" have been created where motorists can wait until they are called on their cell phones to come pick up their passengers.[21] One proposal involves a separate building for initial entry to the airport, where passengers would park their cars and have their luggage screened, and from which passengers and their luggage would then move to the main terminal. (However, this approach would require new systems to transport passengers and their bags.) Designers are considering using garage structures to deflect blasts away from terminals. Another option is to use technologies to screen vehicles before they enter parking structures. One such technology is SecuScan, which scans the undersides of cars as they pass an entry point and also checks their license plates against a database.[22]

As noted earlier, garages are not perceived as safe unless they are perceived as comfortable. And the sense of com-

fort is closely linked to good way-finding: "The ability to orient oneself, both socially and physically, is a major contributor to an individual's feeling of security."[23] It was the advent of the self-park garage that brought way-finding—both for drivers and for pedestrians—to the forefront of garage design. Ramps had to be designed to accommodate drivers with varying levels of skill and familiarity with the structure. Paths had to be created to ensure pedestrian safety. In the Sugarloaf Mountain project of 1924, Frank Lloyd Wright was among the first to recognize the design opportunities created by the self-park garage. His Self-Service Garage in Pittsburgh, designed in 1947, specifically addressed the needs of pedestrians by means of an open, internal, pedestrian-only path through the center of the garage; pedestrian elevators were also provided. As pedestrian movement (and associated issues of lighting and safety) gained increasing importance in garage design, ideas like Wright's continued to be explored, and to affect actual practice.[24]

In 1990, with the passage of the Americans with Disabilities Act (ADA), accessibility moved to the forefront of garage design. Existing buildings that had been funded by, owned by, or leased by the federal government were given the choice of complying with either of two earlier standards: the Architectural Barriers Act of 1968 (ABA) or the Uniform Federal Accessibility Standards (UFAS, an even older standard); all other buildings had to comply with the ADA Accessibility Guidelines (ADAAG). However, in 2004, the ADAAG itself was completely overhauled, yielding higher standards than had ever been in effect before. As of 2006, the revised ADAAG will apply to buildings that were previously subject to the ABA.[25]

At seven garages built by the Bank of America between 1996 and 2001, art was used to create attractive and informative interiors and to assist with way-finding. At one of the largest of these garages, the Seventh Street Station Parking Facility, in Charlotte, North Carolina, each interior level of the facility is linked to some aspect of the history of Charlotte.

Seventh Street Station Parking Facility, Charlotte, North Carolina, 1996–2001. Art can be used to assist with memory and way-finding in parking facilities.

Alewife Intermodal Transportation Facility, Cambridge, Massachusetts, 1985. Especially in the case of airports and multimodal transit facilities, beautiful lobbies and waiting areas allow for easier way-finding.

(Some of the art featured in the facility was created by students from the Charlotte public schools.) At each level in the garage of the Bank of America building at 201 North Tyron Street, also in Charlotte, a text panel near the elevator button describes one decade in the history of the automobile, along with "fun facts" about the car (the building is located on the former site of a Cadillac dealership). Although these approaches brighten what would otherwise be drab interiors, more intuitive and architectural approaches—such as skylights and vividly demarcated pedestrian paths—can also be used successfully to assist garage patrons.[26]

Finding simple and effective ways to guide visitors through the new multimodal transportation hubs is one of the challenges facing these complex systems. Some multimodal facil-

ities may be able to adapt the innovative approaches used by garages. At Chicago's Transportation Center Garage and at O'Hare Airport Garage, music is used to identify each floor. (This method was patented by Myron Warshauer, the former owner, chief executive officer, and president of the Standard Parking Corporation, who first implemented the technique at the 203 North LaSalle Street Garage, in Chicago.) Another Chicago garage, the Theater District Self-Park, built in 1987 by Hammond Beeby and Babka (now known as Hammond Beeby Rupert Ainge), extended the idea of theme music to include related visual images, which appear on panels on the interior columns.[27] In the Paris Las Vegas parking facility, each floor is associated with a different French landmark, such as the Eiffel Tower, to remind users where they have parked. At the garage at Toronto Pearson Airport, visitors can pick up a map at whatever level they park on—virtually a necessity at this facility, which, at the time of its construction, was the largest garage in the world.[28]

Garage Technologies

From the beginning, new technologies—such as the elevator, the turntable, heating systems, automatic sprinklers, and the lightbulb—played a central role in parking garage design.[29] With time, garages gained electronically operated doors and windows, equipment that helped to track and control movement on ramps, and ventilation control mechanisms. Other garage-related technologies include signage, devices for revenue control, and security systems.[30]

A number of garage technologies were associated specifically with the elevator. The most important of these, of course, was the turntable. Where automobile elevators could be accessed directly from the street, there was no need for a turntable: the car would enter the elevator, and once it reached the appropriate floor, would be moved into the garage by the attendant. However, where the elevator was situated on the interior of the garage, a turntable—either within an open area of the garage, or within the elevator itself—made it possible to reverse the direction of the vehicle. Turntables were advertised as being effective both indoors and out, wherever it was necessary to change an automobile's direction in tight conditions. Sales brochures offered detailed drawings of these mechanized systems and cited the number of garages that had purchased particular brands. Turntables were portrayed as being so easy to operate that a child could turn the heaviest car.[31]

Automatic doors were required to prevent fires from spreading in early garages, especially in vulnerable areas such as ramps and elevators. Fire doors had fusible links that melted between 155°and 165° Fahrenheit (between 68.3° and 73.8° Celsius), disconnecting the weights that held the doors open on their sloped tracks, and allowing gravity to slide the doors closed.

Elevator doors were often semi-automatic and made of steel (for fire resistance), even when elevator floors were still made of wood. The pneumatic system that opened and closed the elevator doors could be controlled from a distance by an electrical operating system; such systems were used to operate a number of different types of garage doors, including sliding, overhead, and swinging doors.[32]

Entry Pavilion Parking Structure, Community Hospital of the Monterey Peninsula, Monterey, California, 2004. Top: The interior of a parking facility—including the lighting—can provide an aesthetic experience. Above: Well-designed lobbies and waiting areas are increasingly important amenities.

The "ERNST" revolves with such ease that a CHILD can turn the heaviest car.

Four

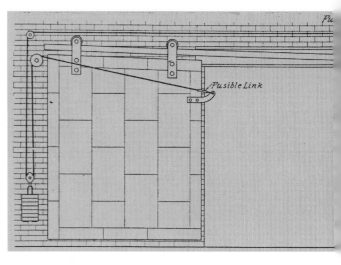

Left: Turntable advertisement, 1911. The turntable, an indispensable element of the garage, was also used to allow cars to turn around in parking lots and narrow streets.

Above: Fire door with fusible links, 1915. Fire was an important concern in the design of early garages.

In early garages, attendants moved between floors by means of elevators, fire poles, or narrow, winding stairs. However, these methods quickly became too slow for the number of cars requiring simultaneous parking and retrieval. The mechanical solution—the man-lift—was a cagelike structure that moved, by means of a chain, along a vertical pole. Although the device did allow one person to move quickly between floors, it provided minimal protection, and could be very dangerous if clothing or a body part protruded even slightly.[33]

Early in the 20th century, nearly all municipalities had stringent regulations to ensure that the oil and gasoline in garages did not enter the sewers. Such protections were especially important beginning in the late 1920s, as garages became larger. Boston's Motor Mart Garage, originally built in 1905 and updated 20 years later, had a two-compartment trap, consisting of a settling tank and a separator tank, that allowed the oil to float to the top and the gasoline vapors to evaporate through a perforated drain. The oil could then be removed. Such tanks were typically made of concrete and were set below the floor, along with the ventilating pipes. Because the Motor Mart's tank could hold up to 10,000 gallons (37,854 liters) of water and oil, it could accommodate the daily runoff for ten to 12 months before requiring cleaning.[34]

The Motor Mart, which had 52,000 square feet (4,830 square meters) on each of its nine floors and accommodated 2,000 cars, was not only an exceptionally large but an exceptionally advanced garage, offering state-of-the-art integrated technologies to support its 18 gasoline stations, 27 oil-distributing stations, 44 stations for filling tires, and sophisticated car-washing facilities. The garage had a fire-alarm system, modern heating and ventilation, and an electrical device that alerted pedestrians by sounding a gong whenever a car entered or exited the building. A parcel room with a parcel lift (similar to a dumbwaiter) was available for the convenience of customers. Gasoline was pumped by means of hydraulic systems. In the unique mechanized washing system, cars were moved automatically along tracks, and 15 could be being cleaned simultaneously. A car wash took only 20 minutes—and, unlike the car washes of today, provided a thorough cleaning of every nook and cranny. The garage also had the equipment to vacuum auto interiors, clean motors, and dry-clean upholstery. Traffic at the Motor Mart was controlled by squads of workers who used "pneumatic tubes as well as telautograph service, call bell signals for quick retrieval, telephones, time clocks, time stamps, and a modified

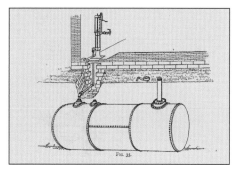

Far left, top: Man-lift, 1950s. Car jockeys used man-lifts to move between the floors of a garage. Although these mechanical devices could be very dangerous, they were the fastest way to park and retrieve automobiles.

Far left, bottom: Gasoline storage system, 1910. Before hotel garages—which provided car storage only—became common, garages had to be designed to ensure proper gasoline storage.

Left: Commodore-Biltmore Garage, New York City, 1927. A typical fueling station, integrated into an early parking garage.

block signal system to control the two different ramp systems for entry and exit to different streets."[35]

Although a number of technologies for revenue control in parking garages were invented between 1910 and 1930, they were not applied until the advent of self-parking. Devices such as the ticket-spitter and the validating meter (an automated parking-validation device), for example, made it possible to automatically document car entrances and exits and to assign appropriate charges to customers, allowing traffic to flow more quickly into and out of the self-park garage (and hastening the disappearance of the car jockey). In 1955, at a garage in Oakland, California, attendants located empty spaces by means of a television. Four years later, a garage in Novara, Italy, used photoelectric cells to keep track of open spaces. At the Dayton Radisson Ramp, in Minneapolis, which was constructed in 1960, a strip placed on the floor counted the number of entering automobiles.[36]

At Cincinnati's Pogue Downtown Garage, built in 1968, the extensive technology was controlled from a central panel in the main office. The garage featured automatic entrance controls, automatic time stamps, and a "differential counter to activate 'full' signs and to direct users to the open side of the garage."[37] At each elevator lobby, drivers could stamp

their tickets with a colored symbol indicating which level the car was on. An excellent example, for its time, of the use of technology, the Pogue even had infrared heaters that kept snow and ice from accumulating on the exterior ramps.[38]

Two of the main issues in garage design—traffic flow and payment—were addressed jointly in a multilevel, 1,159-car municipal garage built in White Plains, New York, in 1972. In an attempt to keep traffic flowing during peak periods, the designers of this garage simply installed parking meters. This approach does not appear to have proliferated in other parts of the country, however, perhaps because of problems with monitoring and collection.[39]

Technology is no less important today than it was in the early garages; in particular, there has been a resurgence of interest in devices that manage traffic flow and indicate the availability of parking spaces. At airports and other large facilities, electronic signs now guide drivers to open spots. Such "smart park" systems are currently in use at the BWI Airport garage, outside Baltimore; on highways in California; and in St. Paul, Minnesota, where real-time electronic signs show drivers the number of available parking spaces in specific garages. In Cologne, Germany, and Dublin, Ireland, among other cities, signs at key entrances to the city direct

Right: Pogue Downtown Garage, Cincinnati, 1968. In this garage, all the available technologies of the time—including heat lamps to melt snow on the ramps—were combined to create the most modern of facilities.

Below left: E.E. Wiezell, stamp- and ticket-vending machine, circa 1910. Revenue control devices were conceived almost as soon as the first commercial parking garages came into existence.

Below right: Hamilton Main Garage, White Plains, New York, 1972. Controlling each parking space with a single parking meter (visible in this photo through the fenestrations in the building) was one solution to the emerging complexities of operating a parking garage.

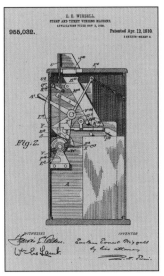

The Parking Garage

drivers to garages that have space available; once a driver arrives at a garage, he or she can then be directed to a particular open space. In the Gary-Chicago-Milwaukee Corridor, an integrated multimodal information system—the PMGS (Parking Management Guidance System)—is being implemented on a pilot basis. Electronic signs will indicate whether the lots and garages at commuter-rail stations are full, and will suggest alternative station locations or parking options. By creating better real-time information about the availability and location of parking, the system will benefit both commuters and transit-system operators—and, it is hoped, encourage the use of commuter rail.[40]

In Baltimore, a parking reservation system (provided by the Baltimore Parking Authority and developed in conjunction with Mobile Parking) is set in motion by a simple cellphone call to a live operator. The driver provides his or her destination, and is then given information on available parking, including cost and directions. The system was developed to alleviate congestion caused by the inefficient distribution of parking during peak periods, which was assumed to be caused by lack of real-time information.[41]

In Seattle and other cities, motorists can now pay for parking in private lots over their mobile phones. Drivers must register to use the service and pay an extra fee of 25 cents each time they park. To activate the service, the driver parks, then simply enters a secret personal identification number over the phone.[42]

In the past few years, garage owners and users alike have benefited from the ability to conduct business electronically. For example, customers can now go online to purchase parking permits and obtain real-time parking data. Albany, New York, has implemented a debit system for parking meters. A similar system is in place at Stony Brook University, which sells "debit keys" that can be used for parking: instead of putting change into a parking meter, students simply insert the key, which automatically debits their account.[43]

Solar technology, used to power both signs and parking meters, is also finding its way into parking garage design. At Phoenix Sky Harbor Airport, drivers are led to available parking spaces by means of wireless, solar-powered roadway signs that are connected to signs on each level of the parking garage and are also integrated into the airport's fiber-optic network.[44]

As research into "intelligent highways" expands, emerging technologies are just beginning to affect the design of the parking garage. Electronic monitoring and analysis of arrival and departure patterns, for example, can facilitate smooth traffic flow within the garage and allow both valet parking and automated systems to function more efficiently. In addition, new technologies, such as personal movement devices, are expanding mobility options and will eventually affect the larger transportation system. Continued overall changes in transportation will inevitably have an impact on the design of parking facilities as well.[45]

The technologies developed for parking access and revenue control (PARC) systems help owners obtain accurate data on how and when the garage is used. PARC systems may offer electronic fee collection, a range of payment options, automatic alerts indicating abuse of the system, pay-on-foot stations, and signs displaying information about available parking. Very new technologies, such as automatic vehicle identification and license plate recognition, which scan either a windshield-mounted tag or the car license plate, can be used to document garage use and to help manage traffic flow (for example, by automatically opening gates and by supporting cashless parking).[46]

Pay-on-foot systems, an updated approach to metering, require garage users to pay at a machine just before returning to their car; to exit the facility, drivers must give a machine (or a cashier) the exit ticket dispensed at the pay station. Similar systems, known as "pay and display" are used for street parking, or in garages where users pay at a central station and then display a time-stamped ticket on their windshield.[47]

Heating and Ventilation

Vast expanses of open space and large doors that were constantly opening and closing made early garages difficult to heat. Nevertheless, proper heating was important for the automobiles, for the drivers, and for the longevity of the building itself. With the ascendance of the open-deck parking ramp, heating disappeared from the discussion. But the issue of ventilation did not.

Because operating and idling cars generate carbon monoxide, it is necessary to monitor the quantity of fresh air in a garage. Initially, attendants counted the number of cars operating in the garage; on the basis of their experience (that is, their sense of how many cars the garage could handle before the windows needed to be opened), the attendants would then manually open and close the windows as needed. As early as 1927, studies had begun to address the exhaust capacity of fans and the number of changes of air per hour

Lloyd Shopping Center, Portland, Oregon, 1970. In the case of an underground garage, the need for ventilation creates a design problem: where and how can the exterior vents be designed above grade?

that were necessary in an enclosed garage. The results of such studies were eventually used as the basis for new building codes; these codes, in turn, added impetus to the development of the open-deck garage, which did not require the added expense of mechanical ventilation systems. Even in open structures, however, particular physical configurations could render natural ventilation inadequate.[48]

Naturally, underground garages were a particular concern. In the 1950s, when Chicago's Grant Park Underground Garage was constructed, there were no standards, so the designers arranged for 16 changes of air per hour. By 1968, in an effort to protect garage employees, state public health departments had set standards for carbon monoxide levels, and new building codes for underground garages reflected the state agencies' recommendations. Some of these codes required only four changes of air per hour (much fewer than had been presumed necessary for the Grant Park Underground Garage), of which two had to be taken from the floor level, where the concentration of carbon monoxide is highest. Some codes from this era also required carbon monoxide detection systems. For example, at Detroit's Cobo Hall Underground Garage, which opened in 1960, automatic fans were supposed to maintain appropriate levels of carbon monoxide; if those levels were exceeded, an alarm would sound. Some early codes had flexible requirements, which the attendants on duty were free to apply as they saw fit.[49]

In the mid-1970s, after a series of dangerous incidents in underground garages, many garages implemented new procedures and undertook corrective actions. These modifications included monitoring and recording of carbon monoxide levels; the installation of alarms, of automatic fans, and of fans with variable-speed motors; and the implementation of specific procedures to assist and direct motorists in unusual situations. Eventually, such modifications became legal requirements; applicable codes continue to evolve today.[50]

The large ventilation shafts that were eventually required for underground garages had to be incorporated into garage design; and, since the shafts were the aboveground portion of the garage, this meant involving landscape architects in the process. In the elaborate and beautiful solution at the Lloyd Center, a shopping center in Portland, Oregon, raised, landscaped pools—complete with sculptures—appear to float above the plaza level, masking the ventilation shafts. Although, as permitted by code, the garage structure was bermed away from the lower floors, creating ventilation without benefit of mechanical devices, the designers felt that

additional ventilation was desirable and created the pools as a means of ensuring airflow into and out of the central portions of the garage.[51]

Today, the facades of open-deck facilities must meet code-based requirements for ratios of open areas to closed areas. A facility that meets these requirements is considered to have enough natural ventilation to avoid the expense of mechanized systems. But traditional approaches to determining these ratios do not take into account the specific geometry of the structure—and since facilities are typically tested after they are built and the ventilation system is already in place, changes or additions are often needed to accommodate the characteristics of specific areas of the garage. Now, however, software is available that can model entire ventilation systems—including airflow, heat transfer, contaminant transport, and thermal comfort—while taking into account the geometry of the building and the effect of stacked, idling cars in various parts of the garage. Because it is now possible to modify the design of ventilation equipment before it is in place, costly postconstruction changes can often be avoided.[52]

Parking Spaces and Parking Methods

Initially, New York and many other cities assumed that stables could easily be converted to garages—as if parking a car were not, after all, very different from stabling a horse. But even the earliest concepts of parking garage design were not necessarily derived from the stable, with its rows of individual stalls. In fact, early garages had neither parking stalls nor aisles: just open space, which was divided into short- and long-term storage areas.[53] As late as 1949, Henry Davis Nadic complained in *The American City* that the municipality of New York had yet to fully grasp the distinction between the garage and the stable: "It is a commercial building. New York City is treating the modern parking garage as though it were a stable in the horse-and-buggy days."[54]

Nadic's comment reflects the complexity of attempting to find space for parking within dense, established city centers. Whatever cities assumed about the ease of converting stables to garages, garage owners knew better. Nevertheless, by the turn of the 20th century, most cities had begun to understand the particular characteristics and requirements of garage structures—thanks, in large part, to the efforts of garage designers, who understood that the parking garage was a unique building that required special design attention—even when it was connected to other building types, and even after it had been separated from the functions of fueling, maintenance, and repair.

As the building type developed, the size of the vehicle became the basis of the overall layout and structure. Within this overall layout and structure, the key elements were the size and orientation of the parking spaces and the width and arrangement of ramps, aisles, and parking bays. And the single most important dimension was—and is—that of the parking space.[55]

Designers use a number of guides to assist them in determining the best layout; such guides take into account both physical variables, such as the anticipated dimensions of the cars, and variables associated with use, such as turnover and the building type being served by the garage. Since the addition or subtraction even a fraction of an inch can affect overall efficiency, auto dimensions naturally have a tremendous impact on the design of parking facilities, and designers must pay close attention to trends in the auto industry. In 1950, the width of a parking space was 8 feet 4 inches (2.5 meters); by the 1970s, spaces were as wide as 10 feet (three meters), and some new garages are still being constructed with spaces that wide. Many industry observers, however, are predicting a downward trend in the size of cars.[56]

The arrangement of parking spaces is also affected by the parking method. For the garage operator, self-parking in single-depth spaces is the most trouble-free approach. Attendant parking, in contrast, allows cars to be parked one deep, two deep, or even three deep. Although single-depth parking arrangements make it easier to service vehicles and to move them quickly and easily, multiple-depth spaces make more efficient use of available space. Attendant-assisted

parking, like attendant parking, allows greater density: in attendant-assisted arrangements, cars are permitted to block each other, and drivers must leave their keys in the car or with the attendant so that their cars can be moved if necessary. Attendant-assisted parking is a good option in exceptionally dense locations: the White House Garage in San Francisco is an example. In a few self-park arrangements, drivers develop a buddy system in which they agree to share a single space by coordinating their departure and arrival times.[57]

Site conditions and structural characteristics sometimes determine which parking method will be used, as the necessity of balancing the available land with parking requirements can demand a particular approach. Where available space and site conditions create extreme constraints, car stackers and other automated systems may be the only means of obtaining an adequate number of spaces. Where conditions are ideal, the appropriate parking method is determined by who will be using the garage: theatergoers, for example, may need

Dimensions of automobiles, 1920. Auto dimensions have a tremendous impact on the design of parking facilities.

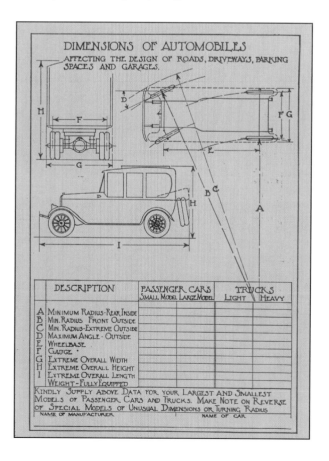

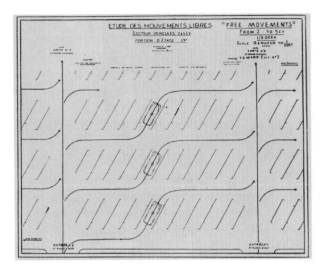

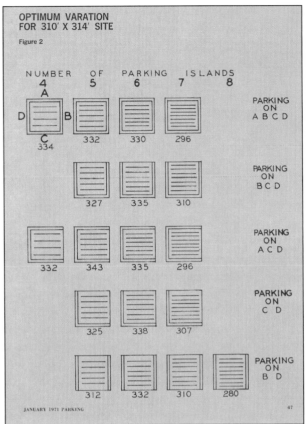

Above: Internal movement system developed by Marcel Froelicher, 1959. Attendants can still be used efficiently in the modern parking facility—for example, to assist with parking systems in which cars only move forward, regardless of whether they are entering or exiting the facility.

Right: Alternative parking layouts, Computer Parking Design Company, 1971. Because they can quickly generate all the possible permutations, computers can be effective tools for identifying the most efficient parking layout for a given situation. The number below each configuration shows the number of parking spots that the plan will yield.

the higher level of service provided by wider parking spaces, or may require attendant parking (to avoid the long walks to and from the vehicle).[58]

Recently, the Disney Resort Garage, in Anaheim, California, introduced a new, low-tech twist on the basic movement pattern of the garage. Since the Disney garage accommodates the simultaneous arrival and departure of a high volume of vehicles, and since forward movement is always the easiest and quickest, attendants have begun directing drivers to pull into pairs of adjacent, end-to-end angled parking spots: the first driver drives through the first spot and parks in the second, and the next driver pulls in behind and parks in the first spot. At the time of departure, both cars can simply pull forward and leave by means of the next aisle. Although attendants are necessary to make the system work, no technology is used, and the result is smoother traffic flow and quicker entering and exiting. Interestingly, this idea was first suggested in 1959, by Marcel Froelicher, of Algiers, as part of his effort to improve parking in his city.[59]

Parking configurations and flow can also be improved by the analysis of driving and parking times for different combinations of ramps and parking layouts. However, such efforts have been driven principally by human brain power, and there is certainly room for greater use of computers in the evaluation of alternatives. As far back as 1970, the Computer Parking Design Company determined that, given all the variables in a garage design, there were 64,000 possible layouts of parking spaces in a 314-foot by 310-foot (96-meter by 94-meter) floor plate. But only a few of these will provide the optimum solution for a given circumstance. The use of computers to rapidly compare solutions, based on unique parameters determined by the designer, should become an integral part of the industry.[60]

Maintenance

Maintenance is important for any building, but is particularly so for the parking facility. The longevity of a garage depends on how it is cared for during its lifespan. A concrete parking facility that is properly designed, constructed, and maintained

The Parking Garage

in accordance with the recommendations of the American Concrete Institute should have a service life of 40 to 50 years. Failure to properly maintain a parking facility puts both property and lives at risk.[61]

Preventive maintenance includes sealing cracks and joints; patching potholes; reapplying sealants and steel coatings; cleaning floors, floor drains, and downspouts; painting; re-pointing; tightening wire restraints (such as guardrail bolts and strands); and regularly inspecting the structure and all of its systems. A parking facility should also be washed down, spring and fall, to rid the structure of accumulated salt and debris.[62]

It is important to repair small cracks or fissures in con-crete in a timely fashion so that they do not expand and allow water to infiltrate the structure. The safety and com-fort of pedestrians requires close cleaning of the interior spaces, and immediate attention to any hazards that might cause tripping or slipping. Supporting equipment, such as fire extinguishers, must be properly maintained, as for any public building.[63]

Parking facilities in colder climates may be exposed to extreme freeze-thaw conditions, similar to those that occur on bridges; they are also subject to rain and snow, and to road salts that are carried in on the tires of cars. Efforts to handle snow buildup—particularly on the top level of garages in cold-weather locations—have led to some in-teresting design solutions. The most common is a large open shaft—a snow chute—that is protected from access by cars or pedestrians. The chute has a gate that can be opened, so that snow can be dumped or shoveled down the shaft to a place where it will be trucked away, mechanically melted, or allowed to melt naturally. In the Blue Cross Blue Shield facility in North Haven, Connecticut, snow chutes are a beautiful part of the design and structure of the facade. On each level of the structure, in the corner of the floorplate, large drainage washes on each level lead to the ground. Al-though the system does not work effectively (because snow tends to freeze in the narrow passages, making them ineffec-tive), the design was a worthy attempt to integrate func-tionality and aesthetics. At a minimum, heavy, rubber-edged snowplow blades are best for moving snow to an empty spot in a garage.[64]

New computer programs apply current knowledge of materials science to predict the effectiveness of different technologies on the longevity of parking structures. These programs can also be used to develop long-term preventive

Blue Cross Blue Shield facility, New Haven, Connecticut, 1990. The design of this garage incorporated oversized downspouts and square snow chutes on each corner.

maintenance programs; to establish repair priorities, given budget constraints; to assess the internal condition of the concrete; and to identify the best technologies and con-struction techniques for the location. Finally, the software can help to ensure that when parking facilities contract for services (maintenance and repair, for example), what has been contracted for is actually being provided.[65]

Construction Practices

New ideas for garage construction are always being explored. When schedule is of primary importance, the design-build approach, in which designers and builders work as a team, can work well. The design-build technique was first imple-mented in the garage industry in the mid-1970s; in subsequent years, efforts were made to improve the design-build process by determining the best approaches to bidding, and by identifying the requirements that would yield the best team for a project. In the mid-1970s, the Parking Consultants Council recommended eliminating from the design-build process any requirements for an architectural rendering or model, which limited the focus of design to pure functionality for the vehicle and assigned less importance to the visual aspects of the facility. The overall effect of the recommendation was to reduce the importance of an integrated design approach. It would be desirable for architectural renderings or models to be restored as part of the design-build approach. Among the early examples of design-build are the parking structures that Watry Engineering (now known as Watry Design) undertook in the early 1980s for transit stations in the San Francisco Bay area. Between 1986 and 1992, the number of design-build garage projects grew by 172 percent; in 2000, the Design Build Institute of America designated design-build as the major trend in the parking industry for that year and beyond.[66]

Many construction technologies used in parking garages lend themselves to design-build, which can result in significant savings. In fact, one of the principal advantages of design-build is that even larger facilities can be constructed as planned, rather than being scaled back because of budget overruns (either on the garage itself, or on the building that it is designed to serve). For example, the successful construction of a 500,000-square-foot (46,452-square-meter) parking garage built by Crescent Resources in Tampa, Florida, in 2002, is largely attributable to the design-build approach, which allows closer management of costs throughout the process. The CSB Parking Garage, in Wilmington, Delaware, was actually built first, for the subsequent addition of a nine-story building; the strict controls on process and pricing that are characteristic of design-build made it possible to construct the main building as planned.[67]

The Penn Street Parking Garage, in Baltimore, was a design-build joint venture undertaken by Desman Parking Associates; BWJ Inc.; Whiting-Turner Contracting Company; Tindall Concrete Virginia, Inc.; and the Consulting Engineers Group. This ten-story, 976-space garage, with office space on the ground level, restored the facade of a historic electric substation, and retained a historic stonemasons' building also located on the site. Through a design-build approach, the project succeeded in using the existing facade to create the architectural appeal of early garage structures. Since the

garage needed to be completed in 15 months, from design to finish, it was constructed using a precast concrete system with over 1,300 precast prestressed components. The tight schedule, restoration of the historic facade and building, new facade detailing, and multiple uses made the project challenging; however, because of the excellent teamwork, the project succeeded.[68]

The Business of Parking

Despite widespread perceptions to the contrary, parking is not free; in fact, it is extremely expensive to provide. Costs associated with parking include land, design, construction, financing, and operating expenses. If these costs are not covered by parking fees, the difference must be made up by the public sector (which means that it is passed on to residents in the form of taxes) or by the private sector (which means that it is passed on to the consumer in the form of higher prices). Every parking facility, regardless of who constructs it or operates it, provides a public service because it is an integral part of the overall transportation system. Most parking facilities are also businesses. Thus, parking garage design, construction, and operation have always reflected the tension between the goals of private enterprise and the quest for the public good.[69]

The operation of the first parking structures involved a good deal of experimentation and no regulation: few garages (other than those owned and operated by automobile clubs) had fixed rates, and it was common practice to provide chauffeurs with commissions in return for bringing cars in for repair. In 1908, auto owners in New York City founded the Co-Operative Garage Company, which was run without commissions and according to honest business principles. The success of the operation challenged the rest of the industry to meet the same standards.[70]

Companies that were in the business of building and operating garages appeared very early, but Detroit Garages, of Detroit, Michigan, was the first major corporation to focus on the design, construction, ownership, and operation of parking garages. Founded in the mid-1920s, as the parking garage was taking on a more standard form, the firm had the expertise and the earning capacity within several years to go national—which it did, adopting the name National Garages. Many other garage corporations followed the lead of National Garages, building and managing commercial garages and parking lots across the country. Allright Parking, for example,

which began in 1926, was the largest garage company in the world by 1977. It is still possible to make a go of the parking business: Central Parking, for example, was begun as a family business and incorporated in 1968. Monroe Carrell Jr. built it into the international operation it is today: it went public in 1995, and is currently listed on the New York Stock Exchange.[71]

In 1941, the federal Defense Highway Act authorized the commissioner of public roads to cooperate with states in the location, development, and construction of off-street parking facilities. Although the legislation was based on the view that parking was an extension of the street system and therefore a public responsibility, parking as a private enterprise continued to make significant contributions to solving the parking problem. Between 1946 and 1954, the car population doubled, and it was expected to double again within the next ten years. By the early 1950s, 94 percent of parking facilities were still being built by the private sector, but municipalities had become increasingly aware

Above left: Apthorp Garage, New York City, 1913. By the second decade of the 20th century, there were thousands of garages all across the country; few, however, were considered completely fireproof, and construction of the standardized commercial garages that are familiar today had yet to begin.

Above right: Co-Operative Garage, New York City, 1908. This was the first garage managed according to sound business principles.

Detroit Garages

In a 1906 photo of Detroit's Broadway and Gratiot streets, the intersection is filled with bicycles, pedestrians, and horses. Fourteen years later, that same intersection is clogged with automobiles. In 1924, 289 traffic fatalities were recorded in the city. One statistic held that on any given day in 1925, almost the entire population of Detroit crossed Campus Martius (voters had failed to approve a subway plan that would have helped alleviate this congestion). In 1926, trolleys, streetcars, jitneys, and motor buses carried 1.5 million passengers daily through the streets of the city.[1]

By the mid-1920s, the traffic problem had become the focus of public discussion in *The Detroiter,* and Mayor Smith had appointed a traffic committee. The committee's recommendations, as reflected in a master plan, included widening existing streets, opening new streets, and constructing 204-foot- (61-meter-) wide superhighways and 120-foot- (37-meter-) wide secondary thoroughfares. A separate effort was made to address congestion by means of traffic regulations.[2]

Although construction regulations for garages were in place beginning in 1915, it was not until 1921 that 13 joint owners—among them Edsel B. Ford—formed Detroit Garages. The company's founders saw Detroit Garages as a solution to the downtown parking problem: as the firm's advertisements pointed out, the garages could assist commuters and shoppers alike by taking cars off the street. The owners also believed that the time was right for parking garages to become successful business ventures, and they set out to prove just that.[3]

To maximize efficiency, the company's first three garages followed the same formula: they were located near hotels, theaters, shopping, and public buildings; they featured the D'Humy ramp system and broad, easily navigable ramps; and they included lobbies, passenger elevators, restrooms, newspaper and cigar stands, public telephones, and taxi stands. Gas and oil stations were located on the corner, outside each garage, and all the garages offered maintenance services. Monthly tenants received enameled medallions to attach to the fronts of their cars, which permitted them to self-park.[4]

Taken together, the first three garages—the East Unit, at Congress and Beaubien streets; the North Unit, at Elizabeth Street, west of Park Boulevard; and the West Unit, on Cass Avenue at Larned—housed 1,500 automobiles, and the owners were prepared to provide unlimited financial backing for expansion into other districts. All three garages opened within three months of each other around the holiday season of 1924–1925. Architecturally, the buildings were of the warehouse type: large, simple concrete frames with expansive metal windows, and little ornamentation of any kind.[5]

A 1924 advertisement in *The Detroiter* for the Detroit Storage Company stated that it had buildings available for auto storage in all parts of the city, which suggests that the owners of Detroit Garages were not the only ones who saw the business potential

of garages and were capitalizing on the opportunity. By 1925, Detroit had nine major garages, three of which were owned by Detroit Garages. Of the six others, some were stand-alone, and several were part of large, high-rise mixed-use projects.[6]

The success of the first three Detroit Garages led the owners to take the business to the national level. The firm then formed National Garages—which, by 1927, owned or operated two units in Pittsburgh; two units in Portland, Oregon; one unit in Syracuse, New York; and one unit in Huntington, West Virginia. National Garages also became associated with subsidiary corporations in many other cities; by 1973, 60 garages around the country were affiliated with National Garages, and the firm had been involved in the design of 500 garages. In each city, the parent company worked with local architects to adapt the basic garage plan to local needs.[7]

George Devlin, who joined National Garages in 1933 as a "parts boy," became the head of the planning division after WW II, and continued with the company well into the century, eventually restructuring it as National Planning. Devlin (who also invented the ticket-spitter) was an inventive force in the industry and trained many important "garage men"—including Richard C. Rich, National Garage's most creative designer. In 1963, Rich formed his own company, Rich and Associates, which designs, constructs, and manages garages across the country, and continues to be a source of innovation in the industry.[8]

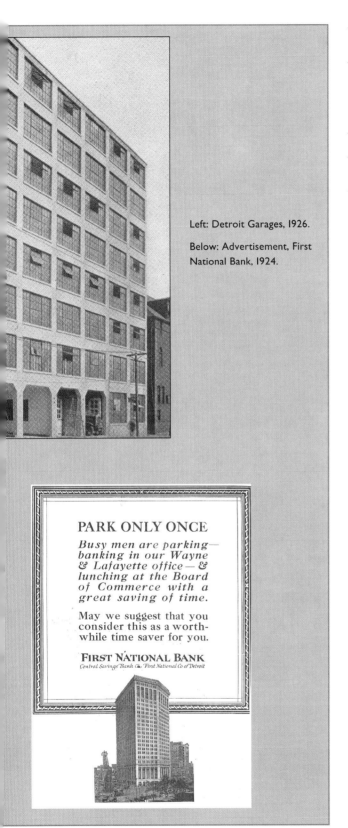

Left: Detroit Garages, 1926.

Below: Advertisement, First National Bank, 1924.

PARK ONLY ONCE

Busy men are parking—banking in our Wayne & Lafayette office — & lunching at the Board of Commerce with a great saving of time.

May we suggest that you consider this as a worthwhile time saver for you.

FIRST NATIONAL BANK
Central Savings Bank & First National Co of Detroit

that the private sector could not meet the demand alone. For one thing, it was more difficult to find equity financing for parking facilities than for other forms of development. Insurance companies, for example, often refused to lend money for parking facilities—and when they did, they required subsidies or risk capital. Private sector firms also found it difficult to compete with subsidized municipal garages. At best, the public and the private sector cooperated in the construction and operation of parking garages. At worst, the public and private sector were in conflict over who should build, where facilities should be built, and how they should be built.[72]

In 1970, 349 parking projects were underway throughout the United States; of these, 38 percent were financed by municipal authorities and 62 percent by the private sector.[73] Municipal funding sources included revenue bonds, general-obligation bonds, special assessments, grants, and parking-meter revenues. Governmental agencies associated with various projects—such as redevelopment corporations, airport boards, highway commissions, and sports authorities—were also drawn into the financing, design, and construction of garages.[74]

When it comes to financing, the parking facility is in a class by itself. Because parking garages are typically constructed as adjuncts to other enterprises, or to serve many different land uses, they are unusually subject to outside influences—including changes in the overall transportation system, in patterns of automobile use, in connected or adjacent properties, and in land use values. Given the range and complexity of the factors that can affect the success of a parking garage, its overall economic viability is difficult to assess: although some parking facilities, such as those in airports, are reliably profitable, economic viability is not necessarily a given in urban environments.

Moreover, parking is an unusual commodity: without parking, few real estate developments—whether public or private—can succeed. And parking is costly to provide. Nevertheless, businesses and governments alike are often reluctant to charge directly (or fully) for parking, for fear of undermining the success of whatever ventures the parking supports. Thus, as noted in a May 1998 *Urban Land* article, "parking facilities frequently are not profitable ventures and therefore must be subsidized. For that reason, parking authorities or city parking departments often become active in their ownership and operation." The article further notes, however, that public sector involvement may lead to pricing distortions, as such involvement is "typically . . . motivated by a desire to encourage economic development by keeping parking rates artificially low."[75]

But the other side of the coin is that just as the actual *costs* of parking may be obscured by the business model that has developed, the *benefits* may not be visible in the form of direct profits. A 1948 article in *The American City,* for example, noted that on the one hand, the decision to build a parking garage should be based on a standard business evaluation: "Does the project provide the service needed? Does the project operate on a cost basis that makes it a sound public or private investment?" But the author goes on to note that the definition of a "sound" investment "does not always imply profit, in the usual sense. . . . The service given by a facility may very well repay a group of private business investors—such as department stores, theaters, hotels—by increasing their total business income through the provision of additional customers." Although this observation was made nearly 60 years ago, it still applies today.[76]

As the parking garage developed, construction and management costs varied considerably. Experiments and advances of the 1940s, 1950s, and 1960s—garages located below parks, mechanized garages, and structurally innovative garages, for example—sometimes increased and sometimes decreased the cost per space. As an example of the wide divergence in costs, Chicago's Grant Park North Underground Garage, built in the 1950s, had 2,359 parking spaces constructed at a cost of $3,515 each; an open-deck Tallahassee garage built at approximately the same time accommodated 230 cars at a cost of $700 per space—and cleverly mitigated a steep slope to boot. Both garages were profitable. In general, the self-park ramp is less costly to manage but more costly to build, because larger driveways, ramps, aisles, and stalls are needed for the convenience of drivers.[77]

Recently, parking garages have begun using advertising as a way to obtain additional revenue. A parking facility in Westwood, California, for example, includes advertising in the valet parking area; advertising can also be found in a facility in Pasadena, California. The addition of other services, such as valet parking and preferred parking areas, can create other potential revenue sources. Past experience with such amenities indicates that they can increase user loyalty and expand profitability.[78]

Changing Functionality

Functionality is important for any building type, but it is paramount for the parking garage. The garage is a utilitarian building designed largely for machines, rather than for human beings; nevertheless, garage designers ignore human needs at their peril.[79]

What are the requirements of a functional parking garage? Convenience of location; efficient use of space; safe, manageable access and circulation for pedestrians and vehicles; and adequate lighting, way-finding, and ventilation. Two factors that are not inherently part of the design, but that are dramatically affected by the design, are also important: efficient operation and careful maintenance.

For the parking facility, functionality has direct implications for land planning and development programming. Even in today's climate, when so much emphasis is being placed on increasing transit use, reliance on the car continues to be almost universal, and parking is therefore crucial to the success of almost any building type or development. Thus, the influence of the parking garage on the built environment—and the complexity of that influence—should not be underestimated.

The definition of functionality for the parking garage has constantly evolved: the first garages were based on existing building types, such as roundhouses, stables, and carriage houses. When fascination with the new technology of the automobile was at its peak, functionality was synonymous with detailed attention to the needs of the car: garages were essentially beauty salons for autos. Nevertheless, the needs of drivers were not ignored: garages provided a range of amenities and services for the comfort of commuters, shoppers, and chauffeurs. With the advent of modernist ideals of "pure" functionality, the garage was gradually transformed into a simple, low-tech, concrete box: designed for self-parking; functional (at least for the auto) on the inside; and not especially appealing on the outside. Today, garages are increasingly required to meet higher expectations: in their role as civic gateways, they must promote holistic and well-designed arrival and departure experiences—and, in keeping with the emphasis on mixed use that shapes much of contemporary development, many characteristics of early garages are reappearing, although in perhaps slightly different forms. For example, facilities for car washing and oil changes are returning to parking facilities across the country, as are services such as dry-cleaning and shoe shines. And new services, such as emissions testing, DVD rentals, and audiotape rentals, are being added. Such use mixes can be found in the Capital City Parking Facility, in St. Paul, Minnesota; at Chicago's O'Hare Airport; at Boston's Post Office Square facility; and in Century City, California.[80]

The reality is that despite considerable changes in both the automobile and the building type that houses it, the garage designers of today confront many of the same issues as their predecessors did decades ago. And although some of the early solutions are obsolete because no longer needed (heat, plate-glass windows, and on-site maintenance facilities, for example), other functional needs—in particular, the dimensions of parking space, driving aisle, and turn-ing radius—continue to drive garage design. The parking facility of today is being transformed into a complex, multi-dimensional building type that is required to meet emerging architectural, urban planning, and transportation needs. In the course of this evolution, the meaning of functionality will continue to expand, as designers seek an ever-better fit—through low-tech solutions, high-tech solutions, and never-before-imagined solutions—between the garage and the humans and automobiles that it serves.

CHAPTER 5

Mechanization
A Taste for Technology

The first efforts to mechanize vehicle storage were spurred by a fascination with technology. The mechanized parking garage was more than a practical way to pack automobiles quickly and densely into a relatively small space: it was a symbol of modern technological power, of the new-found ability to transform an entire building into a machine. The mechanized garage offered just the combination of functionality and excitement that American society craved.

The first garages—whether adaptations of existing buildings or new construction—were practical responses to an immediate need. However, the requirements for parking facilities soon became more complex. Early parking garages relied on elevators and turntables to move vehicles. But elevators had several disadvantages: they were expensive to purchase—and, being subject to breakdowns, were also expensive to maintain. Most important, however, early elevator systems could typically move only one automobile at a time. Although retrieval time was not a crucial matter for early garages, once the number of cars had reached critical mass—and once drivers' perceptions of "speed" had been irrevocably altered by the freedom of zipping around, unencumbered, in automobiles—even a short wait began to seem excessive, and the expectation that parking and retrieval would be both fast and efficient became entrenched.

The evolution of the "parking machine" was accompanied by changes in nomenclature. In the 1920s, the terms *automatic* and *semi-automatic* were used to distinguish between two kinds of systems: in the first, attendants controlled a device that actually parked the cars; in the second, attendants parked the cars while both they and the vehicles were within the however, *automatic* and *semi-automatic* were often used interchangeably. Automatic and semi-automatic systems packed cars densely (often within a building), and typically moved cars in three dimensions. Mechanized systems were mechanical devices that allowed cars to be vertically stacked, typically on a parking lot.

Facing page: Ruth Safety Garage, Jewelers' Building, Chicago, 1926. This mechanized garage, based on a system developed in the early 1920s, featured four centrally located elevators with parking on both sides. This became one of the basic spatial relationships in mechanized parking.

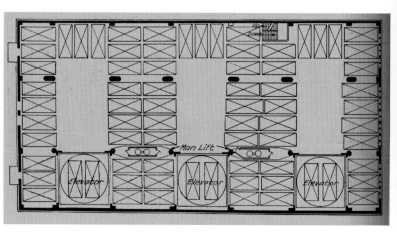

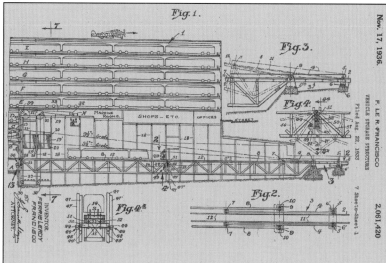

Above left: Garage Rue de Ponthieu, Paris, 1905. This early garage, designed by Auguste Perret, featured a mechanized arrangement that relied on elevators and a sliding, palletlike system.

Top right: Hill Garage, Los Angeles, 1928. In the early 1920s, garage designers were continuing to explore the potential of elevators. In this system, which was patented in 1923, the elevators could open on any of their four sides (although only three were used in this facility), allowing the automobile to move in any direction.

Above right: F. Le R. Francisco, patent drawing, Vehicle Storage Structure, 1936. This patent was a unique combination of airport and mechanized garage.

In this chapter, *mechanized* will be used as the umbrella term for all parking facilities that include a mechanical component, no matter how simple or complex. Today, the three basic types of mechanized facilities are computerized, fully automated facilities, in which the driver need only swipe a card after leaving the vehicle; semi-automatic facilities, in which there is some form of interaction with an attendant (typically, only older mechanized garages are semi-automatic); and car stackers, which are usually found in parking lots, but are now appearing within the traditional ramp garage. Although today's fully automated facilities may still have an attendant, neither the driver nor the attendant is directly involved in parking the car: computers handle the task of "thinking about parking," and machines handle the physical work.[1]

The Beginnings of Mechanization: From the 1880s to 1930

One of the first U.S. patents related to mechanized vehicle storage was granted in 1884, for a machine that parked a buggy above the horse in a stable. Although it was developed at the dawn of the automobile age, this invention presaged later approaches to mechanizing the storage of cars. The first mechanized parking garage in the world, the Rue de Ponthieu Garage, was built by Auguste Perret in Paris in 1905; in this garage, automobiles were moved by means of elevators and trolleys. The Harnischfeger system, which relied on a similar arrangement, was probably created at approximately the same time.[2]

One of the earliest proposals for a mechanized garage in the United States featured a four-sided elevator and turntable combination and a mechanized sloping floor: cars could glide easily from any of the four sides of the elevator to a parking spot. Developed in the early 1920s, the design was a striking example of the interaction of designers' imaginations and new technological capabilities. A 1929 article describing the garage noted that the building was only two stories high, that its incoming capacity was estimated at six cars per elevator per minute, and its outgoing capacity at three cars per minute. The plan required 187 square feet (17 square meters) per car and utilized every portion of the floor plate.[3]

The article also noted that the car jockeys would move through the structure by means of a stairway that was wrapped around a passenger elevator positioned within a two-car bay; however, an actual plan in another article shows only a single stair in the corner of the building, and no passenger elevator; the discrepancy suggests that several different versions of this facility may have been proposed. A garage based on this design was constructed in 1928; a similar approach was also used in the Kent Automatic Parking Garage and in the Hill Garage, both of which are discussed later in the chapter.[4]

By the 1920s, the ramp had begun to overtake the elevator in popularity—and by the 1930s, the ramp was firmly entrenched as the movement system of choice. Nevertheless,

---

- ⇒ The first credit card—the Diners Club Card—was invented by Ralph Scheider in 1950.
- ⇒ The National Parking Association, the first organization to represent the modern parking industry, was formed in the fall of 1951.
- ⇒ The first section of the New Jersey Turnpike opened in 1951.
- ⇒ In 1951, 6.6 million cars were sold; in the course of the decade, roughly 8 million new cars were produced each year.
- ⇒ By 1951, virtually every part of the United States had television reception; by 1953, two-thirds of American families owned televisions.
- ⇒ In 1952, the first passenger jet flew from London to Johannesburg.
- ⇒ In 1953, the Chevrolet Corvette became the first car to have an all-fiberglass body.
- ⇒ By 1953, only 6,000 miles (9,656 kilometers) of the interstate highway system had been completed, of the estimated 40,000 that were needed.
- ⇒ In 1956, the Federal-Aid to Highway/Interstate Highway Act was passed; the legislation was part of a continuing effort to complete the planned interstate highway system.
- ⇒ The hovercraft was invented in 1956.
- ⇒ During the 1950s, William Levitt—of Levittown fame—produced 36 houses a day; in 1950 alone, there were nearly 1.4 million brand-new houses built in the United States.
- ⇒ The solar cell battery was invented in 1954.
- ⇒ The first enclosed shopping center, Southdale, was designed by Victor Gruen and built in 1956 in Edina, Minnesota.
- ⇒ In 1958, President Eisenhower created the National Aeronautics and Space Administration.

Movement Facts of the 1950s

By the 1950s, the country was back on its feet and the economy was in full swing.

Left: Carew Towers, Cincinnati, Ohio, 1931. This garage was one of the many mechanized sky-scraper garages that graced city skylines.

Center: Hill Garage, Los Angeles, 1928. The beaux-arts facade of this garage, as beautiful as that of any other tall building on the street, belied the completely modern, mechanized interior.

Right: Kent Automatic Parking Garage, New York City, 1928. This skyscraper garage was one of several early mechanized garages found around the country. It has been transformed into residential condominiums.

the mechanized garage continued to exert an allure and to address a need. During the late 1920s and early 1930s, mechanized garages were built in several cities, and a number of patents were filed for mechanized garages, although the designs were not constructed. One patented proposal featured an airport on top of a mechanized parking facility.[5] Interestingly, mechanized garages rarely gave any clues about what was within: typically, signage and large entry doors were the sole exterior indications of the building's purpose, and only the owners, the operators, the attendants, and the chauffeurs were aware of the new technology within.

Chicago's Jewelers' Building (now known as the Pure Oil Building), which incorporated the Ruth Safety Garage, was one of the first buildings to combine the skyscraper and the mechanized garage. Built in 1926 and in operation until 1940, the 23-level, 550-car garage was in the center of the building (a space that, at this time, was usually reserved for a light well), and completely surrounded on all four sides by retail and office space. Four automobile elevators were in the center of the garage; there were parking spaces on both sides of the elevators, and cars could exit any of the elevators from either end. An off-ramp of what is now Lake Shore Drive led directly into the lowest level of the Jewelers' Building. An entering automobile would first move into one of the four elevators, which would transport it to the appropriate floor. A gravity-based, electrically operated hydraulic mechanism in the elevator floor allowed the car to roll easily on and off the elevators. The driver, meanwhile, having dropped off the vehicle, was whisked from the lowest level to the shop of his or her choice by any of ten passenger elevators. Although the Ruth Safety Garage was considered automatic at the time, it would now be described simply as an elevator garage. Nevertheless, the central placement of the elevators, the movement system, and the layout of the parked cars in relation to the elevator made the garage a precursor of the semi-automatic garages to come.[6]

Positioning the garage in the very center of the building while providing direct automobile access to Lake Shore Drive created a seamless movement pattern that had the advantage of ensuring the security of the jewelers and their customers, who never had to leave their vehicles until they were completely hidden within the building—a bonus in the Chicago of the 1920s. The well-planned interconnections between the auto, the building, and internal and external movement patterns were very much in the spirit of Daniel Burnham and Edward Bennett's 1909 plan for Chicago, and made a significant contribution to the city's overall transportation system. Chicago was the only city of its time that included parking in its transportation plans.[7]

The first mechanized garages in which cars moved in three dimensions appeared almost simultaneously, in the late 1920s and early 1930s: the Ruth Safety Garage; the Kent Automatic Parking Garages, in New York, Chicago, and Cincinnati; the Hill Garage, in Los Angeles; and the Carew Tower, in Cincinnati. Mechanization offered a single, and simple, advantage: the opportunity to park a large number of cars within a very small space. If a garage is designed as a machine, then theoretically the construction dimensions can be reduced to those of the parked automobile. The Kent Garage was 15 stories high (with one parking level below grade) and could park 1,050 cars on a 50-foot by 200-foot (15-meter by 61-meter) lot. The Hill Garage was 13 stories high and could park 850 cars on a 78-foot by 155-foot (24-meter by 47-meter) lot. The Carew Tower, which operated until 1978, could park 500 cars on its 27 levels.[8] Although the Kent, the Hill, and the Carew Tower garages all used mechanized systems to move the cars, there were variations in approach.[9]

In the Kent Garage, designed by Jardine, Hill & Murdock, the parking operation was controlled by an attendant at a remote station, but machines did all the work. A patented electrical device mounted under the rear axle allowed the attendant to move the car in either direction. The Kent in New York became the prototype for others built in Chicago and Cincinnati, and was in operation well into the 1950s.

Like all skyscrapers in New York, the Kent had to address the zoning requirements for tall buildings. The solution, envisioned by Hugh Ferris and approved by the city of New York, was to step back the upper stories from the streetfront so that the structure's mass and height would not visually overwhelm the street or block light and air. The exterior of the Kent reflected the transition from the beaux-arts to the modern aesthetic: it was relatively austere, but with some ornamentation on the lower street edge and in key places on the facade. The smaller-scale entrance in the two-story portion of the building helped to mediate the gap between the Kent tower and both the surrounding architecture and the human scale at the sidewalk. However, the large electric sign on the top of the garage—easily visible from great distances—placed the structure squarely in the modern age. The first floor of the two-story portion of the building housed space for auto maintenance, and the second provided rooms for car jockeys and chauffeurs to relax and take care of their daily needs.[10]

At the Hill Garage, designed by Kenneth MacDonald Jr. and Company, a specially designed elevator and turntable combination allowed cars to be rotated to face any of four directions to exit the elevator; however, because the mechanism had to be operated by a car jockey within the car, this garage was categorized as semi-automatic. The internal turntable within each elevator could hold two cars at a time—a unique arrangement. The system required only minimal aisle space: car jockeys moved the automobiles along three aisles that led from each elevator to some of the parking areas; other parking spaces had direct access from the elevator. The turntables had electrical push-button controls, and the car jockeys used man-lifts to move between floors.[11]

The beaux-arts facade of the Hill Garage—ornamented in terra cotta and lacking any large, illuminated sign—allowed the building to fit comfortably into the 1920s streetscape. The only thing that set the structure apart was its large automobile entrance. Because the building had flat floor plates and the elevators were positioned on the blank wall that adjoined the neighboring buildings, it was possible to use traditional windows on the front and sides of the facility. Ramps connected the first two parking floors to the street level, and the retail operations on the first floor featured large, ornamented, plate-glass windows.

Car Stackers: A More Modest Approach

A car stacker is a portable, reliable, and relatively inexpensive solution that allows a parking lot to double, triple, or quadruple its capacity with minimal expense; where there is enough ceiling height, car stackers can even be used within garage structures. The idea for such systems appeared as early as 1925, when Peter Lunati built a hydraulic lift for car maintenance and repair that had obvious implications for auto storage.

The first car stacker was patented in 1927, by Max Miller, and was designed to raise parked vehicles above the highway so that the roadway would be unobstructed. Although Miller's design was never built, the car stacker is generally regarded within the parking industry as the first mechanical parking device developed in the United States.[1]

At a time when downtown buildings, including early garages, were being razed and replaced with parking lots, car stackers offered a means of maximizing the number of spaces on lots with a minimal investment of time and money. In 1941, O.A. Light filed a patent for a device that allowed three cars to be parked one above the other. Using a dual-lift system with two hydraulically controlled platforms, the Sky-Park, built in Washington, D.C., in 1954, doubled the available space on a 25-foot by 67-foot (eight-meter by 20-meter) site. The attendant could park or retrieve a car in 22 seconds at the touch of a button. This system, which was manufactured by Simmons Industries, of Albany, New York, was also installed in Detroit in 1956. Other car stackers developed during the 1950s included the Astrolift, the Lift Box, and the B-Box. In 1956, at the Mechanical Handling Exhibition held in London, even a forklift was proposed as a means of lifting cars into a triple-stacker.[2]

The Dubl Park system, used on a very crowded parking lot in downtown Washington, D.C., increased the capacity of that lot by 90 percent. The demountable system was easy to erect and allowed cars to be parked in a parallel parking arrangement on a raised steel platform; the vehicles below were parked in typical, head-in fashion. Because Dubl Park allowed the lot to accommodate both long-term and short-term parking, it increased revenues for the lot. (The Zaha design, which was developed in 1954, worked on a similar principle, but added a conveyor belt to the platform.)[3]

Another solution, Auto-Pak, was derived from aircraft storage and tested and built by All American Engineering Company. In this approach, which was developed in 1959, cars were positioned at a 30-degree angle, which allowed a second car to be parked below the angled vehicle. Car stackers became the mechanized systems of choice from the 1960s through the 1980s; examples included the Space-O-Matic, designed by Fisher, Whitley, and Biddle; the Parkmaster, designed by the Herbst Brothers; the Sky Park, designed by the Simmons Machine Tool Corporation, of Albany, New York; and the DuoPark, designed by Ed Greer. All were self-supporting, portable, and allowed two cars to park in the same

Above: Car stackers in New York City, 2006.

Above: Car stacker, Bellora condominiums, Seattle, Washington, 2004.

Right: M. Miller, patent drawing, Vehicle Parking System, 1927.

space as one. (The DuoPark is among the car stackers that are still being produced today.) In 1969, the Space-O-Mat system—a double car stacker constructed with two units in tandem—was used to double the available space at a parking lot in Long Beach, California.[4]

In the late 1980s, Angelo Fusaro achieved a breakthrough in the design of car stackers: Fusaro's approach placed the parking machine partially below grade, allowing the top car to be retrieved without requiring the bottom car to be moved. This concept, in various configurations, is now a standard part of the industry: instead of being driven off and on the parking machine to allow other vehicles to be retrieved, cars can be automatically shifted. One design even allows the entire system to be underground, with a green space or plaza above.[5]

Another important innovation in the industry was the use of car stackers to meet parking requirements in condominiums. This approach was first used in 1973, in the Menlo Towers project, in Menlo Park, California. At the Bellora Condominiums, in Seattle, Washington, placing car stackers in the existing high-ceilinged garage helped with a parking crunch. And in the new ramp garage currently under construction for Cristalla, another Seattle condominium development, 36 of the stalls will accept stacked parking. Car stackers are being used in crowded cities such as New York and Boston, either on lots or in high-ceilinged garages. Cities in California and new condo projects in Florida are also using the technology to make new condominium projects viable in dense locations and near historic properties, where other parking solutions are not feasible.[6]

Car stackers can be easily disassembled and moved to other locations. Such portability is useful when a parking lot becomes the site of a high-rise residential or commercial building in a desirable downtown location. Today, car stackers—featuring a range of options and advantages—are widely marketed throughout Europe and the United States. They commonly contain one, two, or three movable steel pallets that nest on the ground when not in use. After a car has been driven onto the topmost pallet, it is hoisted upward by means of hydraulic pistons and steel chains or cables. Thus, each 8.5-foot by 17-foot (2.6-meter by five-meter) parking space can accommodate between two and four cars. (Lifts that allow cars to be stacked four high have only recently been introduced.) To increase their capabilities, car stackers are sometimes combined with other movement systems such as turntables, conveyor belts, and mechanisms that allow vehicles to be moved laterally; with such additions, some car stackers are on the verge of being fully automated.[7]

Car stackers are being used to solve many difficult parking problems: Harvard University, for example, installed them in the early 1970s, as did the state of California. Because they provide a convenient means of increasing capacity at an attended facility at low cost, car stackers occupy a growing niche in the list of urban parking options.[8]

After the 1920s, the goal was to create completely automatic systems that did not require the car to be occupied. In the Arthen Auto Storage System, for example, developed in the late 1920s by the Harnischfeger Corporation, of Milwaukee, the driver used crank-type controls or buttons to move the car into a parked position. A patent awarded to E.W. Austin in 1942 became the basis for many later designs (including the Bowser and the Pigeon Hole); it was not until the 1950s and 1960s, however, that the popularity of mechanized parking reached its height, at least in the United States. Austin's design featured an elevator that rose between fixed parking stalls located on both sides; the elevator was positioned within an open "slot" within which it could move vertically or horizontally.[12]

Another early approach to automatic parking, essentially a Ferris wheel for cars, eliminated the building that surrounded the machine and replaced it with a rotating cage. This design made it possible to park many cars on a footprint the size of two or three parking spaces. In the version invented by J.E. Morton, of Sandusky, Ohio, in 1923, cars rested on platforms that were suspended by chains. H.D. James, an engineer at Westinghouse Electric, created a similar system that could be coin operated, and, depending on the design, could house 16 or 24 cars. (More cars could be accommodated by expanding the structure upward, or by placing two systems side by side.)[13]

James believed that his parking machine would address a number of urban problems: the device could be "built into office buildings, hotels, theaters, and public buildings, and set up on convenient locations on vacant lots," in apartment houses, and "at frequent intervals in residential neighborhoods."[14] James believed that the device was also suitable for bus terminals, and that it could revolutionize taxi stands by keeping cruising taxis off the streets. Because of its enormous potential to reduce street parking, the system could eliminate the need for widening streets or tearing down buildings (approaches to creating parking spaces and unclogging streets that were common at the time). James also believed that the machines could be connected to phone systems that would respond immediately if a problem occurred.[15]

In 1929, one of James's systems was built to provide employee parking at the Westinghouse plant in East Pittsburgh. Three years later, two of his systems were built side by side on a Chicago parking lot between State and Dearborn, fronting Monroe Street. The facilities housed 48 cars on a 32-foot by 24-foot (ten-meter by seven-meter) site; the structures rose

Above: Westinghouse auto-
mobile parking machine, East
Pittsburgh, 1929. This parking
machine, based on a system
developed in the early 1920s by
J.E. Morton, had a footprint the
size of just two cars and could
be built to many different
heights. This design eventually
became very popular—within
buildings in Japan.

Right: Harnischfeger system,
circa 1905. The earliest form of
mechanized parking used freight
elevators and a transfer car
mounted on rails.

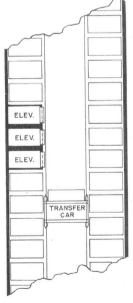

Above: Nash Motors display, Century of Progress Exhibition, Chicago,
1933. This storage system, similar in design to a Ferris wheel, was
encased in glass—thereby both housing and advertising the automobiles within.

The Parking Garage

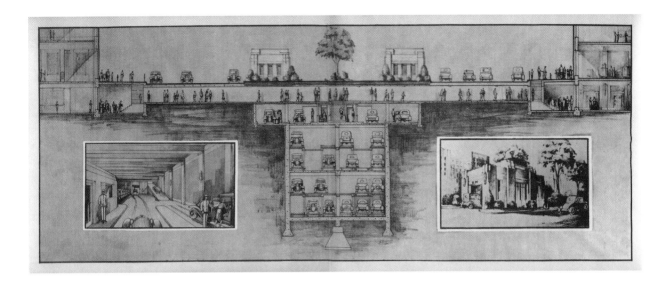

to a height of 105 feet (32 meters). The owner of the car would drive onto the machine, pull a lever, and obtain a check or a key, which would later be used to ensure that only that particular car could be retrieved. Since the system could be coin operated, no attendant was required. The maximum time for a complete retrieval cycle—closing the door of the platform, bringing the car platform to base, and opening the door to the automobile—was one and a half minutes, and the average cycle time was one minute.[16] In 1933, the Nash Motors display at Chicago's Century of Progress Exhibition consisted of a similar system, encased in glass and steel to advertise the colorful wares within, and graced by large "Nash" signs that reflected the elegance of the era.[17]

Mechanization from 1930 to 1950

Between 1930 and 1950, the automatic and semi-automatic garage continued to generate interest, even though few such facilities were actually built. On August 6, 1930, Nolan S. Black and Wilfred W. Casgrain, of Smith, Hinchman, & Grylls, presented the Detroit City Council with a grand scheme that called for the construction of semi-automatic underground garages in the heart of downtown, between "divided roadways such as Washington Boulevard, Madison Avenue, Grand Circus Park, and Cadillac Square."[18] Each facility would have between four and six stories, and the entire system would house between 3,000 and 4,500 cars. Cars would be moved vertically by means of elevators and horizontally by means of conveyor belts. Pedestrian tunnels would give direct access

Above: Nolan S. Black and Wilfred W. Casgrain, proposal for a mechanized underground parking system, Detroit, 1930. Black and Casgrain presented the Detroit City Council with a beautifully drawn pamphlet depicting a new idea: a mechanized underground parking system that would link all of Detroit.

Below: Park-O-Mat, Washington, D.C., 1951. An eyesore by today's standards, the Park-O-Mat was a modern marvel at the time, and would soon be copied around the world.

to some buildings, and drivers would reach the city above by means of stairways. Small-scale, beautifully detailed buildings would mark the entrances to the areas below. One of the advantages of this plan, according to its creators, was that it would eliminate double-parking, and thereby significantly ease congestion on the streets; it was also expected to make a profit. In the early 1930s, when Raymond Hood designed the plan for New York's Radio City Music Hall, he considered a similar system, but it was rejected because the retrieval time was considered excessive.[19]

In 1944, Richard Sinclair, of Los Angeles, designed the Park-O-Mat garage, a 12-story prefabricated structure on a 30-foot by 60-foot (nine-meter by 18-meter) footprint. The first Park-O-Mat actually constructed was built in Washington, D.C., in 1951, and served three hotels: the Washington Statler, the Ambassador, and the Hamilton.[20] Owned by Arthur Dezendorf, the facility was on a 25-foot by 40-foot (eight-meter by 12-meter) lot and had 16 floors above grade and two basement levels. The system's two elevators had fixed hoistways (a hoistway is a shaft in which one or more elevators can travel), and each elevator had two exit doors leading to the parking slots.[21] Cars were moved into and out of the elevators by means of a device connected to the bumper. The automatic system was operated remotely, by an attendant at a control panel on the ground floor, and a car could be parked in 50 seconds with just the push of a button.[22]

Mechanization from 1950 to 1990

During the four decades from 1950 to 1990, inventors of mechanized parking systems explored a range of approaches in an effort to develop a reliable, safe, and efficient "parking machine." The two most popular mechanized parking systems in the 1950s were the Bowser and the Pigeon Hole—but during that decade and the next, many independent inventors created their own variations on the mechanized facility. Designs for parking machines were developed even by elevator companies, and by companies that were involved in shipping and moving goods. Although many of these designs were constructed locally, they did not become as widespread as the Bowser and Pigeon Hole systems.[23]

The Bowser and the Pigeon Hole Systems

Both the Bowser and the Pigeon Hole system were classified as semi-automatic: although the cars were moved by mech-

anized means, some human labor was required. Both systems also relied on elevator platforms that could move both vertically and horizontally within a shaft; thus, a single platform could reach any open parking stall.[24]

In the system designed by V.C. Bowser, of Baltimore, an open shaft runs from top to bottom and end to end in the garage. The movement structure that is suspended within this shaft moves both vertically and horizontally at the same time; in essence, the structure moves diagonally. The parking stalls are on both sides of the open shaft and perpendicular to it; the width of the system is determined by whether the stalls are one deep or two deep. An attendant drives the car into the elevator, then from the elevator drives it into the parking slot. All cars enter from one side of the building and exit on the opposite side, so that no car is required to turn around; this arrangement allows for the smallest possible floor plate and eliminates the need for a turntable. At the base of the structure is a push-button control station, which can theoretically be operated either by the automobile driver or the attendant; however, the machine was typically controlled by the attendant.[25]

The first Bowser system garage, constructed in 1951 by the city of Des Moines, Iowa, was nine stories high and built on a 78-foot by 124-foot (24-meter by 38-meter) lot. Throughout the 1950s and into the 1960s, Bowser garages were built in many large cities—and even in smaller ones, such as Athens, Georgia, which had a population of only 28,000 in 1957, when it got a Bowser garage. By 1956, 14 Bowser garages had been built in the United States (including three in Chicago alone), and one in Mexico. The garages employed a range of construction materials—including steel, glass, reinforced concrete, and precast concrete—and each had a distinctive facade.[26]

In the late 1950s and early 1960s, the engineering firm of Gage and Martinson designed one Bowser system and served as a consultant on another—a garage in the Manhattan theater district. The eight-level, 256-car ShowBiz Garage, on West 45th street, just west of Times Square, had two Bowser elevators. It was constructed by the Balaban-Gordon Construction Company of New York and owned by a 30-person syndicate headed by Sol Goldstein. Still in use round the clock, the Showbiz was refurbished in 2001, at a cost of $1 million. The 10-level, 440-car Velvex Garage, on West 44th street, just west of 8th Avenue, had three Bowser elevators and was built by the Jackbilt Company, of Cedarhurst, Long Island. It also remains in use 24 hours a day. Dur-

ing this era, a number of other automated garages were built in New York.[27]

Bowser system garages were stand-alone structures of either steel or concrete, like those in New York's theater district, or were integrated into other buildings. The 13-story, 500-car garage of the Petroleum Club building, in Oklahoma City, had enough spaces for all the tenants in the building, and the garage floors were linked directly to the offices. The structure, designed by Bailey, Bozalis and Associates, of Oklahoma City, was considered a prototype for the apartment buildings of the future. A Bowser system garage built in Boston in 1957 was designed to have 10-foot (three-meter) floor-to-floor heights so that the building could be converted to office use, should parking demand change in that location.[28]

The pioneer Pigeon Hole system was constructed in Spokane, Washington, in the late 1950s. The Pigeon Hole system was a bolted-steel framework with a 20-foot (six-meter) carrier that contained a two-directional elevator. The carrier moved horizontally on railroad tracks located at the bottom of the hoistway. Cars were loaded into the system by means of mechanical dollies (which many people claimed damaged the undercarriage). Because the dollies had a range of only 20 feet (six meters), positions were available where automobiles could be stored temporarily before being moved into the system.[29]

Attendants operated levers to control the movements of the cars; thus, the system was considered fully automatic

Top left: Bowser system garage, Des Moines, Iowa, 1951. Internal functionality gave this garage—the first facility based on the Bowser system—the look of a modern office building: large horizontal expanses balanced by strong vertical forms.

Top right: Bowser system garage, Athens, Georgia, 1957. Bowser system garages were built all over the country.

Above: City Parking Garage, Chicago, 1956. In this garage, the Bowser system was ornamented by a sculpture—*Chicago Rising Out of the Lake*—created by Milton Horn.

A number of proposals for automatic and semi-automatic garages were based on a round floor plan, which opened up a whole new set of possibilities for layout and design. By 1926, at least two patents existed for round floor systems. The Rotogarage, designed by Albert Buranelli and patented by him in 1954, was a 500-stall system proposed for a 100-foot by 100-foot (30-meter by 30-meter) lot in Manhattan; each floor plate had 28 stalls. The design worked on essentially the same principle as a revolving restaurant: roller-mounted circular steel tracks rotated around a bank of four elevators, which provided the vertical movement for parking. The automobile would ascend on one of the elevators, then a round steel frame on the floor would rotate to an open space so that the car could be driven into a parking slot. The maximum estimated time to park a car in a 650-stall garage of this design was one minute and 24 seconds.[1]

Mechanized Garages with Round Floor Plans

Although Buranelli's design does not appear to have been built, the approach seems to have inspired the creation of other systems along the same lines: examples include projects designed by Guy C. Carr, in 1955, in the United States; the Revolving Lot, built in Düsseldorf, Germany, in 1957; and a system designed in Spain by architect Casto Fernández-Shaw. One proposal, a 1955 design called the Helical Parking System, was a mechanized version of Frank Lloyd Wright's idea for Sugarloaf Mountain.[2]

In 1956, William Zeckendorf and I.M. Pei patented a round multistory garage. But perhaps the most unusual proposal of the era was a round design with parking in concentric circles, illustrated in a 1953 article in *The Architectural Forum*. Within 11 years, however, the idea had become reality: it was constructed in Japan in 1964, by Kawasaki Heavy Industry, and was known as the Wheel Park system.[3]

In 1964, Lee Fraser, of the Diversified Engineering Company, proposed the Tower Hoist Parking Tower, another design based on a round floor. That same year, a prototype of the RotoPark system, designed by Etudes Nouvelles, of Geneva, was built in London. This multilevel system, which was meant to be positioned below grade, had fixed elevators and rotating concentric parking rings. In 1970, Otis placed an advertisement in *The Architectural Record* for a round system called Otis Rotopark, which was designed for use at airports.[4]

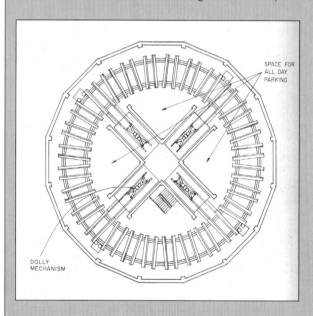

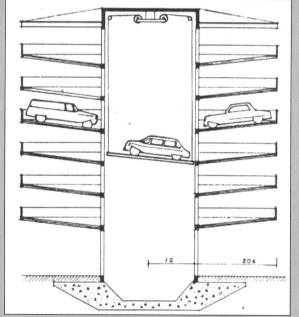

Above: Rotogarage, New York City, 1954.

Right: Lee Fraser, proposal for Tower Hoist Parking Tower, 1964.

The Parking Garage

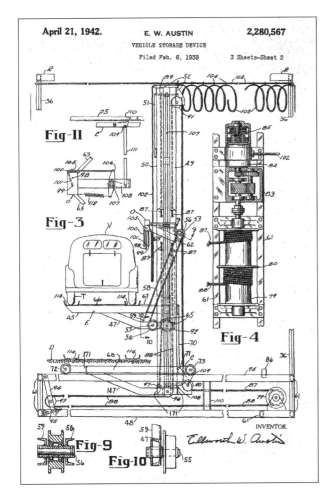

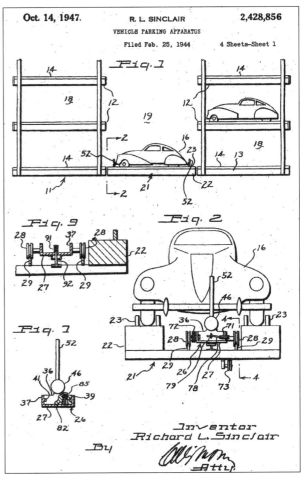

at the time. In 1954, it took one minute and 22 seconds to park a car in a 144-car garage, and the construction cost per space was $400—which was quite inexpensive for mechanized technology, and even less expensive than the ramp garages of the time. By 1954, only six Pigeon Hole garages had been built in the United States, but within three years, 50 had been built, including two in Manhattan alone. One Pigeon Hole garage—with two elevators and room for 350 cars—is still in use in Manhattan's financial district; unlike most Pigeon Hole garages, it is technically a semi-automatic facility.[30]

In 1955, a Pigeon Hole garage was built in Harrisburg, Pennsylvania, on a lot adjoining the Penn Harris Hotel. That same year, a Bowser system garage was built in Mexico City. By 1964, Pigeon Hole garages had been built in many smaller cities in the United States, including Portland, Oregon; Youngstown, Ohio; Lafayette, Louisiana; and Madison, Wisconsin.[31]

Above left: E.W. Austin, patent drawing, Vehicle Storage Device, 1942. This is just one of the many systems for automated parking patented in the mid-20th century.

Above right: R.L. Sinclair, patent drawing, Vehicle Parking Apparatus, 1947. Many inventors explored the issue of how to move the car into position.

Mechanization

Other Systems, 1950–1990

The 1950s and 1960s were a particularly fertile period for the design of mechanized parking systems. Among the many creative proposals was an Italian design based on a conveyor belt. This approach, which was featured in *Parking* magazine in 1956, echoed Black and Casgrain's 1930 proposal for a vast system of underground garages in Detroit. Other designs developed during the same period included the Medway system, the Casgrain system, and the Harnischfeger system—which, although it dated back to the first decade of the 20th century, was still considered viable. The Medway was a rank-and-file system, now often known as puzzle parking. In this approach, individual platforms are arranged in a grid (called a rank and file), and cars are shifted as necessary to make room for incoming vehicles. The Medway required only 210 square feet (20 square meters) per car—the lowest square footage requirement of the three.[32] The Casgrain and Harnischfeger systems were similar to each other, but in the Casgrain approach, the cars were placed parallel to the dolly-and-rail movement system, rather than perpendicular to it, further narrowing the lot size required for parking. In 1954, the McLean brothers and Alan Bigler designed a mechanized garage with a steel frame and an elevator that moved vertically and horizontally through the center of the structure;

like the Casgrain and Harnischfeger systems, this design kept the cars parallel to the movement system. Another patented design was created for the Parkway Motor Lodge, a hotel that had an attached elevator garage.[33]

Other automatic and semi-automatic systems that relied on elevators and transfer systems included the Park-A-Loft, the MinitPark, and the File-A-Way. The Park-A-Loft, a seven-story machine with a 264-car capacity, was designed and built (in prototype form) by the Dresser-Ideco Company, of Columbus, Ohio, in 1955. In the Park-A-Loft, a dolly system was used to move cars into and out of the elevator. The first Park-A-Loft was constructed in 1958, for the parking commission of Parkersburg, West Virginia, one-and-a-half blocks from the town's main shopping district, to help maintain interest in shopping downtown. The exterior of the garage had a clean, modern appearance, not unlike that of a modern office building.[34]

The Washington and Rector Street MinitPark, built in 1960 in Manhattan's business district, was similar in design to the Pigeon Hole system. This garage was the first of a series of 15 to 20 units planned for New York City; the facilities were to have been financed by First Commonwealth Corporation.[35]

The File-A-Way was developed in Portland, Oregon, and patented in 1955. The first File-A-Way was constructed in 1959, by Gunderson Brothers Engineering Corporation, in the

Proposal for storage system, 1956. In this Italian design, conveyor belts allowed storage and movement to be combined.

The Parking Garage

heart of Portland's downtown retail area. The system was push-button-operated and could be designed so that cars were either parallel or perpendicular to the center hoistway. Other examples of this type included the LektroPark, in Milwaukee, Wisconsin; the Squared Circle, in Passaic, New Jersey; the Keypark, in Washington, D.C.; the Push-Button parking system, designed by Detroit industrialist Mervyn G. Gaskin; and the stacker crane system, designed by Fred Miller. The stacker crane system, which originated in Wilmington, Delaware, was based on materials-handling systems that were in operation in many large companies.[36] The stacker crane system was unique in that it had an "electronic brain"—the beginning of computerization.[37] Mechanized approaches designed and constructed in Europe included a system called X-Y parking, designed by Olle Isvén, of Stockholm, in 1961; and the Shoe Lane Car Park, which opened in London in 1963.[38]

In the 1950s, many inventors—including Tom Morrison, of Los Angeles, and Reginald D. Wilson, of Baltimore—developed variations of the Ferris-wheel approach that had first

Above left: Park-A-Loft, Parkersburg, West Virginia, 1958. By the late 1950s, more mechanized systems had begun to appear. This system, a stacking device, was placed within a "horizontal ribbon" building, which was a newly emerging style at the time.

Above right: Blue Pigeon Hole Facility, Portland, Oregon, 1955. Local companies in a number of cities designed and constructed their own mechanized storage systems.

Model of Electro Park, Los Angeles, circa 1950. Many fully functioning models were constructed that represented automated facilities at a miniature scale.

appeared in the 1920s. Ferris-wheel designs were also constructed all over North America; examples included the Electromatic Autopark, built in San Francisco; the Auto Park Towers, designed by P.J. Scott and constructed in Jackson, Mississippi; a stand-alone garage built by William Zeckendorf, on Staten Island; and the Rotary Garage, built in Montreal. (The Ferris-wheel approach was also used in Germany, where it became known as a paternoster.) The Electromatic Autopark was depicted in drawing tucked inside a building, whereas the Autodrome, developed by Herman Glicker, of New York City, was an exposed steel structure situated in an open parking lot.[39]

In 1960, Parking System Engineering, a Denver firm, developed the Vert-A-Park, which was designed by Bob Lichti. A wheel-type parking system similar to the 1929 Westinghouse model, the Vert-A-Park met all building codes and was structurally capable of standing alone. Although it was more than 90 feet (27 meters) high, the footprint was the size of only two-and-a-half cars. The first Vert-A-Park facilities were constructed in Santa Fe Springs, California, and at the Central Bank & Trust Company, in Denver. The Vert-A-Park facility built in 1968 for a Denver car dealership took its cue from a 1948 design developed jointly by the Acme Glass Company and the inventors of the Vert-A-Park system. In this design, large expanses of glass on the beautiful facade of the steel structure gave a full view of the engineering tech-

nology within. Both Parking System Engineering and the Acme Glass Company were eventually owned by Wayne Harding, who continues to produce many types of mechanized systems.[40]

Like the Casgrain system, the Speed-Park system—built in 1963, for Columbia University—parked cars parallel to the carrier system.[41] Created jointly by Speed Park, Inc., and the Otis Elevator Company, and designed by Mihai Alimanestianu, a Romanian-born engineer, the system could be used on a site as small as 24 feet by 24 feet (seven meters by seven meters); the prototype constructed by Otis was eight levels high. "Fork fingers" lifted the car by the tire treads and loaded it sideways into an elevator that moved both horizontally and vertically.[42]

The Columbia University project spanned 200 feet (61 meters)—from street to street, all the way through a city block—and had a 50-foot (15-meter) frontage on both streets. It had the capacity to house 270 cars, from compacts to limousines, and could accommodate 2.7 cars per minute. The facility was advertised as fully automatic; in fact, it was run by a computer. The Speed-Park was demolished in 1980, probably because it had only one operating elevator—which meant that in the case of a mechanical breakdown, customers would have been unable to retrieve their cars. Several proposals combined the Speed-Park system with a hotel; in one, by William Lescaze, the parking mechanism was visible, through

The Parking Garage

Vert-A-Park, Denver, 1968. This facility is yet another exploration of the Ferris-wheel approach.

a glass barrier, from the hotel lobby, so that after leaving their vehicles, drivers could enjoy a view of the technology.[43]

A number of other automatic parking systems appeared in the 1960s; one of the most interesting was the Autosilo, which was eventually known as Silopark. This system, designed by a Swiss engineer, was first built in Germany, in 1955, by the Autosilo Company.[44] This fully automatic system had two main selling points: computerized controls, and built-in redundancies that provided reliability and guaranteed safety for the car, the driver, and the car's contents. The system could be built above or below grade, and cars were moved into and out of the elevator by means of a rubber-wheeled dolly that clamped onto the middle part of the two front tires. According to advertisements for the system, a Silopark

Above: Speed-Park, New York City, 1963. This system moved cars horizontally into their parking spaces, an arrangement that changed plan dimensions and requirements.

Below: Silopark system, Milan, 1968. This system was conceived for use as the foundation for a building.

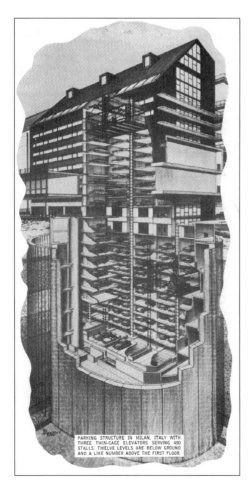

PARKING STRUCTURE IN MILAN, ITALY WITH THREE TWIN-CAGE ELEVATORS SERVING 480 STALLS. TWELVE LEVELS ARE BELOW GROUND AND A LIKE NUMBER ABOVE THE FIRST FLOOR.

garage would require only 20 percent of the land area required by a typical ramp garage. Moreover, because of the compact floor-to-floor heights—which are designed to accommodate vehicles only—a Silopark facility occupies approximately 50 percent of the volume of a ramp garage. As of 1968, 20 installations, totaling 5,000 spaces, had been built around the world, from London to Nairobi to Caracas; many of these are still in operation. Although a Massachusetts company, High-Tech Parking Systems, began marketing the product in the United States in 1984, the one attempt to construct a Silopark system within an older automated facility failed because of the age of the structure's facade. The entire structure was eventually demolished for redevelopment.[45]

It was in the 1970s that mechanized parking really began to take hold, particularly in Asia. Nevertheless, only a few examples were built in the United States. During the 1970s, a Ferris-wheel garage was installed at a hospital in Logan, West Virginia, in order to get the most parking out of a small lot. It received a great deal of use and managed to survive the decade, but was eventually disassembled. Also in the 1970s, Budget Parking announced the construction of a computerized, fully automated garage in Westwood, California. Although this solution was well ahead of its time, it is not surprising that it arose in California, where pressure for parking was intense, and where the greater parking density allowed by mechanized systems would have been appealing.[46]

During the 1980s, the design of mechanized parking garages continued to advance, and computer technology began to make the facilities more efficient and reliable. In Honolulu, for example, rapid growth and severe land constraints led to the construction of two automatic parking facilities, both based on the Ferris-wheel design. One was constructed for an office building at 1946 Young Street and is still in operation; the other, constructed for the Koga Building at the Straub Medical Center, still stands but is unused. Worldwide, most Ferris-wheel systems are constructed within buildings in Japan, but they continue to be the solution of choice in denser, older cities and in modern urban areas all over the world; the United States, however, continues to lag behind in the adoption of this particular approach.[47]

Mechanization Today

Initially, mechanized parking systems were often subject to breakdowns—which is not surprising, given the large number of moving parts. Moreover, it was necessary to rely on

The Parking Garage

Contemporary Systems Outside the United States

Mechanized parking systems are popular worldwide, although perhaps most popular in Japan, which is estimated to have 1.6 million spaces in mechanized facilities. The largest facility in the world, however, is in Greece. Some of the systems are quite advanced: in an office building in Seoul, South Korea, for example, drivers simply leave their cars at the receiving point; a machine reads the driver's pass card, and the completely automated system handles the entire parking and retrieval process.[1]

In a number of older European cities, particularly in Italy, the TreviPark system has been used successfully underground and in the foundations of buildings for many years. A round system that can be adapted to other shapes (and can even be free-form) the TreviPark relies on a center elevator that rotates so that cars can be moved into one of the surrounding open slots. Because the TreviPark can be used to provide the foundation structure for the building above, it is particularly cost-effective.[2]

Although computerized, fully automated facilities can be found throughout Europe, a number of systems happen to have been constructed recently in Germany. The Spiralparkhaus, for example, built in 1996 in a historic district of Augsburg, is an underground facility with a spiral-shaped steel mechanism at it center. The spiral, which holds up to four cars at a time, moves up and down on a rail mechanism, and rotates to place the cars into their parking slots. An elegant solution in a residential neighborhood in Sindelfingen consists of a nine-story, 30-foot- (nine-meter-) wide glass box that holds 120 cars: in effect, the entire structure is a piece of art that changes as the cars are moved. At the Car Park Sindelfingen, a small, triangular piece of land—formerly unused—now offers space for 124 cars in a nine-story structure; movement occurs in three dimensions by means of a simple, automated elevator and pallet system. And in Berlin, the garage portion of an "ecological urban renewal project" consists of two vertical conveyors, or paternosters (a series of parking spots linked on an endless horizontal or vertical chain—similar to a Ferris-wheel design), built directly into the end of a residential unit.[3] Built in 1996, the 12-story facility accommodates 67 cars and makes highly efficient use of the available land area. Another example of the Ferris-wheel design was recently constructed in France, to advertise the Smart Car. Like the Nash Motors display in the United States in the 1930s, the structure combines automation and a glass exterior.[4]

Skyparks, a company that constructs fully automated systems, has many projects all over the world, including a facility at the Foundation Center, in Paris. Westfalia Technologies, which is represented by APT Parking Technologies in the United States, has many projects in Europe—even within historic sites, such as the Palais Coburg, in Vienna. Dubai City is among the latest municipalities to construct a computerized, fully automated facility. The garage is located near the city offices, and customers may charge the parking fee by means of their mobile phones.[5]

Above: TreviPark system, 2007.

Left: Car Towers, Volkswagen Plant, Wolfsburg, Germany, 2005.

human assessment to detect problems: there was no accurate way to monitor, maintain, or repair the systems. In today's computerized, fully automated facilities, however, redundancy and computer monitoring ensure safety and reliability, eliminating the problems once associated with these devices. For example, laser beams can now detect the precise location and workings of every piece of machinery, and software can monitor cumulative hours of use and send alerts to ensure that worn parts are replaced on schedule. In addition, the cost differential associated with the mechanized garage is diminishing, particularly if land costs are taken into account. In fact, in an expensive urban setting, mechanized parking may be more economical, as is clear from the proliferation of car stackers in urban parking lots.

The parking garage has incorporated advanced technologies for moving and storing cars since its inception, and mechanized parking remains the focus of interest and innovation. Inventors continue to file new patents; one granted in 2003, for example, features subtle advancements on designs explored in the 1960s: in this approach, a single drive replaces multiple movement mechanisms. The Web site of the National Association to Restore Pride in America's Capital offers a detailed discussion of the mechanized pallet system. In 2001, Harvard University produced a study comparing automation to other strategies. A 2004 issue of *Metropolis* magazine described the efforts of one young architect to provide parking on a small lot by means of a design based on a Pez dispenser.[48]

What modern approaches to mechanization have in common with the systems of the past is the advantage of safely and efficiently parking a large number of cars in a small area. Thanks to new software, throughput—the number of cars flowing in a single direction that a system can handle in a specified time period—has increased greatly, and garage designers can now accurately assess how a facility will manage peak traffic volumes. Because of suburban

Moskow Architects, proposal, ZipCar Dispenser, 2004. This design, based on a Pez dispenser, is intended to provide parking on a small lot.

The Parking Garage

development patterns, land constraints in the United States have not been serious enough to spur significant construction of mechanized facilities (with the exception of car stackers) since the 1960s; however, growing resistance to sprawl and the return to central cities will certainly lead designers to take a fresh look at mechanized solutions. Three such facilities built in the United States—in St. Louis, Missouri; Hoboken, New Jersey; and Washington, D.C.—offer examples to be emulated. All were designed to serve residential needs in dense, older downtown areas, and to hide the mechanized technology behind or under traditional or existing facades.[49]

In 1984, at the Lennox Apartments, in St. Louis, High-Tech Parking Systems installed the first computerized, fully automated parking garage in the United States; the new system, which relied on a scanner and a coded card, replaced the old mechanized system, which had been unused for many years. Originally connected to the Lennox hotel, the garage was part of a complex being redeveloped by Leon Strauss. However, the garage operated only until 1992, when it was seized and torn down under eminent domain, in order to make room for the expansion of the convention center.[50]

The 324-car, fully computerized Hoboken facility, constructed in 1999, is a public garage designed by Gerhard Haag, of Robotic Parking. Cars are transported and stored on individual pallets, and the three directions of internal movement—along the aisles, into and out of storage bays, and from one level to another—are controlled separately. Because 18 different mechanical movements can occur simultaneously, the system can theoretically handle many cars at once; nevertheless, the garage is not yet functioning smoothly, and the project has been mired in controversy.[51]

The Grand Parc, a 74-space, four-level private parking facility constructed in 1999 under an apartment building in Washington, D.C., uses a stacker crane system manufactured by Wohr-Stopa in Germany, and distributed in the United States by SpaceSaver Parking Systems. In this system, the driver enters a compartment where the car stops and rests on a pallet. The driver then leaves the area and activates the system by means of an electronic card reader located outside the compartment. The stacker crane—a vertical tower that moves vertically and horizontally at the same time—moves the car (which is still on its pallet) into a parking slot, which may be on either side of the tower. A turntable within the transfer compartment is used to face the car in the proper direction for exiting.[52]

Top: Automated facility, Hoboken, New Jersey, 1999. The latest approaches to mechanized parking rely on computer-controlled technology. In an approach that refers back to the garages of the 1920s, the exterior of this facility blends in with the neighborhood.

Above: Grand Parc, Washington, D.C., 1999. The only way to meet all parking requirements for this site was to construct an underground mechanized facility.

New York City's first fully computerized automated facility opened in the spring of 2007, within a luxury condominium project located at 123 Baxter Street. The project is the work of AutoMotion Parking Systems, an American subsidiary of Stolzer Parkhaus, of Strassburg, Germany. AutoMotion is working on another project in New York City.[53]

A number of computerized, fully automated facilities are currently being discussed or planned. One such project is the Buildings at Lovejoy Wharf, in Boston, a project designed by the Architectural Team. Another example is a new system to be located at 1706 Rittenhouse Square, in Philadelphia's Center City district, as part of a proposed 31-story condominium development. Because the lot is too small for traditional underground parking, the best solution is a mechanized facility. The fully automated system will have a throughput of one car per minute and will accommodate 64 vehicles underground, on a steel racking system connected to a conveyor

belt. In this project, the Parkway Corporation, working with the Scannapieco Development Corporation, is using the Multiparker System, manufactured by Wohr of Germany. Other examples of automated facilities are 7 State Circle, in Annapolis, Maryland; 310 Webster Avenue, in Cambridge, Massachusetts; and One York, in New York City.[54]

Recently, several older mechanized parking systems have been modernized, including the New World Tower, a 12-floor Bowser facility in Miami. Thanks to new elevators and a computerized inventory-management system, the facility reduced labor costs and customer waiting times, increased its throughput by 40 percent, and saved $351,279 over a five-year period.[55]

The Future of Mechanized Parking

In the 20th-century American city, as speed became the prerequisite for the success of any endeavor, parking garage designers were compelled to be responsive to that demand, and mechanization was one of the results. Mechanized garages

123 Baxter Street, New York City, 2007. This is the first new automated facility to open in New York since the 1960s.

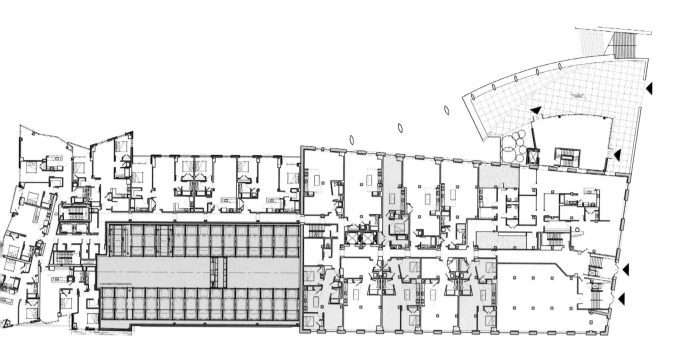

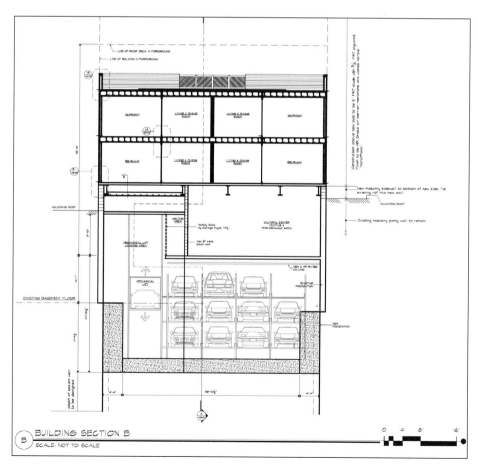

Above: The Buildings at Lovejoy Wharf, Boston, 2007. Automated parking facilities can make it possible to move projects forward despite limitations of project scope and site.

Left: Brazilian Cultural Center, Cambridge, Massachusetts, 2007. Automated facilities can often be accommodated within a small site plan and building floor plate.

Mechanization

7 State Circle, Annapolis, Maryland, 2007. In historic downtowns that have limited available land, automated parking may be the only way to provide parking for development.

eventually became one of the leading parking solutions in Europe and Asia, and are poised to be among the most important solutions for the 21st-century United States.

Today's computerized parking offers a number of advantages over the traditional ramp garage. First and foremost, it can reduce the space allocated to parking by at least 40 percent—in part because it does not require driving ramps or walkways for pedestrians, and in part because the floor-to-ceiling heights need to accommodate automobiles only. Computerized facilities will thus become increasingly important in dense urban areas, or where the use of additional land for parking is impossible or undesirable. Reducing the amount of space required for parking adds more leasable space to a development, creating additional real estate opportunities. Because the facades of computerized facilities can be made to match those of surrounding buildings, they

The Parking Garage

can more easily blend in with existing architectural patterns. Computerization also simplifies the building engineering, allowing a simple frame structure; permits accelerated depreciation; and may qualify a facility for municipal financing.

Because computerized parking is safe and secure for both the car and its owner, these facilities are more valuable as amenities. Dents and scratches are no longer a concern: once the driver leaves the automobile, it will not be driven again until it is retrieved; moreover, throughout the time that the vehicle is in the facility, it will not come into contact with other cars or with the parts of the system itself. Because neither drivers nor passengers enter the facility, computerized garages do not have to grapple with the issue of pedestrian safety. Finally, computerized systems can be flexibly combined with other land uses and building types. For example, underground computerized systems require very little aboveground surface area, and create opportunities for small, parklike pavilions above.[56]

In many cities, older buildings with large floor plates, such as warehouses, are in need of revitalization. Because mechanized parking systems are virtually emissions-free, they can be safely placed in the central core of such buildings—where there is the least natural light—making good practical use of otherwise undesirable space. Similarly, because mechanized parking systems have such a small footprint, they can be located on urban "notch lots"—the small, undeveloped spaces, surrounded by existing buildings, that are often found in older urban centers. The additional parking created through the use of notch lots may be sufficient to make otherwise infeasible commercial projects viable.[57]

As density increases in existing downtowns and edge cities, integrating the automobile—and, therefore, the parking facility—remains a tremendous challenge. The integrative approach, in which the parking facility is conceived as a public space and as an amenity, opens up a wealth of options. The lobby of a computerized facility can be designed as a community gathering space, where drivers and passengers wait for their cars to be retrieved. Thoughtful planning can render such spaces integral to the community: the lobby might incorporate a coffee shop, a newsstand, a post office, a dry-cleaner, daycare, retail shops, and other similar amenities; an automatic car wash would be another natural addition. Here, time would slow down, and the clock would be turned back. What was the norm well into the 1950s—waiting in a beautiful, air-conditioned lobby while your car was being retrieved, sipping a cup of coffee, and catching up on

the latest news—could return as a vibrant, vital part of community life. As it becomes increasingly clear that the "speed" of the self-park garage is more a matter of perception than reality, a mechanized approach begins to looks just as efficient and reliable, if designed properly. By building on the excellent infrastructure that already exists, it is possible to achieve the best of both worlds: dense, pedestrian-friendly environments that also accommodate the automobile, and that support and encourage what is best in urban life.

Past Lessons for the Present and Future

- Mechanized systems, which permit more automobiles to be parked in facilities with smaller footprints and smaller overall volume, have their place in parking garage design.

- The design flexibility afforded by mechanized systems allows them to be integrated inside of buildings or in the center of a block.

- The flat floor plates and smaller overall volumes of mechanized garages offer many design advantages over ramp garages: in particular, the height, mass, and exteriors of mechanized garages can more easily be integrated into the existing streetscape, and adaptive use is often quite easy.

- The lobbies of mechanized garages can be designed as active gathering places, offering convenience and visual appeal and helping to foster a sense of community.

- Mechanized parking provides greater safety for drivers, passengers, and vehicles.

- Combining ramp facilities with car stackers is a cost-effective approach to optimizing space and meeting parking needs.

- Both the smaller, Ferris-wheel garages—first designed in the United States in the 1920s, and since tucked into buildings all over Japan—and the larger, "tower" designs are finding their place in the United States.

- Architects, planners, and parking garage designers view mechanized parking facilities as one means of addressing parking needs within dense environments while preserving mobility choices.

CHAPTER 6

Exploring Structure and Materials
Engineering the Garage

The evolution of the parking garage cannot be understood apart from innovations in structure and materials. Initially, parking garages were built along the lines of warehouses and other habitable structures—facilities that required elevators, open spans, and heating. By the 1950s, garages had become open decks—buildings that were more akin to lightweight bridges. The transition from the warehouse to the bridge was a function of changes in the automobile, advances in construction methods and materials, and the development of the modern aesthetic.

From its earliest beginnings, the parking garage was perceived as a fire hazard. Thus, although wood and steel were among the first construction materials used, concrete quickly became the construction material of choice. Not only was concrete preferable from a fire-safety standpoint, but it also offered much greater potential for creating the longer spans that the parking garage required.[1]

Largely because of concerns about fire, building codes were the primary drivers of parking garage design; nevertheless, because the codes were evolving simultaneously with the building type, there was constant interaction between the two. As priorities changed and new issues emerged, this symbiosis allowed designers to constantly experiment, seeking the best solutions.

Parking garage design thus reflects a continuous interaction between new needs and new solutions to those needs. For example, although the longer spans permitted by new structural forms vastly increased available design options, the result—bridgelike buildings fully exposed to the weather—yielded new problems that had to be addressed: like bridges, open-deck parking structures are exposed to extreme fluctuations in temperature and humidity and to the corrosive effects of road salts. Unlike bridges, however, garages have interior spaces that are used by people as well as vehicles, and must address human needs as well. Architect Cesar Pelli has said, "For me the solid ground ... is given by the basic relationship between the

Facing page: Pike at Rainbow Harbor parking structure, Long Beach, California, 2004. This structure is a recent post-tensioned facility. Post-tensioning is still an important part of the industry.

Movement Facts of the 1960s

The 1960s brought both the Vietnam War and nationwide antiwar protests. Technologies developed for the space program and for national defense began finding their way into everyday life. An orange drink known as Tang and a phenomenon known as the Beatles were all the rage. What cars were admired most? The Love Bug (the Volkswagen beetle) and John Lennon's hand-painted Rolls-Royce.

- The beginning of the 1960s saw the U.S. population reach 180 million.
- At the beginning of the decade, 74 million motor vehicles were registered; by the end, that number had grown to 120 million.
- By 1960, there were over 10 million new homeowners.
- By the 1960s, 720 billion motor-vehicle-miles (1.16 trillion kilometers) were traveled each year—nearly 50 percent in urban areas.
- In the course of the decade, 9,100 miles (14,645 kilometers) of interstate highways were completed.
- The horsepower race that had begun in the 1950s continued: by the end of the 1960s, 400-plus-inch V-8s were being sold, and four-barrel carburetors were becoming common.
- The Seattle World's Fair of 1962 featured the world's first monorail.
- The Federal-Aid Highway Act of 1962 created the first federal requirement for urban transportation planning.
- In 1962, the first downtown pedestrian mall in the United States was completed, in Kalamazoo, Michigan. Minneapolis's Nicollet Mall, the second downtown pedestrian mall, was completed in 1968.
- The Urban Mass Transportation Act, the first significant public transportation legislation, was passed in 1964.
- The National Academy of Engineering was established in 1964.
- In 1964, the Ford Motor Company released the Mustang, inaugurating the era of the "muscle car."
- The first bullet train went into operation in Japan in 1964.
- In 1965, the U.S. Department of Housing and Urban Development was created to authorize grants for comprehensive planning.
- In 1965, after extensive lobbying by Lady Bird Johnson, the Highway Beautification Act was passed.
- The U.S. Department of Transportation was authorized in 1966.
- The profession of parking consultant emerged: parking consultants focused on structural, functional, and operational issues specific to parking garage design.
- To ensure compatibility between the design of roads and the vehicles that used them, new standards for the size and weight of motor vehicles were developed, based on road tests conducted by the American Association of State Highway and Transportation Officials.
- In 1968, the first government safety standards for automobiles became law; emissions controls were still under discussion.
- In 1968, the first rail station ever located at an airport opened in Cleveland.
- The Apollo mission—the first manned flight to the moon—was undertaken in 1969.

The Parking Garage

Left: Service station (city unknown), 1930. Early parking facilities often included fire sprinklers and fire alarms.

Below: Fourth & Yamhill, Portland, Oregon, 1989. Garage designs that resemble early warehouses remain popular.

art of our buildings and their system of construction."[2] This has been one of the many challenges for the parking garage: creating the art within the system of construction.

Fire Safety and Structural Requirements

All construction is driven by zoning and building codes, and the parking garage is no exception. These codes address two principal areas: fire protection and life safety, and structural stability.[3] The codes are designed to protect life and property by (1) allowing occupants to exit quickly and safely, (2) ensuring safe entry and exit for firefighters, and (3) minimizing the spread of fire and of structural instability—both within the building, and to surrounding buildings.

Early code requirements for parking garages emerged from efforts to address the needs of a new and unfamiliar building type. Thus, in the case of fire safety, for example, early codes addressed the activities that were conducted within the building (such as the storage of gasoline) rather than the fire risk inherent in the structure itself, which was actually quite low.

As parking garage designers attempted to respond to changing codes, the building type evolved. One major development was the transformation of the parking facility into a place that only stored automobiles; maintenance and fuel-

ing were carried on elsewhere. Proper documentation of fire safety in current parking facilities, and the creation of codes that reflect realities, rather than assumptions, about the garage, are crucial to the continued development of the building type.

Fire Protection and Life Safety

Because so many cities in the United States had been severely damaged by fires during the late 19th and early 20th centuries, fire protection and life safety were central to the construction of the new American city. Fire sprinklers, which were offered for sale as early as 1875, were used early in the history of the garage, typically within buildings in which wooden or lightweight-steel truss construction had been used.[4] But as early as 1909, it was known that fire sprinklers were not powerful enough to extinguish "a purely local and extremely hot fire" within a vehicle, and were therefore more suited to general storage and stock areas than to areas where cars were parked.[5] Chemical extinguishers and fire alarms were considered of greater importance in providing protection against hot, localized fires.[6]

The early combinations of parking garages and other uses—such as stables, upholstery shops, and repair and maintenance facilities—resulted in hazardous arrangements. As soon as garages appeared, the Sanborn Map Company began to include them on the maps that it created for the fire insurance industry (although such maps did not always include mixed-use structures that combined parking with a stable or an upholstery shop). Because analysis of early garage fires indicated that the gasoline-soaked rags used to clean auto parts were largely responsible, the use of existing, wood-framed buildings (often stables) largely ceased, as did the construction of new, wood-framed garages. In addition, cities gradually developed codes that required automobile storage to be separate from gasoline-pumping facilities and from the provision of maintenance services.[7]

As early as 1907, in an article in *The American Architect* entitled "Motor Garages and Fire Protection," the National Fire Protection Association (NFPA) provided detailed guidelines for the construction of fire-resistant buildings: the article addressed fire walls, pump houses, pumps, vent pipes, filling pipes, and fuel-tank storage. By 1910, over ten cities had regulations in place, of varying strictness, governing garage construction; these regulations generally included mandatory fireproof construction. Under the regulations in effect in Detroit in 1914, for example, (1) a city permit was required to build a garage, (2) no garage could be maintained within the city limits without a permit, (3) garages had to be of fireproof construction, and (4) all trim and interior finishes had to be of metal or nonflammable materials. By 1915, Massachusetts had elaborate regulations that, among other things, specified three-inch- (eight-centimeter-) thick concrete floors, noncombustible construction, and the location of skylights. The Massachusetts regulations divided garages into three classes, each of which had its own set of requirements for construction, fire safety, and location; the stringency of the fire-protection measures was determined by the density of the surrounding area. Only first-class garages, which had to be noncombustible, could be built within the limits of a town. Second-class garages had less stringent building requirements but could be no more than three stories high, and could not be situated within 12 feet (3.6 meters) of any other building. Third-class garages, which were permitted to be of combustible construction, could be no more than two stories high and could not be situated within 50 feet (15 meters) of any other building.[8]

In 1918, when 130 American cities responded to a survey on how street parking affected the ability of fire trucks to reach their destinations, yet another relationship between parking and fire was illuminated. The study, conducted by the New York State Bureau of Municipal Information and a special committee of the State Conference of Mayors, concluded that garages should be permitted "under adequate safeguards, in or near buildings where large numbers of automobile users assemble."[9] Previously, most cities had prohibited garages within 500 feet (152 meters) of a school, place of worship, or place of assembly.[10]

In 1924, statistics reported on 49,156 garages showed that nearly 5 percent experienced serious fires each year. Although the development of the "hotel garage"—a storage facility where maintenance and fueling services were not offered—had helped to decrease the fire risks associated with garages, even hotel garages were not always permitted in downtown business districts. In May 1932, however, an NFPA committee recommended that hotel garages be permitted in or near buildings where large numbers of people assembled, as long as there were sufficient safeguards. Three factors assisted in changing municipal codes: the NFPA recommendation, exceptions to codes that had been allowed by some municipalities, and the implementation of safeguards such as sprinkler systems and fireproof construction. As a result of these changes, garages were permitted to be constructed in locations that would have been unthinkable before, and the possibility arose of combining garages with other uses in a single structure. Nevertheless, mixed-use arrangements continued to be viewed as potentially risky because they might limit firefighters' access to portions of a building, thereby making it harder to fight a fire. This concern was one factor in the eventual popularity of the stand-alone parking structure. To this day, parking professionals and fire safety experts continue to discuss the complexities of fire suppression in mixed-use structures.[11]

Once the parking garage had evolved into a facility whose sole purpose was automobile storage, many of the early concerns about the origins and nature of garage fires came under review. The National Parking Association, which was formed in 1951, advocated nationwide revisions of building codes to reflect the actual experiences of parking garage operators. In 1954, for example, both *Fire Safety in the Atomic Age,* an NFPA publication, and Bulletin Number 267, issued by the National Board of Fire Underwriters, made note of the low level of fire risk in open-air parking facilities. In response to such official statements from respected fire-protection organizations, cities began to reevaluate the construction regulations for parking garages. In Cincinnati, for example, a code that had been in effect since 1933, which required automobiles to be stored in completely enclosed buildings, was changed to allow open-deck garages of not more than five stories that were restricted to passenger vehicles only. Although the open-deck garage had been proposed in Chicago as early as 1913, its eventual acceptance under building codes changed the industry.[12]

The appropriateness of sprinklers in parking garages also continued to be discussed—with the result that, in most jurisdictions, sprinklers were no longer required in open parking decks. (Given that sprinklers cannot be used in the suppression of hot, highly localized fires, the value of requiring sprinklers in garages continues to be questioned.)

A 1972 study conducted by the American Iron and Steel Institute, which was updated and confirmed in 1979, found that between 1911 and the 1970s, among 1,686 parking structures, there had been no fire-related loss of life, and that only six fires had progressed beyond the automobile of origin.[13] As a consequence of these and other studies, codes began to allow the use of steel in garages. Although codes continue to change—for example, unprotected steel, which was prohibited by the earliest codes, is now allowed in certain situations—building regulations still fail to reflect the most recent scientific findings about garage fires.[14]

Since the late 1980s, Dale Denda has been researching fires that have occurred in modern parking facilities: his findings dispel the popular view that there are serious and inherent fire dangers in the multistory parking garage. After evaluating fire service and police records for 400 incidents in 302 jurisdictions, Denda found "no fatalities in any of the 400+ garage fire incidents studied."[15] Moreover, there were only four incidents in which there were any injuries at all, and those injuries were minor and affected a total of five firefighters. Finally, despite reports of extensive smoke, none of the injuries were smoke related. Denda also found that 80 percent of the garage fires were vehicle fires, and were typically (although not always) contained within the vehicle. Of the 20 percent that were not related to vehicles, most were caused by unauthorized storage.[16]

Denda's research has revealed that under virtually all scenarios, the frame and deck systems of the modern garage are noncombustible. However, Denda has identified four factors that can contribute to the spread of fire in a garage: (1) delay in suppressing or extinguishing the fire; (2) the presence of an accelerant; (3) the presence of combustibles

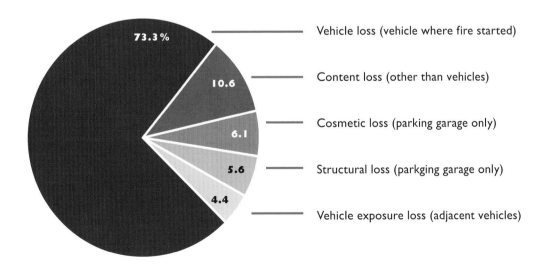

Losses from Parking Garage Fires by Category of Damage

73.3% — Vehicle loss (vehicle where fire started)

10.6 — Content loss (other than vehicles)

6.1 — Cosmetic loss (parking garage only)

5.6 — Structural loss (parkging garage only)

4.4 — Vehicle exposure loss (adjacent vehicles)

(other than vehicles); and (4) unusual weather conditions. The more serious incidents typically result from a combination of delay and a second factor.

Of the weather conditions, wind is the most likely to create risk. Although in most circumstances the open-deck garage is the safest type of facility, if flames are fanned by a breeze, or if a crosswind combines with sprinkler action to create a fog, open-air garages can present the most dangerous conditions for fire. The combination of factors likely to result in an extremely serious fire is highly unlikely, however; according to Denda, when all the parking structures in the United States are taken into account, a single such event may occur every 20+ years.[17]

Despite the fact that building codes typically require fire-separation walls between uses, fears remain that hot automobile fires can spread to adjacent uses. Although 41 percent of the garages in Denda's study shared a common fire wall with another building or use, there were no reports of fire spreading either *from* or *to* adjacent uses or adjacent buildings.[18] Vehicles are the main cause of garage fires, and when a vehicle fire is identified early, it is relatively easy to contain.[19]

In 1913, when gasoline-soaked rags were identified as the cause of garage fires, there was a rational connection between that finding and the codes that resulted. But today, fire codes for garages are no longer related to documented risks. Denda's work was the first to document in detail the actual incidence of fires in various types of facilities, creating a basis for safe and appropriate changes to codes. Because

Denda's research categorized each garage according to a number of different criteria (including structural systems; relationship to other building uses or types; and whether the garage was open, closed, or underground) it was instrumental in the latest revisions to the International Building Code (IBC). In the United States, efforts to standardize codes nationwide, and to bring them into accordance with the IBC, may lead to more realistic construction requirements for garages. Although the IBC currently classifies the parking facility as a low-risk storage use, local codes must remain flexible enough to address specific local conditions and evolving architectural trends.

The single most important component of fire safety in parking facilities is an alarm system, to permit early detection. Interestingly, such systems, first installed in Boston in 1852, were routinely required in the earliest garages. However, in Denda's 1992 report on parking garage fires, 38.9 percent of garages had no fire-detection equipment at all, and only 9.6 percent had systems in which no one needed to be present for a fire to be detected.[20]

Structural Requirements

Structural requirements for the parking garage developed slowly and were linked to a number of other issues, including construction methods and materials. As late as 1952, a survey of 31 cities conducted by the National Parking Association found that only 11 had special building codes for automobile garages.[21]

Types of Fire Detection Systems

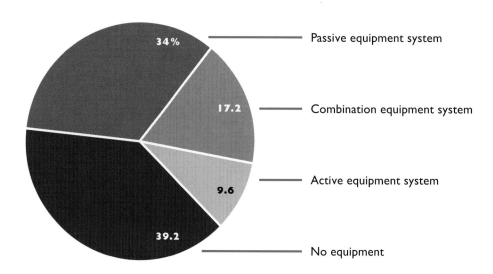

34% Passive equipment system

17.2 Combination equipment system

9.6 Active equipment system

39.2 No equipment

One of the most fundamental concerns in structural design is weight—both the weight of the building, which is known as dead load, and the weight of the building's contents, which is known as live load. In the case of the parking garage, the structural system is the most expensive aspect of the building; since requirements for both live loads and dead loads affect the amount of material used in construction, they can greatly affect overall cost.[22]

The first edition of the *Concrete Designers' Manual*—published in 1921, and one of the first sources for information on concrete design and construction—listed the code requirements for many cities in the United States, along with information on matters such as column spacing and reinforcement. The second edition of the manual, published in 1926, combined the load requirements for parking garages with those for stables and carriage houses. The manual's list of live-load requirements for parking garages indicated wide variations from city to city—75 pounds per square foot (365 kilograms per square meter) in Cincinnati and Seattle, for example, but 120 pounds per square foot (586 kilograms per square meter) in Buffalo. By 1959, Cincinnati and Dayton had the lowest requirement—40 pounds per square foot (195 kilograms per square meter)—which applied only to automobile weight; this was coupled with a maximum floor-to-ceiling height of 6 feet 10 inches (two meters), to ensure that the garage would never be used for any other purpose. In the late 1950s, George Devlin, a Detroit-based expert in parking garage design, suggested a live-load requirement of 50 pounds per square foot (244 kilograms per square meter), which was in line with the Pacific Coast Conference Code.[23] Devlin also pointed out that such a low live-load requirement might require fire protection if steel or other structural options were used.[24]

Early Garage Construction

Early garages were typically small buildings of one or two stories and were constructed in a traditional manner, using whatever local materials were most cost-effective: wood, steel or iron, plus brick on the East Coast and concrete block on the West Coast. Other materials, including fieldstone, terra cotta, and stucco, were also used, and there was some experimentation with poured concrete. Efficiency of movement required large, open spaces that were free of columns. Obtaining the desired 50-foot (15-meter) span between structural supports for roofs was considered a "special prob-

lem" in garage construction; in fact, an entire article in *The Horseless Age* was devoted to the design of roof trusses.[25] Flat roofs—constructed with the Pratt truss, which could easily support the loads of a structure whose width was a multiple of 50 feet (15 meters)—were often used. Since the roofing material had to be fireproof, garage roofs were typically made of reinforced, cast-in-place concrete; thin slabs of precast reinforced concrete; or waterproof cement tile. Connection details and snow loads rounded out the information that was needed to construct a simple, one-story garage for any location in the country.[26]

Unlike stables, which often had floors of soil or wood, garages required floors that would not absorb moisture or become slick. The driving surface consisted of layers of cement mortar, concrete, cinders, and earth. Drainage openings in the floor led to pipes below the surface, which caught oil and gasoline from vehicles and wastewater from car washes. The floors of multistory garages had to be fireproof, and the most widely accepted technique was to construct the upper floors out of concrete that was supported by embedded steel girders. In some areas, semi-fireproof construction—in which the steel girders were unprotected—was accepted, as was heavy timber construction, which was sometimes combined with sprinkler systems. Finally, some early multistory garages were simply constructed of wood: a garage built in San Francisco, in 1909, for the Taxicab Company of California, was an example.[27]

From the beginning of the 20th century, multistory garages could be found in large cities—and even in smaller ones, such as Staunton, Virginia. The facilities were typically constructed using load-bearing masonry-wall construction, the new concrete framing systems that were being employed to construct warehouses, or a combination of the two. Boston's Park Square Garage, built in 1905, was one of the earliest examples of a large, multistory, reinforced concrete garage. (Reinforced concrete is concrete that has been strengthened by the addition of steel or other materials.) This three-story, 47,400-square-foot (4,4036-square-meter) structure was designed by Gaetano Lanza; Edward T. Barker was the architect on the project, and G.H. Brazer was the consulting engineer. The goal was to design a completely fireproof structure of reinforced concrete; the design reflected research that Lanza had conducted in his lab at the Massachusetts Institute of Technology. He had experimented with various concrete mixtures, in order to achieve the necessary strength and span, and with various relationships between the steel rods and the concrete, in

Park Square Garage, Boston, 1905. Experiments with reinforced concrete undertaken at the Massachusetts Institute of Technology, in Cambridge, became reality in neighboring Boston. (The Park Square Garage is the large buiding at center right.)

order to determine the optimum size and placement of the steel rods. The facade was of glass and galvanized iron, and an eight-foot- (2.4-meter-) high fire wall separated the parking area from the commercial space that fronted the street on four of the building's five sides.[28]

Because the building was constructed on fill, it was necessary to employ Gow and Palmer, Boston contractors who had patented the special footings and techniques that were required. The design of the turntables—perhaps the first ever used in a multistory garage—was especially important, because they had to be structurally integrated into the concrete floor system. The turntables were supported around their rim and in the center. The Park Square Garage was in service until the mid-1920s, when it was demolished. It was immediately replaced by a new garage that was taller, but that had exactly the same footprint; that garage is still in use today and underwent an award-winning renovation in 1999.[29]

Experiments with Roof Spans

At the same time that they were exploring new materials, such as concrete, cast iron, and steel, garage designers were experimenting with roof spans, particularly in one-story garages, in order to create the large, unobstructed spaces required for parking. A 1909 parking garage built in Sea Gate, Long Island, featured a square plan and a central wooden pole: the pole supported the wooden roof spans that extended from the center to all four walls. The completely open interior was reminiscent of a roundhouse.

A garage built in Chicago in the late 1920s offers another example of experimentation with roof span. In this building, which housed the delivery vehicles of the Mandel Brothers Department Store, concrete arches were used for roof support. The columns supporting the arches were 16 feet (five meters) apart, allowing the arches to span 103 feet (31 meters). The lower cord (the long horizontal piece connecting the ends of the arch) was a steel rod, which contributed to the truss action. The steel rod was adjusted by turnbuckles, which tightened the wire, counterbalancing the outward compressive pressures of the concrete arches and roof loads. The concrete system allowed monitor skylights to span the entire length of the building and to run perpendicularly in plan to the truss system, fully lighting the space below. The beauty of the design was the light that reached the interior; the difficulty was the susceptibility of the 2.5-inch (six-centimeter) steel rods to fire.[30]

A 1926 garage designed to house motor trucks for Sears, Roebuck & Company had wooden trusses spanning the roof. Although this type of construction was allowed in Chicago, the building had to meet a number of additional code requirements, including brick walls, double steel fire doors, and a sprinkler system. The brick walls and fire doors separated the four 53-foot- (16-meter-) wide bays, and were

The Parking Garage

also positioned between the rest of the building and the 25-foot- (eight-meter-) wide bay that contained the chauffeurs' room, lockers, and restrooms. The 25-foot- (eight-meter-) wide end bay also contained the boiler and fuel rooms and was entered from the outside, as mandated by code requirements. The roof featured three monitor skylights within each bay. The garage areas had to be ventilated, so flues were embedded within the brick walls; registers positioned one foot (0.3 meters) above the floor pulled out the stagnant air.[31]

New solutions continued to emerge even in the late 1940s. In 1948, a combination skating rink, bowling alley, and 300-car garage used concrete barrel arches and semi-domed ends to create a clear span for the skating rink. The square, two-foot by two-foot (0.6-meter by 0.6-meter) columns, placed on a square, 25-foot by 25-foot (eight-meter by eight-meter) grid, supported the dome, allowing three cars to be parked between the columns in each 25-foot- (eight-meter-) grid. On a separate floor, the same column spacing allowed four bowing alleys in each bay.[32]

Multistory Parking Garages

By the 1920s, large, multistory parking garages had become the norm. To meet the needs of these structures—and to attempt to address the requirements of new regulations—architects and engineers experimented with materials and construction techniques. From the beginning, however, concrete technology led the way in the construction of the multistory parking garage, in part because many cities required garages to be fireproof (and concrete was the obvious choice), and in part because the use of reinforced concrete was within the realm of typical construction practices.[33]

By the late 1920s, the elevator garage had largely been left behind, in favor of interior and exterior ramps. But ramps, and the sloped floors that accompanied them, created new structural and fire-safety issues. Because ramps provided opportunities for a blaze to spread upward, some cities required ramps to be enclosed. It was the breakthrough D'Humy ramp, which was developed in 1918, that allowed fire doors to be placed between floors, eliminating the need to enclose ramps for fire protection.[34]

A helical ramp designed in 1919 by Holabird & Roche, an architectural and engineering firm, offers an example of the complex structural needs that had to be addressed within the limitations of flat-slab construction. The ramp, designed for Chicago's Washington Garage, fit into a 40-foot by 70-foot (12-meter by 21-meter) area—along with elevator shafts, ventilating shafts, and a stairway. Girders were used to provide structural bracing, and the ramp was positioned

Sears, Roebuck & Company, Chicago, 1926. These wooden trusses incorporated a sprinkler system that is still familiar today.

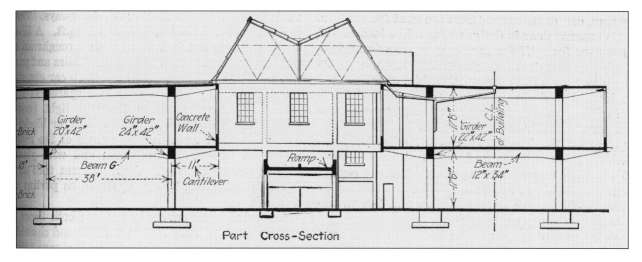

Part Cross-Section

Above: Packard Motor Car Company, Chicago, 1920. Garages with flat floor plates can be adapted to other uses if necessary; some garages were designed specifically with that possibility in mind.

Right: Washington Garage, Chicago, 1919. To minimize the space required by vertical movement systems and to maximize parking space, the designers of this garage created a curved ramp that circled around the elevator, other shafts, and the stairway. This approach would typically be prohibited by today's building codes.

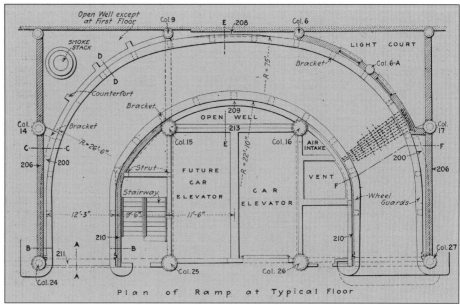

Plan of Ramp at Typical Floor

within the three interior sides of the building. Supporting girders on the inclined curb walls were 51 inches (130 centimeters) deep. The average rise was 11 degrees (13 degrees at the inner curve, and nine at the outer curve), and the inner radius of the curve was 22.5 feet (seven meters). To protect against shocks from runaway cars (a common problem at the time), the ramp had nine-inch- (23-centimeter-) high wheel guards that were braced from the side walls.[35]

A garage constructed in Chicago in 1920, for the Packard Motor Car Company, was an example of experimentation with the possibilities of concrete: this multilevel structure featured a 90,000-square-foot (8,361-square-meter) floor plate

and concrete cantilevers constructed around two large, open light wells. The floor slabs used to construct the ramp were 5.5 inches (14 centimeters) thick, and the roof slabs were four inches (ten centimeters) thick. The North Loop Motoramp Garage, built in Chicago in 1928, was a ten-story structure with a spiral ramp and a brick facade, and was designed specifically so that it could be converted to office use in the future. The structure was so large that a concrete mixing and placing plant had to be constructed on the site, so that the concrete could be poured at the higher levels of the building.[36]

In early multistory garages, the maximum distance between supporting columns was typically about 21 feet (6.5

meters); until structural steel came into use for framing, and until the development of concrete members with longer spans, this measurement remained the limiting factor in garage design. The Fisher Building, however, which was designed by Albert Kahn and constructed in 1928, featured 34-foot (ten-meter) spans on the ground level of the 11-story parking garage. Kahn used steel to keep the size of the columns to a minimum. On the upper parking floors, the aisles are 52 feet (16 meters) wide; this distance is spanned without the use of tie beams between the columns, and with concrete arches that are no deeper than 30 inches (76 centimeters). Concrete beams and slabs were used to form the ramps. On the upper three floors, Kahn used a special aggregate in the concrete that was equal in strength to the typical mix of the time, but had two-thirds the weight.[37]

In the 1950s, basic concrete technology continued to be applied even in mechanized garages: Bowser structures, for example, often had concrete floor slabs. The Texas National Bank and the Medical Arts Garage, mechanized garages built in Houston in the early 1950s, featured a frame of reinforced concrete and a pan joist floor system, which allowed for greater spans. Multistory mechanized garages built in Denver and Chicago in the 1950s were cantilevered structures built from reinforced concrete.[38]

Developments in Concrete

The longer spans and other structural characteristics that would allow the parking garage to evolve and flourish in the course of the 20th century could not have occurred without a give-and-take between structural advances and changes in construction methods, materials, and codes. As noted earlier, concrete was valued for its fireproof qualities, but it did not become widely used in garages until research and experimentation yielded new ways to employ it.

Poured concrete—a mixture of gravel, sand, and Portland cement—was used in construction in New England as early as 1824; in 1835, it was recorded as having been used to erect an "interesting little structure" in New York City.[39] By the turn of the century, cast-in-place concrete (which was poured on the construction site, in its final structural position) was being reinforced with steel rods, matrixes, and cables, which acted together to increase the tensile strength of the concrete.[40] This new construction technology, known as reinforced concrete, was developed to meet new needs, was well suited to the parking garage, and is still in use today. In-

tegral concrete was another type of reinforced concrete used in the first half of the 20th century (in the construction of the Fisher Building parking garage, for example). In this method, structural steel is surrounded by poured-in-place concrete, in a process that takes place entirely in the field.[41]

Almost simultaneously with the introduction of reinforced concrete, a new development emerged—a process known as prestressing. In this process, the steel rods and cables within the concrete are placed in tension, which enables them to act as an invisible column, stabilizing the beam. If the tensile forces are introduced while the concrete is setting or is still liquid, the result is known as prestressed or pretensioned concrete; if the forces are introduced after the concrete has hardened, the result is known as post-stressed or post-tensioned concrete. Concrete can be pre- or post-stressed either in the field or elsewhere, such as in a factory. Post-tensioning, however, is typically undertaken in the field.[42]

Concrete that is poured elsewhere (even on the site, but not in its final position) and then assembled is called precast concrete. There are two main categories of precast concrete: structural precast, which is used for structural purposes, and architectural precast, which is used for aesthetic purposes. Either form can be pretensioned or post-tensioned; however, precast concrete is not necessarily prestressed in any way.

Until the late 1970s, the term *prestressed* was sometimes used to refer either to prestressed or to cast-in-place post-tensioned concrete. Today, *prestressed* refers to pretensioned concrete only—and, because most structural precast concrete is also prestressed, the terms *prestressed concrete* and *precast concrete* have become virtually interchangeable—and are in fact sometimes used in combination: "prestressed precast concrete."[43]

In the United States, experimentation with prestressed concrete (in its early meaning, which referred to either pre- or post-tensioned concrete) began before the turn of the 20th century. In 1886, P.H. Jackson, of San Francisco, patented a method of tightening steel rods in stone and in concrete architectural sections. As early as 1893, precast reinforced concrete was used to create bulkheads in New York City. In Europe, meanwhile, Eugene Freyssinet, a Frenchman who is considered the father of prestressed concrete, developed successful methods for both prestressing and post-tensioning concrete and advocated the use of these techniques.[44]

By 1904, the Joint Committee on Reinforced Concrete had been established to identify, regulate, and disseminate information on concrete research and concrete processes. The

American Concrete Institute (ACI) was founded the following year. In 1906, after three major building failures, serious discussion about the new construction technologies occurred at the meetings of both the International Congress of Architects and the Joint Committee on Reinforced Concrete.[45]

The ACI regards C.A.P. Turner as one of the pioneers of reinforced concrete: in the early 1900s, Turner used his own system of fire protection in the construction of a concrete parking garage. Others experimenting with reinforced concrete included Albert and Julius Kahn—who, also in the early 1900s, developed the Kahn trussed bar. As noted earlier, the Park Square Garage—designed by Gaetano Lanza and constructed in Boston in 1905—incorporated discoveries from Lanza's experiments with reinforced concrete.[46]

By 1907, the Edison Portland Cement Company was manufacturing primary components for buildings; this was the beginning of precast construction. Systematic production of precast reinforced concrete was not patented, however, until 1909, by Ernest L. Ransome, who referred to the process as "unit construction."

In 1912, John E. Conzelman patented what he called the "unit structural concrete method" of precast concrete construction, a technique that was used in 1914 to create 50 pedestrian shelters for the Pacific Electric Railway, in Los Angeles; the structures were still in use in the 1950s. By 1912, tilt-up reinforced concrete (a technique in which a concrete slab is precast on site, then tilted up into position) was being used in Des Moines, Iowa. In 1925, R.E. Dill, of Alexandria, Nebraska, patented a method for manufacturing prestressed concrete posts and slabs by post-tensioning the steel.[47]

Experimentation with various methods of using and reinforcing concrete was accompanied by experimentation with the ingredients. By 1916, the concrete industry had developed standards for Portland cement, the primary ingredient in concrete. In 1925, D.A. Abrams developed the water-cement ratio that yielded high-early-strength concrete—concrete that hardens to its final strength quickly, usually within 72 hours.[48]

In the 1950s, after Gustave Magnel's techniques for prestressing concrete had been brought from Belgium to the United States, Lakeland Engineering and Prestress, Inc., held the first conference on prestressed concrete, in Lakeland, Florida. The Prestressed Concrete Institute was legally chartered in 1954 in Tampa, Florida, by six Florida prestressed-concrete companies, with T.Y. Lin and Harry Edwards as its key researchers. In 1963, prestressed concrete was introduced into the ACI building code. In 1976, the Post-Tensioning Institute formed to advocate post-tensioning. By this time, *prestressed* technically referred only to pretensioned precast structural and architectural concrete.[49]

From Precast to Cast-in-Place Concrete

The development of precast prestressed concrete changed the parking industry. Once the design and construction issues had been resolved, the standardization offered by these new structural forms allowed parking garage construction to be more systematic and cost-efficient. More importantly, however, the parking deck became a totally abstract space: a pure Cartesian grid that had little or no relationship to defined internal spaces. Because of this new structural system, garage designers were free to develop the "purely" functional, highly efficient, self-park garage.[50]

EXPERIMENTATION WITH PRECAST CONCRETE. One of the earliest recorded precast structures was a stable built in Brooklyn, New York, in 1900. In this structure, the roof slabs were four feet (1.2 meters) wide, 17 feet (five meters) long, and two inches (five centimeters) thick, and were reinforced with rods and wires. A car barn and repair shop constructed in Harrisburg, Pennsylvania, in 1909, had precast concrete columns, beams, walls, and roof slabs—over 1,400 pieces in all—and was built in only 33 days. A small storage garage for machinery, built in Cambria, Wisconsin, in 1940, had an arched frame of precast concrete that was divided into three pieces for easy delivery. The arches were field-spliced at the points where the curvature of the arch changed (that is, where the bending moment is zero). Concrete-block walls and hollow, six-inch (15-centimeter) roof slabs were used to enclose the structure.[51]

By the 1940s, several factors had combined to create one of the biggest breakthroughs in the technology of the parking structure: longer floor slabs. These factors were new cement mixtures and processes, new precast shapes, and new reinforcement techniques. Whereas earlier flat floor slabs had been two feet (0.6 meters) wide, 3.5 inches (nine centimeters) deep, and eight feet four inches (2.5 meters) long, the Formigli Corporation, of New Jersey, began manufacturing slabs that were two feet (0.6 meters) wide, six to 12 inches (15 to 30 centimeters) deep, and from 16 to 32 feet (five to ten meters) long. In 1944, the first technical committee on prestressed concrete was organized by the ACI and the American Society of Civil Engineers. By the early 1950s, Arsham Amerikian had designed a five-foot by 18.5-foot (1.5-

meter by 5.5-meter) flat reinforced concrete slab with a thickened edge, and by the mid-1950s, Charles C. Zollman had taken this achievement even farther—to a length of 33 feet, three inches (ten meters). In 1952, the Roebling Company designed a new, seven-wire strand for prestressing steel, further adding to the functionality of prestressed and post-tensioned concrete. At the same time that construction and material technology allowed the manufacture of longer and longer slabs, new equipment made it possible to transport and place heavier and longer precast pieces: jacks had been developed, for example, that could lift 75 tons (68 metric tons) of precast concrete.[52]

In the 1950s, as the precast reinforced concrete floor slab was becoming standard, Perlmutter, Altenberg, and Sachter patented the twin tee, the first precast double tee. The precast prestressed double tee developed by Harry Edwards in 1952–1953 was four feet (1.2 meters) wide, 14 inches (36 centimeters) thick, and 15 feet (4.5 meters) long. At approximately the same time, a six-foot- (1.8-meter-) wide double tee was developed in Colorado, and T.Y. Lin invented the single tee (which was initially known as the Lin tee). Eventually, precast prestressed double tees—the industry standard—had increased in size to a maximum width of 15 feet (4.5 meters) and a maximum length of 80 feet (24 meters); the depth varied according to the relationship between width and length. This size, which first appeared in 1997, is known as a mega-tee.[53]

Precast prestressed floor tees required cast-in-place toppings to seal the joints between the tees and to provide some structural continuity. Today, both pretopped tees, and tees with no topping at all, are found in parking garages.

PRECAST PRESTRESSED CONCRETE IN THE PARKING GARAGE.
By the 1950s, garages were typically constructed from a combination of precast and poured-in-place concrete. In 1953, the first roof parking deck ever constructed of precast prestressed concrete members was installed by Prestressed Concrete of Colorado at the Spitzer Electric Company. The beams, which were either rectangular or I-shaped in cross section, had spans ranging from 17 to 80 feet (five to 24 meters). The garage of the ZCMI Department Store, in Salt Lake City, combined slab construction (cast from the top of the garage down) with precast prestressed concrete columns. This very simple structure, which opened in 1954, had minimal ornamentation except for the concrete floors, which were poured with a sawtooth edge that echoed the new, angled parking pattern. The sawtooth edge was an example of a purely functional design that served an aesthetic purpose. In 1955, Carport, Inc., of Oklahoma City, built a garage of precast reinforced columns and slabs for $800 a space.[54]

In the 1950s, the benefits of precast prestressed concrete were just beginning to be apparent: it was not until the 1960s that the new, long-span construction and erection techniques allowed the modern garage to come into its own. The longer spans not only allowed more design flexibility, but also provided cost savings. The Beverly Hills Garage, for example, completed in 1961, used 75-foot- (23-meter-) long single tees and realized a savings of 24 percent over the typical garage of the period. Most of the savings were derived from the 17 percent reduction in floor area made possible by the construction method. At about the same time, in Asbury Park, New Jersey, a four-story, 350-car Park & Shop was erected in just 11 days. This project, designed by Gage & Martinson, Engineers, cost $1,400 per space: it may not have been the least expensive garage to construct, but it was certainly erected the most quickly—a characteristic that translates into savings, because the structure can begin collecting revenue sooner.[55]

Precast prestressed concrete structures also lowered insurance rates: in 1965, precast prestressed concrete subjected to the Underwriters Laboratories' fire tests for four hours and 50 minutes earned the two-hour fire rating. (Fire tests are run until the product or material fails, or meets standards beyond all expectations.) Precast prestressed concrete was also believed to be inherently watertight, when used in combination with expansive or high-strength cements, eliminating the seepage that typically occurred in concrete garages. At the University of California at Berkeley, in 1961, a turf-covered athletic field was constructed on top of a parking deck; clearly, the designers assumed that the construction would be waterproof.[56]

At an office complex constructed in the 1960s for the Humble Oil and Refinery Company, in Houston, the precast prestressed tees used in the garage had a span of 63 feet (19 meters). The Phoenix Sky Harbor Airport Parking Structure and Terminal, built in 1965, was, at the time, the largest parking facility to rely entirely on precast prestressed concrete for both structural and architectural purposes. Atlanta's First National Bank Garage, constructed in 1968, was a 700-car facility that spanned railroad tracks; it was built with precast prestressed, post-tensioned, and poured-in-place members.

Above: Rodeo Brighton Garage, Beverly Hills, California, 1961. Because of the reduction in floor area allowed by the use of long-span single tees, this early precast garage cost 24 percent less to build than the typical garage of the period.

Right: ZCMI Department Store, Salt Lake City, 1954. The sawtooth edge gave this stripped-down facility a modern feel. The garage was cast from the top down and had flat floor plates.

The precast Lin tees (single tees) used in the structure had a clear span of up to 52 feet (16 meters).[57]

Even with the advent of the fully precast prestressed garage, many parking facilities continued to combine all the available methods of working with concrete. For example, the parking garage at Honolulu's Ala Moana Center, built in 1964, combined precast prestressed concrete and composite cast-in-place concrete. Similarly, the Alcopark, constructed in Oakland, California, in 1963—an oval garage with inner and outer ramps and a 100-foot by 136-foot (30-meter by 41-meter) heliport pad on the roof—combined a double-tee beam structure and cast-in-place concrete.[58]

The parking facility at the Michigan Bank National Association, built in Detroit in 1968, combined precast prestressed and cast-in-place post-tensioned concrete to create a rigid frame structure. The garage featured 94-foot- (29-meter-) long precast prestressed concrete columns and single tees. In an approach known as the Prescon system, the columns and the tees were post-tensioned together by means of tendons that had been precast into the single tees. The columns were post-tensioned after the slabs were in place, creating the rigid frame. (A rigid frame is one way

of resisting structural loads, once grouting is complete.)[59]

The Tridak Parking Structure, in New York, another example of the innovative use of concrete, included an architectural precast facade that enclosed the drainage and electrical systems for the structure. In the early 1970s, this construction technique was used on facades in a number of locations.[60]

Garages constructed in the early 1970s at Boston's Logan Airport and at Hancock Place, also in Boston, used a precast prestressed "pi" system, along with cast-in-place framing. (The pi system was so named because in cross section, the system resembled the Greek letter.) The pi system, which was invented by Othar Zaldastani, of Nichols, Norton and Zaldastani, Inc., was created to address the fact that in single- or double-tee structures, cracks often developed because of insufficient thickness in the required concrete topping, allowing moisture to penetrate. The pi system eliminated the cracks by producing a new kind of joint.[61]

At the Gary National Bank Parking Garage, a 317-car facility built in Gary, Indiana, in 1970, the columns and tee girders were precast prestressed concrete, and the six-inch- (15-centimeter-) thick elevated ramps were poured in place and

T.Y. Lin was a visionary in the world of modern structural engineering. A professor at the University of California at Berkeley, Lin began his research career by working on the Arroyo Seco Pedestrian Bridge, which was built near Los Angeles in 1951. Lin also owned a consulting structural engineering firm called T.Y. Lin & Associates, and was chairman of the Division of Structural Engineering and Structural Mechanics at the University of California at Berkeley. Many of the key garage designers of the past 30 years had their start in his firm.[1]

In 1953, Lin studied under Gustave Magnel, at the University of Ghent, in Belgium. (Magnel had designed the Walnut Lane Bridge, in Philadelphia, the first prestressed concrete structure in the United States, and had developed new methods for prestressing concrete that came into use in the United States during the 1950s.) In 1955, Lin published *Design of Prestressed Concrete Structures*, which had tremendous influence in North America.

In the early 1960s, Lin created the single tee, which was one of the most efficient shapes for spanning the width of a bay. In addition to allowing a completely open span that would accommodate two cars on each side of the driving aisle, the single tee permitted better distribution of light from the fixtures mounted on its underside. The single tee was initially eight feet (2.4 meters) wide and could be manufactured in lengths of up to 110 feet (34 meters); although it was used extensively in early precast pretensioned construction, its shape made it difficult to transport and to install. The "B" parking structure, a ten-story garage in Beverly Hills designed by Lin and built in 1953, was entirely constructed of precast pretensioned single-tee concrete. By 1961, more than 20 buildings of similar construction had gone up; the Beverly Hills structure was the most famous of this group.[2]

In 1954, in Tampa, Florida, the first prestressed-concrete companies joined forces to create the Prestressed Concrete Institute (PCI), which undertook research to expand the shapes, sizes, and capabilities of precast and precast prestressed concrete. This form of concrete was championed not only by Lin, but by Harry Edwards, the founder of Lakeland Engineering and Prestress, Inc. As a result of the work of Lin, Edwards, and others, precast prestressed concrete currently has approximately 45 percent of the market for freestanding parking garages.[3]

During the second half of the 1950s, Edwards created the four-foot by 50-foot by 14-inch (1.2-meter by 15-meter by 36-centimeter) double tee—which, because of its greater width and structural stability, became the industry standard. The double tee was eventually produced in widths from four to ten feet (1.2 to three meters) and in lengths from 30 to 120 feet (nine to 37 meters). The first double tees were topped with concrete; later designs did not require topping or were pretopped at the factory. Among the many examples of garages constructed out of double tees are the Maryland Concert Center Parking Garage, in Baltimore; and the parking garage at Eppley Airfield, in Omaha, Nebraska.[4]

The Precast Concrete Revolution: T.Y. Lin and Harry Edwards

Left: Beverly Hills Garage "B," 1953.

Above: Eppley Airfield, Omaha, Nebraska, 1984.

post-tensioned. The tee girders were then tensioned to the vertical columns as well as to the spandrel walls.[62] Movable form work was also used at the Gary garage, which increased efficiency by allowing the concrete to be poured in large sections.[63]

A three-story precast prestressed garage built in 1972 in Quincy, Massachusetts, set a record: 569 precast prestressed concrete pieces were furnished in 43 working days, and the entire structure was built in eight months. In 1974, a new approach was used at the Baylor Hospital parking structure, in Dallas: precast concrete walls that included haunches to support the floor.[64] Using this method, it is possible to construct solid walls or "lite walls" (walls with punched openings), either of which can act as shear walls.[65]

By the mid-1960s, the modern parking structure was completely exposed to the weather—and, as a result, was closer, as a structural entity, to a bridge than to a building. However, it took some time for this transition to be fully reflected in both construction materials and design details. At approximately the same time, breakthroughs in precast prestressed concrete made it possible for parking garages to span functioning railroad tracks—and, eventually, highways. In other words, parking facilities began to literally function as bridges. In 1967, there was a proposal for a garage that would have spanned the Los Angeles freeway; such a structure was actually built over the streets of San Mateo, California. A portion of Boston's Hancock Place Garage, built in 1972, straddles the Massachusetts Turnpike. In 1978, an air-rights garage was built over Tulsa's loop highway. (As it became more and more difficult to find land for parking in many cities, air rights played an increasing role in parking.) Omaha has a downtown garage, built in 1961 and still in use today, that spans 100 feet (30 meters) over 17th Street.[66]

In 1989, the Sarasota County Parking Garage, a 1,000-space, 300,000-square-foot (27,870-square-meter) parking garage, was designed and erected in 16 months (with an unexpected two-month delay), entirely with precast construction. The unique elevator tower was a free-standing structure designed to withstand lateral forces, such as wind or earthquake loads, and functioned independently from the large shear walls. In 2001, the 11,500-car, $125 million Northwest Airlines Midfield Terminal parking structure, in Detroit, became the largest all-precast concrete parking structure ever built at one time. At the Denver International Airport, which was completed in 1991, K-frames (precast open space frames with steel cross-members) were used instead of solid

shear walls, allowing the interior of the garage to remain open, for pedestrian safety.

In combination with double tees, precast frame systems are also used to resist lateral loads, in an approach that allows the integration of structure and facade. Because different framing systems are appropriate for various conditions, and the choice of framing system will, in turn, affect the appearance of the facade, parking structures built entirely of precast prestressed concrete offer new design strategies for the facade. The advantages—and increasing popularity—of precast prestressed parking structures were reflected in the fact that during a one-year period beginning in 2006 and ending in 2007, approximately 43 percent of garage construction starts used prestressed concrete exclusively; 11 percent were conventional cast-in-place structures; 34 percent were cast-in-place post-tensioned structures; 8 percent were steel; and 4 percent were hybrid structures (typically precast and post-tensioned). (Most freestanding garages are constructed of either precast prestressed concrete, post-tensioned concrete, or a combination of the two.)[67]

Precast concrete allowed for greater quality control throughout the production process, yielding a product that was more resilient and less likely to degenerate in response to typical use. Although the advent of precast prestressed concrete opened up a wide range of design options, the technology has a specific weakness that engineers and designers continue to attempt to address. The principal issue is the connections, which (1) are more subject to temperature fluctuations; (2) may allow penetration by water and road salts, leading to spalling and to the deterioration of the internal steel; and (3) pose problems in the design of structures that are subject to seismic risk. CarbonCast, a recent innovation in precast pre-topped concrete, is a resin-bonded, carbon-fiber grid material that increases the resistance of precast concrete to corrosion, spalling, and cracking; the product allows double tees to be thinner and 66 percent lighter, while providing better long-term performance. In structures that use CarbonCast, conventional steel provides the primary reinforcement, while the new technology provides secondary reinforcement and shear transfer.[68]

Today's precast prestressed concrete is a factory-produced form that is designed to accommodate heavier loads and longer spans. Garages constructed entirely of precast prestressed concrete have many advantages: short construction time, reduced construction costs, and good quality control. Precast pieces may be columns, beams, shear walls, double

Left: Hancock Place, Boston, 1975. As longer spans became common, it became possible to build parking facilities that spanned highways and other structures, such as railroad tracks.

Above: Denver International Airport, Denver, Colorado, 1992. The use of steel and concrete made it possible to replace shear walls with open space frames, allowing for maximum visibility within the parking structure.

tees, or spandrels: the elements are erected at the job site, in Tinkertoy fashion. (Small local companies, such as Iowa Prestressed Concrete, still provide their own systems for parking structures, which are based on simpler precast beams, columns, and slabs.) Because precast prestressed construction is exposed to wide variations in temperature and moisture level, as well as to vibration, the connections are crucial. Stainless steel or epoxy-coated hot-dipped galvanized steel is often used to mitigate corrosion. To ensure the greatest longevity for the structure, any field-applied coatings require complete surface penetration. Typically, the parking garage consists of a prestressed double-tee floor member bearing on a precast frame. The double tee can be pretopped or field-topped, and sometimes no topping is used. The University of Iowa, in Iowa City, was the first to experiment with "untopped" concrete. In 1977, as part of a request from the university to reduce the cost of the hospital garage, a precast deck designed by Carl Walker, Inc., was constructed without a topping, which saved 39 percent on construction costs. The untopped approach is still in use today.[69]

Cast-in-Place Reinforced Concrete

Cast-in-place reinforced concrete—poured-on-site concrete that has steel rods or sections embedded within it—is valued for its flexibility, strength, and longevity. In the 1950s, this proven material was pitted against the newer, longer-span products, which could more easily accommodate the larger car sizes. In the F Street Parking Center, for example, built in 1954 in Washington, D.C., in order to limit the width of the columns to 12 inches (30 centimeters), the designers had to use more steel than was typical in column construction; the narrower columns were necessary to accommodate the Chryslers, Cadillacs, and Lincolns that were popular at the time.[70]

Cast-in-place reinforced garages typically required some of the following: capital columns, beams, drop panels, waffle slabs, pan joists, and bearing columns along the exterior walls. The "smooth ceiling" system invented in 1953 by Walter H. Wheeler, of Minneapolis, eliminated these structural elements. In the 1950s, National Planning, Inc., designed a number of cast-in-place reinforced concrete

Exploring Structure and Materials

parking structures in which pan joists and one-way flat slabs spanned about 20 feet (six meters) between haunched beams, creating clear-spanned parking bays up to 55 feet (17 meters) wide.[71]

Cast-in-place reinforced concrete was also used to cantilever the floor plates of garages. The Hecht Company garage, for example—a self-park, 1,600-car facility constructed in Arlington, Virginia, in 1951—had a flat floor plate with straight, sloped ramps constructed of 10.5-inch- (27-centimeter-) thick reinforced concrete slabs that extended 13.5 feet (four meters) at the sides of the main structure and 15 feet (4.5 meters) at the ends.[72] When it was built, this structure was "the largest of its kind."[73]

During the 1950s, a period marked by extensive exploration in garage design, a facility known as the parketeria was constructed in Philadelphia: in this structure, rigid frames with spans of 54 feet (16 meters), spaced 19 feet (six meters) apart from center to center, were used to create a clear span for the angled parking within. The Parkade Garage, constructed in 1954 in Tulsa, featured a staggered floor system, exterior walls of nine-inch- (23-centimeter-) thick cast-in-place concrete, and cast-in-place floors between five and nine inches (13 and 23 centimeters) thick. This garage is notable because it combined modern construction methods with ground-floor shops, in a design that had rarely been used since the early days of the garage.[74] In 1969, using the tried-and-true building methods that were still widely employed, the city of Chicago constructed an eight-story self-park garage at the corner of Franklin and Madison, choosing poured-in-place concrete to construct a flat-slab, simple post-and-beam garage.[75]

Cast-in-place reinforced concrete still has many advantages over precast concrete, and both have an important place in parking facility design. For example, cast-in-place construction is preferable for underground helical ramps, and when parking is combined with other building types. At the same time, however, the staging requirements and longer construction schedules associated with the cast-in-place method can pose problems, particularly in colder climates.

Post-Tensioned Concrete

Post-tensioning techniques developed in the course of experimentation with methods of strengthening cement and reinforcing concrete. Post-tensioning was also advanced by the lift-slab construction technique and by the Strand PT system, an anchoring system developed in 1962 by Ed Rice,

cofounder and president of T.Y. Lin & Associates.

As noted earlier, post-tensioning involves tensioning of the internal strands after the concrete is poured—typically while the building is under construction. Although it is sometimes combined with various other construction methods, post-tensioned concrete is commonly used as part of a poured-in-place concrete process.[76]

In 1961, the designers of the Denver National Bank Building used post-tensioning and waffle-slab construction to create a unique, long-span structure connected to a cantilevered express ramp. The parking structure's 66.5-foot (20-meter) spans were framed by 24-inch- (61-centimeter-) deep waffle slabs, and the beams required to support the waffle slabs were 30 inches (76 centimeters) deep. The exterior ramp was supported by a horizontal, semicircular beam in which monolithic post-tensioning was used to decrease the deflection and increase the torsional capacity.[77]

Two parking structures built in 1970 in Binghamton, New York, combined post-tensioned concrete beams, post-tensioned concrete floor slabs, and cast-in-place reinforced concrete columns. The beams were cantilevered four to six feet (1.2 to two meters) beyond the exterior columns, creating a covered walkway for the pedestrians below. The slabs were post-tensioned before the beams; because the floors were split-level, it was possible to post-tension the beams from the interior. The Opportunity Park garage, built in Akron, Ohio, in 1972, was, at the time of construction, one of the largest post-tensioned lightweight concrete structures ever built. This project used a new material called ChemComp, which is an expansive cement, and a new method of post-tensioning.[78]

Among the advantages of post-tensioned concrete are lower cost, and resistance to fire, sound, and vibration. Post-tensioning also made it possible to build larger parking garages and to create extended cantilevers, such as those that were used in the two 2,500-car facilities located on the east and west sides of the New Orleans Superdome. These structures, built in 1973, used post-tensioned cast-in-place lightweight concrete.[79]

Although some of the earliest post-tensioned parking facilities were built in Hawaii, the most famous is the Watergate, completed in 1971 in Washington, D.C. In this innovative structure, the use of two-way structural slabs (that is, slabs that are post-tensioned in two directions, rather than in just one) resulted in cost savings. More recent examples are the Pike at Rainbow Harbor parking structure, in Long

Beach, California, and the Consolidated Rental Car Center at Sky Harbor International Airport, in Phoenix.[80]

Other Issues in Concrete Construction

Unusual requirements, such as sites that were extremely constrained, led to experimentation with new construction methods. For example, because the site of the Olympic Hotel parking garage, constructed in Seattle in 1964, was too small for the mobile cranes used to erect precast prestressed concrete, the 17-ton (15-metric-ton), 59-foot- (18-meter-) long pieces were erected by means of a portable bridge crane.[81]

Lift-slab construction was also used at small sites. The height record for lift slabs was set in 1953, by the Tower Parking Garage, in Columbus, Ohio, a 14-level mechanized facility with lift slabs 88 feet (27 meters) above street level; construction required a temporary bracing tower. In the early 1960s, lift-slab construction was being explored at a number of locations around the country. The Park & Lock Garage, a six-level facility constructed in 1961 in Newark, New Jersey, for the Edison Parking Company, consisted of two continuous, overlapping spirals. It was the first parking garage in which lift-slab construction was used to create warped slabs (slabs that slope in two directions).[82]

In many parts of the country—particularly in the San Francisco area—earthquake-resistant design is an important issue. At San Francisco's Downtown Center Garage, built in 1955, a prestressed concrete shear pylon was used in conjunction with reinforced poured-in-place rigid flat-slab construction. In this garage, the fact that the shear wall was placed within the large spiral corner ramp was crucial both to the stability and the usability of the structure.[83]

Even in non-earthquake zones, shear walls are an important part of parking garage design. Although they contribute to structural stability, shear walls can interfere with sight lines and visual safety in self-park facilities. To address this issue, grout-filled steel sleeves have been used in precast moment-frame structures. (This approach was first used in the 1960s, in the Ala Moana project.)[84] In 1972, precast prestressed concrete members were used in the San Bernardino Civic Center Garage, which is in a zone 3 earthquake area. In this structure, cast-in-place techniques were used to create a three-dimensional nonductile space frame with special joinery designed by Victor Gruen and Associates; these special joints provided the necessary stability for the shear walls to

University of Santa Cruz Parking Structure, Santa Cruz, California, 2001. Because cantilevers were used in this structure, the footprint of the original parking lot was the only place where major construction occurred.

be eliminated.[85] T.Y. Lin & Associates were the structural consultants for the facility, and Plumb, Tuckett and Hubbard were the consulting engineers and architects.

Advances in Concrete Technology

For concrete structures, maintenance in cold-weather climates is crucial. In the 1950s, when road salts became the principal means of dealing with ice and snow on highways, the chlorides in these compounds began to cause swift deterioration in parking structures, often within ten years of their original construction. The cracks usually appeared at the intersection of structural members or at changes in plane; water and salt would then penetrate the concrete, corroding the steel on the interior. To prevent penetration and deterioration, modern formulas and construction methods have attempted to increase general protection, as well as to provide greater protection for connection points and areas subject to more exposure.

Air-entrained concrete, sometimes known as cellular concrete, first used in highway construction, has proven to be extremely valuable for protecting open-deck structures from the damage caused by road salts. This type of concrete combines specific cements and other materials to create small air bubbles. The more homogeneous cell structure that results causes air-entrained concrete to be stronger, more durable, and lighter in weight than other forms of concrete. The bays at the Battery Parking Garage, a reinforced concrete building constructed in New York in 1950, were 32 feet by 58 feet (ten meters by 17.6 meters); this was generally the longest length available at the time. Because longer spans are more prone to cracking, air-entrained concrete was used in the structure, along with reinforced steel beams and girders. The facility was one of the most advanced parking structures of its time, and was the first building in the New York metropolitan area to use air-entrained concrete.[86]

At the Downtown Auto Park Garage, built in Minneapolis in 1952, air-entrained concrete was used to prevent the deterioration and cracking associated with the extreme temperature fluctuations of the local climate. In this facility, which used the D'Humy ramp design, 12-inch- (30-centimeter-) thick air-entrained reinforced concrete slabs were cantilevered 14 feet (four meters) beyond the steel columns.[87]

Concrete, Steel, and Sustainability

Concrete has an important place in sustainable construction. Under the Leadership in Energy and Environmental Design (LEED) rating system of the U.S. Green Building Council, which awards points based on specific sustainability criteria, concrete structures may assist with obtaining points for any of the following reasons:

1. Concrete helps to reduce the heat island effect.

2. The rebar embedded within the concrete is made of recycled steel.

3. The cement itself is extracted and manufactured within 500 miles (805 kilometers) of the construction site.

4. The concrete includes recycled content, such as fly ash, silica fume, ground-granulated blast-furnace slag, and aggregates.

5. Low-volatility organic compounds are used to cure the concrete.[1]

Because of its ability to be recycled, steel has also played a role in sustainable design. Steel structures may assist with obtaining points for any of the following reasons:

1. Steel makes it more likely that a building can be adapted to other uses.

2. Steel can be easily separated from construction waste for recycling.

3. Steel is a resource that can be repeatedly recycled.

4. Steel decking, steel joists, and metal studs are typically manufactured within 500 miles (805 kilometers) of construction sites.[2]

Central Park Garage, Austin, Texas, 1996. The use of recycled steel can make newly constructed steel garages eco-friendly.

Downtown Center Garage, San Francisco, 1955. The stability and usability of this structure depended on reinforced, poured-in-place, rigid flat-slab construction; a prestressed concrete shear pylon, and a large spiral corner ramp that incorporated a shear wall.

Recent advances in additives have changed the curing, strength, and longevity of concrete. One additive in particular, however—silica fume—has become crucial to the longevity of both concrete and its interior steel reinforcement. A means of increasing strength and durability and protecting against water penetration, silica fume is also effective in the rehabilitation of deteriorating structures. It was first used in parking garages in the mid-1980s, and had become standard by the mid-1990s. Garages that feature concrete with silica fume include Horne's Garage, in Pittsburgh, where silica fume was used for repair work; the AT&T Garage built in Kansas City, Missouri, in 1985; the Manor Parking Structure, built in Pittsburgh in 1986; the Spruce Tree Parking Structure, built in St. Paul in 1987; and the second phase of the General Mitchell Airport garage, completed in Milwaukee in 1990.[88]

Ultra-high-performance concrete (UHPC), also known as reactive-powder concrete, has been in development since the mid-1980s. A mixture of Portland cement, silica fume, quartz flour, fine silica sand, high-range water reducer (a specialty additive produced by foaming agents), water, and steel or organic fibers, UHPC is less permeable than conventional concrete and can be used to form stronger and stiffer columns, and beams that are capable of spanning longer distances. UHPC can also be used to form uniquely thin shell structures.[89]

Other efforts to increase the longevity of parking structures are focused on improvements in coatings for internal reinforcement, joints and connections, and the concrete itself. One product currently being tested is a metal-ceramic composite coating for steel that works by means of a galvanic process. In addition to forming a barrier, this product has the advantage of being able to seal any cracks that do occur. In the early 2000s, a product called Qualideck was applied to the garage decks at the Toronto Airport. One of several similar products that are on the market, Qualideck is a traffic-coating system that protects concrete decking from penetration by moisture, chemicals, and impact; it is also nonskid, which is helpful in cold or rainy climates. Although some estimates of service life for a standard concrete garage (that is, a garage unprotected by a product such as Qualideck) are as high as 125 years, a 40- to 50-year service life is typical for a structure maintained under the current standards of the American Concrete Institute.[90]

Toronto Airport Garage, Toronto, Canada, 2000. The toppings used in cold-weather climates can be found in any area where exposure to the elements may compromise the integrity of the concrete.

Steel in Parking Garage Design

Although it is believed that the first steel parking deck was constructed by Jerome Stedelin, of St. Louis, during the Great Depression, exposed steel could be found in much earlier parking structures, including the Twentieth Century Garage, which was built in Chicago in 1909. Typically, however, the fire codes that emerged during the first three decades of the 20th century required most areas of parking structures to have a fireproof covering of masonry or concrete. Thus, steel was most often found in combination with other materials. At Toronto's Granite Club parking structure, for example, built in 1956, the frame was steel, and the exterior columns were covered with masonry to provide fire protection; however, in a reflection of the evolving views of fire risks in urban areas, the interior columns were exposed steel. Another common structural combination was precast concrete beams, poured concrete floors, and steel columns. When this combination was used, strippable plywood was employed to form the concrete floors. Because it was advantageous to cut the time involved in attaching the plywood, methods of doing so were often patented.[91]

Steel was used quite early in Atlanta, where it was necessary to span the downtown railroad tracks in order to meet the growing need for parking; steel-framed structures were particularly appropriate for creating the long, clear spans that would reach over the tracks. The parking facility for Rich's Department Store, designed by Stevens & Wilkinson and built in 1955, used steel to do just that. In Springfield, Massachusetts, in 1959, on a parking lot that once served 650 customers a day, Ley Construction Company and C.W. Blakeslee built a 440-space deck that served 2,400 cars a day. The structure, operated by Meyer Brothers Parking, was intended to "fight back against the inroads of the suburban shopping centers."[92] At this time, shoppers were still seeking the downtown experience, and parking was desperately needed. Built as inexpensively as possible, the facility combined steel columns and prestressed concrete tees in an arrangement that yielded clear spans of 55 feet (17 meters). No sooner was the garage complete, however, than it became necessary to add the planned additional level. In 1969, when the six-story reinforced concrete parking facility for Davidson's Department Store, in Atlanta, had to be rapidly expanded in time for the holidays, a three-story steel addition placed on top of the original structure added 50 percent to the amount of available parking.[93]

To compete with the acres of free parking available in the burgeoning suburbs, developers and designers working in

The Structural Aesthetic

One expression of 20th-century modernism was known as the structural aesthetic: this approach, which allowed structure to serve both a functional and an aesthetic role, was a perfect fit for the parking garage. Although the structural aesthetic yielded some parking garages that seemed to go on forever, such large and imposing structures often worked well within the spacious, automobile-generated suburban landscape. The structural aesthetic was less compatible, however, with older urban settings.[1]

An appealing example of the structural aesthetic can be found in the parking structure at Cleveland's Mt. Sinai Hospital: a column shape, repeated with its mirror image, was used to create a pleasing rhythm on the facade. At the seven-level Crown Street Garage, in New Haven, Connecticut, tree columns—single pieces that were 93 feet (28 meters) long and weighed 41 tons (37 metric tons) each—created both structural integrity and a distinctive pattern on the facade. This facility was constructed of single-tee beams and had a cast-in-place spiral ramp. Both the tree columns and the floor tees were exposed, creating a rhythm on the facade.[2]

The hospital parking ramp constructed in 1968 at the University of Iowa, in Iowa City, offers another example of the merger of structure and aesthetics. On the facade of this facility, the precast reinforced columns support the precast spandrels by means of a limblike hook. The combination of exterior columns and exposed supports yield a clean yet compelling facade.[3]

At a parking structure built in 1977 for the city of Rock Island, Illinois, the goal was to use the structural elements—in this case, precast prestressed Vierendeel trusses—to provide the facade with architectural character and a pleasing visual rhythm.[4] As one contemporary observer noted, in the case of the garage, unlike that of other commercial buildings, "use of ornamental skin in general makes the design of a parking structure heavy, expensive and unjustifiable."[5]

A more recent successful effort to use precast concrete as both skin and structure garnered the Prestressed Concrete Institute's 1994 Harry H. Edwards award for advancing the use of this approach. At the USAA Southeast Regional Office, in Tampa, Florida, both the office structure and the parking facility were based on the same five-foot (1.5-meter) grid, creating a handsome combination. A load-bearing ladder-wall system on the facade provided the structure for the pretopped concrete double-tee floor. Inside, standard pretopped double tees were supported by a second ladder-wall system. Spillis, Candela & Partners were the project architects, Walter P. Moore was the engineer, and Coreslab was the precaster.[6]

Left: Tree column, Crown Street, New Haven, Connecticut, 1971.

Below: Vierendeel truss, Rock Island, Illinois, 1977.

urban downtowns had to find ways to build parking structures at minimum cost, while still meeting strict zoning and building requirements; a great deal of experimentation resulted. The K-System, for example, which was developed to lower construction costs for parking garages, uses standard sheets of plywood—two feet (0.6 meters) wide and five-eighths of an inch (1.6 centimeters) thick—between junior beams, and monolithic pouring of concrete. To support the plywood, K-clips are positioned every three feet (one meter) along the beam; wire mesh is then placed over the plywood, and a 2.5-inch (6.4-centimeter) layer of concrete is poured on top. The K-clips and the plywood can be placed and removed without any special tools. In the early 1960s, when the K-System was developed, garages that used the system and had plaster applied to the ceiling side qualified for fire ratings from the National Board of Fire Underwriters, which had tested the system and found it to meet the fire requirements of the time.[94]

In the late 1970s, steel was used in combination with a European construction technique known as filigree wideslab. A five-level, 800-car garage in Bethlehem, Pennsylvania, built in 1977, was one of the largest structures to use this method. In this facility, an eight-foot (2.4-meter) Wideslab panel of 2.25-inch- (six-centimeter-) thick concrete was laid on top of the structural steel; a 5.75-inch (14.6-centimeter) layer of concrete was then poured on top, allowing the steel and the concrete beneath to function as a single structural unit. Filigree wideslab is still used for parking structures, decks, and walls, as in the recently completed garage at Caesars Atlantic City.[95]

Although completely exposed-steel structures were rare, they did exist under certain conditions (for example, if the garage was single story), in certain locations (for example, in some mechanized facilities built in New York in the 1950s and 1960s), or before changes in codes prohibited their construction. In 1948, an exposed-steel garage for trackless trolleys was built in Atlanta, although outside the downtown area. That same year, a four-story, exposed-steel, 650-car facility was erected in Miami, and a welded, rigid-frame garage roof was constructed for a one-story parking garage in Newark, New Jersey. In the District of Columbia, under a 1952 amendment to the building code, garages built after 1953 were permitted to have an exposed-steel framework and 3.5-inch- (nine-centimeter-) thick reinforced concrete floors. In Toledo, Ohio, in 1955, a 270-car self-park garage of welded steel was constructed.[96] The Bethlehem Garage, built in 1960, was the first all-steel garage

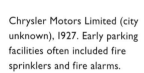

Chrysler Motors Limited (city unknown), 1927. Early parking facilities often included fire sprinklers and fire alarms.

The Parking Garage

in San Francisco. According to Paul L. Lamson, of San Francisco's Metropolitan Corporation, each floor was "like an open parking lot"; as a consequence, the structure had "the lowest operating costs, most efficient service, and the lowest accidental car damage" of any garage in the city. Moreover, Lamson believed the structure to be "the most beautiful garage in San Francisco."[97]

Exposed-steel garages first appeared in significant numbers in the 1970s, when the results of the Scranton Fire Test and of several fire reports undertaken by Underwriters Laboratories helped bring about changes in existing codes. In 1974, for example, exposed steel was used to construct the Easton Parking Authority, in Easton, Pennsylvania. Because the garage exceeded the square footage allowed by code for steel structures and included first-floor retail (another fire-safety concern), local fire officials had to provide special permission for the facility to be built. At the Coliseum Convention Center, built in New Haven, Connecticut, in 1977, exposed-steel construction allowed a 2,400-car garage to be suspended over the sports arena. Placing the garage above the primary structure solved difficult site issues and made it possible for the sports arena and parking garage to have independent structural systems. However, the building did not succeed as a convention center; as a result, it was not adequately maintained. Lack of maintenance, in combination with the use of weathering steel, led to the building's recent demolition.[98] Exposed steel was also used on the parking structure built in Scranton, Pennsylvania, in 1972, where the Scranton Fire Test was performed. (That structure is still in use today.)

Despite unquestionable cost savings and the alleviation of concerns about fire, exposed steel weathered badly in many parts of the country, offsetting lower initial costs with decreased longevity. In the 1970s, however, a new type of steel known as weathering steel came into use in parking structures. Advertised as the most practical framing method, the steel is intrinsically resistant to corrosion (it actually protects itself by weathering), and does not require any painting or maintenance; since weathering steel is also high-strength, the structural members can be lighter and thinner. Weathering steel was used at New York's LaGuardia Airport parking structure and at the Toomey parking structure, in Cleveland (both built in the late 1970s), among others. Nevertheless, weathering steel is not recommended by the American Institute of Steel Construction. Under current industry standards, corrosion-resistant coatings, such as hot-dipped galvanization or high-performance systems, are recommended.[99]

At a commuter parking facility built in Flushing, New York, in 1966, exposed steel was used to create a warped deck. The garage of the St. Clair Memorial Hospital, constructed in Pittsburgh in 1976, had 60-foot- (18-meter-) long castellated steel beams (beams with hexagonal openings). The garage at Pittsburgh's Crickelwood Hill Apartments, a well-known steel structure that was built in 1973 and is still in use today, also has castellated steel beams.[100]

Changes made in 1967 to the Uniform Building Code permitted steel garage structures without fire protection in specific situations; at around the same time, a number of other codes, including the New York State Building Code and the BOCA (Building Officials and Code Administrators) code, were also attempting to address the issue of fire safety in steel garages. The Valet Parking Garage, built at Love Field in 1970, was the first multistory steel parking structure in Dallas that was built without fire protection. Designed by Carter Minor and advertised as a prototype, the facility was built at a cost of $750 per space and was, at the time, one of the most economical garages in the nation. Like many steel garages, however, this one lacked proper steel coatings and also suffered from the deterioration of the concrete slabs; it no longer exists.[101]

In 1973, George Washington University, in Washington, D.C., constructed an 11-story, U-shaped, steel-framed facility with two concentric helical ramps in the center of the structure—one for traffic moving up, and another for traffic moving down. Two parking circuits (the one-way loops that drivers travel while looking for parking spaces) were located above grade, and one was located below. The use of high-strength steel made it possible to reduce the depth of the beams, which in turn allowed an additional level to be built within the height restrictions for the site. The three separate parking circuits and the concentric helical ramps, along with the use of steel, allowed the number of parking spaces to be maximized on this site. One of the largest steel-framed garages constructed during the 1970s was built in Silver Spring, Maryland, in 1976; the facility was constructed of high-strength steel, which allowed clear spans of 18 feet (5.4 meters) by 63.5 feet (19 meters). The first phase had 492 stalls and the second 360; 650 more were built the following year, making the facility the third-largest municipal garage in the country.[102]

After the 1994 earthquake in Northridge, California, many damaged concrete parking structures were rebuilt with steel framing systems. One factor that made this possible was the mild climate: where salts and other deicing chemicals are not

Coliseum Convention Center, New Haven, Connecticut, 1977. Steel construction allowed a 2,400-car garage to be suspended over this sports arena.

used, steel has greater longevity. Steel offered a number of advantages in this case: it saved time and money, obviated the need for fire protection, and easily met the code requirements for an earthquake zone. The Central Park Garage, built in Austin, Texas, in 1996, used the SmartBeam, a 100 percent recyclable steel product that can be used to meet the requirements of the Leadership in Energy and Environmental Design (LEED) rating system of the U.S. Green Building Council. Two parking facilities built in California in 1997—the Station Oaks parking garage, in Walnut Creek, and the Fashion Square Retail Center garage, in Sherman Oaks—featured composite steel decking, which allows for rapid construction and provides superior seismic performance.[103]

Because weathering and exposure to road salts cause exposed steel to deteriorate, recent advances in bridge deck construction—including new coating technologies and hot-dipped galvanization—have been applied to parking structures. A number of other changes are also making the steel parking structure more feasible, including improvements in galvanized fasteners, new strategies for moment connections, intumescent paints for fire protection, and ceramic coatings for protection against corrosion.[104]

A hybrid structure is a steel-column-and-girder system with a precast prestressed long-span floor deck. In the 1980s, Hybrid Parking Solutions, drawing on earlier hybrid projects, created a first-generation project in Cambridge, Massachusetts. The second-generation project, constructed at Becton Dickinson and Company Headquarters, in Franklin Lakes, New Jersey, fully explored the hybrid idea. Each of the garages created for AT&T Lucent, in Warren, New Jersey, and Nortel Networks, in Billerica, Massachusetts, was delivered to the site as a ready-to-assemble kit of parts, an approach that was key to meeting schedules and budgets. New coating technologies and new additives for concrete mixtures will grant longer life spans to hybrid parking systems and ensure them a place in the evolution of the parking facility. A steel-framed system manufactured by Hybrid Parking Solutions has also been used at Portland International Airport and at Yale University.[105]

In a common strategy, steel was used to add six parking levels above an existing garage at the Texas Medical Center, in Houston, in 1996. Because the original garage (which had a cast-in-place frame and single-tee flooring) was the only site available, extensive reconstruction was necessary to accommodate the new composite steel beams and lightweight composite concrete deck. Part of the renovation involved the installation of a glass curtain wall to match the new facade of the adjoining office tower. New entrances were added to several levels of the office building; the addition also featured attractive and inviting lighting and materials. Steel-framed garages were also the choice at JFK, LaGuardia, and Newark airports.[106]

Steel offers a number of advantages in the design of parking structures. Because steel structural members can be

Garage, Crickelwood Hill Apartments, Pittsburgh, 1973. If steel is properly protected and maintained, it can provide a long-lasting parking structure.

East Cambridge Parking Garage, Cambridge, Massachusetts, 1983. The Hybrid system combines steel and precast to create a stable and quickly erected structure.

smaller than those formed from concrete, steel allows for the more efficient use of available space. Moreover, in steel structures, the smaller column sizes, the reduced depth of the beams, and the open quality of castellated beams allow greater light spread and better visibility, increasing both actual and perceived safety for drivers and pedestrians. Where road salts are not used and weather conditions are appropriate, the use of steel bridge grating on internal ramps can reduce costs and increase traction on sloped ramp surfaces. Steel allows a variety of different aesthetic approaches, particularly for the facade. Steel is also invaluable for meeting unique structural requirements, such as those often associated with mixed-use buildings.[107]

When best practices are followed and when all code requirements for open structures are met, a steel parking structure can be functionally and aesthetically successful—and, depending on the current costs of steel versus concrete, it can also be cost-competitive. Steel, precast, and poured-in-place concrete have all been shown to maintain structural stability under the documented scenarios for garage fires. Good parking design means giving the structural engineer the freedom to evaluate the advantages and disadvantages of all possible framing systems—including steel—within the context of specific project needs.[108]

Unit, Prefab, and Demountable Parking Garage Construction

Unit, prefab, and demountable garages are all constructed from a kit of parts. In unit construction, multiples of one or two units are used to create the entire structure. In prefab construction, all the pieces are delivered to the site, ready to assemble. Demountable garages may be erected in various ways, but they are distinguished by the fact that they can be easily disassembled and moved to another site.

The first mention of a demountable garage—which happened to be constructed entirely of steel—was in a 1910 article entitled "Knock Down Garages." Such structures were occasionally referred to in publications of this era, and it is known that in 1915, a barrel-shaped demountable garage was constructed in Spokane, Washington. It was not until the 1950s, however, that efforts to save time and money, and to create longer spans, led to extensive research into nontraditional approaches to garage construction. In 1950, the Blaise Company opened a New Orleans parking garage, built by means of unit construction, that looked very much like a series of tables resting one on top of the other. In 1951, the Miami firm of L.G. Farrant and W.C. Harry, working as consulting engineers, developed a unit building design that reduced construction costs to $400 per space; the approach, which relied on a slab that was reinforced in such a way that it could be 1.5 inches (four centimeters) thick, instead of the typical 12 inches (30 centimeters), widened the possibilities for garage construction. Tierpark, a prototype constructed in 1960 by Tishman Research Corporation, of New York City, was created from precast prestressed concrete units—an approach that made it possible to limit per-space costs to between $1,200 and $1,500.[109]

Unit, prefab, and demountable parking garage construction generally relied on "Tinkertoy" assembly or on a "box" approach (in this approach, the garage is constructed from the largest preassembled members that can be delivered by truck transport). The architect Paul Rudolph summed up these approaches by noting that "the 20th century brick measures 10 feet x 12 inches x 60 feet [three meters x 30 centimeters x 18 meters]"—which, in 1970, was the maximum dimension that most states would allow to be transported on state highways. To minimize the number of pieces

Station Place Garage, Portland, Oregon, 2004. The modern steel garage can provide a lighter, more open aesthetic or a more classical exterior—and, when appropriate coatings are applied, can have a long life.

that had to be moved, designers of unit, prefab, and demountable garages favor units that are as large as possible, and build decks to this maximum dimension.[110]

Several companies, including the Multi-Deck Corporation, experimented with demountable parking structures. One such facility—a short-span structure with a steel deck and frame—was constructed in Beverly Hills in 1950. In 1963, the Port-A-Park—a short-span steel-framed demountable garage with a concrete floor system—was being marketed in the United States. The Can-Park, marketed in Canada, was a short-span demountable garage with a steel frame and deck; each deck was treated with an epoxy compound that was then covered with grit or sand. The structure met the strictest fire and building codes in Canada. In the late 1960s, Portable Parking Structures, Inc., built a short-span demountable garage with an unprotected steel frame and a concrete deck for the city of Los Angeles, and a parking garage in air-rights space over railroad tracks at Washington University, in St. Louis. In Memphis in 1969, an all-steel, three-level, 500-car demountable garage—owned by Alright and designed by Metallic Building Company, of Houston—was constructed; the steel was pretreated before construction, and a waterproofing final surfacing was applied after construction. Even the new precast prestressed concrete structural pieces were often marketed as demountable, depending on the connection technology. For example, the Spanpark system used at the University of Chicago and at several other locations around the country used precast prestressed double-tee deck units, and precast double tees as structural wall panels. According to Carl Walker, some of the Spanpark facilities were taken down and reassembled in other locations.[111]

In 1970, a three-level, 454-car parking facility was erected in a mere 22 days, using the Unicon system, developed by Ray Itaya and Ed Rice. Construction of the facility, which was built at Lockheed Airport, in Burbank California, took six months from contract to occupancy. Advertised as the solution to the airport parking problem, the structure was intended to be demountable, so that it could be moved to another location if the airport needed the land for other uses. Each concrete piece looked like a slant-leg table and was 60 feet (18 meters) long and weighed 17 tons (15 metric tons); the structure required 350 separate components, 300 of which had "legs." The Unicon system uses ChemComp, an expansive cement, and a patented post-tensioning system to ensure a watertight deck.[112]

At the Swedish Hospital Medical Center, constructed in Seattle in 1970, a demountable structure was built from precast concrete structural trees, precast prestressed concrete slabs, and bolts. The hospital opted for a demountable garage because the land was leased from Seattle University, and the garage could be moved whenever the university needed the land. The nine-level parking garage built in 1971 for the Tucson Federal Savings & Loan Association—which combined steel, precast prestressed concrete, and post-tensioned concrete—was intended to be easily demounted. Recently, modular steel systems, advertised as movable parking decks, have regained the popularity they enjoyed in the late 1960s and early 1970s; they are most often used to increase storage capacity at existing parking lots. At $7,500 per stall (the cost in California in the early 2000s), this is a relatively inexpensive way to address a parking shortage until long-term solutions can be found.[113]

Underground Garages

Although underground garages were envisioned as early as 1913—under Grant Park, in Chicago, and under University Park, in Indianapolis—neither of these proposals was realized until years later. In 1926, R.B. Bencker designed the Garden Court Garage, an underground parking structure topped by a garden, for a site in Philadelphia that included a large, multibuilding high-rise residential project. The entrance to the two-level ramped parking facility was situated on the main street, adjacent to a grocery store. In 1927, the construction of underground garages was being explored for the U.S. Senate. Although garages were being constructed under offices and other building types during the late 1920s (the Pacific Mutual Life Insurance Building and the Wilshire Medical building—both in Los Angeles—are examples) it was not until the 1940s that the underground structure became a staple of the building type. Today, in fact, there is tremendous pressure to move garages underground, even though underground structures are more expensive to construct and operate.[114]

Constructing an underground garage is not as straightforward as one might imagine. All the soil must be displaced—and, once the structure is complete, only some will be restored. Efforts are sometimes made to preserve the earlier appearance of the surface of the land, often by installing a landscaped park. A successful underground structure requires sensitively designed entries, exits, and interior

The Parking Lot

Although this book focuses on the parking facility, the parking lot is too important a phenomenon to ignore entirely. For one thing, it is largely the parking lot, with its acres and acres of asphalt, that has given parking in general its bad reputation.

In 1955, it was reported that two-thirds of all parking spaces were in lots (which were then called car parks). But just as the car, the highway, and all the related technologies evolved, so did the car park. First an open area of dirt or grass, the parking lot was subsequently covered with cinders or slag, dust-proofed with calcium chloride, or surfaced with a soil-cement mixture. But asphalt was (and sometimes still is) the material of choice. Asphalt is inexpensive, quickly applied, and easily maintained and repaired; it can also be designed to withstand different weights and types of use. Even the dark color was initially considered an asset because it had low glare, contrasted strongly with the painted markings, and was heat absorbent. Of course, dark surfaces such as asphalt are now considered to be environmentally objectionable because of their contribution to the heat island effect.[1]

In 2000, a religious conference center in West Palm Beach built a 690,000-square-foot (64,103-square-meter) concrete parking lot. Today, concrete is often the material of choice for parking-lot surfaces, principally because it reflects heat and is more aesthetically appealing than asphalt. Moreover, the sometimes higher initial costs of concrete surfacing are offset by better performance and longer life.[2]

Lighting, landscaping, and good drainage have become important aspects of the parking lot. The parking lot is also being discussed as an opportunity for civic uses—a perspective that harks back to the days when public squares and plazas were parking lots for horses and carriages. The main issue for parking lots today, however, is sustainability: given concerns about the heat island effect and water runoff, strategies that will render parking lots more environmentally friendly—such as solar shading and the new, pervious paving materials—should be given serious consideration in parking lot design.[3]

Right: Garage constructed with the Unicon system, Burbank, California, 1970. Because they were quick to erect and could be reused in other locations, demountable garages appeared all over the country.

Below: Pacific Mutual Underground Entry, 1929. Garages under buildings began to appear in the late 1920s.

The Parking Garage

environments for both humans and machines; the designers must also find a way for mechanical exhaust systems to co-exist with the landscape above.

The first underground public parking garage was built in 1942, at Union Square, in San Francisco; placing the garage underground not only made it possible to meet the downtown parking shortage, but to maintain the park above. To preserve the integrity of the structure, the upper columns were 22 inches (56 centimeters) in diameter, and those on the lowest floors were 30 inches (76 centimeters) in diameter. At the foundation, the garage walls expanded from a thickness of 14 inches (36 centimeters) to a thickness of 16 inches (41 centimeters). For the roof, a 12-inch- (30-centimeter-) thick slab was covered with two or more feet (0.6 or more meters) of topsoil.[115]

Many other underground parking structures followed the construction of the Union Square Garage. The Pershing Square Park garage, in Los Angeles, was completed in 1952;

Headquarters, Santander Central Hispano, Madrid, 2006. This large office facility consists of nine buildings, with underground parking for 6,000 cars, and offers landscaped plazas, day-care, a hotel, a training center, and a golf course.

Exploring Structure and Materials

South Street Station, Greenville, North Carolina, 2006. In a cost-saving strategy, the stair and elevator cores were incorporated into this parking facility in such a way that they could also serve the adjoining office building.

because a concrete batch plant could not be constructed on the site, ready-mixed concrete was used. What was then the world's largest underground garage followed two years later, at Grant Park, on Chicago's lakefront. Designed by Ralph Burke Associates, the garage extended 15 feet (4.5 meters) below Lake Michigan. At a construction cost of $3,515 per space, the facility (which is still in use) profitably parked 2,500 vehicles, and yielded a park on land that had most recently been used as a parking lot. By the 1960s, underground parking could be found almost everywhere: in Jersey City, New Jersey, Journal Square featured an underground bus terminal and parking facilities; Detroit had a garage under Washington Boulevard; Boston and Newark had facilities under their greens; Philadelphia had one under Rayburn Plaza; and in Kansas City, underground parking faced the municipal auditorium.[116] At the Health Building Garage, built in Akron, Ohio, in 1969, cast-in-place waffle-slab construction was used to allow longer spans and to accommodate the weight of the plaza above. This structure was designed to hold 300 cars and was eventually expanded to hold 800 vehicles.

Although it is costly to construct an underground garage where the water table is high, some communities choose this approach. At Seaport Village, in San Diego, Hope Architects and Engineers proposed using trenches filled with liquid bentonite to keep the groundwater from seeping into the site; later, the bentonite would be removed and replaced by a three-foot- (one-meter-) thick steel-reinforced concrete wall to resist the perimeter pressure. The retaining walls were to be 50 feet (15 meters) deep, to connect to the hard clay beneath. The unusual features of this parking structure included a hanging garden at the lowest level of the facility, and a glass elevator and pavilion integrated into the park above. A similar approach is currently being used to construct an underground facility in Savannah, Georgia.[117]

At the parking structure built for the Inn of the Mountain Gods, in Rio Deso, New Mexico, steel, rather than poured reinforced concrete, was used for the structural system. The use of steel made it possible for the facility to be completed more quickly, enabling the owner to begin receiving revenues from the completed project. Most of the parking facility is situated below a mixed-use structure, although portions are below terraces or planting areas. For the foundation system, the designers adapted a technique used in highway building, constructing a retaining wall of geofabric wire baskets. A second, precast non-load-bearing interior wall was built to create the enclosure. A steel and concrete-slab structural system within the enclosure wall completed the garage. Intumescent paints, which provide protection by expanding during a fire, were used on the steel.[118]

Materials and Methods

The most expensive aspect of a parking facility is its structure. The development of the parking facility involved the use of many different construction methods and materials, often in combination, as designers attempted to solve emerging technical, structural, and aesthetic requirements. Although much experimentation occurred over the course of the 20th century, concrete and steel, in their various forms, emerged as the primary materials used in garage construction.

Designers can reduce construction costs for parking facilities by carefully determining the most appropriate materials and methods for a given project, by taking advantage of developments in highway technology, and by creating structural innovations. For example, costs are reduced when a parking facility shares its second-most-expensive element (the elevator and stair towers) with an adjoining building. This approach was used at the South Street Station, constructed in 2006 in Greenville, South Carolina—a facility that, even with its elaborate architectural exterior of brick and steel, was built at a cost of only $9,640 per space.[119]

Past Lessons for the Present and Future

⮞ As a stand-alone structure, the parking garage is in a relatively stable position: although individual facilities will always be subject to market forces and to the constraints of the site and the location, general guidelines for structural efficiency and the selection of materials are well established.

⮞ A stand-alone garage can be built in a structurally straightforward and efficient manner; when a garage is combined with other building types, however, conflicting structural demands can arise. Nevertheless, such combinations often create advantages, and should not be avoided simply because of potential complexities. Future research will focus on addressing the various needs that arise when uses are integrated.

⮞ Structure is the key to the functionality of the parking garage. The best practice is always to build for the longevity and flexibility of the structural system, whether the garage stands alone or is combined with other uses.

⮞ Parking garage designers should take full advantage of technological advances that enable structures to resist penetration by water and road salts. For example, improvements in coatings and in joining techniques have given steel greater longevity.

⮞ Parking garage design will place greater emphasis on sustainable, environmentally friendly choices in materials and construction methods.

CHAPTER 7

Man, Machine, and Movement
Reading the Parking Garage

Literal movement is central to survival. Figurative movement—the notion that "tomorrow will be better"—is central to modern culture. The parking garage is linked to both types of movement: it is both a cog in the machinery of how we get from here to there, and a symbol of economic, technological, social, and individual progress.

The emergence of new technologies changed 19th-century movement patterns and spurred the development of a whole new set of building types, including the factory, the railroad station, and the parking garage. Because the great hall of the train station was viewed as an extension of the cathedral and the marketplace—that is, as a locus of social interaction—it was immediately recognized as a civic building type and accepted as an example of "the art of architecture."[1] But not so the parking garage.

Despite early efforts to integrate the garage into the urban fabric, by the mid-20th century, parking garage design was driven primarily by functionality for the automobile; thus, attempts to "read" the garage as if it spoke the language of traditional architectural forms will offer little insight. In fact, by the end of the 20th century, the sense of a common architectural language had begun to disappear altogether, in the face of globalization and rapid social change. And of all building types, it is the parking garage that most vividly reflects this loss.

Although most parking garage design has occurred without explicit reference to architectural theory, the building type is, in fact, the built expression of 20th-century theories about the relationship between man and machine, and lies at the heart of many modern urban forms. Nevertheless, the parking garage has traditionally stood outside the art of architecture, excluded from the pantheon of civic building types deemed worthy of architectural study. But to move forward as a society—to explore new ways of integrating the movement of man and machine—requires recognition of the parking garage as a civic building type that belongs within the art of architecture.

Facing page: Paul Rudolph and Ulrich Franzen, *Evolving City,* 1974. Integrating all forms of movement and every advanced movement technology of the day, this proposal was a prophetic rendition of 21st-century visions.

Why Explore the Garage as a Building Type?

Architects discuss building types and their origins in an attempt to understand how and why people build. The parking garage is a relatively new building type: it has been evolving for only 100 years. But as Peter G. Rowe notes in *Design Thinking,* "type as a shared mental object, the relationship of the one and the many inherent in the type idea has been a subject for profound contemplation and impassioned dispute for centuries."[2] In a book chapter entitled "Types Are Us," Karen A. Frank explains why it is important to consider buildings from the perspective of type:

Types are us because use types support and reinforce our patterns of activities, relationships, and beliefs. They do not simply reflect who we are as individuals, families, and society; they help make us who we are.... Many use types are repeated in highly conventional, standardized, and unexamined ways, and new use types are often adopted without critical reflection. The links between form, use, and meaning are either unrecognized or treated as unbreakable bonds, and the purposes that use types serve and the consequences they have are either invisible or taken for granted.[3]

In other words, types evolve as part of a continuous "dance" with society: as elements in the built world, they are both shaped by, and shape, the "activities, relationships, and beliefs" that give rise to them. And types are both meaningful and mutable: so as a building type evolves, it expresses new meanings. It is by studying the emergence of a new building type, following its progression, and critically reflecting on its development that these meanings—otherwise "invisible or taken for granted"—can be revealed.

But what does it mean, exactly, to talk about the meanings of buildings? Language, whether verbal or nonverbal, is "a complex system of representation in which the basic emotions are structured into an intellectually coherent system."[4] Architecture conveys these unspoken meanings to us

---

Movement Facts of the 1970s

The 1970s brought an oil embargo, gas shortages, and an economic recession. It was during this decade that concerns about energy and the environment moved to the fore.

- In 1970, 65 percent of the world's population was rural.
- In 1970, 5 billion tons (4.5 metric tons) of oil were used worldwide; oil shortages occurred in 1973 and in 1977.
- In 1970, there were 120 million motor vehicles worldwide.
- The first jumbo jet was constructed in 1970.
- The first Earth Day was observed on April 22, 1970.
- Beween 1900 and 1970, the percentage of deaths associated with environmental conditions dropped from 40 percent to 5 percent.
- During the 1970s, acid-producing residues—mainly sulfur dioxide released through industrial processes—emerged as a major environmental issue.
- The Parking Consultants Council, a branch of the National Parking Association whose members design parking structures, was formed in 1972.
- The United Nations Environment Programme was formed in 1972.
- In 1973, 11.4 million automobiles were sold in the United States—a record that was eclipsed only once, in 1986.
- The American Public Transit Association was formed in 1974.
- In 1975, in Morgantown, West Virginia, the first transit agency for an automated guideway system was formed.
- In 1979, President Jimmy Carter restructured the Energy Research and Development Administration, transforming it into the cabinet-level Department of Energy.
- The Corporate Average Fuel Economy law, passed in 1975, when fleets averaged 19.9 miles per gallon (8.5 kilometers per liter), required fleets to obtain 27.5 miles per gallon (11.7 kilometers per liter).

The Parking Garage

in our daily lives. The language of architecture is one of forms, signs, and symbols that reflect the origins and aspirations of a culture. Modern architectural theory is based upon the belief that social systems communicate through design decisions—that is, through the physical act of construction and through the art of architecture. The "central issue" in current notions of architectural type concerns "the ability of a type, which is one thing, to stand for or represent more than one thing."[5]

Buildings that have historically been classified within the art of architecture—churches, city halls, and homes, for example—communicate wordlessly through the architectural language of structure, form, ornament, and space. The human observer "understands" this visual language through his or her emotional, intellectual, and physical response to these complex architectural forms. Thus, every facet of the built world is filled with unspoken messages. These messages are part of what an architect thinks about in the course of the design process, and designing for the parking garage is no exception.

The Parking Garage as a Building Type

In recent architectural theory, the cave, the tent, and the hut are the forms of human shelter that prefigure all other building types. These primal forms were determined by the landscape and by social organization: hunter-gatherers depended on caves, and sought shelter from the existing topography; nomadic herding societies, in need of portable shelters, devised the tent; farming societies had to attend to crops year-round, and needed the greater permanence of the hut. Thus, each of the three primary building types reflects a particular human relationship to the land and embodies particular movement patterns.

At first glance, the parking garage does not appear to fit into any of the three primary building types. However, if one gives prominence to the concept of movement, it is possible to link the parking garage to all three types. The argument for placing the parking garage within the art of architecture is twofold: first, the garage is connected, through literal movement, to all three primal types; second, it expresses architecturally the notion of figurative movement—that is, progress—as a societal goal. Through the concept of movement for positive social progression, the parking garage is linked to the very origin of architecture, and to a phase of human history that predates even the development of language.

Top: The cave in the Ni Mountains, Qufu, China, where Confucius was born. Above: Eugene Girardet, *Bedouin Camp in the Desert Dunes.* Left: Illustration from Marc-Antoine Lauger, *An Essay on Architecture.* Three basic architectural types are grounded in the realities of the land: the cave, which was "found" shelter; the tent, which was connected to a nomadic lifestyle; and the hut, which was connected to cultivation.

The Expression of Movement Is Key

As noted earlier, both literal and figurative movement are the basis of progress within any society—and the idea that the future will bring improvement is one of the foundations of modern culture. The expression of movement is thus important within architectural theory and within the evolution of any building type, but is particularly important for the parking garage, given its role as the physical link between man and machine.

Before oral and written language, there were technological and ornamental or artistic forms of communication, which were centered on ways to express and ensure survival and meaning. Technological communication was linked to science and reason, while ornament and art reflected a culture's understanding of how movement—both literal and figurative—occurs. One ornamental form, the foliated scroll, was based on the cycles of nature; another, the interlaced ornament, found its expression in the weaving of cloth; a third, cave paintings, depicted the relationship between myth and reality. To ignore the importance of primal, nonverbal conceptions of movement and progression is to lose sight of profoundly important aspects of human psychology.[6]

The ability to travel rapidly around the globe, either literally or figuratively, is expanding humanity's horizons ex-ponentially. But superficial visual understanding—"the view through the windshield"—is replacing the multisensory experience of interacting with others and with one's surroundings. The automobile, once a means of escaping from the dirt and congestion of the city to the health of the countryside, eventually became an escape from nature, not an opportunity to interact with it. The ornamental form that is based on the structure of the tire tread is an attempt to nonverbally express the modern movement pattern.[7]

Ironically, the ascent of the ramp garage of the 1930s initiated the disconnection between movement and the immediacy of nature; the self-park garage of the 1950s—essentially a constructed landscape—intensified the lack of connection by eliminating the social interactions embodied in the transition spaces of the great train halls. The result was a false sense of the world, stripped of the deeper meanings traditionally associated with movement and with life. Nevertheless, to eliminate the independent movement permitted by the automobile would be to cut people off from their deepest notions of positive progression. This is the paradox of the parking garage in modern life.[8]

When people spend so much of their time encased in the "private bubble" of the automobile, how is the fabric of social and environmental connection to be maintained? What is needed are new architectural forms and relationships that

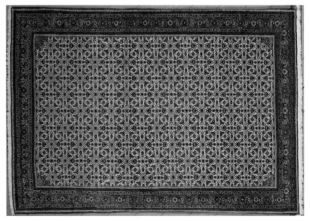

Above: Group of stags, Lascaux Caves, Périgord, Dordogne, France. Above right: Foliated scroll pattern, 16th–7th century B.C. (after Alois Reigl). Right: Ferehan carpet, Persian. Cave paintings and two basic ornamental constructs—the foliated scroll and the interlaced pattern—were nonverbal expressions of movement connected to the cave, the tent, and the hut.

foster, rather than undermine, the sense of connection to others and to nature, while allowing room for individual creativity and advances. Exploring the underlying meanings of architectural forms is a step toward making design choices that better reflect all of society's goals.

Man, Machine, and Movement

Mid- to late-20th-century approaches to "the parking problem" tended to go in one of two directions: total integration, in which the parking garage was just one element in a vast, self-contained structure; or total separation, in which pedestrian and automobile movement were segregated, uses were segregated, and the parking garage was hidden from view, or otherwise disconnected from the surrounding urban fabric and from the civic rituals of arrival and departure. While the first approach remained largely theoretical, it was the second that was actually implemented.

Connection

Throughout the 20th century, architects and others have attempted to conceive new ways for people to interact with nature, with each other, and with the built environment. Movement—in both the practical and metaphorical sense—was central to these proposals. One of the early attempts to completely interweave architecture and the movement of man and machine was undertaken by Edgar Chambless, who in 1910 proposed a streetcar suburb called Roadtown—a combination city and rail line that would stretch, ribbonlike, across the countryside, blending movement and everyday living in a single, linear structure. In a multistory spiral "recreation tower" designed in 1911 by C.K. Knight, movement took the form of a vertical foliated scroll: in Knight's plan, visitors would arrive by car, park on the ground level, then travel up the spiral, by streetcar, to a pavilion and ballroom offering 360-degree views of the city of Cleveland stretched out below. Knight's was one of the first visions to link parking, public transportation, and architecture; the use of the streetcar as a destination in itself was another innovation. (The automobile played only a small part in the promotional drawings: many people are shown arriving by car, and parking appears to be in a one-story, barnlike structure off to the side.) In *The Discopter Port and Harbor Facilities,* a futuristic vision created by Alexander G. Weygers in 1947, every conceivable natural movement system—land, air, and water—is connected. Flying-saucer-

Edgar Chambless, *Roadtown,* 1910. Roadtown was one continuous horizontal ribbon upon the land. But it was also disconnected from the land.

like vehicles are the main form of transportation, but automobiles and their parking garages are also depicted.[9]

None of these projects were ever built, but they exemplified the beginnings of the more integrative proposals that appeared later in the century—particularly in the 1960s and 1970s, when "movement as architecture" became the focus of architectural theory and study. Ron Herron, in his Cities-Moving Project, designed in 1964, offered a new and somewhat unnerving vision of a built world that is in constant motion and completely disconnected from the land. Although Plug-In-City, envisioned in 1965 by Peter Cook, may have seemed unrealistic, it was actually quite similar to Habitat, the Montreal community designed by Moshe Safdie in 1967, and to the Nagakin Capsule Tower, constructed in 1972 in Tokyo; unlike Habitat and the Capsule Tower, however, Plug-In-City had a separate, mechanized parking tower within its core. Another visionary project—which

THE OHIO RECREATION TOWER CO.
C.H. KNIGHT INVENTOR
606 COLUMBIA BLDG. CLEVELAND OHIO.

was actually built and is still in use—is the Atomium, created for the Brussels Expo of 1958. In this project, round spheres for living space are connected diagonally, so that the entire structure has the appearance of a molecule. This structure featured angled and sloped, rather than vertical or horizontal movement—emulating the ramp, the movement system of choice for the car. Sin Center, designed in

1959–1962 by Mike Webb, was a proposed megastructure in which streets flowed inside the building.[10]

Although many of these proposals failed to address parking for individual transportation devices, one scheme did depict an underwater city that consisted of parking ramps for both human and automobile occupation: in *City under the Seine*, proposed by Paul Maymount in 1962, parking appears

The Parking Garage

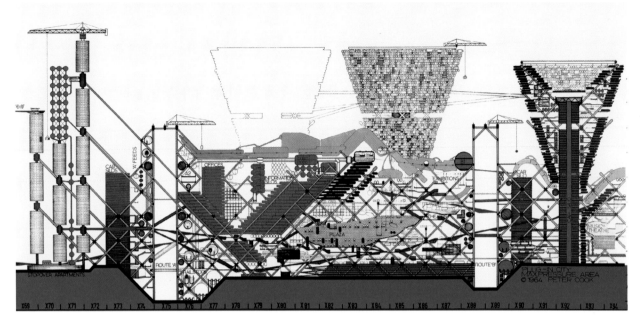

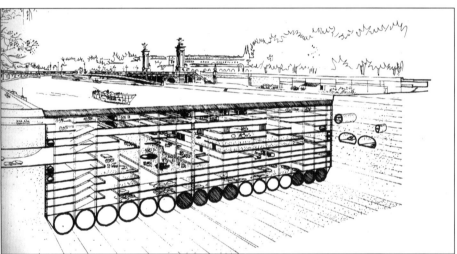

Above: Peter Cook, *Plug-In-City,* 1965. A vision that is now coming to reality: a city where everything is interconnected, and an automated parking facility forms the core of every building.

Right: Paul Maymount, *City under the Seine,* 1962. In this underwater world, parking is integrated with living spaces, and the entire design is based on the structure of the ramp.

at the lowest level of the designer's hidden world. And in *Evolving City,* a 1974 drawing by architects Paul Rudolph and Ulrich Franzen, entire cities are interconnected, parking is integrated into buildings, and parking and buildings are interwoven by mass transit. In this scheme, the interconnectedness of movement, man, and machine is offered as a real-world solution.[11]

Separation

In urban areas at midcentury, the combination of deteriorating buildings and the never-ending influx of automobiles led to development patterns that mimicked those of the suburbs, where the separation of uses was absolute. But segregating the automobile required the construction of large, imposing structures that filled entire urban blocks; that were hidden under buildings, streets, and roads; or that served in some cases as plinths for entire projects. It also created huge, impersonal spaces that prevented drivers and passengers from interacting with the surrounding urban street life.

The parking garage is the piece of architecture that physically connects man and machine, and that connects both to the larger urban fabric. But while architectural theory favored

Many early visions of the urban future were characterized by spatial complexity and a variety of emerging transportation forms. Drawings such as *Visionary City,* a 1908 work by William Robinson Leigh, and *What's to Hinder?,* a 1910 work by Harry Grant Dart, depicted multilevel metropolises where flying machines, wheeled transportation, and other mechanical solutions addressed the complex movement needs of imaginary cities.[1]

At the beginning of the 20th century, Eugene Henard, architect for the city of Paris, imagined a complete, environmentally sensitive system that connected tall buildings, the street, the automobile, and transit. Transit ran below grade, while automobiles went directly up to their owners' apartments. A mechanized system funneled the exhaust away from the interiors of the structures. In 1913, *Scientific American* published a vision of a multilayered city; the designs of Hugh Ferris, Harvey Wiley Corbett, and Francisco Mujica, created in the late 1920s and early 1930s, further explored this approach.[2]

Ebenezer Howard's visions of garden cities, developed at the turn of the 20th century, were realized in experimental New Towns in England. Although Antonio Sant'Elia's 1914 designs depicting stations for trains and airplanes were not fully realized as envisioned, they were in line with transportation strategies implemented later in the century.[3]

Some visionary plans eventually came to life—but only at world's fairs and expositions. In one case, however—the World's Columbian Exposition, held in Chicago in 1893—ideas presented at the exposition were realized 16 years later, in Daniel Burnham and Edward Bennett's plan for the city. The utopian quality of beaux-arts planning and the view of technology as progress found practical expression in the moving sidewalks and elevated trains of Burnham and Bennett's design. The plan combined functionality (such as attention to plumbing and garbage collection) with French planning strategies; it also anticipated multiple forms of transportation and the use of electricity.[4]

It was only natural for innovations in transportation to be a principal focus at fairs and expositions: examples include A Century of Progress, held in Chicago in 1933–1934, and the New York World's Fair of 1939–1940. The Ford exposition, designed by Walter Teague and Albert Kahn, and Futurama, the General Motors pavilion designed by Norman Bel Geddes, both focused on the roadways of the future, and were among the most popular exhibits at the New York World's Fair of 1939–1940.[5]

According to Le Corbusier, "a city made for speed is a city made for success."[6] This paradigm drove the urban plans of the 20th century, but often failed to take into account the car at rest. By the 1930s, Frank Lloyd Wright, Le Corbusier, and Richard Neutra had devised large-scale visions of the urban future that included ideas about how to park the car: in their designs, cars typically resided in streets, in motor courts, and in plazas; parking structures were few and far between. In La Ville Radieuse, however, a 1930 design by Le Corbusier, garages were placed on multiple levels and linked with highways; although this approach ignored the surrounding context, Le Corbusier was at least exploring the impact of large-scale planning projects, and was beginning to think of how best to integrate the car at rest. The fullest exploration of Le Corbusier's urban planning ideas is found in Brasilia, a new town built from the ground up as the capital of Brazil. Brasilia's modern, walkable neighborhoods are a success; but the large-scale highways that connect home and office, although designed for speed, are always filled with traffic, and are the least successful aspect of the city.[7]

Left: *Street Levels,* 1913 (detail). Right: General Motors' Futurama pavilion, New York World's Fair, 1939.

connection, the reality of the built world was very different: parking garages were not designed to evoke any sense of a civic whole, or of arrival and departure as collective social experiences. Instead, in the name of speed and flow, movement systems were separated completely: pedestrians traveled in one sphere, and cars in another.

In a reflection of the push toward separation, many downtown streets were closed to automobiles. The first pedestrian mall was created in Kalamazoo, Michigan, in 1959, and other cities soon followed suit: by 1984, there were more than 100 pedestrian malls in the United States. Eventually, closing streets in the core section of downtown and creating parking in the outer ring became part of the parking strategy even for small communities. Although some pedestrian malls have been very successful, most have been reopened to automobiles, reintegrating man and machine in more sensitive ways.[12]

One example of separation was Victor Gruen's design for the central business district of Fort Worth, Texas, in the 1950s. Originally, Gruen—who was known for his designs of shopping centers—wanted to eliminate the automobile entirely from the pedestrian area of the project, which was on a massive scale. Instead, parking became the base of the entire project, starting at the ring road and reaching into the center, below the pedestrian space. Small electric vehicles would be provided for those who did not enjoy walking in such an expansive urban environment.[13]

The Fort Worth design set the standard that all subsequent projects attempted to emulate. Center cities were gradually transformed along the lines of Paul Rudolph's Boston Center, a late-1960s project that was limited to office buildings and parking, but that incorporated vast open spaces for pedestrians and linked parking directly to the highway. Gruen, meanwhile, continued to design projects of the complexity and scale of downtown Fort Worth, and even created some visionary proposals for residential-only mega-complexes that were designed to rely on advanced mass-transit systems.[14]

Like Gruen, Edward Durrell Stone was working on large-scale plans that separated the automobile and the pedestrian. What Stone's designs for Akron, New Orleans, and Tulsa—completed in the mid- to late 1950s—had in common was large, auto-free plazas in the heart of the city. Stone envisioned parking as a function that could be handled as it

Below left: Fort Worth, Texas, circa 1950. Victor Gruen, among others, connected parking to skywalks and also used the podium strategy to separate vehicles and pedestrians.

Below right: Boston Center, Boston, Massachusetts, circa 1970. Large-scale urban projects continued the tradition of separating work and home; often, the automobile and the parking garage were the only links between uses.

The Parking Garage

is in Venice, where visitors park in the Autorimessa, a huge structure outside of the city, then depart across the waters for the city itself.[15] Stone also used the podium concept, however. At Pittsburgh's Chatham Motor Hotel, constructed in 1962, the base of the building is a solid, four-story city block that can park 2,000 cars; it has only a few openings at sidewalk grade, mainly for automobiles. Perched atop the garage, however, is a landscaped colonnade level for swimming and dining. A recent, award-winning building designed to house the offices of the *New York Times* returned to the podium strategy for parking.[16]

The segregation of the automobile, and of parking, from the flow of everyday life was also reflected in the design of large-scale urban redevelopment projects throughout the country: here, massive interior and exterior spaces were proffered in an attempt to foster the sense of human connection that was being undermined by the automobile. However, the scale of these projects was frequently as overwhelming as that of the monolithic parking garages that were proliferating in downtowns. Opportunity Park, constructed in Akron, Ohio, in the 1970s, was one such redevelopment project; it featured a separate, 2,000-space parking garage that was built to serve the nearby commercial and industrial redevelopment.[17] Co-Op City, constructed in New York in the 1970s, was an equally large, residential-only redevelopment project that required eight massive parking structures.[18]

Integration: Megastructures and Mixed Use

When many building types are integrated at a massive scale—creating what is essentially a city within a building—the result is a megastructure. "Mixed use" means combining uses at various scales, either within a single building or within an entire urban plan. New York City's Rockefeller Center, initiated in 1928, offers 12 acres (five hectares) of land and 14 buildings, including a 725-space garage, and is regarded by some as a model of an urban mixed-use project. One of the most beautiful mixed-use structures, however, is Budapest's Cyclop Garage, which attempted to re-create, for automobile travelers, the experience of the great train halls: on the basis of available photographs, it appears to have succeeded. The structure, built in 1927, featured shops on the street level and hotel rooms on the sixth and seventh floors. But the most striking feature was a central, glass-roofed atrium that rendered visible the movement of all entering automobiles: arriving pedestrians, as well as patrons of the stores and the hotel, could view the cars moving into and through the facility.[19]

Top: Co-Op City, New York City, circa 1970. Large urban redevelopment projects that included residential towers had to grapple with the issue of providing adequate parking.

Above: Cyclop Garage, Budapest, Hungary, 1927. This one-of-a-kind, mixed-use facility maintained the urban form and provided a gathering space that attempted to mimic those of the great train halls.

Top: Frank Lloyd Wright, *Great Arterial Way,* circa 1936. In his Broadacre City project, Frank Lloyd Wright created a suburban vision based on separated uses; parking was integrated into the main highway—the Great Arterial Way.

Above: William S. Mason, proposal for a wholesale showroom complex, Chicago, 1932. Some early parking and building combinations are too remarkable to ignore—such as this ziggurat design for a showroom complex on the current site of the Chicago Merchandise Mart.

Another early version of the mixed-use approach was the 1932 design for a wholesale showroom complex on what is now the site of the Chicago Merchandise Mart. Conceived by the designer, William S. Mason, as a superblock (a structure that consumes an entire block, eliminating the typical street grid), the structure was, for its time, an unusual combination of parking and a commercial building, with parking consuming most of the land area. The open internal parking ramp expands from the center outward to the edges, admitting natural light to each parking level. Automobiles enter through an arch that is nearly five stories high and that breaks the regular rhythm of the factorylike facade. Two towers resembling ziggurats—one at the corner, and the other at the short midblock—rise from the five-level parking base, creating a unique and fascinating structure.[20]

Although in the United States the parking garage was not typically integrated closely with other building types, every other possibility for connectivity was explored: over, under, next to, and in between. Interest in the megastructure and in mixed use also led to explorations of the connections between roads, buildings, and parking. In his proposal for Broadacre City, developed between 1931 and 1935, Frank

Lloyd Wright addressed the connections through the Great Arterial Way, a multilevel connector that incorporated parking, warehouses, and rail travel. In 1957, Laurence G. Farrant imagined an expressway that was combined with off-street parking. *The City in a Bridge,* created by Brian Eldred in 1969, depicts a megastructure suspended above the landscape—an arrangement that was reminiscent of Roadtown. In Eldred's proposal, parking was on the lowest level; the middle was taken up by apartments, shopping, and offices; and there was a ten-lane expressway above.[21]

By the late 1950s in the United States, the idea of a "ribbon city" that linked freeways with parking and office buildings was taken seriously as an example of master planning for downtowns. By the 1990s, direct freeway access to parking garages, as at the Third Avenue North Distributor Garages, outside Minneapolis, was becoming a common strategy. This was in some ways a natural extension of the idea of providing access to garages from more than one street, and from more than one level of attached buildings. Tokyo provides parking—often mechanized—under freeways, utilizing every available piece of land. The most unusual combination, however, can be found in Stuttgart, Germany, where a second-level traffic circle has parking in its center, an arrangement that allows traffic to flow freely below.[22]

Among the projects that actually integrated a road and a building was the Union Carbide facility constructed in 1980 in Danbury, Connecticut: a road runs right through the 4,000-car parking garage in the center of the structure, while the office portion of the project clings to the garage core. Even new architectural projects—such as Zaha Hadid's BMW Plant, where part of the assembly line is elevated above the parking lot, like a catwalk, and appears to be moving into the building—highlight the idea that movement can be used to weave together inside and outside.[23]

True megastructures—integrating parking, roadways, transit, and all building types—never became the planning norm in the United States, as they did in Tokyo. Roppongi Hills, for example, the newest Tokyo megastructure, features a core of automated and ramp parking and is, overall, as interesting and complex as any city. In the United States, megastructures were more likely to take the form of large urban blocks, and were on a much smaller scale. Early projects of this type often altered the street patterns of the surrounding area, cutting off the new developments from the urban context. One example is Santa Monica Place, a solid, four-block area of development completely covered in build-

ing forms. In this project, which was built in 1981, two de-partment stores and two large parking garages are con-nected internally by a covered pedestrian plaza that features stores, bars, and restaurants. The goal of the design was to revitalize the area by removing the automobile and replac-ing the urban street structure with an enclosed pedestrian mall. San Diego's Horton Plaza, another large-scale revital-ization project, included tall buildings and residential units, but very little parking—only 2,800 spaces. Nor did suburbia escape these large developments—in fact, the open land en-couraged them (although in the suburban context, they gen-erally took the form of mixed-use developments rather than megastructures). One of the earliest suburban mixed-use projects was Houston's Galleria, which was started in 1967 and had 9,000 parking spaces.[24]

During the 1960s and 1970s, as cities attempted to retain retail business in their downtown cores, parking was viewed as the problem, and the provision of parking as the solution. Many mixed-use structures were the result: by the 1970s, large-scale mixed-use projects could be found in almost any city in the United States. Atlanta had Atlanta Center and Colony Square, which expanded a growing downtown; in Baltimore, Charles Center helped to revive an older section of downtown. Kansas City's Shoppers Parkade, built in 1970, featured retail shops on the perimeter of the first two lev-els, office space in the center, and six floors of parking above.

Above left: BMW Plant, Leipzig, Germany, 2002. The design strategy that allows automobiles to weave in and out of buildings continues today, and is typically applied to factories.

Above right: Santa Monica Place, Santa Monica, California, 1981. Yet another approach to the parking problem involves closing streets to create a private pedestrian zone, while integrat-ing parking on the periphery.

Even smaller cities, such as Kalamazoo, had successful mixed-used projects. A 1969 mall and office complex in downtown York, Pennsylvania—a community of 120,000 at the time—featured 14 levels with 300,000 square feet (27,870 square meters) of retail, 500 parking spaces, and 3,780 square feet (352 square meters) of office space. Although it must have been shocking when it was first built, the project blends re-spectfully into its surroundings and remains a vibrant part of the community.[25]

In the United States, the parking garage has typically been assigned a supporting role in relation to other building types, and has rarely driven the design process. However, at Pitts-burgh's Stanwix Autopark, built in 1955, an existing parking garage was the driving force for the design of the office build-ing constructed above it, in leased air-rights space. Luckily, the garage had been designed to accommodate another level, and the necessary elevator and shaft were in place for the expansion. Although the Stanwix does not offer the

Parking garage and offices, Culver City, California, 2001. As parking began to drive the design of built forms, finding space for other building types became a challenge; one solution was to add office space on top of an existing parking structure.

beautifully integrated solution of the Cyclop Garage, it is nevertheless an example of a primary structure upon which another building type was constructed, in an arrangement dictated by the necessity of location. This approach was used recently in Culver City, California, where Eric Owen Moss designed offices atop a garage.[26]

In the mixed-use projects of today, the buildings are usually of lower height, and the projects—influenced by the new urbanism—tend to be less dense. In urban and suburban areas alike, the trend is toward retaining the typical urban street grid within the project and creating new connections to the surrounding urban fabric. And, although not on the scale of Roppongi Hills, or even the Kuala Lumpur City Center, large, mixed-use towers—"baby megastructures"—are becoming more common in American cities. Typically, such structures combine many uses vertically and horizontally, which creates structural conflicts when designers attempt to integrate parking efficiently within the tower form. Although many solutions are possible, the structural requirements of the parking garage are the least flexible aspect of a mixed-use project.

Currently, large-scale mixed-use projects are being undertaken in brownfield sites. One example is Atlantic Station, an Atlanta project where all the parking has been placed under the buildings, creating a podium for the city, as in Gruen's design for Fort Worth. The advantage of this arrangement is that the concrete structure and the ventilation required for the parking facility help to address any remaining land contaminants; the disadvantage is that a cavernous parking garage serves as the entry to the new city, creating a feeling of isolation rather than of welcome. Although the underground parking structure attempts to re-create the road structure that is above it, to assist with way-finding, this approach has limited value: people do not respond to street grids or to signs, but to the visual and architectural cues that are woven into the experience of the street and the city. However, the plans for mass transit—and the fact that some residences are within walking distance of the new downtown—may help to keep the sidewalks vital and active, which is rare with podium parking arrangements. Generally, podium arrangements encourage people to park as close as possible to their final destinations and discourage contact with the urban environment.

Function for Both Humans and Machines

It is no wonder that the parking garage inspires ambivalence: it is the built form that most vividly evokes the worst of automobile culture. Automobiles serve the desire for freedom and mobility, but they also pollute the air and water, foster sprawl, contribute to global warming, and require an endless supply of parking spaces. Nevertheless, automobiles are not about to disappear, and the design challenges that they create must be faced head-on.

The parking garage is essentially a functional building

type, meaning that it has been "designed or developed chiefly from the point of view of use."[27] Too often, however, the sole purpose for which the parking garage has been designed is the automobile. Designing for people requires recognition of their primal connections to nature, place, and movement; but as the garage came to be viewed as purely functional— as no more than a place to house the automobile—it lost its role as a civic and ceremonial transition space. Thus, attitudes toward the parking garage have come to reflect a kind of duplicity: although it is perceived as a building that is not occupied by humans, people *do*, in fact, drive through it, walk through it, and look at its mass and form. One way to deal with the ambivalence toward the parking garage is to simply block it from view: many people don't even "see" these structures anymore. Others demand that all garages be hidden underground, or otherwise obscured. But the unavoidable fact is that these facilities shape the modern built environment, people's interactions with that environment, and people's interactions with each other.

How has the garage managed to become a place of unacknowledged transition and unsettling isolation? The design of the building type has been so focused on the technology and the movement of the car that it has mirrored (and perhaps helped to create) a sense of dislocation that is characteristic of modern society. In doing everything for the vehicle, the garage has ignored the human being. It is only by addressing both vehicular and pedestrian movement, and

their interrelationship, that it will be possible to develop an architectural language for the parking garage that honors and responds to both technological and human needs. The passage from the world of speed to a slower pedestrian pace (and back again) needs to be recognized and reflected in parking garage design. New parking facilities have begun to address such issues, bringing fundamental change to the building type.

The Garage as a Connective Building Type

The parking garage functions as a connector in two senses: for the traveler, it marks a transitional point in a movement sequence—the point where drivers and passengers switch to or from the mechanical mode of transportation and the human mode. Although this passage is one of the least explored issues in contemporary architecture, it is central to modern society. At the same time that it is a link in an individual movement sequence, the parking garage is a connector in the larger transportation system. If parking is nonexistent or insufficient, the entire movement chain is obstructed: this is the reality that American cities confronted decade after decade, as the streets became overwhelmed with vehicles and transportation came to a standstill. The parking garage has untapped potential to serve not only as a physical link, but also as a unifying element in both the individual and the larger urban experience of movement.

Temple Street Garage, New Haven, Connecticut, 1963. This garage was originally intended to act as the connector between a new, high-speed roadway and the historic town green.

Espirito Santo Plaza, Miami, 2005. When parking structures are separated from the buildings that they serve, pleasant linkages can provide positive transitions between man and machine.

At the urban scale, New Haven's Temple Street Garage, designed by Paul Rudolph in 1963, was one of the first projects to directly address the role of the garage in the movement sequence. The plan called for a 1,000-foot- (305-meter-) long garage that was to link a new, high-speed road system with the city's historic town green. The driver would enter the garage directly from the new highway and make the transition to the heart of town; to facilitate the transition, the garage was connected to a shopping center along one side. (Ultimately, the project was not built as designed: instead of connecting to the new highway, the garage connected only to the shopping center.)[28]

The goal of the design was to address pedestrians' actual movement patterns while offering a physical connection between a high-speed roadway and a pedestrian environment. However, the built form did not incorporate either the change of scale or the change of physical pace that would have been necessary to reflect this transition. The facility did include separate pedestrian paths along the ramps—along with shrubbery, to evoke the feeling of a natural landscape—but any sense of human scale was overwhelmed by the massive presence of the garage. Despite the intention of providing a physical connection between disparate urban elements, the facility fell far short of addressing the under-

The Parking Garage

lying architectural issues of connection, scale, and pace for man and machine. Nevertheless, the project cast light on the importance of such issues.[29]

A recent project, the Espirito Santo Plaza, which opened in 2003 in Miami Beach, provides a transition space between an otherwise relatively typical garage and a large, mixed-use structure. The space allows pedestrians to progress from one type of movement to another, reflecting some understanding of human needs, although the transition space is not within the parking facility itself. Other projects, such as 1230 Peachtree, in Atlanta, feature a garden space between the parking garage and an office building. However, it is only if both the inside and the outside of the parking facility are designed to reflect its connective, unifying role that the building type can fully address human needs.[30]

The Garage as Landmark

Architecturally, a parking garage is a node: a place where at least two paths of movement intersect. Typically, nodes are distinguished by landmarks. A landmark is set off visually from the surrounding built environment, indicating its importance in the movement sequence and placing it within the realm of the art of architecture. Although garages are sometimes considered landmarks by virtue of their size and scale, they are rarely designed as such—and, hence, rarely function as landmarks. Nevertheless, a garage is a center of connectivity: a place where the paths of man and machine meet. Consciously designing the exterior of the parking garage as a landmark is the first step toward confirming its importance as a transitional space in the experience of arrival and departure. But addressing the interior is also crucial to the evolution of the building type.[31]

Why not accept the parking garage as the important civic statement it can be? Progress for a society, and for its architecture, depends on the structures that are used most frequently. Allowing the parking garage its rightful place in the pantheon of civic building types is a step toward a more holistic view of social organization and the built environment— toward a new architectural language that fully meets the expectations of a city and its people. Ignoring one of the pivotal building types of modern architecture because it does not fit into the traditional sense of the civic structure, or because its paradoxes are disturbing, is in essence denying modern culture, and missing an opportunity to give voice to a new aesthetic language. People—as individuals, and as

members of society—cannot afford to ignore any aspect of relationships, whether individual or collective, especially when creating architecture. Ignoring the complex challenges of the parking facility has never been a professional's choice, and creating a successful parking garage demands the best that professionals have to give.

Through the combined application of technology and aesthetics, architecture expresses cultural needs and relationships and works toward the betterment of society. Thus, it should be a source of balance and structure in a community's life. Successful linkages and places of intersection can occur only through acceptance and understanding of all the building types that define modern life, and that meet genuine social needs. The garage deserves attention as a pivotal piece of civic architecture. Form follows parking.[32]

Past Lessons for the Present and Future

➲ The parking facility needs to be accepted as a unique civic building type that is an appropriate subject for 21st-century architectural discourse.

➲ The meanings associated with movement—both literal and figurative—are important in the design of the parking facility.

➲ Designing the parking facility as a landmark—a building that the public can admire—is a way of acknowledging its role as the place of transition between distinct modes of movement: fast and slow, human and mechanical.

➲ Megastructures offer the opportunity to create complete living environments that integrate man, machine, and nature within a unified structure; however, attention to scale and detail is crucial.

➲ Separation of uses should not be applied without careful consideration: the connections that are lost through separation of uses may never be regained, and the results may dramatically affect the final success of a project and the overall urban environment.

➲ Where uses are separate, transition spaces are crucial and need to be sensitively designed.

➲ Regardless of whether the focus is a megastructure, a mixed-use project, or simply an urban neighborhood, design should allow for growth and flexibility, while providing as many movement options as possible and incorporating elements of both "fast" and "slow" time.

CHAPTER 8

The Aesthetics of the Parking Garage

T he definition of beauty changes with time. During the garage's short history, how has it fit into the concept of the beautiful building? And what does the future hold?[1]

According to Frank Lloyd Wright, a building is not just a place to be; it is a way to be.[2] Architecture is a response to a genuine external need that never subsides: the need for shelter. Yet it also embodies inner needs, experiences, and desires, giving them their expression in the built world, and thereby shaping people's lives. Parking—in some form, for some type of vehicle—will always be a part of life. Embracing the beauty of this evolving typology—the building type that is at the intersection of every modern design issue—means accepting its important aesthetic role.

Facing page: Austin Convention Center parking structure, Austin, Texas, 2005. Lighting on the facade and the innovative use of a metal screen reflect new trends in garage design.

The Garage in the Midst of Aesthetic Change

At the turn of the 20th century, the beaux-arts style was the major influence on design in Europe and the United States. The beaux-arts tradition is most closely associated with public buildings, banks, ministries, museums, and railroad stations; other structures, such as the parking garage, were not necessarily considered "serious architecture," even if clothed in the beaux-arts style.

In Europe, the beaux-arts style was at the center of architectural discussions about morality, social responsibility, and economics. In the United States, which was growing rapidly as it transformed from an agricultural to an industrial economy, the focus of architectural discussion was more on the practical and the necessary; nevertheless, the American ideals of independence, freedom, and equality continued to exert imaginative force. The automobile, the perfect combination of function and desire, reflected the American sensibility. And the garage, the new building type necessitated by the automobile, similarly expressed the sense of progress and of forward movement that dominated American culture. Taken together, these

PUBLIC PARKING CONVENTION CENTER PARKING

Opera House parking facility, Detroit, 2005. A proud civic statement, this facility harks back to the beginning of parking garage design.

two factors led the garage to become a truly American form and space. More than any other building type, the garage came to reflect the struggle to find a new, modern aesthetic that would successfully combine beauty and functionality, and express the changing realities of 20th-century life.

Both the automobile and the parking garage were central to explorations of this new aesthetic: the automobile visibly, and the garage invisibly. The "invisibility" of the garage can be attributed to two factors: first, in the early years of the 20th century, the interior of the garage was hidden, so spatial experiments went on largely behind closed doors; second, the building type was not yet a part of mainstream aesthetic discourse in the architectural community. Thus, parking facility designers had the opportunity to explore all the possibilities of emerging aesthetic traditions long before the building type had begun to receive any serious architectural attention.

Parking garage designers realized early on that the garage could reflect utilitarian principles at the expense of artistic

Movement Facts of the 1980s

Environmental concerns led to new regulations for automobiles; because of these standards, cars became safer, performed better, and polluted less. Although the oil shocks of the 1970s did not recur in the 1980s, the economy had entered a recession by the end of the decade.

⊘ By the 1980s, computers had begun to affect the design process for automobiles.

⊘ In 1980, the San Diego Trolley became the first completely new light-rail system in the United States.

⊘ The United States launched its first space shuttle in 1981.

⊘ In 1983, the Federal Communications Commission approved the world's first portable cellular phone, ushering in a new era in communication.

⊘ In 1983, Congress dedicated one cent of the federal tax on gasoline to the newly established Mass Transit Account.

⊘ In 1986, 100 years after Karl Benz received a patent for his motorized three-wheeler, the automobile celebrated its centennial.

⊘ Miami opened the first commuter-rail transit agency in 1989.

expression. But the garage would not have evolved into an architectural building type in its own right unless some architects, engineers, and designers also understood the importance of an aesthetic. Against a background of rapid and unprecedented change, the garage offered tremendous opportunities for innovation: Frank Lloyd Wright's proposed plan for Sugarloaf Mountain—a design that was eventually brought to fruition, though not for cars, at the Guggenheim Museum—was one example of such explorations. The attempt to balance the aesthetic, the structural, the technological, and the functional was engaged most fully, albeit often invisibly, in the development of the parking garage.[3]

Early Garage Architecture

In 1915, *The Horseless Age* featured an ongoing series dealing with issues in garage design, from the functional to the aesthetic. Noting that there was "as yet no distinct garage architecture," the author, P.M. Heldt, went on to describe the various approaches being used:

In some instances it may be justified to carry through the design strictly on utilitarian principles, without any attempt at ornamentation, and such a tendency is noticeable in the newer parts of the country. But in those sections of the country that have been settled for a longer time, a taste for pleasing, artistic forms has been developed which is taken into account in the design of buildings for even very commonplace purposes. If artistic lines are an asset in factory buildings which are seldom visited by customers, they are certainly more desirable in garages to which the customer or his representative comes every day.[4]

Heldt goes on to note that some architects were guided by local styles: mission facades in the southwest, and "neat and substantial" brick fronts in the northeastern states, for example.[5] And in well-to-do residential districts, typically in the East, elaborately styled and ornamented garages were deemed appropriate. Nevertheless, incorporating local architectural patterns into the design of parking facilities is very different from developing an aesthetic specifically for a building type.

Despite some attention to aesthetics, most of the *Horseless Age* articles dealt with the functional aspects of garage design: automobile movement, light and air requirements, and structural needs. Although the functional requirements of the garage altered the typical architectural relationships of plan, facade, and section found in other building types, and therefore altered the relationship between the garage

Lee Forest Garage, Great Falls, Montana, 1915. The notion of a specific visual aesthetic for the parking garage came under discussion early in the 20th century. The aesthetic solution devised for this structure reflected the outline of a car radiator.

and the surrounding urban context, neither the authors of the *Horseless Age* articles, nor any of those who directly followed, discussed this central issue: how can a garage be designed—with appropriate scale, proportions, and aesthetic presence—within the existing urban fabric? Instead, the articles focused on finding new architectural solutions within the confines of current styles: that is, architectural fashions. But in the architectural world, mere adherence to style is not considered an enduring aesthetic approach.

The Beaux-Arts Facility: Part of an Aesthetic Whole

During the transition from horse-drawn to mechanized transportation, the emerging emphasis on the concept of the machine, combined with the beaux-arts training of the architects, created many beautiful structures that succeeded in visually addressing human needs, the new technology of the automobile, a variety of scales, and the notion of mechanized advancement. Particularly in large cities, stables and garages alike were often constructed with the highest of aesthetic considerations, including elegant chimneys, iron balconies, elaborate brickwork, and the use of limestone and other expensive

Publix supermarket, Miami, Florida, 1998. The ramp is the focus in this parking structure, which takes the Miami Beach aesthetic to a new level.

materials. Typically, designers maintained the human scale of garages by honoring the existing urban context. Except for the large, beautifully detailed street-level opening for automobiles, parking garages were often indistinguishable from the rest of the facades on the street; a passerby would not even have been aware that the structure housed innovative technologies and spatial arrangements for the new machine. Such buildings reflected the view that appropriate housing for the car was as important as housing for humans.[6]

Other early garages had very simple facades, with little ornamentation, but their scale and size were already beginning to overwhelm surrounding buildings. New York's White Motor Cars, for example, which was built in 1910, had a pleasing facade that was compatible with those of the neigh-

boring structures, but its imposing presence hinted at things to come. The facility had two distinct masses on the street-front: a six-story piece and a three-story piece; compared with the adjacent-five story building, however, the six-story section was almost two stories taller, and the garage was, overall, at least twice as long as any other building on the block. Boston's Bowdoin Square Garage, constructed in 1927, although also an imposing edifice, was a classically proportioned tripartite building with columns defining the middle section—an aesthetically impressive structure that was worthy of the new building type. The facility looked much like any public building of the time, and was not incongruous in its location. The facade of a Baltimore public garage—designed by Beecher, Friz & Gregg, and built in 1906—was not

Frank Lloyd Wright and Parking

Like many of his contemporaries, Frank Lloyd Wright was fascinated by the ways in which the automobile was changing the built world, and eager to undertake projects that would integrate the new technology into the emerging modernist aesthetic. Wright's first large-scale design for the automobile was the Gordon Strong Automobile Sugarloaf Mountain Observatory. The client had requested a structure on the top of the mountain as an "objective" for local motor trips, with "the element of thrill, as well as the element of beauty"; Wright provided this and more—perhaps too much for the owner, who never built the project.[1]

Wright was known for a horizontal aesthetic that was based on natural forms. His plan for Sugarloaf Mountain, developed during 1924–1925, featured a spiraling road that provided 360-degree views, plus parking on the descending ramps. This spiral form, fully integrated into the landscape and extending the top of the hill, was a precursor of the modern parking garage. Initially, the design included a dance hall, an auditorium, restaurants, gardens, and parking along the descending ramps; as the project progressed, a theater was substituted for the dance hall, and many other changes were made. Still later, the internal parking was removed, all the spiral roadways were wrapped around a planetarium dome, and separate descending paths were added for automobiles and pedestrians.

Many of Wright's projects incorporated space for the automobile; examples include Broadacre City (1931–1935), Crystal Heights (1939), the Garage and Restaurant for Glen and Ruth Richardson (1943), the Rogers Lacy Hotel (1946), the Pittsburgh Point Civic Center (1947), the Self-Service Garage for Pittsburgh (1949), the Price Tower (1952), the Golden Beacon (1956), the Wieland Motel (1956), and the Mile-High (1956).

All of Wright's garage designs use architectural forms to reflect progression—the movement of both man and machine through nature. The designs also take into account the differences in scale between man and machine, and the transitions from one form of movement to another. The drawings for Broadacre City, a suburban vision fully integrated into the landscape, included the Rogers Lacy Hotel, the Self-Service Garage in Pittsburgh, the Gordon Strong Sugarloaf Mountain Observatory, and the Pittsburgh Civic Center. The Great Arterial Way, also included in Broadacre City, is a multilevel traffic facility, monumental in scale, placed within what is otherwise a low-rise suburban/rural setting. Parking was integrated under the arterial, as the automobile was the primary form of transportation. Wright's vision also included other modes of transportation, such as "atomic barges" and "taxi-copters." Movement and nature drove his design process.[2]

Crystal Heights, an early megastructure, included a hotel, apartment towers, shops, a theater, and parking. The parking structures were terraced in front and had shops lining their edges. Crystal Heights combined many of the qualities of early parking structures with a modern vision (the megastructure), yielding the sense of vitality that is essential to good design. The garage and restaurant for

the Richardsons was for the Wrights' local mechanic, who planned to live above the combination garage and restaurant, on a site with views of the Wisconsin River. The Rogers Lacy Hotel provided basement parking, while the Pittsburgh Point Civic Center included parking on each level, as well as a landing space for helicopters.[3]

Wright's ability to integrate human and mechanical requirements reached its fullest expression in the Self-Service Garage for Pittsburgh, which was to serve the Kauffman's Department Store and the surrounding area. The Price Tower, originally requested by businessman Hal Price as a two-story office building with parking for ten to 15 vehicles, was ultimately built as a 19-story tower with apartments and rental offices, and a roof garden over the parking structure. The Golden Beacon, a 50-story apartment tower, included parking in a three-story structure at its base. At the Wieland Hotel, the parking was partially concealed within and under the second level, so that the building could be set in a gardenlike field. The Mile-High had parking for 15,000 cars and 100 helicopters, and the terraces below featured four separate entrances leading directly from freeways to parking.[4]

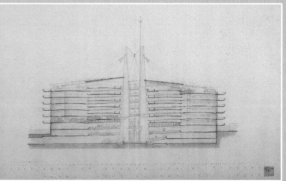

Top: *Gordon Strong Automobile Sugarloaf Mountain Observatory,* 1925.
Above: *Self-Service Garage for Pittsburgh,* 1949.

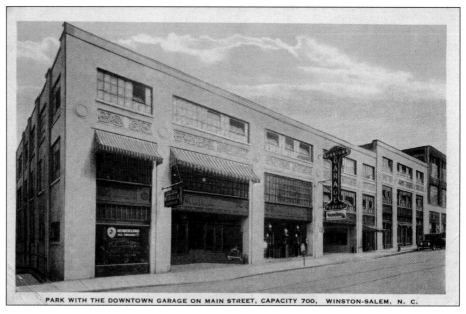

Top left: Public garage, Baltimore, 1906. Many early garages were designed in the manner of other small buildings on the street, and fit easily into their urban surroundings.

Top right: Bowdoin Square Garage, Boston, 1927. Early public garages were designed as handsome civic structures; it was often almost impossible to tell that they were parking facilities.

Right: Downtown Garage, Winston-Salem, North Carolina, 1926. Garages that were designed as civic buildings often became beloved aspects of the urban landscape; many remain in use today, often for other purposes.

PARK WITH THE DOWNTOWN GARAGE ON MAIN STREET, CAPACITY 700, WINSTON-SALEM, N. C.

only beautifully proportioned in itself, but maintained the architectural rhythms and heights of the streetscape. The Baker Garage, designed by Larson and McLaren and built in Minneapolis in 1927, featured a simple, elegant, three-story facade that sat comfortably amid its surroundings.[7]

The alternating rhythms of the typical beaux-arts facade could be used creatively to blend the larger, automobile-scale openings into the building's exterior, and even to blend in other uses that were allowed at this time, such as gas pumps. The flexibility of the beaux-arts tradition allowed experimentation with detail, as a means of ensuring appropriate scale and visual integration with surrounding structures. Nevertheless, some features—such as signs and pumping stations—did give away the interior use of the structure; one example is the Downtown Garage, in Winston-Salem, North Carolina, which opened in 1926. In this case, an elegantly proportioned facade with simple but appropriate ornament was supplemented by large advertising signs and hanging electric lights—expressions of the modern age. Such additions were not seen as incongruous at the time. Like many other parking facilities, this garage fell on hard times in the 1930s and had to offer discounted parking. But it was not demolished: its elegance, scale, and design quality helped it to survive. In 1956, the gas pumping and maintenance areas were moved to a separate facility on a neighboring site, but the parking garage remained in use.[8]

The Parking Garage

In the 1920s, the architecture firm of Lee, Smith & Vandervoort, of Richmond, Virginia, in collaboration with the Auto Ramps Corporation, also of Richmond, produced a number of elegant, beaux-arts–style parking garages that were sensitive to their urban surroundings; some remain in use today. Both the architectural firm and the parking specialists gave thorough attention to practical matters, but the public nature of the garage was not ignored.[1]

By the late 1920s, the Auto Ramps Corporation had achieved a thorough and systematic understanding of the requirements for a commercially successful parking garage. The firm, among others, was cited in a series of articles in *The Architectural Record* that included charts, formulas, and detailed lists of all the factors that had to be taken into account in garage design. For example, the articles outlined ramp choices and offered advice on building height and parking costs (the higher the floor on which the driver parked, the lower the parking fee).[2] However, in the view of *The Architectural Record*, the next challenge was defining a new garage aesthetic:

The appropriateness and character expression for garage design will be attained by architects without conscious effort. Ferro-concrete construction with the demarcation of floor levels, steel sash and the omission of cornice and base will endow the garage with frankness and modernity.

There should be no applied ornament and the surface treatment where concrete is used should be no other than that suggested by the nature of the material.

The garage may well attain a new and distinctly expressive form, indicating its practical function. "Modern architecture of our time seeks to devise form and motives from purpose, construction and materials. If it is to give clear expression to our feelings, it must also be as simple as possible."[3]

Despite the advice proffered by *The Architectural Record*, however, one of Lee, Smith & Vandervoort's beautifully detailed facades—featured on the front page of the article—was created by means of receding layers, classically structured and proportioned, and through the use of tripartite horizontal divisions, contrasting materials, ornamentation, and various massing techniques—all of which were modified, however, to reflect a modern aesthetic. The combination of classical proportions and appropriate detailing gave the building a civic presence, mitigated the bulk of the structure, and created a visually sensitive facade that allowed the facility to fit gracefully into its surroundings. It is still in existence today.[4]

Lee, Smith & Vandervoort

Left: Garage, Richmond, Virginia, 1928.

Above: Model of Richmond Garage, 1928.

Ornament was an important means of visually bridging the transition from the human scale to that of the automobile. In the United States, ornament also became a means of linking the new machine with larger notions of progress, freedom, and hope for the future. Terra cotta, easily molded into decorative forms, was often used on facades and within interiors to capture the spirit of the new technology. Garages bearing such ornamentation are now among the most beloved examples of the early "culture of the car." One of the finest examples was the Capital Garage, a ten-story, 1,000-car garage and showroom built in 1926 in Washington, D.C., and used for nearly 50 years before being demolished in 1974. The facade was filled with terra-cotta reliefs depicting 1920s automobiles and spoked wheels with wings. The structure housed a Nash dealership from 1946 to 1951, and later housed a Chrysler-Plymouth dealership. When the structure was demolished, the ornament was preserved, and is now included in the America on the Move exhibit at the Smithsonian Institution.

The Capital Garage was open 24 hours a day, seven days a week; as was typical at the time, it was steam-heated in the winter. It featured a gas station on the first floor, a service shop on two sublevels, and a complete body and fender shop on the tenth floor. The garage provided pickup and de-livery services to local hotels, such as the Willard. An integral part of Washington life used by notables such as Jacqueline Kennedy, the Capital Garage demonstrated how a practical structure could become a living, aesthetic part of a city, loved and used by all.[9]

The Casey Parkway, another well-designed and beautifully ornamented garage, was built in Scranton, Pennsylvania, in 1926. When it came time to demolish the structure and replace it with a modern parking facility, local residents granted permission for the demolition only on the condition that 18 ornamental medallions—bas-reliefs depicting various motorized vehicles from the period—be reused on the new facility.[10]

It was in the combination showroom and garage, typical in the early evolution of the building type, that ornamentation was at its most elaborate. A 1927 article in *The Architectural Forum* noted that even "in the smaller cities, the casual passer-by cannot fail to be impressed. In the larger cities, the architecture and decoration of show rooms have been carried much further, and their designing and equipment have become significant and highly specialized fields of architectural and decorative endeavor by well known designers."[11] When the Cadillac Corporation announced the opening of its new building in New York, it described the building as "a

Above: Casey Parkway, Scranton, Pennsylvania, 1926. Although this garage was recently demolished, the citizens of Scranton required that the facade ornament be reused on the new facility.

Right: Capital Garage, Washington, D.C., 1926. This garage, which once contained a Nash dealership and was in use for more than 50 years, was a cherished part of the city.

The Parking Garage

permanent salon designed for the presentation of custom built automobiles in the setting and atmosphere of a gallery."[12]

To express the uniqueness and desirability of the cars within, showrooms explored every conceivable architectural style, often featuring lavish and exotically ornamented terra-cotta facades and large, plate-glass windows that allowed full view of the even more elaborate interiors. It was not unusual to find ornamentation on every square inch of both the exterior and the interior. The extensive and fantastical imagery on the facade of the Star Motor Car Company, designed by Morgan, Walls, and Clements and built in Hollywood in 1927, evokes another world entirely. Other showroom-garages, such as Detroit's Packard Motor Car Company's Sales and Service Station, designed by Albert Kahn and built in 1927, and Philadelphia's Ford Motor Company Show Room and Accessory Shop, designed by Philip S. Tyre and also built in 1927, had a more restrained elegance. Smaller cities also had beautiful showroom-garage combinations; one example was the Stephenson Motor Car Company, in Milwaukee, Wisconsin, which was designed by Kirchhoff and Rose in 1910.[13]

Although the beaux-arts tradition was the major early influence on design, some parking garages reflected other stylistic preferences. In the late 1920s and early 1930s, the influence of art deco and streamline moderne was reflected in parking garage design; examples include the Olympic Garage, in Cincinnati, Ohio; Gimbel's Parking Pavilion, in Milwaukee, Wisconsin; and the Towne Park Garage, in Lincoln, Nebraska, a combination bus depot and parking garage. These garages illustrate the transition to the modern aesthetic: brick is used in combination with steel to create a "machine age" feel; the ornament has a mechanized look; and poured concrete is shaped into a streamlined form, giving visual expression to the ascent of technology. At the Plaza Triple Deck Garage, built in 1948 in the Country Club Plaza district of Kansas City, for example, colored stucco was used—along with Mexican tile, decorative urns, and other details—to integrate the design into its urban setting. The structure was an excellent early example of a parking garage designed to be an equal partner in the architectural aesthetic of its surroundings.[14]

The beaux-arts aesthetic language was flexible: it had the capacity to absorb what was new, allowing a transition to the more functional aesthetic that was beginning to emerge. Throughout the 1920s, parking garages remained aesthetically pleasing, civic-minded buildings whose exteriors were com-

Towne Park Garage, Lincoln, Nebraska, 1930. In this structure, the steel casement windows and simple ornamentation combine to create a modern feel.

patible with the surrounding visual context. With the rise of the modernist credo "form follows function," however, the garage was viewed as a perfect opportunity to explore the new aesthetic of "pure" functionality, in which a building's interior functioning was revealed on its exterior. Although the parking garage was rarely deemed worthy of serious architectural attention, the designers of the facilities were struggling to give the building type its own unique expression—to address both functional and social requirements within the context of the emerging modernist aesthetic.

The Garage and the Modernist Aesthetic

The "aesthetic nature of the garage" came into focus as the building type began to assume a unique role as the built embodiment of modernity—specifically, of the automobile age.[15] A 1929 article in *The Architectural Record* noted that "The ferro-concrete construction with the demarcation of

Pike at Rainbow Harbor parking structure, Long Beach, California, 2004. In this modern parking facility, the designers created a visual statement that expressed the unique character of each element in the structure.

floor levels, steel sash, and the omissions of cornice and base will endow the garage with frankness and modernity."[16] In fact, the Garage Rue de Ponthieu, designed by Auguste Perret and built in Paris in 1905, had already taken such an approach, although its aesthetic importance was often overlooked. This structure, whose form appears at first glance to be derived entirely from function, and from the characteristics of the new material, concrete, actually reflected the classical proportions of the beaux-arts aesthetic. To set off the entry and to create a visual transition between the scales of man and machine, the structure featured a large, ornamental form of iron and steel floating within the classical simplicity of its concrete frame. While retaining an element of the old—the tripartite beaux-arts approach to facade design—the building also embraced the new: the honesty and simplicity of its exterior expressed the functionality of its purpose. This combination of old and new often produces a building that stands the test of time.[17]

The Parking Garage

From the beginning, garage designers had to address the conflict between the internal requirements of the building type, such as ramps and longer structural spans, and the demands of the traditional facade. One solution was to hide the ramp from view by attaching it to the exterior on the back of the building. In this arrangement, the main "face" of the building could be freed from the structural role traditionally assigned to it in the beaux-arts aesthetic. Later in the century, the individual functions of the garage were separated and highlighted: for example, in a 1962 sketch of a parking deck for the Rochester Development Company, the streetfront has strong visual appeal—highlighting the ramp, the entry, and the mass beyond—but the remaining three facades feature the "exposed functionality" approach. The same design strategy appeared recently in the Pike at Rainbow Harbor parking structure, in Long Beach, California, which won a 2005 award from the International Parking Institute.[18]

Eventually, the new structural requirements became an area of intense aesthetic exploration in themselves: designers struggled to discover the spatial arrangements that would best meet the unique needs of automobile and driver. Meanwhile, European modernists were calling for "honest" buildings—structures that openly revealed their internal functions and purposes, and that required no ornamentation other than what was inherent in the materials used to construct them. As modernist ideas began to ferment in the United States, the facade became the focus of a debate: Was the beaux-arts style an appropriate expression of the modern age? Many architects and other observers felt that the fast-changing world of technology needed to be captured in the urban form, both inside and out. But how?

Unquestionably, some early garages were "honest" by default: they were built as purely functional structures, as quickly and inexpensively as possible to serve the blossoming need. Boston's Cage Deck, however, built in 1933, was an example of aesthetics driven by functionalism: the facade, rendered unnecessary by the internal structure, was left off entirely, a solution that became the norm for a great many parking decks to follow.[19] The result—a completely exposed structure of stacked slabs and structural columns—lacked any visual appeal whatsoever, and bore no relationship to any other buildings in the city. Neither ugliness nor incongruity was the intent of the modernist aesthetic, and such structures were quickly rejected by designers, who continued to seek other solutions.[20]

The early evolution of the parking garage spanned the transition from the beaux-arts to the modernist aesthetic, and reflected both influences. Nevertheless, as the concept of "pure" functionalism for the parking garage gained ground, the building type became extremely susceptible to design decisions based solely on cost, without so much as a glance at aesthetic value. In essence, the functional approach, pursued single-mindedly, destroyed the ability of the garage to take its rightful place as a piece of civic architecture—a structure that is an essential part of daily life. The "message" of these structures was limited to one of utility: they did not communicate aesthetically with their users or with their surroundings. It is such structures that have given the parking facility a bad name. At best, they are ignored; at worst, their reputation as dark, cold, overwhelming, and potentially dangerous places has led to demands that all parking be banished from view. Even to the casual observer, it is clear that purely functional facilities, conceived without reference to any concern other than cost, are not part of the art of architecture, and do not contribute to the life of the city.

Fortunately, not all garage designers took the dictate "form follows function" to an extreme. More sophisticated explorations of the modernist aesthetic attempted to express the idea of movement itself, on a number of levels: as travel, as change, as speed, and as progress. Because the automobile was so closely tied to prosperity—both in fact and in the popular imagination—the parking garage was a natural place to probe larger connections between aesthetics, social improvement, and architecture. However, these garage designs have not been adequately recognized for their contribution to modernist aesthetics.

Looking beyond Function

It has been said that modern architecture was "founded on the idea that only abstract space is free to follow the exigencies of function."[21] In other words, only when stripped of all reference to the literal can function as an aesthetic truly emerge. The parking garage, as a functional building type created and shaped by the ramp, is the essence of "abstract space." In a drawing entitled *Parking Garage over the Seine,* created in 1925 by Konstantin Melnikov, a Russian architect, the ramp is exposed as the main focus of the nearly nonexistent facade, highlighting the sheer thrill of movement. The stability of Melnikov's first design—an eight-story rectangular garage perched asymmetrically on an exposed, cantilevered, curved ramp rising directly from the street—was

Left: Konstantin Melnikov, *Parking Garage over the Seine*, 1925. In this early proposal, the ramp is the key design element in the parking structure. To appease those who did not understand his vision, Melnikov added a leaning Olympian to the drawing.

Above: Rikes-Dayton Garage, Dayton, Ohio, 1959. Like any other building type, the parking garage reflected the visual trends of the period—in this case, electric signs and low massing.

questioned, so a revision added a leaning muscular Olympian. The drawing expressed the joy of personal movement, highlighting the ease with which an automobile—and its passengers—could climb to new heights.[22]

As the idea of movement became part of the modernist vision, the issue was how to express movement in the design of the parking garage. In the late 1940s and 1950s, with the post–World War II economic boom, interest in the parking garage was reignited, and designers began to actively explore ramp options, the transformation of the facade, and innovative materials and construction techniques. Once again, the garage moved quietly to the forefront of cutting-edge design issues, as exemplified in the Rampark garages, built in Omaha and Lincoln, Nebraska, in the 1950s. The Automobile Hotel, built in Mobile, Alabama, in 1950, illustrates the new and important role of signage and massing on the facade.[23]

Modern art generally takes the view that the only way to understand change is to express it; but the parking garage, like architecture in general, is a static form. Thus, the challenge for the garage was to simulate movement through "pure form" (that is, without realistic ornamental forms),

while simultaneously creating space for the actual movement that occurs within the garage. In other words, the goal was to visually connect and reconcile movement and aesthetics. Space—traditionally the locus of social connection—was being replaced by flow, an individual experience supplied by the ramp. Through the ramp, the parking garage became the first building type to explore modern notions of space and flow. It was Le Corbusier, in his 1930 design for the Villa Savoie, in France, who transferred to a living space—and to the art of architecture—a number of ideas that had already been applied to the parking garage.[24] Constructed of reinforced concrete, a material that was redefining aesthetic sensibilities, the Villa Savoie was raised above the parking area on pilotis (freestanding columns) so that the automobile could travel freely around the structure. More important, the house also featured a roof garden and an integral ramp for human movement.[25]

In the parking garage, meanwhile, the modernist aesthetic was expressed in oblique movement patterns through, in, and around form. For example, at a 700-space parking structure designed in 1940, by Richard Neutra, for a Los Angeles airport, the diagonal ramps that led to the parking within

The Parking Garage

were exposed on two sides of the building—an arrangement that revealed the visual power of the oblique forms but made circulation difficult at best: garage patrons had to navigate the entirety of every single floor in order to move up or down in the garage. The remaining, short sides of the structures were blank walls, foreshadowing the "billboard" facades of later parking structures.[26]

The garage designed by Albert Kahn for Detroit's Henry Ford Hospital, built in 1959, was also a freestanding structure, isolated in the landscape, but was situated next to a highway. The facility featured a facade with a repeating pattern of hyperbolic panels made of precast marble powder—yet another attempt to capture on the exterior of a building the sense of movement within. "Distilling emotion by freezing motion" was becoming an important design approach—a way of expressing, understanding, and coping with modernity.[27]

At Cleveland's Tower East Center garage, built in 1965 and designed by Walter Gropius, the column line was set back from the front facade; as a result, the oblique and subtle shadows of the facade create a floating effect—an exemplary expression of the modernist aesthetic. Interestingly, if internal functionality had been given visual precedence, the "floating" quality would have been lost. Eventually, garage facades that took the form of continuous horizontal strips of concrete would be among the most hated designs; however, in this early version, the result is elegant and sophisticated. At the Murray Lincoln Campus Center, designed by Marcel Breuer and built in 1971 on the campus of the University of Massachusetts at Amherst, the facade eliminated all evidence whatsoever of the underlying structure; instead, the exterior has itself become a screen—a Cartesian grid within the landscape. The result reflects both the Jeffersonian ideal of order and the modernist search for a new order.[28]

By the late 1940s, the parking garage had become more common in the suburbs, where the relationships between buildings were completely different than they were in the city. In a suburban landscape, an exposed ramp—expressing the thrill of movement—was more easily absorbed, and therefore more aesthetically pleasing and appropriate. In the design for the rooftop parking structure of Milliron's Department Store, built in 1949 in Los Angeles, two crisscrossing ramps—one leading up and the other down—serve as the facade, creating a strong visual contrast to the blank wall beyond. The facility, designed by Victor Gruen and Krummeck Associates, faces the suburban parking lot and visually

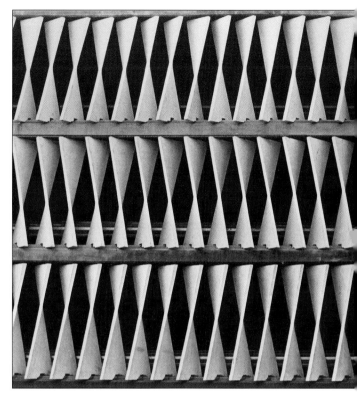

Top: Henry Ford Hospital, Detroit, 1959. Instead of exposing the ramp in order to express movement, this structure uses a modern ornamental strategy: a repeating pattern of twisted hyperbolic columns.

Above: Milliron's Department Store, Los Angeles, 1949. The ramp, the perfect solution for the garage interior, eventually began to appear as the design focus of the exterior.

extends it. The structure is an example of the successful integration of a ramp garage into a suburban landscape.[29]

The Screen as an Aesthetic Tool

The design of an "unnecessary" facade—one that no longer served any structural purpose—became a crucial issue for the parking garage, especially in urban environments. A screen—an ornamental piece that is usually positioned in front of the structural column grid—is a cost-effective means of mediating the scale of parking structures and creating a more pleasing appearance. A screen may be composed of metal, concrete, glass, or any another material; although it is similar to a curtain wall in design, a screen does not need to provide protection from the weather. Screens began to appear in the 1960s and are still found on many parking structures throughout the country; designers continue to experiment with various screening materials, shapes, and forms.[30]

The first example of screening in a parking garage was created by John Joseph Earley, a sculptor, for the window openings of the Evening Star Garage, built in 1940 in Washington, D.C. At this time, architectural precast concrete, which was used for aesthetic purposes only, had just been developed. Earley had experimented with perforated precast concrete panels and created the Earley-Taylor system, a patented technique for forming concrete. At the Evening Star Garage, the lacework screens within the openings of the poured-in-place concrete facade allowed the transfer of light and air, as required by current building codes; more importantly, however, they initiated an architectural aesthetic that became a mainstay of garage design. The ornamental perforated panels created a pleasing facade, allowing the open-deck garage to blend into the surrounding neighborhood.[31]

At Pittsburgh's O'Hare Parking Plaza, designed by Tasso Katselas and built in 1960, the screen takes the form of a modernist painterly composition (think of Mondrian) in which solids and voids provide occasional glimpses of the underlying structure. New York's Bellevue Center Garage, constructed in 1963, used "shocked concrete"—concrete that has been striated within its formwork—to create a complex screen in which one vertical frame is the width of a car, and three represent the width of a bay. At the parking structure of the Minas Department Store, built in Hammond, Indiana, in the 1960s, precast concrete units take the form of ornamental grillwork at a massive scale.[32]

Above left: Evening Star Garage, Washington, D.C., 1940. The sculptor John Joseph Earley, an early experimenter with precast concrete, designed a precast screen for all the openings on this simple, concrete-framed parking structure. This was the first use of the screen for a garage facade.

Above right: University of Pennsylvania parking garage, Philadelphia, 1964. On the long sides of this structure, diagonal bracing is exposed; on the short sides, structure and screen are made one. The blank walls on the short ends of the facility foreshadow the "billboard" approach to facade design.

Right: Exchange National Bank Building garage, Tampa, Florida, 1967. In this structure, one of the largest aluminum screens in existence at the time was used to connect the parking garage with the facade of the bank.

The Parking Garage

At the University of Pennsylvania, a parking garage designed by Mitchell/Giugola and built in 1964 features a side facade in the tradition of "screen as billboard": where the structure meets the urban fabric, the garage is defined by tall, angled, monolithic wall planes. Diagonal bracing stretches from ceiling beam to ceiling beam, providing the required lateral support within a modern aesthetic form: thus, structure and screen become one. The design is an attempt to define "modern" for a civic transportation facility.[33]

Screens—sometimes dense and impenetrable, sometimes light and airy—did not always attempt to hide the underlying structure: occasionally, the function and the contents of the garage were allowed to show through. For several ramp structures built in the 1950s and 1960s in Santa Monica and Beverly Hills, structural engineer T.Y. Lin created veils of metal mesh that floated in front of the garages, softening their appearance and, in effect, creating a new facade. Tampa's Exchange National Bank Building, built in 1967—a nine-story parking ramp with a 13-story bank structure above—had one of the largest aluminum screens in the United States.[34]

One function of the parking facility facade is to prevent the driver from accidentally driving out of the garage; this became particularly important as the open deck—which was very like a "parking lot in the sky"—became the dominant form of the building type. (In 1955 Chicago, for example, parking structures had to be able to restrain a moving force of 40 miles per hour [25 kilometers per hour].) Using screens to restrain vehicles was a means of meeting a functional requirement, but it also allowed the facade of the structure to be as modern as the interior. At Chicago's Public Garage No. 1, built in 1955, stainless-steel turnbuckles and fittings and a twisted strand made of seven stainless-steel wires were used to meet code—but were also part of a decorative screen that, when viewed from a distance, disappeared entirely.[35]

Resistance to the Modernist Aesthetic

When Louis Sullivan coined the term *functionalism,* he was referring to an architecture of engineering—which, while practical, economical, and efficient, was based upon the world of work. Emil Utitz recognized the insufficiency of this approach early on: "Men require warmth and rejoicing, splendor and brilliance . . . elegance . . . the qualities of life appropriate to the hours after work is done."[36] By the mid-1920s, artists, architects, architectural theorists, and cultural critics had begun to criticize the modernist aesthetic.[37] As John Dewey notes in *Art as Experience,*

The living being is characterized by having a past and a present; having them as possessions of the present, not just externally. And I suggest that this is precisely when we get from an art product the feeling of dealing with a career, a history, perceived at a particular point of its development, that we have the impression of life. That which is dead does not extend into the past nor arouse any interest in what is to come.[38]

The building type most likely to reflect functionalist ideals was the parking garage—which meant that, in Dewey's terms, the type was "dying" almost from its inception. According to Penny Sparke, in *An Introduction to Design and Culture in the Twentieth Century,*

It was those critics . . . [who] supported the functionalist ideals of the Modern Movement in the interwar years who helped to perpetuate the myth that "good design" is synonymous with the machine aesthetic, who ignored the meanings that society was to come to associate with that particular design movement, and who thereby turned design into a heroic rather than an everyday concept. However, design . . . plays a fundamental role, both practical and psychological, within daily life.[39]

Once garage design had become purely functional—that is, with its internal purpose reflected on the exterior—the size, location, and design of these ubiquitous structures moved the building type to the forefront of aesthetic controversy. Public reaction reached an all-time low in the late 1980s, when the residents of Des Plaines, Illinois, referred to their garage, which had been constructed in the late 1970s, as the "concrete casket" and the "Berlin Wall," and an alderman nicknamed the garage "the Zit." (The structure has since been torn down.) Although some entrepreneurs, architects, engineers, and planners had always understood the importance of aesthetics in parking garage design, not until the late 1980s did the issue begin to receive broad recognition. In 1988, the American Planning Association issued a report entitled *The Aesthetics of Parking;* as one of the first publications to identify aesthetic issues for parking lots and garages, the report initiated a new era.[40]

At its best, architecture taps the deepest meanings of the past, the present, and the future. A new aesthetic cannot survive unless it expresses and reflects *meaning;* anything less is merely a style. Why not express meaning in a structure such as the parking garage? Why not celebrate daily life by exploring a new aesthetic for a commonplace structure?

Yesterday's Aesthetic Approaches: Today's Best Practices

A look at how scale, visual integration, ornament, and other issues were addressed in the past can offer clues for new solutions—either adaptations of past architectural approaches or, better yet, fresh applications of the skills and traditions of architectural design. The beaux-arts tradition gave designers the tools to mediate differences between the human scale and the machine scale, and to successfully integrate garage structures into the urban fabric. By dividing the monolithic, large-scale facade into multiple layers and distinct visual elements, designers avoided the long horizontal ribbons that typified later parking structures, exaggerating their already excessive size and scale. Although the beaux-arts aesthetic is no longer part of today's living architectural language, elements of the tradition can be successfully applied to modern problems.

Ornament

During the 1980s, as part of the postmodern movement, ornament reappeared, although often in a tongue-in-cheek way.[41] One of the best examples was the facade of Chicago's Lake Street Garage, designed by Stanley Tigerman and built in 1986: a large-scale replica of a 1930s Rolls Royce grille, hood ornament included. The structure, successfully integrated into the urban fabric, is like a found sculpture from the city's past, suggesting that the car itself is an ornament to the city. Interestingly, the facade is similar to a 1915 recommendation for a "radiator facade theme" that appeared in an article on garage design in *The Horseless Age*.[42] In both the 1915 example and Tigerman's garage, visually embedding the car within the surrounding urban architecture becomes a visual metaphor for the challenge of placing parking within urban design.[43]

In the entry pavilion for a hospital in Monterey, California, constructed in 2003–2004, ornament appears in a more serious way: a small band of squares, interspersed with rectangular voids, adds a bit of finish—almost creating a cornice on the otherwise simple design. In downtown Detroit, a handsome parking garage built in 2006 replicates the ornament on the opera house that it serves, creating a parking structure worthy of this automobile city. In an approach that has become relatively common, a parking structure in downtown Orlando, features ornamental ironwork on the facade that complements the brick exterior. More flamboyant (or

Top: Lake Street Garage, Chicago, 1986. With a facade that mimics the front end of a car wedged into the streetfront, this garage pokes fun at the automobile.

Above: Entry Pavilion Parking Structure, Monterey, California, 2004. The simple but serious use of ornament gives this parking structure a beautiful entry.

ironic) uses of ornament still abound: examples include the "Bookbindings" parking garage for the Kansas City Downtown Library; the parking structure for the Boulder Station Hotel Casino, in Las Vegas; and the parking structure for the New York–New York Hotel and Casino, also in Las Vegas. Although ornament enlivens the entire facades of these buildings, it is not integral to the design, as it was in the beaux-arts tradition and in the facades of early showrooms; instead, it appears only as appliqué.[44]

Stairways and Entry Points

The functional elements of garages—such as stairways, elevator cores, and entry points—offer opportunities to bring visual touches to the building type. Many garages designed within the postmodernist tradition address such key design elements.

During the "growth period" of the parking facility, garage designers attempted to accommodate pedestrians by linking parking structures with destinations, often by means of "celebrated stairs." One of the first examples of a celebrated stair was designed by Welton Becket and Associates in the late 1940s, when a double-deck parking facility was constructed on the site of the parking lot of the Bullock's Wilshire department store, in Los Angeles. The designers maintained the existing porte cochere, with its 1929 ceiling fresco painted by Herman Sochs; on the second floor of the new structure, they built a second porte cochere, for pedestrians. A new stairway of white travertine, with walls of flecked, varicolored limestone, connected the lower level of the parking structure to the pedestrian porte cochere. By the 1990s, celebrated stairs had become the norm: the expansive stairway that leads from the parking structure to the beach in Hermosa Beach, California, is just one example.[45]

At a ramp garage designed for Stanford University in 1987, the Watry Design Group created a three-story open space for the automobile entry points, and free-floating stair towers within the structure. By treating the garage as an aesthetic whole, the designers created a feeling of expansiveness for pedestrians and drivers alike. At the Georgia World Congress Center International Plaza, built in Atlanta in 1992, the architecture firm of Thompson, Ventulett, Stainback and Associates created a monumental stairway that rises from the underground garage and runs parallel to a sloping yellow wall; the relationship between the stair and the wall creates a sense of openness and connects the underground parking structure to the sky above. At the University of Cal-

Top: Hermosa Beach parking structure, Hermosa Beach, California, 1999. Stairs are highlighted in this structure, providing a grand and gracious transition to the street and to the beach beyond.

Above: University of California at Davis Medical Center Parking Structure II, Sacramento, California, 1999. In this structure, stairs are an elaborate design element, providing places to stop and reflect as part of the transition experience.

ifornia at Davis Medical Center Parking Structure II, built in 1999, an angled wall is interwoven with the stairs and the elevators—a design that creates balconies and lookouts, assists with way-finding, and celebrates pedestrian access to the garage.[46]

In a direct and relatively simple approach to honoring the pedestrian, stairwells and elevators have often been relocated:

Above left: Gotham Hotel garage, New York City, 1967. Especially at the time this structure was built, integrating a garage into the urban fabric was a difficult proposition; nevertheless, the designers succeeded with a modern yet respectful approach.

Above right: Anchor Shops and Parking, Miami Beach, 2003. This structure is one example of several active and inviting structures created by the firm of Zyscovich, Inc., in downtown Miami Beach. Zyscovich's approach to parking design includes excellent place-making techniques.

Right: Omaha Park Six garage, Omaha, Nebraska, 2002. Although the city did not want responsibility for ground-level shops in this facility, it did want safe and pleasant sidewalks. This is one among several parking structures that have attractive facades and generous landscaping, which combine to soften the sidewalk experience.

moved to the exterior and surrounded with glass, which gives them a presence all their own while maintaining a visual connection to the surroundings. Stair towers, whether simple or flamboyant, have been used to create the sense of a gateway, or to connect garages visually with their surroundings. At the Sarasota County parking facility, for example, built in 1991, a domed tile roof adds a Mediterranean flavor and helps the structure blend in with nearby municipal buildings. The Todos Santos parking center, constructed in 2002 in Concord, California, was designed to complement the historic Todos Santos Plaza, particularly with respect to key elements such as the stairs and the landscaped pathways for pedestrians. At a parking facility built in Winter Park, Florida, in 2005, the exceptional height of the stair towers at the corners of the structure creates a visual focus, and the addition of a lattice cornice helps to visually link the facility to the street corners.[47]

Facades

New York's Gotham Hotel garage, built in 1967, was a successful attempt to incorporate a new facade into the urban fabric while respecting the surrounding streetfront. The facility's aluminum-trimmed windows and dimensional facade created a new architectural statement that was nevertheless compatible with the existing brick- and stone-faced buildings on the block.[48]

In Omaha, a coherent program for integrating garages into the civic tradition has yielded many exciting structures, such as the Omaha Park Six garage, built in 2002. Omaha has also taken a different approach to the sidewalk edge: because the city owns and operates a number of municipal garages, it did not want the added responsibility of dealing with first-floor retail (a now-common approach); instead, garage facades are given special attention through material, scale, ornament, lighting, and landscaping. The result yields a wonderful pedestrian environment.[49]

In Miami Beach, which has recently become something of a laboratory for the parking facility, many garages have been built in an updated version of the South Beach art deco style. The visual quality of these structures—especially the four created by Zyscovich, Inc.—reaches beyond the facilities themselves, revitalizing and rejuvenating this vibrant beach town.[50]

The Screen

As examples earlier in this chapter have demonstrated, expressions of movement have been an essential feature of the urban form. A coexisting impulse, however, has been to bring everything to a stop, and even to move backward, toward an idealized vision of the past. With the end of the load-bearing facade, the appearance of the garage ceased to be grounded in the realities of construction, as it had been in the beaux-arts era. It is now possible to "appliqué" virtually anything to the exterior of a parking structure—including visual touches that hark back to a past that never was. Given modern construction techniques, however, the ideal is to combine structure and screen. For example, the detailed screen on Memphis's Clark Tower garage, built in 1972, combines arches and a curved, suspended ramp to create an unforgettable visual experience. It is the mix of past, present, and future that gives this building life.[51]

The expression of modernity has become synonymous with the repetition of bold, simple, abstract, frozen movement; witness Santa Monica Place, a California mall designed by Frank Gehry in the 1980s. The screen in front of the parking garage features the words "Santa Monica Place" in letters nearly four stories high, angled in such a way that they seem to be flying off the building—an expression of both speed and disconnection.[52]

In a 1991 garage designed for Princeton University by Machado Silvetti Architects, the combination of modern architectural language and beaux-arts traditions yielded a vibrant piece of architecture that is equally suited to the modern world and to the traditional aesthetic of the campus. The impetus for the design was an existing 20-foot- (six-meter-) high brick garden wall originally designed by McKim, Mead, and White. A nonpatinizing double-lattice bronze screen on the three levels of parking above the wall extends the idea of a garden enclosure. The south side of the structure features a simpler screen with ivy growing on it, extending the garden idea further. On the north side, the screen stands free of the wall, creating an arcade for a path that leads to the garage entry. Floating freely beside the stair tower is yet another screen, in this case a copper panel. A cornice reminiscent of the great beaux-arts cornices adds flair to the screen, bringing the parking garage back into the tradition of the civic building.[53]

Sometimes the only way to move forward is to move backward—that is, to pause, take a deep breath, and rediscover abandoned paths. At Ballet Valet, a garage designed by Arquitectonica in the South Beach district of Miami, the screen is a shrub-covered fiberglass trellis that begins at the second level of the structure; the approach to camouflaging the parking facility is reminiscent of the example in chapter 1, in which a barn covered with growing vines advertised itself as a garage. The ground-floor streetfront offers a traditional, small-town shopping experience; meanwhile, greenery rises to the sky above—an effect that is unnatural, to say the least.[54]

The idea of hiding—rather than screening—the garage has also enjoyed a resurgence. Among the most unusual efforts along these lines is a six-story billboard, built in 1999, that faces Atlanta's Centennial Olympic Park. Built after the fact, specifically to hide the garage that stands behind it, the billboard features both a 17-foot by 22-foot (five-meter by seven-meter) video screen for advertisements and a clock whose face is larger than that of London's Big Ben. Unsurprisingly, the notion of advertising looming over a beautiful public park generated controversy.[55]

In the late 1960s, both Dayton's Department Store, in St. Paul, Minnesota, and Quille's Parking, in Baltimore, featured integrated screens. At Dayton's, the design proved to be a mistake: the garage was so well concealed that it took five years for customers to realize that it was there. Nevertheless, facades that make the parking garage look like any other building on the street can be very successful in mediating the issues of scale and size; Chicago's Government Center, built in 2006, is just one of many examples.[56]

Portland, Oregon: Art for the Parking Garage

Portland, Oregon, has always been at the forefront of transportation management.[1] Portland incorporated "design for the automobile" into its master planning in the 1920s and 1930s, and was one of the first cities to do so. By encouraging the private sector to construct parking from the 1940s through the 1970s, Portland continued to be a leader in addressing the parking problem.[2]

Although all cities faced the challenge of ever-increasing automobile use, Portland took an innovative approach earlier than most: in the 1980s, the city used federal highway dollars to build mass-transit systems. Parking in close proximity to train stations was thus an important element in the overall functioning of the system. And as the city became directly involved in the construction of parking facilities, art was integrated into the design process: four parking structures, one of which was built as early as 1979, include artwork.[3]

In the late 1980s, Portland decided, as a matter of policy, to install public art in its downtown parking garages. Since art was already required on all public buildings, this decision effectively recognized the garage as a civic structure. The first piece, *118 Modules*, is part of a 1979 facility located at SW 10th and Yamhill. The work was created by John Rodgers and funded by the Comprehensive Educational Training Act. In 1985, another work—*Electronic Poet*, by Keith Jellum—was added to the same garage, this time through the city's Percent for Art Program, which requires that 1 percent of construction costs for major capital improvement projects be dedicated to art.

In 1990, Bill Will's *Streetwise* and Lee Hunt's *A Human Comedy* were added to the garage at 4th and Yamhill—providing, through both visual communication and the written word, a place to pause and think about the human condition. (And where better to do so than in a parking facility?) The bricks of *Streetwise*, which surround the garage, feature quotations that reflect on time and movement as parts of life. The sculpted images of *A Human Comedy* remind viewers that emotions are universal.

In 1992, two more installations were added. The first, a neon project for the facility on the corner of NW 1st and Davis, brings another dimension to a structure that was already well designed and had successfully engaged the street and the urban experience. At the SW 3rd and Alder facility, Gary Hirsch's *Upstream Downtown* activates the blank spaces of an otherwise fairly typical parking structure: large, brightly patterned fish float in the open voids of the facade.

Portland's decision to integrate art into the parking experience brings life and movement to the city, even for those who do not park.

Top: John Rodgers, *118 Modules*, Portland, Oregon, 1979.

Above: Gary Hirsch, *Upstream Downtown*, Portland, Oregon, 1992.

Parking facility, Gannett headquarters, McLean, Virginia, 2001. A glass facade gives a degree of sophistication to a parking facility.

Other designs—in which, for example, a glass facade completely hides the parking structure—are more elegant: in the early 1950s, the American National Bank, in Austin, Texas, became one of the first structures to feature a beautifully integrated facade for shops, the bank, and parking on the top two floors. At one end of the facility was an elegant composition: the habitable portion of the building featured a glass and metal curtain wall, and the parking garage above featured the same visual aesthetic, rendered in the form of a screen; the other end, however, which faced the street, was a blank wall. The concrete structure of the parking facility is visually related to the concrete columns at the street level. This layering of shapes and textures reflects many lessons from early parking structures, minus the ornament; the result is a "classical" modern building that will stand the test of time. Many new, although not as sophisticated, versions of the glass facade can be found today.[57]

Art in the Parking Garage

Art became common in both commercial and municipal parking garages in the 1990s. Art has a way of engaging peo-

ple with the world, and this is no less true in a parking garage than in a museum. Seventh Street Station, built in 1998, is one of seven public parking garages constructed by Bank of America in Charlotte, North Carolina. Artist Christopher Janney was commissioned to clad the ten-story, 1,600-car facility with a multimedia piece entitled *Touch My Building:* a visitor can press any one of 64 interactive plates on the facade and watch them glow, change color, and emit sounds. Inside, the structure has colorful mosaics designed by StudioWorks, along with 36 tiles, inspired by images of the Earth's strata, that were created by children at local elementary schools. The Bank of America garages are celebratory and interactive environments that explore timeless matters, such as nature and history, as well as more immediate concerns, such as the joy of car travel and the sense of freedom and equality that has become associated with it. Another example of Janney's work, entitled *Maritime Sound,* is featured at the Long Wharf Garage, which was built in New Haven, Connecticut in 2002, for the Fusco Corporation.[58]

At the Nashville International Airport, in a short-term parking garage built in 2001, internationally renowned light artist Michael Hayden has created *Arpeggio,* a lighting installation

Seventh Street Station Parking Facility, Charlotte, North Carolina, 1996. Artwork is often a part of the facade or the interior of parking facilities. The art integrated into this facility was created by Christopher Janney, and allows visitors to control light and sound by touching the building facade.

The Parking Garage

that is designed to continuously change its appearance. Hayden's focus has always been on art in public spaces, and this piece, which is positioned above the moving sidewalks within the parking structure, underscores the idea that the interior of the garage is not only a public space, but an important one: it is the first and the last impression that visitors receive of the airport.[59]

Art for parking garages can be low cost; however, it must create the sense that it is part of a living tradition. When Milwaukee's Second Street Garage was renovated, a bas-relief of the city skyline, with a neon band running through it, was added to the blank north facade. Something as simple as differently colored handrails, combined with panels of alternating textures, reflects a desire to visually engage the user. It is important, however, not to focus on mere visual touches but on the meaning of buildings—what they convey. In *Designs and Their Consequences: Architecture and Aesthetics*, Richard Hill notes that "in Kant's theory, usefulness is not located in our pleasure in the practical adaptedness of buildings, but in the concept of use and aesthetic ideas that bring them to life."[60] Here again is the word *life*—the idea that part of the aesthetic goal is to create something that is alive. Architectural training combines the practical and the artistic, the functional and the aesthetic. But how can a parking garage be beautiful? The answer to this question poses challenges, and offers satisfactions, that architects do not encounter in any other building type.[61]

Preserving the Urban Fabric

Architect J.J.P. Oud wrote in 1918 that "one thing is certain; the aesthetics of modern buildings will not be based on the buildings of the past: they will be shaped by the essential characteristics of modern society and technology, and therefore will be completely different from those of any previous period."[62] But the best art and architecture find a way to bridge the present and the past. To break with the past is to deny the continuity of life.

As historic preservation has become an increasingly vital aspect of architecture and urban design, garages old and new need to be considered in relation to the fabric of the city. Designers have used a number of approaches to weave the parking garage into its surroundings; the best designs complement nearby structures without cloying mimicry of past traditions. In some cases, a historic facade is preserved, but a new parking structure is built behind it. In other cases, new

garages are designed to match their context. In Watsonville, California, the Beach Street Retail and Parking Structure, constructed in 1993, became part of a successful rehabilitation of a downtown that had been destroyed by fire. In other cases, adding brick to a garage facade has been considered gesture enough.[63]

Savannah is an interesting case, as one of its famous green squares was appropriated for a parking facility that not only damaged the city's beautifully planned urban structure, but was visually incongruous as well. The city is now reclaiming this green as open space and moving the garage underground; it has also mandated that new parking structures honor the historic fabric of the city. Savannah's Bryan Street Garage, designed by Carl Walker, Inc., in the 1990s, is a relatively recent example of a parking facility that fits into its surroundings. The approach succeeds by maintaining traditional scale, massing, detail, and relationships between solids and voids on the facade (although additional techniques, such as retail, could have been used to enliven the streetfront). Charleston, South Carolina, offers a number of excellent examples of aesthetic interventions in a historic city.[64]

One of the more successful reinterpretations of the past is a new parking structure that was designed to look as if it had been in its current small-town setting for the past 100 years. Located in Staunton, Virginia, and constructed in 2001, the New Street Garage was designed by Frazier Associates and has won both a Palladio Award (from *Traditional Building*) and an International Parking Institute award for design.

New Street Parking Garage, Staunton, Virginia, 2001. The design strategy for this small-town parking structure was based on the notion, common in the early 20th century, of the garage as civic building.

The Aesthetics of the Parking Garage

Charleston, South Carolina: Revitalization through Parking

If any community grasps the importance of the parking garage for revitalization, it is Charleston, South Carolina. Charleston's history of using parking to reinvigorate the community dates back nearly 40 years—and the current mayor, Joe Riley, remains committed to this approach.[1]

In the early 1970s, when Charleston constructed the first of many new garages, city officials realized that integrating these large and often deadening structures into the historic urban fabric would not be easy. Under the direction of Mayor Riley, however, a coherent philosophy evolved that continues to be successfully implemented today: Charleston parking structures are designed to be attractive, to screen cars, to activate the street, and to be integral elements in revitalization efforts. The city itself has constructed more than ten facilities throughout Charleston and has directed the development of others. Many lessons can be learned from Charleston's sensible, holistic, detail-oriented, pedestrian-friendly approach.[2]

Before 1930, several public garages existed in Charleston, but by the mid-1950s, the city had few parking structures, when compared with other cities of comparable size. Parking was generally relegated to empty lots, or to areas near automobile-related buildings, tenement buildings, or condemned properties. As Charleston's institutions of higher education grew and as the tourist trade blossomed, the parking problem became increasingly severe. Although Charleston is a walkable city, residents, students, and visitors alike were caught up in a pattern of using automobiles even for short trips. Large garages had to be located where open spaces were not necessarily available—which meant integrating them into a walkable, small-scale, historic urban environment. The overall strategy was to preserve the basic structure of this walkable city while incorporating the necessities of modern life for residents, students, and visitors.

An early, pivotal project, the award-winning Charleston Place, was planned and built between 1979 and 1986. Although some older

structures had to be destroyed to make room for this large-scale mixed-use project, some were retained as a means of integrating parking. But the question was how to provide parking.

Charleston Place used a number of successful strategies. To begin with, the entry to the hotel parking structure was positioned in the center of the block, off an existing alley. The alley was then transformed into a beautiful path for pedestrians and automobiles that featured retail, sidewalks, a fountain, and bicycle parking, in addition to the hotel entry. Because automobiles enter and exit the garage from the alley, there is minimal impact on traffic or pedestrian movement on the main street. So that it would not be visible from the street, the 450-space parking garage was positioned 30 feet (nine meters) behind preserved historic storefronts. Finally, the facade on the alley side features louvered openings that mimic those found on many historic Charleston buildings, which helps to create a "main street" ambience.

These strategies—creating an entry off a smaller street or alley, visually integrating the garage with other buildings on the street, and viewing parking as a means of enlivening a public space—were repeated, where possible, on garages constructed later. In the case of some newer garages, where there was no historic fabric to speak of, ground-floor retail was included. Other parking facilities engage the sidewalk through screening and plantings, so that the walking experience is always a pleasant one. Along one very narrow alley, the sidewalk was integrated into the parking structure, providing a safe path for pedestrians. Whether a garage is across from a historic structure or integrated into a larger project, the human scale is always taken into account—the most difficult aspect of parking facility design.

Where it was not possible to position the parking structure off an alley, other approaches were used. For example, at the Francis Marion Hotel, on King Street, the parking facility is not identifiable as such unless one looks very carefully; however, the facility is well marked, and entering or exiting from King Street is easy. Sidewalk retail and a stepped-back upper level, with a usable terrace facing Marion Square, allow the parking structure to blend in between the historic hotel and a historic church, both of which face the city's central urban park.

The Visitor Reception and Transit Center, which was integrated into an old train depot, creates a welcoming experience: planned and built between 1981 and 1991, the facility offers art, retail, a garden courtyard, and a multimodal transportation hub. Tourists are encouraged to walk to the historic center of the city or to park and take transit. Just around the corner is a beautiful, small-scale residential district that has not been affected by the large-scale transportation facility.[3]

Charleston has learned the art of creating parking facilities that balance the needs of man, machine, and movement—and has thrived because of it. The strategies of the past have been melded with present realities in ways that are instructive for every walkable environment, no matter whether historic or brand-new.

Francis Marion Hotel parking facility, 1996.

The elegant composition of the main facade harks back to civic structures of the past; when one turns the corner, however, a different scale emerges: that of the small-town street. Although this particular design approach would never have been applied in the past, the attention to detail and to proportion allows the garage to fit comfortably within its surroundings, while remaining a proud civic statement.[65]

Larger cities offer examples of parking facilities that are virtually indistinguishable from other buildings: it takes more than a glance to realize that they house cars. A downtown facility in Atlanta, for example, mimics the architectural rhythms, proportions, and scale of the surrounding structures, but in different materials. The Bankoh Parking Center, in Honolulu, features a simple, regular rhythm of rectangular openings that complements the various styles on the street.[66]

Efforts are now underway to preserve older garages. Boston's Motor Mart Garage, designed by Ralph Harrington Doane on the site of the 1905 Park Square Garage, was built between 1926 and 1929 and restored in 1999 by Walker Parking Consultants and Bergmeyer Associates. At the time of its original construction, the 2,000-car garage was considered the largest in the world. The facility, which housed many different functions, featured nine level floors above grade; separate, two-way ramps; and street-level shops. Although classical detailing was present on the attic and roof cornice, the finials, and the dentil work, the facade—a simple rhythm of solids and voids—was on the verge of being modernist. The structure, which garnered its original designer the Harleston Parker Award from the Boston Society of Architects, now houses car-rental agencies, upscale restaurants, and, of course, parking.[67]

Other old garages have also found new lives. The Downtown Garage, in Kansas City, built in 1921, was rebuilt in 1949 to include ramps, and the storefronts were remodeled to provide service to the city once again. In Chicago, the Ritz Garage, built in 1929, is now a beloved bank, with beautiful terra cotta depictions of automobiles on its facade. In the 1970s, Boston renovated the Garage (which had first been a stable and then a parking facility), transforming it into a new shopping experience.[68] In Ocala, Florida, the Marion Motor Works, the garage built in the mid-1930s for the Francis Marion Hotel, was renovated in the 1980s (along with the hotel) to provide office space and parking. In Los Angeles, a beautiful eight-story elevator garage—built in 1924, and originally designed by Curlett and Beelman—was converted into lofts (although the few parking spaces that remain are not nearly

Grand Avenue Garage, Los Angeles, 1924. Some historic parking structures, such as this early elevator garage, have been adapted to other uses. This structure, which has been transformed into the South Park Lofts, a condominium project, was protected by the State Historical Resources Commission.

enough for the condominium owners). The structure is listed by the State Historical Resources Commission. In 1998, Boston's Lincoln Street Garage received a face-lift from Brian Healy Architects, a local architecture firm.[69]

Although many older garages were designed beautifully from the beginning and are still able to serve today's needs, others have fared less well. In 2004, Chicago's Hotel La Salle Garage, a stunning beaux-arts structure, was placed on the Chicagoland Watch List of the city's ten most endangered historic places; because it could not be made functional for today's standards, it was demolished the following year. Some garages that have not fallen to the wrecking ball have been subject to questionable improvements: Baltimore's Mid-City Garage is one such example. In other cases, attempts have been made to protect older garage structures.

Stanford University Medical Center Parking Structure 4, Stanford, California, 2003. The sensitively designed entrance and exit to this underground facility consists of a small glass pavilion that sits lightly on the open green.

Chattanooga's Volunteer Parking Garage, constructed in 1927, was nominated for the National Register of Historic Places in 1980—a first for the building type. In San Francisco, efforts have been made to find adaptive uses for two parking structures on Mission and Turk streets.[70]

Because many buildings classified as modern are now 50 years old or more, it is not only the more traditional structures that are becoming the focus of preservation efforts. The New Haven Veterans Coliseum, for example, has been demolished—and with it, a striking parking facility that "floated" high above the coliseum structure.[71]

A Source of Aesthetic Innovation

From its inception, the parking garage has been a source of innovation. Efforts to meet new functional requirements and to address the conflicting needs of man and machine yielded new forms—internal and external, social and spatial—as well as utopian visions that eventually found their way into more "acceptable" building types.

Many cities have recently enacted codes addressing parking garage design; some, in fact, have attempted to define a single acceptable aesthetic for the building type. Zoning codes in Orlando, Florida; Oak Brook, Illinois; and Irvine,

Glendale, and Los Angeles, California, for example, include specific aesthetic requirements for parking garages, while urban design plans in Boulder, Colorado; Ann Arbor, Michigan; and Portland, Oregon, address the appearance, size, scale, and bulk of parking structures. Such codes have helped to restore the sense that the parking garage is a civic structure worthy of aesthetic attention, rather than a block of cement whose design should be dictated solely by the bottom line; at the same time, however, some of the codes are restrictive enough to discourage new visions and creative architectural solutions.[72]

Aldo Rossi notes in *The Architecture of the City* that "aesthetic intention and the creation of better surroundings for life are the two permanent characteristics of architecture."[73] Architects are trained to perform this difficult balancing act—to meet both functional and aesthetic needs. And the parking garage, because of its particular requirements, demands the best that architecture has to offer. The demands of the automobile inevitably and permanently altered the typical architectural relationships between plan, facade, and section. Thus, the need to mediate the scale of man and machine remains the single greatest challenge in parking garage design.[74]

Beginning in the 1990s, the garage—or at least its facade—became once again the focus of aesthetic energy and attention. In many recent parking garages, the design of the facade has made it possible for the bulk and mass of the facility to find its place within the urban fabric; other garages, however, have fallen victim to "facadomy"—the trend toward preserving the facade of a historic structure and demolishing what once lay behind it—or, worse yet, creating a pastiche of historic styles that is disconnected from the original legitimacy of those styles.[75]

As the garage is increasingly recognized as a living part of the built environment, connected to the past and contributing to the future, other issues beyond the facade need to be taken into account—such as the size of the facility, the need to integrate the structure into its surroundings, and the importance of invigorating the life of the street. One positive trend that dates from the mid-1990s is an increasing willingness to pay for an aesthetic approach to parking garage design. An article in the December 2004 issue of *Building Design and Construction,* for example, notes that "clients have asked to be a little more cost effective in other areas, such as structurally, so that they can keep the architectural enhancements."[76] Other articles in the same issue highlighted new parking facilities that had won awards. At the same time, however, there is the recognition that "a parking garage first has to have some integrity to its use, and then make a contribution to the urban landscape."[77]

The decades to come offer a tremendous opportunity to affirm the vital civic role of this building type, to fully integrate the "inside" and "outside" experiences of the user, and to place the garage firmly within the tradition of architectural beauty. No less than any other building, the garage is an aesthetic object: one need only open one's eyes to see this truth. At the Cartier Foundation for Contemporary Art, built in Paris in 1994, for example, vertical glass screens highlight the small, pavilionlike area where the automobile descends to the automated underground parking garage. At the Stanford University Medical Center Parking Structure 4, built in 2003, the simple concrete and glass pavilion used for pedestrian access frames views of the grassy roof of the underground parking structure. And in Miami, a Publix supermarket and parking facility combine to create the ultimate visual and driving experience, reminiscent of Konstantin Melnikov's *Parking Garage over the Seine.* Unfortunately, examples such as these are rare. Cities and suburbs are filled with gaping holes: parking lots and cavernous garages at virtually every corner, creating an aura of unfulfilled expectations. Yet "prettifying" or historicizing the garage is not the answer: "In the consumer society, beauty can also be a smokescreen—a tool for distracting our attention from the bad and the false."[78] The goal, then, is not simply to create better-looking parking garages, but to move on to the deeper issues of the way Americans think and live.[79] Only through examining parking facilities that have met the functional and aesthetic demands of their place and time is it possible to move forward, into a new aesthetic future.[80]

Past Lessons for the Present and Future

- ⮑ Early parking garages were integrated into the urban fabric; this practice is undergoing a resurgence today.

- ⮑ The beaux-arts facade mediated differences in scale, enabling the larger parking facility to appear smaller and more compatible with the surrounding urban setting. It is important for today's architects to learn the techniques of the beaux-arts tradition—not as a stylistic approach, but as part of the art of architecture.

- ⮑ As the perception of movement and of the landscape changed, these shifts found expression in architecture. The thrill of the exposed ramp and the modern evocations of movement are invaluable parts of the American aesthetic.

- ⮑ Stair towers and entry points are logical places to begin to address aesthetic issues.

- ⮑ The facade of the parking facility plays an important role in mediating between the scales of man and machine, individual and civic. To create a design that is pleasing and appropriate from every perspective, all exposed facades need to be considered.

- ⮑ The base of the facade offers an opportunity to create an active pedestrian experience; similarly, lobbies—once neglected—can again be beautifully designed and made an integral part of the parking facility.

- ⮑ Hiding parking behind greenery or moving it underground are valuable approaches in certain settings; nevertheless, they are only two of the many available solutions.

- ⮑ Ultimately, the goal is not to hide the parking garage but to incorporate it into an active, vital aesthetic; it is a living, breathing, civic building type that reflects the entirety of the American experience.

CHAPTER 9

Parking in the Context of Urban Planning

T he relationship between parking and urban design was the pivotal planning issue of the 20th century, and promises to remain one of the crucial issues of the 21st. How a building relates to its surroundings is always of primary importance, and the parking garage is no exception. But the relationship between the garage and the rest of the built environment is particularly intense and interactive because of the centrality of parking to urban planning. As city dwellers discovered early in the 20th century, where parking is inadequate, cars take over the streets, bringing the entire metropolis to a standstill.

How can the car—which functions in many ways as a modern "living space"—be incorporated into urban plans? The early history of the garage offers many lessons on integrating the parking facility into the urban fabric, connecting it to other buildings, and combining it with transit. All these strategies—and more—are necessary if today's urban and suburban environments are to survive.

Facing page: City Center West parking facility, Oakland, California, 1993. The facade of this garage includes steps where people can sit and view public performances—yet another means of integrating parking into a downtown and helping to reinvigorate the area.

The City Comes to a Standstill

In the early years of automobile use, the construction of parking garages was still under debate, and cars were often parked on the street by default. The combination of increasing traffic and parked automobiles created serious problems in many cities: in Los Angeles, for example, during late afternoon rush hour, the streetcars were often rendered immobile. By 1918, garages had proliferated to such an extent that *The Horseless Age,* which published a list of all the new garages in the country, could not keep up. Nevertheless, the need for parking was still not being met. In Boston in the 1920s, publicly owned plots of land were converted into massive parking lots; in nearby Cambridge, drivers insisted on parking on the historic Cambridge Commons. And in Chicago, Grant Park was being used for parking.[1]

In 1920, a survey showed that Los Angeles was one of the worst cities for traffic: it had the largest number of motor vehicles per capita, and, after Columbus, Ohio, the second-smallest ratio of street area to built-up area. That same year, Robert H. Whitten, of the Cleveland City Plan Commission, noted in *The American City* that traffic increases had begun to follow predictable patterns: each time the population doubled, the street traffic tripled, and the number of vehicle trips (including both automobile and transit trips) quadrupled. Between 1910 and 1918, the national increase in the number of private motor cars was "77% times as great as the percentage increase in population."[2] Whitten observed in the same article that on Massachusetts highways between 1909 and 1918, traffic had increased 14.5 times faster than the population.[3]

Meanwhile, two other factors were contributing to congestion: the advent of the tall building, and the use of the new mechanized vehicles to transport goods. The tall building had arrived early in the 20th century, almost concurrently with the automobile, generating numerous conflicts about how the American city should grow. Because tall buildings could house more people—whether workers or residents—on a small plot of land, congestion was inevitable. Some cities responded by limiting building height; others expanded transportation of every kind to meet demand; still others did both. As for motor transport of goods, although it held out the promise of increased prosperity, the delays caused by congestion could easily eliminate any economic advantage. In an article published in *The American City*, F.W. Fenn, of the National Motor Truck Committee and the

Top: State and Madison, Chicago, 1910. At the beginning of the 20th century, the congestion on the streets was even greater than it is today.

Bottom: Grant Park parking lot, Chicago, circa 1920. Until parking garages were constructed, older downtowns made use of large, open areas of land for parking.

Parking in the Context of Urban Planning

Rockefeller Center, New York City, 1930s. Tall buildings and mixed-use structures included parking from the beginning, even when they were built near mass transit.

National Automobile Chamber of Commerce, urged cities to form transportation committees to evaluate the various options for transporting goods, to determine what was best for their community. At the same time, however, Fenn extolled the virtues of motor-trucking goods.[4]

Daniel Burnham and Edward Bennett's 1909 plan for Chicago was the first coherent effort to address a city's transportation system as a whole and to provide multiple transportation options. In other cities, the automobile and its effects were dealt with piecemeal: in 1913, a paper delivered at the Fifth National Conference on City Planning, in Chicago, noted that transportation facilities—including parking—were not being adequately considered in urban plans.[5]

By the close of the 1920s, the number of workers commuting by automobile in some cities—including Washington D.C., Kansas City, and St. Louis—outnumbered those commuting by transit. Especially where the streets had been cleared of parked cars, the faster-moving autos quickly made the streetcar obsolete. Parking lots and garages became essential parts of urban planning and design, and planners, architects, engineers, and entrepreneurs struggled to determine how best to incorporate these facilities. It was

not until after World War II, however, that integrated planning approaches could be put into place at a large scale.[6]

Early Regulatory Efforts

In 1921, for the first time in U.S. history, the percentage of the population living in cities exceeded that living in rural areas. Transportation had become the "keynote of prosperity," and clogged city streets were viewed as a threat to economic progress.[7] As congestion continued to mount, parking became the focus of discussion.[8] A 1923 article in *The American City* suggested that parking garages would not solve the problem of congestion because they "would occupy valuable area," and because those who arrived at work early enough would simply seek street parking near their place of employment.[9]

Thus, although garages continued to be constructed, regulation of street parking was viewed as key to solving the parking problem. In Boston as early as 1899, cars were banned from "the public parks or boulevards" between 10:30 a.m. and 9:00 p.m., and were prohibited from parking at all in certain parts of the city.[10] In many cities, public officials and

218   The Parking Garage

citizens believed that on-street parking would eventually be completely prohibited. In 1920, Los Angeles spelled out parking rules for various locations and times of day and night. (The formation of the Los Angeles Planning Commission, that same year, was largely a response to traffic problems.) In 1923, Columbus, Ohio, implemented parking requirements as part of its zoning code for multifamily dwellings; Columbus is believed to be the first city to have enacted such requirements. In the decades that followed, as the number of cars dramatically increased, and developed areas became more dense, the need to link specific land uses with a particular number of parking spaces became even more pressing.[11] In some cases, parking regulations were not thought through before being implemented: a 1928 Cincinnati ordinance, which allowed local property owners to control the parking on the street area in front of their stores, eventually had to be revoked because "the city has ample power to control the use of the streets, and to regulate travel over the same, . . . but it is elementary that it cannot delegate such powers to an individual."[12]

At the 1923 National Conference on City Planning, held in Baltimore, Hugh Young, of the Chicago Plan Commission, presented the findings of a survey he had conducted of representatives from most of the major cities in the United States.[13] A number of Young's recommendations—including the regulation and enforcement of time limits for parking, the development of economically sound plans for daytime parking in congested districts, and the construction of garages in connection with new building development—are still in use today. That same year, in Boston, at the convention of the Motor and Accessory Manufacturers Association, a proposal was put forth recommending legislation that would require every newly constructed building to incorporate adequate parking: "If department stores have found it advantageous to rent or construct free garages for the benefit of their patrons, the owner of an office building or apartment house would find it equally 'good business.'"[14] A number of organizations and individuals were sympathetic to this point of view. In a 1926 article in *The American City*—"To Park or Not To Park"—a group of traffic and transportation consultants set forth a number of principles that cities could use for "rational city planning and sound municipal finance."[15] Under this set of principles, the right to move a car trumped the right to store a car; thus, streets and thoroughfares should be used for movement first, and for parking second. The article also noted that "if businessmen found these pre-

cepts to be to the disadvantage of business, they should at their own expense provide storage garages and off-street loading facilities."[16] In other words, the provision of adequate parking was the responsibility of the businesses that needed it, not of the municipality.[17]

Miller McClintock, a traffic expert based at Harvard University, was among those who believed that streets were not meant to provide storage for cars. And, although McClintock noted that some municipal parking lots were revenue sources, he concluded that parking for all new establishments should be required by zoning, and that it should be provided by the business owner. McClintock recommended parking under buildings, citing as an example the University Club Building and Pacific Mutual Life Insurance, in Los Angeles, which jointly provided two stories of basement parking for their employees.[18]

By 1929, a number of specific strategies were still being discussed to deal with the parking problem and the resulting congestion: widening the streets; creating parking lots; constructing private or municipal garages; reserving lanes for moving traffic; and reserving lanes for parking only. For their part, city officials believed that by providing parking within the central business district, within a five- or ten-minute walk of the central business district, and outside the central business district, they could solve the parking problem. But cities are living, breathing organisms that, at the time, were expanding rapidly; what may have looked like a perfect solution one day was likely to be outdated the next. And one of the most obvious solutions—mass transit, either alone or in combination with the automobile—was also one of the most controversial.

The mid-1930s brought a new approach to street parking: charging for it. The first coin-operated parking meters, which had been invented by Carl Magee and developed at the University of Oklahoma, were installed in Oklahoma City on July 17, 1935. Two days later, a court challenge was filed alleging the right to the free use of the street; the challenge was dismissed, however, and the meters were reinstalled. Many jurisdictions followed Oklahoma City's example: in the fall of 1935, 1,000 meters were installed in Dallas alone. Although both merchants and the public were initially resistant, they eventually accepted metering; in fact, where the devices had been installed on only one side of the street, municipalities were asked to install them on both sides. Although the initial purpose of the meters was to compel more rapid turnover of the cars on the street, not to make money for the municipality, the advantages of the revenue stream quickly became clear. In some cities, revenue from parking meters (and from fines) partially funded the purchase of parking lots and the construction of much-needed parking decks; in other cities, however, the revenue from the meters became a source of contention.[19]

Although the delivery of goods by means of trucks continued to be a problem, by 1947, most cities had ordinances requiring deliveries to be made very early in the morning, to prevent trucks from impeding rush-hour traffic. The construction of delivery terminals and the inclusion of loading docks within new buildings also helped. Because Cleveland's APCOA 666 Garage, built in the 1950s, included storefronts, it also had separate entrances for trucks.[20]

Roads, Mass Transit, and the First Multimodal Hubs

Despite some support for requiring cars to move at lower speeds—which would have made them the equal of streetcars in efficiency, and allowed the two forms of transportation to continue to exist side by side—cities were more likely to invest in higher-speed thoroughfares for cars than in mass transit. And people everywhere were demanding, and getting, broad thoroughfares. In part, the choice was a matter of economics: as Robert H. Whitten noted in 1920, "for Cleveland the present cost of the necessary street widenings and extensions to provide a complete thoroughfare system will during the next fifty years be saved many times over in lessened expenditure for rapid transit subways."[21]

By the beginning of the 20th century, parkways, first employed by Frederick Law Olmsted in Central Park in 1858, had been built in parks and residential areas across the country—including Boston, Chicago, and Kansas City. However, it was William K. Vanderbilt (who constructed the Long Island Motor Parkway between 1906 and 1911) and Robert Moses (who used 1924 state legislation to construct parkways in New York) who popularized the notion of reserving roads for high-speed motor vehicle travel between the city and the suburbs.[22]

In most cities, in the course of the 20th century, it eventually became easier and faster to drive a car than to use public transit. However, early in the century, in cities such as New York and Chicago—where congestion was most severe, and where no parking was allowed on the streets—transit was more efficient than auto travel, and cars were used only for pleasure, or for business outside of the areas served by public transportation.[23] But transit was more than a practical matter: it was also a political issue—to the point that, during the 1920s, "Chicago's business community worked with others to depoliticize mass transit and remove it from the arena of controversy over social policy."[24]

Although most mass transit had initially been constructed using private capital, this source had dried up by 1930, so solutions tended to focus on the construction of roads and parking garages. City officials believed that, at least from a planning perspective, the parking problem had been solved: the provision of parking was typically mandated through zoning and other ordinances, and supply would eventually catch up with demand. Meanwhile, mass transit—apart from buses—faded into the background for many decades.[25] A 1929 article in *The American City* summed up prevailing attitudes nicely: "And last, but of prime importance, we need a willingness on the part of great foundations and men of means to invest funds in demonstration towns and subdivision developments planned for the motor-age."[26] Some 40 years later, author Studs Terkel explained the relationship between cars and mass transit this way: "I ask how come the emphasis on cars, so little on mass transit? Well, it's a question of power, isn't it? General Motors, I think, has slightly more clout than I as a pedestrian have and that pretty much explains it. There's a bit more moolah there to pass around, is there not?"[27]

Philadelphia was one of the first cities to recognize the value of combining modes of transportation. In the plan initiated in 1925 by the Philadelphia Rapid Transit Company, drivers parked their cars in lots that ringed the central business district, then used streetcars to reach the city center. The three parking areas held 850 cars, and expansion plans were in the works. By 1929, a number of other cities—including Akron, Baltimore, Boston, Chicago, and Poughkeepsie—had built similar suburban parking stations, which succeeded in encouraging the use of mass transit while removing cars from city streets. These systems worked so well, in fact, that St. Louis officials considered a similar arrangement using buses. In Rochester, New York, in 1929, businessmen who lived in an exclusive residential area were transported by bus directly to the commercial district, an arrangement that often made it possible for the family to own only one car.[28]

Supporters of mass transit observed that in the competition between mass transit and the private auto, it was the auto that had been given pride of place: "To appreciate the extent to which the parked automobile has become a parasite on the streets, consider the howl of execration that goes up if a trolley car is parked on a siding!"[29] Given the amount of street area used by autos in proportion to the number of passengers that they carried, those in favor of mass transit found it preposterous when car owners complained of having to wait for three minutes for a stopped trolley car to clear out of the way. In 1926, an article in *The American City Magazine* noted that "the people who complain most about the prevailing congestion… are compelling the wrong kind of transit development that in turn is perpetuating the evil that they themselves are crying out loudest against."[30] A 1927 study of the relationship between automobiles and mass transit in nine major cities, conducted by John A. Beeler, a public utility consultant, found that "the more rapid-transit service a city has, the greater the riding habit and the lower the rate of registration of private automobiles per 1,000 population."[31] As "the cure for our vicious circle," Daniel Turner, a consulting engineer for the New York Transit Commission, recommended "educating the people as to the causes of the trouble and to the necessity of constructing new rapid-transit lines that will decentralize our cities' activities."[32]

By the mid-1940s, 30 cities had transit systems operated by the cities themselves—and although transit continued to be discussed as a means of addressing both congestion and parking needs, increasing interest in highways made transit a tough sell: as a 1944 article in *The American City* noted, "spectacular highway plans can be presented in futuristic panoramas that appeal to the eye and the imagination, for we all like to picture ourselves rolling down a great, broad highway, in a luxurious car, escaping from the cares and restraints of a work-a-day world."[33] The editions of the American Automobile Association's *Parking Manual* published in the 1940s and 1950s described how to undertake a parking survey. Most surveys of the time recommended creating highways through cities; those that offered more sophisticated viewpoints were generally ignored. Nevertheless, Charles Gordon, managing director of the American Transit Association, realized that it would be more economical to provide public transit than to distribute development over a large area.

And so I say there is danger in our planning for tomorrow's cities of getting the cart before the horse; of providing the highways to give city dwellers access to the countryside before we provide the internal transportation systems essential to the very survival of the communi-

ties themselves. Unless this is recognized, we may find too late that we have merely expedited the process of destroying our cities as we know them today, and have distributed their population helter skelter over the surrounding countryside. In such an eventuality, it is hard to visualize how any community can possibly carry the staggering tax burden, of providing over an area expanded ten-fold or more, the necessary municipal facilities and services of a modern urban community.[34]

Gordon also suggested that "helter-skelter" development could potentially be avoided through metropolitan-wide efforts on the part of local planning officials, local transit officials, and highway departments.[35]

Parking as a Municipal Problem

In 1922, in a speech to the City Club of Los Angeles, Carol Aronovici, city planning consultant for Berkeley, California, advocated great buildings to accommodate the need for parking: "A ten-story building, covering two acres [0.80 hectares] of land, will accommodate four thousand cars, or the equivalent of five miles [eight kilometers] of parked cars on both sides of the street."[36] That same year, an article in *The American City* described a scientific approach to the parking problem: the City Plan Commission of Paterson, New Jersey, had undertaken a study to determine how many cars were parked on the main shopping street of the city, and for how long. Based on the findings, the commission determined that the key issues were to provide parking for shoppers, to exclude nonshoppers, and to limit the time cars were allowed to park (all-day business parking was not explicitly mentioned). Merchants in many cities, meanwhile, fought no-parking rules out of fear that such rules would harm business. But merchants and their employees often parked on the street, blocking their own businesses.[37]

Studies undertaken in the late 1920s addressed the problem of street parking. Miller McClintock estimated that a parking prohibition in Boston would remove 10,000 cars from the streets. After numerous studies showed that workers were increasingly dependent on the automobile to get to their jobs—and that parking for workers was therefore required—another study was undertaken to determine when shoppers (the next-largest group of parkers) were parking downtown.[38]

In 1924, Will Rogers wrote that "politics ain't worrying this country one-tenth as much as parking space."[39] In the first several decades of the 20th century, although the parking garage was recognized as a viable, if partial, solution to the problem of congestion, it was also viewed as a problem in itself: crowded city centers often lacked adequate space for garages; it was difficult to integrate garages into other building types; the combination of automobile storage and repair (typical in early garages) created a potential fire hazard; and the building and zoning ordinances that addressed the parking garage often conflicted—which meant that until the conflicts were resolved, garages often could not be constructed where they were needed.[40]

In February of 1929, in an article entitled "The Place of the Garage in City Planning," *The Architectural Record* addressed the most intractable of planning problems head-on. The author, Ernest P. Goodrich, categorized garages into four classes: (1) private garages for one or more families who lived on the same lot as the garage was built on, (2) parking garages within office buildings, (3) public garages whose main function was to provide parking for clients of nearby buildings, and (4) public garages whose main function was automobile repair. The article went on to discuss specific building and zoning code issues for each type, as well as other issues related to the construction of garages. As a result of Goodrich's article, many cities confined auto repair to industrial locations, which solved one of the key issues—fire—associated with parking garages. Other cities prohibited garages from business districts altogether.[41]

Another 1929 article discussed the parking problem from two vantage points: that of older, more established cities such as Boston, Chicago, and New York, and that of rapidly growing West Coast cities, such as Los Angeles and Seattle. But the same solution was proposed for both: building in-town parking spaces and creating broad boulevards connecting to far-flung suburbs. The article also recommended that the cities in the first group follow Chicago's lead by instituting no-parking rules for busy roads, and by amending zoning laws to permit the construction of modern parking garages that did not include repair facilities. Automobile hotels, as these garages designed only for parking were often called, were considered more viable than lots: as a 1929 article in *The American City* observed, "There are a number of such structures, and it is understood they have been uniformly profitable at moderate fees. With proper building laws, there is no reason why such a structure should either add to the fire hazard of the business district or detract from its appearance."[42] Detroit's Fisher Building, which housed 1,200 cars in an 11-story tower, was offered as an example of an excellent modern garage, as was Chicago's Hotel LaSalle Garage.[43]

Hotel LaSalle Garage, Chicago, 1918. This garage—the first that only parked vehicles, and did not provide maintenance—was perceived as the solution to the downtown parking problem.

Although commercial and private garages could meet many public parking needs, local governments realized that they, too, needed to provide space for parking before it became too costly or difficult to do so. However, such efforts led to conflicts with private enterprise. In 1936, the Ohio Supreme Court determined that the city of Cleveland was not entitled to compete with privately owned commercial garages. For a number of years, legal concerns put a stop to the construction of municipally owned garages for public use. It was not until 1949 that Bluefield, West Virginia, constructed what was touted as "the world's first publicly financed, municipally owned automobile parking building" (although Welsh, West Virginia, which built a municipally owned facility in 1941, also claims the honor).[44] Soon, other

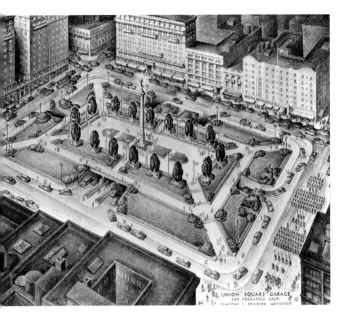

Above left: Union Square Garage, San Francisco, 1942. This was the first underground garage to be built under an existing park in such a way as to preserve the park above; it started a trend in parking solutions.

Above right: Post Office Square, Boston, 1991. An existing above-grade parking facility was replaced by an underground parking garage with a new park above.

cities undertook massive construction programs for parking garages. Buffalo, New York, exempted parking facilities from taxes, and Syracuse followed suit. Minneapolis, Minnesota, and Ann Arbor, Michigan, both parking pioneers, constructed one multilevel parking structure each; Baltimore built 17. By the early 1950s, automobiles were considered the backbone of the peacetime economy—and municipalities felt that they had to accommodate them.[45]

The model for successful public/private cooperation was San Francisco's Union Square Garage, a four-story, 1,700-car underground facility completed in 1942. The garage was built by a nonprofit organization. To reduce the risk to the city, the organization initially paid rent on the facility and covered the associated taxes. Although the city provided no initial funding, after ten years the building became city property. The facility was so popular that the construction debt was paid off 30 years ahead of schedule. The underground location of the garage made it possible to preserve the public park above. The Union Square Garage was so successful that many other underground parking facilities were soon planned for downtowns all across the country. The success of the project also helped contribute to the creation, in 1950, of the San Francisco Parking Authority.[46]

Beginning in the 1930s, many urban buildings, including early parking garages, were demolished by their owners, who would otherwise have been unable to pay the taxes due on the structures. This created vacant land that could then be transformed into parking lots (these lots were called "tax-payers"). Some of these lots had large capacities and a number of extra features: a municipally owned lot in Quincy, Massachusetts, for example, could hold 5,000 cars and had colored, textured pavement; a traffic-control system; dual meters; and lighting. Rochester, New York, was among the jurisdictions that had specific programs to create parking lots on tax-delinquent land. As of 1948, 320 cities with populations of 10,000 or more owned one or more parking lots; many private entrepreneurs flourished as well.[47]

By 1945, downtown off-street parking was recognized as the number-one need in almost every city. "Parking Jam," a 1946 *Architectural Forum* article, noted that all possible methods of housing cars had been tried: rooftop parking lots; multistory ramp garages; mechanical garages within skyscrapers; garages under parks; garages over roads; and garages under roads.[48] The article also noted that "it all needn't have been so bad": "Looking back at the third of a

Parking in the Context of Urban Planning

Parking lot, Stop and Shop Market, St. Louis, Missouri, 1924. Early parking lots were sometimes designed to do more than provide parking.

century in which cities had known the motor car, the traffic doctors pointed out the obvious—if streets and city plans had been tailored to the enlarging needs of a motor age, if buildings had been erected with an understanding of a growing parking demand, the crisis need not have struck. As usual, hindsight was keener than foresight—and as useful as headlights at noon."[49]

Two principal factors intensified the need for parking during the postwar years: first, growing prosperity meant that families could afford to own more than one car, which added to the number of vehicles that were in town during the day. Second, with the exponential growth of suburbs in the post–World War II era, there was an increase in both commuting and shopping trips undertaken by auto. However, increasing prosperity was by no means universal; by the 1940s, many cities were plagued by what became known as urban blight. Nor was growth regarded as entirely benign: citizens and public officials alike began to wonder how population growth, industrialization, and suburbanization would affect their way of life.[50]

In 1947, Los Angeles was the largest city in the United States by area (60 percent larger than New York), its population was already almost entirely dependent on the automobile, and the parking lot was the storage method of choice. Los Angeles was also the first city to address parking as a municipal problem, and the first to experience what would eventually become reality for every other city in the country—namely, autodependence and congestion. Mean-

while, Ann Arbor—which was tiny compared with Los Angeles—was becoming well-known for its attention to the parking problem. In the view of the mayor and the city council, Ann Arbor had three municipal utilities: water, sewage, and parking. The attention to parking led to the construction of three parking lots and a famous new garage, all operating at a profit.[51]

Washington, D.C., acquired its first parking authority in 1947.[52] By 1946, Chicago's central business district had lost 49 parking establishments and 7,800 spaces. In 1950, Chicago created the Bureau of Parking, a new municipal office that was responsible for developing all-day parking away from the urban core. Meanwhile, New York's mayor, William O'Dwyer, was quoted in a 1951 *Architectural Forum* article proposing "paving over the streets and the traffic on them, and starting in clean on a new level eight feet [2.4 meters] higher or flying."[53] That same year, New York created a three-member authority that had the power to buy, construct, operate, and collect fees from parking facilities.[54]

Portland, Oregon, considered itself a parking success story: by 1955, the city had 60 operators and 14,600 spaces, and all parking was privately developed and privately owned—an arrangement that plumped up city revenues from both property and payroll taxes. For the success of its approach, the city credited the members of the municipal staff who had chosen to handle parking and mass transit through private enterprise. Portland's city engineer was considered one of the top parking experts in the nation.[55]

Despite the example of Portland and other cities, however, parking continued to be a problem. By the 1950s and 1960s, parking garages in some cities were replacing older historic buildings; in Dallas, for example, a 1916 church was demolished to make room for a parking facility, creating resentment among citizens and changing life in downtown Dallas forever.[56] The title of a 1966 article in *Nation's Cities* said it all: "Parking Gains Status: Now Regarded as Major Urban Problem."[57]

Cities, Suburbia, and Parking

Both mass transit and the automobile shaped the development of cities in the early decades of the 20th century. Ironically, however, both had the same effect: decentralizing the city. As the population began to move outward from city centers, driving downtown to stores became an increasingly difficult proposition, so the stores followed the people by moving to the newly forming suburbs. In Los Angeles, the link between shopping and parking had developed by the mid-1920s, directly contributing to that city's particular growth pattern. Some observers, including Clarence Dykstra, commissioner of water and power in Los Angeles, were not only untroubled by that city's outward spread, but reveled in it. A 1926 article in *The American City Magazine* quoted Dykstra:

Rapid transit—congestion—relief—is a delusion and a snare as far as sound city planning is concerned. A population can be spread out without rapid transit or streetcar facilities. The private automobile and the bus have turned the trick so far as transportation is concerned. The development of the motor truck and the availability of electric power for manufacturing will continue to decentralize the industrial district. There can be developed in the Los Angeles area a great city population which for the most part lives near work, has its individual lawns and gardens, finds its market and commercialized recreation facilities right around the corner, and which because of these things can develop a neighborhood with all that it means.

Under such conditions city life will not only be tolerable but delightful—infinitely more desirable and wholesome than the sort induced and super induced by the artificially stimulated population center which constantly must reach higher and higher into air for light, air and a chance to see the sun. It will be a city in which children will not be discriminated against.[58]

In keeping with Dykstra's prediction, the separation of urban land uses did lead to what is now known as suburbia.

In Los Angeles and elsewhere, suburban land was plentiful, so the typical parking solution was the parking lot. Until cars could be safely exposed to the elements, parking lots were more prevalent in warmer parts of the country. The first "car park" in Detroit—which was developed by Max Goldberg, who made "California tops"—opened in 1917. Typically, land would be used for a parking lot until the surrounding uses required more spaces than the lot could handle. Although parking lots initially helped to sustain suburban growth, continued development at almost any scale eventually generates parking shortages.[59]

As early as the 1930s, urban downtowns were reaching out to let people know that they could indeed find a place to park for work and shopping. In Spokane, Washington, the Hospitality Club and the Merchants Parking Association published a pamphlet that clearly stated all the city's parking regulations; maps were also distributed to guide drivers to available parking. This effort was considered one of the best in the country. Merchants' associations in downtown Newark, New Jersey; Milwaukee, Wisconsin, and elsewhere attempted to solve their customers' parking problems by arranging discounted parking at garages and lots.[60]

The flow of business to the suburbs led to a decline in urban property values that, in some cities, began as early as 1939. In Detroit, for example, an unfinished, tax-delinquent structure close to the business district became a storage space for automobiles. The building's owner was quoted as saying, "From here in, let 'em use mass transportation."[61] In 1946, in Winston-Salem, North Carolina, a man named Bill Reynolds tore down an unfinished, tax-delinquent structure that he owned, then offered to build a parking center instead, provided that the city would manage it.[62]

Cities saw an opportunity: using their condemnation powers, they acquired properties (many of which were tax-delinquent), then sold them to entrepreneurs, who used the land to construct multistory parking garages. The goal was twofold: to address the parking problem and to revitalize the decaying urban core. This approach to urban redevelopment was not always successful, however, and often had unintended results: for example, parking structures meant for only one use were often empty on nights and weekends, creating gaping holes in formerly walkable areas.[63]

However, by the middle of the 20th century, the difficulty of ensuring adequate parking for their customers was not the only problem for downtown shopkeepers. Instead, it was the competition from the suburban shopping mall, with its many shops clustered together and its acres of "free" parking. Competition from suburbia led city garages to provide various amenities, including babysitting (offered, for example, at the Sioux City Park and Shop, which was constructed in 1955). It became clear that if merchants were to keep shoppers downtown, the link between parking and retail had to be more than architectural.[64]

Efforts to provide safe and efficient parking, in order to keep downtowns vital, led to some unusual proposals. For example, it was suggested in 1949 that Gary, Indiana, use a "pair-parking" system. Because this configuration would allow an eight-foot (2.4-meter) gap between each pair of cars, pedestrians could pass safely between vehicles, and drivers could parallel park easily and quickly. However, enforcing such a pedestrian-friendly configuration was next to impossible: parking was so scarce that drivers would be inclined to squeeze more vehicles into the available space.[65]

Between 1959 and 1965, in 49 cities in 20 states, three out of four parking meters were removed. Although the removal of the meters sometimes allowed a more free flow of traffic (because parking was prohibited), it also created an additional need for structured parking facilities. Meanwhile, as some cities lost population—and businesses—they reinstated free parking, in an effort to survive.[66]

Two Parking Philosophies

Broadly speaking, the years from 1940 to 1970 were dominated by two solutions to the parking problem: one was based on protection, and the other on integration. Protection involved containing cars on the fringes of the city (and providing mass transit so that drivers could get downtown); integration involved clearing developed land or using otherwise unbuildable land to provide parking downtown, right where it was needed. "Parking: The Crisis Is Downtown," an article published in 1963 in *The Architectural Forum,* noted that "if attempts to store vehicles on the fringes of the city are successful, they will take much of the pressure off the authorities to provide further parking facilities in the downtown."[67] This was the presumed advantage of the "protection" approach.[68]

The "integration" approach was reflected in the *Rotival Report,* issued in 1941 for New Haven, Connecticut. According to the report, "a city which loses its traffic is no more a city in the proper sense of the word.... By letting the main traffic pass outside the city limits, the city reduces its impor-

Section, Market Street East, Philadelphia, circa 1960. Edmund Bacon, the planner for the city of Philadelphia, believed that redeveloping cities should incorporate parking into walkable environments, balancing the needs of automobiles and pedestrians in a new, modern way.

tance to . . . one of a small local center and therefore must accept the consequences."[69] The goal of Mayor Richard Lee, Edward Logue, New Haven's development administrator, and Maurice Rotival, the city's redevelopment director, was "to lift New Haven . . . into the twentieth century." Under Lee and Logue's direction, New Haven was to "become the first slumless city, a truly new New Haven."[70] One effort in this direction involved the construction of the $5 million Temple Street Garage, which linked a major new road to the city's historic center square. The facility, designed by Paul Rudolph in 1963, was envisioned as a sculpture in the round, and its many technological innovations included a web of electric wires that kept the ramps warm in winter, and a signal system that could change the direction of traffic flow on the ramps. The structure also provided direct access to the main department store in the city. (Although it was viewed by some as the ideal parking garage, the facility did not save the city—nor was it accepted as a gateway to the metropolis.)[71]

Integration was also the model followed in Philadelphia in the 1960s. Under the guidance of Edmund Bacon, the executive director of the Philadelphia Planning Commission, parking garages found their way into the city center and into the central zone of Market Street East; they were also interwoven into other parts of the city in multidimensional ways.[72]

Whether parking should be located on the fringes of a city or integrated into the urban fabric remains a matter for debate. In a survey undertaken in 2000 by the Pittsburgh *Post-Gazette,* Pittsburgh was compared with 14 other cities

The Parking Garage

and found to be near the low end in numbers of downtown parking spaces. In response, city officials elected to construct new garages downtown, one of which will link to a new light-rail system. Officials also intend to increase the capacity of surface lots in the fringe areas, which will eventually be linked to downtown via light rail. Like the approach taken early in the 20th century in Chicago and other cities, the plan addresses parking from several perspectives and provides multiple options for citizens.[73]

Multilevel Solutions

Early designers imagined resolving the parking problem by separating pedestrian and automobile movement. As early as 1910, Eugene Henard, architect for the city of Paris, had envisioned an entirely new urban transportation structure in which one level would be reserved for automobile travel, and other levels would be reserved for trucks, public transportation, and utilities: thus, a six-story building might be served by as many as five levels of street. Moreover, parking was to be located within buildings, leaving the streets available for other uses. In 1924, the Beeler Organization proposed a plan for Atlanta that featured wide, aboveground streets for cars, and automated belowground platforms for transit. Both levels were to be lined by broad pedestrian sidewalks.[74]

A plan for traffic relief in Chicago involved two distinct levels—both above grade, but with pedestrians above and vehicles below; cars and people would access buildings at different levels. Chicago's Union Station, completed in 1925, was among the first buildings to incorporate streets—an arrangement that was consistent with Burnham and Bennett's plan for the city. The notion of merging street and garage, to create a direct connection between the automobile and the tall building, appeared in many cities, and remains a viable solution today.[75]

In 1928, Druar and Milinowski, a municipal engineering firm, suggested a 100-foot- (30-meter-) wide raised highway that would use "aerial rights over railroad yards and tracks for nearly two miles [three kilometers] around the business section of St. Paul"; below the highway, within easy reach of the city's business district, would be enough space for 3,000 cars.[76] In 1931, businessmen Nolan S. Black and Wilfred V. Casgrain proposed to the Detroit City Council the construction of public underground mechanized parking garages.[77] That same year, Thomas Adams's *Regional Plan of New York and Its Environs* included this vision: "The whole aspect becomes that of a very modernized Venice, a city of arcades, plazas and bridges, with canals for streets, only the canal will not be filled with water but with free-flowing motor traffic, the sun glittering on the black tops of the cars, reflecting on this waving flood of rapidly moving vehicles."[78]

The *World's First Automobile City,* a 1934 proposal for the waterfront area of Portland, Oregon, also separated pedestrian and auto traffic: automobile traffic was on a lower level, and parking was located under buildings. Each building featured two lobbies: one at the main level, for pedestrians, and one below, to serve the garage. This was one of the earliest schemes to include parking within a movement system that

Druar and Milinowski, proposal for a raised highway and parking, St. Paul, Minnesota, 1928. Integrating parking and highways was an early solution that eventually became common in Tokyo.

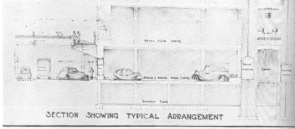

Theron R. Howser, *World's First Automobile City,* a proposal for the development of the Portland, Oregon, waterfront, 1934. Portland's waterfront was considered one of the first to be designed specifically for the automobile.

Cobo Hall, Detroit, 1960. With its massive parking deck on Detroit's downtown waterfront linked directly to a main highway, Cobo Hall was a typical 1960s model for integrating large convention centers into urban downtowns.

separated pedestrian and automobile traffic. Several other schemes also proposed separate lanes and streets for transit, in an attempt to address the parking problem by encouraging the use of transit.[79]

Perhaps the most beautiful images of separate movement systems for the 20th-century city were produced by Hugh Ferris, an architect known for his evocative drawings of New York City and for his setback ideas for skyscrapers. Ferris's *Avenue of the Future* featured three separate levels: one for trucks, one for cars, and one for pedestrians (at the top, for access to light). Large cities, such as New York and Chicago, were able to implement some of Ferris's ideas. Separate paths for man and machine—when conceived as part of ac-

tive and vital designs for cities—remain viable as a means of solving complex urban design issues.[80]

The earliest proposals for expressways date from the early 20th century; the idea was that enabling traffic to flow freely around and through city centers could prevent traffic jams. It was not until the 1940s, however, that virtually all major cities actually began to construct these high-speed roadways. In Detroit in 1960, as part of the redevelopment of the waterfront, the architectural firm of Giffels and Rossetti created a new form of collector: a three-lane spiral ramp that led directly from the expressway to the garage for Cobo Hall, a convention center. In Atlanta at about the same time, rapid growth made it necessary to try every possible parking

The Parking Garage

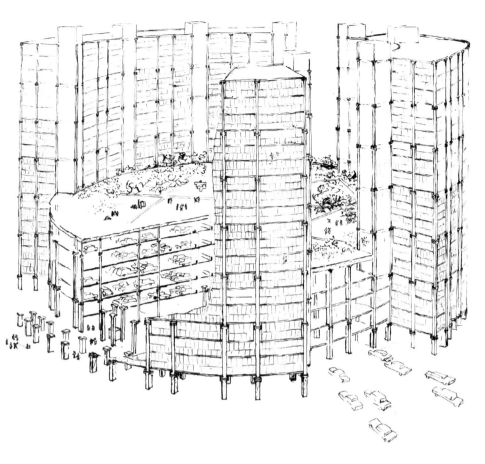

Above: Louis Kahn, proposal for a combination housing and parking structure, Philadelphia, circa 1950.

Left: Louis Kahn, traffic study, Center City, Philadelphia, 1952.

To remove the automobile from the city, Louis Kahn designed large circular towers, combining residences and public parking, that would surround and protect the city from the onslaught of cars.

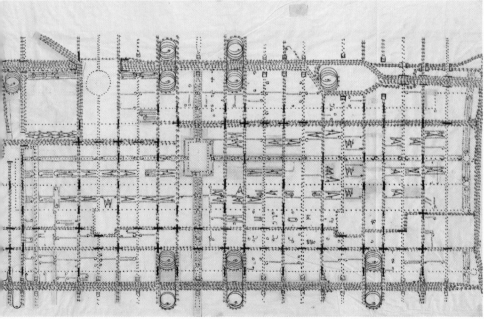

solution for downtown—including a large supply of free or low-cost parking. Nevertheless, none of these efforts were enough to ensure that urban downtowns—large or small—remained vital centers for shopping and work.[81]

By the mid-20th century, many architects had come to view the automobile as a threat to the urban centers that they loved. Louis Kahn envisioned an arrangement in which large concrete towers would surround the city, as if to defend it from the onslaught of cars. These massive forms were habitable buildings in staggered, multilevel arrangements that interlaced parking with residential uses, yielding growing space for trees and terraces for people. The centrality of the parking garage in Kahn's vision illustrates the power of the car—both in motion and at rest—in shaping the architectural future of cities.[82]

In the 1960s and 1970s, what had once seemed like visionary ideas for multilevel living began to be implemented: in a number of cities, enclosed skywalks or pedestrian bridges began to appear, floating above the streets. Two cities—Minneapolis, Minnesota, and Des Moines, Iowa—developed an entirely new pedestrian level above the ground, linking shopping, working, living, and parking. In both cities, the skywalks and the street level have remained active and viable pieces of the urban fabric. Skywalks were also built at a much smaller scale, between buildings, in several locations around the country: Pittsburgh's 1963 Gateway Garage, for example, was linked to other buildings by means of skywalks.[83]

Urban and Suburban Revitalization

In the 1960s, when urban renewal was the focus in many cities, parking garages were typically incorporated into redevelopment plans. In White Plains, New York, the location of one of the largest urban renewal projects in the state, a 1,200-space garage was built in 1965 in the airspace between two main thoroughfares. A 70-acre (28-hectare) shopping complex built as an urban renewal project in New Rochelle, New York, in 1968, included a 1,900-space parking garage. In Akron, Ohio, in 1969, "a parking deck formed the nucleus for a 'new downtown,'"[84] and in Dayton, Ohio, a combination 1,500-car parking garage, bus terminal, and airline ticket office constructed in 1972 became the focal point of downtown renewal.[85]

Cascade Superblock, Akron, Ohio, 1970. Urban renewal efforts included parking, typically on a massive scale.

The Parking Garage

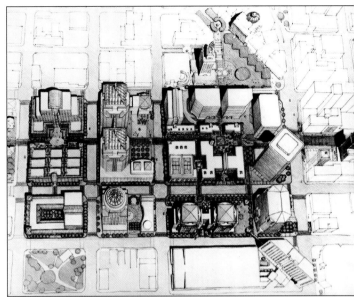

Collaborations of various types were undertaken in urban renewal areas: in Akron in 1969, for example, Parsons Brinckerhoff and the city government collaborated on a project involving the Health Building Garage, the University Concourse, the Cascade Superblock, and the University of Akron. An existing highway was moved under the concourse, as was the parking garage for the Health Building (a decision that led to a new design for the Health Building). The concourse bridged existing railroad tracks, and also served as the roof of the underground garage. The design linked the city's new Cascade Superblock with the university, creating the pedestrian flow that the community desired.[86]

In Hartford, Connecticut, urban renewal efforts were focused on the Gateway Center, the Hartford Center, and the US Gypsum Building. Although sufficient parking was available to meet zoning requirements for these facilities, it was still insufficient to meet demand, and Hartford's renewal plan called for existing parking lots to be converted into multideck parking facilities.[87]

The parking garage has always supported revitalization. In the 1970s, some cities, including Atlanta, San Francisco, and Washington, D.C., constructed heavy-rail systems linked first to parking lots, and later to parking garages. After 1980, at least 19 cities or metro areas built new transit lines, many of which were linked to parking facilities or lots. Between 1973 and 1988, as a result of new rail systems, public transit ridership increased by 13 percent, and the average number of

Above left: High Falls Garage, Rochester, New York, 1991. In the 1990s, parking facilities were again being used to help rejuvenate older sections of cities. In this structure, built to provide parking for a revitalized downtown, a modern industrial aesthetic links old and new.

Above right: City Center West site plan, Oakland, California, 1993. A structured parking facility was integrated into this mixed-use plan, creating a vibrant urban core.

vehicle-miles traveled per household (both for work and nonwork trips) decreased—in part because transit-oriented development encouraged greater density, making it possible to walk between destinations.[88]

Currently, the primary users of transit are people who live in the suburbs but work in the central city; however, the number of intersuburban commuters is on the rise, and meeting that demand—and reducing congestion—will be one of the principal challenges of the coming years. Currently, the Metro system in Washington, D.C., operates more parking spaces than Central Parking; the synergy between transit and parking will continue to be an important one.[89]

In outlying locations, transit stops are typically connected to lots; in downtowns, however—of which Portland, Oregon, is an example—parking facilities are important elements in a cohesive transportation system. As suburbia grows and matures, suburban parking lots are

Country Club Plaza retail and parking facility, Kansas City, Missouri, 2001. This street-friendly retail and parking facility, with parking integrated above and behind the retail, was part of the revitalization of Country Club Plaza.

combines an outdoor theater, a gathering space, retail, and a garage that serves the GSA Federal Building, Preservation Park, and local businesses. Placing other uses (not necessarily retail) on all or parts of the perimeter of the parking facility is an excellent strategy: not only is it good design, but it may also render a project financially feasible.[91]

Recent Approaches to Suburban Revitalization: Smart Growth and the New Urbanism

In many metropolitan areas, the suburbs—once the symbol of a better life—are plagued by the problems once associated only with central cities: crowding, congestion, aging infrastructure, and economic decline. Planners, developers, and architects are exploring a range of approaches to address these issues: strip malls, parking lots, vacant land, and aging suburban centers are being redesigned in attempts to restore quality of life. Two of the major influences on current urban and suburban revitalization efforts are smart growth and the new urbanism. Although they start from slightly different perspectives—smart growth has more of a regional planning emphasis, and the new urbanism tends to focus on community design—both approaches share an emphasis on choice: choice about where (and how) to live, where to work, where to shop—and, inevitably, how to get there.[92]

SMART GROWTH. Broadly speaking, smart growth is an approach to planning that discourages growth beyond the boundaries of current development until all of the places and spaces that exist within the boundaries are fully utilized. The principal national organization associated with the smart growth movement is Smart Growth America, which supports "citizen-driven planning that coordinates development, transportation, revitalization of older areas and preservation of open space and the environment."[93] In practical terms, smart growth means carefully evaluating development decisions in terms of their regional sustainability. Parking is a part of that decision-making process.[94]

Some suburbs and edge cities are subject to increasing pressure from growth. Although growth poses problems—in particular, infrastructure that was designed for much lower levels of demand—few areas have a choice: they must accommodate or risk stagnation. Parking is an essential element in the efforts of suburban and edge communities to reinvent themselves. Tyson's Corner, Virginia, for example, a suburb of Washington, D.C., plans to double the size of its shopping center over the next ten to 12 years.

becoming ripe for development, and for the expansion of parking availability.

Ideally, when a new parking garage is brought into an established neighborhood, it will become a source of community cohesion rather than dissent. Sensitive integration into the existing urban fabric is often the key to success. The High Falls Garage, in Rochester, New York, for example, is one of the most interesting parking structures built in the 1990s as part of an urban revitalization effort. Designed by William Rawn and LaBella Associates, the facility features a modern industrial aesthetic that contrasts with the historic mill buildings that surround it. The colorful steel structures of the elevator and stairs celebrate technology, and a simple brick triangle serves as a visual focal point for the conventional garage behind it. The engaging juxtaposition of the industrial aesthetic and the nearby historic structures showcases the past, the present, and the future, visually invigorating the area.[90]

The City Center West parking facility, constructed in Oakland, California, in 1993, is another excellent example of the integration of place and parking in an urban environment. This complex, in the heart of downtown Oakland,

Parking is a crucial element in every current approach to planning and architectural design, and smart growth is no exception. Applied to parking, smart growth is a particularly broad and comprehensive approach.

A recent publication of the Maryland Governor's Office of Smart Growth, *Driving Urban Environments: Smart Growth Parking Best Practices*, expresses concern about the amount of land needed for parking under current patterns of segregated zoning, and about the effect of that demand on quality of life:

Parking requirements now drive many site designs, and are often the make or break issue for financing new developments. Too many quality smart growth projects remain on the drawing board because they simply cannot solve the parking dilemma. We need parking, but we need to re-think parking design, parking financing, and parking supply and demand to better meet the needs of communities, developers, and users.[1]

Parking and Smart Growth

This report offers many practical suggestions, including guidelines for minimum parking requirements, maximum parking requirements, areawide zoning caps, shared parking, and parking districts; it also incorporates a parking checklist that can assist planners and developers to evaluate parking options.[2] However, advocates of smart growth also recognize that reducing parking demand is a necessary complement; strategies for reducing demand include transit-oriented development, traditional neighborhood design policies, programs that manage overall transportation demand, parking pricing strategies, and "unbundling" parking from residential rent and purchase prices.[3]

The report also addresses some basic issues in parking garage design, and provides suggestions for street parking, parking lots, and parking facilities. Among the key objectives highlighted in the report are minimizing runoff from parking facilities and encouraging vibrant street-level activity.[4]

Driving Urban Environments can serve as a basic guide to solving to complex issues related to development, planning, transportation, architecture, and parking.

Site plan, Bethesda Row, Bethesda, Maryland, 2007.

The expansion will include additional retail, residential and office uses, and multiple plazas; the nearby Metro station will also be expanded. The key planning principles identified for the Tyson's Corner redevelopment project are focused on sustainability.[95]

Plans to redevelop Midvale Plaza, a half-vacant shopping center in an older suburb of Madison, Wisconsin, are currently awaiting city council approval. The shopping center would be transformed into a four-story condominium and retail project that would also include parking and a branch library. Although the redevelopment project will be more dense than the surrounding neighborhood of one-story homes, many residents support the proposal: because the project is located along a major travel route, it is viewed as

Parking and the New Urbanism

In the early 1990s, a number of architects who were concerned about sprawl founded the Congress for the New Urbanism (CNU), an organization that hopes to redefine American life as "one interrelated community-building challenge."[1] New Urban News, a newsletter put out by the CNU, features a "technical page" that discusses specific design strategies, including parking.[2]

According to the CNU charter, the organization advocates

the restructuring of public policy and development practices to support the following principles: neighborhoods should be diverse in use and population; communities should be designed for the pedestrian and transit as well as the car; cities and towns should be shaped by physically defined and universally accessible public spaces and community institutions; urban places should be framed by architecture and landscape design that celebrate local history, climate, ecology, and building practice.[3]

In short, integrating, rather than separating, all the functions of life is key to the new urbanist approach.

The new urbanism recognizes the central role of parking in determining the dimensions of architecture and urban design; however, new urbanist strategies put the pedestrian first, then integrate the automobile. For example, a traditional neighborhood development (another term for new urbanist development) may offer the same number of parking spaces as a conventional suburban development, but the placement of parking will alter the ambience of the project and the pedestrian experience. Generally, the new urbanist approach relies on buildings to mask the presence of the automobile, although on-street parking is also deliberately encouraged in some settings, where it can be used to slow traffic and to protect pedestrians from traffic.[4]

Communities across the country have embraced the new urbanism: examples include Kentlands, in Gaithersburg, Maryland; Kiss Harbour, in Memphis, Tennessee; Laguna West, in Sacramento, California; Rio Vista West, in Mission Valley, California; and Seaside Village, in Seaside, Florida. One of the most recent projects is Seabrook, in Pacific Beach, Washington, the first full-scale traditional neighborhood development on the West Coast.[5]

New urbanist principles can also be applied to the development (or redevelopment) of office parks and shopping centers. Integrating structured parking into such projects may be feasible from a financial perspective, but it does create more complex design issues if the tenets of new urbanism are to be realized.[6]

Variations in parking, housing, and block configurations.

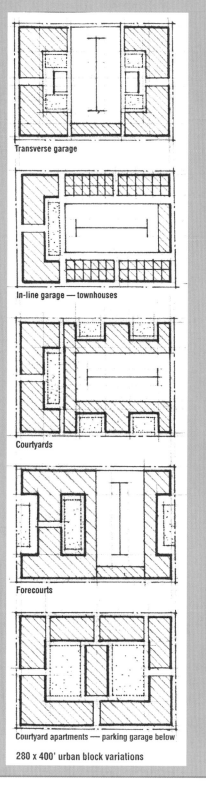

Transverse garage

In-line garage — townhouses

Courtyards

Forecourts

Courtyard apartments — parking garage below

280 x 400' urban block variations

sustainable. Meanwhile, the Madison South and Roseway Neighborhood Association of Portland, Oregon, is fighting the construction of a traditional shopping center surrounded by a parking lot—a project that could be described as the antithesis of smart growth.[96]

The smart growth strategy, which calls for intensifying development where appropriate, is a useful one for many areas of the country. In Atlanta, for example, under the Livable Centers Initiative, the Atlanta Regional Council is encouraging mixed-use development with access to public transportation on tracts of land within the city environs. The designers will need to integrate parking structures into these projects. When Washington Township, a rural New Jersey municipality, decided to create a new town center, it relied on smart growth principles to create an environment that would have a higher quality of life than what arises from typical suburban zoning. The project, which was undertaken in partnership with the development community, had two goals: avoiding strip malls and creating a sense of place. The town center features a mix of housing types and conserves open space. On the basis of the figures that are available so far, the town appears to have succeeded in achieving a balance between public and private investment.[97]

THE NEW URBANISM. The new urbanism is an approach to urban design that embraces participatory planning; walkable, mixed-use, and transit-oriented development; a variety of housing choices; open-space preservation; and an appropriate mix of jobs and housing. A movement that has captured the imaginations of many architects, urban planners, public officials, and citizens, the new urbanism draws on the best of traditional planning practices to create welcoming, distinctive, pedestrian-friendly environments. The principal national organization associated with the new urbanism is the Congress for the New Urbanism, and the leading newsletter on the subject is *New Urban News.*[98]

The sprawling development patterns that the new urbanism attempts to address were facilitated by the automobile. Although new urbanist design encourages transit—because it reduces dependence on cars and fosters compact, walkable development—the new urbanist approach acknowledges that the automobile is crucial to the success of any project, whether greenfield or redevelopment; at the same time, however, new urbanist design tends to minimize the role of the automobile within the urban plan. What matters is *connectivity*—creating vibrant and active links between uses, building types, and transportation options. Such connectivity is the key to encouraging pedestrian use, and to creating a sense of place. Every aspect of a new urbanist development—from pavement widths to pedestrian crossings, street furniture, parking, and traffic speed—is appropriate to the scale and size of the street, and is designed with the pedestrian in mind.[99]

Working from the "village" model, new urbanists are reviving patterns of land use that were characteristic of the pre-automobile era. Designs for residential areas, for example, often feature alleys—convenient, functional, and even attractive spaces for small garages and for necessary activities such as trash pickups. In Charleston, South Carolina, alleys have been used extensively to address parking needs in an elegant way: they have been transformed into places that people would want to be. In new urbanist developments, residences are within walking distance of shopping, which cuts down on the number of cars. (In fact, the quest for compact development has revived the idea of "living above the store"; second-floor apartments are not only convenient, but often overlook pleasant alleys or vibrant main streets.)

The successful placement and design of parking garages requires attention to the entire pedestrian experience—including where, how, and why pedestrians travel after they leave their cars. For example, the currently popular solution of hiding parking structures in the interior of a block is by no means a panacea: because this strategy encourages people to go directly from their cars to their destinations, it often undermines the pedestrian-friendly environment that planners are currently attempting to create. As Joel Garreau notes in *Edge City: Life on the New Frontier,* "Parking lots spread buildings apart. The farther apart buildings are, the less willing people are to walk between them. The fewer people there are within walking distance of any one place, the less able that place is to support civilization as measured by the existence of restaurants and bookstores."[100] Understanding that the parking facility can be a beautifully designed structure that is integrated into, and supportive of, its environment allows more subtle and complex solutions to emerge.

In areas where large numbers of people congregate, but at different times of day and for different reasons, shared parking allows spaces to be used around the clock, and permits growth to occur without the proliferation of new parking spaces. Shared parking arrangements are very much in the spirit of both smart growth and the new urbanism. At the Circle Center project, constructed in Indianapolis in

1996, shared parking made it possible to reduce by 3,100 the number of parking spaces that would have been required under zoning for separate uses. Shared parking is an example of intelligent design for a city—of thinking in terms of integration, rather than separation.[101]

Multimodal Hubs and Transit Villages

All building types have a symbiotic relationship with parking. J.B. Jackson—author, educator, landscape architect, and founder of *Landscape* magazine—has said that "if the landscape is to be truly human it ought to reflect the kind of people we are.... For Americans that means recognizing and accepting our national landscape for what it is: something very different from Europe.... Because Americans so value change, our landscape must be fluid and capable of sudden change."[102] The parking garage has already demonstrated that it can be gracefully combined with a range of uses and building types, yielding the fluidity that is needed to support 21st-century civic design.

Interest in mass transit began to revive in the late 1960s, especially in cities with congested downtowns. In 1975, Richard Beebe, a parking consultant, wrote an article in *Parking* magazine that set forth the crucial role of the parking industry in creating "sub-center parking stations"—attractive facilities that would link transit and automobiles.[103] As noted earlier, new rail systems were constructed in a number of cities during the 1970s. In addition, many old systems were improved, and transit was planned even in historically auto-dependent cities. The revival of interest in mass transit, and the recognition that transit would in many cases coexist with, rather than replace, auto travel, meant that transportation was again viewed as one of the defining factors in urban form.[104]

Multimodal structures, designed to accommodate various forms of transportation—including buses, autos, intercity rail, light rail, and heavy rail—were often stunning displays of urban engineering. One example was the parking garage and transit station, built in 1971, that spanned the tracks of the Quincy-Boston rail line. In many cities, transportation centers played a crucial role in urban renewal: in Dayton, Ohio, for example, a transportation center constructed in 1972 offered parking for 1,500 cars and included skywalks connecting to other buildings.[105]

Today, the focus on transit continues, and transit centers are an important emerging building type. A transit center may be a link within a suburban environment, or may be integrated into a downtown setting. One of the first such centers constructed during the past several decades is Chicago's

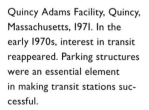

Quincy Adams Facility, Quincy, Massachusetts, 1971. In the early 1970s, interest in transit reappeared. Parking structures were an essential element in making transit stations successful.

The Parking Garage

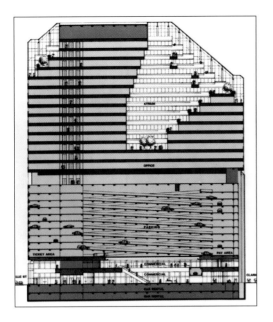

Loop Transportation Center, designed by Skidmore, Owings & Merrill and built in 1984. The construction of the building was preceded by a 12-year ban on the construction of parking in the city; like many of the structures built in the wake of the ban, the center is mixed use. The complex includes both a multipurpose office tower and the transportation center. The center consists of two below-grade levels and 12 above-grade levels, and features restaurants, retail shops, airline ticket counters, car-rental firms, and direct access to the city's rapid-transit system. Floors three through 12 and the two underground levels are parking; the large number of spaces is appropriate to such a dense urban area.[106]

Parking garages have been incorporated into new multimodal centers at many scales, from the 400-space Riverfront Parking Facility, built in 2004 in Wilmington, Delaware, to the 1,700-space garage at Amtrak's 30th Street Station, in Philadelphia—the second-busiest station in the Amtrak system.[107] The Riverfront facility was designed so that passengers waiting for trains can view the adjacent park and the river beyond. The structure also blends into the fabric of the surrounding historic buildings, which were designed by Frank Furness.[108]

Even small towns are constructing multimodal transportation facilities: in 2001, for example, Wilkes-Barre, Pennsylvania, with fewer than 45,000 people, constructed a facility with more than 400 parking spaces, a daycare center, a restaurant, and a fire station. Larger cities, such as Des Moines, Iowa, with a population of nearly 200,000, are also creating multimodal facilities. The Center Street Park and Ride, designed by Herbert Lewis Kruse Blunck and constructed in 2001, offers a restaurant, a daycare center, a small retail and service area, and bus links to downtown. The integration of uses, easy access for drivers and pedestrians alike, and direct bus connections to downtown and the suburbs combine to create a successful, holistic solution that supports peoples' daily lives.[109]

Cities are also beginning to understand the importance of multiple transportation options. Many downtowns, including Portland, Oregon, and Seattle, Washington, have met the challenge by adding new transportation technologies, such as light-rail systems, to city streets. In the 1980s, Portland made an innovative choice: using federal highway dollars to create a new mass-transit system. Portland's Old Town Parking Garage, designed by SERA Architects and constructed in the 1990s, is but one example of Portland's successful linking of

Above left: Loop Transportation Center, Chicago, 1984. Large, multimodal transportation centers typically integrate parking into the use mix.

Above right: Riverfront Parking Facility, Wilmington, Delaware, 2004. Parking structures can be integrated into transit facilities in many ways. In this case, it was critical to design a parking garage that was compatible with the historic station.

Center Street Park and Ride, Des Moines, Iowa, 2001. This complex, consisting of a modern parking facility linked with bus transit, also features a daycare center, a dry cleaner, a video shop, and other services.

Old Towne Parking Garage, Portland, Oregon, 1991. In Portland, which has led the country in designing for transit, parking and transit are linked to create a seamless transportation system.

parking and mass transit: in addition to housing a stop along the new rail line, this facility visually balances an ultramodern office building and surrounding historic structures. The garage at 4th and Yamhill, a traditional urban building positioned diagonally across the street from a transit station, was constructed in the early 1990s; the facility features street-level retail and excellent lighting, which combine to create an attractive and inviting structure. These and other Portland parking facilities have successfully rejuvenated the surrounding neighborhoods and have also forged architectural links between new development and historic structures.[110]

Examples of even more strikingly innovative multimodal strategies have been proposed throughout the country. It was at the Disney parks, of course, that breakthrough transportation environments—where the entire complex was designed around the transportation system—first appeared. Gradually, however, what Disney created in the spirit of fun became a part of everyday life. In 1984, for example, the Dallas suburb of Las Colinas constructed a five-mile (eight-kilometer) personal transit system that runs on a curved, elevated guideway. In 1990, a monorail link was proposed for Burbank, California, between Douglas Plaza and John Wayne

The Parking Garage

Transit Villages

The ideas behind the transit village are not new: in many ways, today's transit villages are reminiscent of the early streetcar suburbs, such as Roland Park, outside Baltimore, and Country Club Plaza, outside Kansas City. Parking has always been essential to the planning of such communities.[1]

One advantage of clustering parking at transit stations is a reduction in building costs: it is much less expensive to construct an office building, for example, if it does not include parking for employees. In addition, the higher density typical of transit villages encourages lower automobile ownership and can increase housing affordability (because homeowners do not have to budget for car ownership). In fact, when housing is constructed near rail stations, it is often possible to lower the parking requirements, because residents of dense, transit-accessible areas tend to own fewer cars.

Much research on transit villages originated with Peter Hall, director of the Institute of Urban and Regional Planning at the University of California, Berkeley; Hall's efforts were subsequently continued by Michael Bernick and Robert Cervero. Hall encour-

Fruitvale Village, Oakland, California, 2003.

aged the establishment of a research forum to study the link between mass transit and urban development; the result was the National Transit Access Center (NTRAC), founded at Berkeley in 1991. NTRAC has led research on transit-oriented development and on the use of paratransit and electric mini-cars. NTRAC was the first organization to advocate eliminating free parking for office workers because it discourages the use of mass transit; NTRAC also promotes the construction of alternative methods of transportation.[2]

Pleasant Hill Station, begun in 1995 in Walnut Creek, California, and Fruitvale Village, completed in 2003 in Oakland, California, were among the first projects to be based on transit-village principles. The park-and-ride lots that initially surrounded these stations became their biggest asset: as development continues around transit stations, parking lots become "banked land," allowing the construction of additional housing, commercial projects, and structured parking.[3]

American Plaza, built in 1991 in San Diego, is one of the few transit villages in the country that required no direct public funding. This "vertical transit village" includes a multimodal transfer station. The multideck parking structure that serves the facility is across an open plaza from the main building. Transit villages with an entertainment focus, such as Millennium Pleasant Hill, constructed in 1995 in Walnut Creek, California, have also proved successful. Such projects draw on both automobile and transit users, and make use of shared parking arrangements.[4]

There are a number of options for integrating parking facilities into transit villages. Two strategies that should be avoided, however, involve using the parking garage as a podium or hiding it behind buildings. Both approaches discourage pedestrians from interacting with the street by allowing them to arrive directly at their destination. It is far preferable to integrate the parking facility into the surrounding urban environment.

Airport. A similar connection is planned between a 3,500-acre (1,416-hectare) planned community and Dallas's rapid-rail system. In 2002, Seattle residents voted to expand the maglev system that was originally constructed for the Seattle World's Fair, in 1962; however, residents reversed the decision approximately one year later because of concerns about cost. In Mystic, Connecticut, in 1996, a parking garage and transit station were linked by a people mover; however, the device was eventually removed, as it was found that the people mover was no more effective than walking, for the short distance that was involved. However, in 1997, a peo-

ple mover was installed to connect the Getty Center and its parking facility; the arrangement has been very successful. A new multimodal center in Pittsfield, Massachusetts, will connect four forms of travel: bicycle, auto, bus, and rapid transit. It may not be long before such facilities will need to accommodate revolutionary transit devices, such as the Segway, as well.[III]

Building on the ideas described by Christopher Alexander, Sara Ishikawa, and Murray Silverstein in *A Pattern Language: Towns, Buildings, Construction,* which was published in 1977, Michael Bernick and Robert Cervero chose the term transit village to refer to an environment that links transit and mixed-use development. A transit village is an urban or suburban setting that has easy access to transit; the transit station serves as the gateway to the village. Transit villages are pedestrian-friendly places that improve mobility and public safety, expand options for living and working, revitalize neighborhoods, and create opportunities—and reasons—for public celebration.[112]

Bernick and Cervero found that the two most important determinants of rail use were trip destination and the availability of free parking. Rail use increased if both ends of the trip—home and work—were easily accessible by rail. And free parking at the user's destination led to a decline in the use of rail. Many studies—of Edmonton, Alberta; Toronto, Ontario; Washington, D.C., and cities in California—found that office workers were more likely to commute by rail if they lived near rail, commuted long distances, had to pay for parking, and owned relatively few cars.[113]

Interestingly, beginning in 1991, the federal government began to subsidize commuting costs for federal employees; and until 1992, federal tax policy encouraged companies to provide free parking for workers by offering tax credits to

People mover, Las Colinas, Texas, 1987. Parking has been linked to trains and buses for many years, and is often integrated into facilities that feature advanced forms of mass transit.

firms that offered this benefit. In 1992, however, limitations were imposed on tax-free employee benefits such as free parking, and the maximum value of the tax-free benefit for public transportation was tripled.[114]

To encourage transit use, BART (Bay Area Rapid Transit) controls the cost of parking at its transit stops—a strategy that sometimes makes it difficult to cover costs; in fact, several new transit villages in California have failed to take in the revenues that they need to meet the bottom line.[115] Atlanta's Lindbergh Station, another transit village, is also struggling financially. Nevertheless, available data indicate that transit villages may be the best means of encouraging transit use. Holly Lund, Robert Cervero, and Richard Willson found that people who work adjacent to transit stops will ride transit if it is fast and convenient and if driving is expensive. They are more likely to change their habits, however, if they live near a good transit stop. For example, almost half of the residents who live near the Pleasant Hill BART station take BART.[116]

Multimodal facilities, new transportation options, and transit villages do not obviate the need for parking: instead, they create opportunities for new synergies and solutions. As the context of the parking garage changes, project plans that sensitively integrate parking become all the more important.[117]

Infill Development

Along with large-scale urban redevelopment, smaller-scale infill projects are underway all across the country. Parking is of course a key component of such projects. However, the timing is often tricky: although the amount of parking is often driven by code—that is, by assumptions about the minimum number of spaces needed by a hotel, condominium, shop, or office—a structured parking facility is not always feasible in the early stages of a project. Peter Calthorpe notes in The Next American Metropolis that where structured parking is not financially feasible at the outset, plans should specify how it can be phased in later. Although this is a good approach in theory, it is more difficult in practice.[118]

Calthorpe observes that if the construction of a parking facility is planned for a later phase of a project, it leaves a gap in the space and form of the project, creating a sense of incompleteness and an unwelcoming environment. On the rare occasions that it is feasible to use a parking lot as a placeholder for later structured parking, such an approach is most likely to succeed if the lot is carefully designed: it should include landscaping and attractive paving, and could

The Parking Garage

perhaps incorporate other elements, such as small pavilions, benches, or pieces of sculpture. For redevelopment and in-fill sites, Calthorpe strongly recommends structured parking; where there is a choice between aboveground and underground parking, Calthorpe prefers the latter—which, of course, is even more expensive once the buildings have gone up. Thus, when all is said and done, a well-designed parking facility, properly integrated into the surrounding context, is the best solution.[119]

If parking is to be integrated into a building at a later date, then the only feasible solution, unless appropriate space has been left elsewhere, is on the top of the structure—an arrangement that must be planned for early in the design process. Because of the constraints associated with delaying the construction of a parking facility, parking is usually completed first, with the number of spaces based on zoning and other municipal requirements. No developer wants to be caught short—with insufficient space for customers, residents, or employees—or to attempt to launch a project that seems incomplete.[120]

In the historic centers of European cities, paved plazas that are enclosed and defined by architectural edges support parking both above and below grade; in these arrangements, the parking facilities are often linked to other forms of transportation. Such mixed-use urban spaces are a viable option for the United States as well. Why not create a pedestrian plaza that is surrounded by buildings on all sides, and make it available for limited parking and for slower-moving vehicles? Courtyards and forecourts can also be designed with parking in mind: the visual impact of a paved courtyard used for parking is very different from that of the ubiquitous asphalt parking lot.

For a public garage constructed in 1970 in Evanston, Illinois, the designer created spandrel panels that hid the sloping floors, creating a more typical visual rhythm on the facade that fronted the side alley. While this approach was a good attempt to integrate the garage into its surroundings, the facade on the street side was a blank brick wall—a foreboding presence looming over the streetscape. By the 1990s, the Evanston Parking Authority wanted to improve the facade on the street side, enlivening the adjacent sidewalk and bringing to this section of the street the same vibrancy that permeated the rest of the town.[121]

Newport News, Virginia, is currently developing its new city center within an existing suburban office park, transforming the park into a walkable town center. In an another

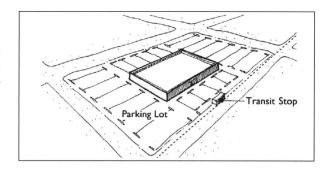

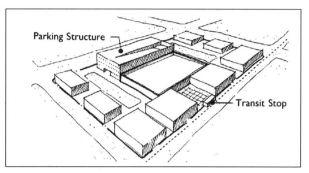

Proposal for the redevelopment of a parking lot, Calthorpe, 1993.

intriguing suburban project being undertaken at the Georgia Institute of Technology, two professors (Michael E. Gamble and W. Jude LeBlanc) and their students designed "thin" buildings to line the 60- to 75-foot (18- to 23-meter) setbacks between strip malls and the street. In this approach, known as "incremental urbanism," parking is sandwiched between the original strip mall and a row of small retail buildings, which are oriented toward the sidewalk and the street. In one proposal, the new row of buildings is only 20 feet (six meters) deep (the depth of a parking space) and consists of an arcade with retail and business uses above. The strategies of Newport News and Georgia Tech increase density, create more walkable places, and integrate parking into the existing suburban fabric.[122]

Modern Regulatory Efforts

In 1947, the Eno Foundation surveyed the use of zoning to set parking requirements, and found that the greater the population of the city, the more likely it was to have zoning ordinances that addressed parking. Among cities with populations of 100,000 or more, 28 percent had such ordinances, while among cities with populations between 10,000 and

Left: *Liner: The Oreo Deck,* Atlanta, Georgia, 2005. Thin buildings, like those shown in this proposal, are among the strategies for transforming suburban strip centers into pleasant, walkable environments.

Right: Pearl Street Parking Garage, Boulder, Colorado, 2000. Boulder, Colorado—a university town—embraced transit and parking as a means of fostering synergy between town and gown.

25,000, only 7 percent did. Such ordinances generally required new buildings to provide off-street parking spaces, but did not necessarily include residential uses in the requirement. The Eno Foundation report also noted that parking requirements for residential uses tended to be lower in the East than in the West.[123] The report concluded, however, that the "advantages of zoning for parking will ultimately be recognized by all cities."[124]

It requires effort to find solutions that balance automobile dependence and responsible land use. Beginning in 1968, citizen commissions in Boulder, Colorado, began work on a comprehensive land use plan designed to manage growth. In 1982, another commission was formed to address energy and transportation needs. As a result of such efforts, Boulder has succeeded in providing just enough parking to meet needs, while managing growth and embracing other transportation choices. New facilities, such as the Pearl Street Parking Garage, which was built in 2000 and has won several awards, are well planned and well located within the downtown urban fabric.[125]

A number of organizations—including the American Planning Association, the Eno Transportation Foundation, the In-

stitute of Transportation Engineers, the National Parking Association, and the Urban Land Institute—conduct research to help communities determine how many parking spaces are required for various types of land uses. Through such efforts, the complex relationships between land use and parking—in both urban and suburban contexts—are being documented in detail. In many communities, the parking lot will continue to be an important part of the picture; however, shared parking, structured parking, integrated parking, and park-and-ride arrangements are all solutions that should be explored.[126]

Traditional zoning regulations set minimum parking standards for various land uses. But developers often exceed the requirements because they know that the availability of parking can make or break a project—especially a retail project, and especially during the holidays. The resulting problems—poor stormwater drainage because of excessive paved areas, and parking facilities that sit empty most of the year—have generated interest in setting maximum parking standards. Such standards are already in place in Gresham, Oregon; Jefferson County, Kentucky; and San Antonio, Texas. For locations near transit stations, San Francisco, Seattle, and other municipalities are using various incentives to encourage the construction of fewer parking spaces.[127]

Several jurisdictions, including Austin, Texas; Bellevue, Washington; Hamden, Connecticut; Irvine, California; and Prince George's County, Maryland, have instituted zoning incentives for builders. For example, a builder who provides structured or underground parking instead of surface parking may be allowed to include extra height or additional square footage, or to cover an additional percentage of the site with other building types. Another option is to require developers to maintain unpaved green space that can be converted to parking during periods of peak demand; this approach softens the visual and the environmental impact of parking areas. Under the SmartCode, a new urbanist model code developed by Duany Plater-Zyberk and Company, the inclusion of high-quality mass transit allows the number of required parking spaces to be reduced by 30 percent; however, even without transit, shared parking arrangements for mixed-use projects can still significantly reduce parking needs.[128]

Zoning regulations shape the pace, direction, and appearance of development. Thus, they offer an ideal opportunity to foster intelligently designed, well-integrated parking facilities that support, rather than undermine, a vibrant and pedestrian-friendly street life. Form-based zoning, for example, which was developed to address the sprawling,

"placeless" environments that proliferate under traditional zoning, focuses on regulating urban form rather than land use. Under this approach, parking requirements are required to be compatible with pedestrian scale.[129]

In addition to encouraging shared parking and setting maximum parking standards, many updated zoning codes reflect some of the best practices that have been described in previous chapters: street-level retail, staggered setbacks, and compatibility with surrounding structures. Such regulations may add to the structural and aesthetic complexity of garage design; however, the results—attractive garages that support the community's architectural and social goals—are worth it.

By the mid-1960s, traffic engineers had become part of municipal transportation departments, and were carefully studying automobile and pedestrian movement to increase traffic flow. And during the mid-1980s, transportation man-

Place Making

Smart growth, the new urbanism, and the development of transit villages all have one thing in common: an interest in place making. Simply defined, place making is a matter of creating livable urban environments: such environments are socially, economically, and environmentally sustainable; offer multiple mobility options; feature diverse housing types and opportunities; are pedestrian-friendly; and include a mix of uses, while preserving the community's character. Successful place making involves creating a shared vision, then implementing that vision through zoning and regulatory approaches that support compact, vibrant, welcoming communities. Parking is, of course, one of the fundamental building blocks in place making.[1]

One of the foremost practitioners of place making is Peter Calthorpe, winner of the 2006 ULI J.C. Nichols Prize for Visionaries in Urban Development.[2] Even when others have advocated heroic visions of modern utopias, Calthorpe has taken a more multidimensional and humanistic approach: his four basic principles are diversity, building on a human scale, a focus on restoring and preserving buildings, and taking a regional perspective. From these core principles, true places emerge that allow the best of the past, present, and future to combine. These principles, along with "green" infrastructure, yield places such as Stapleton, a new planned community on the site of a former airport in Denver. Calthorpe's approach to parking is to omit parking lots, in order to allow more compact, walkable development.

Place making means just what it says: creating places that are distinctive, that have a viable public realm, and that will stand the test of time. "Real" places allow people to form connections—to interact with each other and with the surrounding environment, now and in the future.

Above: Site plan, Mizner Park, Boca Raton, Florida, 2007.

Below: Site plan, Country Club Plaza, Kansas City, Missouri, 1922.

agement associations evolved to help the private sector—including developers, employers, and managers of office buildings or office parks—deal with traffic flow, encourage transit use, and support pedestrians. As a result, some employers developed shuttle services or coordinated with local governments to provide parking. But until recently, the complex movement patterns of modern daily life had never been scientifically analyzed at a large scale. In a major project currently being undertaken by the University of California, Irvine, and the California Department of Transportation (Caltrans), the automobiles of volunteers have been linked to a Caltrans computer, which is tracking all their movements. The data obtained through the study will provide a good starting point for scientifically analyzing how, when, and where people travel and park; ultimately, the project findings will be used to support the design of intelligent transportation systems in the state. Ideally, this study and others like it will eventually include the pedestrian experience as well. Careful analysis of movement patterns can be used to create new synergies between parking, pedestrians, and the built environment.[130]

Constructing new facilities and taking advantage of technology (such as systems that tell drivers where the empty spaces are) can help, but the real goal is to change the way that people think about land use and transportation: this means encouraging walkable development and supporting transportation methods (car pooling, bicycling, and mass transit) that reduce automobile dependence.

Site and Size in Modern Garage Design

In dense, older European cities, separating the movement patterns of man and machine was of major importance. In the United States, however, where land was abundant and cities were being designed around the needs of the automobile, the costly solutions proposed for European cities seemed less necessary. Instead, parking garage designers focused on maximizing the number of spaces provided within each structure and on moving the auto through the facility as efficiently as possible.

The issues related to appropriate site selection include access to other transportation choices, access for pedestrians and service vehicles, and environmental concerns. Topography—including natural features, surrounding structures, and the relationship between the garage and the street—is another consideration that must be addressed in an overall design strategy. Typical architectural issues (such

as setbacks and yard clearances) will also affect design. Both topographical and architectural concerns are more complex in dense urban areas, where land is scarce but large parking facilities may be needed. Efficiently accommodating the maximum possible number of cars is important, but it is essential to take the surrounding context into account.[131]

Various studies have attempted to determine how best to maximize parking within a typical urban street grid. In the 1960s, for example, 140 feet by 175 feet (43 meters by 53 meters) was viewed as the minimum lot size for a 350-space self-service garage; smaller lots were regarded as impractical for the new self-park facilities. However, the particular size and structure of a given downtown often limited the possible parking solutions.

Three times in the past century—between 1910 and 1930, between 1950 and 1960, and beginning in the late 1990s and continuing today—the garage has undergone tremendous physical expansion, both in its dimensions (to accommodate larger cars), and in the number of spaces provided. Most of the parking structures built in the 1960s had between 500 and 700 spaces, but the average garage built in 2000 had between 800 and 1,000 spaces.[132] According to Dale Denda, director of research for Parking Market Research Company, between 1996 and 2000, "garage construction starts increased by 72 percent, and the average size of garages grew by 24 percent."[133] Denda also found growth in construction starts for parking facilities with between 90 and 200 spaces. Interestingly, however, in 2000 alone, the number of starts for smaller garages (those with fewer than 400 spaces), was almost double the number of starts for larger garages. California leads the market in the construction of smaller garages.[134]

Smaller facilities present both challenges and opportunities in efforts to support denser urban fabrics. Because ramp garages are not as cost-effective for facilities with a smaller number of spaces, some ramp garages are being constructed with higher floor-to-floor heights so that they can accommodate mechanical stackers. These new hybrid facilities provide the required number of parking spaces but can be more easily integrated into dense areas. It may not be long before the Ferris-wheel–type parking facilities—invented in the United States in the 1920s and currently tucked neatly into buildings all over Tokyo—reappear in the United States.

According to Denda, the number of medium-sized garages—those in the 400- to 600-space range—has peaked. With the shift in planning strategies in urban areas (including form-based zoning, new urbanist approaches, and an em-

Medford Downtown Retail and Parking Structure, Medford, Oregon, late 1990s. Smaller downtowns can pose some of the greatest challenges when it comes to providing parking that does not overwhelm the city, but that is adequate for its needs.

phasis on historic preservation), garages of this size are often used to support the denser urban fabric typical of older cities. Although many land uses—such as airports, universities, and medical centers—may require mega-garages, these large structures are usually difficult to integrate into pedestrian-friendly urban environments.[135]

The Best Buy complex in the suburban environment of Richfield, Minnesota, offers perhaps the largest number of parking spaces for any corporate headquarters in the United States. Built in 2003, the complex provides 7,500 on-site parking spaces (five spaces per 1,000 square feet [93 square meters], as specified in the zoning requirements): 6,750 in the parking structure and 750 in surface lots. An enclosed L-shaped passageway links the parking facility to four office buildings, creating a common space and ensuring secure connections between the garage structure and the office buildings. Although this arrangement easily accommodates traffic flow (from multi-lane highways into the parking garages), it is possible only because of the spaciousness of the site.[136]

The Parking Facility as a Civic Building

Early garage designers, working in the beaux-arts tradition, designed the parking garage as a civic building because they understood that every building type must contribute to the harmony of the whole. Later garage designs, shaped by modernist notions of functionality (and later by cost considerations), visually challenged the very concept of civic architecture.

Fellow-architect Carlo Aymonino, speaking of Aldo Rossi, once said that if Rossi were to create a new city,

I am convinced that his project would resemble the plans made 200 years ago upon which many American cities were based: a street network that permits division of property, a church that is a church, a public building whose function would be immediately apparent, a theater, a courthouse, individual houses. Everyone would be able to judge whether the building corresponded to his ideal—a process and structure that would give confidence as much to the designer as to those who use it.[137]

For the parking garage, the challenge is to design a civic structure "whose function is immediately apparent."

Several parking firms recognize the parking facility as an important civic building type, and believe that community participation is a crucial element in the design process. The Medford Downtown Retail and Parking Structure, constructed in the late 1990s in Medford, Oregon, is the result of one such process. The building not only offers an attractive architectural presence, but also provides 3,250 square feet (302 square meters) of retail space, a retail arcade that links parking to an adjacent retail block, and a second pedestrian corridor connecting to Medford's main street. The forms surrounding the main entry to the building evoke Mondrian's work, while custom lighting and finishes give the garage a civic air, even at night.[138]

The Oregon facility cost more than the standard garage design, but many communities are willing to pay: more and more jurisdictions are recognizing the positive effects of pedestrian interaction, increased attention to detail, and mixed-use structures. Moreover, better-designed and better-integrated parking facilities may release creative synergies, through connections with other uses and other buildings, that can help to cover the additional costs; one example is the Greenville South Street Station Project, designed by Carl Walker, Inc., and constructed in Greenville, South Carolina, in 2006, in which the building and the parking facility share the stair and elevator cores. Jurisdictions are now realizing the value of taking the long view: they are seeking opportunities not only to provide parking, but also to create civic buildings that will enhance the community for years. As a community gateway, the parking garage deserves this level of attention.[139]

Typically, the parking facility is considered the least valuable form of land use—a view that reinforces its less-than-important status in the overall plan. But as the past century has demonstrated, failing to plan for parking is a risky business. Making parking an essential element in the urban plan generates more transportation choices and better living environments. Understanding the parking garage as a civic building type is a first step in understanding the relationship between the movement of man and machine. Automobiles, mass transit, and pedestrians can successfully coexist when each is treated with the respect it deserves. Design follows parking.[140]

Around and Around We Go

The relationship between man, machine, and movement is one of the core issues in planning and architecture, and requires sensitive and complex solutions. It is essential to understand the potential synergies among transportation systems, and the integral role of the parking garage in solving the problems of the modern urban form.

Location, location, location has been and always will be the key to parking, whether in congested urban areas or small rural towns. But a sustainable vision is not built on a single focus: it is built on multiple options. As the link between options, the parking facility can play a unique role. In the coming years, fresh visions—some of which will draw from the best practices of the past—can subtly and sensitively integrate the parking garage into its surroundings. It is important to remember, however, that simply changing the placement of parking (or hiding it) does not guarantee the success of a project, let alone the success of a community. Instead, the designer must achieve a thorough understanding of the complexities (both physical and social) of a particular location, then develop a solution that will address specific needs and create the intended result. When the parking facility is *designed* to be part of a vibrant street life, it will rise to the occasion.[141]

In determining what the best solution for a given situation might be, context is all. For example, in the case of historic architectural styles, imitation is not always flattery: how a building looks, and how it relates to its surroundings, create an aesthetic whole that people intuitively grasp as relevant (or irrelevant) to their own time and place. Paraphrasing Aldo Rossi, architect Peter Rowe has noted that the "city type" reflects "the collective memory of its people made up of objects and spaces . . . a memory which in turn shapes the future."[142] And as Rossi himself has observed, "The relationship between the locus (the collective memory) and the citizenry then becomes the city's predominant image, both of architecture and of landscape. . . . In this entirely positive sense great ideas flow through the

Chicago Millennium Park, Chicago, 2006. Situated atop a new underground garage, this park offers green space, sculpture, entertainment areas, a bicycle garage, and solar entries to the parking facility.

The Parking Garage

Past Lessons for the Present and Future

⊃ Designers integrated early garages into the urban fabric by complementing the surrounding architecture and respecting the pedestrian and the streetfront. The inclusion of storefronts or other active pedestrian uses along the sidewalk edge of a garage has always been a good strategy.

⊃ By the second decade of the 20th century, the automobile had begun to redefine the way people lived: eventually, older, pedestrian-centered design strategies gave way to newer, auto-centered approaches. However, there is increasing interest, among new urbanists and others, in reviving some of the characteristics of traditional town planning—in particular, by providing people with multiple choices of how and where to live.

⊃ Changes wrought by the automobile compelled municipalities to create parking and planning commissions. Eventually, citizens—concerned about the behemoths that garages had become—demanded that municipalities address the design and placement of parking.

⊃ To combat urban sprawl, architects, designers, and developers are creating new, pedestrian-friendly places that evoke pre–World War II development patterns. These environments are often focused on transit, but also accommodate the automobile.

⊃ Properly designed, alleys can become active, pedestrian-friendly spaces where cars can enter and exit garages freely, without impeding street traffic. Moving entrances and exits to alleys also makes it easier to visually integrate the street-facing portions of the garage.

⊃ Integrating loading areas for delivery trucks into the parking facility can help keep street traffic flowing more smoothly.

⊃ Linking parking and transit can be a win-win arrangement. The point, however, is not merely to add parking spaces, but to sensitively integrate parking as a civic building type that supports the entire master plan. Transit-oriented development has the potential to reduce dependence on automobiles and to increase housing affordability.

⊃ Shared parking arrangements enable communities to take round-the-clock advantage of parking spaces—and to avoid brilliantly lit, empty eyesores that detract from the nighttime streetscape.

⊃ The parking facility is a natural generator of pedestrian activity—but only if it is fully integrated into the overall plan, rather than being hidden within a block or a building.

⊃ Public/private partnerships can be successful in parking facility design: for example, the municipality can select the location and participate in the design process, and institutions and private enterprise can contribute funding.

⊃ Citizen engagement is particularly important in public/private development projects: community residents should be informed of all the options that are available in the design of parking facilities.

⊃ Integrating other uses into the parking facility—from daycare centers to dry-cleaners to coffee shops—is not only a convenience for users, but can also cut down on additional auto trips, saving gas and helping to protect the environment. Lining the sidewalk edge of the garage with ground-floor shops is an "old" idea that is appearing again today.

history of the city and give shape to it."[143] Although mimicry of the past—no matter how lovely the older buildings in question—is not always the best choice, modern reinterpretations of past architectural approaches can often sit very comfortably alongside the real thing.

Although it has been said that "individualism in the form of the automobile, fights the formation of society and community and civilization," individual and group movement systems have coexisted since the invention of the wheel and even before.[144] The goal is not to eliminate the automobile, but to study and plan for the interweaving of movement systems in the new "modern age." Parking is not free to con-

struct, and it is expensive to maintain: thus, the key is to create the right amount of parking in the right places. Utopia is beyond reach, but it is still possible to plan for growth, while attempting to ensure that as many people as possible enjoy lives that are as happy and full as possible. Parking is a crucial element in that quest.

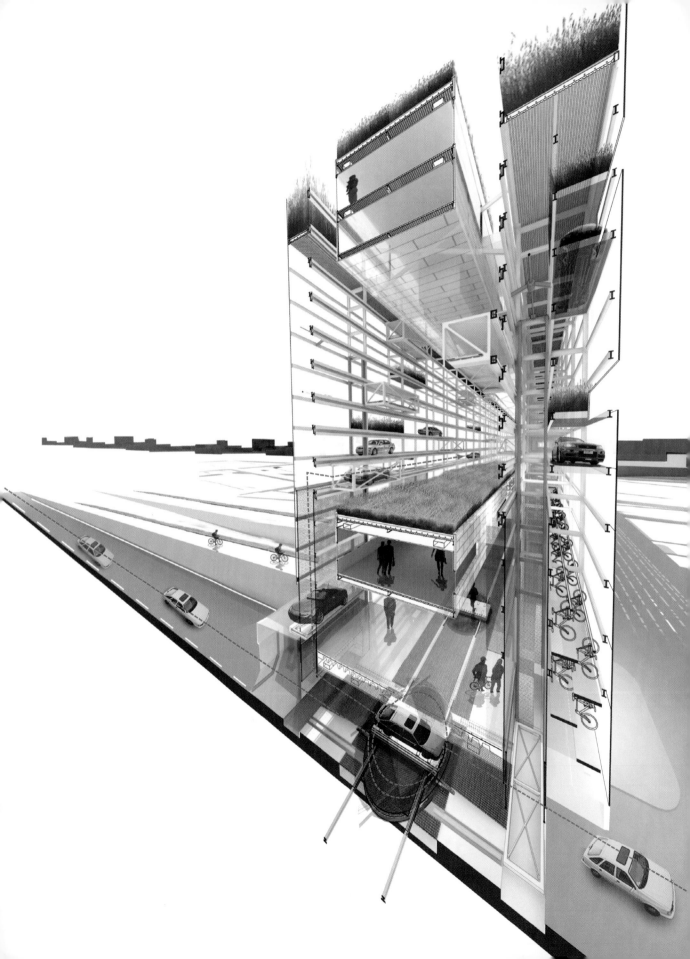

CHAPTER 10

An Evolving Building Type

P arking has been a key determinant of the form of urban settlements since at least the seventh century B.C., when the Assyrian king Sennacherib decreed that anyone parking a chariot so as to obstruct the royal road "should be put to death with his head impaled on a pole in front of his house."[1] As Joel Garreau points out in *Edge City: Life on the New Frontier,* "Twenty-seven hundred years later, the pivot of urbanity and civilization . . . is still, as it turns out, parking."[2]

The parking facility is the place where movement stops, and true connections begin. Yet "no one expects a parking ramp to chart bold new architectural paths . . . . Our expectations for these behemoths are so low that we treat them as throwaways. The result: anti-landmarks that blight entire neighborhoods, deaden street life and destroy a sense of place."[3] Although the parking garage is a locus of physical transition and connection, it is regarded as a place of "noninteraction." Nevertheless, the garage has the potential to become a place of communication and cohesion: consider the example of Evanston, Illinois, where the parking garage is transformed once a year into the site of a community garage sale.[4]

How is it that the parking garage has come to represent people's deepest fears, instead of their dreams? And how can the garage—the "lightning rod" building type—become the gateway to a better future for all?

It All Started in a Garage

Everyone has heard stories of thriving companies that were started in a garage. But how did the garage—the building out back, the one that no one notices—become a place of experimentation, innovation, and even revelation? Perhaps because it is a transitional space—a private environment where time and space merge, and the mind is free to explore.[5] Or perhaps the modern garage, because it is associated with the auto and personal mobility,

Facing page: Leven Betts Studio, *Filter Garden,* 2003. In this entry for a Chicago parking-design competition, two tall, automated glass parking structures situated over the highway clearly signal where to park, and a landscaped garden allows a transition from the world of speed to the urban environment.

Above left: Model of the Guggenheim Museum of Art, New York City, 1959. Designing for the people who will be experiencing the building is always the best approach.

Above right: Robbert Flick, photograph from the Arena Series (detail), 1977. The work of Robbert Flick, a respected Los Angeles photographer and a keen observer of the modern world, reveals Flick's fascination with the internal spaces and geometry of the parking garage.

represents some of the most sacred American ideals: the belief in individual freedom and a better future.[6] In "Landscapes Redesigned for the Automobile," John A. Jakle discusses how the automobile fit perfectly into the values that formed, and that continue to sustain, the United States: "At base was belief in individual freedom of action as well as respect for change as progress. Basic also was the pursuit of privatism, utilitarianism, and egalitarianism, values honed by pioneer circumstances."[7] Yet those pioneer circumstances also bred interdependence: newcomers to American shores have always relied on each other to survive.

This tension—between individualism and interdependence, freedom and social ties—is embodied within the parking garage. When designed as a discrete object, the building type emphasizes separation and segregation; but when designed as part of a whole, the garage celebrates and confirms relationships and connections. Many facilities of the past half-century have emphasized the individual at the expense of the communal: as Karen A. Franck and Lynda H. Schneekloth note in *Ordering Space: Types in Architecture and Design,* "segmentation of use types and efforts to arrange our lives and landscapes into independent categories have allowed many of us to avoid conflict, to escape demanding or unpleasant experiences, to remain ignorant of the problems of others, and to conceal or deny our own. We have not only escaped, we have been anesthetized."[8]

What Makes a Great Parking Place?

First and foremost, a parking facility must serve the user. Consider, for example, the Newark restaurant owner who, in 1956, used a portable air-conditioner to cool off cars that had been sitting in the lot of his restaurant, so that their interiors would be pleasant when the vehicles were returned to their drivers. A focus on the people who use the parking facility always yields the most innovative and the most lasting solutions.[9]

The Parking Garage

Milwaukee Art Museum, Milwaukee, Wisconsin, 2001. This underground garage is such a beautiful structure that architect Santiago Calatrava designed it to be visible from inside of the museum.

Of course, a parking facility must also meet the needs of the machine, the place, the owner, and the operator. Here, as in every other architectural project, one size does not fit all. Nevertheless, many of the best practices described in this book share certain guiding principles. The key principle is respect for the experience of arrival and departure. At the Milwaukee Art Museum, constructed in 2001, architect Santiago Calatrava created such a beautiful structure for the underground garage that on the lower level of the museum, the garage is visible through a glass wall, for all to admire and reflect on. Arrival and departure evoke a range of emotions: about the individual and the group; about change, movement, and progression; and about preparing for the new and reflecting on the old. Good garage design engages these emotions, creating a unique space that allows users, however unconsciously, to fully experience the present, and to explore what lies ahead and what has been left behind.[10]

Sustainability

It has been said that America's biggest export is its culture—and that includes, of course, the culture of the automobile. In countries around the world, new-found pros-perity has led to an explosion in ownership of personal vehicles: in 2003, China alone added 1.8 million cars to its roads. (If car ownership patterns in China matched those in the United States, China would have to accommodate 600 million cars—more vehicles than there are currently in the entire world.) But in China and other developing nations, the combination of industrial expansion and the proliferation of automobiles is leading to environmental degradation—a pattern that, to observers of the past 50 years of American history, is all too familiar.[11]

Worldwide environmental risks must be addressed before they overwhelm the planet. Sustainability is key to such efforts. According to the 1997 Task Force for the President's Council on Sustainable Development, sustainable communities are those that "flourish because they build a mutually supportive, dynamic balance between social well-being, economic activity, and environmental quality."[12] The phrase "dynamic balance" reflects the interconnectedness of all things. People must again consider themselves part of the natural world—and must realize that changes in the built environment have potentially devastating global effects. The challenge today is to connect the rural and the urban in a new paradigm, one that reaches far beyond anything ever envisioned by Frederick Law Olmsted. The technology is available, but the will is essential.[13]

Cars and the Environment

Auto usage is a key source of greenhouse gas (GHG) emissions and poor air quality in the United States and in many other parts of the world. A 2003 report by the Federal Transit Administration noted that "reducing emissions from the transportation sector is one of the most urgent actions needed to stabilize U.S. emissions."[14] Tests undertaken by the Center for Neighborhood Technology, in Chicago, and by TransManagement, Inc., in Washington, D.C., came to similar conclusions. Reducing greenhouse gases should simultaneously improve air quality and human health while decreasing dependence on fossil fuels. Such actions will allow the United States to look forward to a more sustainable future.[15]

A 2000 analysis of greenhouse gas emissions by sector found that transportation contributed 27 percent of all such emissions; it was second only to electricity generation.

Transportation emissions grew 20 percent between 1993 and 2004; during the same period, total emissions rose only 10 percent. In 1997, transportation surpassed industry as the leading source of carbon dioxide (CO_2) emissions in the United States. The use of petroleum in transportation exceeds the use in industry by 8 million barrels a day.[16]

Insufficient, poorly planned, and poorly located parking contributes to the excessive use of fossil fuels. After analyzing statistics from selected cities worldwide, Donald Shoup, a professor of planning at the University of California at Los Angeles, estimated that "cruising time"—the average time taken to find a parking space—has been 7.7 minutes since 1965.[17] It has also been calculated that since 1927, an average of 30 percent of traffic in downtown urban areas consists of cars looking for a parking spot rather than traveling to a destination. Especially as rates of vehicle ownership increase and cars become larger, this unnecessary driving time quickly compounds GHG emissions. Thus, well-located parking must be part of any efforts to address the environmental risks associated with fossil fuel use. Such efforts must be flexible and

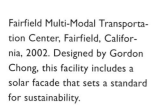

Fairfield Multi-Modal Transportation Center, Fairfield, California, 2002. Designed by Gordon Chong, this facility includes a solar facade that sets a standard for sustainability.

The Parking Garage

multidimensional: a society subject to rapid change needs an unprecedented range of transportation options. Urban planners and architects will play a crucial role in new initiatives, creating built environments that allow people to meet their daily needs and that are socially, economically, and environmentally sustainable.[18]

Sustainable buildings are also an element in environmental solutions. The Fairfield Multimodal Transportation Center, in Fairfield, California, a mixed-use complex designed by Gordon Chong and Associates and completed in August 2002, sets a new standard for sustainability that should be emulated across the country. The parking facility features solar collectors on its facade. Solar panels can also be found on the facade of a 2005 garage designed by Stanley Saitowitz for the University of San Francisco at Mission Bay; the panels complement the unique glass system on the facade. The building provides almost all its own energy and even offers a shaded rooftop, which reduces solar gain on both the vehicles and the rooftop. A gracious pedestrian stairway serves as the entry to the campus. In still another example, a 2006 garage built for Connecticut Transit incorporates a photovoltaic system.[19]

Changes in design and construction materials are moving the parking garage in the direction of greater sustainability. Because the standards of the LEED (Leadership in Energy and Environmental Design) rating system of the U.S. Green Building Council are based on human occupancy, freestanding parking facilities can rarely obtain enough points to be eligible for LEED certification; however, garages built in conjunction with other building types can add qualifying points that will enable the overall structure to obtain LEED certification.[20] A parking garage completed in 2007 in Santa Monica, California, will be the first freestanding garage to receive certification (the building does have some occupied space on the lower level). Photovoltaic panels on the roof and on the east and west facades meet all the energy needs of this remarkable structure, which offers stunning views of the Pacific Ocean and the city.[21]

Tall buildings in dense urban environments with good public transportation systems have been on the cutting edge of green design; however, such structures do not always include parking (an example is One Bryant Park, a LEED-certified building started in 2004 in New York). In some locations outside the United States, megastructures, which address all the needs of both man and machine, are the appropriate solution for highly dense environments. Roppongi Hills, for example,

Top: Parking facility, University of San Francisco at Mission Bay, San Francisco, California, 2005. This structure is another example of the trend toward solar-powered facilities.

Above: Santa Monica Civic Center Parking Structure, Santa Monica, California, 2007. This facility will be the first freestanding parking garage to qualify for certification under the LEED (Leadership in Energy and Environmental Design) rating system of the U.S. Green Building Council.

Roppongi Hills, Tokyo, 2003. In Roppongi Hills, one of the newest megastructures in Tokyo, everything one could possibly need—including both automated and ramp parking—is integrated into a single environment.

a megastructure recently constructed in Tokyo, offers multiple living, working, and transportation choices—including 2,700 ramp and automated parking spaces—and an integrated natural landscape. Such environments can provide an excellent quality of life for people of all ages.[22]

Integrating Parking and the Landscape

Integrating parking and the landscape is one way to preserve (or create) green space while meeting urban needs. Combining parking with amenities such as tennis courts, gardens, playgrounds, and swimming pools changes the community's perception of the garage and increases the value of the land use. In a visionary design by V.P. Batista and Associates, for example, parking and a landscaped rooftop community center are tucked into an embankment, while highway traffic flows below.[23]

Although rooftop gardens are nothing new (New York's Astor and Waldorf-Astoria hotels had roof gardens before the end of the 19th century), it was not until the 1920s that a garden was placed on the top of an underground garage: Philadelphia's Garden Court. San Francisco's Union Square Garage, completed in 1942, was built under an existing park—an arrangement that became common throughout the country. At Boston's Post Office Square, a 1,500-car underground garage replaced an aboveground facility that had been built 20 years before, reclaiming the land for trees, lawns, and

pavilions, and creating a pleasant green space amid the downtown skyscrapers. This strategy is still a good one today.[24]

Making a garage roof a part of the urban landscape—allowing it to replace the original natural site, only several stories higher—can help lessen the amount of open space that is lost to automobile uses. As early as 1950, a garage with a landscaped roof was proposed by the New York Life Company, in New York City. In 1969, Ashen & Allen Architects collaborated with T.Y. Lin to create a playing field, with 18 inches (0.45 meters) of turf, on top of a garage in Berkeley, California (the facility was recently replaced, minus the playing field). But it was the Kaiser Center Garage, in Oakland, California—designed by Theodore Osmundson and built in 1961—that featured the largest continuous roof garden in the world. In an area where 90 percent of the land was covered by buildings, Osmundson created a semi-public park (although the land was owned by a private company, public access was provided), and ensured that 60 percent of that same area would be covered with plantings.[25]

The Kaiser Center demonstrated how the natural environment could be preserved even in dense areas, and marked the beginning of the green roof movement. Today, rooftop gardens large and small can be found on parking garages throughout the country: examples include those at Cambridge Center and at the University Green, both in Cambridge, Massachusetts. Although transforming a garage

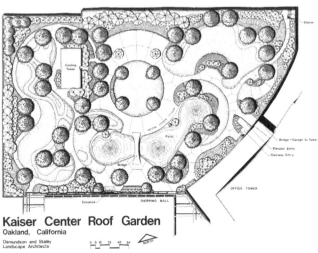

Left: Proposed parking facility for the New York Life Company, New York City, 1950. This design for a parking garage included a landscaped roof.

Below: Entry Pavilion Parking Structure, Monterey, California, 2004. Nestled into the hillside, this parking structure interacts gently with the land.

Bottom: Kaiser Center Garage, Oakland, California, 1961. This garage, designed by Theodore Osmundson, a landscape architect, marked the beginning of the green roof movement.

Kaiser Center Roof Garden
Oakland, California
Osmundson and Staley
Landscape Architects

roof into a park or a playground is most common in dense urban environments, the strategy is worth considering even in suburban areas, where parking lots contribute to excessive stormwater runoff and to the heat island effect.[26]

Often, the combination of parking facility and public park is commercially viable: for example, Barney Allis Plaza, a park and underground garage that serves the Kansas City Convention Center, also attracts members of the general public. At Northpark Town Center, built in 1991 in a suburb of Atlanta, the parking garage is a series of stepped-back rooftop terraces nestled within a hillside, an arrangement that provides beautiful views and easily accessible parking for the entire complex. Many facilities have featured plantings on the facade, sometimes in combination with a stepped-back facade, which yields a pleasing, natural effect within the built environment. This approach was used at parking garages constructed in 1991 at Ronald Reagan Washington National Airport, in Arlington, Virginia.[27]

The 1,400-car parking facility for Blue Cross/Blue Shield in North Haven, Connecticut, built in 1990, features interior landscaping, which visually softens the structure and supports way-finding. Users are naturally drawn to the central atrium, where the main stairway and a skyway linking the parking facility to the office complex are clearly visible. Although the combination of landscaping and open space within the interior of a garage is not yet a common approach, it creates a

Top: Parking facility, Ronald Reagan Washington National Airport, Arlington, Virginia, 1991. At this facility, stepped landscaping helps integrate the garage into the natural environment.

Bottom: Northpark Town Center, Atlanta, Georgia, 1991. At this office center, the garage was integrated into the landscape.

The Parking Garage

more pleasant arrival and departure experience and can help to soften the sometimes harsh interiors of modern open-deck structures, allowing them to become places of transition. Richard C. Rich's design for a 1968 facility in Cedar Rapids, Iowa, which included a light core (a multilevel open space that often includes plantings and other amenities), is one of the earliest examples of this approach.[28]

At the University of California at Santa Cruz, a campus known for its environmental sensitivity, Watry Design situated a new garage on the footprint of an existing parking lot, in order to disturb as few as possible of the redwood trees that hug the site. Integral paths enhance the pedestrian experience and connect the facility to the surrounding natural paths. The parking facility is now well hidden behind the trees, demonstrating that parking and trees can coexist—even without a landscaped roof.[29]

New Links between Parking and the Community

A number of studies have looked at driving patterns in the United States—in particular, at whether people drive by choice or out of necessity—and the results point to a paradox: "People drive more than they would like to yet they are not doing so entirely out of need."[30] Changing this pattern is one of the most difficult challenges that planners, designers, and public officials face.[31]

Many European cities have mastered the art of creating "walkable urbanity"—and in the United States, the revived interest in living, working, and playing downtown is creating a growing demand for walkable places. Such environments offer a number of advantages: they provide built-in exercise, which may help to stem the tide of obesity in the American population; they allow seniors and others who have limited mobility to engage fully in community life; and they help to support more sustainable development patterns. The automobile is still a part of this mix; as growth occurs, however, perhaps parking spaces can be managed in a more sustainable way.

The design of the street, and the design and placement of the parking garage, are of course key to the creation of walkable environments. It is important to remember, however, that walkability is not a panacea: successful transportation management requires a broad range of movement options. Turning directly to the community for guidance, through charrettes or other participatory approaches, can

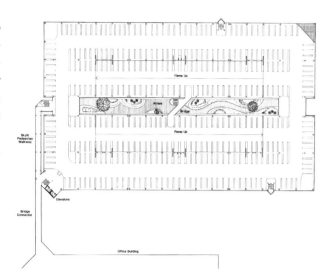

Top: Blue Cross/Blue Shield facility, North Haven, Connecticut, 1990. The design of this facility brought the landscape inside—an approach that softened the harsh interior, added natural light, and provided a natural way-finding system.

Above: Parking facility, University of Santa Cruz, Santa Cruz, California, 2001. In an example of extraordinary design finesse, Watry Design replaced a parking lot with structured parking, while disturbing only a few of the surrounding mature redwoods.

An Evolving Building Type

open the way to new synergies and possibilities. Ideally, such an initiative would begin with a blank slate, allowing the participatory process to become a shared learning experience.[32] In a quest for what might be called "extreme walkability," London is currently experimenting with a "naked street"—one devoid of markings, traffic lights, and even curbs. The idea is to calm traffic by placing responsibility on the users, pedestrians and drivers alike.

Newly developed (or redeveloped) walkable places are drawing visitors from far beyond the immediate neighborhood. Somewhat ironically, many (if not most) of these visitors arrive by car. Although the influx of pedestrian traffic is good for local businesses, automobile traffic—and the accompanying surge in parking needs—is another story. A number of jurisdictions have found positive strategies for handling intermittent increases in parking needs; in fact, some of these strategies have actually encouraged local residents to move downtown. Shared parking, thoughtful pricing strategies, and the integration of transit into urban design are among the approaches used to address temporary surges in parking needs. Another option is to return to the use of demountable garages and temporary parking lots.[33]

When supported by planning, low-tech solutions such as bicycles and car sharing become viable. Although getting around by bicycle has historically been more common in Europe—as early as 1946, a bicycle garage was built in Copenhagen for the office and factory workers of G.M. International—bicycling has also found a place in the United States. In 1959, Fairbanks, Alaska, opened a 200-bicycle lot to alleviate sidewalk congestion. In 1970, the APCOA division of ITT, the nation's largest parking firm, began offering free parking for all nonmotorized bikes in 116 cities across the country; these were the first garage spaces for bicycles in the United States. Two years later, the National Parking Association initiated a similar program, in which 26 downtown parking garages in the nation's capital participated. Space for bicycles can now be found integrated into parking facilities in many different ways—from small bike racks to large "caged" bike rooms. In Japan, high-tech bicycle parking has been part of the transportation mix since the 1980s: in 1989, the peak year for the construction of bicycle parking facilities in Japan, 55 automated facilities were built to shelter 40,446 bicycles. A facility near Ohfuna Transit Station, in Yokohama, includes ramp parking for automobiles, a separate parking structure for motorcycles, a nine-story automated facility for bicycles, and small lots for additional bicy-

cles. The facility—a truly multimodal hub—also offers bus connections and is within walking distance of rail.[34]

Although providing space for bicycle parking appears to be straightforward—a matter of creating dedicated areas for bikes in existing garages—as bicycle use increases, and as cities add code requirements for bicycle spaces, conflicts may arise between bicycle users and automobile drivers. Some facilities have addressed this issue by separating bicycle parking from automobile parking; nevertheless, the combination of bicycles and cars will continue to create design challenges.

Some newer parking facilities for bicycles provide bikers

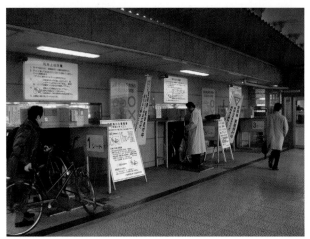

Top: Bicycle-parking facility, Copenhagen, 1946. In this early bicycle-parking facility, created for the office and factory workers of G.M. International, a retaining wall created the shape that optimized the space available for bicycles.

Above: Automated bicycle-parking facility, Yokohama, Japan, circa 1990. The automated bicycle facilities that can be found all over Japan store the maximum number of bicycles in the minimum amount of space.

The Parking Garage

Bikestation, Long Beach, California, 2006. Today, some bicycle-parking facilities include showers and lockers, and are designed to complement the architecture of the community.

with other services as well. For example, in addition to secure bicycle storage, Bikestation—a nonprofit, California-based organization—offers lockers, showers, rentals, sales, and repair. The first station opened in 1996, in Long Beach; three more have been built in Berkeley, Palo Alto, and Seattle; and others are now in the planning stage for Union Station, in Washington, D.C., and in conjunction with the Granada Garage, in Santa Barbara. Chicago's Millennium Park Bicycle Station, which opened in 2004, provides 300 indoor, heated spots for bicycle parking, as well as lockers, showers, and bicycle maintenance services. In Fruitvale Village, a transit-oriented development in Oakland, California, residents opted to relocate the proposed automobile garage because it would have blocked pedestrian access to the transit stop. Ultimately, the parking facility was constructed on the other side of the tracks, and a long-desired bicycle-parking station—with a 200-bicycle capacity—was built within 100 feet (30 meters) of the northeast transit exit. Retail, a health clinic, offices, a library, lofts, and a community resource center are now situated on the site originally proposed for the parking garage.[35]

Carpooling, car sharing, and other low-tech solutions have so far not met with a great deal of support outside of a few areas. However, if such arrangements were to become community owned and supported, the tide might turn, reviving the notion of the "neighborhood parking garage"—the sort of convenient, centrally located facility that was a part of life in the early 20th century, and that was perhaps best exemplified by the Dupont Garage, in Washington, D.C. Such neighborhood garages could also support the new car-sharing programs—short-term car rentals that, in some cases, may obviate the need for a second car, or even any car at all.[36]

Urban planners face daunting challenges in their efforts to accommodate the modern lifestyle. People are more mobile—both professionally and geographically—than ever before; household arrangements are more diverse; the population is aging; and demands for sustainability are increasing. As a result, transportation needs are constantly changing, and planners must provide as many options as possible. Although new planning approaches are certainly necessary, planning cannot singlehandedly solve parking, land use, and environmental problems; the overall movement system must change as well. Planners and architects must learn to integrate all aspects of movement, and every conceivable form of transportation, in new ways. The future depends on it.[37]

Improving the Pedestrian Experience

Even with the transition to the self-park garage, the pedestrian experience was not ignored. Merchants Parking, for example, a facility completed in Indianapolis in 1966, provided an attractive lobby where packages could be delivered, and where drivers and passengers could wait safely

Top left: Economy Garage, Tampa International Airport, Tampa, Florida, 2007. Gracious waiting rooms and pedestrian areas were a part of early parking garages. These features are starting to reappear in some modern parking facilities.

Top right: Entry Pavilion Parking Structure, Monterey, California, 2004. Attention to architectural detail provides a calming pick-up and drop-off space for people at a hospital entry.

Right: Cincinnati Union Terminal, Cincinnati, Ohio, 1933. At this train terminal, the design attention given to the bus ramp was equal to that given to every other part of the structure.

and comfortably. The Georgia-Pacific Garage, constructed in Portland, Oregon, in 1970, also included a welcoming transition place for travelers.[38]

A pleasant pedestrian experience depends largely on the preservation—or creation—of a human scale within the parking facility. Cincinnati's Union Terminal, built in 1933, featured beautifully detailed bus ramps and pedestrian walkways to the main hall. This same level of attention to design within the parking facility would improve the pedestrian arrival and departure experience tremendously.[39]

A range of architectural approaches can be used to support way-finding, to engage users' senses, and to increase

awareness of the intersections between pedestrians' and drivers' movement paths. A number of garages built since the 1990s feature dedicated pedestrian paths along the outside edges of the floor plate—the part of the structure that offers the most natural light and the best sight lines. Examples include a 1992 garage designed by Machado & Silvetti for Princeton University; the University of Iowa's Newton Road Parking Ramp, designed by Herbert Lewis Kruse Blunck and completed in 2001; and the Emory University Clairmont Campus Parking Deck, completed in 2002.[40]

It is important to remember, however, that even the most carefully planned walking paths within the garage cannot

The Parking Garage

eliminate the conflict between pedestrian and automobile movement patterns; paths should therefore be designed with care, especially in high-turnover facilities. In addition, unless all automobiles turn into the garage from alleyways, and unless pedestrians are limited to the sidewalk, garage design must take into account the complex interactions between street, sidewalk, auto, and pedestrian.[41]

Unique Visions

As the population increases and the desire for mobility expands, the only true answer to the parking problem is to create a movement system that disappears the moment one is finished using it. Since this seems unlikely, the goal is to create a range of widely accessible movement systems—and, as necessary, places to arrive, depart, and park.

It was Eugene Henard, architect for the city of Paris, who first imagined a totally integrated, environmentally sensitive combination of building and street: in a 1910 Henard design, the transit system flowed below street level, emissions were ventilated through the tall buildings above, and automobiles were moved by elevator directly to apartments: essentially, the car was parked in the home. Decades later, a portion of Henard's vision was realized through arrangements in which each floor of a parking garage connected directly to a floor of an office or hotel. At the CarLoft, in Berlin, which is scheduled for completion in 2007, cars will be parked on the balconies of an apartment tower. And at a recent condominium project in New York, designed by Annabelle Selldorf, vertical elevators for cars will allow residents to have private garages up in the sky, next to their homes.[42]

Above: Parking facility, Princeton University, Princeton, New Jersey, 1992. To create a more pedestrian-friendly experience within the garage, some newer parking facilities are providing separate pedestrian walkways.

Right: Newton Road Parking Ramp, University of Iowa, Iowa City, 2001. This facility features transit links, pedestrian walkways, and pedestrian amenities.

An Evolving Building Type

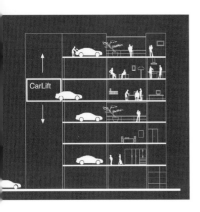

CarLoft, Berlin, 2007. Parking that is adjacent to a home in the sky has become reality.

Union Carbide Headquarters, Danbury, Connecticut, 1980. This corporate headquarters places office buildings directly adjacent to the central parking structure, allowing tenants to easily park near the building and floor where they work.

NL Architects, *Parkhouse Carstadt*, Amsterdam, 1995. Entirely new visions of parking are emerging that integrate man and machine.

In 1995, NL Architects, of Amsterdam, created a new parking form: Parkhouse/Carstadt, an ingenious roadlike structure that twists, turns, and overlaps itself. Situated on an angled site intersected by a road, the facility provides the maximum amount of parking that can be achieved on the site, and features apartments, stores, a hotel, and restaurants. NL Architects has also proposed a design called Roof Road, in which driveways are positioned on the tops of row houses, offering a panoramic view and allowing the ground level to be car-free and child-friendly. In Verona, Italy, Gabellini Associates, of New York, replaced an aging plaza with an underground parking facility that features a waterfall

at the entry. Light filters down into canted spaces on the periphery of the garage.[43]

A 2003 competition—the Stop Go, Chicago Portal Project—asked designers to create a 1,000-car garage between Madison and Monroe, spanning the expressway. Most of the proposals focused on hiding the garage with landscaping or using other amenities to distract from it. One of the first-place winners, however, celebrated the garage: the design, entitled *Filter Garden*, consisted of two 130-foot- (40-meter-) tall automated parking towers separated by a "filtering garden" for bicycles and pedestrians. The towers would serve as visual gateways to the city, and would also provide clues, for the speeding cars below, as to the location of parking. A similar vision was realized in Copenhagen, through a 50/50 partnership between the city government and a housing development company. Each automated parking tower houses 700 vehicles and offers users a wonderful interior waiting area. The activated space between the towers features a public garden and a skate park. The successful provision of parking is not merely a question of where, what type, and how much, but of imagination, innovation, and appropriate focus on the architectural challenges and opportunities posed by the building typology.[44]

As these recent proposals demonstrate, the parking facility is capable of moving closer to the social and civic role of the great train halls of the past. In fact, the parking garage may actually move beyond the train station, as the car begins to travel throughout the entire interior of a mixed-use facility, entering the types of spaces previously reserved for human occupation and bringing movement into otherwise

The Parking Garage

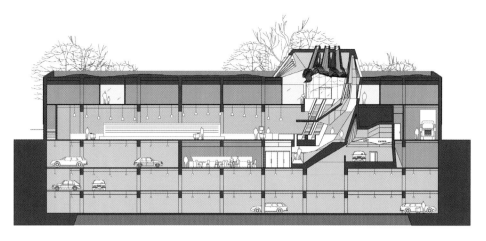

Above: SHoP, VMall virtual project, 2000. In this approach to integrating man and machine, the automobile is incorporated into the center of a multistory mall.

Below: Lewis. Tsurumaki. Lewis. (LTL) Architects, Park Tower virtual project, 2005. This concept fully integrates a variety of uses, including parking, in a tower envisioned for any city.

static interiors. In VMall, for example, a virtual project created in 2000 by SHoP (Sharples Holden Pasquarelli), cars move through a central atrium, completely integrating the parking ramp into the architectural experience. The lower floors of the five-story structure are for parking only, and the upper floors include parking, ramps, and retail. The roof features a miniature-golf course.[45]

As the building type continues to evolve, more architectural, cost-effective, and environmentally friendly methods to engage the pedestrian will transform the gateway experience of the parking facility. This is the challenge of the garage: to become humanized.

Transformations in Movement

The car was the catalyst for much of 20th-century design. But the car of today is unlikely to be the car of tomorrow, and the 21st century is already upon us.[46]

No sooner had the automobile appeared than inventors were attempting to improve it. The Curtiss Autoplane, designed in 1917, was the first car-plane combination. Self-parkers (fold-up cars) first made their appearance in 1927 (the fold-up bicycle—one version of which was patented in 1955—remains popular today). At the Century of Progress exhibit at the Chicago World's Fair of 1933, cars that looked like airplanes were presented as the vehicles of the future. The Fulton Airphibian, designed by Robert Fulton in 1946, could be transformed from auto to flying machine by one person in five minutes; the U.S. Department of Air Commerce developed variations on this design. By midcentury,

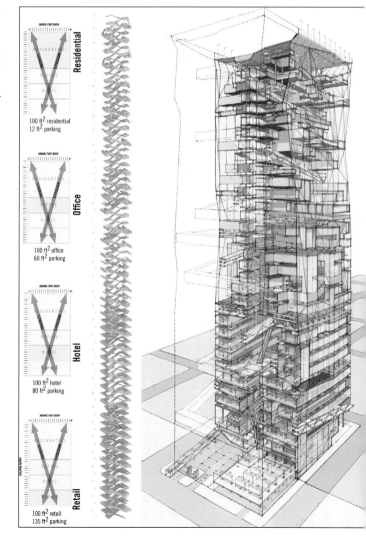

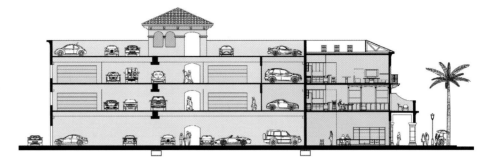

Southwest Florida mixed-use project, 2006. Integrating parking with mixed uses can pose challenges with respect to design and building codes, but it can be undertaken successfully.

many architects, including Buckminster Fuller and Frank Lloyd Wright, had created their own designs for cars.[47]

Today, the National Aeronautics and Space Administration, the U.S. Army and Navy, and a firm in Israel are competing to develop vehicles capable of vertical takeoff and landing. Moller International, in Davis, California, has already flight-tested a four-passenger vehicle known as the Skycar—which is just one among many futuristic versions of the car that are currently being developed. But even hovering vehicles like the Skycar will have to land *somewhere*—unless, like the "hood over heels" patented in 1926, the car of the future can be made to fly *and* to collapse when it is not needed.[48]

Anderson Miller's "Nonsense about the City of Tomorrow," published in the September 1943 issue of *The American City,* offers an eye-opening assessment of what the future may bring—and of why it is important to look at all the possibilities, as the outcome is always unknown. At the City of Tomorrow, airplanes were envisioned as the solution to the parking problem. Will technology fulfill its promise, and will people soon be flying about by means of power packs on their backs? And will this actually solve the parking problem?[49]

Meanwhile, real changes are finally coming to the automobile. With rising fuel prices, sales of hybrid-powered cars are increasing rapidly. Hybrid-powered buses are also coming into wider use: the 235-bus fleet of the Seattle Transit Authority saves an estimated 750,000 gallons (2.8 million liters) of fuel annually. Smaller cars, such as the Smart Car, are now becoming more popular. Fuel-cell technology, first developed in the mid-20th century, currently has a number of applications in transportation and can also be used to power buildings. In Tokyo, architect Kiminobu Kimura's home turns "hydrogen power into electricity and hot water into cold."[50] And in Edison and Parsippany, New Jersey, two Sheraton hotels meet their basic power needs by means of 250-kilowatt fuel cells; Sheraton plans to ex-

pand this program to more hotels. Through the Freedom-CAR Partnership, a joint effort of the U.S. Department of Energy and the U.S. Council for Automotive Research (representing Ford, General Motors, and DaimlerChrysler) fuel-cell-powered vehicles are now operating in Washington, D.C. In Ann Arbor, Michigan, the Environmental Protection Agency (EPA) and DaimlerChrysler operate a hydrogen fueling station at the EPA's National Vehicle and Fuel Emissions Laboratory. The EPA and DaimlerChrysler are also collaborating with UPS to put hydrogen-powered vehicles into service in Michigan. Use of fuel-cell technology is likely to expand, as part of a growing hydrogen economy. Other energy sources, such as biofuels, offer potential, although not the synergy between energy use and architecture that is associated with fuel cells. Moreover, changing energy sources requires tremendous upfront investment: infrastructure and vehicles may need to be redesigned to accommodate new fuel sources.[51]

As Daniel Burnham said, "Make no little plans." Advanced movement technologies will eventually reshape transportation, urban planning, and, of course, the parking garage. The role of parking can be crucial in this transformation, as long as planners, designers, developers, and citizens understand its potential to positively engage man and machine.

A Holistic Approach

Utopian visions for the future have often centered on movement—which, "at high speed and in its latest technological manifestation, is seen as a symbol of life, dynamism and strength."[52] Because the parking garage represents the vehicle at rest, the imaginative solutions of parking facility designers have rarely received the attention they deserved. Nevertheless, "they also serve who only stand and wait."[53] Even though a parking garage may not be as evocative and romantic as a speeding vehicle, it has no less importance in the fabric of a successful society.[54]

By the late 1930s, with the installation of the first parking meters, all the primary ways to park a car were available: street parking, surface parking lots, ramp parking garages, and mechanized garages. Creative solutions for *locating* parking continued to proliferate, however: under parks and buildings, over highways, on off-shore barges, and even underwater. Parking on the street is the least costly solution. Surface lots, though inexpensive to create, accommodate the smallest number of cars for the amount of space required. Ramp garages allow more efficient use of space than lots; however, mechanized parking can provide two or three times the number of parking spaces in the same land area.[55]

The most important task today in garage design is to determine the unique needs of a particular location—not just now, but for the future—and to respond to those needs holistically: with an understanding of past solutions, a willingness to innovate, and a respect for the aesthetics, the functionality, and the social fabric of the surroundings. In the 1970s, the preferred solution was one in which parking was physically separated from other uses, but in close proximity to the principal associated use. Although there is no question that this arrangement allows for the most efficient garage design, it has become outdated, and increasing emphasis is being placed on integrating the garage into the community.

As the parking lot is less and less likely to be the "easy" solution, more sophisticated and sensitive approaches are becoming all the more important. Kyocera's Solar Grove Parking Lot is one example of how a parking lot can be transformed into a clean electrical generator while also shading cars. When people's needs for transportation and for places to live, work, and shop are considered holistically, the solutions that are devised are more sustainable and lead to improved quality of life. And, as always, parking is at the center of the equation.[56]

Among the factors that need to be taken into account in parking garage design are changes in the automobile. The car, initially viewed as a force for environmental change, may yet achieve that goal. The automobile of the future will no longer depend on fossil fuels; it will be quiet; it will not emit pollutants; and it will require minimal effort on the part of the driver. Even the materials used to construct cars will eventually be completely recyclable. The car of the future

will once again transform the world, interweaving the movement of man and machine. And as the vehicle changes, every aspect of the parking facility will be affected.

At the same time, greater understanding of the unique nature of the parking facility will allow fire, building, and zoning regulations to evolve, yielding new combinations of building types and new use mixes. Currently, codes based on other building types are still being applied to parking facilities, especially when the facilities are combined with other uses.[57] As a result, some use mixes that would otherwise be highly desirable are too costly to construct. Eventually, however, more rational codes—based on scientific study of current conditions, on the special characteristics of the parking garage, and on new developments in the building type—will evolve.[58] One result will be greater support for mixed use.[59]

Visions within Reach

Sustainability depends on a mix of high-tech and low-tech strategies: after all, freedom of choice is the American way. Integrated approaches—characterized by multiple transportation choices, a range of living options, walkability, and interconnectedness—have already been implemented in new communities; in revitalized parts of small cities and towns; and in dense, older urban environments such as Chicago, New York, and San Francisco. Although visions of urban sustainability still provoke skepticism, they have also given rise to carefully tempered optimism about the future of the city. The history of 20th-century industrialization and development—and the attendant pollution—need not be repeated.[60]

Although not everyone desires the intensity of New York City, increasing urbanization may help the environment because city dwellers tend to use resources more efficiently. Thus, more complex urban development is likely to play a crucial role in the future. Within such systems, some form of parking is the linchpin—the connector between multiple forms of transportation, higher densities, and diverse land use options.

Technology and nature *can* coexist. Brownfield sites in older downtowns, for example, are being transformed into models of sustainable development: Atlantic Station, discussed in chapter 8, is just one example. Even parking garages and streams and wetlands can coexist: at the new Emmet Street parking garage, at the University of Virginia, in Charlottesville, a stream on the site was retained within

Top: Proposed design for Speedwalk, 1954. One of the first proposed urban applications for moving walks was to connect buildings and parking structures.

Bottom: Hedges Garage (location and date unknown). Garages for electric vehicles were the first parking garages in this country. Integrating services for electric vehicles into parking garages is an approach that makes sense for today's commuters.

its existing channel, and the garage was built above—preserving the natural habitat for fish, birds, and native plantings.[61]

Moving Sidewalks and Elevators

The moving sidewalk is among the technologies that have the potential to reshape architecture, planning, and the parking structure. The idea is not new: in 1874, Harold Speer envisioned an elevated moving sidewalk as a means of transporting pedestrians along lower Broadway, in New York City. In 1889, Eugene Henard proposed a moving platform for pedestrians; such a platform was actually built for the Paris Exposition of 1900. In the United States, the first pedestrian conveyor was built for the World's Columbian Exposition, held in Chicago in 1893. The device did not become commercially available, however, until 1954.[62]

Automated movement technologies for pedestrians have been linked to the parking garage for decades. In 1954, a moving sidewalk was envisioned to connect parking lots, buildings, and shopping centers in Jersey City, New Jersey; the first such sidewalk that was actually constructed linked Jersey City's Erie Railroad terminal with a station on the Hudson and Manhattan transit line. A moving sidewalk constructed in 1955 was designed to connect the Sam Houston Coliseum, in Houston, Texas, to a 2,000-car parking structure. Also in 1955, the University of Washington considered constructing a moving sidewalk to link the parking garage to the campus center. In 1970, a "horizontal elevator" was planned to connect a high-rise hotel and a 2,000-car parking garage in Columbus, Ohio. In 1984, Otis shuttles were built to connect a number of building types in Harbour Island, a master-planned community in Tampa. A number of airports across the country now feature such shuttles, some of which are connected to parking structures—as is the case at Tampa International Airport.[63]

Today, people movers have the potential to create entirely new linkages between man and machine. One new system—the Odyssey elevator, which is currently not being marketed— is capable of moving people sideways, as well as up and down, and can even move them in and out of buildings. Such systems may bring to life the kinds of connections envisioned by Henard, whose 1910 drawing *Street of the Future* features pedestrian movement systems that bring residents and vehicles right to their doors. As the automobile and other forms of transportation change, interconnectivity among individual and collective movement systems will become reality.[64]

Electric Vehicles

The electric cab was central to the advent of the commercial parking industry, and electric vehicles were quite popular during the first decade of the 20th century, when the automobile was still regarded as an environmental savior. After a hiatus of more than four decades, electric vehicles became available again in the 1960s. In 1967, behind an Allentown office building occupied by Pennsylvania Power and Light, Colonial Parking opened a "plug-in-and-park" facility for electric cars. In Tucson, Arizona, in 1975, the Downtown Shoppers Garage was among 30 facilities in the area to offer free recharging for electric cars. Electric vehicles—available, in some form, for the past three decades—are enjoying a resurgence. Will the electric car again lead the way to the future?[65]

Today, many educational institutions and other entities that require large, campuslike settings use electric vehicles to conserve energy and protect the environment. Electric-powered GEMs (Global Electric Motorcars)—small, street-legal vehicles that cannot exceed 25 miles per hour (40 kilometers per hour)—are gaining popularity for brief, in-neighborhood trips. In 1959, Peachtree City, a planned community in Atlanta, was designed around the use of electric golf carts for neighborhood trips. In Palo Alto, California, the High/Alma South Parking Facility, built in 2003, includes recharging stations for electric vehicles. GE Lofts, a condo conversion project developed in Atlanta in 2000, features solar panels and electric-vehicle charging stations, and has even provided some homebuyers with electric bicycles. Electric school buses are running in Napa Valley, California. Park-

ing garage designers, accustomed to meeting the unique functional needs of the automobile and the individual desires of drivers, will be challenged anew to address the needs of electric vehicles.[66]

Automated People Movers

Since the late 19th century, world's fairs have offered futuristic visions of how people could and would live. The monorail is among the visions that have became reality: Detroit has two (one downtown and one at the airport), and Seattle and Las Vegas have one each. The Seattle system, built for the 1962 World's Fair, features inclined moving sidewalks that link pedestrians to the tracks and platforms; the 1.2-mile (1.9-kilometer) trip from downtown Seattle to the fairgrounds takes 95 seconds.[67]

Although most people connect monorails with world's fairs and amusement parks, there is no reason to limit advanced transit technology to such environments. For many land uses—such as airports, medical centers, and colleges—automated people movers have tremendous potential to address congestion, increase connectivity, mitigate parking shortages, and provide links to parking.

One technology within the people mover category that offers great potential to change movement, architectural, and planning paradigms is personal rapid transit (PRT)—a network of small, automated vehicles that run on guideways, providing on-demand, nonstop service to the chosen destination. In the level of service they provide, PRT systems are akin to taxicabs. What gives PRT its flexibility and efficiency is the concept of the off-line station: instead of progressing in linear fashion, stopping at every station, PRT vehicles automatically take passengers directly to their final destination; all other stations are bypassed. The first PRT system in the country—built in Morgantown, West Virginia, in the 1970s—still offers safe and secure cars; nonstop, point-to-point travel; and little or no waiting times for West Virginia University.[68]

A PRT network allows movement to be quicker and more efficient: because passengers are delivered directly to their desired location, with no stops in between, PRT allows more people to be moved within a given time period than conventional transit. PRT offers other advantages as well. Because of its human scale, PRT allows the pedestrian experience to be preserved—minus the traffic and congestion. It can also provide a more flexible link between man and machine: because it so small, quiet, and light (compared with conventional transit), PRT can be adapted to a wider array

Above: ULTra Parking Connection, Heathrow Airport, London, 2007. A personal rapid transit system is being installed to connect parking lots and terminals at Heathrow Airport.

Right, top and bottom: StarrCar, circa 1960. The StarrCar was designed to serve either as a transit car or as a private vehicle, depending on the situation.

of environments. Although PRT does not eliminate the need for parking, it does offer opportunities to change the parking paradigm. In an automated parking facility, for example, PRT vehicles could easily change direction or move between levels within a small space.

PRT systems can provide excellent transit coverage for urban or suburburban areas; such a system would be ideal, for example, in locations such as Destiny USA—the environmentally sensitive entertainment, shopping, and technology project currently under construction in Syracuse, New York. PRT would be equally appropriate in more traditional urban locations, particularly as a link between parking and other land uses. Heathrow airport is currently installing such as system to link the terminal to remote parking. The system,

The Parking Garage

CyberCab, Floriade, Hoofddorp, Netherlands, 2002. A new transportation company, "2getther," provides completely new forms of automated transit. The CyberCab shown here was created for temporary use at a horticultural show.

known as ULTra (Urban Light Transport), is expected to be in place by 2008. As part of a larger effort to explore the transformation of office parks into transit villages, Cities21, a nonprofit research organization based in Palo Alto, California, is completing an EPA-funded study of the environmental benefits of a PRT system within the Hacienda Business Park. In November 2006, the citizens of Fresno, California, voted to spend $36 million to establish a fund to begin a PRT effort in their downtown. New PRT products, such as Sky-Web Express, are being developed around the world.[69]

In the 1960s, William Alden designed the StarrCar, a vehicle that could function independently, on the road, or on dedicated tracks, as part of a transit system. At the time, technology had not yet caught up to Alden's vision, although part of Alden's concept was the basis for the Morgantown PRT system. Today, however, with advanced automotive technology, Alden's vision is almost within reach. Within a system that allowed vehicles to be taken off the tracks as needed, for example, PRT vehicles may be used to pick up drivers at their parking spots and take them to their next destination. The parking facility could both provide space for traditional vehicles, and become an active participant in new approaches to transit and movement.[70]

A number of technologies developed to help drivers— including automated braking, parking-assistance systems, and highway-guidance systems—may eventually affect parking garage design as well. An automated braking system senses when something is in the path of a car and causes the car to stop, which can be helpful when visibility is poor or when the car is backing up. A parking-assistance system senses the parameters of a parallel parking space and guides the automobile and the driver to a perfect fit. Highway-guidance systems are being studied as a means of keeping cars evenly spaced when they are traveling at high speeds. As automotive technologies advance, moving in the direction of "cars that drive themselves," it may be possible to drop off a car at a garage and have the car park itself. As PRT, automated vehicles, and other high-tech transportation options become integrated into the overall transportation system, they will affect parking garage design in ways that cannot yet be imagined.[71]

Beauty, technology, function, engineering, and civic purpose: the pieces are all in place. But determining the solutions of the future—whether urban, suburban, or rural— will mean connecting, at a deeper level, to the ways in which people relate to the world around them. It will be through these deeper connections that new solutions will emerge.[72] Horst Bredekamp, in an exploration of the phenomenon of

Garage, Litton Industries Corporate Headquarters, Beverly Hills, California, 1975. In this early approach to environmentally friendly design, the garage was visually integrated into the surrounding environment.

the Kunstkammer—the cabinets of art and curiosities that were the precursors to modern museums—notes that

No one wants to return to the deliberate chaos of the Kustkammer as museums. But the boundaries between art, technology, and science are beginning to break down in a similar manner as has been demonstrated by the Kunstkammer. In view of this fact, their lessons of visual association and thought processes which precede language systems take on a significance which might even surpass their original status. Highly technological societies are experiencing a phase of Copernican change from the dominance of language to the hegemony of images.[73]

Gateway to the Future: 21st-Century Transformations

The costs of sprawl are reaching the breaking point. As the search for affordable land and housing pushes development farther and farther into the countryside, massive infrastructure costs—for roads, sewers, utilities, and schools—inevitably follow.[74] Moreover, the cost of unfettered outward expansion falls most heavily on those who can least afford it: households with incomes under $27,176 spend 25.3 to 40.2 percent of their after-tax incomes on transportation;

among households with household incomes above $44,462, the corresponding figures are 13.1 to 18.2 percent. And in Europe, 6 percent of household income is spent on transportation; in the United States, the figure is 19 percent.[75]

Thus, much of the future depends on curbing sprawl, while preserving—and even expanding—choice: using existing infrastructure efficiently, increasing density, providing as many travel options as possible, decreasing automobile dependency, improving the distribution of jobs and housing, maintaining housing affordability, and protecting the environment. Inevitably, the parking structure will play a key role in such efforts.

The parking garage is a civic building type: needed by all, used by all. It is not a transient phenomenon but a permanent feature of everyday American life—and, as such, has the potential to contribute to the quality of that life. After all, "communities live in time as well as space."[76] The past century offers a wealth of solutions and alternatives—for transportation, for housing, and for parking. To give communities what they need, designers must study the best of the past and provide inspiration for the future. Properly conceived and designed, and visually and spatially connected to the deeper meanings of life, the parking facility can serve

The Parking Garage

as a community link: offering a range of services to meet daily needs and featuring a range of amenities, from child care to stroller rentals, package delivery, books-to-go, films-to-go, and pedestrian paths.[77]

Environmentally friendly construction can help support the community's sustainability goals. The focus should not be on short-term financial gains but on the long-term advantages offered by technology and by various movement systems. Planners, architects, designers, and developers need community support and understanding in order to create complex and sensitive solutions. In the coming years, the parking structure will not go away: it will evolve, and it will continue to drive design. The question is how best to guide this evolution—to ensure that the parking structure realizes its potential as a link between different forms of movement, and to ensure that it relates to its surroundings in ways that are aesthetically, functionally, and socially supportive.[78] As architecture critic Herbert Muschamp has noted, "There is nothing ignoble about the idea that architecture, as a public art, should share elements of a common language. By the same token, the ideal of a common language depends on the willingness to learn one."[79]

The back cover of a 1946 issue of *Amazing Stories* magazine invited readers to "Trade Your Trouble for a Bubble"; the idea was that the coming years would bring so much leisure that everyone would live in a "pleasure bubble" that would move constantly across the landscape.[80] Instead, modern industrial society is a complex, interconnected, fast-moving web, where leisure is limited and traffic congestion increases by the minute. Instead of retreating into a bubble, the United States needs to face the challenges ahead and to lead the way to new, sustainable ways of living. One of the earliest examples of such efforts was the 1975 garage designed by Paul Williams and built for Litton Industries' corporate headquarters, in Beverly Hills. Designed to meet new local requirements that addressed land use and aesthetics, the structure reflected what was then a new understanding of the complex role of the parking facility within the community.

Zoning, building, architecture, transportation, and planning practices will change to support new movement technologies—which will, in turn, increase sustainability. The parking facility must be a part of that change. Parking design must look to its entire history for inspiration, but remain open to future innovations and to new, synergistic solutions that will improve people's lives. For the parking facility and for a sustainable future, good architecture makes good sense.[81]

Emerging Visions

➲ A sustainable future depends on environmental approaches to every aspect of design, from the scale and placement of buildings, to transportation linkages, to the selection of construction materials.

➲ Changes in the automobile—lower emissions, better mileage, greater safety, and new energy sources, to name a few—will transform the parking facility into one element in an integrated and sustainable transit system.

➲ By linking multiple movement options, the parking facility can help lead the way toward sustainable living.

➲ The lobbies of parking structures can be reconceived as community centers that offer amenities (such as child care and package delivery), and that support services such as car sharing and car pooling.

➲ Garages can be designed specifically to integrate bicycles and other forms of personal transportation.

➲ Eventually, technology will integrate the automobile and the building itself, creating a self-sustaining power loop.

➲ In a fully integrated environment for man and machine, the needs of the pedestrian will be as carefully addressed as those of the car.

➲ Nature and technology play a crucial role in the creation of new forms of movement, and in the perception and acceptance of new movement systems.

➲ Community-owned and community-supported shared parking could become a way of life.

➲ New synergies will expand living choices, helping to invigorate the environment and community life.

➲ Parking will continue to drive design.

NOTES

Epigraph

This poem appeared in Herbert Ridgeway Collins, "If I Can't Make the White House I'll Take the Garage," *Parking* (July 1975), 16; Collins found the words painted on a fence.

Introduction

1. Robert M. Fogelson, *Downtown: Its Rise and Fall, 1880–1950* (New Haven: Yale University Press, 2001), 21.

2. Ibid.

Chapter 1

1. *Ideas and Actions: A History of the Highway Research Board, 1920–1970* (Washington, D.C.: Highway Research Board, 1970), 187–188; Clay McShane and Joel A. Tarr, "The Centrality of the Horse in the 19th-Century American City," in Raymond A. Mohl, ed., *The Making of Urban America* (Wilmington, Del.: Scholarly Resources, 1997), 116, 118.

2. McShane and Tarr, "Centrality of the Horse," 105–130; Benjamin C. Marsh, "Transportation and Urban Health," *American City* 7, no. 6 (December 1912): 510; Gerald Carson, "Goggles and Side Curtains," *American Heritage* 18, no. 3 (April 1967): 33–39, 108–111; "Stables Breeders of Disease," *Horseless Age* 4, no. 3 (May 3, 1899): 6.

3. *Ideas and Actions*, 188.

4. McShane and Tarr, "Centrality of the Horse," 123; Marsh, "Urban Health," 510; *Ideas and Actions*, 187; Clyde L. King, ed., "The Automobile: Its Province and Its Problems," special issue, *Annals* 116 (November 1924): 1–10; Gorman Gilbert and Robert E. Samuels, *The Taxicab: An Urban Transportation Survivor* (Chapel Hill: University of North Carolina Press, 1982), 33; Lee Iacocca, "Henry Ford," *Time*, December 7, 1998, 76–77; Steven Watts, *The People's Tycoon* (New York: Knopf, 2005); E.D. Kennedy, *The Automobile Industry* (New York: Reynal & Hitchcock, 1972), 1–6; Reynold M. Wik, *Henry Ford and Grass-Roots America* (Ann Arbor: University of Michigan Press, 1972); Alfred H. Kirkland, *A Century of Progress in Electricity, Transportation and Communication*, World's Fair Series, Bulletin No. 4 (Chicago: A Century of Progress International Exposition, n.d.).

5. "The Growth of the Garage Business," *Horseless Age* 15, no. 17 (April 26, 1905): 477–478.

6. Daimler-Benz Aktiengesellschaft, Archiv-Geschichte-Museum, and Museum of Science and Industry, Illinois, *The First Century: A Social View of the Automobile* (Stuttgart: Daimler-Benz Aktiengesellschaft, Archiv-Geschichte-Museum, 1986), 30; *Ideas and Actions*, 188; King, "Province and Problems," 1–10; "Effect on Land Values and the Distribution of Population," *Horseless Age* 1, no. 5 (March 1896): 1.

7. "How the Jacksonville Motor Co., at Jacksonville, Texas, Made Nature Assist in Providing an Attractive 'Front' to Its Garage," *Horseless Age* 37, no. 8 (April 1916): 14.

8. Peter Geoffrey Hall, *Cities of Tomorrow: An Intellectual History of Urban Planning and Design in the Twentieth Century* (Oxford, U.K.: Blackwell, 1988), 276.

9. *Ideas and Actions*, 187; James J. Flink, *The Car Culture* (Cambridge, Mass.: MIT Press, 1975), 178; Howard L. Preston, *Automobile Age Atlanta* (Athens: University of Georgia Press, 1979). Tremendous battles over where automobiles could drive and park were an early part of the change to automobile use; see "Excluded from Chicago Parks," *Horseless Age* 4, no. 12 (June 21, 1899): 6; "Anti-Motor Legislation in Chicago," *Horseless Age* 4, no. 14 (July 5, 1899): 1; "Barred from Bar Harbor," *Horseless Age* 4, July 5, 1899, 6; "Motor Carriages Excluded from Boston Parks between 10:30 A.M. And 9 P.M.," *Horseless Age* (March 1899): 7.

10. "Notes and Clippings: The Louvre as a Garage," *American Architecture and Building News* (July 1905): 4.

11. "Notes from Paris," *Architectural Review* 24 (1908): 136, 138–139; Karla Britton, *Auguste Perret* (New York: Phaidon, 2001), 20–21.

12. "Stables Taken Over by Garage Firm," *Horseless Age* 24, no. 6 (August 11, 1909): 167; McShane and Tarr, "Centrality of the Horse," 105–130; "The Joscelyn

Garage, New York," *Horseless Age* (May 3, 1912): 765–766; Robert A.M. Stern, Thomas Mellins, and David Fishman, *New York 1880: Architecture and Urbanism in the Gilded Age* (New York: Monacelli, 1999), 57; "Parking Pioneer Retires," *Parking* (July 1970): 29.

13. McShane and Tarr, "Centrality of the Horse," 105–30.

14. "Modern American Public Garages," *Horseless Age* 29, no. 18 (May 1, 1912): 755; "Minor Mention," *Horseless Age* 5, no. 7 (November 15, 1899): 11; "Stables Taken Over," 167. Although many multistory fireproof garages already existed, many were fire hazards—especially when automobiles were housed in stables and other structures originally intended for other uses. See "Liability of Fire and Work for the Automobile Club," *Horseless Age* 5, no. 2 (October 11, 1899): 5; J.E. Jennings, "The Garage as a Conflagration Risk," *Horseless Age* 22, no. 21 (November 18, 1908): 682; "Liability of Fire," *Horseless Age* 5, no. 2 (October 11, 1899): 5; King, "Province and Problems," 1–10; Peoples Garage and Auto Livery Company to the Roberts Oxygen Company; P.M. Heldt, "The Garage Business—Buildings, Equipment, Methods," *Horseless Age* 36, no. 10 (October 15, 1915): 394–395.

15. *Brickbuilder* 16, no. 12 (December 1907): 232–233 (images).

16. Collins, "White House," 16–20, 35.

17. Heldt, "Garage Business," 394. Like stables, early car barns for electric and steam vehicles were often a source of fires; see Thomas H. Shanks, *From Horse Car to Red Car to Mass Rapid Transit: A Century of Progress* (Virginia Beach, Va.: Donning, 1991). For a good general history of electric railways, see George W. Hilton and John F. Due, *The Electric Interurban Railways in America* (Stanford, Calif.: Stanford University Press, 1964). For a good history of the trolley barns, see LeRoy O. King Jr., *100 Years of Capital Traction: The Story of Streetcars in the Nation's Capital* (Washington, D.C.: Taylor, 1972).

18. "First Motor Emporium in Boston," *Horseless Age* 4, no. 8 (June 1899): 6; Mary Van Meter, "The Cyclorama Building and Its Neighbors" (Massachusetts Historical Commission, January 1972); *Manassas Panorama Building*, Library of Congress G-3640X, James M. Goode Collection, "Lost Washington," courtesy of Craig Morrison, Detroit Urban Conservation Project, Center for Urban Studies, Lot #11800-N1, 48202.

19. "First Motor Emporium," 6.

20. James J. Flink, *America Adopts the Automobile, 1895–1910* (Cambridge, Mass.: MIT Press, 1970), 217; "Displaying Horseless Vehicles for Sale," *Horseless Age* 4, no. 21 (August 23, 1899): 24.

21. Catherine G. Miller and Irwin-Sweeney-Miller Foundation, *Carscape: A Parking Handbook* (Columbus, Ind.: Washington Street Press, 1988), 10; Lonnie Hackman and Norene D. Martin, *The Parking Industry: Private Enterprise for the Public Good* (Washington, D.C.: National Parking Association, 1969), 1–2.

22. "Our Electric Cab Station," *Horseless Age* 3, no. 6 (September 1898): 1.

23. "Central Station of the Electric Vehicle Company," *Horseless Age* 3, no. 6 (September 1898): 9; Heldt, "Garage Business," 394–395; H. Maxim, "Electric Vehicles and Their Relation to Central Stations," *Horseless Age* 3, no. 12 (March 1899): 17–19; "Electric Vehicle Companies for Every State and Territory," *Horseless Age* 4, no. 8 (May 24, 1899): 17–19.

24. "Garage Building, Detroit, Mich.," *American Architect* 111, no. 2160 (May 16, 1917): 301–314; "Minor Mention," 19; Gilbert and Samuels, *Taxicab*, 19–60; William A. Schnader, "The Taxicab: Its Service and Regulation," *Annals* 116 (November 1924): 101–106; "The Illinois Company's Purchase," *Motor Age* 1, no. 2 (September 19, 1899): 33; "Charging Station for $12," *Motor Age* 1, no. 6 (October 17, 1899): 110. Because they did not require cranking to start, the first electric cars were referred to as the "car for women."

25. Maxim, "Electric Vehicles," 19.

26. Gilbert and Samuels, *Taxicab*, 30–33; Maxim, "Electric Vehicles," 17–19; Schnader, "Taxicab," 101–106; "Illinois Company's Purchase," 33; "Charging Station," 110.

27. "Motor Livery at Pittsburg," *Horseless Age* 5, no. 12 (December 20, 1899): 9.

28. "Sport and Utility," *Automobile Topics* 4, no. 11 (June 28, 1902): 491; "Charging Station," 110.

29. "Electric Vehicle Storage and Charging Rates," *Horseless Age* 31, no. 19 (May 7, 1913): 842.

30. "The Edison Electric Garage, Boston, Mass.," *Horseless Age* 31, no. 19 (May 7, 1913): 841–842.

31. Flink, *Car Culture*, 178; Kennedy, *Automobile Industry*, 1–6; Kirkland, *Century of Progress*, 11.

32. "Prior to 1888," *Horseless Age* 1, no. 1 (November 1895): 9.

33. Personal visit, Royal Automobile Club of Australia, Sydney. The original group of men who built the first parking garage in Sydney went on to build a more elaborate garage in the mid-1920s that included a ballroom, sleeping rooms, and meeting rooms, and featured ramp parking in the interior. The facility is still in use today. George S. May, "The Thanksgiving Day Race of 1895," *Chicago History* 11, no. 3 (Fall and Winter 1982): 175–183;

Stephen Sennott, "Chicago Architects and the Automobile, 1906–26," in Jan Jennings, ed., *Roadside America: The Automobile in Design and Culture* (Ames: Iowa State University for the Society for Commercial Archeology, 1990), 158; "Automobile Club Organized," *Horseless Age* 4, no. 11 (June 14, 1899): 6–7; Flink, *America Adopts the Automobile*, 218; "Automobile Club of America," *Horseless Age* 4, no. 11 (June 14, 1899): 1.

34. "Prejudice of Livery Stable Keepers," *Horseless Age* 4, no. 12 (June 21, 1899): 6.

35. "Garage Notes," *Horseless Age* 4, no. 23 (August 23, 1899): 13. In the automobile club, the earliest example of a mixed-use structure incorporating parking, fire was a key concern; see "Liability of Fire and Work," 5;

36. "Successful Opening of Boston Club," *Motor Age* 1, no. 2 (January 9, 1902): 2, 3; Flink, *America Adopts the Automobile*, 217, 218; F.C. Donald, "The Chicago Club's Attitude," *Motor Age* 1, no. 2 (January 9, 1902): 1–3; "Chicago Automobile Club" (construction image, 1907), Chicago Historical Society, #78253; Sennott, "Chicago Architects," 159–160; "Hartford Club to Build Modern Official Garage," *American Motorist* 12, no. 5 (May 1920): 46; "Jonathan Club Drive-In," *Parking* (Summer 1954): 11. A 1925 garage built on the premises of the Jonathan Club was expanded in 1954 and is still in use.

37. "Automobile Storage and Repair Facilities," *Scientific American* 86 (March 29, 1902): 226 (quoted in Flink, *Car Culture*, 217).

38. "Public Garages," *Horseless Age* 31, no. 19 (May 7, 1913): 793–839; "Examples of Modern Public Garages," *Horseless Age* 25, no. 18 (May 4, 1910): 647–685; Heldt, "Garage Business," 394–395; "Garage Notes: New Garages Built and Building," *Horseless Age*, ongoing column; "Blue List," *Garage* 1, no. 3 (January 1911): 59–62; "Just What You Need," in *Automobile Owner's Guide and Chauffeur's Manual* (Chicago: John J. McKenna, 1919); Andrew S. Dolkart, Columbia University School of Architecture, unpublished report on the Monterey Garage, July 2002.

39. "Metropolitan Storage Stations," *Automobile* 6 (June 21, 1902): 2; Flink, *Car Culture*, 220.

40. "Public Garages: The Dupont Garage, Washington, D.C.," *Horseless Age* 31, no. 19 (May 7, 1913): 793.

41. "A Large Southern Garage," *Horseless Age* 14, no. 8 (August 24, 1904): 189; Heldt, "Garage Business," 493; "Demarest and Peerless Co.," *Brickbuilder* 18, no. 9 (September 1909): 196; *American Architect* 111, no. 2160 (May 16, 1917): image; "A Tennessee Garage," *Horseless Age* 14, no. 13 (September 28, 1904): 306; Flink, *America Adopts the Automo-*

bile, 219; "Two New Garages for Detroit," *Horseless Age* 35, no. 1 (January 6, 1915): 28.

42. Carl W. Mitman, *An Outline Development of Highway Travel, Especially in America* (Washington, D.C.: Smithsonian Institution, 1935), 344.

43. "Motor Transportation," in *Polk's Detroit City Directory* (Detroit: R.L. Polk, 1934); "Varied Uses of Motor Trucks by Municipalities, Contractors, and Public Utility Corporations," *American City* 8, no. 5 (May 1914): 522–524.

44. Mohl, *Urban America*, 105.

45. "Two Modern Types of Fire Stations," *American City* 13, no. 2 (August 1915): 114; "Illustrations of Provision for Fire Protection in Two Cities," *American City* 13, no. 6 (December 1915): 540–541.

46. W.S. Lloyd, "A Municipal Garage," *American City* 15, no. 2 (August 1916): 172–173.

47. Flink, *America Adopts the Automobile*, 219.

48. Flink, *America Adopts the Automobile*, 219; Heldt, "Garage Business," 394–395; "Storage and Repair Stations in New York," *Horseless Age* 8, no. 6 (May 8, 1901): 122.

49. Flink, *America Adopts the Automobile*, 218–220; Heldt, "Garage Business," 394–395; "New Winton Garage," *Garage* 1, no. 2 (December 1910): 18.

50. Flink, *America Adopts the Automobile*, 220; "Parking Editorial Page: The Department Store Was Once New," *Parking* (Spring 1954): 6.

51. Sennott, "Chicago Architects," 169n8; *Architectural Review* (February 1904): 124.

52. "Class 'B' Project Problem in Design: An Automobile Garage," *American Architect* 98, no. 1825 (December 14, 1910): 197–200; Tyler Stewart Rogers, "The Automobile and the Private Estate," *Architectural Forum* (April 1920): 171–174.

53. "The Brickbuilder Competition for a Public Garage, Automobile Sales and Service Building," supplement, *Brickbuilder* 22, no. 3 (March 1913).

The Parking Garage and the Train Station

1. "Just What You Need," in *Automobile Owner's Guide and Chauffeur's Manual* (Chicago: John J. McKenna, 1919); "Uptown Garage," *Garage* 1, no. 2 (December 1910): 7; "Garage," *Garage* 1, no. 1 (November 1910): 6–8.

2. Nikolaus Pevsner, *A History of Building Types* (Princeton, N.J.: Princeton University Press, 1976); P.M. Heldt, "The Garage Business—Buildings, Equipment, Methods," *Horseless Age* 36, no. 10 (October 15, 1915): 394–395. For good gen-

Notes

eral histories, see George W. Hilton and John F. Due, *The Electric Interurban Railways in America* (Stanford, Calif.: Stanford University Press, 1964); and Thomas H. Shanks, *From Horse Car to Red Car to Mass Rapid Transit: A Century of Progress* (Virginia Beach, Va.: Donning, 1991). For a good history of trolley barns, see LeRoy O. King Jr., *100 Years of Capital Traction: The Story of Streetcars in the Nation's Capital* (Washington, D.C.: Taylor, 1972).

Women Drivers and the Parking Garage

1. Gerald Carson, "Goggles and Side Curtains," *American Heritage* 8, no. 3 (April 1962): 35; "A Modern Parking Garage in a Central Metropolitan District," *American City* (December 1930): 143.

2. "For Women Automobilists," *Automobile* (December 1909): 992–995; Daimler-Benz Aktiengesellschaft, Archiv-Geschichte-Museum, and Museum of Science and Industry, Illinois, *The First Century: A Social View of the Automobile* (Stuttgart: Daimler-Benz Aktiengesellschaft, Archiv-Geschichte-Museum, 1986), 30; "Women in Parking," *Parking* (Winter 1955): 39–40.

Garages for the Landed Gentry

1. "Class 'B' Project Problem in Design: An Automobile Garage," *American Architect* 98, no. 1825 (December 14, 1910): 197–200; Tyler Stewart Rogers, "The Automobile and the Private Estate," *Architectural Forum* (April 1920): 171–174.

Chapter 2

1. Although self-parking did not become widespread until the 1950s, it was available as early as the 1920s for parkers who held monthly permits, and for members of automobile clubs, which often had their own parking garages. Cars that had monthly permits were identified by special decals. *Convenience Personal Parking Privileges,* a brochure for Chicago's Fisher Building, which was constructed in 1928, noted that patrons were permitted to park their cars on their own. Garry Sommer, of APCOA parking, provided the author with a copy of this brochure.

2. William Phillips Comstock, comp., *Garages and Motor Boat Houses* (New York: William T. Comstock, 1911), 63–69, 70–74; "Public Garages," *Horseless Age* 31, no. 19 (May 7, 1913): 819, 832.

3. Harold F. Blanchard, "Ramp Design in Public Garages," *Architectural Forum* (November 1921): 172, 175; "Public Garages," 832. For a number of reasons, the totally mechanical approach to parking garage design never gained wide acceptance in the United States: these included expense; mechanical limitations; the lack of connection to the emotions evoked by driving an automobile; and the ready availability of open land, which prompted other, less compact solutions. The notion of the car and the garage as a single, integrated machine lived on, however, in the experiments with fully mechanized garages discussed in chapter 5. One example of a late elevator garage is the System Park garage, constructed in Chicago in 1925, which had valets and used elevators for vertical movement. See Ronald E. Schmitt, "The Ubiquitous Parking Garage: Worthy of Preservation?" (paper presented at Preserving the Recent Past 2, a conference sponsored by the National Park Service, Philadelphia, October 9–13, 2000), 2–194.

4. Efficient ramp construction also required the solution of a number of technical problems in forming concrete; for example, creating a surface that was flat but sloped (and often curved as well) required specific skills in working with concrete.

5. "The New Garage of the New York Taxicab Company," *Horseless Age* 23, no. 8 (February 24, 1909): 269–273 (republished under the same title on April 21, 1909).

6. Edward Wells, "Design of a Taxicab Garage for 175 Cabs," *Horseless Age* 23, no. 16 (April 21, 1909): 574–576.

7. James M. Hunnicutt, "Old Time Parking Garages," *Parking Professional* (August 1989): 26–29.

8. "The New Fenway Garage, Boston, Mass.," *Horseless Age* 31, no. 19 (May 7, 1913): 826.

9. "Types of Garages," *Horseless Age* 36, no. 14 (December 15, 1915): 531; "A Garage Building Built with a Purpose," *Horseless Age* (September 15, 1915): 295–296.

10. "Types of Garages," 531.

11. Blanchard, "Ramp Design," 169–175; "Loop's First Parking Garage Gets Landmark," *Parking Professional* (July 2002): 8–10. Much to the frustration of preservationists, who realized the historical importance of this building type, the Hotel LaSalle Garage was recently demolished.

12. Blanchard, "Ramp Design," 169–175.

13. Ibid.

14. Blanchard, "Ramp Design," 169–175; Harold F. Blanchard, "The Layout of Automotive Buildings," *Architectural Forum* (March 1927): 281–288. Although the 100-foot by 100-foot (30-meter by 30-meter) floor plate was used as the basis for analysis, this base dimension did not address all possible site configurations and characteristics, and did not take into account the dimensions of the automobile itself. Until the ramp structure had evolved further, and the urban plan could be based on the automobile's dimensions, early ramp designs could not always maximize the numbers of cars parked and provide easy access for self-parking.

15. Blanchard, "Ramp Design," 169–175; Blanchard, "Automotive Buildings," 281–288; Harold F. Blanchard, "Comparison of Ramp and Elevator Type Garages," *Bus Transportation* (June 1922): 331–335. D'Humy and Moe formed the first consulting design firm for parking garages, which later became the Ramp Buildings Corporation, of which Harold Blanchard was a part.

16. Albert O. Larson, "An Analysis of Garage Design," *Architectural Forum* (March 1927): 213–216; Robert O. Derrick, "The City Parking Garage," *Architectural Forum* (March 1927): 233–240; "Technical News and Research: Garages," *Architectural Record* (February 1929): 177–195.

17. This list does not include the parking garages in which the entire floors sloped; this design became popular much later.

18. "Technical News," 183.

19. Blanchard, "Ramp Design," 171–172.

20. Blanchard, "Ramp Design," 172–173; "Technical News," 177, 182–183; Lee Eastman, "The Parking Garage Merits Encouragement as an Important Factor in Traffic Relief," *American City* 11, no. 1 (January 1929): 157; Thomas Earl Larose, "Babylon South: The Building of the Richmond Loew's Theater and the Richmond Garage, 1925–1928, *Arris* 13 (2002): 55–71; Gary Robertson, "A Parking Garage with Style," *Richmond Times-Dispatch*, February 27, 2003, B1, B5.

21. Larson, "Garage Design," 214.

22. Anne Whiston Spirn, C. Ford Peatross, and Robert L. Sweeney, *Frank Lloyd Wright: Designs for an American Landscape, 1922–1932* (New York: Harry N. Abrams in association with the Canadian Centre for Architecture, the Library of Congress, and the Frank Lloyd Wright Foundation, 1996), 83. See the feature box on Frank Lloyd Wright in chapter 8.

23. Library of Congress, Frank Lloyd Wright: Designs for an American Landscape, 1922-1932, http://lcweb.loc.gov/exhibits/flw/flw01.html; Steve Thompson, "The Wright Stuff," *AutoWeek*, May 26, 1997, 22–23; *Frank Lloyd Wright Collected Writings,* ed. Bruce Brooks Pfeiffer (New York: Rizzoli; Scottsdale, Ariz.: Frank Lloyd Wright Foundation, 1992), 310.

24. "Garage with Warped Floor Areas Connecting Ramps," *Engineering News-Record* 95, no. 6 (August 6, 1925): 230–231.

25. "Technical News," 178–195; Eastman, "Garage Merits Encouragement," 157;

26. Arthur Comey, "Present Tendencies in the Widths of Motor Trucks," *Landscape Architecture* 1, no. 4 (July 1911): 184–185; Tyler Stewart Rogers, "The Automobile and the Private Estate: Part II. Dimensions of Automobiles," *Architectural Forum* (April 1920): 171–174; "Technical News," 182.

27. Blanchard, "Automotive Buildings," 281–288.

28. "Technical News," 182.

29. "Technical News," 177–198. The only system that was found to be more efficient than the D'Humy was not a ramp system at all, but a four-way elevator system (discussed in chapter 5 of this book) that required 187 square feet (17 square meters) per car and had an efficiency rating of 59.5 percent. The *Architectural Record* article also considered the new Kent Automatic Garage, a fully mechanized garage, but did not provide a full comparison.

30. Sealed-beam headlights, however, did not appear until 1940; see Chip Lord and Ant Farm, *Autoamerica: A Trip Down U.S. Highways from World War II to the Future; A Book* (New York: Dutton, 1976), 29.

31. "Garages Grow Up," *Architectural Forum* (February 1953): 120–123; Hunnicutt, "Old Time Garages," 26–29; "From the Parking Archives, Winter 1954: Evolution—What Is Past Is Prologue," *Parking* (March 2003): 36–38; "Pioneer Wall-Less," *Parking* (Summer 1954): 42.

32. R.C. Diefenbach, "New Car Syndrome," *Parking* (Spring 1964): 19; Dietrich Klose, *Metropolitan Parking Structures; A Survey of Architectural Problems and Solutions* (New York: Praeger, 1965), 51, 228–231. Other unique examples of self-parking can be found; see, for example, "Louisville's Self- Parking Garage," *Parking* (Fall 1954): 20; "Self-Parking in Wichita," *Parking* (Winter 1955): 38; R.B. Bowser, "Self-Parking . . . Is It a Bargain?" *Parking* (Spring 1956): 14; "Four Streets Are Access Ramps to Store Garage," *American City* 72, no. 1 (January 1957): 134.

33. "Ramp Types," *Parking* (Winter 1954): 35–37; "Design Analysis," *Parking* (Fall 1958): 8–10; "Interfloor Travel Patterns for Self-Service Parking," *Parking* (Fall 1958): 11–14; "Unique Garage Plan," *Urban Land* 7, no. 10 (November 1948): 4. See the feature box on Country Club Plaza in chapter 3.

34. "Spiral Garage Permits High Space Use," *Engineering News-Record* (July 22, 1948): 78; "Parking Garage," *Architectural Forum* (September 1949): 90–91; V. Lankovsky, "New Staggered-Floor Garage Design Cuts Cost," *Engineering*

Larose, "Babylon South," 55–71; Robertson, "Parking Garage with Style." See the feature box on Lee, Smith & Vandervoort in chapter 8.

News-Record (August 15, 1940): 51–52; John J. Waferling, "The Williams Parking Deck," Parking (Spring 1954): 11–13; Geoffrey Harold Baker and Bruno Funaro, Parking (New York: Reinhold, 1958), 148–151.

35. Larry Donoghue, Larry Donoghue and Associates, discussions with author, 2005–2006; Henry G. Kramer, "Traffic Control," American City (June 1955): 166–171; "Downtown Center Garage Prestressed Pylon to Resist Earthquake," Architect and Engineer (April 1955): 9–15. See chapter 6 for more information about Grant Park.

36. "Denison Parking," Parking Today (November 2000): 12; Robert Ketring, "New Denison Garage Is Formally Opened," Parking (Summer 1954): 12.

37. Donoghue, discussions with author; "Self Parking," Parking (Winter 1954): 47; William Girgash, "Conversion to Self-Parking: Case History," Parking (April 1977): 40–41; "Self-Park System," Parking (Winter 1954): 48. Once self-parking had eliminated the need for attendants to park the cars, garage operators saw an opportunity to reduce operating expenses further by replacing the remaining attendants with a new machine: the "ticket spitter," which was championed by George Devlin, and had actually been imagined many years before. The device monitored garage use and charged for the time parked.

38. M.R. Beckstrom, "New Design," Parking (Fall 1955): 18; Philip R. Weary, "Circ-L-Park," Parking (Winter 1966): 28.

39. "Art Students Design Garages," Parking (Winter 1965): 15–17; Bruce Brooks Pfeiffer, Frank Lloyd Wright Drawings (New York: Abrams, 1990), 153. Beginning with Albert Kahn's experiments with different ramp designs for the Fisher Building, which were undertaken to ensure ease of access for all drivers, every attempt was made to find the "best" solution for self-parkers—although no one but Kahn created test ramps.

40. "Interfloor Travel Patterns," 11–14; John Brierley, Parking of Motor Vehicles (Essex, U.K.: Applied Science Publishers, 1962), 167; "Ramp Types," 35–37; Klose, Metropolitan Parking Structures, 170–171.

41. Carl Hooper, "Parking Palace, New Garage at Allen Center Could Become Model," Parking (July 1979); Jerome Gottesman, "Parking Concept Checklist," Parking (April 1970): 4, 48–54; "Design," Parking (Spring 1962): 24–27; "New 'Four-in-One' Garage," Parking (Fall 1968): 20; Daniel Locitzer, "A Parking Garage Helps Revitalize a Deteriorating Downtown," American City (June 1970): 94.

42. George Devlin, "Design and Construction of the Parkade," Parking (Summer 1960): 8–9; "Design," 24–27; "News in Photos," Parking (April–May 1969): 10; Eric Lipton, "At Dated Mall, Nothing Gaudy But Sales Figures," New York Times, February 2, 2000, New York Report, A21.

43. William B. Gleckman, "Two New Parking Systems," Traffic Quarterly (July 1961): 391–400; "The William Brower," Parking (Winter 1954): 46.

44. Gleckman, "Parking Systems," 397.

45. Ernest Coler, "Parking the Car Up in the Clouds," American Motorist 12, no. 1 (January 1, 1920): 26, 46.

46. Nick Watry, founder, Watry Engineering (now known as Watry Design, Inc.), discussions and e-mail exchanges with author, 2001–2006.

47. Parking (October 1979): cover; Seymour Gage Associates, "The Geometry of Parking Structures," Parking (Fall 1967): 30–32; Richard C. Rich, "How to Solve the Hospital Parking Problem with a Deck," Parking (April–May 1969): 38–42; "Planning a Downtown Parking Deck," Architectural Record (May 1965): 177, 182.

48. In Parking Structures: Planning, Design, Construction, Maintenance and Repair, 3rd ed. (New York: Springer, 2001), Anthony Chrest, Mary Smith, and Sam Bhuyan discuss a number of ramp configurations, although with slightly different names than those used here. All the designs, however, are based on the early ones discussed in this chapter. Other books also cover the topic of ramp design and codify the relationships between cost, efficiency, and use. For a general list of reference books on parking, see the "Parking" section in the list of further readings at the end of this book.

Albert Kahn (1869–1942)

1. National Park Service, "Fisher Building," Detroit: A National Register of Historic Places Travel Itinerary, www.cr.nps.gov/nr/travel/detroit/d31.htm.

2. Grant Hildebrand, The Architecture of Albert Kahn (Cambridge, Mass.: MIT Press), 1974; Federico Bucci, Albert Kahn: Architect of Ford (New York: Princeton Architectural Press, 1993); Detroit Institute of Arts, The Legacy of Albert Kahn (Detroit: Detroit Institute of Arts, 1970); Great Buildings Online, "Albert Kahn," www.greatbuildings.com/architects/Albert_Kahn.html; Ralph W. Hammett, "Detroit's Machine-Age Architecture," MSA Bulletin (March 1957); Albert Kahn's file of newspapers and journals, Box #7 (1905–1908), Albert Kahn Collection, Bentley Historical Library, University of Michigan at Ann Arbor.

3. Great Buildings Online, "Albert Kahn."

4. Great Buildings Online, "Albert Kahn"; "New Garage for the Standard Auto Co. at Woodward and Garfield Will Be Most Elaborate Structure of Its Kind in the City," Kahn's file of newspapers and journals, coll. 122-G, Box #7 (1905–1908), Albert Kahn Collection; "Kahn Realty Garage," Job #488, Albert Kahn's personal cost ledger, Box #9 (1907–1913), Albert Kahn Collection.

5. "Sales Garage for the Chicago Motor Car Company, Chicago," Brickbuilder 19, no. 6 (June 1910): 150.

6. Current management of the Detroit Athletic Club, discussions with author, September–October 2006; drawings from the Detroit Athletic Club, Job #672C, Drawer 14, Folder 12, Sheet SM No. 1, 19-6, April 9, 1921; Job #672, Drawer 14, Folder 7, Sheet #4, Sheet #2, 1915; Job #672B, construction drawings, Sheet #2S, 1919.

7. "Skyscraper Garage Open," Kahn's file of newspapers and journals, coll. 122-G, Box #7 (1920–1923), Albert Kahn Collection; Architecture (May 1931): 269–272 (illustrations).

8. "Industrial Architecture Showing That Even a Garage May Have Dignity and Beauty," Kahn's file of newspapers and journals, coll. 122-G, Box #7 (1931), Albert Kahn Collection.

9. Kahn's personal cost ledger, Box #9 (1907–1913), Albert Kahn Collection; Kahn's file of newspapers and journals, Box #7, Albert Kahn Collection.

The Elevator Garage: A New Old Idea

1. Richard Rich, founder, Richard Rich and Associates, discussions with author, 2006; "The Lofts of Merchants Row," www.loftsofmerchantsrow.com. Another consequence of the proliferation of self-park ramp garages is that garages cannot be adapted to other purposes. Because old elevator garages had standard floor-to-floor heights and level floors, many were easily converted to residential use—and, because the cost of doing so was comparatively low, there was greater ease in obtaining financing. For early designers of parking garages, flexibility of conversion—whether from garage to residential use, or the reverse—was an important issue.

Chapter 3

1. By the 1960s, mall parking lots had become so large that the walking distance from parking to the shops was being discussed as a design issue.

2. Recently, a number of municipalities, including Chicago, passed ordinances that determine every detail of parking garage design, bringing it completely under the city's control. Given that flexibility is key to solving the complex issues related to parking, it is unfortunate that some local governments are moving in this direction.

3. "Kids Profit from Theater and Arts Center in Maryland Parking Facility," Parking Today 6, no. 5 (May 2001): 38–42; Benjamin Forgey, "Injecting Imagination into a Drab Urban Form," Washington Post, May 17, 2003, C1.

4. "Garage and Salesroom," Horseless Age 24, no. 18 (May 1, 1912): 821; "Here and There among Garages and Salesrooms," Horseless Age (August 15, 1916): 142; "Garage and Salesroom," Horseless Age 35, no. 23 (June 9, 1915): 787; "Modern American Public and Corporation Garages," Horseless Age 33, no. 19 (May 7, 1913): 793–842. A used-car showroom called the People's Auto Market, where owners sold directly to each other, with no commission applied, also appeared very early. See "No-Commission Auto Market Is Here," American Motorist 7, no. 11 (November 1915): 681.

5. "The Locomobile Salesroom, Atlanta, Ga.," Horseless Age 31, no. 19 (May 7, 1913): 800.

6. "A Large Southern Garage," Horseless Age 14, no. 8 (August 24, 1904): 189; "Garage of Wm. F.V. Neumann and Co., Detroit," Horseless Age 23, no. 13 (March 31, 1909): 447–448.

7. "Sales Garage for the Chicago Motor Car Company," Brickbuilder 19, no. 6 (June 1910): 151.

8. William F. Wharton, "Architecture and Decoration of Automobile Show Rooms," Architectural Forum (March 1927): 305–313.

9. "On the Boards: Vertical Auto Mall; Kanner Architects," Architecture (May 1998): 67; David Wethe, "Car Dealerships Face the Great Homogenization," New York Times, January 11, 2004; Jack Snyder, "Car Dealer Will Park Showroom Downtown," Orlando Sentinel, August 15, 2001, A1, A6; "On the Boards: Acura Dealership Prototype; Oliver + Ray Architects with Deiss and Associates," Architecture (May 1998): 67.

10. "Boys Club House," American Architect 97, no. 1795 (May 18, 1910): 196–197; E.H. Bartelsmeyer, "New Headquarters and Gymnasium Occupied by St. Louis Police Department," American City (June 1929): 105–107; Joseph Johnson, "The Modernization of the New York Fire Department," American City 5, no. 3 (September 1911): 154; "Transforming an Eyesore," American City 10, no. 4 (April 1914): 378; American City 5, no. 5 (November 1911): 318; American City 7, no. 5 (November 1912): 438; "New Equipment for Dover, N.J.," American City 8, no. 2 (February 1913): 199; "Kanawha Chemical Fire Engine Mfg. Co.," American City 5, no. 1 (July 1911): 173.

11. Arthur S. Aungst, "Automobile Fire Stations," American City 7, no. 1 (January 1915): 57.

12. Aungst, "Fire Stations," 57; "Two Modern Types of Fire Stations," *American City* 7, no. 2 (August 1915): 114.

13. "Types of Fire Stations," 114; "Fire Protection," *American City* 7, no. 1 (July 1912): 50–51; "Illustrations of Provision for Fire Protection in Two Cities," *American City* 8, no. 6 (December 1915): 540–541; Louis Pujol, "The Modernizing of New Orleans' Fire Department," *American City* 11, no. 4 (October 1914): 303.

14. Edmund Crinnion, "A Systematized Municipal Garage," *American City* 14, no. 4 (April 1, 1916): 258–260.

15. W.S. Lloyd, "A Municipal Garage," *American City* 15, no. 2 (August 1916): 172–173; Guy Bartlett, "A Modern Municipal Garage," *American City* 35, no. 1 (January 1928): 163; Raymond A. Williams, "Garage and Repair Space for the Street Equipment," *American City* 68, no. 9 (September 1953): 104–105; A.M. Littlefield, "New Municipal Garage and Bandshell at Hollywood, Fla.," *American City* 67, no. 2 (February 1952): 171.

16. Ralph Harrington Doane, "The Mechanical Equipment of the Garage," *Architectural Forum* 46 (March 1927): 277, plate 55; *American City* 5, no. 5 (November 1911): 318 (illustration).

17. "Bus Garage," *Progressive Architecture* (February 1952): 98–101.

18. "Port Authority Bus Terminal," *American City* 64, no. 5 (May 1949): 70.

19. "Parking Space for Auditoriums a Necessity," *American City* 65, no. 1 (January 1950): 7.

20. "Hartford Plans an Attractive Parking Plaza," *American City* (May 1954): 125–127.

21. "Parking Space for Auditoriums," 7.

22. Many cities were adopting similar strategies. See "A City Parking Garage Invites Patrons," *American City* (October 1962): 118.

23. "Manhattan Gets a Municipal Garage," *American City* 76, no. 1 (January 1961): 82; C.W. Ennis and T.J. Feagins, "Mountain View Parking Complex," *Parking* (January 1976): 24; "Knock Down Garages," *Garage* 1, no. 2 (December 1910): 25; "Unit Building Design Lowers Cost of New Orleans Parking Garage," *American City* 66, no. 4 (April 1951): 161; "Prefab Can Park Geared to Mod Design," *Parking* (Spring 1968): 16; T.Y. Lin, "Demountable Parking Structures," *Parking* (October 1969): 26–33; "News in Photos," *Parking* (October 1970): 8; "County Dedicates New Portable Parking Garage in Civic Center," *Parking* (October 1969): 40–41; "The Portable Garage," *American City* 85, no. 1 (January 1970): 108–110; "Parking Relief for Cities: A Relocatable Garage," *American City* (July 1969): 55; "Automobile Garage Located under the Bleachers of a Baseball Park," *Automobile* (December 2,

1909): 980. The difficulty of providing parking for large events continues to be an issue in the parking industry today. See Jerry S. Marcus and Matthew L. Feagins, "Prime-Time Parking," January 10, 2002, Stadia Showcase Special 2002, www.stadia.tv/archive/user/archive_article.tpl?id=2002110111112835.

24. "City of Orlando/Orlando County Courthouse Parking Garage Expansion," *Ascent* (Fall 2001): 32.

25. "A Parking Ramp Is Part of the Solution," *American City* (January 1967): 118–20; Mary S. Smith et al., *Shared Parking*, 2nd ed. (Washington, D.C.: ULI– the Urban Land Institute, 2005); Greg W. Sylvester, "Two Brief Case Studies: Developing a Shared Parking Model for Urban Hotel/Office Developments," *Parking Professional* (December 2001): 16–20.

26. Blair Kamin, "A Subterranean Parking Garage Reveals a Museum's Beauty and Excitement," *Chicago Tribune*, July 16, 1998, Tempo section, 1, 4; William Mullen, "Museum Counting on Garage for Revival," *Chicago Tribune*, June 25, 1998, Metro Chicago section, 1–2.

27. Rodd Cayton, "Who Will Replace Amtrak?" *Lincoln Journal Star*, March 17, 2002, 1F–2F; Carl Walker Parking, brochure.

28. "Category II Award of Excellence," *Parking Professional* (August 1999): 20–21; International Parking Design, *The Art of Parking* (brochure).

29. John Van Horn "The Art of Parking," *Parking Today* (May 1999): 12–13; "A Parking Garage for a Boat?" *Parking* (June 2002): 11.

30. City planners and parking officials, Lodi, California, discussions with author, 2006.

31. Leo A. Daly, *Department of Water and Power: Lincoln Heights District Headquarters* (brochure); visit by author to Minneapolis Energy Center, spring 2005.

32. "Kids Profit," 38–42; Benjamin Forgey, "Injecting Imagination," C1.

33. "Parking Facilities for Industrial Employees," *American City* (September 1924): 239.

34. Curtis C. Myers, "A Garage at the Office Door," *Horseless Age* (August 15, 1916): 141–142.

35. Harold F. Blanchard, "Ramp Design in Public Garages," *Architectural Forum* (November 1921): 169–175.

36. "Facilities for Industrial Employees," 239.

37. "Industrial Plant Parking," *Urban Land* 18, no. 5 (May 1959): cover, 3–7; Dorothy A. Muncy, "Planning Guidelines for Industrial Park Development," *Urban Land* 29, no. 11 (December 1970): 3–10. Zoning codes produced many new combinations of garage, office space,

and manufacturing. See "Warehouse of Wilkinson, Gaddis and Co., Newark, N.J.," *American Architect* (March 1916): 194. All of the following items were viewed at the Chicago Historical Society: *Tower Garage* (Chicago: Tower Automobile Corporation, n.d.); *Gateway Garage* 25 (October 1941); *Gateway Garage* 20 (December 1941). The following are advertisements for garages, also viewed at the Chicago Historical Society: "Plymouth Court Garage," "The Dearborn-Lake Garage," "The Place to Park Your Car!" and "South Loop Motoramp Garage."

38. The building was also intended to be linked to a planned subway system, but the system was never built.

39. Documents and photographs from the Fisher Building Archives, Bentley Historical Library, University of Michigan at Ann Arbor; original advertisements for the Fisher Building and for the Fisher Building garage (provided by the Farbman Group); "The Fisher Building," *American Architect* 135 (February 1929): 187–267; National Park Service, "Fisher Building," Detroit: A National Register of Historic Places Travel Itinerary, www.cr.nps.gov/nr/travel/detroit/d31.htm.

40. "Other Concepts," *Parking* (Winter 1954): 21; Geoffrey Harold Baker and Bruno Funaro, *Parking* (New York: Reinhold, 1958), 90–91; C.T. McGavin, "Teamwork Can Solve the Downtown Parking Problem," *Urban Land* 9, no. 7 (July–August 1950): 3–9.

41. "Industrial Plant Parking," cover, 3–7; "Preserving the Industrial Base of Detroit," *Urban Land* (July–August 1957): 1–5; Muncy, "Planning Guidelines," 3–10; "Johns Manville World Headquarters," *Process:architecture 1980*, no. 19, 46–55, 161. One advantage of workplace parking is the fact that the same employees use the same facility five days a week: seasoned drivers can handle the more unusual and complex configurations that maximize available space and increase traffic flow.

42. "Income, Expense Analysis of Parking Garages," *Parking* (Winter 1965): 18–19; Norene Dann Martin, "Report of the Executive Vice President," *Parking* (July 1973): 11–12; Joe Farrell, Architects Hawaii Limited, discussion with author, December 19, 2000; "Award for Excellence in Parking Design and Program Innovation," *Parking Professional* (July 1986): 10–13. Early parking garages were often built using warehouse construction techniques, and looked very much like warehouses. Later, warehouses were often adapted for use as parking garages.

43. Jo Allen Gause et al., *Office Development Handbook*, 2nd ed. (Washington, D.C.: ULI–the Urban Land Institute, 1998), 47.

44. Ibid., 228–233.

45. Ibid., 234–239.

46. The solution implemented in Los Angeles, in the late teens, was the parking lot—but Los Angeles had more available land than the older cities in the East and Midwest.

47. G.H. Brazer, "Reinforced Concrete Building for the Park Square Motor Mart, Boston," *Engineering News-Record* 52, no. 21 (November 18, 1905): 573–577; Highway Research Board, *Parking Principles*, Special Report 125, Subject Area 53 (Washington, D.C.: National Academy of Sciences, 1971), 109; "The Gala Garage," *AIA Journal* (August 1968): 71–73; "A Gala Garage," *Parking* (Winter 1969): 36–40.

48. James J. Flink, *America Adopts the Automobile, 1895–1910* (Cambridge, Mass.: MIT Press, 1970), 220; "The Department Store Was Once New," *Parking* (Spring 1954): 6; Daniel J. Boorstin, *The Americans: The Democratic Experience* (New York: Random House, 1973), 443; Kenneth L. Hess, "The Growth of Automotive Transportation," www.klhess.com/car_essy.html.

49. L.R. Bowen, "Union Market and Garage," *American City* 34, no. 4 (April 1926): 414–415.

50. "Drive in Banks," *Parking* (Spring 1954): 46. Examples of bank and parking combinations abound: see "Multi-Level Banking by Car," *Parking* (Fall 1962): 54–55; "First National Parking Garage," *Parking* (Fall 1957): 23–26; "Gary National Bank," *Parking* (October 1970): 44; "Design Analysis," *Parking* (Fall 1957): 23; "First National Bank Garage," *Parking* (Winter 1961): 46–47.

51. Meyer also supported the idea of relieving traffic congestion by bringing shopping centers closer to residential neighborhoods; this was a planning technique that had been used in Los Angeles in the late teens.

52. "A New Move in Seattle," *American City* 43, no. 1 (July 1930): 143. "Roof Parking to Relieve Street Overcrowding," *American City* 52, no. 1 (January 1937): 44. "Department Store Builds First Parking Ramp for Wilkes-Barre," *Parking* (Spring 1954): 5; "American National Bank of Austin, Texas," *Parking* (Fall 1954): 38–39; "World's First Roof-Top Drive-On Bank to be Opened," *Parking* (Summer 1954): 45.

53. "Rooftop Parking," *American City* 65, no. 3 (September 1950): 143; Baker and Funaro, *Parking*, 108–109; "Roof-Parking in Queens," *American City* (June 1948): 167.

54. "Tomorrow's Parking Today," *Parking* (Winter 1959): 30–31.

55. J.C. Nichols, "Developing Outlying Shopping Centers," *American City* 41, no. 1 (July 1929): 98.

56. Bernard H. Prack, "Provisions and Parking," *Architectural Forum* 58, no. 5 (May 1933): 378–380.

57. Thomas Smith, *The Aesthetics of Parking* (Chicago: American Planning Association, 1988), 38; Baker and Funaro, *Parking*, 60; "San Francisco Builds a Garage under a Park," *American City* 57, no. 11 (November 1942): 66.

58. S.A. Carrighar, "Built Down Instead of Up: The Union Square Garage, San Francisco," *Architect and Engineer* (August 1942): 19–29.

59. "Hub Shopping," *Parking* (Winter 1954): 3; John Brierley, *Parking of Motor Vehicles* (London: Applied Science Publishers, 1972), 173; Dietrich Klose, *Metropolitan Parking Structures: A Survey of Architectural Problems and Solutions* (New York: Praeger, 1965), 196–197; "Self-Parking Downtown Center Garage," *Architect and Engineer* (April 1955): 9–24.

60. "Nation's Largest Parking Building Completed," *Engineering News-Record* (July 10, 1952): 34–39; "A 2,000-Car Parking Garage," *American City* 66, no. 11 (November 1951): 143; Willard A. Kemp, "550-Car Parking Garage for Salt Lake City Store," *American City* 70, no. 6 (June 1955): 173; Klose, *Parking Structures*, 43; Baker and Funaro, *Parking*, 68–71.

61. "Parking News," *Parking* (Winter 1963): 4; Larry Donoghue, Larry Donoghue Associates, discussion with author, 2006; "Gala Garage Opening, Harrisburg, Pennsylvania," *Parking* (July 1970): 32–33.

62. E.A. Scotton, "Thirty-Eight Merchants Produce Parking Space," *American City* 65, no. 1 (January 1950): 119; "Department Store Parking Services Grow," *American City* 80, no. 12 (December 1965): 1; "Plan-itorial . . . ," *Urban Land* 17, no. 7 (July–August 1958): 2; Abraham Marcus, "Shopping on Wheels," *Parking* (Winter 1967): 16–24. The founding of the International Council of Shopping Centers was announced in 1964: see "Shopping Center Parking," *Urban Land* 23, no. 8 (September 1964): 2.

63. "Parking News," *Parking* (Winter 1963): 4; Jack H. Pearlstone Jr., "Deck Parking at a Regional Shopping Center," *Parking* (April 1971): 43–44; visits by author to Old Orchard Shopping Center, and observation of the construction of the decks; Walker Parking Consultants, fact sheet, Aventura Shopping Mall parking facility; J. T. Stegmaier, "Parking and Its Relationship to Business," *Urban Land* (May 1956): 3–7; Coreslab Structures, brochure.

64. John Graham, "Prestressed Concrete in the Northwest and Hawaii," *PCI Journal* (April 1964): 63–66; Michael D. Beyard and W. Paul O'Mara, *Shopping Center Development Handbook*, 3rd ed. (Wash-

ington, D.C.: ULI–the Urban Land Institute, 1999), 248–249.

65. Macerich Company, "TysonsFuture.com," www.tysonsfuture.com/vision/index.html.

66. Beyard and O'Mara, *Development Handbook*, 316–317.

67. Although most people would think of the Mall of America as a suburban site, its design prompted its inclusion as a URE.

68. Mary Smith, "Circle Center," *Parking* (September 1996): 25–33.

69. Geoffrey Booth et al., *Transforming Suburban Business Districts* (Washington, D.C.: ULI–the Urban Land Institute, 2001), 115–117, 225; Dean Schwanke et al., *Mixed-Use Development Handbook*, 2nd ed. (Washington, D.C.: ULI–the Urban Land Institute, 2003), 181, 215.

70. Charles C. Bohl, *Place Making: Developing Town Centers, Main Streets, and Urban Villages* (Washington, D.C.: ULI–the Urban Land Institute, 2003), 174–179.

71. "Garage of Andrew Carnegie," *American Architect and Building News* 89, no. 1587 (May 26, 1906); *American Architect* 110, no. 2115 (July 5, 1916); "Garage, John W. Aitken," *Architecture* 105, no. 1990 (February 11, 1914): 60 (illustration); Catherine G. Miller and the Irwin-Sweeney-Miller Foundation, *Carscape: A Parking Handbook* (Columbus, Ind.: Washington Street Press, 1988), 10; A.T. North, "The Residential District Garage," *Architectural Forum* (September 1930): 379–384. The relationship between housing and transportation has been the focus of much research and discussion, in an effort to seek the best solutions for as many people as possible. See Henry C. Wright, "The Interrelation of Housing and Transit," *American City* 10, no. 1 (January 1914): 51–53; *Zoning, Parking and Traffic* (Saugatuck, Conn.: Eno Foundation for Transportation, 1972), 14.

72. H.M. Cauley, "The Massellton," *Atlanta Journal-Constitution*, May 16, 1999, Homefinder section, 12.

73. Visit by author, 2002.

74. Klose, *Parking Structures*, 244–247; *Parking* (October 1980): cover; *Mixed-Use Developments: New Ways of Land Use*, Technical Bulletin 71 (Washington, D.C.: ULI–the Urban Land Institute, n.d.), 113–117.

75. Sharon Stangenes, "Value of a Parking Space Skyrockets amid Chicago's Residential Boom," *Chicago Tribune*, June 28, 1998, real estate section, 1, 7; Sherman W. Griselle, "Parking Related to Residential Development," *Urban Land* (April 1965): 7–8; Kerry Miller, "The Priciest Places to Park," BusinessWeek online, July 19, 2006, www.businessweek.

com/autos/content/jul2006/bw2006 0718_694993.htm?chan=search.

76. Vincent Lawrence Dixon, "The Parking Condominium: Has Its Time Arrived?" *Parking* (Spring 1983): 63–68; "Parking Condo Works in Brooklyn," *Parking Professional* (April 1987): 10; "Prime Space, No View," *Parking Professional* (September 2001): 9–11; Vail Resorts Development Company, "Founders Garage and Parker's Green," www.newvail.com/vailfrontdoor/vvpark.cfm; Scott N. Miller, "Ground Broken on Village Parking Structure," *Vail Daily News*, May 22, 2004, www.vaildaily. com; Michele Wendler, principal, Watry Design Group, e-mail message to author, 2006.

77. Kevin M. Hagerty, Gordon H. Chong, and Sam Nunes, "Commercial Neighborhood Parking Garages: An Integrated Approach," *Parking Professional* (June 1991): 14–20.

78. "Making for Better Neighbors," *Multifamily Trends* (Spring 2002): 35–37, 57; Steven Fader, *Density by Design: New Directions in Residential Development*, 2nd ed. (Washington D.C.: ULI–the Urban Land Institute, 2000), 100–119.

79. In new downtown condominiums, a buyer generally chooses how many parking spaces to purchase along with the condominium, but typical suburban apartment dwellers still expect parking to be free.

80. See Smith et al., *Shared Parking*, for design details for a successful project.

81. Gary Bolton, "The Smart Answer," *Modern Steel Construction* (April 2001); Steel Institute, *Jefferson at Lenox Park: Atlanta, Georgia*, Steel Parking Structure File F003–02 (promotional brochure).

82. Adrienne Schmitz et al., *Multifamily Housing Development Handbook* (Washington, D.C.: ULI–the Urban Land Institute, 2000): 244–249.

83. "Condos Break the Sound Barrier," *New York Times*, February 17, 2005, D10; Handel Architects, LLP, www.Californiaarchitects.com; Dave Barista, "Last Curtain Wall: Plenty of Light, But Is It Sound Tight?" Building Design and Construction, May 1, 2006, www.bdcnetwork.com.

84. "Kirk's Garage, New Haven, Conn.," *Horseless Age* 33, no. 19 (May 13, 1914): 756–757; Henry Sage, "In and About New Haven, Connecticut," *American Motorist* 3, no. 7 (July 1911): 390. In an approach that is still considered a best practice today, garages were often located near train stations because they were considered an integral part of the larger transportation system.

85. "Georgian Service Garage, Atlanta, Ga.," *Horseless Age* 31, no. 19 (May 7, 1913): 803–804.

86. Ibid.

87. "Pioneers in Parking," *Parking* (Fall 1955): 10.

88. "Biltmore Garage," *Architectural Forum* (March 1927): 299, plate 62. The newer Biltmore garage did not have the elegance of the old. See "Make the Most of Your Site," *Parking* (Winter 1954): 24.

89. "Hotel Statler Garage," *Architectural Forum* (March 1927): 231–232, plate 40; American Automobile Association, *Official Hotel Directory: Restaurants and Storage Garages* (American Automobile Association, 1932).

90. One example is "Coral Court: The No-Tell Motel with a Touch of Class," www.coralcourt.com (reference provided to author by Andrea Talley, May 2006).

91. Norman Katen, "A Hotel You Can Drive To," *Parking* (Winter 1966): 13; Klose, *Parking Structures*, 234–235; "Hotels Need Parking," *Parking* (Fall 1954): 25–26.

92. "Howard Johnson Motor Hotel Set for Chicago Loop," *Parking* (October 1969): 20; "Parking News," *Parking* (Winter 1960): 2. Another of many examples is described in "The Indianapolis Hilton," *Parking* (October 1969): 42.

93. "Automated Parking," *Innkeeping* (January 1965): 32–34.

94. Gerald Salzman, "Hotel Parking: How Much Is Enough?" *Urban Land* (January 1988): 14–17; Susan Stellin, "It's Not the Gas, It's the Parking," *New York Times*, July 18, 2004, travel section, 4.

95. Timothy Haahs and Associates, *Turning Stone Casino Resort—Oneida Indian Nation Parking Garage* (brochure); Duncan B. Crowther, "Caesars Hotel/Casino Builds Garage Fit for an Emperor," *Parking* (March 1991): 22–25; Tom Hudak, "Parking in Las Vegas: How It's Changed," *Parking Professional* (May 2001): 18–21.

96. Adam Steinhauer, "Group Plans Big Garage Complex," *Las Vegas Review-Journal*, July 9, 1997; William Taaffe, "Las Vegas Monorail Rolls above Strip Traffic," *New York Times*, July 25, 2004, 3; John Deiner, "A Test Ride (and Walk) on Vegas Monorail," *Atlanta Journal-Constitution*, September 5, 2004, 15; Vegas.com, the Official Vegas Travel Site, www.vegas.com/transportation/parking garages.html.

97. Harry Wolfe, architect of the Disney Garage, discussion with author, 2001. Universal City, in Orlando, Florida, has also constructed a mega facility: see Howard Linders and Mary S. Smith, "Redefining the Mega Parking Structure," *Parking* (July 1996): 23–29.

98. Larry Donoghue, "United States Airports Parking Statistical Analysis," *Parking Professional* (October 2001): 18–25;

"Aviation and Urban Land," *Urban Land Institute Bulletin* 2, no. 12 (December 1943): 1; "Residents Resist Airport Parking Plan," *Parking Professional* (July 1989): 30–31; E. William Arons, "Parking 'Blooms' in the Garden," *Parking Professional* (December 2000): 20–23; Richard C. Rich, "The History of Airport Parking," *Parking Professional* (June 2004): 20–23; Carl Walker Parking, fact sheet, Louisville International Airport; "San Francisco Airport Automated People Mover Debuts," *Parking* (June 2003): 9. Even in the 1970s, designers of airport parking facilities understood that it was important to provide open, skylit passageways for pedestrian movement from the garage to the terminal. See "Parking Structure Enhances Beauty of Major International Airport," *Parking* (April 1979): 20–23.

99. RAC stand for rental automobile center, and CONRAC and CRCF stand for consolidated rental car facility.

100. Jerry Marcus and Blair Hanuschak, "An Idea Whose Time Has Come," *Passenger Terminal World*, Annual Technology Showcase Issue, 2000; Hartsfield-Jackson Atlanta International Airport, "Consolidated Rental Agency Complex (CONRAC)," www.atlanta-airport.com/default.asp?url=http://www.atlanta-airport.com/ecc/conrac.htm; Walter Briggs and Ben Young, "Design for Parking," *Parking* (Summer 1967): 20; Los Angeles World Airports, "Remote Airline and Baggage Check-in," www.lawa.org/lax/laxremotecheckin.cfm.

101. Marcus and Hanuschak, "An Idea"; John Burgan and Vlasta Poch, "Airport Parking Garage Design Takes Off," *Parking Professional* (June 2001): 24; Richard C. Rich, "A New Approach That's Taking Flight," *Parking Today* 5, no. 9 (October 2000): 28–30.

102. Coolidge, Shepley, Bulfinch and Abbott, Architects, "The Designing Procedure," *Architectural Forum* 58, no. 2 (February 1933): 87–93.

103. "Parking Garage/Future Hospital Ancillary Building," *PCI Journal* (July–August 1981); Channing C. Edington, "Medical Building Parking," *Parking* 43, no. 2 (March 2004): 49–52.

104. "2003 International Parking Awards," *Parking Professional* (August 2003): 35.

105. Adrian Lao, "Parkades and the Therapeutic Garden," *Parking Professional* (March 2001): 24–27.

106. Rick Kinnell and Jarman Word, "A Driving Force Behind Campus Expansion," *Parking Professional* (November 2001): 22–25.

107. "Parking under a Library," *American City* 86, no. 9 (September 1971): 124–125; "Parking Garages over Freeways," *American City* 81, no. 8 (August 1966): 134; C.D. Mullinex, "Parking under an

Island," *American City* 81, no. 9 (September 1966): 164–168; "Abandoned Piers Downtown Converted from City Liability into Assets," *Parking* (October 1970): 13.

Preserving Early Showrooms

1. Christopher Gray, "The Car Is Still King on 11th Avenue," *New York Times*, July 9, 2006, real estate section.

2. Albert Kahn, "Sales and Service Buildings, Garages and Assembly Plants," *Architectural Forum* (March 1927): 209.

3. Kahn, "Garages and Assembly Plants," 209–289; William F. Wharton, "Architecture and Decoration of Automobile Show Rooms," *Architectural Forum* (March 1927): 305–313.

4. Bob Wilkinson, "End of an Era," *Parking* (January 1974): 16–17; "News in Photos," *Parking* (April 1974): 16; "Going . . . Going . . . Gone," *Parking* (April 1974): 16; McCaffery Interests, "Georgetown Centre—Washington, D.C.," www.mccafferyinterests.com/content/completed/georgetown_centre.

5. "Sales Garage for the Chicago Motor Car Company," *Brickbuilder* 19, no. 6 (June 1910): 151; David Mendell, "City Out to Preserve Its Auto Past," *Chicago Tribune*, April 5, 2000, Metro section, 1; Tracie Rozhon, "Windy City Asks, Past or Progress?" *Atlanta Journal-Constitution*, November 12, 2000, D12.

The Fisher Building, 1937 to the Present

1. National Park Service, "Fisher Building," Detroit: A National Register of Historic Places Travel Itinerary, www.cr.nps.gov/nr/travel/detroit/d31.htm.

2. Kay Houston and Linda Culpepper, "Rearview Mirror," detnews.com (Detroit News Online), http://detnews.com/apps/pbcs.dll/frontpage; Randall Fogelman, *Detroit's New Center* (Charleston, S.C.: Arcadia Publishing, 2004).

3. Houston and Culpepper, "Rearview Mirror."

4. "The Fisher Building," *American Architect* 135 (February 1929): 187–267; construction photos of the Fisher Building, Burton Historical Collection, Detroit Public Library.

5. "Fisher Building," 187–267; *The Fisher Building Garage* (brochure). Many thanks to Garry Sommer, of APCOA, for providing a copy of this brochure.

6. "Fisher Building," 187–267; *Fisher Building Garage*.

7. "Technical News and Research: Garages," *Architectural Record* (February 1929); Fisher Building promotional booklet, Fisher Building Archives, Bentley Historical Library, University of Michigan at Ann Arbor. Many thanks to Robin Zohoury, of the Farbman Group, for provid-

ing copies of original materials advertising the opening of the Fisher Building.

Country Club Plaza: From the 1920s to the Present

1. Geoffrey Booth et al., *Transforming Suburban Business Districts* (Washington, D.C.: ULI–the Urban Land Institute, 2001), 115–116; J.C. Nichols, "Developing Outlying Shopping Centers," *American City* (July 1929): 98; *Urban Land Institute Bulletin* 12, no. 12 (December 1943): cover; J.C. Nichols, "Parking and Downtown Stability," *Urban Land* (March 1949): 3.

2. "Tributes to Developer," *Urban Land* 4, no. 9 (October 1945): 2; "Concrete Proves Versatile for Ramp, Mechanical-Type Parking Facilities," *Parking* (Spring 1955): 18–23.

3. Ibid.

4. Community Builders' Council, *The Community Builders' Handbook* (Washington, D.C.: ULI–the Urban Land Institute, 1947), 110; Davis K. Jackson, "Long-Span Triple-Deck Parking Station," *Engineering News-Record* (August 19, 1948): 111–113; "Unique Garage Plan," *Urban Land* (November 1948): 4; "Central Business District Panel Session—Taxes, Transit, and Off-Street Parking," *Urban Land* 8, no. 3 (March 1949): 1–3.

5. Booth et al., *Suburban Business Districts*, 117.

6. Many thanks to Gayle Terry, of Highwoods Property Company, for sharing information on the two newest parking structures in Country Club Plaza—Saks and Valencia Place.

Unique Proposals and Initiatives

1. Walter H. Kilham Jr., *Raymond Hood, Architect* (Toronto: Saunders, 1973), 12.

2. Rem Koolhaas, *Delirious New York* (New York: Monacelli, 1994), 173.

3. "Minor Mention," *Horseless Age* 8, no. 7 (May 15, 1901): 161; "Parking News: Dallas Has It," *Parking* (Summer 1954): 5; Leo A. Daly, *Trammell Crow Square 429* (brochure); Michael Szkatiski, "Parking Garage Is Just the Ticket for Chicago Church," *Parking* (September 1990): 25–29.

4. "Parking Sidelines," *Parking* (Spring 1954): 51; "Budget Rent-A-Car," *Parking* (Winter 1962): 9; "Share-A-Cab," *Parking* (July 1977): 21. Another rent-a-car operation was started by the Kinney Service Corporation, a publicly traded company that included a parking division. See Ira U. Cobleigh, "Kinney Service Corporation," *Parking* (Winter 1963): 21, 24.

5. Anne Whiston Spirn, C. Ford Peatross, and Robert L. Sweeney, *Frank Lloyd Wright: Designs for an American Landscape, 1922–1932* (New York: Harry N.

Abrams in association with the Canadian Centre for Architecture, the Library of Congress, and the Frank Lloyd Wright Foundation, 1996), 179.

6. Dick Parker, *What'll Ya Have: A History of the Varsity* (Singapore: Looking Glass Books, 2003), 72.

Parking at Colleges and Universities: A Unique Opportunity

1. Robert Brecklin, "A Different Angle on Parking," *Parking Today* (April 2001): 20–23.

2. Clark Kerr, *The Uses of the University*, 4th ed. (Cambridge, Mass: Harvard University Press, 1995), 138.

3. John R. Kleberg, "A Look at College Parking," *Parking* (Fall 1967): 26–28; Spencer M. Hurtt, "The Impact of Institutional Growth on Urban Land Use," *Urban Land* (January 1968): 3–10; "Appearance Belies Vast Dimensions of Newly Completed UCLA Parking Structure," *Parking* (Spring 1968): 22–23; "Pulling Out of a Parking Jam: Colleges Shift into Action," *Parking* (January 1971): 20–24; Kris Anderson and Al Carroll, "University Parking Structures Come of Age," *Parking* (August 2003): 53–57.

4. Ed Ellis, "Getting Around Campus," *American School and University* (May 2003): 40–44; David Jay Lieb, "Cornell University Takes a Holistic Approach to Transportation Demand Management," *Parking* (August 2002): 25–30; Richard C. Rich, "Colleges Build Up—and Down—in Search for Parking Space," *Parking* (Winter 1969): 44–49.

5. "Parking Structures That Enrich a City and Influence Its Emerging Urban Patterns," *Architectural Record* 156, no. 1 (July 1974): 112–118.

6. "Magnetic Levitating Train," *Parking Professional* (May 2003): 36–37.

7. Jan Pero, "City of Tampa and Hillsborough Community College Pool Resources for Parking Facility," *Parking Today* (April 2003): 36, 37; "Creative Parking Solutions," *Parking Professional* (October 2000): 16–23; Jerry Marcus, "The Fernando Noriega Jr. Palm Ave. Garage: A New Feature in Ybor City," *Parking Today* (September 2003): 30, 31; Roxanne Warren, *The Urban Oasis: Guideways and Greenways in the Human Environment* (New York: McGraw-Hill, 1998), 167–168; "36 Hours: Morgantown, W. Va.," *New York Times*, May 9, 2003, D4; Ellis, "Getting Around Campus," 40–44; "Emory University—Home to Award-Winning Parking Design," *Parking* (May 2002): 27–28.

8. Walker Parking Consultants, *The Driving Force* (brochure); "Category One: Award of Merit," *Parking Professional* (August 1997): 19.

9. Tim Haahs, *University of Pennsylvania: Hamilton Square, Philadelphia, Pennsylvania* (brochure).

10. "Unique Soccer Facility Sits Atop Garage at St. John's University," *Parking Today* (November 2002): 30–31; "Award of Excellence: Rose Garden Parkade," *Parking Professional* (August 1996): 27; Joedy Hoogner, "University of Kansas: Design Tempered with Function," *Parking Today* 17, no. 4 (April 2002): 24–27.

11. Dennis Burns and Todd Litman, "Integrated University Access Management Programs," *Parking* (January 2007): 16–23.

Chapter 4

1. "The New Fenway Garage, Boston, Mass.," *Horseless Age* 31, no. 19 (May 7, 1913): 826–827.

2. "A Garage for Motor Trucks," *American Architect* (September 1918): 296–301.

3. P.M. Heldt, "The Garage Business—Buildings, Equipment, Methods," *Horseless Age* (March 15, 1916): 234–236; "Fenway Garage," 826; "Concrete Cantilever Construction in Chicago Garage," *Engineering News-Record* 85, no. 3 (September 23, 1920): 609–611. The twin requirements for space and light spurred connections between the built form of the garage and the material used to construct it: it was not until arch and truss roof construction became typical, freeing large areas from structural supports, that it was possible to create windows large enough to admit significant amounts of natural light into the interior. The quest for space and light also led to more experimentation with reinforced concrete, which could span even longer distances than typical wooden post-and-beam construction.

4. A foot-candle (equivalent to 10.764 lux) is a measure of the amount of light on a surface.

5. Heldt, "Garage Business," 234–236. Supplemental lighting was needed because early garages often had space for long-term storage on the top floor, which made it difficult for skylights to bring natural light into the lower floors; supplemental lighting was also needed so that mechanics could do their work.

6. Heldt, "Garage Business," 234–236.

7. Ben W. Young, "Conversion of Parking Facilities: Attendant to Self-Park," *Parking* (April 1974): 28.

8. "A Modern Parking Garage in a Central Metropolitan District," *American City* (December 1930): 143. A similar approach is still in use in Germany, where spaces dedicated to women are often located close to pedestrian entry points, in areas that are well lit and open to public view. Men who park in these spaces receive a citation. Such passive approaches to garage security are complementary to architectural approaches such as good lighting and way-finding.

9. "Women in Parking," *Parking* (Winter 1955): 39–40.

10. Young, "Conversion of Parking Facilities," 28; E.H. Shaefer, "Lighting Packs Profits into Night Business," *Parking* (Fall 1955): 21; "Why Lighting for Self-Service Parking?" *Parking* (Fall 1963): 22–23; "Free Lighting Advice for Parking," *Parking* (Fall 1956): 23; George Devlin, "Self-Service Parking," *Parking* (Summer 1957): 39–44; F.W. Callison, "Self-Service Parking," *Parking* (Summer 1957): 32–36; George Applegarth, "Design and Operation of World's Largest Self-Service Parking Facility," *Parking* (Summer 1957): 37.

11. Jon T. Lang, *Creating Architectural Theory: The Role of the Behavioral Sciences in Environmental Design* (New York: Van Nostrand Reinhold, 1987), 135.

12. Bill Collier, director of parking, Emory University, discussion with author, August 2005.

13. "Custom Engineered Luminaries," *Parking* (Spring 1961): 36–37; "Engineered Lighting for a 750-Car Parking Garage," *American City* 76, no. 6 (June 1961): 124–125.

14. Steven Straiger, Energy Innovation Group, e-mail message to author, April 16, 2004; Don Monahan, vice president, Walker Parking Consultants, e-mail message to author, April 12, 2004; Jim Hunnicutt, GaragePark, e-mail correspondence with author, August 12, 2006; Donald R. Monohan, "Parking Facility Lighting Design, Measurement and Maintenance," in *Parking Management: The Next Level* (Fredericksburg, Va.: International Parking Institute, n.d.) 260–297.

15. Shannon Sanders McDonald, "Bus Shelters to Parking Structures," *Parking Professional* (March 2005), 12–16; "50 Years of Parking Innovations," *Parking* (May 2001): 29.

16. "A Lighting Primer," *Parking* (June 1998): 26–27; "You Can Use Prismatic Lighting for Appearance and Security," *Parking Today* 8, no. 1 (January 2003): 16–18; Holophane, "Lighting for Parking Garages," www.holophane.com/school/tecg/pdl.htm.

17. Lee E. Gray, "From Elevator Boy to Automatic Elevators," *Construction Specifier* (August 2004): 40–46; Buck Simpers, "Making Safety a Priority in Parking Garages," *Parking Today* 8, no. 11 (November 2003): 20–21; visit by author to Western Michigan Community College, fall 2005. The first glass elevator appeared in 1956, when San Diego's El Cortéz hotel was renovated and expanded.

18. "T.V. Parking Attendant," *Parking* (Summer 1955): 31; "Design Analysis," *Parking* (Winter 1958): 8–9; "Parking Security," *Parking* (Fall 1969): 34–35; Frank Abram, "Video Surveillance Technology Makes Parking Facilities More Secure," *Parking Today* 8, no. 6 (June 2003): 34–36; "Security First in This Parking Structure," *American City* 86, no. 1 (January 1971): 74; Richard C. Rich, discussions with author, fall 2005; "Emergency Phones: An Intelligent Choice at BWI," *Parking* (September 2003): 13.

19. James I. Johnson Associates, "Security in Parking Facilities" (presentation, Parking Industry Exhibition, Chicago, April 2, 2001); Sharon Easley et al., "September 11th Attacks: Impacts on the Parking Industry," *Parking Professional* (May 2002): 20–25; "The Impact of September 11, 2001, on Airport Parking in the United States," *Parking* (March 2002): 28–31; Helen Vaughn, "Parking Lot Security at Nashville International Airport," *Parking* (March 2002): 32; Harold Matthews, "Security," *Parking* (January 1974): 35–39; TCS International, product information sheet on SecuScan. The most recent available version of *Recommended Security Guidelines for Airport Planning, Design and Construction* is dated June 15, 2006.

20. Visits by author to Hartsfield-Jackson Atlanta International Airport.

21. Christopher Elliott, "Airports Use the Cellphone to Ease Traffic Congestion," *New York Times*, January 9, 2005, TR2.

22. "Stop! Step Forward and Be Sniffed," *New York Times*, August 30, 2004, A17; "GIS: Public Safety Agencies Plug in to High-Tech Mapping," *Atlanta Journal-Constitution*, August 22, 2004; TCS International, www.tcsintl.com/products.htm; SecuScan, www.secuscan. com.

23. Lang, *Architectural Theory*, 135.

24. Bruce Brooks Pfeiffer, *Frank Lloyd Wright Drawings* (New York: Abrams, 1990), 136–137, 153; Library of Congress, "Frank Lloyd Wright: Designs for an American Landscape," www.loc.gov/exhibits/flw/flw.html.

25. Mary Smith, "ADAAG/ABAAG Update," *Parking* (January–February 2006): 36–37; Mary Smith, "Complying with the new ADAAG" (paper presented at International Parking Institute annual conference, Fort Lauderdale, Florida, 2005); "Access Board Issues New Guidelines for Accessible Design," *Parking* (September 2004): 36–37.

26. Dennis Burns and Becky Hannum, "A New Canvas: Wayfinding Graphics and Art to Enhance Parking Facility Design," *Parking Professional* (April 2006): 44–47; Becky Hannum, owner, ART Everywhere, e-mail exchanges with author, January 9, 2006.

27. Jim Wilhelm, "Ambiance in Parking at Chicago's O'Hare International Airport," *Parking* (August 1996): 56–59; Larry Donoghue, Donoghue and Associates, telephone conversations with author, 2005–2006; "Musical Theme Garages Are Grammy Winners with the Public," *Standard Parking Newsletter*, n.d.; Jonathan Abarbanel, "Is Your Theater Defunct?" Performink Stories, www.performink.com/archives/news/LoopTheatreParkingGarage.htm.

28. Www.vegas.com/transportation/parking garages.html; Walker Parking consultants, *The Driving Force in Creative Parking Solutions* (brochure); Lou Cook, *50 Years of the National Parking Association* (Washington, D.C.: National Parking Association, 2001), 53.

29. In fact, the extended lightbulb changer that is still in use today was created for use in the garage.

30. P.M. Heldt, "The Garage Business—Buildings, Equipment, Methods," *Horseless Age* (January 15, 1916): 76–78; P.M. Heldt, "The Garage Business—Buildings, Equipment, Methods," *Horseless Age* (February 15, 1916): 152–153; Charles L. Hubbard, "Heating, Ventilating and Mechanical Equipment of a Garage," *Horseless Age* 25, no. 18 (May 4, 1910): 631–643; Gamewell Company, "The Sprinkler Watchman" (advertisement) *American City* 42 (January 1930); Motor World, *Automobile Repairshop Short-Cuts*, 4th ed. (New York: U.C. Book Company, 1918), 132.

31. "The Private Garage," *Automobile* (December 23, 1909): 1083–1084; Heldt, "Garage Business" (January 15, 1916): 76–78; "Motor-Driven Equipment for Garages," in *Westinghouse Motor Applications,* Catalogue 3002-A, Section 3226 (East Pittsburgh, Penn.: Westinghouse Electric and Manufacturing Company, n.d.), National Automotive Collection, Detroit Public Library.

32. P.M. Heldt, "The Garage Business—Buildings, Equipment, Methods," *Horseless Age* (January 15, 1916): 76; Heldt, "Garage Business" (February 15, 1916): 152–153; P.M. Heldt, "The Garage Business—Buildings, Equipment, Methods," *Horseless Age* (April 1, 1916): 266–267; "Opening Garage Doors by Push Button," *Scientific American* (January 5, 1918): 25; Ralph Harrington Doane, "The Mechanical Equipment of the Garage," *Architectural Forum* (March 1927): 259–264. With the evolution of the building type, design changes have largely eliminated fire doors.

33. Leo J. Pothetes and Ehrsam and Sons, "Belt Manlift Safety in Parking Garages," *Parking* (Fall 1962): 57–58; "Other Recent Innovations: Manlifts," *Parking* (Winter 1955): 23.

34. Doane, "Mechanical Equipment," 259–264.

35. Ibid. A telautograph was a device that allowed handwriting and drawings to be reproduced by an electronically controlled pen.

36. E.E. Wiezell, Stamp and Ticket Vending Machine, U.S. Patent 955,032, filed November 2, 1909, and issued April 12, 1910; G.F. Day, Ticket Vending Apparatus, U.S. Patent 954,787, filed March 10, 1909, and issued April 12, 1910; J.L. Gore, Automatic Ticket Dispensing Machine, U.S. Patent 1,337,837, filed November 25, 1915, and issued April 20, 1920; H.M. Hirsch et al., Automatic Gate, U.S. Patent 1,629,790, filed October 29, 1925, and issued May 24, 1927; J. Andreatte, Pay as You Enter Gate or Turnstyle, U.S. Patent 1,221,268, filed September 19, 1914, and issued April 3, 1917; S.E. Test, Traffic Control System for Multifloor Garages, U.S. Patent 1,823,008, filed September 19, 1914, and issued April 3, 1917; "Modern Parking Garage," *Parking* (Winter 1960): 12–13; Jean M. Keneipp, "New Developments in Automatic Equipment," *Parking* (July 1973): 52–53; "Parking Garages Join Self-Service," *Parking* (October 1973): 34–35; R.C. Ringholz, "The Valometer . . . Story of an Invention," *Parking* (Fall 1963): 19; "Self-Service Parking," *American City* 68, no. 5 (November 1953): 85; Josef Diamond, "After-Hour Controls," *Parking* (Summer 1960): 46–49; Leonard Dickerson, "Automatic Gate Control," *Parking* (Summer 1960): 49–51; "Control System Gives High Speed and Accuracy for St. Louis Operator," *Parking* (Winter 1961): 40–43; "Airtubes Speed Parking Turnover," *American City* 69, no. 4 (April 1954): 138; "Mechanical Parking Attendant," *American City* 72, no. 6 (June 1957): 156; "The Grant Park Garage System," *American City* 70, no. 6 (June 1955): 166–171; "Ticket Spitter with Appeal," *Parking* (April 1970): 36; "T.V. Parking Attendant," 31; "Numbered Stalls Assigned," *Parking* (Fall 1959): 4.

37. "Pogue's Downtown Garage Is Tremendous Success," *Parking* (Winter 1968): 13–14.

38. "Pogue's Heated Ramps," *Parking* (July 1970): 22–25.

39. Edward J. Conroy, "Metered Garages Best . . . For a Meter-Oriented City," *American City* 87, no. 4 (April 1972): 80.

40. John Van Horn, "Parking Is Easy at BWI," *Parking Today* (February 2005): 16–18, 24–25; "First Parking Guidance System Installed at the Baltimore/Washington Airport," *Parking Today* (May 2001): 36–37; "Smart Parking Eases Congestion in Bay Area," *Parking* (January–February 2005): 11; Eric Glohr, "Lansing Community College: Parking Smart Card Trailblazer," *Parking Professional* (June 2002): 36–40; "Daktronics Introduces New Line of Parking Displays," *Daktronics, Inc., Quarterly Publication* (Spring 2001); "Recent Daktronics

Parking Installations," *Daktronics, Inc., Quarterly Publication* (Winter 2002); National Aeronautics and Space Administration, Small Business Innovation Research, "Merritt Systems, Inc.: Orlando, Florida; Parking Garage Automation System," http://sbir.gsfc.nasa.gov/SBIR/successes; Kenneth Orski, "Best Space Scenario," *Traffic Technology International* (February–March 2003): 54–56.

41. "Parking News," *Parking* (Winter 1964): 4; Jason Boseck, "MobileParking and the Transformation of Transient Parking in Baltimore," *Parking* (September 2003): 61–64; "Park by Phone," *Parade*, July 31, 2005, 7; "High-Tech Mapping," *Atlanta Journal-Constitution*, August 22, 2004, B2; Evelien Krabben, "Groningen: The First City to Introduce High-Tech Parking," *Parking Professional* (January 2002): 14–16; Jethro Mullen, "For Those in Paris about to Park, a Service That Tells Them Where," *New York Times*, November 20, 2006, C12.

42. Neal Podmore, "Pay to Park with Your Mobile Phone," *Parking Today* 7, no. 5 (May 2002): 26–27.

43. Albany Parking Authority, www.parkalbany.com; Michael Klein et al., "Get Your Customers Off-Line by Going On-Line" (presentation, International Parking Institute Conference, May 23, 2000); Michael Klein, executive director, Albany Parking Authority, email exchanges with author, December 15, 2005.

44. "Sun Powers Parking Signs at Phoenix Sky Harbor," *Parking Today* 7, no. 5 (May 2002): 38.

45. BCC Research, "The Intelligent Highway," www.SAnewsletters.com; brochures from Alphatech, Inc., Rohwedder, and TagMaster, Inc.

46. Ami Shattenstein, "An Innovative Traffic and Parking Access Control/Management System for Campuses" (paper, Bar-Ilan University, Ramat Gan, Israel); Tim Phillips and Dick Beebe, "Airport Parking Revenue Control System Procurement," *Parking Today* 7, no. 10 (October 2002): 18–21; Bernard Shapiro, "Automated Revenue Control: Controlling Monthlies Enhances Traffic Control and Increases Revenue," *Parking* (January–February 2002): 24–26; "License Plate Recognition at Phoenix Sky Harbor," *Parking Today* (February 2000). The Parking Garage Automation system is based on technology developed by NASA; see http://sbir.gsfc.nasa.gov/SBIR/successes.

47. Laura Longsworth, "Technology-Driven Parking Structure Becomes National Prototype for Garage of the Future," *Parking* (July 1998): 24–26; "Using Credit Cards Wisely," *American City and County* (August 2005): 52; Theresa Hagerty, "A Pay-and-Display Payoff in Portland," *Parking Today* 9,

no. 1 (January 2004): 20–22; Raul Ragalado and Clyde B. Wilson Jr., "Paystations in the Airport and Urban Parking Markets, Part I," *Parking Professional* (July 2000): 50–53; Raul Ragalado and Clyde B. Wilson Jr., "Paystations in the Airport and Urban Parking Markets, Part II," *Parking Professional* (December 2000): 14–19; Raul Ragalado and Clyde B. Wilson Jr., "Paystations in the Airport and Urban Parking Markets, Part III," *Parking Professional* (April 2001): 50–63.

48. Walter Tusch, "Heating and Ventilating of Garages," *Architectural Forum* (March 1927): 257–258; "Don't Start Your Motor in a Closed Garage," *American Motorist* 11, no. 1 (February 1919): 19.

49. Donald F. Roos, "Ventilation System Control of Underground Parking Garages," *Parking* (Fall 1968): 21–23; "Carbon Monoxide Analyzer," *Parking* (Fall 1968): 24–25; "Ventilation for Cobo Hall Garage," *Parking* (Fall 1961): 20.

50. Starks W. Lewis, "Carbon Monoxide (CO) Emergency Procedures," *Parking* (October 1973): 36–41; Charles Boldon, "On Ventilation for Parking Facilities" (paper presented at the annual convention of the National Parking Association, Orlando, Florida, May 20, 1985).

51. Carl Gohs, "Parking in Lloyd Center," *Parking* (July 1970): 48.

52. Heejin Park, "High-Performance Ventilation Systems," *Parking* (May 2002): 20–23; Lewis, "Emergency Procedures," 36–40.

53. In early parking garages, "short-term" and "long-term" didn't refer to one hour versus ten hours, but to hourly or daily storage versus storage for several months.

54. Henry Davis Nadig, "A Garage Is Not a Stable," *American City* 64, no. 9 (September 1949): 175.

55. Tyler Stewart Rogers, "The Automobile and the Estate: Part II. Dimensions of Automobiles," *Architectural Forum* (April 1920): 171–174; Richard F. Roti, "On Changing Automobile and Parking Stall Sizes," *Urban Land* (January 1983): 26–27; Michael Janofsky, "Small Cars Losing the Parking-Space War," *New York Times* on the Web, June 18, 2002.

56. Architects Collaborative, *A Design Manual for Parking Garages* (Cambridge, Mass.: Architects Collaborative, 1975), 15–21; National Consultants Council, National Parking Association, *Recommended Guidelines for Parking Geometrics* (Washington, D.C.: National Parking Association, 1989); Channing C. Edington, "Self-Parking Operations," *Parking* (Summer 1954): 38–39; F.W. Callison, "Self-Service Parking," *Parking* (Summer 1957): 32–36; Richard B. Bowser, "Car Sizes and the Parking In-

dustry," *Parking* (Fall 1955): 15; "New Cars Will Get Bigger, Ramblerman Romney Says," *Parking* (Summer 1957): 78–82; Edward Turner, "Case of the Shrinking Car Space," *Parking* (Winter 1958): 5–6; Roy Drachman, "A New Parking System," *Urban Land* (September 1974): 30; "Parking Design," *Urban Land* (May 1975): 75–76.

57. Richard Roti, *Methods of Parking an Automobile* (National Parking Association and International Parking Design, 1984).

58. For further general references on parking, see the list of further readings at the end of this book.

59. Harry Wolfe, designer of the Disney parking facility in Anaheim, California, discussion with author, spring 2002; Bill Hillis, "Planning That Special Event: Disney Style," *Parking Professional* (May 2002): 26–29; "Around the World: Paris–Algiers," *Parking* (Winter 1959): 24. The approach used at the Disney Resort Garage is successful in speeding up parking and facilitating pedestrian safety. Another idea about entering and exiting parking spaces is proposed in "Benefits of Back-in Angle Parking," *Parking* (August 2004): 11. The article suggests that this approach might be a way of increasing safety in the context of low-speed, low-volume street parking.

60. Clint L. Lefler, "An Introduction to Computer Parking Design," *Parking* (January 1971): 41–54. A new version of this idea is called ParkCAD; see Craig Van Alstyne, "Case of the Week for Parking: Software Helps Develop City of the Future," *Roads and Bridges* (January 20, 2006).

61. American Concrete Institute, "Guide for the Design of Durable Parking Structures" and "Guide for Structural Maintenance of Parking Structures," in *Manual of Concrete Practice* (American Concrete Institute, 2006).

62. David Monroe, "The Structural Maintenance of Parking Garages," *Parking* (November 2001): 19–21; Jim Staif, "Parking Industry Exhibition 2001" (paper presented at Parking Industry Exhibition Conference, Chicago, April 3, 2001); Mark T. Taylor, "How to Build Longevity and Security into Your Next Parking Garage and Keep It That Way," *Parking Today* 8, no. 6 (June 2003): 32–33.

63. Jim Staif, "Parking Structures: Housekeeping, Preventive Maintenance, and Repairs" (paper presented at Parking Industry Exhibition Conference, Chicago, April 3, 2001); Cathy Duncan, Marc Nouri, and John Burgan, "Developing a Parking Facilities Management Plan," *Parking Professional* (September 2002): 18–22.

64. Carl Walker, "Design Fundamentals for Durable Parking Structure Floor Slabs," *Parking* (March–April 1986): 25–30;

Leap Ledger, *Minimizing Maintenance at Your Parking Structure?* (brochure); "Blue Cross, Blue Shield," *PCI Journal* (January–February 1990): 30–33; "Municipal Parking Garage Products," *American City* 85, no. 1 (January 1970): 121–123.

65. Materials Service Life, *Asset Preservation Specialist for Parking Structures* (brochure); "Corrosion Program Weighs Prevention," *Engineering News-Record* (January 15, 2001).

66. Ben Young, "The Design/Construct Method," *Parking* (July 1973): 48–50; Carl Walker, "Multi-Level Parking Facilities Developed by the Design/Build Process," *Parking* (April 1975): 17–18, 43, 44, 47; Nick Watry and Michele Winder, Watry Design, discussion with author, 2005; Design-Build Institute of America, www.dbia.org; Craig A. Shutt, "How to Profit from Design/Build," *Ascent* (Summer 1996): 14–19; "Design/Build Industry Trend for the Year 2000 and Beyond," *Leap Ledger* (April 1998). The first discussion of the design-build approach in parking was in "Turnkey Parking in a Movable Structure," *American City* (Summer–Fall 1971): 162.

67. Kimberly Izenson, "A Holistic Approach to Garage Construction," *Parking Today* (April 2002): 38–41; "One for the Record Books," *Leap Ledger* (April 1998).

68. Keith D. McCartney et al., "The Penn Street Parking Facility," *PCI Journal* (November–December 1995): 40–47; Desman Associates, Penn Street Parking Garage, project fact sheet.

69. Carl Walker, *Industry Insights* (March–April 2006); Alva Williams, "Free Parking in Downtown? You're Kidding!" *Parking* (October 1975): 26–27, 43; "Free Parking???" *Parking* (January 1976): 27, 34.

70. "Joscelyn Again Urges Higher Garage Rates," *Horseless Age* (November 11, 1914): 713; "Uniform Garage Rates," *Horseless Age* (December 7, 1904): 585; Peter V. Hoyt, "The Co-Operative Garage," *Garage* 1, no. 1 (November 1910): 4–5; "The Growth of the National Garage Association," *Horseless Age* (May 12, 1915): 634–635.

71. Robert O. Derrick, "The City Parking Garage," *Architectural Forum* (March 1927): 233–240; Tyler Whitley, "Parking Personalities," *Parking* (Fall 1964): 43; Audee Seeger, "Designer for One of the Country's Largest Garage Chains Offers a Solution to a Universal Problem," *Parking* (July 1970): 44–46; "Economics: Private Industry Must Operate at a Profit," *Parking* (Winter 1954): 15–17; Joseph F. Blasi, "The Place of Parking in Our Present-Day Economy," *Parking* (Fall 1954): 10–12; "The Basis of Parking Rates," *Parking* (January 1970): 36–38; John Walker, "Carparking Economics," *Parking* (Winter 1967): 44–48; "Parking Industry Statistics," *Parking*

(December 2001): 13; Carl Hooper, "Business 'All Right' for Parking Baron," *Parking* (July 1977): 37.

72. "Evolution—What Is Past Is Prologue," *Parking* (Winter 1954): 18–20; Walter Briggs, "Impact of the Motor Car on Real Estate," *Parking* (Fall 1954): 18–19, 48; John M. Bruce, "The Cost of Motoring," *American Motorist* 1, no. 5 (August 1909): 202–203; William D. Heath et al., *Parking in the United States: A Survey of Local Government Action* (Washington, D.C.: National League of Cities, 1967).

73. "Parking Construction Hits New High," *American City* 85, no. 5 (November 1970): 102.

74. "Revenue Bonds for Parking Sites," *Urban Land* (May 1952): 5.

75. John W. Dorsett, "The Price Tag of Parking," *Urban Land* (May 1998): 66–70. For a more detailed discussion of these issues, see Todd Litman, "Parking Management: Strategies, Evaluation and Planning," www.vtpi.org.

76. Fred W. Moe, "What Is a Practical Parking Facility?" *American City* 63, no. 6 (December 1948): 14. In a well-researched book, Donald Shoup has proposed that it is detrimental not to charge for the actual cost of parking. See *The High Cost of Free Parking* (Chicago: Planners Press, 2005).

77. Arvah B. Hopkins, "$700 per Car Space Builds Tallahassee Garage," *American City* 72, no. 4 (October 1957): 149–151; "Shepard Plans Facility in Tallahassee," *Parking* (Fall 1956): 25–26; "Ramp Garage Cost $800 per Parking Space," *American City* 70, no. 5 (May 1955): 158; Bernard J. Gorman, "Ample Garage Space for $10 per Foot," *American City* 84, no. 3 (September 1969): 136–138; "The Grant Park Garage System," *American City* 70, no. 6 (June 1955): 166–171; W.H. Ellison and T.Y. Lin, "Parking Garage Built for $5.38 per Sq. Ft.," *Civil Engineering* (June 1955): 37–40; "Income, Expense Analysis of Parking Garages," *Parking* (Winter 1965): 18–19; Evan Jones, "Garage Design and Operation," *Parking* (Summer 1961): 40–48. In 2004, a garage comparable to the one in Tallahassee would have cost between $6,000 and $7,000 per space.

78. Paul S. Kitsakos, Parsons Corporation, e-mail exchanges with author, January 12, 2006.

79. John J. Cleary, "Parking Chief Puts People before Cars," *Parking* (October 1969): 16; "The Principles of Partnering," *Parking* (October–November 2003): 67–68; Dennis Burns, "Parking Principles," *Parking Professional* (December 2001): 28–30.

80. "Parking Heaven: Try Using One of the New Garages," *Parking Professional* (February 2002): 14–15.

Detroit Garages

1. Milo Milton Quaife, *This Is Detroit: 1701–1951, Two Hundred and Fifty Years in Pictures* (Detroit: Wayne State University Press, 1951), 156; "Can You Guess Detroit's Busiest Corner?" *Detroiter*, March 9, 1925, 8; Robert W. Adams, "Where Are Detroit's Death Traps?" *Detroiter*, March 9, 1925, 1, 8; "Voters to Pass on Rapid Transit," *Detroiter*, November 2, 1925, 1, 18.

2. Robert W. Adams, "Detroit's Traffic Problem—?" *Detroiter*, February 16, 1925, 1, 6.

3. "Garages Help Parking Problem," *Detroiter*, December 1, 1924, 23.

4. "Detroit Garages Are Ramp Types," *Detroiter*, February 23, 1925, 27; "Now Open," *Detroiter*, February 16, 1925 (advertisement).

5. "Announcing the Opening of the East Unit of Detroit Garages, Inc.," *Detroiter*, December 1, 1924, 25 (advertisement); "Detroit Garages, Inc., Open Another Unit," *Detroiter*, January 26, 1925, 19.

6. "Detroit Storage Co.," *Detroiter*, October 27, 1924, 19 (advertisement); "February Figures Show Increases Over 1924," *Detroiter*, March 23, 1925, 8; "How Downtown Detroit Changed in 1924," *Detroiter*, February 2, 1925, 30–31; "Detroit's New $500,000 Garage Unit," *Detroiter*, April 5, 1926, 38; "Park Only Once," *Detroiter*, November 3, 1924, 4 (advertisement).

7. Robert O. Derrick, "The City Parking Garage," *Architectural Forum* (March 1927): 233–240; "Parking Personalities," *Parking* (Fall 1964): 43.

8. "Parking Garages Join Self-Service," *Parking* (October 1973): 34–35; Audee Seeger, "Designer for One of the Country's Largest Garage Chains Offers a Solution to a Universal Problem," *Parking* (July 1970): 44–47; Fred Olmsted and E. Kenneth Bloom, "Parking Controls," *Parking* (July 1971): 29; George Devlin, "Design and Construction of the Parkade," *Parking* (Summer 1960), 3; Bill Smith, "50: An Industry Pioneer's Golden Anniversary," *Parking Professional* (May 2003): 28–30.

Chapter 5

1. John Van Horn, "Automated Garages," *Parking Today* (March 2003): 50–53.

2. Motor World, *Automobile Repairshop Short-Cuts*, 4th ed. (New York: U.C. Book Company, 1918), 13; "From the Parking Archives, Winter 1954: Evolution—What Is Past Is Prologue," *Parking* (March 2003): 36–38; Auto Space, *Q and A on Mechanical Parking Systems* (brochure), 1–3; Karla Britton, *Auguste Perret* (New York: Phaidon, 2001), 20–21; Vincent Scully Jr., *Modern Archi-*

tecture (New York: Braziller, 1986), plate 51; Robert Mallet-Stevens and Jacques Roederer, "Notes from Paris," *Architectural Review* 24 (September 1908): 136–138.

3. "Plan of Four-Way Elevator Parking Garage: A Patented Arrangement," *Architectural Record* (February 1929): 193 (illustration); "Semi-Automatic," *Parking* (Winter 1954): 40. C. Kehr also patented a hexagonal version of the elevator and turntable: Storage Building, U.S. Patent 1,465,135, filed November 3, 1922, and issued August 14, 1923.

4. "Semi-Automatic," 40; "Parking Archives," 36–38.

5. F. Le R. Francisco, Vehicle Storage Structure, U.S. Patent 2,061,420, filed August 22, 1933, and issued November 17, 1936.

6. R. Stephen Sennott, "Chicago Architects and the Automobile, 1906–26," in Jan Jennings, ed., *Roadside America: The Automobile in Design and Culture* (Ames: Iowa State University for the Society for Commercial Archeology, 1990), 166–168; "Parking Archives," 36–38; Carl W. Condit, *Chicago: 1910–1929* (Chicago: University of Chicago Press, 1973), 104, 114–115; "Semi-Automatic," 41.

7. Sennott, "Chicago Architects," 166–168; "Fully Automatic," *Parking* (Winter 1954): 38–40; Condit, *Chicago*, 114–115.

8. According to Robert H. Field II, of High-Tech Parking Systems (in e-mail exchanges and discussions with author, September 2006), there were attempts to replace the older Carew system within the original structure, but they did not succeed, and the structure was torn down.

9. Geoffrey Harold Baker and Bruno Funaro, *Parking* (New York: Reinhold, 1958), 117; "Kent Automatic Parking Garage, New York," *American Architect* (June 20, 1928): 835–837 (illustrations); "The Hill Garage," *American Architect* (April 5, 1928): 480 (photograph and drawing); Museum for the Preservation of Elevating History, "Timeline," www.theelevatormuseum.org/timeline.htm; Donald R. Monahan, "Mechanical Access Parking Structures," in Anthony P. Chrest, Mary S. Smith, and Sam Bhuyan, *Parking Structures*, 3rd ed. (Norwell, Mass: Kluwer Academic Publishers, 2001); "Semi-Automatic," 40; "Carew Garage Opens February 14," *Cincinnati Post*, January 21, 1931, 3–4; "The Carew Tower Car Jam and How It Was Broken," *Elevator World* (September 1958): 14–20, www.elevator-world.com; "Autos Marooned 'Way Up,'" *Cincinnati Enquirer*, July 23, 1949; "Mechanical Parking to End," *Cincinnati Enquirer*, June 6, 1953; "$36,976 Asked in Suit against Parking Garage," *Cincinnati Enquirer*, September 13, 1959; "Emery May Turn

Notes

Garage into Tower Apartments," *Cincinnati Enquirer,* December 5, 1962.

10. "Kent Garage," 836–837 (illustrations); "Semi-Automatic," 40.

11. "Hill Garage," 480 (photograph and drawing); "Technical News and Research: Garages," *Architectural Record* (February 1929): 191.

12. E.W. Austin, Vehicle Storage System, U.S. Patent 2,280,567, filed February 6, 1939, and issued April 21, 1942; Wayne Harding, "Mechanical Parking: The New Generation; Part One," *Parking* (May 1992): 27–32; *Elevator World* (February 1953), cover.

13. "Semi-Automatic," 38; "Parking Archives," 36–38; "Five Mechanical Garages," *Architectural Forum* (February 1953): 136; "Eight Cars Housed on Ground Space Formerly Required By Two," *Electric Journal* 26, no. 10 (October 1929): 479; "Automobile Parking Machine Developed," *American City* 41, no. 5 (November 1929): 100; "Vertical Parking Machines," *American City* 45, no. 2 (August 1931): 135.

14. "Parking Machine," 100.

15. "Parking Machine," 100; "'Ferris-Wheel' System," 44.

16. The current term for this process is *retrieval cycle,* although the term *throughput* is also used.

17. "Vertical Parking Machines," 135; "Eight Cars Housed," 479; "Parking Machine," 100; "Garages Grow Up," *Architectural Forum* 98 (February 1953): 123; "Automatic Parking Elevator Installed in Chicago," *Engineering News-Record* (March 17, 1932): 396–397; *Base of Parking Tower—1935,* image neg. #29564, Chicago Historical Society; Folke T. Kihlstedt, "The Automobile," in Jan Jennings, ed., *Roadside America: The Automobile in Design and Culture* (Ames: Iowa State University for the Society for Commercial Archeology, 1990), 11–12; Ken Hedrich, *Nash Motors: Century of Progress; Chicago 1933,* image neg. #HB-00770, Chicago Historical Society; American Institute of Steel Construction, *Successes in Steel-Framed Parking Structures* (Chicago: American Institute of Steel Construction, 2002).

18. Nolan S. Black and Wilfred V. Casgrain, *A Plan for the Construction of Underground Mechanical Garages in Downtown Detroit* (Detroit: 1930), I. Smith, Hinchman, & Grylls is still in existence today; it is now known as SmithGroup.

19. "Shall Motor-Cars Be Parked Underground?" *American City* 44, no. 1 (January 1931): 133; Walter Kilham, *Raymond Hood, Architect* (New York: Architectural Book Publishing Company, 1973), 133–134. The Apiarium system, developed three decades after Black and Casgrain made their proposal, was another mechanized approach to underground parking. In this system, cars

would enter a below-grade, hollowed-out space through a seven-foot by 17-foot (two-meter by five-meter) hatch that would open in the street surface, interrupting road traffic for about three minutes. The cars would be drawn into the garage by means of mechanized chains. Alternatively, the hatch could be placed in an off-street location.

20. The Washington Statler also had its own 400-car garage and service center, which was connected directly to the hotel.

21. In the design of mechanized parking facilities, fixed hoistways would eventually be replaced by movable hoistways, which allow both vertical and horizontal movement.

22. Joseph Nathan Kane, Steven Anzouin, and Janet Podell, *Famous First Facts: A Record of First Happenings, Discoveries, and Inventions in American History,* 5th ed. (New York: Wilson, 1997), 387; "Semi-Automatic," 42; "Robot Parker," *Life,* January 21, 1952, 64; "Automobile 'Automat,'" *American City* 59, no. 5 (May 1944): 105; "Hotels Need Parking," *Parking* (Fall 1954): 25–26; Charles W. Lerch, "Garages: Automatic Parking," *Elevator World* (June 1962): 16–29; R.L. Sinclair, Vehicle Parking Apparatus, U.S. Patent 2,428,856, filed February 25, 1944, and issued October 14, 1947; "Push-Button Parking," *Urban Land* 11, no. 4 (April 1952): 4; "Fifteen-Story Elevators," *Architectural Forum* (February 1953): 137; George Hansen, ed., *Parking: How It Is Financed* (New York: National Retail Dry Goods Association, 1952), 16; Today in Science History, "December 5," www.todayinsci.com/12/12_05.htm; "Pigeon Hole Garage," *Popular Mechanics* (May 1952); Lourie W. Reichenberg, "50 Years of Parking Innovations," *Parking* (May 2001): 26–29.

23. Carlton Robinson, "Mechanical Parking," *Parking* (Summer 1959): 48–49; Charles W. Lerch, "Vertical Parking," *American City* 68, no. 12 (January 1954): 143; "Semi-Automatic," 38; "Progress in Vertical Stacking," *Parking* (Spring 1955): 6; Edward Hillman, "The Modern Elevator Garage," *Parking* (Summer 1954): 31, 48; "Pigeon Hole," *Parking* (Summer 1954): 33; "Municipal Parking Garages Can Pay Their Way," *American City* 74, no. 6 (June 1959): 124–125; Lerch, "Automatic Parking," 16–20, 28, 29; "Garages Grow Up," 142, 143. Mechanized systems have been used to manage and store goods, shipping containers, and even boats. Some of these systems were adapted for automobile storage— a trend that continues today.

24. *American City* 72, no. 4 (April 1957): cover; W.H. Fielder, "Mechanical Parking," *Parking* (Summer 1957): 74–75; J.M. Tippee, "Des Moines' Self-Sustaining Municipal Garages," *American City*

66, no. 5 (November 1951): 145; Harold Hallock, "Pigeon Hole Parking," *American City* 69, no. 6 (June 1954): 151; "Mechanical Parking: Push-Button Parking," *Parking* (Spring 1960): 24; Dietrich Klose, *Metropolitan Parking Structures; A Survey of Architectural Problems and Solutions* (New York: Praeger, 1965), 56–87; Baker and Funaro, *Parking,* 116–117.

25. "Rising to the Occasion," *Elevator World* (February 1999): 102–103; Dick Bowser, "A Little Bit of History," *Elevator World* (February 1999): 104–105; Baker and Funaro, *Parking,* 154–163; R.B. Bowser, "Self-Parking Bargains?" *Elevator World* (March 1957): 9–11; "Passenger Conveyors: Automatic Parking," *Elevator World* (July 1956): 14, 21.

26. Tippee, "Self-Sustaining Garages," 145; "Skyparking in Business Districts," *American City* 71, no. 8 (August 1956): 113; Frank B. Hallagan, "Bowser Elevator-Crane Units to Operate Parking Garage," *American City* 65, no. 5 (May 1950): 153; Al Gallo, "40th Birthday for a Toughie," *Elevator World* (May 1997): 76–78; Chenoweth-Kern, "First Bowser System Garage," *Elevator World* (February 1953): 2–8; Hansen, *Parking,* 50–51; "Bowser Parking System," *Parking* (Spring 1955): 24 (advertisement); "In February 1953," *Elevator World* (February 2002): 58; "Self-Parking Bargains?" *Elevator World* (March 1957): 9–11; "First for New York City," *Parking* (Fall 1957): 14; "Park in the Office," *American City* 71, no. 11 (November 1956): 220; "Oklahoma City Bank Goes Bowser," *Parking* (Spring 1957): 10–11; "Bowser Parking System," *Parking* (Winter 1955): 15 (advertisement); "Bowser Parking System," *Parking* (Winter 1959): 7 (advertisement); "Macon/a Hotel/a Motel," *Parking* (Fall 1959): 37–39; "Bowser Builds in Houston," *Parking* (Spring 1955): 36; "Park It, Retrieve It in 120 Seconds," *American City* 77, no. 1 (July 1962): 123–124; "Elevator Parking on Biscayne Boulevard," *American City* 76, no. 1 (July 1961): 129; "Fully Automatic Parking System Developed in California," *Parking* (Spring 1960): 26; "Another Bowser System Garage," *Parking* (Spring 1956): 8; "Fastest Elevator in City Speeds Cars to Top of Athens's Tallest Building," *Parking* (Spring 1957): 16 (advertisement); "Mechanical Parking in City of 28,000," *American City* 72, no. 2 (August 1957): 161; Fielder, "Mechanical Parking," 74–75; Baker and Funaro, *Parking,* 154–163.

27. "First for New York City," 14; Gallo, "40th Birthday," 76–78; Sy Gage, Martinson and Gage Engineers, e-mails and discussions with author, September 2003; "Now You Can Own," *Parking* (Winter 1959): 7.

28. "Park in the Office," 220; "Bank Goes Bowser," 10–11; "Bowser Garage Able to Become Office Building," *American City* 72, no. 6 (June 1957): 180; *Parking*

*(Fall 1958): 19 (advertisement featuring a letter from Meyers Brothers).

29. "Pigeon Hole Parking Means Greater Profit," *Parking* (Winter 1961): 3 (advertisement); "Pigeon Hole," *Parking* (Summer 1954): 33; Hallock, "Pigeon Hole Parking," 151; Hansen, *Parking,* 15.

30. "The Pigeon Hole Parking System: How It Works, What It Does," *Parking* (Spring 1954): 59 (advertisement); "Greater Profit," 3; J. Rayburn Bertrand, "Thirteen Stories of Parking Pleasure," *American City* 79, no. 1 (July 1964): 113; "News in Photos," *Parking* (Spring 1956): 4; Hansen, *Parking,* 13, 15. Philadelphia had an early Pigeon Hole garage: see "Philadelphia Pigeon-Hole," *Parking* (Spring 1960): 25. In New York, the use of dollies was eventually discontinued because of problems aligning the elevator and the garage floors, so attendants rode in the cars and controlled the movements of the elevator by reaching out to the control panel from the driver's seat—a practice that is still in use today in New York's older mechanized garages (Sy Gage, e-mails and discussions with author, September 2003).

31. "Penn Harris Pigeon Hole Parking," *Parking* (Summer 1955): 18; "VNB Car-Park Reports . . . ," *Parking* (Winter 1955): 25; "Bowser Parking System," 24; "Pigeon Hole Parking," 59; Bertrand, "Parking Pleasure," 113.

32. The Baldwin system was another puzzle parking system. See Wayne Harding, "Mechanical Parking: The New Generation; Part Two," *Parking* (June 1992): 46–51.

33. "Conveyor Belt Garage," *Parking* (Fall 1956): 2; Reichenberg, "Parking Innovations," 26–29; "Semi-Automatic," 39; "Skeletonized," *Parking* (Winter 1954): 45; A.H. Bowles, Parkway Motor Lodge, U.S. Patent 2,763,381, filed September 16, 1955, and issued September 18, 1956.

34. Frank Gove Jr., "New Mechanical Parking Features Safety," *American City* 73, no. 12 (December 1958): 110; "Park-A-Loft," *Parking* (Spring 1955): 2 (advertisement); "Park-A-Loft," *Parking* (Fall 1959): 2 (advertisement); "First Commonwealth Builds Mechanicals," *Parking* (Winter 1962): 30–31; "File-A-Way: A New Mechanical Parking System Boasts Lowest Per Car Unit Cost," *Parking* (Spring 1955): 46–47; "MinitPark," *Parking* (Spring 1955): 1 (advertisement); "Parking News," *Parking* (Fall 1960): 4; "New York's Newest and Tallest Garage for Wall Street," *Parking* (Fall 1960): 4.

35. "First Commonwealth," 30–31.

36. Another design that appears to be related to materials-handling systems is described in "The Auto Park System," *Parking* (April 1975): 45.

37. Another early system that called for an electric brain was the Slater system; see "Semi-Automatic," 43.

38. "File-A-Way," 46–47; Evan Kennedy, "Portland File-A-Way," *Parking* (Spring 1959): 8–11; "File-A-Way," *Parking* (Spring 1955): 35 (advertisement); "Parking News," *Parking* (Spring 1954): 3; "Mechanical Parking Is Here To Stay," *Parking* (Fall 1954): 1 (advertisement); "Lektro-Park," *Parking* (Summer 1954): 33; "Announcing Lektro Park," *Parking* (Spring 1954): 1 (advertisement); "Passaic May Go Foreign," *Parking* (Spring 1956): 2; "24 Cars in Space of 3," *Parking* (Spring 1965): 15 (advertisement); "Mechanical Developments: Push-Button Parking," *Parking* (Spring 1960): 24; Hansen, *Parking*, 30; "The Stacker Crane Parking Device," *Parking* (Summer 1954): 32 (advertisement); "Parking News," *Parking* (Spring 1955): 4; "The Stacker Crane Parking Device," *Parking* (Spring 1954): 55 (advertisement); "The Miller Stacker Crane," *Parking* (Winter 1954); "Swedes Invent New Automatic Garage," *Parking* (Winter 1961): 4; "Shoe Lane Car Park," *Parking* (Spring 1963): 31–34.

39. "News in Photos," 4; "Parking News" (Spring 1955): 5; "Parking News," *Parking* (Fall 1956): 2; "Parking News," *Parking* (Spring 1957): 3; "Parking News," *Parking* (Winter 1959): 3; "Semi-Automatic," 38–40; "Automatic Parking System," 26; Dominik Dlouhy, "Rotary Garages and Elevators," *Parking* (Fall 1956): 30; Reichenberg, "Parking Innovations," 26–29; "Other Recent Inventions: Autodrome," *Parking* (Winter 1955): 23. A variation of the Ferris-wheel approach—the Hico-Park—was constructed in Milan. See "Parking News" (Fall 1960): 2.

40. "Vert-A-Park," *Parking* (Fall 1968): 32–33; Harding, "Mechanical Parking: Part One," 27–32; Harding, "Mechanical Parking: Part Two," 46–51; "Rotating Parking Unit Will Be Denver Product," *Denver Post*, October 17, 1968; "Ferris Wheel Parking Setup Due Downtown," *Denver Post*, October 6, 1968; Alan Huff, "Vertical Parking Structure Boosted," *Topeka Capital-Journal*, 1968.

41. The Speed-Park system was originally known as the Alkro System. See "Semi-Automatic."

42. "Speed-Park," *Parking* (Winter 1962): 17–22; "Parking News: Columbia University to Build Automatic Garage," *Parking* (Winter 1958): 2–3; Lerch, "Automatic Parking," 16–29; "Garages Grow Up," 141. This system was also constructed in Canada. See "News in Photos," *Parking* (Spring 1968): 6.

43. "Parking: The Crisis Is Downtown; Mechanized Garage Run by a Computer," *Architectural Forum* 98 (February 1963): 102–103; "Parking Garage Can Receive 2.7 Cars a Minute," *American City* (May 1962): 132, 135; Sy Gage, discussions with author, September 2003;

"Automated 'Lobby Parking,'" *Parking* (Spring 1963): 17; "Automated Parking," *Innkeeping* (January 1965): 32–34.

44. The first facility to use the name Silopark was built in Milan, in the early 1960s. The system rights are now owned by SiloParking Systems, Inc., of Beverly, Massachusetts.

45. Patricia Carter-Roberts, "Rising to the Occasion," *Elevator World* (February 1999): 103; Vince Dixon, "New Computerized Electro-Mechanic Parking System Introduced," *Parking* (November–December 1984): 29–32; "News in Photos," *Parking* (April 1970): 6; "Silopark—A European Favorite," *Elevator World* (August 1970): 12–16; "News in Photos," *Parking* (Fall 1968): 8; William M. Bulkeley, "What's New: Garages," *Wall Street Journal*, March 13, 1986; Gail Ignacio, "Great Product Ideas: Robot Parking," *Venture* (March 1987): 105; "Vanishing Valet," *Robb Report* (November 1986): 81; "Computer Automates Parking," *Civil Engineering* (June 1986): 14; High-Tech Parking Systems, brochure; Field, discussions with author, September 18, 2006. Developer David Shusett planned a new automated system, to be constructed of aluminum, for Los Angeles; see "Parking News" (Fall 1960): 2.

46. "Mystery Photograph Was Peculiar and Scary 'Ferris Wheel' Parking Contraption Near Guyan Valley Hospital," *Logan Banner*, 2004; "Construction of the First of a Worldwide Series," *Parking* (April 1973): 8; "Automated and Mechanical Parking Seminar," Parking Industry Exhibition 2001, Chicago, April 4, 2001; Norene Dann Martin, "Report of the Executive Vice President: Garage Construction—1972," *Parking* (July 1973): 11–12.

47. Visits by author to Tokyo and Honolulu; Isamu Koshimidzu, "Report on Parking in Tokyo," *Parking* (Spring 1964): 22–27; "News in Photos," *Parking* (April 1971): 6; Donald R. Monahan and John Van Horn, "A Few Notes on Automated Parking in Korea and Japan," *Parking Today* (March 2002): 44–45. Many thanks to Hal Reilly, of Hawaii Pacific Realty, and to Joe Farrell, principal, Architects Hawaii, for providing information on the Honolulu facilities.

48. "Patents: Parking Garage Elevator System," *Elevator World* (February 2004): 122; William S. Payne, Parking Garage Elevator System, U.S. Patent 6,641,351, filed May 2, 2001, and issued November 4, 2003; National Association to Restore Pride in America's Capital, "High-Density Metro Parking: The Missing Link in Public Transit—Public Parking," www.narpac.org/METROPRK.HTM; Frederick H. Abernathy and R. Victor Jones, "Engineering Sciences 96: Parking at Harvard; Addressing New Demands Associated with Campus Development"

(unpublished report, Harvard University, 2001); Kira L. Gould, "Car Tricks," *Metropolis* (July 2004): 68.

49. C.J. Hughes, "An Urban Parking Perk: The Automated Garage," *New York Times*, December 6, 2006, C10; "Automatic Parking: A Major Technology Coming to the U.S.," *Parking Today* (November 2000): 18; Gil Smart, "Robotic Parking Plan Would Save Space," Lancaster Online, December 17, 2005, http://local.lancasteronline.com/4/19363; Gary Cudney, "Automated Parking: Is It Right for You?" *Parking Today* (May 2003): 17–21; Field, discussions with author, September 18, 2006; Shannon Sanders McDonald, "Mechanized/Automated Parking: Part I—A History," *Parking* (October 2005): 38–44; Shannon Sanders McDonald, "Mechanized/Automated Parking: Part II—Today," *Parking* (November 2005): 24–30. For an alternative view of the feasibility of automated structures, see Leslie Griffy, "Parking Garage May Be Just That," [San Luis Obispo] *Tribune*, July 14, 2005.

50. Carter-Roberts, "Rising to the Occasion," 103; Dixon, "New System Introduced," 29–32; Bulkeley, "What's New: Garages"; Ignacio, "Robot Parking," 105; "Vanishing Valet," 81; "Computer Automates Parking," *Civil Engineering* (June 1986): 14; High-Tech Parking Systems, Inc., brochure; Field, discussions with author, September 18, 2006.

51. Antoinette Martin, "Space-Age Garages That Save Space," *New York Times*, September 21, 2003, section 11, 1; "Automatic Parking: A Major Technology Coming to the U.S.," *Parking Today* (November 2000): 18; Smart, "Robotic Parking Plan"; Michael Maurer, "Hoboken Almost Online," *Parking Today* (March 2002): 30; Cary Kopczynski, "Tight Site Parking Problem? Stack Those Cars," *Seattle Daily Journal of Commerce*, Urban Development Special Section, October 2, 2003, www.djc.com/news/co/11149494.html; Paul Lew, "Automated Parking Takes Its Place in the United States," *Parking* (January–February 2003): 21–31; Scott Barancik, "Pinellas Park's Garage of Tomorrow," *St. Petersburg Times*, July 30, 2001; "Parking Made Easy," *ABC World News Tonight*, March 12, 1999; Robotic Parking, brochures and Web site (www.robopark.com). At the time of writing, the Web site of Robotic Parking indicated that several new garages were in the planning stages, and that the technology was under consideration for the Lancaster Press building, in Lancaster County, Pennsylvania.

52. SpaceSaver Parking Company, brochures and Web site (www.spacesaverparking.com); "Spacesaver System in the Final Test Stage," *Parking Today* (March 2002): 50; Josh Levin, "The Valet You Don't Have to Tip," Slate,

April 1, 2004, www.slate.com/id/2098136/; Jacqueline L. Smith, "Automated Valet Parking," *Elevator World* (April 2003): 79; Donald R. Monahan, "Automated Valet Parking Debuts in the U.S.," *Parking* (September 2002): 45–46.

53. "First Fully Automated Garage Opens in Manhattan in January," *Parking Today* (January 2007): 14; "New York to Have First Robotic Garage," *Atlanta Journal-Constitution*, January 30, 2007, C6; Hughes, "Parking Perk," C10; American Development Group, www.adgorg.com; Phil Patten, "Parking as a Destination," *New York Times*, February 25, 2007, automobile section.

54. The Buildings at Lovejoy Wharf, www.architecturalteam.com; John Osborne, "Still Waiting for Sunshine," *Issue 250* (February 2007): 30–32; Natalie Kosteini, "Parking Cars the Sci-Fi Way," *Philadelphia Business Journal*, August 25, 2006, http://philadelphia.bizjournals.com.

55. "Elevator Dynamics Project for New World Tower," *Elevator World* (May 1999): 118–125.

56. It will soon be possible for a driver to call a mechanized facility in advance so that the automobile will be ready by the time the driver arrives. Such arrangements would be particularly useful in dense urban environments, and at car rental agencies at large metropolitan airports. Integrating mechanized facilities into the master plan for a dense area would create opportunities for better land use, especially if the facilities were linked to other transportation systems and included an advance-notice system for retrieval.

57. Auto Space, *Resolving the Developer's Dilemma: Case Study 13; The Large Floor Plate* (brochure); Jim Myers, "The Basic Economics of Automated Parking" (paper presented at the Parking Industry Exhibition, Chicago, April 4, 2001); Auto Space, *Resolving the Developer's Dilemma: Case Study 12; The Urban Notch Lot* (brochure).

**Car Stackers:
A More Modest Approach**

1. Peter Lunati, Lifting Device for Motor Vehicles, U.S. Patent 1,552,326, filed November 29, 1924, and issued September 1, 1925; Wayne Harding, "Mechanical Parking: The New Generation; Part One," *Parking* (May 1992): 27–32; M. Miller, Vehicle Parking System, U.S. Patent 1,619,360, filed March 21, 1925, and issued March 1, 1927.

2. Harding, "Mechanical Parking, 27–32; "Parking in the Air: Skypark Doubles the Capacity and Is Movable," *Parking* (Winter 1954): 40–41; "Parking News," *Parking* (Summer 1956): 3; "Skele-

tonized," *Parking* (Winter 1954): 45; Earle Brown, "Parking Operators Are Trying New Ideas, New Techniques," *Parking* (Winter 1955): 41; "Parking News," *Parking* (Summer 1956): 4; Wayne Harding, "Mechanical Parking: The New Generation; Part Two," *Parking* (June 1992): 46–51.

3. "Dubl Park," *Parking* (Fall 1968): 34; "Fully Automatic," *Parking* (Winter 1954): 43.

4. "Aircraft Storage System Works for Cars," *Parking* (Fall 1959): 18; Lourie W. Reichenberg, "50 Years of Parking Innovations," *Parking* (May 2001): 29; "Two-Tier Car Parking System Doubles Capacity on Same Ground Space," *Parking* (April 1973): 47–49; Brown, "Trying New Ideas," 41; "Sky Park," *Parking* (Spring 1955): 13 (advertisement); "Park Two Cars Where You Now Park One," *Parking* (July 1974): 53 (advertisement); Harding-AFG, *Stackable" Parking Since 1968* (brochure); "News in Photos," *Parking* (October 1969): 8.

5. Harding, "Mechanical Parking: Part Two," 46–51.

6. Cary Kopczynski, "Tight Site Parking Problem? Stack Those Cars," *Seattle Daily Journal of Commerce*, Urban Development Special Section, October 2, 2003, www.djc.com/news/co/11149494.html; Richard Spalding, "City Front Terrace May Use Mechanical Auto Stack System," *San Diego Daily Transcript*, May 13, 1992; Klaus Parking, *Park and Smile* (brochure).

7. Sy Gage, Martinson and Gage Engineers, e-mail exchanges and discussions with author, September 2003; Donald R. Monahan, "Mechanical Access Parking Structures," in Anthony P. Chrest, Mary S. Smith, and Sam Bhuyan, *Parking Structures*, 3rd ed. (Norwell, Mass.: Kluwer Academic Publishers, 2001); Raju Nandwana, "Design of Automated Parking in Structures," *Parking Professional* (June 2006): 14–16.

8. Harvard University, for example, installed car stackers in the early 1970s, as did the state of California.

Mechanized Garages with Round Floor Plans

1. A.F. Buranelli, Garage, U.S. Patent 2,676,714, filed March 1, 1960, and issued April 27, 1954; "Semi-Automatic," *Parking* (Winter 1954): 40; "Automatic Parking Garage," *Architectural Forum* (February 1951): 108–109, 162; "Garages Grow Up," *Architectural Forum* 98 (February 1953): 140.

2. "Carr Parks Cars," *Parking* (Winter 1955): 4; "Revolving Lot: Duesseldorf, Germany," *Parking* (Spring 1957): 3; "Parking Around the World: Spain," *Parking* (Winter 1954): 9; John L. Becker, "The Helical Parking System," *Parking*

(Spring 1955): 48. Inventions abounded: see, for example, "Combination Ferris Wheel–Beehive," *Parking* (Spring 1955): 5.

3. W. Zeckendorf et al., Multistory Building Structure, U.S. Patent 2,698,973, filed December 22, 1949, and issued January 11, 1955; Isamu Koshimizu, "Report on Parking in Tokyo," *Parking* (Spring 1964): 22–27.

4. Lee Fraser, "Here Comes the Future," *Parking* (Fall 1964): 41–42; E.R. Drucker, *Parking in Urban Centres* (Ottawa: A.M.I. Company Publishing, 1973), 10–12; "Rotopark," *Architectural Record* (August 1970): 141. Designs for automated round garages were appearing everywhere; see "Parking Tour Auto," *L'architecture d'aujourdhui* 58 (October–November 1963): 110.

Contemporary Systems Outside the United States

1. Shannon Sanders McDonald, "Bicycles, Automobiles, and Automation in Japan," *Parking* (October–November 2004): 17–21; Isamu Koshimizu, "Report on Parking in Tokyo," *Parking* (Spring 1964): 22–27; "News in Photos," *Parking* (April 1971): 6; Don Monahan, "A Few Notes on Automated Parking in Korea and Japan," *Parking Today* (March 2002): 44–45; Barbara Chance, president and chief executive officer, Chance Management Advisors, Inc., e-mail exchanges with author, August 30, 2006.

2. "Emerging Construction Technologies," Division of Construction Engineering and Management, Purdue University, www.new-technologies.org; Larry J. Cohen, "How I Spent My Vacation . . . Visiting Parking Garages in Italy," *Parking Professional* (June 2000): 22–23; Donald R. Monahan, "Mechanical Access Parking Structures," in Anthony P. Chrest, Mary S. Smith, and Sam Bhuyan, *Parking Structures*, 3rd ed. (Norwell, Mass: Kluwer Academic Publishers, 2001).

3. International Iron and Steel Institute, *Innovations in Steel: Parking Structures around the World* (brochure), 11.

4. International Iron and Steel, *Innovations in Steel*, 11; "Smart Car of America," www.smartcarofamerica.com/; Phil Patten, "Parking as a Destination," *New York Times*, February 25, 2007, automobile section.

5. Westfalia Automated Parking Systems, "Palais Coburg," www.westfaliausa.com/products/parking/WTI-Parking-PalaisCoburg.html; "Skyparks Automated Parking Solutions," www.skyparks.com; John Osborne, "Still Waiting for Sunshine," *Issue 250* (February 2007): 30–32; Zaigham Ali Mirza, "Dubai to Have Robotic Car Parks Soon," *Khaleej Times*, September 14, 2005, www.khaleejtimes.com.

Chapter 6

1. Roger H. Corbetta, "Evolution of Concrete Construction," *Journal of the American Concrete Institute* (February 1954): 500–511.

2. Peter C. Papademetriou, "Pattern and Principle," *Progressive Architecture* (July 1985): 86.

3. Fire protection concerns the building and its contents (property); life safety concerns the occupants. The particular building type typically drives decisions about how to balance these two forms of protection.

4. A truss is made up of smaller, interconnected pieces of steel, iron, or wood that act together to created compressive and tensile force.

5. "Fire Protection Apparatus in Garages," *Horseless Age* 23, no. 16 (June 1909): 594–595. Nor could sprinklers extinguish liquid fuel fires. Options for extinguishing such fires included sand and bromium. Although bromium could extinguish gasoline, benzoyl, or turpentine fires in open or enclosed spaces without producing offensive gases, the material was difficult to handle because it had strong corrosive properties and released dangerous vapors until it was combined with the gasoline, benzoyl, or turpentine. Bromium was sold in small glass vials (about the size of an egg) that contained enough of the liquid to suppress a typical engine fire. See "A New Method of Extinguishing Fires," *Horseless Age* 24, no. 7 (August 19, 1909): 192.

6. Joseph A. Anglada, "Some Notes on Garage Building Construction," *Horseless Age* 23, no. 17 (April 28, 1909): 614–615; Mary Bellis, "Fire Sprinkler Systems," http://inventors.about.com/library/inventors/blfiresprinkler.htm.

7. J.E. Jennings, "Garage as a Conflagration Risk," *Horseless Age* 22, no. 21 (November 18, 1908): 682; "Storage of Gasoline," *Horseless Age* 5, no. 13 (December 27, 1899): 1, 10; "Disastrous Garage Fire," *Horseless Age* 14, no. 23 (December 7, 1904): 585; John P. Fox, "Public Garages and Filling Stations: Their Proper Location and Legal Control," *American City* 41, no. 2 (August 1929): 134–136; "Gasoline Stations Become Architectural Assets," *American City* 41, no. 5 (November 1929): 98–99; John A. Jakle and Keith A. Sculle, *The Gas Station in America* (Baltimore: Johns Hopkins University Press, 1994).

8. "Municipal Garage Regulations," *Horseless Age* 25, no. 18 (May 4, 1910): 686–687; "New Detroit Garage Regulations January 1," *Horseless Age* (November 11, 1914): 711; P.M. Heldt, "The Garage Business—Buildings, Equipment, Methods," *Horseless Age* (April 1, 1916): 266–267. As the car increasingly shaped the city, such building requirements obvi-

ously affected spatial patterns of urban development: it is not difficult to see, for example, how the requirements for the location of third-class garages might foster low-density development.

9. William P. Capes, "To Eliminate Fire Hazards Resulting from Parking Automobiles," *American City* 30, no. 3 (March 1924): 290.

10. Heldt, "Garage Business" (April 1, 1916): 266–267; P.M. Heldt, "The Garage Business—Buildings, Equipment, Methods," *Horseless Age* (April 15, 1916): 320–324; Capes, "Fire Hazards," 290; "Parked Cars as Handicaps to Fire-Fighting," *American City* (January–February 1930): 21.

11. "One Fire Each Year for Every Twenty-One Public Garages," *American City* 31, no. 7 (July 1924): 35; "N.F.P.A. Committee Recommends Changes in Garage Regulations," *American City* 46, no. 4 (April 1932): 17; "Off-Street Loading Facilities and 'Hotel Garages' Recommended for Business Districts," *American City* 41, no. 3 (September 1929): 133; John P. Fox, "Public Garages and Filling Stations: Their Proper Location and Legal Control," *American City* 41, no. 2 (August 1929): 134–136.

12. S.G. Langefels and F.S. Buchanan, "Building Codes," *Parking* (Fall 1954): 23; "Building Codes," *Parking* (Spring 1954): 52; B.L. Wood, "Steel Offers Answer to Parking Needs," *Parking* (Spring 1955): 32–34; "Chicagoans Propose Open Air Garage," *Horseless Age* (August 27, 1913): 353.

13. In 1972, Richard Gewain, a fire engineer, published the results of a voluntary survey of parking garage owners, but he failed to link each fire to the type of garage. See R. Gewain, "Survey of Fire Experience in Automobile Parking Structures," *Parking* (October 1972): 47–49.

14. American Institute of Steel Construction, *Successes in Steel-Framed Parking Structures* (Chicago: American Institute of Steel Construction, 2002); American Institute of Steel Construction, *Steel Parking Decks* (n.p., n.d.; ca. 1970); American Iron and Steel Institute, *Innovations in Steel Parking Structures around the World* (Belgium: International Iron and Steel Institute, 2001), 12–13; "Garage Fire Guts Cars at Houston Airport," *Parking Today* (May 2003): 49.

15. Dale Denda, "What About Parking Garage Fires?" *American Fire Journal* (February 1993): 22–27.

16. Unauthorized storage typically introduces combustibles into the garage. As the parking garage gains increasing respect for the importance of its role in the built environment, it may no longer be perceived as a place to deposit whatever is unwanted. Then again, the code

has yet to be written that will not, at some point, be violated.

17. Denda, "Parking Garage Fires"; Dale Denda, *Parking Garage Fires (A Statistical Analysis of Parking Garage Fires in the United States: 1986–1988)* (McLean, Va.: Parking Market Research Company, April 1992); Dale Denda, "Parking Garage Fires: A 10-year Perspective on the Findings" (paper presented at the International Parking Institute conference, Las Vegas, June 2001).

18. The fire walls in Denda's study were not categorized by type or rating.

19. Most vehicle fires in garages are reported as such, rather than as structural fires; however, patterns in reporting can lead to confusing data about the spread of fires in garages. Perhaps new reporting categories need to be created to help address this issue. (Dale Denda's work was the first to take into account the different ways in which fires in garage structures are reported.)

20. L.E. Lowry, "Fire Protection: The Development of the Electric Fire Alarm System," *American City* 4, no. 2 (August 1911): 88–90; Denda, *Parking Garage Fires*, 1–159.

21. Langefels and Buchanan, "Building Codes," 23–24.

22. The complexities of loading conditions continue to be studied; see A.A.G.B. Aswad, "Point Load Test on Double Tee Flanges," *PCI Journal* (July–August 1991): 66–73; Predrag L. Popovic, Peter J. Stork, and Richard C. Arnold, "Use of Hydraulics for Load Testing of Prestressed Concrete Inverted Tee Girder," *PCI Journal* 36, no. 5 (September–October 1991): 72–78.

23. The requirement was the minimum weight that was supposed to be taken into account in designing the structure; however, the design rarely called for the minimum to be exceeded, because structures capable of withstanding more weight are more costly.

24. George A. Hool and Charles S. Whitney, *Concrete Designers' Manual* (New York, McGraw-Hill, 1926), 267 (copy of book provided by Ronald G. Van Der Meid, Renaissance Engineering); Ashley T. Carpenter, "The Architect and Garage Design," *Parking* (Summer 1959): 6–8. For a list of recent books covering these issues, see the list of further readings at end of this book.

25. P.M. Heldt, "The Garage Business—Buildings, Equipment, Methods," *Horseless Age* 36, no. 11 (November 1, 1915): 422–424; P.M. Heldt, "The Garage Business—Buildings, Equipment, Methods," *Horseless Age* (November 15, 1915): 454–456; P.M. Heldt, "The Garage Business—Buildings, Equipment, Methods," *Horseless Age* (October 15, 1915): 394–395.

26. P.M. Heldt, "The Garage Business—Buildings, Equipment, Methods," *Horseless Age* (December 1, 1915): 492–493; Anglada, "Garage Construction," 614; J.L. Peterson, "History and Development of Precast Concrete in the United States," *Journal of the American Concrete Institute* (February 1954): 483.

27. "Frequently Asked Questions About Concrete," *Parking* (May 1998): 23–26; "Taxicabs in San Francisco," *Horseless Age* 24, no. 10 (September 8, 1909): 269. In fact, heavy timber and glue-lam (large sections of wood created by gluing many smaller pieces together) are extremely fire-resistant (heavy timber is even more fire resistant than steel) and are allowed under contemporary codes; nevertheless, they are rarely used.

28. G.H. Brazer, "Reinforced Concrete Building for the Park Square Motor Mart, Boston," *Engineering News-Record* 52, no. 21 (1905): 573–577; "The Motor Mart, Boston," *Horseless Age* (April 21, 1909): 513. The building had five sides because it filled an oddly shaped lot.

29. Brazer, "Motor Mart," 573–577; Mark A. Zelepsky, project manager, Walker Parking Consultants, Boston office, discussions with author; Walker Parking Consultants, "Parking Structure Maintenance and Repair" (PowerPoint presentation, Build Boston conference, Boston, November 16–18, 1999); "Motor Mart in Boston Wins ICRI and IPI Awards," *Parking Today* 6, no. 1 (January 2001): 32; "Category Three/Four: Award of Excellence," *Parking Professional* (August 2000): 29.

30. "The Sea Gate Garage," *Horseless Age* 24, no. 21 (November 24, 1909): 592–593; G.E. Warren, "Novel Concrete Arches for Garage Roof Supports," *Concrete* 16, no. 5 (May 1920): 210–212.

31. George C. Nimmons, "Motor-Truck Garage for Sears Roebuck and Company," *American Architect* 113, no. 1 (February 1918): 169–170.

32. "Arch Roof with Dome-Ends Provides Unobstructed Area for Skating," *Engineering News-Record* (July 8, 1948): 110–112.

33. M.N. Bussell, "The Era of the Proprietary Reinforcing Systems," in *Early Reinforced Concrete*, ed. Frank Newby (Burlington, Vt.: Ashgate, 2001); "Concrete: The Year Past," *Architectural and Engineering News* (April 1959): 15–18.

34. Harold F. Blanchard, "Comparison of Ramp and Elevator Type Garages," *Bus Transportation* (June 1922): 331–335.

35. "Curved Drive for Automobiles in Six-Story Garage," *Engineering News-Record* 83, no. 4 (July 24, 1919): 188–189.

36. "Concrete Cantilever Construction in Chicago Garage," *Engineering News-Record* 85, no. 13 (September 23, 1920): 609–611; "Compact Mixing Plant on Ten-Story Reinforced Concrete Garage Job," *Engineering and Contracting* (November 1928): 533–534.

37. Albert Kahn, Inc., Architects, "Fisher Building Garage," *American Architect* (February 20, 1929): 187–267.

38. "Concrete Proves Versatile for Ramp, Mechanical-Type Parking Facilities," *Parking* (Spring 1955): 18–23; Geoffrey Baker and Bruno Funaro, *Parking* (New York: Reinhold, 1958), 116–117.

39. Ada Louise Huxtable, "Historical Survey," *Progressive Architecture* (October 1960): 144.

40. Although concrete offers significant compressive strength, it has lower tensile strength.

41. William A. Maples and Robert E. Wilde, "A Story of Progress," *Journal of the American Concrete Institute* (January 1954): 415; Amy E. Slaton, *Reinforced Concrete and the Modernization of American Building, 1910-1930* (Baltimore: Johns Hopkins University Press, 2001).

42. R.M. Dubois, "Development of Prestressed Concrete in the United States," *PCI Journal* (September 1958): 55–62; L. Coff, "Prestressed Concrete: An Inflation Antidote in the Municipal-Construction Field," *American City* 62, no. 9 (September 1947): 112–113; August E. Komendant, "Possibilities," *Progressive Architecture* (October 1960): 174–185; Prestressed Concrete Institute, *Reflections on the Beginnings of Prestressed Concrete in America* (Chicago: Prestressed Concrete Institute, 1981).

43. "Explanation of Common Terms in the Precast and Prestressed Concrete Industry," *PCI Journal* (November–December 1984): 28–29.

44. Peterson, "Precast Concrete," 477–499; Charles C. Zollman, "The End of the 'Beginnings,'" *PCI Journal* (March–April 1980): 96–117; Corbetta, "Concrete Construction," 500–511; Ada Louise Huxtable, "Concrete Technology in USA," *Progressive Architecture* (October 1960): 143–191.

45. Huxtable, "Historical Survey," 144.

46. Maples and Wilde, "Story of Progress," 415; Bussell, "Reinforcing Systems," 8, 11; Slaton, *Reinforced Concrete*, 143; Brazer, "Motor Mart," 573–577.

47. Peterson, "Precast Concrete," 483; Huxtable, "Historical Survey," 144; Zollman, "End of 'Beginnings,'" (March–April): 96–117; Peterson, "Precast Concrete," 483–484; 491; "U.S. Progress in Prestressed Concrete," *Architectural Record* (August 1951): 148–155.

48. Huxtable, "Historical Survey," 149; Maples and Wilde, "Story of Progress," 424; Slaton, *Reinforced Concrete*, 85.

49. G. Magnel, "The Principles of Prestressed Concrete," *Engineering Journal* (March 1947): 110–112; Charles C. Zollman, "Magnel's Impact on the Advent of Prestressed Concrete: Part I," *PCI Journal* (May–June 1978): 23–47; Charles C. Zollman, "Dynamic American Engineers Sustain Magnel's Momentum: Part 2," *PCI Journal* (July–August 1978): 31–62; "50 Years and Growing," *Leap Ledger* (March 2001): 1–4; J. Rex Farrior Jr., "What Is P.C.I.?" *PCI Journal* 1, no. 1 (May 1956): 2; Harry Edwards, "The Innovators of Prestressed Concrete in Florida: Part 3," *PCI Journal* (September–October 1978): 14–43; Harry Edwards, "The Innovators of Prestressed Concrete in Florida: Part 3," *PCI Journal* (November–December 1978): 19–35; Precast/Prestressed Concrete Institute (PCI), "1954–2004, Celebrating Milestones of an Industry and Its Organization," www.pci.org.

50. This shift can be thought of as a reflection, in built form, of the way in which the American landscape was altered when grids were placed across the land without consideration for the topographical forms beneath.

51. Peterson, "Precast Concrete," 482, 483; Joseph J. Weiler, "Field-Spliced Precast Concrete Arches," *Engineering News-Record* (November 21, 1940): 56–57.

52. Charles C. Zollman, "The End of the Beginnings," in Prestressed Concrete Institute, *Prestressed Concrete*, 308–331; Dubois, "Prestressed Concrete," 55–63; PCI, "Celebrating Milestones"; Zollman, "End of 'Beginnings,'" *PCI Journal* (January–February 1980): 124–145.

53. PCI, "Celebrating Milestones"; Zollman, "Magnel's Momentum," 31–62; McLeod C. Nigels, "The Bill Dean We Knew," *PCI Journal* (September–October 1978): 14–43; Edwards, "The Innovators of Prestressed Concrete in Florida: Part 3," *PCI Journal* (September–October 1978): 14–43; Zollman, "End of 'Beginnings'" (March-April): 96–117; George C. Hanson, "Early History of Prestressed Concrete in Colorado: Part 6," *PCI Journal* (May–June 1979): 16–39; "Quick Public Acceptance Gained in Parking Structure with 110-Foot Spans," *Parking* (Winter 1963): 16–20; Charles C. Zollman, "The End of the 'Beginnings,'" (January–February 1980): 124–145; "Precast Concrete Tees," *School Construction News* (October 2004): 37; "High Honors for High Concrete," *Parking* (October–November 2004): 14; Thomas A. Holmes and George Burnley, "New Mega Tee Passes Load Testing," *PCI Journal* (March–April 1997): 136–139.

54. Hanson, "Prestressed Concrete," 173; "Parking Decks Built from the Top Down," *Architectural Forum* (May 1955): 164–167; "Wall-Less Garage Built from Top Down," *Engineering News-Record*

(December 9, 1954): 44–47; "Dramatic New Facility Now Open in Salt Lake," *Parking* (Winter 1955): 26–27; "Concrete Proves Versatile," 18–23; Baker and Funaro, *Parking*, 68–71; "Ramp Garage Cost $800 per Parking Space," *American City* (May 1955): 158.

55. T.Y. Lin, "Revolution in Concrete," *Architectural Forum* (May 1961): 121–127; Albert C. Martin Jr., "Creative Prestressed Concrete Design Techniques in the Western United States," *PCI Journal* (April 1964): 58–62; Edward K. Rice and Richard W. Wickert, "Longspan Prestressed Concrete . . . Dynamic New Principle for Parking Structure Construction," *Parking* (Fall 1961): 11–12; "Precast Rigid Frame for a Bargain," *Engineering News-Record* (May 11, 1961): 38–39; H.L. Hurlburt, "A Fresh Idea in Parking-Structure Design," *American City* 76, no. 12 (December 1961): 80–82; Dietrich Klose, *Multi-Storey Car Parks and Garages* (New York: Praeger Architectural, 1965), 156–159.

56. Zollman, "End of 'Beginnings,'" in *Prestressed Concrete*, 332–360; "50 Years," 1–4; Rice and Wickert, "Longspan Prestressed Concrete," 11–12.

57. Klose, *Car Parks and Garages*, 219; John Van Horn, "It Works! License Plate Recognition at Phoenix Sky Harbor," *Parking Today* (February 2000: 20); "Sky Harbor Implements Vehicle Tracking System with RFID, GPS," *Parking* (July 2005: 15); "1st National Bank Parking Garage," *Parking* (October 1970): 61–62.

58. J. Graham, "Prestressed Concrete in the Northwest and Hawaii," *PCI Journal* (April 1964): 63–67; "Precast TTs Deck Spiral Garage," *Engineering News-Record* (September 26, 1963): 36–37.

59. "Michigan Bank National Association Parking Facility," *Parking* (Fall 1968): 26–27.

60. "Tridak Parking Structure," *Parking* (April 1970): 18; "Precast Prestressed Concrete Paves the Way to Big Savings," *Parking* (January 1970): 41–42.

61. "News in Photos," *Parking* (Winter 1969): 4; Michael J.A.H. Jolliffe, "Large Precast Prestressed Concrete Decks over Air Rights," *PCI Journal* (March–April 1975): 74–86.

62. On a building facade, spandrel walls are the flat, vertical areas between the top of the structure of one story and the bottom of the structure of the story above.

63. "Gary National Bank Parking Garage," *Parking* (October 1970): 44; H.J. Walocha, "Parking Structure Solutions in a Seismic Zone," *PCI Journal* (July–August 1972): 60–64.

64. A haunch is a structural element that is thicker and deeper, so that it can support another structural member.

65. "Baylor Hospital Parking Structure," *Ascent* (Winter 2004): 22. A shear wall is designed to brace parallel planes in such a way that they remain in position when subjected to shear forces such as wind, blast, or earthquake.

66. Donald H. Olson, "Parking Ramps on Air Rights over Freeways," *Parking* (Spring 1968): 17–19; Paul N. Bay, "Air Rights Help to Solve a Parking Problem," *American City* (November 1967): 84–85; Jolliffe, "Decks over Air Rights," 74–91; "Design and Typical Details of Connections for Precast and Prestressed Concrete," *PCI Journal* (January–February 1989): 172; W.H. Bruder, "This Parking Garage . . . Uses Airspace, Architectural Excellence, Automated Efficiency," *American City* 80, no. 6 (December 1965): 98–100; *Parking* (July 1975): 31; "News in Photos," *Parking* (July 1972): 10; "Air Space Used," *Parking* (Fall 1961): 10; *Parking* (July 1972): 10.

67. J. Zekany, Ede Vessey, and William M. Bollinger, "Sarasota County Parking Garage," *PCI Journal* (May–June 1991): 34–39; "Northwest Airlines Midfield Terminal Parking Structure," *Ascent* (Winter 2004): 29; Rocky Mountain Prestress, *Denver International Airport* (brochure); "Hurricane Andrew: The Good News?? The Bad News!!" *Leap Ledger* (January 1993): 1–4; George Southworth, "Precast Concrete Frames," *Leap Ledger*. These statistics are based on urban garages with between 265 and 5,000 parking spaces. The data do not accurately reflect certain market areas, such as those subject to seismic hazards or particular weather conditions. For more specific data, see Dale Denda, *Parking Garage Construction 2000: A Statement of Market Conditions* (Parking Market Research Company, February 2001).

68. Altus Group, brochure on CarbonCast, www.altusprecast.com/. Forces such as wind can cause two parallel vertical sections of a structure to slide; *shear transfer* refers to the transfer of such forces, so that sliding does not occur.

69. Andrew Pinneke, project manager, Iowa Prestressed Concrete, Inc., discussion with author, 2002; Consulting Engineers Group, *Research Project #7: Survey of Precast Prestressed Concrete Parking Structures* (Chicago: Prestressed Concrete Institute, 1986); Precast Prestressed Concrete Institute, *Parking Structures: Recommended Practice for Design and Construction* (Chicago: Precast Prestressed Concrete Institute, 1997); "Innovative Building System Meets Strict Requirements of Atlanta's MARTA System," *Parking* (August 1998): 30–31; "What Are the Symptoms of Corrosion?" *Leap Ledger*, 1–4; Carl Walker, e-mail discussions with author, September 19, 2005; William C. Arons, "University of Iowa Saved 39% with

New Parking Ramp Design," *Parking* (January 1977): 26, 28. For a description of an early attempt to eliminate cracking by using a different slab system, see "The Modern Garage on Display," *Parking* (July 1971): 21.

70. "Design Analysis of the 1416 F St. Parking Center, Washington, D.C.," *Parking* (Spring 1954): 43–45; R.B. Bowser, "Car Sizes and the Parking Industry," *Parking* (Fall 1955): 15; Edward Turner, "Case of the Shrinking Car Space," *Parking* (Winter 1958): 5–7; Gary Cudney, "Pre-Cast vs. Cast-in-Place: How Do They Compare?" *Parking* (May 1998): 27–30. The F Street Parking Center also had another interesting feature: it was constructed with a banked spiral, meaning that the spiral floor plate was warped one foot toward the exterior, which allowed moisture to drain into two master outlets.

71. Peterson, "Precast Concrete," 477–499; "Two New Private Parking Garages in Minneapolis," *American City* 68, no. 1 (January 1953): 143. "Design Analysis," *Parking* (Winter 1958): 8–9. A one-way flat slab is a slab that is reinforced in one direction only. A haunched beam is thicker and deeper under the ends of what it is supporting—in this case, the slab.

72. "Garages Grow Up," *Architectural Forum* (February 1953): 132–133; George Hansen, ed., *Parking: How It Is Financed* (New York: National Retail Dry Goods Association, 1952), 9; Baker and Funaro, *Parking*, 140–141.

73. "Nation's Largest Parking Building Completed," *Engineering News-Record* (July 10, 1952): 34–39.

74. "New Parketeria Makes Full Use of Hilly Site," *Parking* (Spring 1955): 14–15; "Concrete Proves Versatile," 19–23.

75. "Award Winning Self-Park Garage in Chicago," *Parking* (October 1969): 47–48.

76. "Rice Inducted into Post-Tensioning Hall of Fame," www.concretemonthly. com/monthly/art.php?I523; U.S. Patent 3,813,835, issued June 4, 1974.

77. Carroll S. Delaney and Neil R. Runyan, "A Monolithic Post-Tensioned Parking Structure," *PCI Journal* (December 1961): 53–59; "Design Analysis," 8–9; "News in Photos," *Parking* (October 1971): 4. Torsional capacity refers to the amount of stress a structural member can withstand along its longitudinal axis when it is being twisted.

78. "News in Photos," *Parking* (October 1970): 4; "Parking Facility Award Winner," *American City* (July 1971): 88; "Opportunity Park: Post Tensioning," *Parking* (October 1972): 23–31.

79. R. Meenen, "Parking Garages for New Orleans Superdome," *PCI Journal* 19, no. 2 (March–April 1974): 98–111; Delaney

and Runyan, "Monolithic Parking Structure," 53–59; Ivan J. Miestchovich and Wade R. Ragas, "Stadium Parking Attracts Office Developers in New Orleans," *Urban Land* (June 1986): 14–17.

80. Theodore L. Neff, "Post-Tensioning Parking Projects throughout the United States Showcase the Benefits and Acceptance of the Method," *Design Cost Data* (July–August 2006): 10; A. Kennerly, "Prestressing and Its Function in Architecture," *PCI Journal* (December 1960): 60–73.

81. Graham, "Prestressed Concrete," 63–67; "Wall-Top Traveler Erects Big T-Beams," *Construction Methods* (February 1964): 92–93.

82. J. Ford, "Height Record Goes Up Again for Lift-Slabs in the U.S.," *Engineering News-Record* (July 3, 1958): 30–39; "Design Analysis: New Garage Gives Department Store Row a 'Lift,'" *Parking* (Winter 1961): 31–36; R.E. Harbaugh, "Lift-Slab Construction," *American City* 77, no. 3 (September 1962): 143–145; "Latest Methods Cut Lift-Slab Costs," *Western Construction* (November 1956): 28–29; "Parking Garage for Oshkosh," *American City* (June 1960): 130.

83. "Design Analysis: 9-Story Self-Parking Garage in San Francisco Designed to be 'Quake' Proof," *Parking* (Summer 1955): 14–15; W. H. Ellison and T.Y. Lin, "Parking Garage Built for $5.38 per Sq. Ft.," *Civil Engineering* (June 1955): 37–40; T.Y. Lin, "Self-Parking: Downtown Center Garage," *Architect and Engineer* (April 1955): 9–15.

84. A moment force is a force that produces movement around a point or axis. Moment-frame structures rely on the connections between the framing pieces to resist moment forces.

85. Alvin C. Ericson and Cloyd E. Warnes, *Precast Prestressed Concrete Parking Structures: Framing Systems and Connection Technology* (brochure sponsored by Walker Parking Consultants and Carl Walker Engineers, Inc.); H.J. Walocha, "Parking Structure Solutions in a Seismic Zone," *PCI Journal* (July–August 1972): 60–64. The term *nonductile* refers to structures that are not capable of stretching or deforming in any way.

86. "Concrete Proves Versatile," 18–23; Edward L. Friedman, "Cast-In Place Technique Restudied," *Progressive Architecture* (October 1960): 157–175; John J. Dwyer, "Garage to Relieve New York Traffic Jam," *Engineering News-Record* (May 18, 1950): 44–45.

87. "Garages Grow Up," 134–135; "Concrete Proves Versatile," 18–23.

88. Tarif M. Jaber, *Project Report: Spruce Tree Parking Structure; A New Concept in Concrete Durability* (brochure sponsored by Elkem Materials and Braun/ Intertec); Thomas G. Weil, "Address-

ing Parking Garage Corrosion with Silica Fume," in Transportation Research Board, *Portland Cement Modifiers* (Washington, D.C.: Transportation Research Board, 1998), 8–10; Tom Kuennen, "Silica Fume Resurges," *Concrete Products* (March 1996); Silica Fume Association, *What Is Silica Fume?* (Fairfax, Va.: Silica Fume Association, n.d.); L. Rocole, "Silica-Fume Concrete Proves to Be an Economical Alternative," *Concrete Construction* 38, no. 6 (June 1993): 441–442.

89. Frank Owens and Sreenivas Alampalli, "Increasing Durability of Decks Using Class HP Concrete," *Concrete International* (July 2000): 33–35; Tony Kojundic, "HP Concrete Flexes Its Muscles," *Roads and Bridges* (April 1997); U.S. Department of Transportation, Federal Highway Administration, "High Performance Concrete (HPC) for Bridges," www.tfhrc.gov; Susan C. McCraven, "High-Performance Concrete Today: Nothing Routine," *Concrete Construction* 47, no. 6 (June 2002): 29–36; William C. Panarese, "Celebrating Twenty-Five Years of CTT," *Concrete Technology Today* 26, no. 1 (April 2005): 1–8; "Plastiment Increases Workability of Lightweight Concrete," *PCI Journal* (December 1961): 42 (advertisement).

90. Paul Brienza, "Waterproofing a Parking Garage," *American City* 82, no. 3 (September 1967): 142–143; "Toronto Airport Project Uses Watson Bowman System," *Parking Professional* (July 2002): 44; Frank Kuchinski, Triton, e-mail exchanges with author, March 2005; American Concrete Institute, *Guide for the Design of Durable Parking Structures*, ACI 362.1R-97 (Farmington Hills, Mich.: American Concrete Institute, August 1997); Advanced Polymer Technology, "Qualideck," www.advpolytech.com/ navigation/protect.htm#qualideck; Tarek Alkhrdaji and Jay Thomas, "Techniques and Design Considerations for Upgrade of Parking Structures," *Parking* (June 2002): 24–25, 28; Richard C. Rich, "The History of Airport Parking," *Parking Professional* (June 2004): 20–23.

91. J. Cross, "Building Tomorrow's Parking Structures Today," *Parking Today* (August 2001): 18–20; "Edwin L. Mead," *Parking Today* (August 2006): 33. One system for attaching plywood was the K-System, designed by A.M. Kinney: see "Costs Come Down," *Parking* (Spring 1961): 26; "Construction News," *Parking* (Fall 1957): 34. Another similar system was created by Mulach Parking Structures (*The Mulach Answer: A Quality Parking Facility at Budget Prices* [brochure]).

92. "Design Analysis," *Parking* (Spring 1961): 17–22.

93. "Parking News," *Parking* (Winter 1963): 4; Wood, "Steel Offers Answer," 32–34; "News in Photos" (Winter 1969): 6.

94. Junior-beams are a category of shaped I-beam made from hot-rolled steel. "K-System," *Parking* (Spring 1961): 26; "Costs Come Down," 26.

95. "New Construction Method Cuts Three Months Off Construction Time," *Parking* (July 1977): 16–17; Midstate Filigree Systems, "The Filigree Method of Concrete Deck Construction," www. filigreeinc.com; Midstate Filigree Systems, "About Midstate Filigree Systems Inc.," www.filigreeinc.com.

96. Another 1950s steel garage, the Sioux City Park and Shop, used steel bridge grating for the ramps.

97. Wood, "Steel Offers Answer"; "Bus Garage," *Progressive Architecture* (February 1952): 98–100; "Erected in 22 Days," *Engineering News-Record* (October 14, 1948): 76; "Welded Rigid-Frame," *Engineering News-Record* (October 7, 1948): 10; "Parking News: New Type of Structural Steel Garage Now Open in Washington, D.C.," *Parking* (Summer 1954): 5; "Design Analysis: Here Is a Low Cost Garage Designed for High Turnover, Low Rates," *Parking* (Fall 1955): 12–13; "Bethlehem Garage: San Francisco," *Parking* (Fall 1962): 42–43.

98. "News in Photos," *Parking* (April 1973): 7; "Novel Concept in Parking Structure Design Saves Taxpayers $100,000," *Parking* (April 1974): 36–37 (advertisement); "Weathering Steel," *Parking* (July 1978): 34–35 (advertisement); *Parking* (April 1973): 41–42 (advertisement).

99. "Steel-Framed Coliseum Provides 2,400-Car Facility within Its Structural Framework," *Parking* (April 1973): 43 (advertisement); "Weathering Steel," 34–35; "Code Change Lets Detroit Build Its First Exposed-Steel Parking Deck," *Parking* (July 1977): 38–39 (advertisement); Charles H. Churches, Emile W.J. Troup, and Carl Angeloff, *Steel-Framed Open-Deck Parking Structure Design Guide No. 18* (Chicago: American Institute of Steel Construction, 2004), 77; "Exposed-Steel Parking Combines with Rentable Space for Economy and Quicker Amortization," *Parking* (January 1972): 18–19 (advertisement).

100. "Warped Deck Cuts Costs of New Parking Structure," *American City* 81, no. 1 (January 1966): 132; "Embedded-Flange Beams, Reusable Forming System Produce Construction Economies with Steel," *Parking* (January 1977): 24–25 (advertisement); "Steel Parking Structures: A 25-Year Perspective; An Interview with Charles Churches," *Modern Steel Construction* (March 2002): 53–58; American Institute of Steel Construction, *Steel-Framed Parking Structures*; American Institute of Steel Construction, *Open-Deck Steel-Framed Parking Structures* (Chicago: American Institute of Steel Construction, 2003).

101. "Dallas Airport Garage," *Parking* (October 1970): 46; "Symptoms of Corrosion," 1–4.

102. "Unique Steel-Framed Structure Solves University Parking Problem," *Parking* (July 1973): 30–31; "Steel-Framed Garage Will Be One of the Nation's Largest," *Parking* (January 1970): 21.

103. Scott Kennedy, "Rebuilding after Northridge," *Modern Steel Construction* (November 1997); American Institute of Steel Construction, *Steel-Framed Parking Structures*, 66–72; SMI Steel Products, *Project Profile: Central Park Garage, Austin, Texas* (SMI Steel Products, 1996); SMI Steel Products, *SMI Smartbeam: The Intelligent Alternative* (brochure); "Pacific Parking," *Modern Steel Construction* (March 2002): 46–51; American Institute of Steel Construction, *Fashion Square Retail Center: Sherman Oaks, California*, Steel Parking Structure File, F008-02 (Chicago: American Institute of Steel Construction, n.d.).

104. Ericson and Warnes, *Concrete Parking Structures*. Moment connections are particularly important for resisting gravity and wind loads in structures such as parking garages, which do not always include shear walls.

105. Alan H. Simon, "Unique Steel-Framed Solution to Parking," *Modern Steel Construction* (April 2001); American Institute of Steel Construction, *Steel-Framed Parking Structures*, 10–13, 20–22, 26–28; "Hybrid Parking Structure Cuts Costs," *Modern Steel Construction* (December 1996); American Institute of Steel Construction, *Nortel Networks, Billerica, Massachusetts*, Steel Parking Structure File F006-02 (Chicago: American Institute of Steel Construction, n.d.); J. Cross, "Building Tomorrow's Parking Structures Today," *Parking Today* (August 2001): 18–20; "Parking with Class," *Modern Steel Construction* (March 2002): 24–27.

106. "Parking Revolution Arrives First Class," *Parking* (January 1977): 20–21; David H. Sadeghpour, "Vertical Expansion," *Modern Steel Construction* (June 1996); American Institute of Steel Construction, *Steel-Framed Parking Structures*, 14–19, 44–46, 58–61; Joseph Englot, *On Parking Garages* (brochure sponsored by the American Institute of Steel Construction).

107. Craig Totten, *Portland International Airport, Portland, Oregon*, Steel Parking Structure File F004-02 (Chicago: American Institute of Steel Construction, n.d.). As noted in chapter 8, steel and other metals have also been used successfully as visual screens. One current example of the aesthetic use of steel is at the Portland International Airport, where a 220-foot by 530-foot (67-meter by 162-meter) steel-and-glass canopy spans a four-lane highway between the parking structure and the

terminal; steel was also used for two pedestrian bridges at the airport.

108. Joey D. Rowland, "An Inconvenient Truth," *Industry Insights* (January–February 2007): 1.

109. "Knock Down Garages," *Garage* 1, no. 2 (December 1910): 25; "Barrel-Shaped Garage," *Horseless Age* 35, no. 7 (February 17, 1915): 231; H.H. Brown, "A Tent or Portable Garage," *Horseless Age* 24, no. 13 (September 29, 1909): 356; "Unit Building Design Lowers Cost of New Orleans Parking Garage," *American City* 66, no. 4 (April 1951): 161; Klose, *Car Parks and Garages*, 106–110.

110. T.Y. Lin, "Demountable Parking Structures," *Parking* (October 1969): 28; "Concrete: The Material That Can Do Almost Anything," *Architectural Forum* (September 1962): 78–101; Baker and Funaro, *Parking*, 145–147.

111. Lin, "Demountable Parking Structures," 26–32; "Prefab Can Park Geared to Mod Design," *Parking* (Spring 1968): 16; "The Portable Garage," *American City* 85, no. 1 (January 1970): 108–110, "Portable over Air Space," *Parking* (October 1970): 16; "Parking Relief for Cities: A Relocatable Garage," *American City* (July 1969): 55; Carl Walker, e-mail exchange with author, September 19, 2005.

112. "Airport Parking Problem Solved—Modular Structure Erected in 22 Days," *Parking* (October 1970): 40–42; "Unicon Structure for California," *Parking* (April 1972): 10–11; "New Parking Structure at Los Angeles International Airport 'Topped Out,'" *Parking* (October 1969): 34–36; *Unicon: Parking Structures* (brochure provided by Edward K. Rice, former president of T.Y. Lin and Associates).

113. "Movable Garage Designed," *Parking* (January 1970): 20–21; "Portable Planned Parking Garage Is Permanently Placed," *Parking* (October 1971): 14–16; "News in Photos," *Parking* (October 1970): 8; "County Dedicates New Portable Parking Garages in Civic Center," *Parking* (October 1969): 40–41; *Modular Steel Systems, Inc.* (brochure). Leasing parking decks rather than owning them eventually became an increasingly important option; in 1969, for example, to meet the parking needs for its civic center, the city of Los Angeles leased a garage from Portable Parking Structures.

114. "Underground Garage to Relieve Chicago Street Congestion," *Horseless Age* (May 21, 1913): 949; "Underground Garage for Indianapolis Proposed," *Horseless Age* (December 10, 1913): 993; A.T. North, "The Residential District Garage," *Architectural Forum* 53, no. 3 (September 1930): 379; Lonnie Hackman and Norene D. Martin, *The Parking Industry; Private Enterprise for the Public*

Good (Washington, D.C.: National Parking Association, 1969), 3; Miller McClintock, "Parking—When, Where and Why?" *American City* (April 1924): 361; "Technical News and Research: Garages," *Architectural Record* (February 1929): 192.

115. S.A. Carrighar, "Built Down Instead of Up: The Union Square Garage, San Francisco," *Architect and Engineer* (August 1942): 19–29; Thomas Smith, *The Aesthetics of Parking* (Chicago: American Planning Association, 1988), 38; Klose, *Car Parks and Garages*, 46–47, 172–191; Baker and Funaro, *Parking*, 60–63, 142–144; "Shall Motor-Cars Be Parked Underground?" *American City* 44, no. 1 (January 1931): 133; "San Francisco Builds a Garage under a Park," *American City* 57, no. 11 (November 1942): 66; "Concrete Proves Versatile," *Parking* (Spring 1955): 18–23.

116. "Underground Garage Walls Built Last," *Engineering News-Record* (March 6, 1952): 30–31; Gib Clark, "Ready-Mix Used on Big Underground Garage," *Concrete* (February 1952): 18–20; Baker and Funaro, *Parking*, 60–63, 66–67; Klose, *Car Parks and Garages*, 184–197, 190–191, 204–207; "World's Largest Garage Now Being Built in Grant Park," *American City* 68, no. 1 (July 1953): 128; "Parking 5,000 Cars a Day," *American City* (June 1955): 166; "The Health Center in the 21st Century," *Parking* (July 1976): 21–23; "Health Building Garage: A Parking Facility and a Redevelopment Hub," *Parking* (October 1970): 36–38. Among the many articles on underground garages are the following: V.B. Steinbaugh, "Underground Parking for Detroit," *American City* 61, no. 2 (February 1946): 112; "Underground Terminal Planned in Jersey City," *American City* 62, no. 4 (April 1947): 122; "Find the City's Garage," *American City* 72, no. 6 (December 1957): 127; Edmond T. Keenan, "1,450 Cars to Park under Boston's Common," *American City* 81, no. 2 (August 1960): 84; "Newark Gets Underground Parking Garage," *American City* 80, no. 2 (February 1960): 137; Paul L. Heineman, "Parking under the State Capitol Grounds," *American City* 81, no. 3 (March 1966): 96–97; "Toronto's 1,320-Car Underground Garage," *American City* 72, no. 3 (September 1957): 155; "Kansas City Gets Green Light for Improvement Program," *American City* 63, no. 1 (January 1948): 5; Harry Hewes, "Underground Parking in Kansas City," *American City* (August 1946): 105; Electus D. Litchfield, "Parking under Parks," *American City* (August 1946): 109.

117. "Seaport Village, San Diego: California Hope Architects and Engineers," *Architecture* (December 1991): 81; Chris Morill, city manager, City of Savannah; Susan Broker, assistant city manager, City

of Savannah; Jerry Lominack, Lominack Kolman Smith Architects; and others on the Ellis Square project team, discussions with author, November 2005.

118. "Inn of the Mountain Gods," *Metal Architecture* (August 2005): 10; Dean Abbondanza, "Changing the Economics of Underground Parking Structures," *Parking Professional* (February 2005): 22–25; William L. Pascoli, national project director, American Steel Institute, discussions with author, August 2004; Robert Pyle, Southwest Region, American Institute of Steel Construction, discussions with author, August 2004; Charles Stubbs, structural engineer, discussions with author, August 2004; Skyline Steel Systems, www.skylinesteel.com.

119. Carl Walker Parking, *South Spring Street Garage* (project information sheet); "Best Parking Structure, Co-winner," *PCI Journal* 51, no. 5 (September–October 2006): 55; Fred Laughlin, John Dorsett, Margie Schnelle, and John Hicks, "Operating Costs for Parking Structures Vary Significantly," *Parking* (May–June 1997): 18–20; James M. Hunnicutt, "So You're Going to Build Your First Parking Garage," *Parking Professional* (August 2000); Gary L. Cudney and Edmund L. Baum, "Precast vs. Cast-In-Place: Is There a Difference? And What about Steel?" (presentation, International Parking Conference and Exposition of the International Parking Institute, Toronto, June 3, 2002).

The Precast Concrete Revolution: T.Y. Lin and Harry Edwards

1. T.Y. Lin, "Symposium on Prestressed Concrete," *PCI Journal* (September–October, 1976); T.Y. Lin, "Revolution in Concrete," *Architectural Forum* (May 1961): 121–127; "Tung-Yen (T.Y.) Lin, 1912–2003," *Ascent* (Winter 2004): 8.

2. G. Magnel, "The Principles of Prestressed Concrete," *Engineering Journal* (March 1947): 110–112; Charles C. Zollman, "The End of the 'Beginnings,'" in Prestressed Concrete Institute, *Reflections on the Beginnings of Prestressed Concrete in America* (Chicago: Prestressed Concrete Institute, 1981), 349; Edward K. Rice and Richard W. Wickert, "Longspan Prestressed Concrete . . . Dynamic New Principle for Parking Structure Construction," *Parking* (Fall 1961): 11–19; Edward K. Rice, "Quick Public Acceptance Gained in Parking Structure with 110-Foot Spans," *Parking* (Winter 1963): 16–20; T.Y. Lin, "A New Concept for Prestressed Concrete," *PCI Journal* (December 1961): 36–52; H.L. Hurlburt, "A Fresh Idea in Parking-Structure Design," *American City* 76, no. 12 (December 1961): 80–82; Lin, "Revolution in Concrete," 121–127; Perry Scott, "Santa Wouldn't Provide 2,000 Free Parking Spaces," *American City*

(May 1969): 145–146; Dietrich Klose, *Multi-Storey Car Parks and Garages* (New York: Praeger Architectural Press, 1965): 156–159; "Beverly Hilton Parking Structure," *Ascent* (Winter 2004): 15; A.C. Martin Jr., "Creative Prestressed Concrete Design Techniques in the Western United States," *PCI Journal* (April 1964): 60. To allow the building to withstand earthquakes, the Beverly Hills garage also had vertical prestressing that extended through the building down into the foundation; the purpose of this design was to transfer the horizontal forces of an earthquake to the vertical supports of the structure. And the structure did indeed withstand several earthquakes during the 1950s, without any sign of weakness.

3. "50 Years and Growing," *Leap Ledger* (March 2001): 1–4; Parking Market Research Company, *Parking Garage Construction 2000: A Statement of Market Conditions* (Parking Market Research Company, February 2001). For an excellent history of the Prestressed Concrete Institute, see Prestressed Concrete Institute, *Prestressed Concrete*.

4. "Precast Prestressed Concrete Paves the Way to Big Savings," *Parking* (January 1970): 41–42; "Maryland Concert Center Parking Garage," *PCI Journal* (January–February 1984): 159.

Concrete, Steel, and Sustainability

1. Martha Vangeem and Medgar Marceau, "Using Concrete to Maximize LEED Points," *Concrete International* (November 2002): 69–73; Jim Parsons, "Concrete for a Sustainable Future," *Architecture* (November 2000): 70–71; Colin Lobo, "An Initiative Toward Performance-Based Specifications for Concrete," *Concrete Technology Today* 24, no. 3 (December 2003): 3.

2. American Iron and Steel Institute, Washington, D.C., Steel Recycling Institute, Pittsburgh, Penn., and American Institute of Steel Construction, Chicago, *Steel Takes LEED with Recycled Content* (brochure); American Institute of Steel Construction, *Structural Steel Sustainability* (Chicago: Modern Steel Construction, 2003).

The Structural Aesthetic

1. Burton H. Holmes, "Exposed Concrete Today," *Progressive Architecture* (October 1960): 150–157.

2. "Mt. Sinai Hospital, Cleveland," *PCI Journal* (July–August 1982): 120–126; Philip R. Pastore, "Crown Street Parking Garage: Design Fabrication and Erection of Tree Columns," *PCI Journal* 17, no. 1 (January–February 1972): 21–28; "Crown Street Garage," *Parking* (October 1971): 18–21.

3. "Fact Sheet: Hospital Parking Ramp, University of Iowa," *Parking* (July 1970): 55.

4. "Rock Island Parking Structure Wins Award," *Parking* (April 1979): 18. A Vierendeel truss is an open web truss in which the top and bottom cords are connected by vertical members only; there are no diagonal members.

5. Pradeep H. Shah and Howard R. May, "Vierendeel Trusses," *PCI Journal* (July–August 1977): 24–39.

6. "USAA Southeast Regional Office Parking Structure, Tampa, Fla.," *Ascent* (Fall 1994): 26–27.

The Parking Lot

1. "Dustproofing the Car Park," *Parking* (Fall 1955): 25–28; "Soil-Cement for Parking Areas," *Parking* (Fall 1955): 27–29; John Coyne, "NPA 2001: Facility Development; Case Study of a Surface Parking Lot" (handout, National Parking Association conference, Orlando, Florida, 2001); "World of Asphalt Named One of 50 Fastest Growing Trade Shows," *Roads and Bridges* (August 31, 2004).

2. "Parking Can Be Beautiful," *Parking* (July 1971): 14–20; Jean Feingold, "West Palm Beach Boasts Area's Largest Parking Lot," *Parking Today* 5, no. 9 (October 2000): 20–22.

3. Mark Childs, *Parking Spaces* (New York: McGraw-Hill, 1999); Leopold Kohr, "From Vacant Lot to Car Park," *American City* (November 1945): 119–121; Heather Brown, "Concrete Parking Lot Design Seminar" (presented at the Georgia Concrete and Products Association meeting, Atlanta, March 30, 2005); Paul D. Tennis, Michael L. Leming, and David J. Akers, *EB203 Pervious Concrete Pavements* (Skokie, Ill.: Portland Cement Association, 2004); Bradley T. Burke, "A Concrete Advantage," *Construction Bulletin*, June 18, 2004, 27–28; Thomas A. Phillips Jr., "Designing a Parking Lot for Maximum Efficiencies: A Small Operator's Perspective," *Parking* (May 2003): 22–26. Today there is even the option of a temporary solution that can be laid down in rolls on top of grass.

Chapter 7

1. In his 1976 book *A History of Building Types*, architectural historian Nikolaus Pevsner discusses nearly every building type—including train stations and "air halls" (where dirigibles landed). But even at such a late date, this prominent typological history makes no mention of the parking garage. Curiously, Pevsner does discuss warehouses as the building type dedicated to storage, but he does not consider storage of the automobile. Moreover, he ends the book by noting that "what the effects of automation will be remains to be seen"—

as if automation had not already transformed society. See Nikolaus Pevsner, *A History of Building Types* (Princeton, N.J.: Princeton University Press, 1976), 288.

2. Peter G. Rowe, *Design Thinking* (Cambridge, Mass.: MIT Press, 1987), 190.

3. Karen A. Franck and Lynda H. Schneekloth, eds., *Ordering Space: Types in Architecture and Design* (New York: Van Nostrand Reinhold, 1994), 350.

4. Alan Colquhoun, "Typology and Design Method," *Arena* 83 (June 1967): 22–14.

5. Rowe, *Design Thinking*, 190. In *Quatremère De Quincy and the Invention of a Modern Language of Architecture* (Cambridge: MIT Press, 1992), Sylvia Lavin examines the theoretical basis for a linguistic understanding of type. De Quincy, a leading French theorist of the early 19th century, was instrumental in developing the fundamental concepts of modern architecture, and he remains influential today. It is largely through his work that the role of type in architecture has come to be viewed as analogous to the role of type in language.

6. Christian Norberg-Schultz, "Meaning in Architecture," in *Meaning in Architecture*, ed. Charles Jenks and George Baird (New York: Braziller, 1969), 214–219; Charles Jencks, "History as Myth," in Jenks and Baird, *Meaning in Architecture*, 245–265; Alan Colquhoun, "Typology and Design Method," in Jenks and Baird, *Meaning in Architecture*, 266–277. Architecture is directly linked to this preverbal era in human development: although the language of architecture is neither spoken nor written, meanings are deeply embedded in its built forms. The cave, the tent, and the hut all arose from the need for shelter, but each has a different physical form, elicits different human emotions, and embraces different ideas about how movement progresses. The expression of movement—that is, how a given group of people perceive both literal and figurative movement to occur—is fundamental to the notion of civic progress. The art of architecture embraces both continuity with the past and the positive progression that is associated with the future. Art and ornament were both early, nonverbal forms of communication, and both held deeper meanings that were connected to the idea of movement. Cave paintings, depicting both the mythic and the real, were an attempt to express, reveal, and explore all that was being absorbed in the course of daily life. The interlaced ornamental patterns of weaving reflected the nomadic existence, where all movement was interwoven, and were directly connected to the technology of the tent, which was constructed of rugs or fabrics. The foliated scroll, a visual expression of repetitive, cyclical movement, was traditionally

linked to farming cultures, and to their unique connection to the land. Art and ornament reflect how humans understand movement; at the same time, they communicate how movement—both literal and figurative—occurs.

7. "Caserne de pompiers à Maastricht, Pays-Bas," *L'architecture d'aujourd'hui* (March–April 2001): 74.

8. In the late 1940s and 1950s, architects began to discuss these disconnections. However, books such as Siegfried Giedion's *Mechanization Takes Command* and *Space, Time and Architecture* simply assumed movement to be positive; they failed to attempt a broader investigation of the psychology of movement and its theoretical implications for architecture.

9. Anne Whiston Spirn, C. Ford Peatross, and Robert L. Sweeney, *Frank Lloyd Wright: Designs for an American Landscape, 1922–1932* (New York: Harry N. Abrams in association with the Canadian Centre for Architecture, the Library of Congress, and the Frank Lloyd Wright Foundation, 1996), 174, 175; Joseph J. Corn and Brian Horrigan, *Yesterday's Tomorrows: Past Visions of the American Future*, ed. Katharine Chambers (Baltimore: Johns Hopkins University Press, 1996), 97.

10. Peter M. Wolf, *The Future of the City: New Directions in Urban Planning* (New York: Watson-Guptill, 1974), 100–101, 102–103; Aaron Betsky, "Flashback to the Future," *Architecture* 88, no. 4 (April 1999): 59–62; Reyner Banham, *Megastructure: Urban Futures of the Recent Past* (London: Thames and Hudson, 1976), 40, 84–103, 104–111; Botond Bognar, *The Japan Guide* (Princeton: Princeton Architectural Press, 1995); Stephanie Whitlock, review of a lecture delivered by Eric Mumford at the Graham Foundation, December 5, 2001, "Two Phases of Modern Urbanism: CIAM and Team 10," www.grahamfoundation.org/messagePopup.asp?msgID=40; Banham, *Megastructure*, 104–111; Ted Smalley Bowen, "Structure," *New York Times*, October 20, 2005, D3; Atomium, www.atomium.be; Peter Cook, *Archigram* (Boston: Birkhauser, 1991), 12–13, 21–22.

11. Banham, *Megastructure*, 63; Paul Rudolph and Ulrich Franzen, *The Evolving City* (New York: American Federation of the Arts, 1974), 74–75.

12. "Parking News," *Parking* (Spring 1962): 2; "Wondering about Pedestrian Malls," *Urban Land* (July 1984): 40; Wolf, *Future of the City*, 34.

13. Wilfred Owen, *Cities in the Motor Age* (New York: Viking, 1959), 66–69; Banham, *Megastructure*, 42; "The Fort Worth Plan," *Urban Land* (September 1956): 7; Geoffrey Baker and Bruno Funaro, *Parking* (New York: Reinhold, 1958), 41.

14. Owen, *Motor Age*, 66–69; "Another Major Project for Boston," *Progressive Architecture* (February 1964): 62–64; Paul Rudolph drawings, Prints and Photographs Division, Library of Congress; Wolf, *Future of the City*, 174–175; Banham, *Megastructure*, 73–76.

15. Stone and Gruen both referred to the idea of fringe parking in poetic terms, as being related to nature and to the flow of water.

16. Edward Durell Stone, *Evolution of an Architect* (New York: Horizon, 1962), 146–147, 272–273; "Cascade Plaza," *Parking* (October 1972): 16–21; Baker and Funaro, *Parking*, 60; Herbert Muschamp, "A Rare Opportunity for Real Architecture Where It's Needed," *New York Times*, October 22, 2000, Arts and Leisure, 1.

17. The garage, which used post-tensioning techniques and expansive cement, was both innovative and cost-effective. Both sections of the structure were directly linked to arterial highways. In 2003–2004, one 1,000-car section was replaced (maintaining direct highway access), and the other was torn down, although the open space that remains could be used for parking again.

18. "Opportunity Park Garage: A Sophisticated Piece of Machinery," *Parking* (October 1972): 23–31; Seymour Gage Associates, "Co-Op City," *Parking* (July 1970): 34–37.

19. Urban Land Institute, *Mixed-Use Developments: New Ways of Land Use*, Technical Bulletin 71 (Washington, D.C.: ULI—the Urban Land Institute), 3–16, 21–27; Dean Schwanke et al., *Mixed-Use Development Handbook* (Washington, D.C.: ULI—the Urban Land Institute, 1987), 182–191, 222–223; "Rockefeller Center," *Urban Land* (December 1989): 24; "Landmark," *Smithsonian* (March 2004): 112; Francesco Andreani, *Garages* (Rome: Gangemi Editore, 1997), 32. Cost and code issues would make the level of integration used in the Cyclop virtually impossible in the United States today.

20. "Radical Ways of Relieving Parking Congestion," *American City* (March 1932): 107.

21. Banham, *Megastructure*, 41; "Highways of the Future," *Parking* (Fall 1957): 3; "News in Photos," *Parking* (October 1969): 4.

22. "Highways of the Future," *Parking* (Fall 1957): 3; William R. McConochie, "Freeways Can Save Urban Transit," *Urban Land* (September 1957): 1–4, "News in Parking," *Parking* (Fall 1961), 4; Gregory A. Finstad, "Garages: The Key to a Successful Transportation System," *ITE Journal* (May 1996): 38–42; Highway Research Board, *Parking Principles*, Special Report 125, Subject Area 53 (Washington, D.C.: National Acad-

emy of Sciences, 1971), 92–93; Bognar, *Japan Guide*; "Golden Gate Garage Meshes Automation and Aesthetics," *Parking* (July 1970): 26–27; "Second-Story Traffic—Stuttgart, West Germany," *Parking* (Fall 1961): 3; "Downtown Masterplanning," *Parking* (Winter 1959): 6; Urban Advisors to the Federal Highway Administration, *The Freeway in the City* (Washington, D.C.: U.S. Government Printing Office, 1968), 47–53.

23. "The Union Carbide Corporation World Headquarters, Danbury Connecticut, 1976–1982," *Architecture and Urbanism* (August 1987): 120–129; Nicolai Ouroussoff, "The Assembly Line Becomes a Catwalk," *New York Times*, May 22, 2005, Arts and Leisure, 21–29; Folke T. Kihlsted, "A Bridge between Engineering and Architecture," in Jan Jennings, ed., *Roadside America: The Automobile in Design and Culture* (Ames: Iowa State University for the Society for Commercial Archeology, 1990), 10; Jane Holtz Kay, "A Brief History of Parking: From Main Street to Megastructures, and Back Again," *Architecture* (February 2001): 76–79.

24. Barbara Goldstein, "A Place in Santa Monica: Santa Monica Place," *Progressive Architecture* (July 1961): 84–89; "Santa Monica Place, Santa Monica, California, 1981," *GA Document*, no. 5 (1982): 82–87; "Santa Monica Place," *Architecture and Urbanism* (January 1982): 122–128; Gerald M. Trimble and Stuart L. Rogel, "Horton Plaza," *Urban Land* (July 1983): 15–19; Donald C. McElfresh, "Parking and the Investment Developer," *Parking* (April 1973): 21–23; "ULI's First Annual Award of Excellence Goes to the Galleria," *Urban Land* (November 1979): 10–13; Wolf, *Future of the City*, 120–121.

25. Urban Land Institute, *Mixed-Use Developments*, 104–109; Frank E. Jacob and Michael W. Seitz, "A Parking Garage, Mall and Office Complex," *American City* 84, no. 2 (August 1969): 108–109, 138.

26. "One Step from Car to Desk," *Parking* (Winter 1956): 33; Eric Owen Moss, "Parking Garage and Offices," *GA Document: Global Architecture* (May 2001): 74–79.

27. *Merriam-Webster's Collegiate Dictionary*, 11th ed. (Springfield, Mass.: Merriam-Webster, Inc., 2003); Adolf Behne, *The Modern Functional Building* (Santa Monica, Calif.: Getty Research Institute, 1996).

28. Paul Rudolph, *Architecture of Paul Rudolph* (New York: Praeger, 1970); "A Future," *Architectural Record* (February 1963): 145–150; Bernard P. Spring and Donald Canty, "Concrete: The Material That Can Do Almost Anything," *Architectural Forum* (September 1962): 89–90.

Notes

29. "Rudolph's Roman Road," *Architectural Forum* (February 1963): 104–109; "Landscaping to Give the Sense of a Hill," *L'architecture d'aujourd'hui* (October–November 1963): 34–37; Rico Cedro, *Modern Visions: Twentieth-Century Urban Design in New Haven* (New Haven, Conn.: City Art Gallery, 1988); air rights photographs, Oak Street Connector files, New Haven Colony Historical Society.

30. "Miami—The Magic City," *Between the Lines* (Winter 2003): 1–2; "Espirito Santo Plaza," www.espiritosantoplaza.com.

31. Jon T. Lang, *Creating Architectural Theory: The Role of the Behavioral Sciences in Environmental Design* (New York: Van Nostrand Reinhold, 1987), 137.

32. N.J. Slabbert, "John Dewey: Philosopher of Community," *Urban Land* (November–December 2006): 150–155.

Past Visions of the Future

1. Joseph J. Corn and Brian Horrigan, *Yesterday's Tomorrows: Past Visions of the American Future*, ed. Katharine Chambers (Baltimore: Johns Hopkins University Press, 1996), vii, 34.

2. Peter M. Wolf, *The Future of the City: New Directions in Urban Planning* (New York: Watson-Guptill, 1974), 20, 23, 26–27; Henry Harrison Suplee, "The Elevated Sidewalk," *Scientific American* (July 26, 1913): cover; Corn and Horrigan, *Yesterday's Tomorrows*, 40–43.

3. Robert Hughes, *Shock of the New* (New York: Knopf, 1981), 170–172; Wolf, *Future of the City*, 23; Reyner Banham, *Megastructure: Urban Futures of the Recent Past* (London: Thames and Hudson, 1976), 19.

4. Chicago History Museum, "Antecedents and Inspirations," Encyclopedia of Chicago, www.encyclopedia.chicagohistory.org; Cynthia R. Field, "Burnham Plan," Encyclopedia of Chicago, www.encyclopedia.chicagohistory.org; Chicago History Museum, "The Plan Comes Together," Encyclopedia of Chicago, www.encyclopedia.chicagohistory.org; Chicago History Museum, "Reading the Plan," Encyclopedia of Chicago, www.encyclopedia.chicagohistory.org; Chicago History Museum, "Infrastructure," www.encyclopedia.chicagohistory.org.

5. Wolf, *Future of the City*, 28; Folke T. Kihlsted, "A Bridge between Engineering and Architecture," in Jan Jennings, ed., *Roadside America: The Automobile in Design and Culture* (Ames: Iowa State University for the Society for Commercial Archeology, 1990), 10.

6. Le Corbusier, *The City of To-Morrow and Its Planning* (Mineola, N.Y.: Dover, 1987), 179.

7. Ian Tod and Michael Wheeler, *Utopia* (New York: Harmony Books, 1978), 126–147; Wolf, *Future of the City*, 24; Edmund N. Bacon, *Design of Cities* (New York: Viking, 1967), 214–227; Hughes, *Shock of the New*, 209–211.

Chapter 8

1. The definition of aesthetics—the study of beauty—as a theoretical or philosophical enterprise changes with time. Beauty's concrete expression in the visual realm—"an aesthetic"—also changes. Generally speaking, an aesthetic is a readable visual language that has identifiable characteristics and is connected to a specific time, place, and culture. An architectural aesthetic encompasses the inside and outside of a building and all the connections between structural, spatial, and visual form. Over time, some forms of architectural expression become codified and are given a name—and, in many cases, continue to be built long after the period in which they were created. Architectural styles can be thought of as brief, narrower expressions of a particular time and place; like fashion, they are constantly changing, and are not associated with the deeper visual meanings of an aesthetic. In the architectural world, mere adherence to style is commonly understood as a fleeting event and is not considered an enduring aesthetic approach. At its highest level, architecture seeks to define a new aesthetic, while maintaining a visual and experiential link to the past, present, and future.

2. Frank Lloyd Wright Foundation, www.frankloydwright.org.

3. Jennifer Harper, "In America, Form No Longer Follows Function," *Washington Times*, November 29, 2005.

4. P.M. Heldt, "The Garage Business—Buildings, Equipment, Methods," *Horseless Age* 36, no. 13 (December 1, 1915): 492–493.

5. Ibid.

6. "Editorial Comment and Selected Miscellany," *Brickbuilder* 18, no. 9 (September 1909): 232–233.

7. "White Company Garage in New York City," *Horseless Age* (May 4, 1910): 647; Albert Kahn, "Sales and Service Buildings, Garages and Assembly Plants," *Architectural Forum* (March 1927): 265, plate 49; *Brickbuilder* 15, no. 10 (1906): 214; Albert O. Larson, "An Analysis of Garage Design," *Architectural Forum* (March 1927): 212–216; Robert O. Derrick, "The City Parking Garage," *Architectural Forum* (March 1927): 233–239.

8. Harold Ellison, "First In North Carolina," *Parking* (Spring 1961): 27–31.

9. "The Capital Garage, Washington, D.C.," *American Architect* 121, no. 2522 (June 5, 1927): 761–763; Bob Wilkin-son, "End of an Era," *Parking* (January 1974): 16–17; "Going . . . Going . . . Gone," *Parking* (April 1974): 16.

10. Lynne Slack Shedlock, "Council Moving to Transfer Casey Parkway Ownership," *Times Shamrock*, June 4, 2004; Coney Island Lunch, "The Casey Garage Project," www.texas-wiener.com/garage_project.htm; Jim Wintermantle and Joan Sparrow, Scranton Parking Authority, discussions with author, May and June 2004.

11. William F. Wharton, "Architecture and Decoration of Automobile Show Rooms," *Architectural Forum* (March 1927): 305–312.

12. Ibid., 309.

13. "An Automobile Sales Building," *American Architect* (September 1918): 301–303; Kahn, "Sales and Service Buildings," 299–302; Wirt C. Rowland, "Architecture and the Automobile Industry," *Architectural Forum* (June 1921): 199–206; J.L. Snow, "The Brickbuilder Competition for a Public Garage, Automobile Sales and Service Building," supplement, *Brickbuilder* 22, no. 3 (March 1913); William Phillips Comstock, comp., *Garages and Motor Boat Houses* (New York: William T. Comstock Company, 1911), 63–69.

14. Ronald E. Schmitt, "The Ubiquitous Parking Garage: Worthy of Preservation?" (paper presented at Preserving the Recent Past 2, a conference sponsored by the National Park Service, Philadelphia, October 9–13, 2000), 2–194; Whitney Gould, "If You Can't Take the Garage Out of the City, Take the Ugly Out of the Garage," February 20, 2005, JSOnline, www.jsonline.com; Gordon Scholz, "Historic Art Deco Bus Depot in Downtown Lincoln Restored," *Newsletter of the Preservation Association of Lincoln, Nebraska* (Winter 1997): 12; "Concrete Proves Versatile for Ramp, Mechanical-Type Parking Facilities," *Parking* (Spring 1955): 18–23.

15. Unfortunately, the modernist vision of social equality through free and independent movement for all failed to address the thorny issue of what happens when the movement device is at rest. Although the parking garage may seem to have little to do with traffic or communication, it is actually the crucial element in a well-functioning movement system and is an integral part of American culture and society—not to mention the American landscape.

16. "Technical News and Research: Garages," *Architectural Record* (February 1929): 177–193.

17. Reyner Banham, *Theory and Design in the First Machine Age*, 2nd ed. (New York: Praeger, 1960), 40–41; "Notes from Paris," *Architectural Review* 24, no. 142 (September 1908): 136–138; Henry-Russell Hitchcock, *Architecture, Nineteenth and Twentieth Centuries* (New Haven: Yale University Press, 1987), 422–433; Peter Collins, *Concrete: The Vision of a New Architecture* (Montreal: McGill–Queen's University Press, 2004), 184–185; Vincent Scully, *Modern Architecture* (New York: Braziller, 1986), 23; Siegfried Giedion, *Space, Time and Architecture* (Cambridge, Mass.: Harvard University Press, 1956), 329; Karla Britton, *Auguste Perret* (New York: Phaidon, 2001), 20–21, 24; "Parking News," *Parking* (Fall 1962): 2.

18. "Parking News," *Parking* (Fall 1962): 2; International Parking Design, "IPD Wins IPI Awards," July 2005, www.ipd-global.com.

19. New codes for fire and ventilation also encouraged the disappearance of the facade.

20. "Garages Grow Up," *Architectural Forum* (February 1953): 120–123; James M. Hunnicutt, "Old Time Parking Garages," *Parking Professional* (August 1989): 26–29; "Evolution—What Is Past Is Prologue," *Parking* (Winter 1954): 18–20; "Pioneer Wall-Less," *Parking* (Summer 1954): 42.

21. Robert Maxwell, "The High Museum: Atlanta, Georgia," *AA Files* (September 1984): 73.

22. Anne Whiston Spirn, C. Ford Peatross, and Robert L. Sweeney, *Frank Lloyd Wright: Designs for an American Landscape, 1922–1932* (New York: Harry N. Abrams in association with the Canadian Centre for Architecture, the Library of Congress, and the Frank Lloyd Wright Foundation, 1996), 181; S. Frederick Starr, *Melnikov* (Princeton: Princeton Architectural Press, 1978), 103–107.

23. Highway Research Board, *Parking Principles*, Special Report 125, Subject Area 53 (Washington, D.C.: National Academy of Sciences, 1971), 109; John F. Hendon, "Private Enterprise in the Parking Field," *Urban Land* 9, no. 10 (November 1950): 1.

24. Soon after the Garage Rue de Ponthieu was constructed, Le Corbusier began to work in Auguste Perret's atelier.

25. Geoffrey H. Baker, *Le Corbusier: An Analysis of Form* (Wokingham, U.K.: Van Nostrand Reinhold, 1984), 141–159; Alan Colquhoun, "Displacements of Concepts in Le Corbusier," *Architectural Design* 43 (April 1972): 236.

26. Francesco Andreani, *Garages* (Milan: Gangemi Editore, 1997), 33–37.

27. Dietrich Klose, *Metropolitan Parking Structures; A Survey of Architectural Problems and Solutions* (New York: Praeger, 1965), 114–117.

28. Andreani, *Garages*, 45.

29. Klose, *Metropolitan Parking Structures*, 114–117; Geoffrey Baker and Bruno Fu-

naro, *Parking* (New York: Van Nostrand Reinhold, 1958), 133–135; "Parking News," *Parking* (Summer 1955): 4.

30. In the course of the 20th century, the shift from load-bearing walls to floors supported by columns and beams brought about the realization that the facade could float free of the building's structure. The new, non-load-bearing facades were called curtain walls.

31. "Concrete Lace Curtains for Walls," *Engineering News-Record* (June 6, 1940): 73–74; Frederick W. Cron, *The Man Who Made Concrete Beautiful* (Fort Collins, Colo.: Centennial Publications, 1977), 58.

32. William B. Foxhall, "Building Types Study: Airports," *Architectural Record* (October 1972): 127–142; "Airport Departures," *Architecture* (August 1993): 48; Klose, *Metropolitan Parking Structures*, 132–135, 168–169; "Low-Cost Garage Structure Shows Design Finesse," *Architectural Record* (January 1964): 164–166; "News in Photos," *Parking* (Winter 1960): 4.

33. "University Parking Garage," *Progressive Architecture* (December 1964): 151–154.

34. Klose, *Metropolitan Parking Structures*, 156–159; Albert C. Martin Jr., "Creative Prestressed Concrete Design Techniques in the Western United States," *PCI Journal* 9, no. 2 (April 1964): 58–62; Harvey L. Hurlburt, "A Fresh Idea in Parking-Structure Design," *American City* (December 1961): 80; Jacob Frank and Michael W. Seitz, "A Parking Garage, Mall and Office Complex," *American City* 84, no. 8 (August 1969): 108–109, 138; "Urban Parking Garages," *American City* (January 1970): 91; "Parking News," *Parking* (Winter 1967): 6.

35. Michael Brawn, "Parking Terminals," *Architectural Review* 128, no. 762 (August 1960): 124; "New Construction Technique," *Parking* (Summer 1955): 32–33; Klose, *Metropolitan Parking Structures*, 60–63; Baker and Funaro, *Parking*, 155–157.

36. Quoted in Barbara Miller Lane, *Architecture and Politics in Germany, 1918–1945* (Cambridge, Mass.: Harvard University Press, 1968), 131.

37. Lane, *Architecture and Politics*, 131. Emil Utitz and Paul Schultze-Naumburg, among others, began to voice criticism of the modernist aesthetic for the anonymous quality of its expression and for its reliance on abstract qualities that did not connect with the full range of human emotions.

38. John Dewey, *Art as Experience* (New York: Minton Balch, 1934), 176.

39. Penny Sparke, *An Introduction to Design and Culture in the Twentieth Century* (London: Allen and Unwin, 1986), xxi.

40. Thomas Smith, *The Aesthetics of Parking* (Chicago: American Planning Association, 1988), 26.

41. Although postmodern architecture attempted to revive some earlier architectural forms and approaches, these efforts were not always serious. Architecture is a complex combination of past forms and current ideas, materials, and building practices, and is always striving for new visions; thus, even "basic" issues, such as scale, are rooted in deeper concerns. But postmodern structures rarely explored such concerns. Instead, forms from the past were often presented playfully or ironically.

42. Heldt, "Garage Business," 492–493.

43. Blair Kamin, "Parking Places," *Chicago Tribune*, December 28, 2004.

44. "Category One: Award of Excellence," *Parking Professional* (August 2004): 18; Mat Jobin and Patrick Hager, "A New Architectural Jewel," *Parking Professional* (January 2007): 24–27; "Kansas City Downtown Library Book Bindings; Idea Awards, Bronze 2005, Environments," Business Week online, http://images.businessweek.com; "Library District Parking Garage," *Ascent* (Fall 2005): 36; Coreslab Structures, brochure for Coreslab.

45. "Los Angeles Has a 'Parking-Minded' Architect," *Parking* (Spring 1954): 48–49; Sam Nunes with Evan Reminick, "Breaking Out of the Box," *Parking Professional* (June 2000): 24–28.

46. Nick Watry, Watry Design, Inc., discussions with author, spring of 2001; John Morris, ed., *Urban Spaces* (New York: Visual Reference Publications, 1999), 269; Gordon H. Chong and Partners, *UC Davis Medical Center Parking Structure II, Sacramento, CA* (brochure).

47. Andrew J. Zekany, Ede Vessey, and William M. Bollinger, "Sarasota County Parking Garage," *PCI Journal* (May–June 1991): 34–39; "Design Secrets of Success: The Award-Winning Todos Santos Parking Center," *Parking* (May 2003): 17–21; Craig A. Shutt, "RTKL Focuses on Context, Social Interaction," *Ascent* (Winter 2005): 14.

48. "Parking News," *Parking* (Winter 1967): 6.

49. Greg Peterson, City of Omaha Planning Department, discussions with author, summer of 1992; "Category Two Award of Merit," *Parking Professional* (August 2002): 23; AGA Consultants, 2002 International Parking Conference and Exposition (brochures, June 2002). Omaha has an approach to parking that encourages good design; see Grace Shim, "A Pinch of Parking Pizzazz," *Omaha World-Herald Business*, October 18, 2001, D1–D2.

50. Laura Cerwinske, "South Beach: The Nation's Urban Laboratory for Parking Facility Design," *Parking Professional* (August 2001): 36–39; Bernard Zyscovich, "Parking or Urban Place Making?" *Multifamily Trends* (Spring 2004): 34–37.

51. "Clark Tower Parking Garage," *Parking* (January 1973): 29–31.

52. Barbara Goldstein, "Santa Monica Mall," *Progressive Architecture* (July 1981): 84–89; "The Play of Roles," *Domus* 620 (September 1981): 12–18; "Santa Monica Place," *GA Document* (January 1982): 82–87; "Santa Monica Place," *A&U* (January 1982): 122–128; Rita Fitzgerald and Richard Peiser, "Development (DIS)Agreements at Colorado Place," *Urban Land* (July 1988): 2–4; Neal I. Payton, "Architects Are Taking a Second Look at Parking Garages," *Parking* (May 1993).

53. Machado and Silvetti, "Scrim-Side Parking," *Progressive Architecture* (December 1992): 66–67.

54. Michael D. Beyard and W. Paul O'Mara, *Shopping Center Development Handbook*, 3rd ed. (Washington, D.C.: ULI—the Urban Land Institute, 1999), 120; McCarthy, *Parking Structures* (brochure).

55. David Firestone, "Critics Cry Foul on Sign for Atlanta Sports Arena," *New York Times*, August 26, 1999, National Report, A11; Julie B. Hairston, "Architect Wary of Garage Facade," *Atlanta Journal-Constitution*, September 2, 1999, JN2.

56. Audee Seeger, "Designer for One of the Country's Largest Garage Chains Offers a Solution to a Universal Problem," *Parking* (July 1970): 44–46; Desman Associates, "The Government Center Self-Park," July 22, 2005, www.desman.com/hotproperty/task,view/id,38/Itemid,189/.

57. Klose, *Metropolitan Parking Structures*, 226–228; Baker and Funaro, *Parking*, 81–87; Heather West, "Park Your Business Here," *Glass Magazine* (November 2005): 62–66.

58. Catherine Fox, "Charlotte's New Devotion to the Arts," *Atlanta Journal-Constitution*, January 9, 2000, L1; Becky Hannum, principal, ART Everywhere, e-mail exchanges with author, January 2006; Dennis Burns and Becky Hannum, "A New Canvas: Wayfinding Graphics and Art to Enhance Parking Facility Design," *Parking Professional* (April 2006): 44–47; John Van Horn, "Maritime Sound Created for New Haven's Long Wharf Garage," *Parking Today* (August 2002): 40–41. This project was commissioned by Lynn Fusco, the president of the corporation and a strong supporter of Janney's work.

59. "Art in a Parking Garage," *Parking Today* (March 2001): 38; "Arts in the Airport," *Parking Professional* (June 2001): 25.

60. Richard Hill, *Designs and Their Consequences: Architecture and Aesthetics* (New Haven: Yale University Press, 1999), 188.

61. John Burgan and Jeff Carlson, "Restored Parking Garage Benefits Milwaukee," *Parking Today* (June 2001): 8–10; Gould, "Take the Ugly Out."

62. Hill, *Architecture and Aesthetics*, 225.

63. Chong and Partners Architecture, marketing brochure (further information provided by Morgan Jones, marketing department, Chong and Partners).

64. Susan Broker, assistant city manager, City of Savannah, Chris Morrill and Jerry Lominack, Lominack Kolman Smith Architects, and others involved with the underground garage, discussions with author, November 2005; "Bryan Street Garage—Designing for Historical Districts," *Carl Walker Newsletter* (December 1997): 1–2; Yvonne Fortenberry and Eddie Bello, Department of Design, Development, and Preservation, Charleston, South Carolina, discussions with author, fall 2005; Bill Stephens, Parking Operations Division, Charleston, South Carolina, discussions with author, fall 2005.

65. Palladio Awards, "Parking Takes a Turn for the Better," 2002, www.traditional-building.com/Palladio.

66. Architects Hawaii, *Bankoh Parking Center, Honolulu, Hawaii* (brochure).

67. Mark A. Zelepsky, project manager, Walker Parking Consultants, Boston office, discussions with author; "Parking Structure Maintenance and Repair" (PowerPoint presentation, Build Boston conference, Boston, November 16–18, 1999); "Motor Mart in Boston Wins ICRI and IPI Awards," *Parking Today* 6, no. 1 (January 2001): 32; "2000 International Parking Awards, Category Four Award of Excellence," *Parking Professional* (August 2000): 29.

68. A garage in downtown Atlanta was converted for use by the University of Georgia, and a 1950s automated faculty in downtown Athens is now a condominium. These types of conversions can be found all over the country: see "Downtown Garage in Kansas City," *Parking* (Winter 1958): 23; "The City Quiz," *Chicago Tribune Magazine*, August 28, 2005, 8; "Preservation and Change in the Individual Building," *Architectural Record* (December 1974): 110–111.

69. Sally G. Oldham and H. Ward Jandl, "Francis Marion Hotel," *Urban Land* (March 1982): 9; LAObserved.com, "New L.A. Landmark," August 6, 2004, www.laobserved.com; Bob Pool, "Lofty Designation for a Downtown Garage," *Los Angeles Times*, August 7, 2004; Mary Beth Klatt, "Car Culture," Preservation Online, October 8, 2004, www.nationaltrust.org/magazine/archives/arch_story/100804.htm; "Lincoln Street Garage: Brian Healy Architects," *Architecture* (May 1998): 69.

70. Jamie Francisco, "Downtown Garage Built in 1918 Suited Model T's but Shows Age in Day of SUV's," *Chicago Tribune,* April 1, 2002; "City File," *Chicago Reader,* April 6, 2001, section 1, 6; Landmarks Illinois, "Chicagoland Watch List Archive, 2002–2006," www.landmarks.org/watch_list_archive.htm; "Loop's First Parking Garage Gets Landmark," *Parking Professional* (July 2002): 8–10; "Here and There among Garages and Salesrooms: Harry Newman's Scripps-Booth Establishment on Michigan Avenue," *Horseless Age* (February 15, 1916): 174; "News in Photos," *Parking* (Fall 1966): 2; "Historic Garage," *Parking* (April 1980): 33; "Preservation Notes: 225–265 Turk St. and 1601 Mission," *Heritage Newsletter* 19, no. 3 (Summer 1991): 5–6.

71. "Big Changes on the Horizon for New Haven's Downtown," *Yale ELIne* 5, no. 1 (September 2004).

72. As an example of one such ordinance, see Chicago Department of Planning and Development, Office of the Mayor, *A Guide to the Chicago Parking Garage Ordinance* (draft, July 11, 2001).

73. Aldo Rossi, *The Architecture of the City* (Cambridge, Mass.: MIT Press, 1982), 21.

74. The increasing size of the automobile has only intensified concerns about proportion and scale; one can only hope that the trend toward ever-larger vehicles will eventually reverse.

75. Paul O'Mara, "Rutabagas and Real Estate: Facadomy," *Urban Land* (September 1983): 36–37.

76. C.C. Sullivan, "Decks and Context," *Building Design and Construction* (March 1, 2001); C.C. Sullivan, "Technology for City Cars," *Building Design and Construction* (March 1, 2001); C.C. Sullivan, "Parking Panacea," *Building Design and Construction* (March 1, 2001); Roger K. Lewis, "Aesthetics Need Not Take a Back Seat in Public Garage Design," *Washington Post,* January 6, 2007, F14.

77. Sullivan, "Decks and Context"; Sullivan, "Technology for City Cars"; Sullivan, "Parking Panacea."

78. Herbert Muschamp, "A Happy, Scary New Day for Design," *New York Times,* October 15, 2000, AR39A.

79. The parking garage should definitely be included in the Infrastructure Beautiful movement; see Fred A. Bernstein, "In My Backyard, Please: The Infrastructure Beautiful Movement," *New York Times,* February 27, 2005, Architecture section, 37; Blair Kamin, "Parking Places," *Chicago Tribune,* December 28, 2004; Christopher Knight, "Intersection of Car and Camera," *Los Angeles Times,* September 17, 2004, E1–E26, E27.

80. Oliver Boissiere, *Jean Nouvel* (Boston: Birkhauser, 1996), 163–165; the Fondation Cartier, www.fondation.cartier.fr/flash.html; Watry Design, Inc., *Stanford University Medical Center Parking Structure 4* (brochure); "Haar-Win Parking Helps Beautify Baltimore," *Parking* (Spring 1957): 32–33; Howard Kozloff, "The Destruction of Memory: Architecture at War," *Urban Land* (November–December 2006); Keith Schneider, "Making a Parking Garage Look Nicer Than a Parking Garage," *New York Times,* October 26, 2005.

Frank Lloyd Wright and Parking

1. Ann Whiston Spirn, C. Ford Peatross, and Robert L. Sweeney, *Frank Lloyd Wright: Designs for an American Landscape, 1922–1932* (New York: Harry N. Abrams in association with the Canadian Centre for Architecture, the Library of Congress, and the Frank Lloyd Wright Foundation, 1996), 82–100; Bruce Brooks Pfeiffer, ed., *Frank Lloyd Wright Collected Writings* (New York: Rizzoli; Frank Lloyd Wright Foundation, 1992), 136–137; Steve Thompson, "The Wright Stuff," *Autoweek,* May 26, 1997, 22–23; Library of Congress, Exhibitions, "Frank Lloyd Wright, Designs for an American Landscape, 1922–1932," http://lcweb.loc.gov/exhibits/flw/flw01.html.

2. Reyner Banham, *Megastructure: Urban Futures of the Recent Past* (London: Thames and Hudson, 1976), 41; Pfeiffer, *Wright Collected Writings,* 165; Bruno Zevi, *Frank Lloyd Wright* (Bologna, Italy: Zanichelli Editore, 1979), 142–147.

3. Justin Davidson, "Wright's Lofty Dreams: Exhibit Shows the Suburban Genius Had Rarefied Hopes for Cities, Too," *Newsday,* October 6, 2004, B04; Pfeiffer, *Wright Collected Writings,* 153, 192, 251, 260–261.

4. Pfeiffer, *Wright Collected Writings,* 115–118, 120–121, 202, 258, 263, 318; "Frank Lloyd Wright's Mile-High Rise," *New York Times,* October 17, 2004, 31.

Lee, Smith & Vandervoort

1. Lee J. Eastman, "The Parking Garage Merits Encouragement as an Important Factor in Traffic Relief," *American City* 40, no. 1 (January 1929): 156–157; Thomas Earl Larose, "Babylon South: The Building of the Richmond Loew's Theater and the Richmond Garage, 1925–1928," *Arris* 13 (2002): 55–71; Italo William Ricciuti, "Garages and Service Stations," in *Building Types,* vol. 4 of *Forms and Functions of Twentieth-Century Architecture,* ed. Talbot Hamlin (New York: Columbia University Press, 1952), 615–621.

2. "Technical News and Research: Garages," *Architectural Record* (February 1929): 177–193.

3. "Garages," 178. (The quotation within the quotation was not sourced in the original article.)

4. Greg Will, "Community Development Authority Kicks Poor Off Broad Street," *Richmond Independent Media Center,* July 7, 2003.

Portland, Oregon: Art for the Parking Garage

1. Many thanks to Casey Jones, City of Portland, and Peggy Kendellen, public arts manager, Regional Arts and Culture Council of Portland, for providing both information and images for this feature box.

2. Theron R. Howser, "A Plan for a City Built to Fit the Automobile," *American City* (July 1934): 56–57; Ralph Kadderly, "Portland Parking-Privately-Progressively," *Parking* (Spring 1955): 37.

3. Frank Coffey and Joseph Layden, *America on Wheels* (Los Angeles: General Publishing Group, 1996), 290; National Trust for Historic Preservation, "Old Town Parking Garage," Solutions Database, September 30, 1998, www.nthp.org/preserve_link; John Morris Dixon, *Urban Spaces No. 2* (New York and Washington, D.C.: Visual Reference Publications; ULI–the Urban Land Institute, 2001), 98–99; Urban Land Institute, "Fourth & Yamhill Parking Garage," Project Reference File 20, no. 18 (October–December 1990); Melvin B. Meyer, "Eighth Annual IMPC Awards," *Parking Professional* (September 1990): 21.

Charleston, South Carolina: Revitalization through Parking

1. Yvonne Fortenberry and Eddie Bello, Department of Design, Development, and Preservation, Charleston, South Carolina, discussions with author, fall 2005; Bill Stephens, Parking Operations Division, Charleston, South Carolina, discussions with author, Fall 2005; Pinckney Seabrook Wilkinson, "Our Own Desert Places: Charleston's Parking Garages," *Charleston City Guardian,* May 2003, 9.

2. "Building on Success: The Pride of Joseph P. Riley, Jr.," ULI J.C. Nichols Prize for Vision in Urban Development, www.uli.org; David Slade, "Loan," *Post and Courier,* November 21, 2001, 11A; Robert A. Weant and Herbert S. Levinson, *Parking* (Westport, Conn.: Eno Foundation for Transportation, 1990), 133, 183.

3. Robert Gehre, "Opening of 'Garage Mahal' Nears," *Post and Courier,* April 11, 1995, 17A.

Chapter 9

1. "Traffic Regulation through the Centuries," *American City* (December 1931): 97–98; "How Traffic Regulation in Paris Is Being Revolutionized by an American," *American City* (January 1914): 41; William Phelps Eno, *Street Traffic Regulation* (New York: Rider and Driver Publishing, 1909), 62–63; Milo R. Maltbie, "Transportation and City Planning," *American City* (October 1928): 586–590; Miller McClintock, "Parking—When, Where and Why?" *American City* (April 1924): 360; "The Historic Cambridge Common and the Automobile Parking Problem," *American City* (August 1928): 132; Paul Barrett, *The Automobile and Urban Transit: The Formation of Public Policy in Chicago, 1900–1930* (Philadelphia: Temple University Press, 1983), 135; McClintock, "Parking," 361; G. Gordon Whitnall, "No Parking of Autos," *American City* (May 1920): 484; Thomas P. Smith, *The Aesthetics of Parking: An Illustrated Guide,* Planning Advisory Service Report Number 411 (Chicago: American Planning Association, 1988), 2; "Where Shall They Park?" *American City* (March 1928): 130. Because autos were not yet dependable under all weather conditions, abandoned vehicles also contributed to the crowding on the streets.

2. Robert H. Whitten, "Unchoking Our Congested Streets," *American City* 23, no. 4 (October 1920): 353.

3. Whitten, "Congested Streets," 354.

4. Daniel L. Turner, "Is There a Vicious Circle of Transit Development and City Congestion?" *American City Magazine* (September 1926): 314–315; F.W. Fenn, "Transportation: The Keynote of Prosperity," *American City* 23, no. 12 (December 1920): 598–599; "Highways Taking the Place of Railway Tracks," *American City* 18, no. 6 (December 1917): 504.

5. Maltbie, "City Planning," 569–590; Nelson Lewis, "The Automobile and the City Plan," *American City* (July 1916): 80–81; "Raised Sidewalks and Traffic Separation Urged for Chicago," *American City Magazine* (September 1926): 334–336.

6. Peter Geoffrey Hall, *Cities of Tomorrow* (Oxford, U.K.: Blackwell Publishers, 1988), 276.

7. Fenn, "Transportation," 598–599.

8. "The Parked Car as a Community Expense," *American City* 40, no. 2 (February 1929): 133.

9. Harold W. Slauson, "Two Suggestions for Relief of Municipal Traffic Congestion," *American City* 29, no. 10 (October 1923): 421.

10. "Motor Carriages Excluded from Boston Parks between 10:30 A.M. and 9 P.M.," *Horseless Age* 3, no. 12 (March 1899): 7. Prohibitions on parking and on automobile access appeared periodically in many cities and can still be found today.

11. G. Gordon Whitnall, "No Parking of Autos," *American City* (May 1920): 484; Catherine G. Miller, *Carscape: A Parking Handbook* (Columbus, Ind.: Published for the Irwin-Sweeney-Miller Foun-

dation by Washington Street Press, 1988), 10.

12. A.L.H. Street, "The City's Legal Rights and Duties," *American City Magazine* (December 1928): 667–669.

13. By the mid-1920s, there was a great deal of discussion about what traffic surveys should include; see J. Rowland Bibbins, "Thinking Ahead for the Relief of Street Traffic Congestion," *American City Magazine* (March 1924): 302–303.

14. Slauson, "Municipal Traffic Congestion," 421.

15. "To Park or Not to Park," *American City* 35, no. 4 (October 1926): 461–462.

16. Ibid.

17. "Parking Regulations," *American City* (February 1929): 139–140; "New Type of Suburban Shopping Area Proposed," *American City* (August 1926): 214–216; "Consolidated Delivery Service: Storage Garages—Decentralization," *American City* (October 1926): 463; "To Park or Not to Park," 461–462; Hugh E. Young, "Day and Night Storage and Parking of Motor Vehicles," *American City* (July 1923): 44–46.

18. Miller also championed traffic control; uniform traffic codes; the use of streets around the clock; grade separation; superhighways (which, by the mid-1920s, when Miller was writing, already existed in three cities); visionary solutions, such as tunneling under the Hudson River; and a change in public psychology. See Miller McClintock, "Remedies for Traffic Congestion," *Society of Automotive Engineering* 23, no. 5 (November 1928): 443–446; and McClintock, "Parking," 360–361.

19. "50 Years . . . and Still Ticking," *Parking Professional* (October 1984): 7–10; McClintock, "Parking," 361; "Son of the Father of Parking Meters," *American City* (December 1949): 137; O.M. Mosher, "Our Experience with Parking Meters," *American City* (January 1936): 97; C.G. Beckenbach, "Dallas Installs 1,000 Parking Meters," *American City* (January 1936): 95; "A Promising Solution of the Parking Problem," *American City* (August 1936): 59; "Meter Revenue Builds Parking Garages," *American City* (February 1969): 142; "Our Municipal Notebook," *American City* (November 1936): 7; "Parking Meters," *Urban Land* (April 1953): 6.

20. Theodore M. Matson, "Who Takes the Initiative in Parking and Truck-Loading Facilities?" *American City* (November 1948): 143; "APCOA's 666 Garage in Downtown Cleveland," *Parking* (April 1970): 33–34.

21. Whitten, "Congested Streets," 354.

22. Hall, *Cities of Tomorrow*, 110, 277.

23. Whitten, "Congested Streets," 352; "Rapid Transit, Street Cars, Busses and Private Automobiles," *American City* (October 1928): 112; Barrett, *Public Policy in Chicago*, 161; "Cleveland Seeking to Untangle Traffic," *American City* (December 1916): 702; "New York to Have a $13,500,000 Elevated Express Highway," *American City* 35, no. 7 (July 1926): 8–10.

24. Barrett, *Public Policy in Chicago*, 163.

25. Ibid.

26. "Ultimate Remedies for the Traffic Problem," *American City* (July 1929): 135–136.

27. Quoted in Frank Coffey and Joseph Layden, *America on Wheels* (Los Angeles: General Publishing Group, 1996), 290.

28. "Philadelphia's Parking-Riding Plan Extended," *American City* (July 1926): 7; Leon R. Brown, "Suburban Parking Stations, with Street-Car or Limited Bus Service, as Aids in Solving Parking and Traffic Problems," *American City* 40, no. 2 (February 1929): 81–82; "For All-Day Parkers," *American City* (October 1946): 131; G.J. MacMurray, "Parking Places at Electric Railway Stations Help to Relieve Downtown Congestion," *American City* (December 1930): 142.

29. Walter Jackson, "Why Give the Streets Away When Public Transport Is Available?" *American City Magazine* (October 1926): 463.

30. Turner, "Vicious Circle," 314–315.

31. John A. Beeler, *Report to the City of Atlanta on a Plan for Local Transportation* (New York: Foote and Davies, 1927).

32. Turner, "Vicious Circle," 315; Jas R. Bachman, "An Unusual Report on Local Traffic and Transportation Problems," *American City Magazine* (February 1925): 148–149.

33. Charles Gordon, "A Modern City's Transportation Needs," *American City* (November 1944): 99–101.

34. Ibid., 99–101.

35. "What about Parking?" *American City* (November 1945): 139; Wolfgang Sachs, *For Love of the Automobile* (Berkeley: University of California Press, 1992), 87; "Providing Parking Spaces in Downtown Business Districts," *American City* (June 1945): 135; "Studies: Let's Get the Facts," *Parking* (Spring 1954): 28–29; "A Parking Resolution," *American City* (December 1940): 99; "Logical Relief of Downtown Congestion," *American City* (March 1948): 133–134; Philip E. Geissal, "Kansas City Sees Expressways Preventing 1970 Traffic Jams," *American City* (March 1952): 141–142; "Expressways and Off-Street Parking," *Urban Land* 10, no. 4 (April 1951): 2; "Freeways and Parking," *Parking* (Spring 1961): 38–39; Donald H. Olson, "Parking Ramps on Air Rights over Freeways," *Parking* (Spring 1968): 17–19; Herman E. Olson,

"Cities Must Deal with Transit," *American City* (December 1943): 93; John J. Hassett, "Mass Transit and Private Parking Have Same Aims," *Parking* (Fall 1953): 38–41; Harry C. Koch, "Finance Transit!" *American City* (March 1939): 99–103; William R. McConochie, "Freeways Can Save Urban Transit," *Urban Land* 16, no. 8 (1957): 1–5; "Thirty-Three Cities Have Municipal Transit Systems," *American City* (October 1946): 129; "Metropolitan Transit Authority Proposed for Chicago," *American City* (March 1945): 113; "Program for Improved Transit and Parking," *American City* (September 1945): 147; G.W. Wilson, "Good Transit Makes Cities More Liveable," *American City* (March 1946): 123; G.J. MacMurray, "Parking Places at Electric Railway Stations Help to Relieve Downtown Congestion," *American City* (December 1930): 142; Carl L. Gardner, "Blighted Vacant Land," *Urban Land* 9, no. 8 (1950): 1, 3–5; "Potential Blight," *Urban Land* 11, no. 10 (October 1943): 1; "Visualized Proposal for Rebuilding a Kansas City Blighted Area," *Urban Land* 11, no. 6 (June 1943): 1; "Moving People," *Urban Land* 13, no. 11 (December 1954): 1–8; Boyd Barnard, "A Business Man Looks at Transit," *Urban Land* 14, no. 10 (November 1955): 1–6; Gordon, "Transportation Needs," 99, 101; "Transportation Plans," *American City* (September 1944): 119; "Cartoons Dramatize Need for Regional Cooperation," *American City* (April 1947): 123; George W. Anderson, "Let's Make Room for Everybody," *Parking* (Spring 1954): 22–23; "Parking in the Bay Area," *Parking* (Fall 1957): 19–22; Ernest B. Goodrich, "Traffic Planning for the Motor Age," *American City* (February 1930): 173.

36. "Great Municipal Garages Advocated to Relieve Street Congestion," *American City* (January 1928): 139.

37. Herbert S. Swan, "Our City Thoroughfares—Shall They Be Highways or Garages?" *American City* 27, no. 6 (December 1922): 496–300; "Will It Come to This?" *American City Magazine* (January 1926): 45 (cartoon); "Where Do We Park?" *American City* (December 1928): 19.

38. McClintock, "Parking," 361; Robert H. Nau, "No Parking—A Year and More of It," *American City* 40, no. 3 (March 1929): 85–88; "How Many Shoppers Park Autos in Streets?" *American City* (February 1928): 163; "Traffic Congestion, Parking Facilities, and Retail Business—II," *American City* (July 1926): 62–65; "Devouring the Parking Problem," *American City* (December 1939): 65; Barrett, *Public Policy in Chicago*, 162.

39. Will Rogers, *Will Rogers' Weekly Articles*, ed. James M. Smallwood and Steven K. Gragert (Stillwater: Oklahoma State University Press, 1980). The comment

appeared in Rogers's column on January 6, 1924.

40. Some cities, including Boston, wanted to abolish automobile parking entirely, as a fire-protection measure. Concern about the relationship between fire and parking continued well into the 1940s; see "Abolition of Automobile Parking in Downtown Boston as a Fire Protection Measure," *Urban Land Institute Bulletin* (December 1942): 2.

41. Ernest Goodrich, "The Place of the Garage in City Planning," *Architectural Record* (February 1929): 198.

42. McClintock, "Parking," 361.

43. "Off Street Loading Facilities and Hotel Garages Recommended for Business Districts," *American City* 41, no. 3 (September 1929): 133; "Garage Men Protest against '50-Foot Rule' in New York," *Horseless Age* 35, no. 4 (January 27, 1915): 138; Nau, "No Parking," 85–88; Lee J. Eastman, "The Parking Garage Merits Encouragement as an Important Factor in Traffic Relief," *American City* 40, no. 1 (January 1929): 156–157.

44. "Bluefield Makes Money on Municipal Parking Building," *American City* (October 1949): 139; Joseph Nathan Kane, Steven Anzouin, and Janet Podell, *Famous First Facts: A Record of First Happenings, Discoveries, and Inventions in American History*, 5th ed. (New York: Wilson, 1997), 387.

45. "The City's Legal Rights and Duties: Municipal Buildings," *American City* (1936): 103; K. Vaughan-Birch, "Adequate Parking a Municipal Utility," *American City* (November 1949): 135; "Arguments against Municipal Ownership of Off-Street Parking," *Urban Land* 10, no. 1 (January 1951): 6; William G. Barr, "Private vs. Municipal Parking," *Parking* (Winter 1965): 10–11; "Buffalo Exempts Parking Facilities from Taxes," *American City* (February 1953): 143; "Parking Garages Tax-Exempt in Syracuse," *American City* (July 1954): 119; "New Garage Construction in Minneapolis," *American City* (February 1951): 145; "Ann Arbor Close to Sufficient Parking Facilities," *American City* (December 1951): 12; "Minnesota Authorizes Creation of Central Business District Authorities to Operate Downtown Parking and Transportation Systems," *Urban Land Institute Bulletin* 2, no. 5 (May 1943): 4; "17 Parking Garages for Baltimore, Md.," *American City* (July 1943): 143; "Parking Plan to Restore Baltimore's Downtown Values," *American City* (April 1946): 127; "City Loans for Parking Garages," *Urban Land* 9, no. 10 (November 1950): 2; "Parking Clinic in Kansas City," *Urban Land* 5, no. 9 (October 1946): 1, 3–4; David R. Levin, "Needed: Better Enabling Laws on Parking Facilities," *American City* (February 1947): 113; "More Cities Construct Parking Garages," *Urban Land* (May–

June 1951): 6; "What Cities Are Doing about Parking Facilities," *American City* (October 1946): 129; "Which Big Cities Are Most Traffic-Conscious?" *American City* (October 1947): 135, 137.

46. S.A. Carrighar, "Built Down Instead of Up: The Union Square Garage, San Francisco," *Architect and Engineer* (August 1942): 19–29; Thomas Smith, *The Aesthetics of Parking* (Chicago: American Planning Association, 1988), 38; Dietrich Klose, *Multi-Storey Car Parks and Garages* (New York: Praeger Architectural Press, 1965): 46–47, 172–191; Geoffrey Baker and Bruno Funaro, *Parking* (New York: Van Nostrand Reinhold, 1958), 60–63, 142–144; "Shall Motor-Cars Be Parked Underground?" *American City* 44, no. 1 (January 1931): 133; "San Francisco Builds a Garage under a Park," *American City* 57, no. 11 (November 1942): 66; "First Downtown Underground Garage Reverts to City," *Urban Land* 20, no. 3 (March 1961): 8; Lisa Findley, "San Francisco Union Square Opens after Redesign to Enhance Public Space," *Architectural Record* (November 2002): 38; "San Francisco Has Parking Authority," *Urban Land* 8, no. 11 (December 1949): 6. So that the Union Square Garage could also serve as a wartime shelter, the U.S. Army assisted in planning the facility. The pattern of public/private cooperation in the development of an underground garage was successfully repeated in Boston's Post Office Square project: see "Friends of Post Office Square," *Parking* (May 1995): 38–43 (reprinted from *ULI Project Reference File* 4, no. 3, 1994); Charity Brown, "Park Above, Park Below," *Parking* (May 1991): 44–50; "One Post Office Square," *ULI Project Reference File* 13, no. 9.

47. Joseph H. Hughes, "Mammoth City-Owned Metered Parking Lots," *American City* (June 1950): 153; William J. Deegan Jr. and Parker Webb, "The Quincy Story," *Urban Land* (March 1955): 1, 3, 4–6; "Rochester's Nine Parking Lots All Metered," *American City* (December 1949): 135; "Municipal Parking Lots Metered in 28 Cities," *American City* 64, no. 8 (August 1949): 16; "Rochester's Parking Program," *Urban Land* 8, no. 8 (September 1949): 1, 3–4; William A. Kennedy, "4,500 Cars Use 216-Car Lot in a Day," *American City* (January 1951): 125; "New York City to Buy First 1,500 Parking Meters," *American City* (June 1951): 135; "Hackensack Untangles Its Business District," *American City* (April 1951): 159; "Municipal Ownership of Off-Street Parking," *Urban Land* 10, no. 1 (1951): 2; L.M. Lovejoy, "Courtesy Nickel in Gordon, Neb.," *American City* (June 1952): 153; Francis A. Murray, "Two Meters per Post at Summit's New Lot," *American City* (March 1950): 143, 145; "Parking Meters Are Just an Aspirin Not a Cure," *Urban Land* (July 21, 1941): 2; John F. Hendon, "Private Enterprise in

the Parking Field," *Urban Land* 9, no. 10 (November 1950): 3–5; "Municipal Programs for Off-Street Parking Facilities," *Urban Land* 8, no. 9 (October 1949): 1–4.

48. "Parking Jam," *Architectural Forum* 85 (September 1946): 8–10.

49. Ibid., 10.

50. Theodora Kimball Hubbard and Henry Vincent Hubbard, "It Pays to Plan," *American City* 41, no. 4 (October 1929): 85–86.

51. C.B. Horrall, "Everybody Is Solving It," *American City* (August 1947), 111; "Stop Fooling with the Parking Problem," *American City* (December 1949): 133; "Retraction: The Ann Arbor Story," *Parking* (Fall 1953): 26; "What Can Be Done to Conserve and Revitalize Our Downtown Business Areas?" *Urban Land* 4, no. 9 (October 1945): 1; "Plan for Rebuilding Part of Los Angeles," *Urban Land Institute Bulletin* 2, no. 5 (May 1943): 1; "The Cost of Wichita's Growth," *Urban Land* 2, no. 8 (August 1943): 1; "Is Your City Tired of Congestion?" *American City* (October 1954): 153. Parking continues to be a core element in revitalizing Ann Arbor: see David M. Feehan, "A Tale of Three Cities: Ann Arbor, Battle Creek and Kalamazoo Are Proving Downtowns Can Be Revitalized," *Parking* (October 1993): 26–30.

52. The first Urban Land Community Builders Institute handbook, prepared by the ULI Community Builders Council to assist in planning parking and mixed-use projects, also came out in 1947; see Community Builders Council of the Urban Land Institute, *The Community Builders Handbook* (Washington D.C.: ULI–the Urban Land Institute, 1947), 110–115.

53. "Automatic Parking Garage," *Architectural Forum* (February 1951): 108.

54. "Automobile Storage Facilities in Chicago's Business District," *American City* (March 1937): 109; Milton C. Mumford, "A Review of the Parking Problem," *Urban Land* (June 1947): 1–4; "Parking Plan for Chicago," *Urban Land* 9, no. 6 (June 1950): 4; George Hansen, ed., *Parking: How It Is Financed* (New York: National Dry Goods Association, 1952); "Big-Time Parking on the Increase," *American City* (August 1951): 137; David R. Levin, "The Effectiveness of Parking Agencies" (paper presented at the 31st annual meeting of the Highway Research Board, January 17, 1952).

55. Ralph Kadderly, "Portland Parking Privately Progressively," *Parking* (Spring 1955): 37.

56. "Self Park Structure for Dallas," *Parking* (Spring 1963): 24; "Report," *Parking* (Winter 1955): 8, 30–31.

57. Harry Vaughan, "Parking Gains Status: Now Regarded as Major Urban Problem," *Nation's Cities* (February 1966): 12–13.

58. "And This from Los Angeles," *American City Magazine* (September 1926): 315.

59. Lewis, "City Plan," 80–81; "Pioneers in Parking: Max Goldberg . . . Had Faith in Free Enterprise," *Parking* (Winter 1954): 11–12; "Free Parking Space for Kansas City," *American City* (December 1924): 588; Hal Burton, *The City Fights Back* (New York: Citadel, 1954); Paul C. Petrillo, "The Case against Banning the Car in the Central Business District," *Parking* (January 1973): 8–21.

60. "Hospitality to Parkers," *American City* (December 1937): 91; "Educating Newark Shoppers to Parking Garages," *American City* (January 1930): 155; "Pioneers in Parking," *Parking* (Spring 1955): 11–12; William G. Barr, "Executive Director Reports 'It Can Be Contagious,'" *Parking* (Winter 1960): 5–7; Norene Dann Martin, "Park and Shop in 1968: Case Histories," *Parking* (Winter 1969): 16–29; "What's New in Park and Shop," *Parking* (Fall 1958): 28–41; Don Jones, "Downtown Park and Shop," *Parking* (Summer 1959): 32–33; "Park and Shop, Ride and Shop," *Parking* (Summer 1960): 56–63; "Allentown's Parking Program Nears Completion," *Parking* (Winter 1959): 32–34; "Fargo Inaugurates Ride-Park-Shop," *Parking* (Winter 1959): 36–37; "Park 'N Ride in Rhode Island," *Parking* (Winter 1955): 34–35; "Sioux City Park and Shop," *Parking* (Fall 1955): 8–9; "Parking Sidelines," *Parking* (Fall 1954): 40. The idea of discounting parking resurfaced in the years following Word War II, when dying downtowns had a surplus of vacant lots. Of course, the practice of "parking validation"—a stamp on the back of a parking garage ticket that entitles a shopper to free or discounted parking—continues to this day.

61. "Our Municipal Notebook," *American City* (March 1939): 7.

62. Charles T. Stewart, "The Rationing of Automobiles, Tires, and Gasoline Is Expanding Municipal Ownership of Public Transportation," *Urban Land Institute News Bulletin* (August 1942): 4; "Publicly Owned Motor Vehicles in the United States," *American City* (December 1939): 64–65; Alfred G. Ivey, "Turns a Fumble into a Touchdown," *American City* (September 1954): 127–128.

63. Hendon, "Private Enterprise," 3–5; William G. Barr, "Downtown America Is Being 'Planned to Death,'" *Parking* (Winter 1961): 6–7; William G. Barr, "Let's Get the Facts," *Parking* (Winter 1959): 15–19; William G. Barr, "Executive Director's Report: Private vs. Municipal Parking," *Parking* (Winter 1965): 10–11; "Legal Aspects of Municipal Park-

ing Facilities," *American City* (September 1941): 93.

64. "Sioux City Park and Shop," 8–9; "Parking Sidelines," 40; Barton-Aschman Associates, Inc., "Parking Demand at the Regionals," *Urban Land* (May 1977): 3–11.

65. William G. Barr, "On-Street Parking," *Parking* (Spring 1959): 16–17; "Are Your Streets Overloaded? . . . Use These Charts," *American City* (June 1950): 151.

66. *Urban Land* 9, no. 3 (March 1950): cover; Community Builders Council of the Urban Land Institute, *Community Builders Handbook*, 110–115; "Meters Buy Seven Parking Lots in Visalia," *American City* (November 1949): 135–136; "Parking News: Removal of Meters," *Parking* (October 1970): 4; Herbert B. Kimzey, "How Not to Install Parking Meters," *American City* (February 1951): 145; E.R. Drucker, *Parking in Urban Centres* (Ottawa, Canada: Accredited Mortgage and Investment Corporation, 1973), 32–33.

67. "Parking: The Crisis Is Downtown," *Architectural Forum* 118 (February 1963): 100–103.

68. Richard C. Rich, "Planning a Downtown Parking Deck," *Urban Land* (October 1965): 6; Ronald J. Lenney, "Private Parking Facilities Needed," *Parking* (July 1972): 51–53.

69. Rico Cedro, *Modern Visions: Twentieth-Century Urban Design in New Haven* (New Haven, Conn.: City Art Gallery, 1988): 17. An article published years earlier in *The American City* took very much the same view: "Street traffic is the life-blood of a city. The city's pulse can best be watched by checking periodically the flow of traffic. In what better manner can we reduce congestion and prevent hardening of the arteries than by keeping close check on the movement of this life-blood?" See "Effect of Street Widening on Traffic Flow," *American City* (November 1929): 169.

70. Allan R. Talbot, *The Mayor's Game* (New York: Harper and Row, 1967), 88.

71. Hall, *Cities of Tomorrow*, 230–231; Paul Rudolph, *Architecture of Paul Rudolph* (New York: Praeger, 1970); "A Future," *Architectural Record* (February 1963): 145–150; Bernard P. Spring and Donald Canty, "Concrete: The Material That Can Do Almost Anything," *Architectural Forum* (September 1962): 89–90; "Rudolph's Roman Road," *Architectural Forum* (February 1963): 104–109; "Landscaping to Give the Sense of a Hill," *L'architecture d'aujourd'hui* (October–November 1963): 34–37; Cedro, *Modern Visions*; air rights photographs, Oak Street Connector files, New Haven Colony Historical Society; Peter M. Wolf, *The Future of the City: New Directions in Urban Planning* (New York: Watson-

Guptill, 1974), 50. Even though the size of the Temple Street facility was ultimately cut in half (which meant that it did not connect directly to the expressway), the cost of the garage was twice what would have been budgeted for a typical municipal garage offering the same number of spaces.

72. "Restructuring Philadelphia," *Parking* (July 1976): 18–21; Louis I. Kahn, "Toward a Plan for Midtown Philadelphia," *Perspecta* 2 (1953): 10–27; "The Gallery," *ULI Project Reference File* 8, no. 4 (February 1978): 21; Edmund N. Bacon, *Design of Cities* (New York: Viking, 1967), 243–271.

73. Tom Barnes, "New Parking Garages May Lure More Visitors," *Pittsburgh Post-Gazette*, December 31, 2000, business section; "Fringe Parking on Way Out," *American City* (December 1949): 137; George W. Anderson, "Let's Make Room for Everybody," *Parking* (Spring 1954): 22–23.

74. Beeler, *Report to Atlanta*, 83; Bachman, "Traffic and Transportation Problems," 148–149. Interestingly, although Eugene Henard foresaw subways and elevated expressways, he did not anticipate today's pervasive parking lots.

75. "Raised Sidewalks," 334–336; R. Stephen Sennott, "Chicago Architects and the Automobile, 1906–26," in Jan Jennings, ed., *Roadside America: The Automobile in Design and Culture* (Ames: Iowa State University for the Society for Commercial Archeology, 1990), 162–165.

76. "Proposed Plan to Relieve Traffic Congestion in St. Paul and Provide Parking Space for 3,000 Automobiles," *American City* (April 1928): 87.

77. William F. Streich, "A Plan for Multiplying the Utility of Business Thoroughfares," *American City* (March 1913): 275–276; Hall, *Cities of Tomorrow*, 156–159, 164–166; Nolan S. Black and Wilfred V. Casgrain, *A Plan for the Construction of Underground Mechanical Garages in Downtown Detroit* (Detroit, 1930), 1–10; "Shall Motor-Cars Be Parked Underground?" *American City* 44, no. 1 (January 1931): 133. Although the mechanized facilities proposed by Black and Casgrain were not constructed, underground ramp garages were eventually constructed in the same locations.

78. Chip Lord and Ant Farm, *Autoamerica: A Trip Down U.S. Highways from World War II to the Future; A Book* (New York: Dutton, 1976), 91.

79. Theron R. Howser, "A Plan for a City Built to Fit the Automobile," *American City* (July 1934): 56–57; Wolf, *Future of the City*, 26–28.

80. Harvey Wiley Corbett, "Different Levels for Foot, Wheel, and Rail," *American City* (July 1924): 2–6; Harvey Wiley Corbett, "The Problem of Traffic Con-

gestion, and a Solution," *Architectural Forum* (March 1927): 202–208; "Raised Sidewalks," 334–336; Wolf, *Future of the City*, 27.

81. "Arena for the Auto Age," *Architectural Forum* 115 (October 1960): 98–100; John B. Rae, *The Road and the Car in American Life* (Cambridge, Mass: MIT Press, 1971): 314–315; Robert F. Dennis, "Atlanta Trailways Parking Garage," *Parking* (Spring 1968): 14; "Freeways and Parking," 38–39; "Atlanta," *Parking* (Winter 1956): 18–19; Marshall F. Reed, "Parking Costs," *Parking* (April 1973): 24–26. The second-largest facility in Atlanta at the time was the parking garage over the Trailways Bus Terminal.

82. D. Brownlee and D.G. DeLong, *Louis I. Kahn* (New York: Rizzoli, 1991), 417; Kahn, "Plan for Midtown Philadelphia," 10–27; Wolf, *Future of the City*, 30–31.

83. "Gateway Garage," *Parking* (Spring 1963): 12; Thomas F. Murray, "The Resurgence of Downtown," *Urban Land* (July–August 1964): 1–6; "The Gallery," *ULI Project Reference File* 8, no. 4 (February 1978): 21; Stuart L. Rogel, "Plaza of the Americas," *Urban Land* (April 1983): 16–19.

84. "Downtown Parking a Force in Rehabilitating 'Downtown,'" *Parking* (April–May 1969): 49–51.

85. James Alkire, "A Parking Garage Built to Give Downtown a Lift," *American City* (August 1970): 65–67; "The Status of Urban Redevelopment: A Symposium," *Urban Land* 7, no. 9 (October 1946): 1, 3–8; Thad E. Murphey, "Syndication of Parking Garage," *Parking* (Spring 1961): 15–16; W.H. Bruder, "This Parking Garage . . . Uses Airspace; Architectural Excellence; Automated Efficiency," *American City* (December 1965): 98–100; Daniel Locitzer, "A Parking Garage Helps Revitalize a Deteriorating Downtown," *American City* (June 1970): 94; Perry Scott, "Santa Wouldn't Provide 2,000 Free Parking Spaces," *American City* (May 1969): 44–46; "Transport Center Focal Point for Downtown Renewal," *American City* (August 1972): 82.

86. William Wisser, "The Health Center in the 21st Century," *Parking* (July 1976): 21–23; "Health Building Garage—A Parking Facility and a Redevelopment Hub," *Parking* (October 1970): 36–38; Richard C. Rich, "Colleges Build Up—and Down—in Search for Parking Space," *Parking* (Winter 1969): 44–49.

87. "Parking Jam," *Architectural Forum* 85 (September 1946): 8–10.

88. Robert T. Dunphy, "Travel Trends and the Transportation Impacts of New Projects," *Urban Land* (July 1986): 20–23; Robert T. Dunphy, "Urban Traffic Congestion: A National Crisis," *Urban Land* (October 1985): 6; Robert Dunphy, Senior Resident Fellow, Transportation,

Urban Land Institute, e-mail exchanges with author, September 2006.

89. Raul Garcia, "Project-Based Traffic Mitigation," *Urban Land* (August 1991): 21–23; Richard Ward, "Planning for Growth in Arlington County, Virginia," *Urban Land* (January 1991): 2–6; "Parking Development Coming into Its Own," *Urban Land* (July 1991): 30–31; Harbridge House, Inc., "The Future of the Auto in City Transportation," *Parking* (October 1980): 46–50.

90. Carl Walker Parking, *High Falls, Rochester, New York* (fact sheet).

91. Melvin B. Meyer, "IMPC's 1994 Awards for Excellence," *Parking Professional* (August 1994): 32; International Parking Design, *City Center West* (brochure); Dolores Palma and Doyle Hyett, "Special Events, Cool Downtowns, and Parking," *Parking* (September 2003): 48–50.

92. Douglas R. Porter, "The Future Doesn't Work," *Urban Land* (June 1987): 34–35; Roy Drachman, "U.S. Cities Are Stuck with the Automobile," *Urban Land* (October 1988): 38–39; Robert T. Dunphy, "Traffic Slowdown in Suburbia," *Urban Land* (December 1986): 36; "Vacant Lots Shouldn't Be Eyesores: Parking Areas Need to be Enhanced, Replaced," *Dallas Morning News*, February 14, 2002.

93. Smart Growth America, "What We Do," www.smartgrowthamerica.com/whatwedo.html. Of course, there are other approaches to dealing with growth; see Douglas R. Porter, "Growth Management Texas Style," *Urban Land* (December 1986): 32–33; Jim Heid, "Greenfield Development without Sprawl: The Role of Planned Communities" (working paper, ULI–the Urban Land Institute, 2004).

94. Governor's Office of Smart Growth, "Driving Urban Environments: Smart Growth Parking Best Practices," www.smartgrowth.state.md.us, 28; Lourie W. Reichenberg, "Suburban Sprawl: Shouldn't Smart Growth Include Parking as Well as Parks?" *Parking* (August 2000): 22–25.

95. Neil Adler, "Tysons Corner Task Force Announces Principles for Future Development," *Washington Business Journal*, September 27, 2006, http://washington.bizjournals.com; Jen Haberkorn, "Tyson's Expansion Seen Enhancing Fairfax," *Washington Times*, October 6, 2006; Peter Whoriskey, "Fairfax's Elusive Downtown," *Washington Post*, April 1, 2001, A1; Patricia Kirk, "Mid-Atlantic Boom," *Urban Land* (March 2005).

96. Mike Ivey, "Midvale Makeover Commission OKs Condo, Retail Development Plan," *Capital Times*, June 20, 2006, business section, D8; Amy Jennigies, "Shop Right," *Portland Mercury*, December 28–January 3, 2007, www.portland

mercury.com; "Roseway Neighborhood Association," www.roseway.org.

97. "Focusing Growth amid Sprawl: Atlanta's Livable Centers Initiative," www.atlantaregional.com/qualitygrowth; Janet Frankston, "Smart Growth Proposal Rewarded in Chamblee," *Atlanta Journal-Constitution*, October 25, 2001, B3; "The Real Jersey Devil? Sprawl," *New Urban News* (March 2003): 10; Tom Bell, "Metro Atlanta Outlook," *Urban Land* (May 2004): 100; Ken Belson, "In Success of 'Smart Growth,' New Jersey Town Feels Strain," *New York Times*, April 9, 2007.

98. Congress for the New Urbanism, "Charter," www.cnu.org/aboutcnu/index.cfm?formAction=charter.

99. Andrés Duany, Elizabeth Plater-Zyberk, and Jeff Speck, *Suburban Nation: The Rise of Sprawl and the Decline of the American Dream* (New York: North Point Press, 2000); Peter Katz, *The New Urbanism* (New York: McGraw-Hill, 1994); Andrés Duany, ed., "The Timeline of the New Urbanism Online," www.nutimeline.net.

100. Joel Garreau, *Edge City: Life on the New Frontier* (New York: Doubleday, 1991), 245.

101. Mary S. Smith, *Shared Parking*, 2nd ed. (Washington, D.C.: ULI–the Urban Land Institute, 2005); Barton-Aschman Associates, Inc., "Shared Parking Demand for Selected Land Uses," *Urban Land* (September 1983): 12–13; Reichenberg, "Suburban Sprawl," 22–25; Antoinette Martin, "Can 'Smart Growth' Cut Parking Needs?" *New York Times*, August 3, 2003, New Jersey region.

102. Quoted in D.W. Meinig, "Reading the Landscape," in *The Interpretation of Ordinary Landscapes: Geographical Essays*, ed. D.W. Meinig (New York: Oxford University Press, 1979), 231.

103. Richard Beebe, "Parking and Transit: A New Role?" *Parking* (July 1975): 30–31, 37, 44.

104. Edgardo Contini, "Recycling of Urban Land," *Urban Land* (April 1976): 7–17; National Building Museum, *On Track: Transit and the American City* (exhibit brochure, 2002); "Transport Center," 82; "News in Photos," *Parking* (October 1971): 4; E. Crichton "Kite" Singleton, "Kansas City's Love Affair with Transportation," *AIArchitect* (August 2001).

105. "News in Photos," 4; Alfred J. Pacelli, "A Highway/Transit Joint Development Project for a 2,000-Car Parking Garage," *American Society of Civil Engineers* (October 1979), preprint 3667; "Transport Center," 82; Alkire, "Give Downtown a Lift," 65–67.

106. "Chicago's Loop Transportation Center," *Parking* (November–December 1984): 38–39; General Parking Corpo-

ration, "Parking Development Coming into Its Own," *Urban Land* (July 1991): 30–31. For many air travelers, the Loop Transportation Center is the first or last stop on the way to or from O'Hare Airport.

107. The architecture of the 30th Street Station was the work of Frank Furness, a well-known Philadelphia architect who worked in the late 19th and early 20th centuries.

108. James A. Tevebaugh, "Public-Private Collaboration Resolves Parking Inadequacies in Historic Riverfront District," *Parking* (March 2005): 26–35; "Riverfront Parking Deck," *Design Cost Data* (May–June 2005): 44–45; "Tim Haas Engineers · Architects," www.timhaahs. com.

109. Thomas D. McGroarty, mayor, Wilkes-Barre, Pennsylvania, memorandum, August 2001; "Parking Structures," *Architecture* (February 2001): 90–94; David Rich, "Realizing the Promise of Multi-Modal Design," *Parking Professional* (October 2001): 23–25; Perceptics Corporation, "Pittsfield Gets New Intermodal Transportation Center," *Transportation Management and Engineering* (September 9, 2003); Pat Dawe, "Parking's Key Role in FasTracks," *Parking* (July 2005): 32–37; Timothy Tracy, "Intermodal: The Parking Perspective" (paper presented at the Transportation Issues in Parking seminar, International Parking Institute, Hallandale Beach, Fla., January 2002).

110. "Solutions Database," Old Town Parking Garage, Portland, Oregon, www.mainstreet.org/preserve_link/solutions/solutions410.htm, 1–3; Coffey and Layden, *America on Wheels*, 290; "Fourth and Yamhill Parking Garage," *ULI Project Reference File* 20, no. 18 (October–December 1990); Thomas H. Shanks, *From Horse Car to Red Car to Mass Rapid Transit: A Century of Progress* (Virginia Beach, Va.: Donning, 1991), 132; Julian Wolinsky, "Passenger Rail: Strong, Stable, Secure," *Railway Age* (January 2000): 64–67.

111. William R. Eager, "Innovative Approaches to Transportation for Growing Areas," *Urban Land* (July 1984): 6; Shanks, *Century of Progress*, 132; "Seattle Monorail Project," www.elevated. org/; Roxanne Warren, *The Urban Oasis: Guideways and Greenways in the Human Environment* (New York: McGraw-Hill, 1998), 120–121; Perceptics Corporation, "Pittsfield."

112. Christopher Alexander, Sara Ishikawa, and Murray Silverstein, *A Pattern Language: Towns, Building, Construction* (New York: Oxford University Press, 1977).

113. Michael Bernick and Robert Cervero, *Transit Villages in the 21st Century* (New York: McGraw-Hill, 1997), 121–126. For

a complete discussion of, and more current data on, transit-oriented development and parking, see Richard Willson, "Parking Policy for Transit-Oriented Development: Lessons for Cities, Transit Agencies, and Developers," *Journal of Public Transportation* 8, no. 5 (2005): 79–94; William Fulton, "Living and Working Adjacent to Rail Sounds Great, But Where Do We Park?" *California Planning and Development Report* 20, no. 2 (February 2005): 1, 16; "California Transit-Oriented Development (TOD) Searchable Database," http://transitorienteddevelopment.dot.ca.gov.

114. American Public Transportation Association, *APTA 2001 Public Transportation Fact Book*, 52nd ed. (Washington, D.C.: APTA, 2201), 168.

115. According to Kevin Hagerty, manager of BART's customer access department, when developers redevelop parking lots owned by BART, problems arise for both the developers and for BART. Replacing parking lots with parking garages is "costly and oftentimes results in the development not penciling out." Moreover, even though the construction of residential uses near transit stations is expected to increase ridership—and, therefore, revenue for the transit system—that increased revenue will not offset the loss of parking revenue from the redeveloped lots. However, if BART attempts to recoup some of the lost revenue by increasing parking fees, that has the perverse effect of discouraging transit use (e-mail exchanges and discussions with author, 2001–2007).

116. Willson, "Parking Policy," 79–94; Fulton, "Where Do We Park?" 1, 16. For a good discussion of the difficulties inherent in mixed-use development, see Elsa Brenner, "A Piazza for a Maryland Suburb," *New York Times*, November 22, 2006, C7.

117. Pat Dawe, "Parking's Key Role in FasTracks," *Parking* (July 2005): 32–37.

118. Peter Calthorpe, *The Next American Metropolis: Ecology, Community, and the American Dream* (Princeton, N.J.: Princeton Architectural Press, 1993): 108–112.

119. Ibid.

120. Another option is to use flat floor plates, which can be used either for human habitation or for parking cars.

121. Ronald E. Schmitt, "The Ubiquitous Parking Garage: Worthy of Preservation?" (paper presented at Preserving the Recent Past 2, a conference sponsored by the National Park Service, Philadelphia, October 9–13, 2000), 2–200.

122. Burrell F. Saunders, "New Urban Center," *Urban Land* 63, no. 8 (August 2004): 44; Kirk, "Mid-Atlantic Boom"; Michael E. Gamble and W. Jude LeBlanc,

"Incremental Urbanism," *Harvard Design Magazine* (Fall 2004–Winter 2005): 51–57; Mary Beth Corrigan et al., *Ten Principles for Smart Growth on the Suburban Fringe* (Washington, D.C.: ULI–the Urban Land Institute, 2004).

123. "New Buildings Provide Parking," *American City* (May 1947): 15; Charles S. LeCraw Jr. and Wilbur S. Smith, "Tackling Parking through Zoning," *American City* (February 1947): 109–111; David Witheford and George Kanaan, *Zoning, Parking, and Traffic* (Saugatuck, Conn.: Eno Foundation for Transportation, 1972), 14; "Use These Charts," 151–152; Charles T. Stewart, "New Building Sites in the District of Columbia Must Contain Off-Street Parking Space," *Urban Land Institute News Bulletin* (August 1, 1942): 1. One of the first people to address traffic issues at the turn of the 20th century was William Phelps Eno, who spent his entire life (and his personal fortune) supporting traffic safety. Eno also founded the Eno Foundation for Highway Traffic Regulation, which is still in existence today.

124. LeCraw and Smith, "Tackling Parking," 109–111.

125. Sandra Cooper, "Growth Control Evolves in Boulder," *Urban Land* (March 1980): 13–18; Patric Dawe, "New Urbanist Parking Concepts," *Parking* (March 2004): 38–44.

126. Shelley L. Smith, "The Stuff of Parking," *Urban Land* (February 1990): 36–38; Jason Wittenberg, "Parking Standards in the Zoning Code," *Zoning News* (January 2003): 1–4; Michael Davidson and Fay Dolnick, *Parking Standards* (Chicago: American Planning Association, 2002). For up-to-date information on parking and zoning requirements, check with your local municipality; a number of national organizations, including the American Planning Association, the Urban Land Institute, and the Institute of Transportation Engineers, also have resources: in particular, see Smith, *Shared Parking*; Institute of Transportation Engineers, *Parking Generation* (Washington, D.C.: ITE, 2004); David Bergman, *Off-Street Parking Requirements: A National Review of Standards*, PAS Report 432 (Chicago: American Planning Association, 1991); Robert T. Dunphy, "Traffic and Parking: A New Generation of Information," *Urban Land* (May 1988): 6–10.

127. Alan Ehrenhalt, "Curbing Parking," *Governing* (June 2005); R.T. Gregory, "Economics of Downtown Parking," *Parking* (April 1976): 16–17, 44–46; Maryland Governor's Office of Smart Growth, "Driving Urban Environments," 5; Todd Litman, "Parking Management," Victoria Transport Policy Institute, www. vtpl.org; Diane R. Stepp, "No Parking Zones," *Atlanta Journal-Constitution*, May 8, 2001, B1–B6; U.S. Environmental

Protection Agency, "Parking Spaces/Community Places: Finding the Balance through Smart Growth Solutions," EPA 231-K-06-001, January 2006, www.epa. gov/smartgrowth/parking.htm; John R. Meyer and José A. Gómez-Ibáñez, *Autos, Transit, and Cities* (Cambridge, Mass.: Harvard University Press, 1981). In *The High Cost of Free Parking* (Chicago: American Planning Association, 2005), Donald Shoup discusses parking standards in detail, noting that the amount of space required under zoning regulations is often quite disproportionate to actual need. There are many additional sources of information on smart parking and zoning strategies, a number of which are included in the list of further readings at the end of this book; two that are accessible online are International City/County Management Association, "Getting to Smart Growth: 100 Policies for Implementation," http://smartgrowth.opg; Susanna McBee et al., *Downtown Development Handbook*, 2nd ed. (Washington, D.C.: ULI–the Urban Land Institute, 1992), 101–104.

128. Smart Growth Network and the International City/County Management Association, "Getting to Smart Growth: 100 Policies for Implementation," www. smartgrowth.org/pdf/gettosg.pdf, 70; Robert Steuteville et al., *New Urbanism: Comprehensive Report and Best Practices Guide*, 3rd ed. (Ithaca, N.Y.: New Urban News, 2003): 17-5–17-6; "SmartCode Now Free of Licensing," *New Urban News* (April–May 2005): 3. There are many sources of information on parking strategies, a number of which are included in the list of further readings at the end of this book. Three useful sources are Urban and Economic Development Division, Environmental Protection Agency (EPA), *Parking Alternatives: Making Way for Urban Infill and Brownfield Redevelopment*, EPA 231-R-99-00 (Washington, D.C.: EPA, November 1999), 1–65; William R. Eager, "Innovative Approaches to Transportation for Growing Areas," *Urban Land* (July 1984): 10; Urban Land Institute, *12 Tools for Improving Mobility and Managing Congestion* (Washington, D.C.: ULI–the Urban Land Institute), 3–12.

129. Phil Langdon, "Form-Based Coding Needs a Place," *New Urban News* (March 2003): 2; Form-Based Codes Institute, www.formbasedcodes.org; Jo Anne Stubblefield, "Using Architectural Design Guidelines in the Planned Community," *Practical Real Estate Lawyer* (November 1966): 83–89.

130. Ann Benson, "Cars and Development Projects," *Urban Land* (April 1987): 38; Kenneth C. Orski, "Transportation Management Associations," *Urban Land* (December 1986): 2–5; Dave Haley, "Long-Range Transportation Planning," *Urban Land* (November 1988): 36–37;

Kenneth C. Orski, "Private Sector Involvement in Transportation," *Urban Land* (October 1982): 3–5; Malcolm D. Rivkin, "Can Transportation Management Reduce Traffic in the Suburbs? Ask the Nuclear Regulatory Commission," *Urban Land* (November 1988): 18–20; Terry Jill Lassar, "Sharing the Benefits and Costs of Growth Management in Minneapolis," *Urban Land* (February 1991): 20–25; Urban Land Institute, *12 Tools for Improving Mobility and Managing Congestion* (Washington, D.C.: ULI-the Urban Land Institute, 3–12.

131. "Urban Design Guidelines," *Urban Land* (September 1983): 30–31.

132. The largest parking structure built during the 1960s was at the Glendale Galleria Shopping Center, in California: it had 4,300 spaces, and was one of only two of this size in existence at the time.

133. Dale Denda, research director, Parking Market Research Company, unpublished research. These statistics apply to facilities with at least 400 spaces and less than 5,000. See Parking Market Research Company, *Parking Garage Construction 2000* (February 2001).

134. Richard F. Roti, "The Trend to Larger Parking Facilities," *Parking* (July 1977): 22–24; Norene Dann Martin, "Report of the Executive Vice President: Garage Construction," *Parking* (July 1972): 11–12; Michael Janofsky, "Small Cars Losing the Parking-Space War," *New York Times*, June 18, 2002. Denda analyzed the statistics on smaller facilities separately from those on larger facilities because the two groups could not be accurately compared in terms of configuration, typical construction methods, or manner of use.

135. Dale Denda, Parking Market Research Company, discussions with author, 2001–2007.

136. William C. Arons, "The Best? Who Knows . . . The Biggest? They Think So!" *Parking Today* (September 2002): 30–33. Connecting parking to highways is not a new approach in Minneapolis; see Melvin B. Meyer, "IMPC's 1994 Awards for Excellence," *Parking Professional* (August 1994): 36–37.

137. Aldo Rossi, *Architecture of the City* (Cambridge, Mass.: MIT Press, 1982), 15.

138. Sam Nunes, with Evan Reminick, "Breaking Out of the Box," *Parking Professional* (June 2000): 24–28.

139. Carl Walker Parking, *South Spring Street Garage* (project information sheet); "Best Parking Structure, Co-winner," *PCI Journal* 51, no. 5 (September–October 2006): 55.

140. Trisha Riggs, "Developing Inner-City Projects: 'It's about Inclusivity, Not Gentrification,'" *Parking Today* (May 2003): 44–46. On rare occasions, a parking

garage has been deemed the highest and best use for a site; this was the case in 1968, for the First National Bank garage in Atlanta; see "First National Bank Garage," *Parking* (Fall 1968): 35–36.

141. John D. Edwards, "Planning and Developing New Parking Facilities," *Main-Street* (January 1995): 1–5; "Downtown Parking—A Guide for Municipalities," *Parking* (August 1998): 16–17. For strategies for incorporating parking structures into downtown settings, see Cy Paumier, *Creating a Vibrant City Center: Urban Design and Regeneration Principles* (Washington, D.C.: ULI–the Urban Land Institute, 2004).

142. Peter G. Rowe, *Design Thinking* (Cambridge, Mass.: MIT Press, 1987), 191–192.

143. Aldo Rossi, *Architecture of the City* (Cambridge, Mass.: MIT Press, 1982), 130.

144. Joel Garreau, *Edge City*, 245.

Parking and Smart Growth

1. Maryland Governor's Office of Smart Growth, "Driving Urban Environments: Smart Growth Parking Best Practices," www.smartgrowth.state.md.us.

2. Although the checklist is useful, the idea of locating parking behind buildings is problematic: as is discussed extensively elsewhere in this book, the parking facility does not need to be hidden or isolated; it simply needs to be appropriately designed as an integral part of the urban fabric. In many cases, hiding parking structures often impedes the synergies and connections that are central to smart growth and the new urbanism.

3. Maryland Governor's Office of Smart Growth, "Driving Urban Environments." For examples of smart growth efforts across the country, see National Association of Local Government Environmental Professionals and the Smart Growth Leadership Institute, "Smart Growth Is Smart Business: Boosting the Bottom Line and Community Prosperity," www.sgli.org/downloads/others/smartbusiness.pdf.

4. Maryland Governor's Office of Smart Growth, "Driving Urban Environments." For further reading on smart growth, see Smart Growth Network and the International City/County Management Association, "Getting to Smart Growth: 100 Policies for Implementation," www.smartgrowth.org/pdf/gettosg.pdf; U.S. Environmental Protection Agency, "Parking Spaces/Community Places: Finding the Balance through Smart Growth Solutions," EPA 231-K-06-001, January 2006, www.epa.gov/smartgrowth/parking.htm.

Parking and the New Urbanism

1. Congress for the New Urbanism, "Charter of the New Urbanism," www.cnu.org/aboutcnu/index.cfm?formAction=charter.

2. Andrés Duany, Michael Morrissey, and Patrick Pinnell, "The Technical Page: Urbanism and Infrastructure I. Parking: Introduction," *New Urban News* (April–May 2003): 16; Andrés Duany, Michael Morrissey, and Patrick Pinnell, "The Technical Page: Urbanism and Infrastructure II. A. Basic Considerations," *New Urban News* (June 2003): 16.

3. Congress for the New Urbanism, "Charter."

4. The new urbanism has also approached the parking issue from the perspective of codes; see Robert Steuteville et al., *New Urbanism: Comprehensive Report and Best Practices Guide*, 3rd ed. (Ithaca, N.Y.: New Urban News, 2003).

5. "Land Use: Sprawl versus Communities," *In Business* (May–June 1995): 21; Roger M. Showley, "Old-Fashioned Urban Design Is Touted as Making Life Happier," *San Diego Union-Tribune*, April 3, 1994, H3; Nadine M. Post, "Putting Brakes on Suburban Sprawl," *Engineering News-Record* (May 9, 1994): 32–39; Victor Hull, "Alternative Developments Strive for a Small-Town Feeling," *Sarasota Herald-Tribune*, July 10, 1994, 1A; Marian Stinson, "'New Urbanism' Built on Old Values," *Report on Business* (July 4, 1994): 1-B2; "Transect Applied to Regional Plans," *New Urban News* (September 2000), www.newurbannews.com; Jim Heid, "Greenfield Development without Sprawl: The Role of Planned Communities" (working paper, ULI–the Urban Land Institute, 2004).

6. Andrés Duany, Elizabeth Plater-Zyberk, and Jeff Speck, *Suburban Nation: The Rise of Sprawl and the Decline of the American Dream* (New York: North Point Press, 2000); Peter Katz, *The New Urbanism* (New York: McGraw-Hill, 1994); Andrés Duany, ed., "The Timeline of the New Urbanism Online," www.nutimeline.net.

Transit Villages

1. J.C. Nichols, "Developing Outlying Shopping Centers," *American City* (July 1919): 98–100. For general information on transit villages, see Hank Dittmar and Gloria Ohland, eds., *The New Transit Town* (Washington, D.C.: Island Press, 2003); Robert Dunphy et al., *Developing around Transit: Strategies and Solutions That Work* (Washington, D.C.: ULI–the Urban Land Institute, 2004); Robert Steuteville, "Transit-Oriented Development Is Going Strong, According to Study," *New Urban News* (October–November 2004), www.newurbannews.com/TransitorientedOct04.html.

2. Michael Bernick and Robert Cervero, *Transit Villages in the 21st Century* (New York: McGraw-Hill, 1997).

3. William R. Eager, "Innovative Approaches to Transportation for Grow-

ing Areas," *Urban Land* (July 1984): 10; "Fruitvale Village Replaces Park-and-Ride," *New Urban News* (April–May 2005): 10–11; "Fruitvale Village," www.unitycouncil.org/fruitvale/overview1.htm; Steuteville, "Transit-Oriented Development," 1–5.

4. Details on all California projects are available through the California Transit-Oriented Development Searchable Database, http://transitoriented development.dot.ca.gov.

Place Making

1. For examples of other communities that have successfully used place-making techniques, see Charles C. Bohl, *Place Making: Developing Town Centers, Main Streets, and Urban Villages* (Washington, D.C.: ULI–the Urban Land Institute, 2002).

2. Peter Calthorpe, *The Next American Metropolis: Ecology, Community, and the American Dream* (Princeton, N.J.: Princeton Architectural Press, 1993); Trisha Riggs, "2006 Winner New Urbanist Pioneer," www.uli.org.

Chapter 10

1. Joel Garreau, *Edge City: Life on the New Frontier* (New York: Doubleday, 1991), 19.

2. Ibid.

3. Whitney Gould, "New Airport Parking Structure Need Not Be Another Bland Box," *Milwaukee Journal Sentinel*, March 8, 1999, 3.

4. Jeffrey Tumlin and Adam Millard-Ball, "The Mythology of Parking," *American Institute of Architects San Francisco Online Magazine* 2, 2003, www.linemag.org/_line/.

5. The garage is experienced as a void between events, where the mind can reach toward new visions—if we allow it to.

6. Jon Christensen, "A Small Family Business That Started, of Course, in a Garage," *New York Times*, February 22, 2005, 4; Annie Gowen, "The Garage Where Secrets Were Parked," *Washington Post*, July 1, 2005, C1; "Restored: 1924 Hewlett-Packard Garage," Preservation Online, March–April 2006, www.nationaltrust.org/magazine/.

7. John A. Jakle, "Landscapes Redesigned for the Automobile," in *The Making of the American Landscape*, ed. Michael Cozen (London: HarperCollins Academic, 1990), 308–309.

8. Karen A. Franck, "Types Are Us," in *Ordering Space: Types in Architecture and Design*, ed. Karen A. Franck and Lynda H. Schneekloth (New York: Van Nostrand Reinhold, 1994), 363.

9. "Restaurateur Hits on Cool Idea," *Parking* (Summer 1956): 45.

10. Milwaukee Art Museum, "The Building," www.mam.org/thebuilding/index.htm; "2002 Solutia Design Awards," *Glass Magazine* (July 2002): 51.

11. Jasper Becker, "China's Growing Pains," *National Geographic* (March 2004): 80; Jim Yardley, "Bad Air and Water, and a Bully Pulpit in China," *New York Times*, September 25, 2004, A4; Yishi Song Chang Junwang, "Urban Parking in China," *Parking Professional* (July 2001): 36–42; John J. McKetta, "The 8 Surprises or Has the World Gone to Hell?" *Parking* (April 1975): 19–23, 52–55; Peter G. Koltnow, "The Automobile and Energy," *Parking* (October 1975): 30–34; Evan V. Jones, "The Environment and Parking," *Parking* (January 1974): 41–44; "NPA and the Clean Air Act: Our Side," *Parking* (July 1974): 26–27; Edward M. Whitlock, "A Suggested Common-Sense Approach to Parking for the EPA," *Parking* (July 1974): 22–39; Fred C. Hart, "Rational Approach to Clean Air," *Parking* (July 1974): 19–21; "EPA Proposals: A Position Statement by the International Downtown Executives Association," *Parking* (July 1974): 32–35; James E. McCarthy and Fred C. Hart, "Energy Costs of Business Relocation from Urban Center to Suburbs," *Parking* (October 1977): 14–17; Urban Land Institute, *Shopping Center Development Handbook* (Washington, D.C.: ULI–the Urban Land Institute, 1977), 242–244; George Devlin, "Cars Are Here to Stay," *Parking* (April 1970): 26; "Bigger Pickups, Laden with Amenities, Are Selling at a Fast Clip," *New York Times*, July 31, 2003, A1; Phillip L. Longman, "American Gridlock," *U.S. News and World Report*, May 28, 2001, 16–22; S.M. Bruening, "The Future of the Parking Industry," *Parking* (October 1969): 21–24.

12. Federal Transit Administration, *Travel Matters: Mitigating Climate Change with Sustainable Surface Transportation*, Transit Cooperative Research Program Report 93 (Washington, D.C.: Transportation Research Board, 2003), 28.

13. "Special Edition: Sustainability," *The Angle* (May 22, 2006); William McDonough Architects, "The Hanover Principles: Design for Sustainability," downloaded from http://myhero.com; David Ivey, "National Land Use Planning? Yes," *Parking* (July 1974): 14; Rice Odell, "Can We Afford to Maintain Our Urban Infrastructure?" *Urban Land* (January 1982): 3–8; "Financing Local Infrastructure in a Time of Fiscal Constraint," *Urban Land* (August 1983): 16–21; Albert Fein, *Frederick Law Olmsted and the American Environmental Tradition* (New York: Braziller, 1972); Katie McDermott and Ann Mladinov, "Moving Beyond Conflict" (paper prepared for the Center for Transportation and the Environment, Institute for Transportation Re-

search and Education, North Carolina State University).

14. Federal Transit Administration, *Travel Matters*, 57.

15. Federal Transit Administration, *Travel Matters*, 57; TravelMatters, www.TravelMatters.org; Neal Peirce, "Britain Works on Cities, U.S. Doesn't," *York Daily Record,* June 26, 2005.

16. John A. Riggs, ed., *A Climate Policy Framework: Balancing Policy and Politics*, (Washington, D.C.: Aspen Institute, 2004), 32; Bureau of Transportation Statistics, *Pocket Guide to Transportation: 2006* (Washington, D.C.: Bureau of Transportation Statistics, 2006): 13, 44–47; U.S. Department of Transportation (DOT), *Transportation Statistics Annual Report* (Washington, D.C.: DOT, 2006).

17. Donald Shoup, *The High Cost of Free Parking* (Chicago: Planners Press, 2005): 290.

18. Donald Shoup, "Gone Parkin,'" *New York Times*, March 29, 2007, A19; Shoup, *Free Parking*, 290; Anthony Downs, "Traffic: Why It's Getting Worse, What Government Can Do," Policy Brief #128, www.brookings.edu/comm/policybriefs/pb128.htm; Kim O'Connell, "Cities Offer Incentives for 'Green' Vehicles," *American City and County* (March 2006): 12–13.

19. "Architect of the Month: Gordon Chong," *Archiworld* 133 (2006): 20–29; Stanley Saitowitz, Stanley Saitowitz | Natoma Architects, Inc., discussions with author, 2005–2006; Susan DeGrane, "States Offer Incentives to Expand Solar Power," *American City and County* (February 2006): 8, 10; "California City Turns Sunlight into Savings with a New Solar Canopy," March 2006, www.buildings.com.

20. Harry T. Gordon, "Sustainable Design: A Journey through the Nautilus Shell," *AIA Journal of Architecture* (August 2004); Steven Kellenberg, "Where Is the Green in Green Communities?" *Urban Land* (May 2003): 1–12.

21. Planetizen Radar, "Santa Monica Parking Garage Nearly Done," February 9, 2007, http://radar.planetizen.com; Moore Ruble Yudell, www.mryarchitects.com; International Parking Design, www.ipd-global.com. The LEED program is considering additions to its basic categories; one such addition, called Cold/Dark Shell, would allow LEED ratings to be applied to parking garages (Kim Hosken, U.S. Green Building Council, discussions with author, spring 2007).

22. Barnaby J. Feder, "Environmentally Conscious Developers Try to Turn Green into Platinum," *New York Times*, August 25, 2004, C5; Ellen Rand, "Commercial Real Estate: A Space Odyssey," *New York Times* advertising supplement,

2000; "Is Tall Beautiful?" www.ctbuh.org; Robin Pogrebin, "How Green Is My Tower," *New York Times*, April 16, 2006, section 2, I; floor guide to Roppongi Hills; James Brooke, "Tokyo's City within a City," *New York Times*, January 4, 2004, travel section, 5, 6; James Pygman, "Tall Office Buildings," *Urban Land* (January 1986): 32–33.

23. "Parking News," *Parking* (Winter 1955): 4.

24. A.T. North, "The Residential District Garage," *Architectural Forum* (September 1930): 379–384; S.A. Carrighar, "Built Down Instead of Up: The Union Square Garage, San Francisco," *Architect and Engineer* (August 1942): 19–29; Thomas Smith, *The Aesthetics of Parking* (Chicago: American Planning Association, 1988), 38; Dietrich Klose, *Multi-Storey Car Parks and Garages* (New York: Praeger Architectural, 1965), 46–47, 172–191; Geoffrey Baker and Bruno Funaro, *Parking* (New York: Reinhold, 1958), 60–63, 142–144; "Shall Motor-Cars Be Parked Underground?" *American City* 44, no. 1 (January 1931): 133; "San Francisco Builds a Garage under a Park," *American City* 57, no. 11 (November 1942): 66. "Friends of Post Office Square," *Parking* (May 1995): 38–43 (reprinted from ULI Project Reference File 4, no. 3 [1994]); Charity Brown, "Park Above Park Below," *Parking* (May 1991): 44–50; "One Post Office Square," ULI Project Reference File 3, no. 24, January–March 1994. The park above the underground garage at Post Office Square was the first privately funded park in Boston's history constructed within the city's financial core. All profits from the operation of the garage are used to maintain parks in the city of Boston.

25. "Public-Private Cooperation to Provide Park-Topped Garage," *American City* 64, no. 4 (April 1950): 89; "Garage Roof Doubles as Turfed Playfield," *Architectural Record* (April 1969): 168–169; Theodore Osmundson, *Roof Gardens: History, Design, and Construction* (New York: Norton, 1999), 92–95.

26. Osmundson, *Roof Gardens*, 39–40, 44–46.

27. Osmundson, *Roof Gardens*, 62–64; "Stacking the Decks," *Architecture* (December 1991): 81–85; Kelli Quinn, Hartman-Cox Architects, e-mail exchange with author, February 2007.

28. Harry Ellensweig, M.V. Ravindra, H.W. Hagen, and Robert Vitelli, "Blue Cross and Blue Shield Parking Facility," *PCI Journal* (January–February 1990): 26–36; Richard C. Rich, discussions with author, 2001–2007.

29. Nick Watry, Watry Design, Inc., ongoing discussions with author, 2001–2007; Paul Napolitano, "The Parking Structure People," *California Construction Link* (November 2001): 1–2.

30. Susan L. Handy, Lisa Weston, and Patricia Mokhtarian, "Driving by Choice or Necessity: The Case of the Soccer Mom and Other Stories" (paper presented at the annual meeting of the Transportation Research Board, Washington, D.C., January 15, 2003), 21.

31. Christine Cosgrove, "Travel for the Joy of It," *Institute of Transportation Studies Review* 29, no. 1–4 (June 2003): 2–5; Patricia L. Mokhtarian, Ilan Salomon, and Lothlorien S. Redmond, "Understanding the Demand for Travel: It's Not Purely 'Derived,'" *Innovation* 4, no. 4 (2001); Howard Frumkin, "Traveling toward Health" (lecture, Center for Transportation and the Environment, Atlanta, Georgia, October 15, 2004); U.S. Environmental Protection Agency (EPA), "Parking Spaces/Community Places: Finding the Balance through Smart Growth Solutions," EPA 231-K-06-001, January 2006, www.epa.gov/smartgrowth/parking.htm; Samuel R. Staley, "Suburbanites, Don't Give Up Hope," *Atlanta Journal-Constitution*, October 5, 2004, A9.

32. Shelley Emling, "Street to Go 'Naked,'" *Atlanta Journal-Constitution*, February 13, 2005, B6; Mary S. Smith and Thomas A. Butcher, "Parkers as Pedestrians," *Urban Land* 53, no. 6 (June 1994): 9–11; Brian S. Bochner, "Traffic Sensitive Site Design," *Urban Land* (February 1988), 13; "U.S. Traffic Problems Said to Worsen," *New York Times*, September 8, 2004, A16; Jeff Morrisey, "Want to Fit In?" *Parking* (August 2000): 27–29; Nick Watry, "Gaining Community Acceptance of Parking Facilities" (paper presented at the International Parking Conference and Exposition of the International Parking Institute, Las Vegas, Nevada, June 5, 2001); Christopher B. Leinberger, "The Shape of Downtown," *Urban Land* (November–December 2004): 68–75.

33. Glen Weisbrod, "Can Ma and Pa Compete Downtown?" *Urban Land* (February 1983): 20–23; Dolores Palma and Doyle Hyett, "Special Events, Cool Downtowns, and Parking," *Parking* (September 2003): 48–52; "Parking Heaven: Try Using One of These New Garages," *Parking Professional* (February 2002): 14–15; Maria Saporta, "Fixing 'Little Things' Inspires Big Dreams," *Atlanta Journal-Constitution*, June 16, 2003, E6.

34. Transportation Research Board, "Car-Sharing: Where and How It Succeeds," Transit Cooperative Research Program Report 108, www.trb.org/news/blurb_detail.asp?ID=5634; Moshe Safdie and Wendy Kohn, *The City after the Automobile: An Architect's Vision* (New York: Basic Books, 1997); Cathy Lang Ho, "Pooled Cars," *Architecture* (October 2000): 76–77, 142; "International Builds a Better Mousetrap," *General Motors World* (May–June 1946): 6–7; "Parking in the 49th State," *Parking* (Fall 1959): 3;

"Garages Park Bikes," *Parking* (January 1972): 6; "Fair Air Pair, APCOA Division," *Parking* (July 1970): 6; Shannon Sanders McDonald, "The Bicycle Parking Garage: An Idea Whose Time Has Come," *Parking* (January–February 2004): 47–49; Shannon Sanders McDonald, "Bicycles, Automobiles, and Automation in Japan," *Parking* (October–November 2004): 17–21. Bicycle parking in Japan is partially supported through lottery funds: see "Funding Infrastructure by Lottery," *Urban Land* (March 1983): 26–27. Many thanks to the following organizations for the personal tour of, and information on, Ohfuna Transit Station: Koyo Automatic Machine Company, the Bicycle Parking Facilities Development and Management Foundation, the Japan Bicycle Facilities Promotion Organization, the Japan Bicycle Promotion Institute, the Corporation of Construction and Management of Bicycle Parking Lots, and the Department of the Built Environment at the Tokyo Institute of Technology, Yokahama.

35. Brian Faegans, "Commute Takes Turn for Better," *Atlanta Journal-Constitution*, November 1, 2004, D5; Chris Dixon, "Taking Hills in a Single Glide," *New York Times*, December 31, 2004, D7; "Commuting by Bicycle: The Prospect Could Give Parking Operators Nightmares," *Parking* (October 1993): 39–41; "Parking News," *Parking* (Winter 1956): 2; "Bikestation," www.bikestation.org; Office of Transportation, City of Portland, "Bicycle Parking Facilities Guidelines," www.portlandonline.com/transportation/index.cfm?a=fieaj&c=deibd; "Millennium Park Bicycle Station More Than Doubles Available Parking with High-Capacity Racks," *ED+C eNews*, August 18, 2004, www.edcmag.com; "Fruitvale Village I," ULI Development Case Study #C035004, 2005, www.casestudies.uli.org; Morris Newman, "A Neglected Neighborhood Builds Itself a Village," *New York Times*, August 11, 2004, C7; "Alameda Bicycle," http://alamedabicycle.com.

36. Putsata Reang, "High-Tech Car-Sharing Program to Start in San Francisco," *Atlanta Journal-Constitution*, December 27, 2000, A9; "Neighborhood Garage Promotion," *Parking* (Winter 1961): 18–19; Ho, "Pooled Cars," 76–77, 142; C. Kenneth Orski, "Automobiles for Future Communities," *Urban Land* (September 1980): 3–4; "Car-Free Housing Now an Option in Europe, San Francisco," *Parking* (May 1998): 16.

37. Larry Lipman, "Nation Faces Crisis of Nondrivers," *Atlanta Journal-Constitution*, April 18, 2004, B4; Larry Lipman, "Maine City Responds to Elders' Transit Needs," *Atlanta Journal-Constitution*, April 18, 2004, B4.

38. "Merchants Parking, Indianapolis," *Parking* (Winter 1966): 30; Carl Gohs, "Georgia-Pacific Garage," *Parking* (October 1970): 59.

39. "Union Terminal, Cincinnati, Ohio," *Architectural Forum* 58, no. 6 (June 1933): 453–455; Carl W. Condut, *The Railroad and the City: A Technological and Urbanistic History of Cincinnatti* (Columbus: Ohio State University Press, 1977), 215–285.

40. Machado & Silvetti, "Scrim-Side Parking," *Progressive Architecture* (December 1992): 66-69; "Parking Structures," *Architecture* (February 2001): 98–100; "Emory University Home to Award-Winning Parking Design," *Parking* (May 2002): 27, 28.

41. Harlow Landphair, "Simulating Pedestrian Behavior," *Texas Transportation Researcher* 38, no. 4 (2002), available at http://tti.tamu.edu.

42. Peter M. Wolf, *The Future of the City: New Directions in Urban Planning* (New York: Watson-Guptill, 1974), 20; Klose, *Car Parks and Garages*, 234–235; Baker and Funaro, *Parking*, 60–63, 142–144; "Shall Motor-Cars Be Parked Underground?" 190–91; "Carloft," www.carloft.de; "New York Condominium to Provide Elevated Garages," *Parking* (March 2007): 11; "Urban Lofts for the Car Enthusiast," May 19, 2006, www.MetropolisMag.com.

43. NL Architects, "Parkhouse/Carstadt Amsterdam, 1995," *Lotus International* 106 (2000), 46–49; "Parkhouse Carstadt," www.archiprix.nl/e/1996/carstadt_eng.html; NL Architects, e-mail exchanges with author, fall 2006; Giazza Isolo, "Gabellini Associates," *Architecture* 88, no. 4 (April 1999): 70–73.

44. Lynn Becker, "Vehicular Visions," *Chicago Reader*, June 27, 2003, section 1, 8–11; Chicago Architectural Club, 2003 Chicago Prize Finalists, www.chicagoarchitectureclub.org; Ove Bjorn Petersen, "Danish Automated Parking," *Parking* (October 2006): 45-48.

45. Ned Cramer, "On the Boards," *Architecture* (March 2000): 52–53. Another interesting project, the Park Tower, was exhibited at the Venice Biennale, September–November, 2004.

46. Christopher Hawthorne, "Design for (Better) Living," *New York Times*, October 24, 2004, 30; "Flying Boats of Commerce," *American City* 60, no. 2 (February 26, 1945), cover; Ken Johnson, "Yesterday's Tomorrows: Past Visions of the Future," *New York Times*, May 11, 2001, B36; Bill Husted, "It's All History Now," *Atlanta Journal-Constitution*, December 26, 1999, C1; Osamu Hirao, "Human Engineering and the Automobiles of the Future," *Parking* (April 1970): 38–42; "News in Photos," *Parking* (April 1973): 6. See also www.retrofuture.com, www.wfs.org, and http://technologyfuture.info.

47. Eric Lefcowitz, "The Original Futurama: The Only Car That Flies; The Convaircar," Retro Future, www.retrofuture.com; "Folding Parker," *Parking* (Spring 1955): 2; "Self-Parkers," *Parking* (October 1972): 50–53; Alex Marshall, "The Need for Speed," *New York Times Magazine*, January, 23, 2000, 12; Todd Krieger, "Too Tipsy to Drive? Call in the Cavalry," *New York Times*, October 24, 2004, 9–10; "Freewheeling on the New Lightweight Fold-Ups," *New York Times*, September 15, 2005, E12; George P. Blumberg, "Not So Sedate: Sidecars Fitted for Speed," *New York Times*, April 30, 2004, D9; Joseph J. Corn and Brian Horrigan, *Yesterday's Tomorrows: Past Visions of the American Future*, ed. Katharine Chambers (Baltimore: Johns Hopkins University Press, 1996), 94, 99; Douglas Martin, "Robert E. Fulton Jr., an Intrepid Inventor, Is Dead at 95," *New York Times*, May 11, 2004, A25; Bruce Brooks Pfeiffer, *Frank Lloyd Wright Drawings* (New York: Abrams, 1990), 246.

48. Katrina C. Arabe, "Flying Cars Try to Land on the Market," ThomasNet.com Industrial Market Trends, http://news.thomasnet.com/IMT/archives/2003/06/flying_cars_try.html?t=archive; Christopher McDougall, "Going Way Off-Road," *New York Times Magazine*, September 26, 2004, 66–69; David Carr, "Some Highish Brows Furrow as a Car Critic Gets a Pulitzer," *New York Times*, April 8, 2004; "Hood Over Heels," *Motor Trend* (May 1958): 82; "Self-Parkers," 50–53.

49. John Anderson Miller, "Nonsense about the City of Tomorrow," *American City* 58, no. 9 (September 1943): 113–115; Chip Lord and Ant Farm, *Autoamerica: A Trip Down U.S. Highways from World War II to the Future; A Book* (New York: Dutton, 1976), 96; "Flying Boats of Commerce," *American City* 60, no. 2 (February 26, 1945): cover; Johnson, "Yesterday's Tomorrows," B36; Bill Husted, "It's All History Now," *Atlanta Journal-Constitution*, December 26, 1999, C1. Parking garages are even designed with heliports on their roofs: see "The Ten Ten Parking Garage," *Parking* (Summer 1956): 9–11; "Houston's New Parking Garage," *Urban Land* 15, no. 7 (June 1956): 6. For information about the Segway, see Rachel Metz, "Oft-Scorned Segway Finds Friends among the Disabled," *New York Times*, October 14, 2004, E5; Ed Ellis, "Will It Really Have an Impact on Mobility in Atlanta?" *Georgia Engineer* (February–March 2002): 52; Max Alexander, "Wow, Isn't That Cool!" *Smithsonian* (September 2003): 95–97; Matt Feagins, "A Modest Proposal to Help Save the Earth," *Parking Today* (November 2006): 52–53.

50. Martin Fackler, "The Land of Rising Conservation," *New York Times*, January 6, 2007, B1.

51. Danny Hakim, "New Mainstream Hybrids Offer Comfort with a Clearer Conscience," *New York Times*, October 27, 2004, G1; "All Aboard the Magic Bus," *New York Times*, August 2, 2004, A7 (advertisement); Katrina C. Arabe, "Hybrid Fleets Take City Streets," ThomasNet.com Industrial Market Trends, July 20, 2004, http://news.thomasnet.com/IMT/archives/2004/07/hybrid_fleets_t.html?t=archive; press release, Starwood Hotels and Resorts, July 11, 2007, www.csrwire.com; "Hydrogen and Fuel Cell Vehicle R&D: FreedomCAR and the President's Hydrogen Fuel Initiative," *Federal Research News* (December 14, 2004); Stephen Bennett, "The Power of Hydrogen," *National Petroleum News* (June 2004): 36–38; Jonathan Rubin, "Driving to New Sources of Transportation Energy," *TR News* (May–June 2003): 16–23; EPA, "Fuel Cells & Vehicles," www.epa.gov/fuelcell/; Katrina C. Arabe, "Fuel Cells May Power Subway Trains," ThomasNet.com Industrial Market Trends, August 27, 2003, http://news.thomasnet.com/IMT/archives/2003/08/fuel_cells_may.html?t=archive; "Energy Department Joins Drive for Fuel Cell Cars," CNET, March 30, 2005, http://news.com.com/2100-1047_3-5647258.html; Terrence Belford, "Fuel Cell Technology Energizing Real Estate," *Globe and Mail*, September 21, 2004, www.theglobeandmail.com; "Hydrogen Gas Station Operating in Iceland," *Atlanta Journal-Constitution*, April 25, 2003, A17; Danny Hakim, "George Jetson, Meet the Sequel," *New York Times*, January 9, 2005, section 3, 1–4; Danny Hakim, "Taking the Future for a Drive," *New York Times*, November 2, 2005, C1; "Futuristic," *Parking* (Fall 1961): 2; "Conserve Energy with Fuel-Efficient Cars? What a Laugh!" *New York Times*, June 24, 2004, C1; Matthew L. Wald, "Both Promise and Problems for New Tigers in Your Tank," *New York Times*, October 26, 2005, E1; Duncan Mansfield, "Tennessee Campus Pulls the Plug on 'Green Power,'" *Atlanta Journal-Constitution*, May 29, 2004, B6; Keith Reid, "Making the Switch," *National Petroleum News* (June 2004): 48–53; Teresa Riordan, "Patents," *New York Times*, June 21, 2004, C4; "World's First Biogas Train Makes Maiden Voyage in Sweden," October 24, 2005, www.terradaily.com/reports/Worlds_First_Biogas_Train_Makes_Maiden_Voyage_In_Sweden.html.

52. Thomas A. Markus, *Visions of Perfection: Architecture and Utopian Thought* (Glasgow: Third Eye Center, 1985), 13.

53. John Milton, "On His Blindness," in *The Poems of John Milton*, ed. John Carey and Alastair Fowler (New York: Norton, 1972).

54. Richard Guy Wilson, Dianne H. Pilgrim, and Dickran Tashaian, *The Machine Age in America* (New York: Abrams,

1986), 184–188; Jakle, "Landscapes Re-designed," 309; Edgardo Contini, "Transportation and the Recycling of Urban Land," *Urban Land* (April 1978): 6–11; "Urban Reliance on Motor Vehicles," *Parking* (October 1978): 40–41.

55. The idea of parking cars underwater has recently reappeared at the Acte-Park, in Gothenburg, Sweden; see Ann Geracimos, "Out to Sea for a Parking Solution," *Washington Times*, February 24, 2007, B1.

56. "Kyocera's Award-Winning Solar Grove," www.renewableenergyaccess.com; "Kyocera Solar Grove Parking Lot," July 10, 2005, www.greencar congress.com/2005/07/kyocera_solar_g. html.

57. These include codes that are applicable to high-rise residential buildings, that address how far inhabitants must travel to exit a building, and that are related to sprinkler use; see Richard C. Rich, "Parking Design and Requirements for High Rise Buildings," *Parking* (October 1972): 54–62.

58. Two recent developments in the evolution of the building type are completely enclosed facilities and garages with smaller floor plates. One use mix that will benefit from new developments in the building type is the combination of automated parking and advanced transit options. In 1976, the Fairlane Town Center and the Dearborn Hyatt, in Dearborn, Michigan, were linked in a prototype urban transit system.

59. Michael Moukalian, Richard C. Rich, M. Franco, and P.W.B. Kruger, "Parking," in *Monograph on Planning and Design of Tall Buildings*, vol. PC, *Planning and Environmental Criteria for Tall Buildings* (New York: American Society of Civil Engineers, 1981), 639–678.

60. "Urban Reliance on Motor Vehicles," *Parking* (October 1978): 40–41; "Vehicles Are Reaching a Saturation Point," *Parking* (April 1998): 13; Williamson Day, "A Glimpse of the Future," *Parking* (July 1973): 21–24.

61. Christine Cosgrove (with Phyllis Orick), "The Future That Never Was," *Institute of Transportation Studies Review Online* 1, no. 3 (Spring 2003): 2–5; "Yesterday's Tomorrows: Past Visions of American's Transportation Future" (session presented at the annual meeting of the Transportation Research Board, Washington, D.C., January 14, 2003); Jim Heid, "Greenfield Development without Sprawl: The Role of Planned Communities," Urban Land Institute Working Paper on Land Use Policy and Practice (Washington, D.C.: ULI–the Urban Land Institute, 2004); Mary Hughes, university landscape architect, University of Virginia, e-mail exchanges with author, February 28, 2007; Urban and Economic Development Division, Environmental

Protection Agency (EPA), *Parking Alternatives: Making Way for Urban Infill and Brownfield Redevelopment*, EPA 231-R-99-00 (Washington, D.C.: EPA, November 1999).

62. Wolf, *Future of the City*, 69, 74–75; Brian Richards, *Future Transport in Cities* (London: Spon Press, 2001), 103–105.

63. "Conveyor Belts for Pedestrians," *Urban Land* (June 1954): 1–3; "Moving Sidewalk between Times Square and Grand Central Station," *Parking* (Summer 1955): 34–35; "Speedwalk," *Parking* (Spring 1954): 14; "First Speedwalk, " *Parking* (Summer 1954): 4; Sven Tynelius, "European Architects Look at American Parking Progress," *Parking* (Spring 1957): 39; "Don't Walk, Ride to the Nearest Exit," *Parking* (Spring 1955): 2; "College Belt," *Parking* (Winter 1955): 2; *Parking* (July 1970): 6 (drawing of horizontal elevator); "Parking News," *Parking* (Spring 1955): 2; "Harbour Island in Tampa," *Urban Land* (July 1984): 8; "Building Types Study: Airports," *Architectural Record* (October 1972): 127–142.

64. Eric Taub, "Elevator Technology: Inspiring Many Everyday Leaps of Faith," *New York Times*, December 3, 1998, D12; "Introducing Odyssey," in *The Elevator World Source, 1997–1998* (Mobile, Ala.: Elevator World, 1998), 370–372; "Cars: A Special Section," *New York Times*, October 26, 2005, E1–E40.

65. "First 'Plug-in and Recharge' Parking Facility," *Parking* (Fall 1967): 8; John Bret Harte, "Park-Charge Will Rekindle Your Batteries," *Parking* (July 1976): 23; Rich Parker, "Driving with Ms. D.C. Sparks," *Parking* (July–August 1993): 44–45; "Electric Car News," *Parking* (August 2000): 12; N.R. Kleinfield, "Study Supports 900 Extra New York Cabs," *New York Times*, January 1, 2004; "Imagining the Taxi's Future, with a Nod to Checkers Past," *New York Times*, November 14, 2005, D10; "Electric Car Update: 249 Miles without Recharge," *Parking* (July 1997): 13; Jason Pontin, "A New Battery Takes Off in a Race to Electric Cars," *New York Times*, March 11, 2007, 3. Electric cars have even been proposed as a means of generating energy, and will perhaps power the homes or office buildings of the future.

66. David Colman, "The Roadster as Electric Bubble," *New York Times*, August 22, 2004, 9; Christopher Quinn, "Cars of the Future Ready to Roll," *Atlanta Journal-Constitution*, November 21, 1999, C2; Chris Dixon, "Cute, Clean, Quiet and Pulling into Traffic," *New York Times*, June 4, 2004, D6; Barry Lynn, "Alternative Autos," *American Way* (March 15, 2002): 64–73; Fred Hartley, "16,000-Acre Dream City Planned in Fayette County," *Atlanta Journal-Constitution*, August 2, 1959, 12D; City of Palo Alto,

"Opening Celebration for High/Alma Parking Structure," www.city.palo-alto.ca.us/press/archive/20030923.html; Jill Elizabeth Westfall, "GE Lofts," *Atlanta Journal-Constitution*, April 16, 2000, Homefinder section, 12; Warren Brown, "Tech Race Will Quickly Date Current Hybrid Cars," *Atlanta Journal-Constitution*, December 16, 2005, G5; John Kelly, "Batteries Included," *CVX* (Third Quarter 2003): 26–29; Danny Hakim, "Smokestack Visionary," *New York Times Magazine*, September 29, 2002, 100–101; "Car Struck," *Architecture* (July 1997): 19. As an added advantage, GEMs are much smaller than traditional vehicles—which means that more can be parked in existing parking facilities, delaying by a few years the onset of a parking crisis.

67. John Deiner, "A Test Ride (and Walk) on Vegas Monorail," *Atlanta Journal-Constitution*, September 5, 2004, L5; William Taaffe, "Las Vegas Monorail Rolls above Strip Traffic," *New York Times*, July 25, 2004, TR3; *Official Guide Book: Seattle World's Fair, 1962* (Seattle: Acme Publications, 1962), 141; "Designing Success," *Northwest Airlines World Traveler* (October 2003): 18; "A Monorail for Los Angeles," *Urban Land* (June 1954): 5.

68. Roxanne Warren, *The Urban Oasis: Guideways and Greenways in the Human Environment* (New York: McGraw-Hill, 1998), 167–168; "36 Hours: Morgantown, W. Va.," *New York Times*, May 9, 2003, D4. The Advanced Transit Association is the principal advocate for the development of PRT; see www.advanced transit.org.

69. Amanda Griscom Little, "The Mall That Would Save America," *New York Times Magazine*, July 4, 2005, 19–20; Steve Raney, James Paxson, and David Maymudes, "Major Activity Center PRT Circulator Design: Hacienda Business Park" (Transportation Research Board Paper #07–3063, presented at the National Transportation Reseach Board meeting, Washington, D.C., January 2007); Cities21, "Transportation Demand Management," www.cities21.org/tdm.htm; Cities21, www.cities21.org; "Transforming Office Parks into Transit Villages," http://es.epa.gov/ncer/publications/meetings/12_5_2006/transitvillages.pdf; Dennis Manning, Fresno resident, discussions with author, 2004–2007; "PRT Clarion Call," www.cprt.org/Newsletters/Jun2003.pdf; "Goodbye, Gridlock," *Parking* (June 2003): 10; Brian Richards, *Future Transport in Cities* (London: Spon Press, 2001); William R. Eager, "Innovative Approaches to Transportation for Growing Areas," *Urban Land* (July 1984): 6–7.

70. Richards, *Transport in Cities*, 124–127; Bruening, "Parking Industry," 21–24.

71. Sharon Easley, "Can't Parallel Park?" *Parking Professional* (July 2004): 44–47; Sharon Easley, "EPS for Parking: How You Pay May Be Determined by Where You Live," *Parking Professional* (May 2004): 22–27; Paul Sharke, "Smart Cars," March 2003, Mechanical Engineering Online, www.memagazine.org; Alok Jha, "Robot Car: Streets Ahead in Cities of the Future," *Guardian*, December 29, 2005.

72. *The Citizens Transportation Coalition (CTC) Position Paper on the Comprehensive Plan* (Lincoln, Neb.: 2002).

73. Horst Bredekamp, *The Lure of Antiquity and the Cult of the Machine: The Kunstkammer and the Evolution of Nature, Art, and Technology* (Princeton, N.J.: M. Wiener Publishers, 1995): 113.

74. In Cherokee County, Georgia, for example, where a family can purchase a typical three-bedroom home for $150,000, that same family would have to purchase a $800,000 home before their taxes would pay for the services they actually use. It's no wonder that for local officials attempting to balance their budgets, the childless family has become the most sought-after demographic group.

75. Jeffrey H. Dorfman, "The Rural/Urban Interface: Preserving Farmland in the Atlanta Metropolitan Region—The Economics of Growth, Sprawl, and Land Use Decisions" (paper presented at a meeting of Southface, Atlanta, March 2003); Robert Dunphy, "Housing and Traffic," *Urban Land* (February 2004): 76–80; Surface Transportation Policy Project (STPP), "Transportation Costs and the American Dream: Why a Lack of Transportation Choices Strains the Family Budget and Hinders Home Ownership," July 2003, www.transact.org/library/decoder/american_dream.pdf; Urban Markets Initiative, Metropolitan Policy Program, Brookings Institution, "A UMI Innovation: The Housing and Transportation Affordability Index; Understanding What Makes Housing Truly Affordable," online scheduled chat, January 19, 2006; Keith Bradsher, "Nice House, Great Neighborhood. But Honey, It Has Only a 3-Car Garage," *New York Times*, November 12, 2000, BU16. According to the STPP report, "Only recently has transportation comprised such a large share of the family budget. The proportion of household expenditures that is devoted to transportation has grown from under 10 percent in 1935 to about 14 percent in 1960, to almost 20 percent from 1972 through today."

76. Herbert Muschamp, "Fitting into History's True Fabric," *New York Times*, May 6, 2001, AR4.

77. "Sioux City Park and Shop," *Parking* (Fall 1955): 8–9; "Child Care Service in Joliet,"

The Parking Garage

Parking (Fall 1962): 20–21; "Parking Sidelines," *Parking* (Fall 1954): 40.

78. Interestingly, a book on sustainable development in Canada predicts that by 2030, "70 percent of Canadian households will have one small electric car, with 10 percent having two electric vehicles and 20 percent having no motorized vehicles at all." Such a prediction may be appropriate for Canada, where the majority of the population is clustered in urban areas. The population of the United States, however, is not only much larger but much more dispersed, suggesting other solutions. See Ann Dale and John Bridger Robinson, eds., *Achieving Sustainable Development: A Project of the Sustainable Development Research Institute* (Vancouver: UBC Press, 1996), 14.

79. Muschamp, "History's True Fabric," AR4.

80. Corn and Horrigan, *Yesterday's Tomorrows*, 10; "U.S. Problems Said to Worsen," *New York Times*, September 8, 2004, A16.

81. Charles M. Bolden, "Environmental Impact on Parking," *Parking* (January 1975): 22–34; N.J. Slabbert, "John Dewey: Philosopher of Community," *Urban Land* (November–December 2006): 150–155; "The Economic Contribution of Architecture," *Urban Land* (December 1982): 14; Patricia Panchak, "Stuck in the Slow Lane," *Industry Week*, May 1, 2003, www.industryweek.com; C.H. Claudy, "The Motor Car of the Future," *Scientific American* (January 5, 1918): 1, 28; "Gateway Garage," *Parking* (Spring 1963): 12–13; Nancy Egan, "Shifting Gears," *Urban Land* (November–December 2004): 112–119; Richard G. West, "Tomorrow's Transportation Today," *Parking* (July 1976): 33–48; Neal I. Payton, "Architects Take a Second Look at Parking Garages," *Parking* (May 1993): 37–43; "Parking Is Power," *Urban Land* (February 2001): 53; Robert T. Dunphy, "Big Foot," *Urban Land* (February 2003): 82–85; Gary Cudney, "Good to Great Parking Structure Design" (paper presented at Visions New Orleans, International Parking Institute Conference, New Orleans, June 21, 2004).

FURTHER READING

Parking

Baker, Geoffrey Harold, and Bruno Funaro. *Parking*. New York: Reinhold, 1958.

Burrage, Robert H., and Edward G. Mogren. *Parking*. Saugatuck, Conn.: Eno Foundation for Highway Traffic Control, 1957.

Chrest, Anthony P., Mary S. Smith, and Sam Bhuyan. *Parking Structures*. 3rd ed. Norwell, Mass.: Kluwer Academic Publishers, 2001.

Comstock, William Phillips, comp. *Garages and Motor Boat Houses*. (New York: William T. Comstock, 1911).

Davidson, Michael, and Fay Dolnick. *Parking Standards*. Chicago: American Planning Association, 2002.

Edwards, John D. *Parking: The Parking Handbook for Small Communities*. Washington, D.C.: Institute for Transportation Engineers; National Main Street Center; National Trust for Historic Preservation, 1994.

Hackman, Lonnie, and Norene D. Martin. *The Parking Industry; Private Enterprise for the Public Good*. Washington, D.C.: National Parking Association, 1969.

Jakle, John A., and Keith A. Sculle. *Lots of Parking: Land Use in a Car Culture*. Charlottesville: University of Virginia Press, 2004.

Klose, Dietrich. *Metropolitan Parking Structures; A Survey of Architectural Problems and Solutions*. New York: Praeger, 1965.

Komendant, August E. *Prestressed Concrete Structures*. New York: McGraw-Hill, 1952.

Lew, I. Paul, and Robert S. Engle. *Planning Guidelines for Intermodal Parking*. Washington, D.C.: National Parking Association, 1997.

Luiz, Christian R., Mary S. Smith, John Burgan, and Dewey Hemba. *Guidelines for Parking Geometrics*. Washington, D.C.: National Parking Association, 2002.

McCluskey, Jim. *Parking: A Handbook of Environmental Design*. London: Spon Press, 1987.

Shoup, Donald. *The High Cost of Free Parking*. Chicago: American Planning Association, 2005.

Smith, Mary S. *Shared Parking*. 2nd ed. Washington, D.C.: ULI—the Urban Land Institute, 2005.

Smith, Thomas P. *The Aesthetics of Parking*. Chicago: American Planning Association, 1988.

Urban Land Institute and National Parking Association. *The Dimensions of Parking*. Washington, D.C.: ULI—the Urban Land Institute, 2000.

Weant, Robert A., and Herbert S. Levinson. *Parking*. Westport, Conn.: Eno Foundation for Transportation, 1990.

Architecture

Bachelard, Gaston. *The Poetics of Space*. Boston: Beacon Press, 1964.

Banham, Reyner. *The Architecture of the Well-Tempered Environment*. London: London Architectural Press, 1969.

_____. *Megastructure: Urban Futures of the Recent Past*. London: Thames and Hudson, 1976.

_____. *Theory and Design in the First Machine Age*. New York: Praeger, 1960.

Behne, Adolf. *The Modern Functional Building*. Santa Monica, Calif.: Getty Research Institute for the History of Art and the Humanities, 1996.

Bloomer, Kent. *The Nature of Ornament: Rhythm and Metamorphosis in Architecture*. New York: Norton, 2000.

Bredekamp, Horst. *The Lure of Antiquity and the Cult of the Machine: The Kunstkammer and the Evolution of Nature, Art, and Technology*. Princeton, N.J.: M. Wiener Publishers, 1995.

Britton, Karla. *Auguste Perret*. New York: Phaidon, 2001.

Collins, Peter. *Concrete: The Vision of a New Architecture*. 2nd ed. Montreal: McGill—Queen's University Press, 2004.

Detroit Institute of Arts. *The Legacy of Albert Kahn*. Detroit: Detroit Institute of Arts, 1970.

Dewey, John. *Art as Experience*. New York: Minton Balch, 1934.

De Zurko, Edward Robert. *Origins of Functionalist Theory.* New York: Columbia University Press, 1957.

Fader, Steven. *Density by Design: New Directions in Residential Development.* 2nd ed. Washington, D.C.: ULI—the Urban Land Institute, 2000.

Fein, Albert. *Frederick Law Olmsted and the American Environmental Tradition.* New York: Braziller, 1972.

Franck, Karen A., and Lynda H. Schneekloth, eds. *Ordering Space: Types in Architecture and Design.* New York: Van Nostrand Reinhold, 1994.

Franzen, Ulrich, and Paul Rudolph. *The Evolving City.* New York: American Federation of the Arts, 1974.

Giedion, Siegfried. *Mechanization Takes Command, a Contribution to Anonymous History.* New York: Oxford University Press, 1948.

_____. *Space, Time, and Architecture: The Growth of a New Tradition.* Cambridge, Mass.: Harvard University Press, 1956.

Gissen, David, ed. *Big and Green: Toward Sustainable Architecture in the 21st Century.* New York: Princeton Architectural Press, 2002.

Hamlin, Talbot, ed. *Building Types.* Vol. 4. *Forms and Functions of Twentieth-Century Architecture.* New York, Columbia University Press, 1952.

Heschong, Lisa. *Thermal Delight in Architecture.* Cambridge, Mass.: MIT Press, 1979.

Hughes, Robert. *The Shock of the New.* New York: Knopf, 1981.

Kant, Immanuel. *Observations on the Feeling of the Beautiful and Sublime.* Berkeley: University of California Press, 1960.

Krauss, Rosalind E. *The Originality of the Avant-Garde and Other Modernist Myths.* Cambridge, Mass.: MIT Press, 1986.

Langer, Susanne K. *Mind: An Essay on Human Feeling.* Baltimore: Johns Hopkins University Press, 1967.

Lavin, Sylvia. *Quatremère De Quincy and the Invention of a Modern Language of Architecture.* Cambridge, Mass.: MIT Press, 1992.

Le Corbusier. *Towards a New Architecture.* New York: Dover, 1931.

McDonough, William, and Michael Braungart. *Cradle to Cradle: Remaking the Way We Make Things.* New York: North Point Press, 2002.

McHarg, Ian L. *Design with Nature.* New York: Wiley, 1992.

Misa, Thomas J. *A Nation of Steel.* Edited by Merritt Roe Smith. Studies in the History of Technology. Baltimore: Johns Hopkins University Press, 1995.

Neutra, Richard. *Survival through Design.* New York: Oxford University Press, 1954.

Newby, Frank, ed. *Early Reinforced Concrete.* Aldershot, U.K.; Burlington, Vt.: Ashgate/Variorum, 2001.

Osmundson, Theodore. *Roof Gardens: History, Design, and Construction.* New York: Norton, 1999.

Pfeiffer, Bruce Brooks, ed. *Frank Lloyd Wright Collected Writings: Volume 4 (1939–1949).* New York: Rizzoli, 1994.

_____. *Frank Lloyd Wright Drawings: Masterworks from the Frank Lloyd Wright Archives.* New York: Abrams, 1990.

Safdie, Moshe, and Wendy Kohn. *The City after the Automobile: An Architect's Vision.* New York: Basic Books, 1997.

Semper, Gottfried. *The Four Elements of Architecture and Other Writings.* Cambridge: Cambridge University Press, 1989.

Slaton, Amy E. *Reinforced Concrete and the Modernization of American Building, 1900–1930.* Baltimore: Johns Hopkins University Press, 2001.

Spirn, Ann Whiston, C. Ford Peatross, and Robert L. Sweeney. *Frank Lloyd Wright: Designs for an American Landscape, 1922–1932.* New York: Harry N. Abrams in association with the Canadian Centre for Architecture, the Library of Congress, and the Frank Lloyd Wright Foundation, 1996.

Tod, Ian, and Michael Wheeler. *Utopia.* New York: Harmony Books, 1978.

Virilio, Paul. *The Aesthetics of Disappearance.* New York: Semiotexte, 1991.

Wilson, Richard Guy, Dianne H. Pilgrim, and Dickran Tashjian. *The Machine Age in America, 1918–1941.* New York: Brooklyn Museum of Art in association with Abrams, 1986.

Wittkower, Rudolph. *Architectural Principles in the Age of Humanism.* New York: Norton, 1962.

Wright, Frank Lloyd. *Frank Lloyd Wright Collected Writings.* Edited by Bruce Brooks Pfeiffer. New York: Rizzoli; Scottsdale, Ariz.: Frank Lloyd Wright Foundation, 1992.

Wright, Frank Lloyd. *The Living City.* New York: New American Library, 1958.

Zevi, Bruno. *Architecture as Space: How to Look at Architecture.* New York: Horizon Press, 1957.

Urban Planning

Alexander, Christopher, Sara Ishikawa, and Murray Silverstein. *A Pattern Language: Towns, Building, Construction.* New York: Oxford University Press, 1977.

Bacon, Edmund N. *Design of Cities.* New York: Viking, 1967.

Bailey, James, ed. *New Towns in America: The Design and Development Process.* New York: Wiley, 1970.

Barnett, Jonathan. *The Fractured Metropolis.* New York: HarperCollins, 1995.

_____. *Redesigning Cities: Principles, Practice, Implementation.* Chicago: Planners Press, 2003.

Beatley, Timothy, and Kristy Manning. *The Ecology of Place: Planning for Environment, Economy and Community.* Island Press, 1997.

Bohl, Charles C. *Place Making: Developing Town Centers, Main Streets, and Urban Villages.* Washington, D.C.: ULI—the Urban Land Institute, 2002.

Booth, Geoffrey, et al. *Transforming Suburban Business Districts.* Washington, D.C.: ULI—the Urban Land Institute, 2001.

Brosterman, Norman. *Out of Time: Designs for the Twentieth-Century Future.* New York: Abrams, 1999.

Calthorpe, Peter. *The Next American Metropolis: Ecology, Community, and the American Dream.* New York: Princeton Architectural Press, 1993.

Cervero, Robert. *The Metropolis.* Cambridge, Mass.: MIT Press, 1968.

_____. *Suburban Gridlock.* New Brunswick, N.J.: Center for Urban Policy Research, 1986.

Conzen, Michael P. *The Making of the American Landscape.* Boston: Unwin Hyman, 1990.

Corn, Joseph J., and Brian Horrigan. *Yesterday's Tomorrows: Past Visions of the American Future.* Edited by Katharine Chambers. Baltimore: Johns Hopkins University Press, 1996.

Corrigan, Mary Beth, et al. *Ten Principles for Smart Growth on the Suburban Fringe.* Washington, D.C.: ULI—the Urban Land Institute, 2004.

Dale, Ann, and John B. Robinson, eds. *Achieving Sustainable Development: A Project of the Sustainable Development Research Institute.* Vancouver: UBC Press, 1996.

Davis, Mike. *City of Quartz: Excavating the Future in Los Angeles.* New York: Verso, 1990.

Dittmar, Hank, and Gloria Ohland, eds. *The New Transit Town.* Washington, D.C.: Island Press, 2003.

Duany, Andrés, and Elizabeth Plater-Zyberk, *Towns and Town-Making Principles.* Cambridge, Mass.: Harvard University Graduate School of Design; New York: Rizzoli, 1991.

Duany, Andrés, Elizabeth Plater-Zyberk, and Jeff Speck. *Suburban Nation: The Rise of Sprawl and the Decline of the American Dream.* New York: North Point Press, 2000.

Ewing, Reid. *Best Development Practices: Doing the Right Thing and Making Money at the Same Time.* Chicago: American Planning Association, in cooperation with the Urban Land Institute and the Florida Department of Community Affairs, 1996.

Fogelson, Robert M. *Downtown: Its Rise and Fall, 1880–1950.* New Haven, Conn.: Yale University Press, 2001.

Garreau, Joel. *Edge City: Life on the New Frontier.* New York: Doubleday, 1991.

Girardet, Herbert. *Creating Sustainable Cities.* Totnes, Devon, U.K.: Published by Green Books for the Schumacher Society, 1999.

Hall, Peter Geoffrey. *Cities of Tomorrow: An Intellectual History of Urban Planning and Design in the Twentieth Century.* Oxford, U.K.: Blackwell, 1988.

Jackson, John Brinkerhoff. *Discovering the Vernacular Landscape.* New Haven, Conn.: Yale University Press, 1984.

Jackson, Kenneth T. *Crabgrass Frontier: The Suburbanization of the United States.* New York: Oxford University Press, 1985.

Jacobs, Jane. *The Death and Life of Great American Cities.* New York: Random House, 2002.

Kaplan, Robert D. *Empire Wilderness: Travels into America's Future.* New York: Vintage Departures, 1998.

Katz, Peter. *The New Urbanism: Toward an Architecture of Community.* New York: McGraw-Hill, 1994.

Kunstler, James Howard. *The Geography of Nowhere: The Rise and Decline of America's Man-Made Landscape.* New York: Simon and Schuster, 1993.

_____. *Home from Nowhere: Remaking Our Everyday World for the Twenty-First Century.* New York: Simon and Schuster, 1996.

Langdon, Philip. *A Better Place to Live: Reshaping the American Suburb.* Amherst: University of Massachusetts Press, 1994.

Le Corbusier. *The City of To-Morrow and Its Planning.* New York: Dover, 1929.

Longstreth, Richard. *City Center to Regional Mall: Architecture, the Automobile, and Retailing in Los Angeles, 1920–1950.* Cambridge, Mass.: MIT Press, 1997.

Lynch, Kevin. *Site Planning.* Cambridge, Mass.: MIT Press, 1962.

McBee, Susanna, et al. *Downtown Development Handbook.* 2nd ed. Washington, D.C.: ULI–the Urban Land Institute, 1992.

Moe, Richard, and Carter Wilkie. *Changing Places: Rebuilding Community in the Age of Sprawl.* New York: Henry Holt, 1997.

Mohl, Raymond A., ed. *The Making of Urban America.* 2nd ed. Wilmington, Del.: Scholarly Resources, 1997.

Mollenkopf, John H. *The Contested City.* Princeton, N.J.: Princeton University Press, 1983.

Owen, Wilfred. *Cities in the Motor Age.* New York: Viking, 1959.

Paumier, Cy. *Creating a Vibrant City Center: Urban Design and Regeneration Principles.* Washington, D.C.: ULI–the Urban Land Institute, 2004.

Reps, John W. *The Making of Urban America.* Princeton, N.J.: Princeton University Press, 1965.

Rusk, David. *Cities without Suburbs.* 2nd ed. Washington, D.C.: Woodrow Wilson Center Press, 1995.

Schreiber, Kenneth, Gary Binger, and Dennis Church. *Higher-Density Plans: Tools for Community Engagement.* San Jose, Calif.: Mineta Transportation Institute, College of Business, San Jose State University, 2004.

Schwanke, Dean, et al. *Mixed-Use Development Handbook.* 2nd ed. Washington, D.C.: ULI–the Urban Land Institute, 2003.

Scott, Mel. *American City Planning Since 1890.* Berkeley: University of California Press, 1969.

Smart Growth Network. *Getting to Smart Growth: 100 Policies for Implementation.* Washington, D.C.: Smart Growth Network and International City/County Management Association.

Steuteville, Robert, et al. *New Urbanism: Comprehensive Report and Best Practices Guide.* 3rd ed. Ithaca, N.Y.: New Urban News, 2003.

Stilgoe, John R. *Borderland: Origins of the American Suburb, 1820–1939.* New Haven, Conn.: Yale University Press, 1988.

_____. *Outside Lies Magic: Regaining History and Awareness in Everyday Places.* New York: Walker, 1998.

Teaford, Jon C. *The Rough Road to Renaissance: Urban Revitalization in America, 1940–1985.* Baltimore: Johns Hopkins University Press, 1990.

Urban Land Institute. *The Community Builders Handbook.* Washington, D.C.: ULI–the Urban Land Institute, 1947.

Wilson, Chris, and Paul Groth, eds. *Everyday America: Cultural Landscape Studies after J.B. Jackson.* Berkeley: University of California Press, 2003.

Wolf, Peter. *Eugene Henard and the Beginning of Urbanism in Paris, 1900–1914.* The Hague: International Federation for Housing and Planning; Paris: Centre de recherche d'urbanisme, 1968.

_____. *The Future of the City: New Directions in Urban Planning.* New York: Watson-Guptill, 1974.

Transportation

American Public Transportation Association. *APTA 2001: Public Transportation Fact Book.* Washington, D.C.: American Public Transportation Association, 2001.

Barrett, Paul. *The Automobile and Urban Transit: The Formation of Public Policy in Chicago, 1900–1930.* Philadelphia: Temple University Press, 1983.

Bernick, Michael, and Robert Cervero. *Transit Villages in the 21st Century.* New York: McGraw-Hill, 1997.

Coffey, Frank, and Joseph Layden. *America on Wheels.* Los Angeles: General Publishing Group, 1996.

Dunphy, Robert T. *Moving Beyond Gridlock: Traffic and Development.* Washington, D.C.: ULI–the Urban Land Institute, 1992.

Dunphy, Robert T., and Ben C. Lin. *Transportation Management through Partnerships.* Washington D.C.: ULI–the Urban Land Institute, 1990.

Dunphy, Robert T., et al. *Developing around Transit: Strategies and Solutions That Work.* Washington, D.C.: ULI–the Urban Land Institute, 2004.

Durning, Alan Thein. *The Car and the City: 24 Steps to Safe Streets and Healthy Communities.* Seattle: Northwest Environment Watch, 1996.

Feigon, Sharon, et al. *Travel Matters: Mitigating Climate Change with Sustainable Surface Transportation.* Washington, D.C.: Transportation Research Board of the National Academies, 2003.

Flink, James J. *The Automobile Age.* Cambridge, Mass.: MIT Press, 1988.

_____. *The Car Culture.* Cambridge, Mass.: MIT Press, 1975.

Gilbert, Gorman, and Robert E. Samuels. *The Taxicab: An Urban Transportation Survivor.* Chapel Hill: University of North Carolina Press, 1982.

Jennings, Jan, ed. *Roadside America: The Automobile in Design and Culture.* Ames: Iowa State University Press for the Society for Commercial Archeology, 1990.

Kay, Jane Holtz. *Asphalt Nation: How the Automobile Took over America, and How We Can Take It Back.* New York: Crown, 1997.

Kennedy, Marla Hamburg, ed. *Car Culture.* Salt Lake City: Gibbs Smith, 1998.

Kirsch, David. *The Electric Vehicle and the Burden of History*. New Brunswick, N.J.: Rutgers University Press, 2000.

Kuzmyak, J. Richard, et al. *Traveler Response to Transportation System Changes*. Washington, D.C.: National Academy Press, 2003.

Lewis, Lucinda. *Roadside America: The Automobile and the American Dream*. New York: Abrams, 2000.

Lord, Chip, and Ant Farm. *Automerica: A Trip Down U.S. Highways from World War II to the Future; A Book*. New York: Dutton, 1976.

Ministry of Transport, Great Britain. *Traffic in Towns; A Study of the Long-Term Problems of Traffic in Urban Areas*. London: H.M. Stationery Office, 1963.

Mitman, Carl W. *An Outline Development of Highway Travel*. Washington, D.C.: Smithsonian Institution, 1935.

Morris, Marya, ed. *Creating Transit-Supportive Land-Use Regulations*. Chicago: American Planning Association, Planning Advisory Service, 1996.

Motavalli, Jim. *Breaking Gridlock: Moving toward Transportation That Works*. San Francisco: Sierra Club Books, 2001.

Newman, Peter, and Jeffrey R. Kenworthy. *Sustainability and Cities: Overcoming Automobile Dependence*. Washington, D.C.: Island Press, 1999.

Pisarski, Alan F. *Commuting in America II: The Second National Report on Commuting Patterns and Trends*. Lansdowne, Va.: Eno Transportation Foundation, 1996.

Pline, James L., ed. *Traffic Engineering Handbook*. 4th ed. Englewood Cliffs, N.J.: Prentice Hall, 1992.

Project for Public Spaces. *The Role of Transit in Creating Livable Metropolitan Communities*. Washington, D.C.: National Academy Press, 1997.

Rae, John B. *American Automobile Manufacturers: The First Forty Years*. Philadelphia: Chilton, 1959.

———. *The Road and the Car in American Life*. Cambridge, Mass.: MIT Press, 1971.

Richards, Brian. *Future Transport in Cities*. London: Spon Press, 2001.

Rose, Albert C. *Historic American Roads: From Frontier Trails to Superhighways*. New York: Crown, 1976.

Shanks, Thomas H. *From Horse Car to Red Car to Mass Rapid Transit: A Century of Progress*. Virginia Beach, Va.: Donning, 1991.

U.S. Bureau of Transportation Statistics. *Pocket Guide to Transportation: 2006*. Washington, D.C.: Bureau of Transportation Statistics, 2006.

Warren, Roxanne. *The Urban Oasis: Guideways and Greenways in the Human Environment*. New York: McGraw-Hill, 1998.

Wollen, Peter, and Joe Kerr, eds. *Autopia: Cars and Culture*. London: Reaktion Books, 2002.

The following organizations and publications are useful resources for information on parking.

American Concrete Institute: www.concrete.org

American Planning Association: www.planning.org

American Society of Civil Engineers: www.asce.org

Eno Transportation Foundation: www.enotrans.com

Institute of Transportation Engineers: www.ite.org

National Parking Association: www.npapark.org

New Urban News: www.newurbannews.com

Parking Today: www.parkingtoday.com

Post-Tensioning Institute: www.post-tensioning.org

Precast/Prestressed Concrete Institute: www.pci.org

The International Parking Institute: www.parking.org

Smart Growth Network: www.smartgrowth.org

Transportation Research Board: www.trb.org

U.S. Environmental Protection Agency: www.epa.gov

Urban Land Institute: www.uli.org

ILLUSTRATION CREDITS

The author has made every effort to acknowledge all sources for the images in the book and to ensure the accuracy of this information; the author has also engaged in exhaustive efforts to obtain permission to use these images. Any errors or omissions are the responsibility of the author.

Credits are listed by page number, project name, and source.

Frontispiece

ii.   Nash Motors display—Chicago History Museum; photographer Ken Hedrich, Hedrich-Blessing, HB-00770-H.

Introduction

2:    Motor Mart Garage—Courtesy of the Boston Public Library, Fine Arts Department. No restrictions on use.

Chapter I

6:    Palmer & Singer Manufacturing Co. garage—William Phillips Comstock, comp., *Garages and Motor Boat Houses* (New York: William T. Comstock, 1911), 70.

8:    Joscelyn Garage—"The Joscelyn Garage, New York," *Horseless Age* (May 3, 1912), 765.

9:    Hoyt & DeMallie Garage—Courtesy of the Detroit Public Library, National Automotive History Collection.

10:    New York City, circa 1900—Courtesy of the Detroit Public Library, National Automotive History Collection.

Detroit, circa 1920—Campus Martius, Library of Congress, Washington, D.C., Prints and Photographs Division, LC-D4-500951.

11:    Jackson Motor Company—"How the Jacksonville Motor Co., at Jacksonville, Texas, Made Nature Assist in Providing an Attractive 'Front' to Its Garage," *Horseless Age* 37, no. 8 (April 1916): 14.

Garage Rue de Ponthieu—"Notes from Paris," *Architectural Review* 24 (1908): 138.

13:    People's Garage and Livery—"Modern American Public Garages," *Horseless Age* 29, no. 18 (May 1, 1912): 755.

14:    Presidential garage—Courtesy of William Howard Taft National Historic Site.

15:    Cyclorama—Courtesy of the Bostonian Society/Old State House: Boston Streets Photograph Collection ca. 1855–1999. Cyclorama Building at 539 Tremont Street, February 1, 1965.

Electric Vehicle Company garage—Courtesy of the Detroit Public Library, National Automotive History Collection.

Moutoux Automobile Garage—Courtesy of the Detroit Public Library, National Automotive History Collection.

17:    Chicago Automobile Club—Stephen Sennott, "Chicago Architects and the Automobile, 1906–26," in Jan Jennings, ed., *Roadside America: The Automobile in Design and Culture* (Ames: Iowa State University for the Society for Commercial Archeology, 1990), 160.

19:    Acton Garage—"Garages and Motor Boat Houses," William Phillips Comstock, comp., *Garages and Motor Boat Houses* (New York: William T. Comstock, 1911), 77.

Dupont Garage—"Public Garages: The Dupont Garage, Washington, D.C.," *Horseless Age* 31, no. 19 (May 7, 1913): 793.

Clinton Garage—"Modern American Public Garages," *Horseless Age* 29, no. 18 (May 1, 1912): 756.

20:    Fire station—Courtesy of Amarillo (Texas) Public Library.

21:    Times Square Auto Company—Courtesy of the Detroit Public Library, National Automotive History Collection.

23:    Entry for a 1913 design competition—"The Brickbuilder Competition for a Public Garage, Automobile Sales and Service Building," supplement, *Brickbuilder* 22, no. 3 (March 1913).

The Parking Garage and the Train Station

12:    Grand Central Station—Photography Collection, Miriam and Ira D. Wallach Division of Art, Prints and Photographs, the New York Public Library, Astor, Lenox and Tilden Foundations.

Women Drivers and the Parking Garage

18:    Postcard—Courtesy of the National Automobile Museum, the Harrah Collection.

St. Paul Garage—Courtesy of the Baltimore Museum of Industry.

Garages for the Landed Gentry

22: First-prize entry, design competition—"Class 'B' Project Problem in Design: An Automobile Garage," *American Architect* 98, no. 1825 (December 14, 1910): First Mention

Chapter 2

24: Eliot Street Garage—Courtesy of the Boston Public Library, Fine Arts Department.

26: White Garage—"White Company Garage in New York City," *Horseless Age* (May 4, 1910): 647.

Old Post Road Garage—"Garage Items," *Horseless Age* 24, no. 18 (November 3, 1909): 507.

28: Plan of White Garage—"The Garage Situation in New England," *Horseless Age* 23, no. 16 (April 21, 1909): 511.

Plan of Waterville Garage—"Waterville Garage, Waterville, Me.," *Horseless Age* 31, no. 19 (May 7, 1913): 832.

Boulevard Auto Company garage—William Phillips Comstock, comp., *Garages and Motor Boat Houses* (New York: William T. Comstock, 1911), 67.

29: Portland Street Garage—Harold F. Blanchard, "Ramp Design in Public Garages," *Architectural Forum* (November 1921): 175.

30: Fenway Garage—"The New Fenway Garage, Boston, Mass.," *Horseless Age* 31, no. 19 (May 7, 1913): 826.

New York Taxicab Company garage—"The New Garage of the New York Taxicab Company," *Horseless Age* 23, no. 8 (February 24, 1909): 271.

Brown Garage—"A Garage Building Built with a Purpose," *Horseless Age* (September 15, 1915): 295.

31: A.C.A. Annex Garage—"Types of Garages," *Horseless Age* 36, no. 14 (December 15, 1915): 531.

32: D'Humy ramp system—Harold F. Blanchard, "Ramp Design in Public Garages," *Architectural Forum* (November 1921): 174.

D'Humy ramp, section—Harold F. Blanchard, "Ramp Design in Public Garages," *Architectural Forum* (November 1921): 174.

34: Baker Garage—Norton & Peel, 10/2/1929, Minnesota Historical Society.

35: Commodore-Biltmore Garage—Museum of the City of New York, the Bryon Collection, 93.1.1.5826.

Eliot Street Garage, plan—Harold F. Blanchard, "Ramp Design in Public Garages," *Architectural Forum* (November 1921): 172.

37: Kehler Garage—"Garage with Warped Floor Areas Connecting Ramps," *Engineering News-Record* 95, no. 6 (August 6, 1925): 231.

Fort Shelby Garage—Photo courtesy of the offices of Albert Kahn Associates, Inc.

40: Examples of garage layouts—Harold F. Blanchard, "The Layout of Automotive Buildings," *Architectural Forum* (March 1927): 282.

41: Advances in the automobile—Reprinted from AUTOMERICA with permission of Chip Lord Projects.

Cage Garage—Shepley Bulfinch Richardson and Abbott.

42: Garage, Miami—Photograph: Ezra Stoller © Esto. All rights reserved.

Self-park ramp designs—"Ramp Types," *Parking* (Winter 1954): 36.

43: Parkit design—M.R. Beckstrom, "New Design," *Parking* (Fall 1955): 18.

Circ-L-Park—Philip R. Weary—Structural Engineer.

Entry for a 1965 competition—"Art Students Design Garages," *Parking* (Winter 1965): 15.

44: Silo proposal—William B. Gleckman Architect.

Park-A-Back prototype—William B. Gleckman Architect.

Grand Rapids Community College Garage—Grand Rapids Community College Archives.

46: Current ramp designs—Springer and Kluwer Academic Publishers: *Parking Structures: Planning, Design, Construction, Maintenance, and Repair,* Anthony P. Chrest et al., 3rd ed., 2001, drawings page 61. With kind permission of Springer Science and Business Media.

Albert Kahn (1869–1942)

38: Detroit Athletic Club—Job #672 (1915), Drawer 14, Folder 7, Sheet #4, West End Elevation, Bentley Historical Library, University of Michigan, Albert Kahn Associates, Inc., and Detroit Athletic Club.

S.S. Kresge Administration Building—Box #7, Albert Kahn Collection: Newspapers and Journal, Bentley Historical Library, University of Michigan, and Albert Kahn Associates, Inc.

39: Fort Shelby Garage—Manning Brothers Historic Photographic Collection: Library of Congress, Washington, D.C., Prints and Photographs Division, LC-USZ62-129076.J257196 U.S. Copyright Office.

Evening News Garage (also known as the Detroit Garage)—"Structural Fire Prevention for Large Garages," *Architectural Forum* (April 1927): 342.

The Elevator Garage: A New Old Idea

45: Lofts of Merchants Row—Photos courtesy of Art Kreiss.

Current Perceptions of Time and Space

47: Lobby, Downtown Center Garage—San Francisco History Center, San Francisco Public Library.

Chapter 3

49: Saks Fifth Avenue parking facility—© Mike Sinclair and Gastinger Walker Harden Architects.

50: 1180 Peachtree Street—1180 Peachtree © 2006 Jonathan Hillyer.

54: Vertical auto mall—Kanner Architects.

55: Boys Club House—"Boys Club House," *American Architect* 97, no. 1795 (May 18, 1910): 197.

Fire station, Ocean City—© Ocean City Historical Museum.

56: Port Authority Terminal—Courtesy of the Port Authority of New York and New Jersey.

Forbes Field—"Automobile Garage Located under the Bleachers of a Baseball Park," *Automobile* (December 2, 1909): 980.

57: Museum of Science and Industry (top)—*Chicago Tribune* Photo by Walter Kale. All rights reserved. Used with permission.

Museum of Science and Industry (bottom)—*Chicago Tribune* Photo by Bill Hogan. All rights reserved. Used with permission.

58: Queensway Bay Parking Structure (both images)—© Erhart Pfeiffer 2007.

59: Minneapolis Energy Center—Photograph by Franz Hall; image provided by NRG Energy Center, Minneapolis, Minnesota.

62: Cafritz Office Building—A Morris Cafritz project, featured in Geoffrey Harold Baker and Bruno Funaro, *Parking* (New York: Reinhold, 1958), 91. Leroy L. Werner, designer.

63: Rampark Garage—Photo courtesy of Shannon Sanders McDonald Architects.

Union Market—Photograph by J. W. Oldfield, ca. 1925. Missouri Historical Society Photographs and Prints Collections. NS35410. Scan © 2007, Missouri Historical Society.

Gala Garage—Warren C. Heylman, FAIA.

Illustration Credits

100: Internal movement system—"Around the World: Paris–Algiers," *Parking* (Winter 1959): 24.

Alternative parking layouts—Clint L. Lefler, "An Introduction to Computer Parking Design," *Parking* (January 1971): 41-54.

101: Blue Cross Blue Shield facility—© Paul Gobeil Photography 1990; photo provided courtesy of Ellenzweig.

103: Apthorp Garage—216 West 80th Street, Museum of the City of New York, Print Archive.

Co-Operative Garage—Peter V. Hoyt, "The Co-Operative Garage," *Garage* I, no. 1 (November 1910): 5.

Detroit Garages

104: Detroit Garages—Robert O. Derrick, "The City Parking Garage," *Architectural Forum* (March 1927): 233.

105: Advertisement, First National Bank—*Detroiter*, November 3, 1924, 4.

Chapter 5

109: Ruth Safety Garage—Chicago History Museum; photographer Kaufmann & Fabry, ICHi-38515.

110: Garage Rue de Ponthieu—"Notes from Paris," *Architectural Review* 24 (1908).

Hill Garage—"Hill Garage," *American Architect* (April 5, 1928): 480.

F. Le R. Francisco, patent drawing—U.S. Patent 2,061,420: filed August 22, 1933; issued November 17, 1936.

112: Carew Towers—Cincinnati Museum Center—Cincinnati Historical Society Library.

Hill Garage—"Technical News and Research: Garages," *Architectural Record* (February 1929): 191.

Kent Automatic Parking Garage—Delta Progressive Inc., New York in Photos. Currently known as Sofia Apartments.

116: Westinghouse automobile parking machine—Courtesy of George Westinghouse Museum. Thanks to Roger White, Associate Curator, Transportation Collections, Work and Industry, National Museum of American History, Smithsonian Institution.

Harnischfeger system—"Semi-Automatic," *Parking* (Winter 1954): 39.

Nash Motors display—Chicago History Museum; photographer Ken Hedrich, Hedrich-Blessing, HB-00770-H.

117: Proposal for a mechanized underground parking system—Nolan S. Black and Wilfred V. Casgrain, *A Plan for the Construction of Underground Mechanical Garages in Downtown Detroit* (Detroit: 1930).

Park-O-Mat—Copyright *Washington Post*; reprinted by permission of the DC Public Library.

119: Bowser system garage, Des Moines—Print and Picture Collection, the Free Library of Philadelphia.

Bowser system garage, Athens—Heery International, Inc.

City Parking Garage—Chicago History Museum; photographer unknown, ICHi-50395.

121: Patent drawing—U.S. Patent 2,280,567: filed February 6, 1939; issued April 21, 1942.

R.L. Sinclair, patent drawing—U.S. Patent 2,428,856: filed February 25, 1944; issued October 14, 1947.

122: Proposal for storage system—© 1956 The Associated Press.

123: Park-A-Loft—Artcraft Studio, Parkersburg, W.V.

Blue Pigeon Hole Facility—Oregon Historical Society, CN_007357_.

124: Electro Park—Security Pacific Collection/Los Angeles Public Library.

125: Vert-A-Park—Reliable Parking, Image, Courtesy Colorado Historical Society (John Post negative collection). All Rights Reserved.

126: Speed-Park—"Speed-Park," *Parking* (Winter 1962): 18. A Mihai Alimanestianu project.

Silopark system—© Elevator World.

128: Proposal, ZipCar Dispenser—Moskow Architects Inc., Boston, Mass.

129: Automated facility—Photo courtesy of Shannon Sanders McDonald Architects.

Grand Parc—Summit Properties, Camden Development Inc.

130: 123 Baxter Street—AutoMotion, www.automotionparking.com.

131: The Buildings at Lovejoy Wharf—Architect: The Architectural Team, Inc. Developer: Ajax Investment Partners, LLC.

Brazilian Cultural Center—2004–2007 A Point Design, Inc. and DiLullo Associates, Inc.

132: 7 State Circle—Siena Corporation, Bohl Architects, Lasater/Sumpter Design.

Car Stackers: A More Modest Approach

114: Car stackers in New York City—Photo courtesy of Shannon Sanders McDonald Architects.

Car stacker, Bellora condominiums—Cary Kopczynski & Company.

Patent drawing—U.S. Patent 1,619,360: filed March 21, 1925; issued March 1, 1927.

Mechanized Garages with Round Floor Plans

120: Rotogarage—"Automatic Parking Garage," *Architectural Forum* (February 1951): 108.

Proposal for Tower Hoist Parking Tower—Lee Fraser, "Here Comes the Future," *Parking* (Fall 1964): 41.

Contemporary Systems Outside the United States

127: TreviPark system—Pictures appear courtesy of MitchCo, Inc., exclusive licensee for Trevipark in the United States, www.mitch-co.com.

Car Towers—Reuters/Christian Charisius.

Chapter 6

134: Pike at Rainbow Harbor parking structure—Copyright © 2007, John Linden.

137: Service station—Courtesy of the Detroit Public Library, National Automotive History Collection.

Fourth & Yamhill—Zimmer Gunsul Frasca Architects/Credit: Strode Eckert.

139: Losses from parking garage fires by category of damage—Dale Denda, *Parking Garage Fires: A Statistical Analysis of Parking Garage Fires in the United States: 1986–1988*, 2nd printing (McLean, Va.: Parking Market Research Company, 1995).

140: Types of fire detection systems—Dale Denda, *Parking Garage Fires: A Statistical Analysis of Parking Garage Fires in the United States: 1986–1988*, 2nd printing (McLean, Va.: Parking Market Research Company, 1995).

142: Park Square Garage—Courtesy of the Boston Public Library, Fine Arts Department.

143: Sears, Roebuck & Company—George C. Nimmons, "Motor-Truck Garage for Sears Roebuck and Company," *American Architect* 113, no. 1 (February 1918): 169.

144: Packard Motor Car Company—"Concrete Cantilever Construction in Chicago Garage," *Engineering News-Record* 85, no. 13 (September 23, 1920): 609.

Washington Garage—"Curved Drive for Automobiles in Six-Story Garage," *Engineering News-Record* 83, no. 4 (July 24, 1919): 188.

148: Rodeo Brighton Garage—Conrad Associates.

ZCMI Department Store—Used by permission, Utah State Historical Society, all rights reserved.

151: Hancock Place—Zaldastani Associates, Inc., Michael Jolliffe, Engineer in Charge.

Denver International Airport—Rocky Mountain Prestress, Inc.

153: University of Santa Cruz Parking Structure—Photo courtesy of Watry Design, Inc. Photography by Matthew Millman.

155: Downtown Center Garage—Moulin Studio #131591-2 and San Francisco History Center, San Francisco Public Library.

156: Toronto Airport Garage—Rich and Associates Photo Archives.

158: Chrysler Motors Limited—Courtesy of the Detroit Public Library, National Automotive History Collection.

160: Coliseum Convention Center—Courtesy of Kevin Roche John Dinkeloo and Associates.

161: Garage, Crickelwood Hill Apartments—Copyright © American Institute of Steel Construction, Inc. Reprinted with permission. All rights reserved.

East Cambridge Parking Garage—Zaldastani Associates, Inc., 1st Hybrid Parking Structure; Michael Jolliffe, Engineer in Charge, Completed 1992; Vittols Associates Architect.

162: Station Place Garage—Strode Photographic LLC.

164: Garage constructed with the Unicon system—Conrad Associates.

Pacific Mutual underground entry—Security Pacific Collection, Los Angeles Public Library.

165: Headquarters, Santander Central Hispano—Courtesy of Kevin Roche John Dinkeloo and Associates.

166: South Street Station—Carl Walker, Inc.

**The Precast Concrete Revolution:
T.Y. Lin and Harry Edwards**

149: Beverly Hills Garage "B"—Conrad Associates.

Eppley Airfield—Rich and Associates Photo Archives.

Concrete, Steel, and Sustainability

154: Central Park Garage—Bruce Glass Photography.

The Structural Aesthetic

157: Tree column—Desman Associates.

Vierendeel truss—Photo provided by the city of Rock Island, Ill.

Chapter 7

168: *Evolving City*—Paul Rudolph and Ulrich Franzen, *The Evolving City* (New York: American Federation of the Arts, 1974), 74–75.

170: Cave where Confucius was born—Werner Forman/Art Resource, N.Y.

Bedouin Camp in the Desert Dunes—Bridgeman-Giraudon/Art Resource, N.Y.

Illustration from *An Essay on Architecture*—Marc-Antoine Laugier, *An Essay on Architecture*, ©1977, Hennessey + Ingalls, Santa Monica, Calif., cover.

172: Group of stags, Lascaux Caves—Art Resource, N.Y.

Foliated scroll pattern—Drawing by Rebecca Smith, after Alois Reigl, *Stilfragen*, for Kent Bloomer.

Ferehan carpet—Art Resource, NY.

173: *Roadtown*—Fisher Fine Arts Library, University of Pennsylvania Architectural Archives.

174: Ohio Recreation Tower Co.—Library of Congress, Washington, D.C., Prints and Photographs Division, G38482, August 28, 1911, LC-USZ62-117373.

175: Atomium—© asbl Atomium vzw. ©2007 Atomium/Artists Rights Society (ARS), New York/SABAM, Brussels.

176: *Plug-In-City*—Archigram Archives.

City under the Seine—Reyner Banham, *Megastructure: Urban Futures of the Recent Past* (London: Thames and Hudson, 1976), 63.

178: Fort Worth, Texas—Courtesy Victor Gruen Papers, American Heritage Center, University of Wyoming.

Boston Center—Aerial Photos of New England, Boston Redevelopment Authority Photograph Collection, City of Boston Archives.

179: Co-Op City—RiverBay Corporation.

Cyclop Garage—Francesco Andreani, *Garages* (Rome: Gangemi Editore, 1997), 32.

180: *Great Arterial Way*—Reyner Banham, *Megastructure: Urban Futures of the Recent Past* (London: Thames and Hudson, 1976), 41.

Proposal for a showroom complex—"Radical Ways of Relieving Parking Congestion," *American City* (March 1932): 107.

181: BMW Plant—Aerial view of the Zaha Hadid Architects BMW Central Building, Leipzig, Germany; courtesy of BMW.

Santa Monica Place—Photograph © Tim Street-Porter/Esto. All rights reserved.

182: Parking garage and offices—Eric Owen Moss Architects.

183: Temple Street Garage—Photograph Ezra Stoller © Esto. All rights reserved.

184: Espirito Santo Plaza—Kohn Pedersen Fox, Woodruff & Brown Architectural Photography.

Past Visions of the Future

177: *Street Levels*—*Scientific American* (July 26, 1913): cover.

General Motors pavilion—General Motors Corp. Used with permission, GM Media Archives.

Chapter 8

187: Austin Convention Center parking structure—Architect: Barnes Gromatzky Kosarek Architects. © 2005 McConnellPhoto.net.

188: Opera House parking facility—Rich and Associates.

189: Lee Forest Garage—P.M. Heldt, "The Garage Business—Buildings, Equipment, Methods," *Horseless Age* 36, no. 13 (December 1, 1915): 492.

190: Publix supermarket—© Jeff Goldberg/Esto. All rights reserved.

192: Public garage, Baltimore—*Brickbuilder* 15, no. 10 (1906): 214.

Bowdoin Square Garage—Albert Kahn, "Sales and Service Buildings, Garages and Assembly Plants," *Architectural Forum* (March 1927): 265, plate 49.

Downtown Garage—Courtesy of the Forsyth County Public Library Photograph Collection.

194: Casey Parkway—School bus medallion from the facade of the Casey Parkway, Adams Avenue, Scranton, Penn. *Times-Tribune* Archives, June 2004.

Capital Garage—Library of Congress, Prints and Photographs Division, photograph by Commercial Photo Co., Washington, D.C., LC-USZ62-92374.

195: Towne Park Garage—Photo courtesy of Shannon Sanders McDonald Architects.

196: Pike at Rainbow Harbor parking structure—Copyright © 2007, John Linden.

198: *Parking Garage over the Seine*—Frederick Starr, *Melnikov* (Princeton, N.J.: Princeton Architectural Press, 1978), 105.

Rikes-Dayton Garage—Rich and Associates Photo Archives.

199: Henry Ford Hospital—Photo courtesy of the offices of Albert Kahn Associates, Inc.

Milliron's Department Store—Courtesy Victor Gruen Papers, American Heritage Center, University of Wyoming.

200: Evening Star Garage—Copyright *Washington Post;* reprinted by permission of the DC Public Library. Walter Hoban, Jerry on the Job C Negative R-8.

University of Pennsylvania parking garage—University of Pennsylvania Architectural Archives.

Exchange National Bank Building garage—Courtesy of George K. Denison (Tampa Bay History Center).

202: Lake Street Garage—Tigerman McCurry Architects.

Entry Pavilion Parking Structure—Photo courtesy of Watry Design, Inc. Photography by Matthew Millman.

203: Hermosa Beach parking structure—David Wakely, photographer; Chong Partners Architecture.

University of California at Davis Medical Center Parking Structure II—Russell Abraham, photographer; Chong Partners Architecture.

205: Gotham Hotel garage—William B. Gleckman Architect.

Anchor Shops and Parking—Steven Brooke, photographer; Zyscovich Architects.

Omaha Park Six garage—AGA Consulting, Inc.

207: Parking facility, Gannett headquarters—Kohn Pedersen Fox, Timothy Hursley.

208: Seventh Street Station Parking Facility—Photo Courtesy of Bank of America. © 2007 Bank of America Corporation. ©2007 PhenomenArts, Inc., Christopher Janney, Artistic Director.

209: New Street Parking Garage—Jason Hottel Photography; Frazier Associates Architects.

211: Grand Avenue Garage—Martin Building Company/martin-building.com.

212: Stanford University Medical Center—Photo courtesy of Watry Design, Inc. Photography by Matthew Millman.

Frank Lloyd Wright and Parking

191: *Gordon Strong Automobile Sugarloaf Mountain Observatory*—Drawings of Frank Lloyd Wright are Copyright © 2007, The Frank Lloyd Wright Foundation, Taliesin West, Scottsdale, Ariz.

Self-Service Garage for Pittsburgh—Drawings of Frank Lloyd Wright are Copyright © 2007, The Frank Lloyd Wright Foundation, Taliesin West, Scottsdale, Ariz.

Lee, Smith & Vandervoort

193: Garage, Richmond—Dementi Studio, Richmond, Virginia; neg #ID-1874, November 1949.

Model of Richmond Garage—"Technical News and Research: Garages," *Architectural Record* (February 1929): 184.

Portland, Oregon: Art for the Parking Garage

206: *118 Modules*—Courtesy Regional Arts and Culture Council, Portland, Oregon.

Upstream Downtown—Courtesy Regional Arts and Culture Council, Portland, Oregon.

Charleston, South Carolina: Revitalization through Parking

210: Francis Marion Hotel parking facility—Photo courtesy of Shannon Sanders McDonald Architect.

Chapter 9

214: City Center West parking facility—International Parking Design, Inc. Photographer: Ashok Nandwana.

217: State and Madison, Chicago—Chicago History Museum, photographer unknown, ICHi-04788.

Grant Park parking lot—Chicago History Museum, photographer unknown, ICHi-19437.

218: Rockefeller Center—Milstein Division of United States History, Local History and Genealogy, the New York Public Library, Astor, Lenox and Tilden Foundations.

222: Hotel LaSalle Garage—Chicago History Museum, photographer unknown, ICHI-51081.

223: Union Square Garage—Moulin Studio #131591-2 and San Francisco History Center, San Francisco Public Library.

Post Office Square—© Steve Rosenthal, Photographer. Photo provided courtesy of Ellenzweig.

224: Parking lot, Stop and Shop Market—*American City Magazine* (December 1924): 588.

226: Market Street East—University of Pennsylvania Architectural Archives.

227: Proposal for a raised highway and parking—"Proposed Plan to Relieve Traffic Congestion in St. Paul and Provide Parking Space for 3,000 Automobiles," *American City* (April 1928): 87.

228: *World's First Automobile City*—Theron R. Howser, "A Plan for a City Built to Fit the Automobile," *American City* (July 1934): 56.

Cobo Hall—Courtesy of the Detroit Public Library, National Automotive History Collection.

229: Proposal for a combination housing and parking structure—Louis I. Kahn Collection, University of Pennsylvania, and Pennsylvania Historical and Museum Commission.

Traffic study—Digital Image © the Museum of Modern Art/Licensed by SCALA/Art Resources, N.Y. Permission also granted by William Whitaker, Collections Manager, Architectural Archives, University of Pennsylvania.

230: Cascade Superblock—Bruce S. Ford/City of Akron.

231: High Falls Garage—David Lamb/David Lamb Photography.

City Center West—Site plan by VBN Architects.

232: Country Club Plaza retail and parking facility—© Mike Sinclair and Gastinger Walker Harden Architects.

236: Quincy Adams Facility—H.W. Moore Associates and Vitols Associates, Joint Venture Architect/Engineers.

237: Loop Transportation Center—Skidmore, Owings & Merrill LLP, architects; Stein & Company, developer; Crane General and Newberg/Paschen, contractors.

Riverfront Parking Facility—Jim Tevebaugh, Tevebaugh Associates.

238: Center Street Park and Ride—HLKB Architecture and photographer Cameron Campbell.

Old Towne Parking Garage—Copyright Eckert & Eckert. 6/18/07.